HANDS
IN CLAY

CHARLOTTE F. SPEIGHT

HANDS IN CLAY
An Introduction to Ceramics

Second Edition

John Toki, Technical Advisor / Collaborator

Mayfield Publishing Company
Mountain View, California

Speight, Charlotte F.
    Hands in clay : an introduction to ceramics /
Charlotte F. Speight. —2nd ed.
        p.   cm.
        Bibliography: p.
        Includes index.
        ISBN 0-87484-848-2
        1. Pottery craft.   I. Title.
    TT920.S685   1989
        738—dc19   88-13796
                CIP

Manufactured in the United States of America
10   9   8   7   6   5   4   3   2

Mayfield Publishing Company
1240 Villa Street
Mountain View, California 94041

Sponsoring editor, Janet M. Beatty; production editor,
Linda Toy; manuscript editor, Suzanne Lipsett; text
and cover designer, Cynthia Bassett; illustrators, John
M. Casey (Part I), Danute J. Bruzas (Part II). All
photographs not otherwise credited are by the author.
The text was set in 10/12 Janson and printed on 60#
Stora Matte by W. A. Krueger Co., Inc.

Frontispiece: Arnold Zimmerman, U.S.A. *Courtesy
the artist*.

To the Student

Hands in Clay tells the story of how human hands—past and present—have formed and transformed clay into beautiful, evocative, and useful objects. The book grew out of my life-long interest in clay and my excitement about the special relationship that people in all cultures and eras have developed with this malleable material. Through the creativity of countless humans who shaped these objects, we can form a greater understanding of cultures far removed from our own in time or place. Whether a pot, a brick, or a sculpture, each ceramic object formed by human hands bears an imprint of its maker's spirit and represents its culture's aesthetic taste and utilitarian needs. In presenting the continuity of human involvement with clay, I also offer you a broad range of methods, so that you may find your individual style of working in clay.

At the same time, I want to demystify what at times appears to be an intimidating technology by showing how for thousands of years potters and sculptors experimented with the simplest materials and methods, building up a body of knowledge that enabled them to fill their practical needs and to communicate their feelings with clay. The technical innovations that resulted in new ceramic forms were developed only through persistent experimentation, and it is this spirit of "try it and see" that I wish to emphasize in the book.

By beginning with history, and opening Part 2 with a new chapter, "The Artist's Vision," I stress the importance of the imaginative and aesthetic aspects of ceramics, and the depth of human feeling and commitment that is such an important part of creativity in clay. My hope is that these glimpses into the spirits, hearts, and minds of ceramists will encourage you to draw on your own inner sources as you work with clay. In addition, my aim has been to give you the technical information you need without overwhelming you. I wish you joy as you find pleasure, satisfaction, and creativity through working with your hands in clay.

To the Instructor

After rereading the first edition of *Hands in Clay*, and in response to the many helpful suggestions from teachers, students, reviewers, and artists, I decided to expand the book, incorporating a number of new features to help the beginning and continuing ceramics student.

NEW TO THIS EDITION

In Part 1, I have added two new chapters. The first (Chapter 7) focuses on the development of ceramics in the United States, giving the reader an understanding of the eclectic background from which contemporary ceramics derives. The second (Chapter 8) highlights worldwide innovations in ceramics in the last three decades (1950s–1980s), providing the student with an overview of the influences that have shaped contemporary artists. These two chapters lead into Part 2, where the new Chapter 9, "The Artist's Vision," and the following method chapters discuss many contemporary approaches to ceramics. Thus, by first absorbing the historical background, then by trying a variety of processes, the student will come to appreciate the continuity of clay as well as become aware of how artists today continue to use or modify techniques from the past.

To support the textual emphasis on the aesthetic aspects of ceramics, the black and white photographs present an extensive array of historical and contemporary examples, and I have increased the number of color plates to illustrate 44 examples of ceramic art, giving special emphasis to contemporary pottery and sculpture. These examples range from delicate glazed vases to china-painted sculptures to massive architectural installations.

The process section (Part 2) now includes more information on ceramics methods. There are also more detailed instructions for building with slabs and coils, a wider variety of wheel forming methods, new material on working with molds, and an additional integrated section on mixing and testing clays and glazes. As students read the text and study the illustrations of people working with clay, they will be introduced first to the basic hand building methods and then progressively to more complex techniques. A new chapter, Chapter 14, surveys the process of creating large-scale sculpture and architectural works, introducing the student to the process of planning and installing such works.

As I reworked the technical sections with my collaborator, John Toki, we decided to offer students more experience in mixing and testing clays and glazes. To do this, he formulated some simple *Hands in Clay* clay and glaze recipes that use only a few ingredients. This project grew in scope until it became a complete unit. The recipes for these clays and glazes are in the appendixes, along with additional information to help students run the tests. If students work through this sequence, they will learn much about the basic function of ceramics materials and the all-important interaction between clay and glaze. They will then be ready to test some of the more complex recipes shared with us by a number of ceramists and go on to develop their own clays and glaze recipes. Those who care to may continue further with the analysis and calculation of glazes using chemistry, and many formulas are provided in the appendix.

Health and safety in the ceramics studio figures prominently in this edition, and this visual sign in the margin alerts readers to the need for precautions. In addition, the materials list in the expanded appendixes rates ceramic materials according to their toxicity. Some commercial sources of materials, as well as sources of current information on health and safety, are also listed there. The most up-to-date research in the field of ceramics forms the foundation of this text, and every effort has been made to provide appropriate warning throughout the text where potentially hazardous substances or procedures are involved. Anyone following these procedures should use his or her best judgment and common sense.

The first usage of unfamiliar words in the text appears in bold type, indicating that the word will be found in the glossary, and the expanded reading list is now organized by subjects to make it easier for the reader to find the names of books giving historical, technical, and health and safety information.

ACKNOWLEDGMENTS

I am grateful to the many dedicated people working in clay today who have inspired and delighted me with their creations. A number of these are represented in the book in photographs or through the technical information they contributed. But the spirits of hundreds of other artists and craftspeople have guided me. I am also indebted to the artists, editors, and curators whose advice helped me shape the first edition. They are still an important part of the book, and I would like to thank them once again, especially Larry Murphy, technical adviser for that edition.

My heartfelt thanks go to John Toki, sculptor, teacher, and friend for his knowledge, creative sensitivity, and encouragement. John joined me first as technical adviser, but as it became clear that our perceptions and ideas meshed to a remarkable degree, his contributions to the second edition grew in scope, depth, and detail. We became collaborators in many areas of the book, and John was responsible for the conception and realization of the unit on testing clays and glazes. Much credit also goes to him for his guidance as I worked on presenting in a clear manner the technical information that the learner needs to progress comfortably in ceramics. His father, Rayer Toki, was also drawn into the project, and I am grateful for his generous sharing of years of experience with clay and glaze materials. He provided a rich source of information on which we drew.

Many thanks are also due John Casey who recreated the historical drawings, and Danute Bruzas, who drew the kiln sections for Part 2. Their skill and dedication added greatly to the clarity and attractiveness of the new edition.

Many excellent suggestions were made by the reviewers of the text: Von Allen, Brigham Young University; Art Haney, East Carolina University; Katherine L. Ross, School of the Art Institute of Chicago; Marion Weiss-Munk, Middlesex County College; and Julian A. Waller, M.D., M.P.H., University of Vermont, whose special expertise as a doctor and potter expanded my awareness of health and safety considerations. I am grateful for their thoughtful suggestions, and for those of the teachers who responded to a questionnaire about the proposed new edition.

It requires the efforts of many skilled people before a book like *Hands in Clay* finally comes to life. I would like to express my personal thanks to those at Mayfield Publishing Company who made this edition possible: Boyce Nute, president; Janet M. Beatty, sponsoring editor; Linda Toy, production editor; Cynthia Bassett, designer; as well as the supporting staff for their part in the long, exhaustive process that created this new edition.

My daughter Martha and many friends nourished my spirit during the months of work, and I am deeply grateful to them.

Contents

5   Sources of Health Information, Materials, and Equipment

Let us honor clay, the impressionable and responsive art media; the naturally plastic and textured architectural media; the most lasting when fired into vitreous ceramic; the most brilliant and finely textured when glazed with colors of the mineral oxides; the most direct and colorful sculptural voice and the most exciting.

Weylande Gregory, U.S.A. 1905–1971

A Hopi woman in Arizona at the turn of the century, ▶
seated outside her home, worked with local materials
and simple tools. A lump of clay to form the pot, a
basket for support, a container of water, and a half
circle of dried gourd for smoothing the clay were all
she needed to create beauty from the earth. Arizona,
c. 1900. *Courtesy Field Museum of Natural History (Neg.
#133), Chicago.*

SHAPING THE PAST

1
An Introduction to Clay

One might almost say that, if all the rest of his activity were to vanish, man might still be known by his pottery.

Germain Bazin*

Clay feels soft and pliable in your hands. Pick up a lump of it, let your fingers respond to its **plasticity,** and as you pinch and poke it, the clay seems to have a life of its own, to which your fingers respond. Perhaps you will find yourself forming a human figure, an animal, or a small pot.

By responding to the clay's plastic quality with these pinching gestures, you are repeating the actions of untold numbers of humans who have worked with clay even as far back in time as the Ice Age, thirty-seven thousand to twelve thousand years ago. The earliest known examples of clay objects formed by human hands are representations of animals modeled on a clay bank in a cave in France and some fired clay animal figures and a female human figure found at an Ice Age site in what is now Czechoslovakia.

*The Loom of Art, Simon & Schuster, N.Y. Thames and Hudson, London, 1962.

Female figures made of clay have been found in quantity in many areas of the world. This one, formed from the mud of the Nile River about six thousand years ago in Egypt, is believed to be a bird deity. Fired at a very low temperature, these early Egyptian figures are usually grey in color. Ht. 11½ in. (29.3 cm). *Courtesy the Brooklyn Museum.*

Figure 1-1
We do not know the exact use of the female figures, but most were probably fertility figures or representations of nature goddesses. This one was made during the Middle Kingdom period in Egypt, c. 1800 B.C. Ht. 5⅜ in. (13.5 cm). *Courtesy the Trustees of the British Museum, London.*

Figure 1-2
Another goddess or fertility figure, from excavations at Tureng Tepe, Persia, shows the scratched and applied details that so often decorated these figures wherever they are found. (5-2). *Courtesy the University Museum, University of Pennsylvania (Neg. #21863).*

This very early use of fire to harden clay, though it predated the oldest **pottery** yet found, was apparently localized. Not until around 6000–4000 B.C. did the knowledge of how to fire clay become widespread and the craft of **ceramics** develop in a number of areas. Nevertheless, among the simple pots found in excavations of early sites around the world, archaeologists have frequently dug up small fired clay figures of women similar to the Ice Age figure, images that are believed to have had a magical or religious purpose linked to fertility worship (see page 2, 1-1, 1-2).

The new craft of ceramics depended on the exploitation of several intrinsic qualities of clay—its plasticity, its ability to hold the shape into which it is formed as it dries, and the fact that heating it to **maturity** transforms it into a new, permanently hard substance (1-3). Learning to

Figure 1-3
The name Jōmon, meaning "cord pattern," is applied to a type of early Japanese pottery that was decorated, as is this pot, with incised lines and applied clay. Ht. 3⅞ in. (10 cm). Japan, late Jōmon period. *Courtesy the Trustees of the British Museum, London.*

3

Figure 1-4
The Sumerians used slabs of damp clay as writing surfaces, and the impression of the marking tool that a clerk pressed into a tablet around 2100 B.C. is still legible. This tablet records the prescription of a local doctor: "Pulverize the seed of the 'carpenter plant,' the gum resin of the markasi-plant, and thyme; dissolve it in beer; let the man drink." *Courtesy the University Museum, University of Pennsylvania (Neg. #55887).*

control fire and using it to create this new material was one of humanity's first great technical achievements. In many cultures, ceramics developed along with the craft of metallurgy, with the discoveries in each technology aiding the other.

The knowledge and technique necessary to transform damp clay into a ceramic material developed at various times in different cultures, but no matter where the craft evolved, it influenced the development of that culture. For example, the knowledge of ceramics allowed villagers to make vermin-proof storage jars, which meant they could store grain against future crop failures and accumulate surpluses with which to trade with neighboring communities.

A RECORD OF HUMANITY IN CLAY

The close relationship between human hands and clay, along with the fact that a ceramic object is indestructible unless it has been crushed into such minute fragments that it cannot be repaired, has made it easier for archaeologists and historians to reconstruct how people lived in cultures that have long since disappeared (1-4). Even if a clay pot or sculpture has been broken, its **shards** can often be put together again. Or, if the fragments are too scattered, the archaeologist can still study the type of clay in the remaining shards, the nature of the decoration on the fragments, and the shape of a pot or sculpture as suggested by the preserved sections. From these ceramic remains, it is possible to learn a considerable amount about a society—its degree of technical development, the extent of its trade, and its exposure to migrations of other peoples that may have introduced new ceramic techniques. For example, pottery from six thousand years ago found in Sian, China, reveals techniques and painted designs similar to those in older pottery found in Russian Turkistan in western Asia, showing that interchanges occurred between the peoples of these areas.

Ceramics aids archaeology in another important way. Since most archaeological sites are rich in pot shards, through modern dating methods the excavator can often establish a pottery sequence that allows the dating of other materials found in the same stratum. But an archaeologist may spend years establishing such a sequence and rarely have the luck to stumble on a dramatic discovery.

Masada: An Early Drama Revealed

In the 1960s, however, Dr. Yigael Yadin, professor of archaeology at Hebrew University in Jerusalem, Israel, unearthed a clay artifact that evoked a moment of great human drama. Dr. Yadin was directing the excavation of a large fortress and palace built by Herod the Great on top of the Rock of Masada, a massive outcrop that towers 1,300 feet above the Dead Sea plain. In A.D. 73, this rock had been the site of an heroic last-ditch stand made by a thousand Jewish rebels against their Roman rulers. These Zealots of Masada, as they are called, withstood three years of siege, but finally realizing that a Roman breakthrough was imminent, they decided to die by their own hands rather than surrender. Each man first killed his wife and children; the survivors chose ten men by lot to be their executioners. According to the historian Josephus, the men "offered their necks to the stroke of those who by lot executed that melancholy office." The last ten then drew lots among themselves to decide who would kill the other nine, and this last man finally killed himself.

Almost two thousand years later, members of Dr. Yadin's Masada expedition found eleven pottery *ostraca*, or lots, lettered with the names of men (1-5). One of them bore the name of the Zealots' leader, Eleazar ben Ya'hir'. Were these pieces of clay the tragic lots described by Josephus? We know that lots like these were also used on Masada to ration food and assign duties, so even if these were not the Zealots' death lots, they are still a dramatic record of the last-ditch stand of the Zealots, substantiating the written word of Josephus.

Clay Artifacts in Burials

Given the facts that pottery and clay images played important roles in many cultures and that ceramic containers did not disintegrate as did

Figure 1-5
Found by the Masada Expedition in Israel, this *ostraca*, or lot, may be one of those used to determine the order of death of the Zealots of Masada, patriots who chose to die by their own hands rather than surrender to the Romans. Their bravery inspired the modern Israeli cry, "Masada shall not fall again." Masada, A.D. 73. *Courtesy Israel Exploration Society. Photo: Y. Yadin.*

those made of wood, it is not surprising that ancient peoples frequently buried their dead in ceramic vessels. They also buried with them small ceramic containers of oils and perfumes and clay reproductions of servants and objects they believed the deceased might need in the afterlife. Through study of these burial finds, archaeologists are able to theorize about a culture's religious beliefs and attempt to reconstruct its daily life. Looking at these records of life preserved in clay, we can identify with the human feelings, needs, and beliefs of people who lived in widely separated places and in times far removed from our own. Anthropologists can even learn much about

Figure 1-6
A potter who lived on Crete about fourteen hundred years ago left the enduring mark of his thumb in the damp clay of a large *pithos*, or storage jar. Mallia, Crete. *Photo: James McGann.*

Figure 1-7
With the same gesture, a Cretan village potter today pressed his thumb in the damp clay when he attached the handle to a smaller version of the ancient jar. These two prints, spanning thousands of years, symbolize the long-continuing tradition of human hands working in clay.

the physical makeup of a people from fingerprints preserved in clay (1-6 and 1-7).

For example, the artifacts discovered in digs can help us visualize the Sumerian doctor dictating his pleasant-sounding remedy to a scribe (1-4), or feel the joyous excitement of two children swinging in ancient Veracruz (5-3). Talented early sculptors captured in clay the gestures of women performing household chores (1-8), the details of house and temple architecture (1-9), the trappings of a war horse (3-20), and the exploits of heroes (2-20).

THE ORIGINS OF CLAY

Just what *is* this substance called **clay,** which tells us so much about the past? What is there in

the makeup of this material that is responsible for its unique qualities? And where does clay come from?

The fertile areas of the earth are covered with a layer of topsoil that is rich in rotted organic matter. Under this soil, or sometimes under a layer of rock, lie deposits of various types of clay. You can see these clay beds in highway cuts or at construction sites where they have been exposed by earth-moving machines. As rivers erode and cut into their banks, they also reveal beds of clay.

The earth's surface was formed from melted rock that cooled and solidified. Over millions of years, the weathering action of alternating freezing and thawing, along with the grinding of glaciers, the pounding of rain, the flow of rushing streams, and the probing of tree roots, slowly breaks down the earth's crust into boulders, then into stones, then pebbles, and finally into the

Figure 1-8
Grinding corn on a metate, unaware of her child trying to steal a tortilla from her lap, this figure shows us an aspect of family life in the Colima area of Mexico around A.D. 300–900. To an expert, a realistic clay figure like this also tells much about the culture's agriculture, cooking and eating habits, clothing and jewelry, as well as its custom of binding the heads of babies in order to achieve an elongated skull. *Courtesy Museo Nacional de Antropologiá, Mexico.*

Figure 1-9
An earthenware model of a house from Peru shows how the Moche people built their homes around A.D. 400. From clay pots, figurines, and representations of habitations like this, archaeologists can reconstruct almost every aspect of a society, from its religious rituals to how its people waged war and made love. Ht. 5¾ in. (14.8 cm). North Coast, Peru. *Courtesy Linden-Museum Stuttgart. Photo: Didoni.*

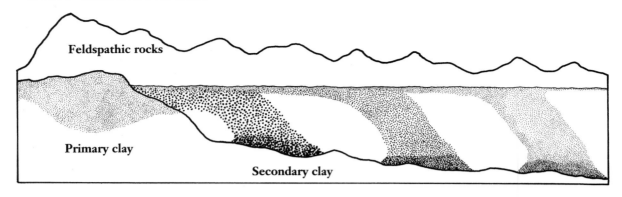

Feldspathic rocks

Primary clay

Secondary clay

Figure 1-10
Rain, snow, wind, and water wear down the earth's feldspathic rock, causing it to decompose in place to become primary clay. Particles are also moved by the action of water to be deposited elsewhere, forming beds of secondary clay. Different types of clay such as stoneware, earthenware, or ball clay are dug from these deposits to be transformed by human hands into vessels or sculptures.

small particles that make up different types of clay (1-10).

At the same time, chemical changes take place as oxygen combines with minerals to form oxides. **Feldspar,** the most abundant element on the earth's surface, is an essential component of granite rocks and is the basis of clay. Made up for the most part of the oxides silica and alumina combined with such **alkalies** as potassium and some so-called impurities such as iron, it is this feldspathic origin of clay that makes it possible to fire it to a dense and permanent hardness and cover it with impermeable coatings of a glasslike material called **glaze.** Just as the intense heat of a volcano can fuse the elements in certain rocks into the glassy substance obsidian, so can the heat of the fire fuse and transform the mineral components of clay into ceramic. To be capable of producing ceramic, a clay must contain, along with other components, a **flux** and a heat-resistant material, or **refractory.** The amount of flux a clay contains in relation to the refractory material is one factor that controls the point at which a clay reaches its optimum density, or maturity.

Types of Clay

To fuse and mature, each type of clay requires a different heat level and duration in the fire. Some, like low-fired **earthenware** clay, never do become as dense and **vitreous** (glassy) as high-fired clays like **stoneware** and **porcelain.** The variations in size of the clay particles and the varying temperatures at which clays reach maturity account for the differences in texture and appearance between, say, a white porcelain vase and a reddish flowerpot. Color variations are produced by the presence or lack of coloring oxides such as iron or manganese. Potters refer to the particular types of clay they use as **clay bodies.** The clay a potter uses may consist of clay as it was found in its natural state, but the term *clay body* usually refers to a combination of materials that the potter, sculptor, or supplier has formulated for a specific purpose. In later chapters you will learn more about the composition of clays and the appropriateness of each type to a particular type of work, but in Part I we are primarily concerned with understanding how the characteristics of the material affected ceramic technology as it developed in various areas of the world.

The Plasticity of Clay

If you stop to think about the difference between fired and unfired clay, you will realize what an amazing material clay is. Dampened with water, it is easy to form, holding together as you shape it. Air-dried, it is fragile, crumbling easily. But when subjected to the heat of a **kiln,** it becomes hard and permanent, capable of keeping its form for thousands of years.

Clay's plasticity when damp is mainly due to the fineness of its particles (or platelets), to their flat shape, and to the action of the water between them. In addition, the organic materials that have become mixed with the clay in its journey from rock to riverbed play their part in making it malleable. Leaving damp clay to age for a period of weeks, months, or even years increases its plasticity—an advantage when the clay is used to throw on the wheel but less critical for building sculpture.

When water is absorbed by dry clay, the film it forms between the platelets lubricates them so that they slip against each other. The water film also makes them cling together, just as smooth pieces of glass both cling to and slide against each other when they are wet.

Clays differ greatly in their degree of plasticity. Some are so sticky they are almost impossible to shape; others, which might work well when used in a semiliquid **slip** state for casting, would never hold together if used damp for shaping on a potter's wheel. And a clay that is a joy to shape on the wheel may not be successfully modeled into a large sculpture. Thus, the clay worker must take into account the properties of each clay in relation to the desired results. These variations in clay as well as the local availability of specific clays had an important effect on how the craft of ceramics developed in different areas of the world.

EARLY USES OF CLAY

When people found that they could domesticate animals and store wild seeds for food, they began to exchange their nomadic lives for life in reasonably settled communities. The campfire now became a homefire. Traces of the changes that took place during such transitional periods have been found recorded in clay. For example, around 9000 B.C. in a transitional village that was located at a spring near what would later become Jericho, the simple houses contained clay-lined pits in which wild grains were stored, a fact that

indicates that the people who lived there were developing an agricultural society. In Jarmo, in northern Mesopotamia, excavators discovered that by the seventh millennium B.C., clay-lined pits in the floors were used as hearths. Some of these excavated pits contained stones, suggesting that hot stones may have been placed in them for cooking. However, the lack of any pottery shards at this site plus the presence of unbaked clay figures there and in Jericho indicate that the deliberate firing of clay to harden images or pots was as yet unknown in this area. On the other side of the world, however, deliberately fired pottery, examples of which have been found at sites in Japan, Taiwan, and China, is believed to have appeared between 11,000 and 10,000 B.C.

There is always the possibility that archaeologists will discover other sites that will fill in some of the gaps in our knowledge of the history of ceramics, but we will probably never be able to set an exact date for when some human first discovered that clay became hard when exposed to fire and that this newly found material could be used to make receptacles for holding water and cooking or storing food. Perhaps pottery making was discovered when a hut burned down and the clay floor was accidentally fired. Or perhaps someone built a fire in a clay-lined pit, thus unintentionally firing it. One theory that has been widely accepted but is now considered unlikely by some experts is that a woman in a prehistoric community lined a basket with clay to keep out mice, let it sit too near a fire, and discovered that the clay had hardened when the basket burned. In whatever manner the discovery was made that fire changed clay into a solid substance, and whether it was made in one place and spread or, as is more likely, in several different areas independently, the finding initiated the long exploration of ceramics technology—an exploration that still continues in both the potter's workshop and the space laboratory.

The discovery of ceramics must have changed the domestic life of women wherever it occurred, and eventually it led to changes in the complex fabric of society. Once people could substitute pots for woven or leather containers, they could cook in a clay pot over a fire instead of having to drop hot stones into a basket of water to create cooking heat. Also, they could carry water more easily from the spring and could store grains, which enabled them to become even more firmly established in one place and to take advantage of the changing seasons to cultivate foodstuffs.

As time went on, permanent settlements in various parts of the world grew larger and life became more complex. Simultaneously, surpluses of food and other necessities accumulated. As a result, trade based on these surplus commodities developed, leading to the exchange of ideas and technologies. Scholars suggest that it was at this point in the development of a society that the craft of pottery became specialized and that the men rather than the women became the potters, producing wares for trade as well as for local use. Even today in some traditional cultures, however, the potters are women and the men are forbidden to make pottery.

In most early cultures, clay was so much a part of everyday life that we might say these early communities existed in a Clay Age, just as later eras have been classified as Iron and Bronze Ages because of their wide use of those metals. At any rate, these periods did not follow each other in a direct line as historians tend to present them. Rather, overlapping technologies and time lags in the technological developments meant that they appeared at different times in different areas.

EARLY CERAMIC TECHNOLOGY

Any reconstruction of history involves educated guesses, so we cannot say for certain how the earliest potters actually made their pots. However, experts can learn a good deal about their methods both through the microscopic examination of the ceramics found in excavations and the study of methods of potters whose techniques are believed to be similar to those of the earliest cultures. By watching a village potter in Africa or the American Southwest, we can hope to learn something of the problems encountered and the processes worked out by our earliest potting ancestors. For this reason, ceramic historians and archaeologists are making every effort to record these methods before metal and plastic

utensils become universal and pottery for regular domestic use is no longer made by hand.

Gathering the Material

For the early potter, the first step in making a pot would naturally have been the gathering of the necessary material (1-11). A village potter who had no cart or pack animal would have tried to find a clay source near enough to the village so that the clay could have been carried back in baskets or leather bags. Sometimes, however, a particular clay would have to be brought from quite a distance. But pottery was apparently important enough to the village to make even a difficult trip worthwhile. For example, in the Hebrides Islands, off the Scottish coast, in the second millennium B.C., clay and the wood for firing it were scarce, and both had to be fetched from across the open water by dugout canoe.

Early potters, like all agricultural peoples, felt their dependence on the earth, and in many cultures the potters would not dig the clay without proper religious observances. To them the earth was a sacred mother on whom they depended for life and health. In the American Southwest, for example, potters had so much respect for the earth that they asked its permission to remove the clay before digging it out with a stick. Mothers taught their daughters the required rituals, calling the earth Mother Clay, and to this day, some of the potters of New Mexico scatter cornmeal on the ground as an offering before digging their clay.

Adding Temper to Clay

When people first started making pottery, they probably used the clay just as it came from the riverbank or hillside (1-12), merely picking out the larger impurities. But at some point, they discovered that a pot made of coarse-textured clay was less likely than one made of fine-grained clay to burst or crack in firing because the vapors could escape more readily through the pores. Sand, pounded rock, mica, ground-up seashells, volcanic ash, and similar materials open the pores

Figure 1-11
The photo shows Julian Martinez digging clay from an exposed bed on a mesa in New Mexico in the 1940s. Maria Martinez recalled that in her grandmother's day the digger always scattered grain as an offering before digging the clay—a custom that is still practiced by some potters in the Southwest. New Mexico, c. 1940. *Courtesy Collections in the Museum of New Mexico. Photo: Wyatt Davis.*

Figure 1-12
After digging and transporting the clay to the village, the early potter sometimes used it as it came from the earth, but it often required cleaning or aging. This clay, stored outside a workshop in Thrapsanon, Greece, is being dried before being broken up and soaked in water. Once thoroughly wet again, it will be spread in the sun until it reaches throwing consistency.

of clay. Some clays already contain a natural **temper,** so no other addition is needed, but as potters observed what happened in the kiln, they learned to add these and similar materials to the natural clay. The general term for this added material is temper, while the term **grog** refers to one type of commercially prepared temper widely used today.

If one potter changed and altered a local clay by adding a particular temper and her pottery became the best in the village, her knowledge about where to go for clay and what materials to add and in what amount would be copied by others. From then on the other potters in the village would use the same mixture. This fact has helped archaeologists; experts can often tell the origin of a piece of pottery by noting what tempering material was used. For example, around 6000 B.C. in some areas of the Middle East, potters mixed straw in their clay to open the pores, while in certain parts of the American Southwest traditional potters still use volcanic rock or sand as temper.

Early Forming Methods

After carrying the clay home, mixing it with temper, and working it to the right consistency, the potter was ready to shape a pot. Local clays, local tempering materials, local firing methods, and even local climate would all have their effect on how a potter worked.

Nowadays we can control humidity and drying by artificial means, but the early potter was at the mercy of the climate. In hot, dry Mesopotamia, for example, the work of building up a pot would have had to be done quickly, before the evaporation of moisture made the clay unmanageable, but that difficulty would not have existed for the Bronze Age potter in misty Scotland (1-13). There, getting the pots dry enough to fire safely would have been the problem, and the potter would probably have had to dry them beside a fire for a long time before the moisture in their walls was completely driven out.

Pinching   If you pick up a lump of clay, let your thumb sink into it, turning it while pinching and pulling up the sides, pinching and compressing the walls as they grow between your fingers and thumb, you will find it quite easy to shape the clay into a rough, thick-walled but quite serviceable pot. The very earliest pots, simple containers, were probably made this way by women pinching the clay into shape (1-14). However, it takes considerably more skill to shape a thin-walled, aesthetically pleasing pot using the pinching method. If the clay is stretched too much during the pinching process, it tends to crack, or the walls may collapse. It is also difficult when pinching to control the shape of the pot—for example, narrowing in a neck from a swelling body or opening it out into a flaring bowl. For this reason, some potters found it easier to build up the walls of a pot using rolls of clay that they spiraled up in a method called coiling.

Coiling   In the coiling method, coils had to be attached to some type of a clay base to form

Figure 1-13
In Great Britain, where clay deposits are abundant, pottery has been made for well over five thousand years. Early pots, like this Bronze Age urn from Scotland, were made of local clays fired to a low temperature. Similar linear decoration, scratched on the walls while the clay was still damp, appeared on early pots around the world. Ht. 5¾ in. (14.6 cm). Terradale, Scotland, Bronze Age (1700–1300 B.C.). *By courtesy of the Board of Trustees of the Victoria & Albert Museum.*

Figure 1-14
As we look at this woman in New Guinea, building a pot on her lap using thick, damp coils, it is easy to imagine how the world's earliest potters pressed pieces of clay together to make roughly constructed pots. Lokanu, New Guinea. *Courtesy Field Museum of Natural History, (Neg. #32000), Chicago.*

the bottom of the pot (see Part 1 Opening photo and 5-15) before the walls could be built. It is possible to make a base from a roll of clay coiled on a flat surface and smoothed out or a slab of clay pounded flat. But to form a pot with a rounded bottom, the potter would have been more likely to pat some clay out over a smooth rock or press it into half a dried gourd, a basket, a broken pot, or even a hollow tree stump used as a **mold** (4-10). In order to keep the damp clay from sticking to this simple mold, the potter might have placed leaves or ashes under the clay (1-15). Special baked clay molds were sometimes used in which to form the base. In the Tewa culture of the American Southwest, these molds were called

puki, a word that has been adopted into our ceramics vocabulary.

Once a base was formed, the potter rolled out coils between her hands or on a flat surface and then attached them to the base to build up the walls. This is the most common pottery-building method still used in traditional cultures, and it was probably the most common one used by the Neolithic potter. Turning the pot constantly as the coils were added, she would push the coils together to make them stick to each other, smoothing them on the inside and outside as she went along (5-17). By doing this, the potter could not only shape the pot, but also could make the walls thinner and stronger by forcing the clay par-

Figure 1-15
Resting their pots on bases of grasses and leaves, potters in the Fiji Islands form them with flat slabs of clay, which they will later shape through paddling. The paddling will also meld the slabs together. *Courtesy Fiji Museum, Suva, Fiji.*

Figure 1-16
Once the pot is built, the potter pounds it into shape with a wooden paddle while holding a round stone against the inside of the walls. Sometimes wooden paddles are carved or wrapped with matting to produce a textured surface on the damp clay walls. *Courtesy Fiji Museum, Suva, Fiji.*

ticles together. Whether the pot was built up of coils or slabs, paddling also helped to force the clay particles together (1-16). Methods of coiling undoubtedly varied in different areas of the world just as they do today. In parts of Southeast Asia, for instance, instead of turning the pot itself, people in a line holding a long coil of clay walk around a pot placed on a stand, building the coil up into a spiral that is then pounded into shape. And in one area of Africa, a potter starts the pot in a hollow tree stump and then walks around it backwards adding the coils.

Sometimes, in the process of making a large pot through coiling, a potter might find that so much clay has been built up on the base that the walls have collapsed under its weight. As a solu-

tion, she might build up her next pot only part way, and set it aside to harden somewhat before adding more damp clay (4-9). Whatever the method of applying the coils, the process of coiling has played an important role in the history of ceramics and is still used by potters everywhere (11-18, 11-21, 11-26).

Finishing   As the coiled walls rose up under the potter's hands, she would thin the walls and scrape and smooth the inside and outside with a tool made from a natural material—perhaps a piece of dried gourd or a shell. Sometimes this was all the finishing that she would do to a pot before it was fired. But if the potter wanted an even smoother surface, she could **burnish** the

S H A P E

Once potters had learned to make basic vessels, they let their imaginations range, drawing ideas from the world around them to create an infinite variety of shapes. Some of the forms they developed were based on containers made from other materials (1-17). Some were humorous adaptations to specific functions (1-18). Still others resulted from the potter's sensitive attention to the relationship between the rim and base of a pot and the manner in which they both were related to the body of the pot (1-19).

The early potters who lived close to the earth, planting, reaping, sorting, and grinding their food, had responsive fingers, and their pottery reflected this sensitivity. Living in a world where nature was part of everyday life, they were also alert to the stances and movements of the animals that shared their lives, so they sometimes shaped their pots into simplified, exaggerated, or distorted images of those furred and feathered creatures (1-20, 1-21, 1-22). Animal vessels like these were often buried with the dead or used to hold liquid offerings at a grave. Even if the early potter was making a vessel that might hold a ritual libation, his work could still be lively and inventive within the limits set by tradition, showing keen observation and often humor.

Figure 1-17
A Bronze Age jar from Yortan, Anatolia, is shaped for safe carrying and the easy pouring of liquids. Its linear decoration was probably derived from the thongs or cords that were laced around gourds or pottery vessels in order to carry them. Ht. 9¾ in. 24.8 cm). Third millennium B.C. *Courtesy the Trustees of the British Museum, London.*

Figure 1-18
The shape of this earthenware feeding vessel is emphasized by the painted face, which must have helped a harried mother keep her child amused at mealtime. Cyprus, tenth or eleventh century B.C. *By courtesy of the Board of Trustees of the Victoria & Albert Museum.*

Figure 1-19
Mesopotamian potters made their urns and jars in a variety of shapes, many of them decorated with earth colors applied in bold linear patterns that accentuated the curves of the vessels. Ht. 4½ in. (11.5 cm). Nineveh, Mesopotamia, third millennium B.C. *Courtesy the Trustees of the British Museum, London.*

Figure 1-20
Bird-shaped pottery vessel from Africa—perhaps a guinea fowl? The neck of the lifelike bird forms the spout and its head becomes the vessel's stopper. Ht. 10 in. (25.4 cm). Suto, Lesotho. *Courtesy the Trustees of the British Museum, London.*

clay when it had stiffened but was still damp—a consistency called **leather hard.** To do this, the potter took a smooth pebble, a piece of bone, or a shell, and with rhythmic gestures stroked the surface of the pot, polishing the surface to a glossy finish. To burnish the surface of a pot made of coarse clay, the potter might paint the pot with a coating of fine clay soaked in water—called slip—and then burnish this to a smooth surface.

Burnishing forces the particles of clay on the surface closer together, while coating the pot with a finer slip before burnishing fills more of the pores. However, this treatment did not make low-fired earthenware impervious to water, because earthenware clay was not fired high enough to become impervious. In addition, in the early days of ceramics the technology of applying glazes that would seal the pores had not yet been developed.

Early potters used various methods to try to close the pores of the clay to make it more watertight or to give it a smooth surface on which to paint decoration. Sometimes, in an attempt to solve the problem of porosity, potters treated their fired pots with a mixture made by boiling certain plants; alternatively, they coated the still-hot pots with pitch from native trees. (This technique is believed to account for the origin of the retsina wine of Greece, which took on its pinelike taste when stored in jars coated with natural resin.) Cooking in earthenware over a period of time also helps to make it less porous, as does soaking it for a long time in water. The porosity of earthenware can, however, be an advantage in hot climates, where water is usually stored in unglazed earthenware jars so that evaporation through the pores of the clay cools it.

Figure 1-21
Although the legs of this bull-shaped vessel are stubby and the pouring spout eliminates the animal's features, an Amlash potter's depiction of the domesticated animal is lifelike. Ht 6⅞ in. (17.4 cm). First millennium B.C. *Courtesy the Trustees of the British Museum, London.*

Figure 1-22
Potters of the Old Silla dynasty in Korea frequently modeled vessels in the shape of animals or people. The realistic heads of these duck-shaped vessels rest on abstract bodies that served as stands. Fifth or sixth century A.D. *Courtesy National Museum of Korea, Seoul.*

Figure 1-23
The rough, decorative texture on the lower pot carried on the head of a Bozo woman from Mali was probably added to make it less slippery to lift when it was wet. *Courtesy National Museum of African Art, Eliot Elisofon Archives, Smithsonian Institution. Photo: Eliot Elisofon.*

Figure 1-24
Burnishing with a smooth stone while the clay is stiff but still damp gives the pot an attractive glossy surface. It also serves to press the clay particles together, making the earthenware less porous. Smooth stones, like the one this potter in Ndola, Zambia, is using, were treasured possessions, often handed down through several generations. Ndola Rural. Chipulukusu Compound. *Courtesy Zambia Information Services, Lusaka, Zambia.*

Decorating the damp clay   Some pots were left plain or burnished, but others were decorated with awareness, imagination, and restraint. The simplest decoration consisted of incised lines, scratched or punched while the clay was damp by means of natural tools chosen to achieve texture and pattern. A fingernail repeatedly pushed into the clay to form a design, holes poked into it with a stick, lumps or coils of clay pressed onto it, the serrated edge of a shell combed across it, a corn cob rolled over it—any of these methods might be

used on the damp clay. Sometimes this decorative texture served a function, as on a water vessel that would otherwise be slippery and difficult to carry when wet (1-23). Early potters had a keen sense of the relationship between a pot's decoration and its shape, often solving a basic design problem with discernment and obvious pleasure. For example, a potter in ancient Japan might decorate his pot with a combination of texture and carving (1-3), while a Bronze Age potter in Scotland might combine simple cross-hatching and hori-

Figure 1-25
Based on an Egyptian carving of the god Khum, this drawing shows him using an early kick wheel. Early myths from many cultures tell of gods or goddesses forming humans from clay, while others recount the discovery of pottery making in legendary terms.

DECORATION

Once a pot was finished, the potter often took the time to decorate it, especially if it was to be used for ritual or burial. Making art was not seen as an activity separate from daily life, and the impulse that led early humans to decorate their tools, their clothing, and even their bodies reached into every facet of life. Even the gods were not considered above working at the potter's craft; indeed, the Greeks believed that the goddess Athena taught them how to make pots, while the Egyptians honored the god Khum as the first potter (1-25). When clay crafters discovered that certain pigments could make colored decorations on their fired ware, they often washed their pottery over with a red color and painted it with geometric designs using various minerals. These early painted decorations ranged from stylized human figures, fishes, or birds in the Panpo culture of China to intricate abstract rosettes in Mesopotamia. Many of the early painted pots from widely separated cultures carry similar designs, leading some scholars to speculate about an as yet unconfirmed common decorative ancestry. It is possible that these symbols did have common origins, but more likely the shapes of the pots themselves suggested the motifs. There is a strong similarity among the spiral designs seen on pots around the world. Scratched on a pot in ancient Japan (1-3) or painted on an early Chinese (1-26) or Egyptian vessel before 3000 B.C. (1-27), or on a Cretan jar (1-28), the spirals could have had a religious significance, but it is also possible that the potters used these swirls and spirals because their rhythms were particularly appropriate to the curving profiles of the vessels.

zontal lines into effective decoration, or a woman in Africa might burnish a pot, using the same gesture that women potters there use today (1-24).

The scratched or applied decoration was enriched by the color of the clay body, which could range from buff to reddish, from light to dark brown, or from gray to black, depending on its mineral composition or the firing methods used. Some pots, owing to uneven firing, came out of the fire with dark and light red and black splotches on the outside, a decorative effect still sought by many potters.

Figure 1-26
Elegantly decorated with spirals painted in red and
black, this earthenware vessel was found in a
cemetery in Hanzu, China. Ht. 13 in. (33 cm). Pan
Shan culture, 2500–1500 B.C. *Courtesy Collection Haags
Gemeentemuseum, The Hague.*

Figure 1-27
Spirals of purple painted on its surface relate to the
bulbous shape of a pot made in Egypt sometime
before 3000 B.C. Ht. 7½ in. (19 cm). *Courtesy the
Trustees of the British Museum, London.*

Figure 1-28
The spiraling abstract, wavelike design on a large urn
from the palace at Phaistos carries our eyes around the
jar's form. Crete 2000–1700 B.C.

Figure 1-29
A clay disk is one of the earliest pottery-turning devices found. Used by a potter in Ur around 3500 B.C., it may have pivoted on an axle in a stone socket similar to those used today in Thrapsanon, Crete. Diameter 29½ in. (75 cm). *Courtesy the Trustees of the British Museum, London.*

Early Potter's Wheels

We have seen how early potters built up their pots with coils, shaping them as they turned them in their hands or on a base mold. To understand how the potter's wheel evolved, picture yourself kneeling or squatting in the sun outside a mud-daubed hut sometime around 6000 B.C., coiling a pot in your lap. Perhaps you have started the base in an old broken pot, and as you smooth the coils you turn it to keep the walls rising evenly all around it. Tiring of holding it, you might set the pot and base down on a stone, finding that you can turn it more easily there.

Eventually, someone had the idea of using two stones, the top stone revolving on the lower. Then it probably took several generations before someone thought of shaping the stones to fit together. Made from a smooth stone like ba-salt, such shaped turntables could revolve quite quickly and smoothly, making it much easier to coil, smooth, and polish a pot evenly (1-29). Other early turntables were made of stone, wood, or clay disks that revolved on wooden shafts fitted into a stone (1-30, 1-31).

At some point, a potter probably put an assistant to work spinning the turntable (2-15) and found that the work of shaping a pot became easier as the wheel revolved faster. A true potter's wheel must turn quickly enough—at least one hundred revolutions per minute—to give the necessary centrifugal force to the lump of clay so that only a comparatively light pressure of the hands is needed to make the walls rise. The main energy comes from the wheel rather than from the potter's hands.

The development of the potter's wheel was a technological advance of great importance, mark-

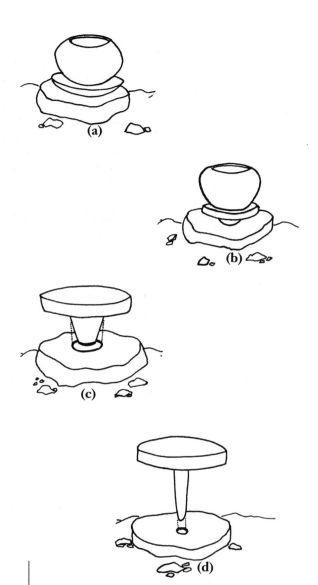

Figure 1-30

This stone pottery-wheel bearing would have turned a disk—probably made of clay or wood—on which a pot was placed, making the forming of the pot easier and quicker. Beth Shan, Israel, c. A.D. 500. *Courtesy Israel Department of Antiquities & Museums.*

ing the beginning of thrown as opposed to hand-built pottery. At some point—we don't know exactly where or when—the simple turntable evolved into a true potter's wheel. Neither do we know exactly what type of wheel it was or exactly when or where someone added a lower disk that could be kicked by the potter's foot to start it whirling. Archaeologists have studied the characteristic finger marks on pots thrown on true wheels and have set probable dates for the first known use of a kick wheel at around 3500 B.C. in Mesopotamia, 2300 B.C. in Sumer, and after 2750 B.C. in Egypt and China. Even with the introduction of this more efficient way to produce uniform pots, many potters continued to use turntables, and in some areas, such as preconquest America, the kick wheel was never used. Turntables are still used in many traditional potteries (2-5), and contemporary potters often use modern adaptations of them in handbuilding (11-22).

Figure 1-31

The diagram shows various types of turntables from a variety of cultures. **(a)** A broken bowl resting on a stone helps the potter turn the pot as it is built. **(b)** A specially shaped clay base swivels on a rounded protrusion. **(c)** A turntable with two stones shaped to fit together made it easier for the potter or an assistant to turn it. **(d)** Some village potters still use this type of turntable, which pivots on a wooden axle in a socket (2-5a).

Figure 1-32
Potters in Ogbomosho, Nigeria, warm their pots by burning straw in them before subjecting them to the heat of the fire. *Courtesy Field Museum of Natural History (Neg. #70026), Chicago.*

Firing

Whatever method was used to shape the vessel or sculpture, the piece eventually had to be fired before it would be changed permanently into ceramic. The earthenware clay used in ancient workshops was fired at a comparatively low temperature, reaching maturity in a relatively short time. This was due to the large amounts of iron in it that acted as a flux, making it possible for the refractory components to melt at a low temperature. Thus, it was the earthenware clay's natural mineral content that made it possible for early potters to develop their firing technology. Used throughout the world in most periods of history for making domestic ware, this low-fired clay body still supplies the bulk of cooking and storage containers in areas where industrial products have not taken over the potter's market.

Open firing The first earthenware was undoubtedly fired in **open firing,** or in pits, much as it is still done in villages in Africa (4-12), Fiji (1-33), and parts of the Middle East and the American Southwest (5-19). Before firing, the potter would have air dried the pots and perhaps, to speed the drying process and drive out all the water from the clay, would have burned dried grass or dung inside the containers (1-32). This process would also have heated the pots slowly, minimizing the **thermal shock** that could have caused them to crack in the fire.

Figure 1-33
The earliest potters undoubtedly fired their pots in open fires, just as many village potters do today, using a local source of fuel. In Fiji the pots are stacked together with palm fronds and grasses piled over them. Pots undergoing this type of firing can be damaged by gusts of wind that suddenly cause the fire to burn hotter. *Courtesy Fiji Museum, Suva, Fiji.*

Once the pots were thoroughly dry, they were stacked along with the fuel. This might be wood, dung, sugar cane, peat, rice straw, palm fronds, or any combustible material that could be gathered locally in the necessary quantity (1-33).

How to stack the pots, how much straw or wood to use, how long to burn the fire, when to cool the pots were all technical decisions that were worked out slowly through experimentation. A potter may have found that in her area the best time for firing was in the evening when the wind dropped or that a certain time of the year was best for digging the clay. This would become a habit and then a tradition unquestioned by potters of later generations. Similar empirically learned techniques have been the basis of the potter's craft throughout history, passed on within potting families and through the apprentice system.

Early kilns   Where the firing was done in pits instead of on top of the ground, the potters realized that they had more control over the fire, and found that wind was less of a problem. By 4000 B.C. in a Neolithic village in Panpo, China, the potters constructed perforated floors in their firing pits, which meant that the pots could be separated from the fire. The next step was to build clay walls up around the pits to shelter the fire more fully. This increased control of the fire and cut down on breakage owing to erratic winds that caused abrupt temperature changes. By around 2900 B.C., in what is now Israel, potters were building enclosed kilns. By the same date in China, a more efficient type of kiln was developed with a tunnel that led to a beehive-shaped chamber, creating a forced draft and resulting in an improved use of fuel. In Mesopotamia, kilns were built with domed roofs and perforated floors that gave potters still more control over the firing (1-34).

The earthenware fired in these early kilns was fired for varying periods of time, depending on fuel and kiln type and the number of pieces being fired. After the pots matured and the fire was allowed to die down, the pots were taken out and set aside to cool (5-8).

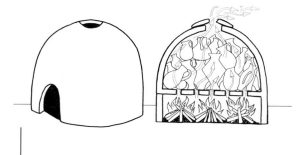

Figure 1-34
Potters in Mesopotamia around 4000 B.C. built vertical kilns that gave greater control over the fire. Similar kilns, in which the heat rises from a firing chamber under a perforated floor, are still used in Crete today (2-8).

EVOLVING TECHNIQUES

Because we must depend on excavations to supply information about early forming and firing methods, there are gaps in the story of the development of ceramics. Much of the story is built on conjecture based on studies of traditional methods still in use today, but one thing is certain—later generations of potters built directly on the discoveries made by the earliest potters. In this overview of the beginnings of ceramics, we have compressed thousands of years and the experiments of untold numbers of individual potters in isolated villages.

The techniques described evolved at different times and in different places. At times, the migrations of peoples or the capture of slaves would bring new potters into an area. They would then teach the local potters new techniques. New ideas were generally absorbed slowly, however, and it took hundreds of years for modifications and refinements to be developed. In some cultures, pottery techniques were so well adapted to the local needs and local ecology that the processes stayed the same almost indefinitely.

Our contemporary ceramics technology, which makes use of space-age kiln insulation and computer-controlled kilns, gives the modern potter a wider range of techniques and methods from which to choose than that open to our early potting ancestors, but no matter how complex modern ceramics has become, a handmade pot is still made of decomposed rock and is still formed by human fingers responding with sensitivity to the plastic quality of clay.

2
The Mediterranean World

Many of the Greek pot shapes remained essentially the same for centuries, because they were so well-suited to the needs of Greek society; and the potter thus had to express his changing sense of form through variations within a fairly narrow range.

Arthur Lane*

Famous black-figure amphora by potter-painter Exekias shows Achilles and Ajax playing a game during a lull in the siege of Troy. Exekias drew the detail on their flowered cloaks, the curls of their hair, and the decorated armor by scratching through the slip with a fine point, skillfully subordinating the detail to the dignified figures of the heroes and to the curving form of the vase. 540–530 B.C. *Courtesy the Vatican Museums.*

As early agricultural societies evolved into more complex ones, new skills and crafts emerged alongside the older crafts of weaving and pottery. In many cultures, metal working and ceramics developed around the same time, each borrowing techniques from the other. In fact, it has been suggested that the idea of using heat to produce workable metal may have occurred to an observant fire tender who saw how the impurities in

*Greek Pottery, Faber & Faber, London, 1947.

Figure 2-1
(a) In a potter's shop in ancient Egypt, workers mix the clay with their feet, while two apprentices load the vertical kiln. **(b)** A helper carries finished pots in baskets; at his feet another wedges more clay. The master potter appears to be removing a pot from a hump of clay on the wheel, steadying the turntable with his hand. **(c)** Two potters surrounded by finished ware form vessels. Mural in Tomb 2, Beni Hasan, Egypt, c. 1900 B.C. *Courtesy Library of the Egyptian Museum, Egyptian Service of Antiquities, Cairo.*

clay fused when the clay was fired. These technical developments in metallurgy and ceramics occurred at different times around the world. Clay techniques in the Orient, for example, quite often predated or paralleled those in the Mediterranean world, so we could equally well continue our survey of ceramic history there as in the Mediterranean area. However, since in the Western Hemisphere we have been accustomed to taking a Western-oriented approach to art history, it seems logical to start this historical survey with the Mediterranean cultures.

Once settled village life was well established around the shores of the Mediterranean Sea and on its many islands, trade routes developed, towns appeared along the trade routes, and kingdoms and empires grew, flourished, declined, and disappeared. On the mainland of western Asia, in the Fertile Crescent between the Tigris and Euphrates rivers, a succession of cultures built elaborate cities based on the irrigation of crops and on trade with neighboring communities, while along the Nile River, the Egyptians constructed temples and tombs using the labor of thousands of slaves.

In some of these areas where there was little good building stone, only sun-dried clay bricks were used for construction of temples and palaces, but in others fired and glazed clay tiles were applied to the surface to cover the sun-dried bricks. And throughout the Mediterranean area, potters continued to produce earthenware vessels for both ritual and domestic use. The surface of the pots was left plain on utilitarian ware and painted with earth colors when the vessels were made for ritual or aristocratic use.

EGYPT

In Egypt, pottery making was carried on in workshops under the supervision of master potters who formed the ware while their assistants mixed the clay, loaded the kilns, and stacked the fired ware (2-1). Since the pharoahs and priests used vessels of expensive alabaster or even gold rather than earthenware for their oils and perfumes, the bulk of the ceramic production was low-fired domestic ware for everyday use and vessels for storing the inventory of merchants and the wealth of the ruling class. Some small luxury items, however, glistened with a blue-green **glaze.**

Egyptian Glazes

The discovery that clay could assume such brilliance was Egypt's most important contribution to the story of ceramics. The potters there had, apparently accidentally, discovered the first ceramic glaze. Glazes are compounds of glass-forming minerals that fuse in the heat of the kiln and adhere to the clay body, coating it with what is essentially a thin layer of glass. Glazes, like clay, are of geological origin. They consist essentially of the refractories (heat-resistant materials) silica and alumina and a flux to make the ingredients fuse. Sand and flint (or quartz) are almost pure silica, and if they are heated to 3270°F/1798.8°C, they will fuse and form glass. At that temperature, however, the clay under them would also melt, so a flux is necessary to make lower firing feasible.

The very first Egyptian-glazed ceramics, known as Egyptian paste (or sometimes, incorrectly, as faience), were not coated with an applied glaze. Rather, the glaze was actually formed by ingredients in the clay body itself that were carried to the surface with the water as it evaporated, creating a shiny blue-green coating. This integral glaze was probably discovered by accident when desert sand containing soda ash and potash happened to be mixed into the clay as temper. When such a piece was fired, the **soluble** sodium would have fused with the glass-forming minerals in the sand, and particles of copper contained in the clay body would have given its characteristic color. Once this glaze-forming clay body was discovered and potters realized what caused the color to appear, the Egyptians learned to add alkaline salts deliberately to the clay body to produce the colored, glassy surface. Obtained in the lakes formed by the alkaline springs in the Nile Valley, the salts became an article of commerce whose revenues went to the pharoahs. The glaze-producing clay body was used mostly for small sculptures, ceremonial vessels, and jewelry, but given the number of these objects found in tombs, the revenues the pharoahs realized from the mining operations must have been considerable. The Egyptian method of making small objects with integral glazes became known through trade to the potters in Crete, where small statuettes, along with jewelry and luxury items, were made of the same type of clay body containing glass-forming minerals.

The Egyptians were expert at glass making, and it is possible that their first applied glazes were discovered when glass workers saw how the melted glass coated the pottery crucibles in which it was heated. By the middle of the second millenium B.C., the Egyptians had learned to apply an **alkaline glaze** that fired blue-green owing to the copper it contained, but since this applied alkaline glaze did not adhere well to the surface of fired clay or to the soapstone on which they also applied it, they used it only for small sculptures and other nonutilitarian objects. The Egyptian use of applied glaze probably became known through trade in western Asia, where the exploration of this technique was carried further.

WESTERN ASIA

Sun-baked, arid, but with fertile areas along its rivers, western Asia was a center of civilization from the earliest times. That the early peoples there gave an honored place to the malleable qualities of clay is testified to by the ancient *Poem of Creation*. In this work, the creation of men, deities, kings, mountains—in fact, everything—was ascribed to the god Ea, who pinched them out of clay.

From the most primitive sun-dried goddess figures (1-1, see also page 2 and 1-2) to domestic ware in a variety of shapes (1-17 to 1-19), and to tablets on which were recorded inventories of possessions, medical prescriptions (1-4), and even ceramic glaze formulas, the early societies of western Asia used clay for numerous objects, both domestic and ritual. Theories abound on how the knowledge of clay firing was discovered, but among many suggestions, a particularly logical one is that which suggests that the experience of drying and hardening clay bricks using the heat of the sun, along with the process of learning how to mix, form, and bake grains into bread in ovens, may have given humans in this area the necessary background to start developing ceramics technology. In addition, it has been suggested that since plaster was used to model vessels and skulls in this part of the world, the process of making plaster by heating gypsum, grinding it, then adding water to create a paste that could be shaped and dried may also have stimulated the development of ceramics. Whatever theories are put forward to explain how humans in western Asia first acquired a knowledge of ceramics, archaeological studies tell us that in several places there the firing of pottery had developed by at least 6500 B.C., and by around 4000 B.C. some form of potter's wheel was in use (1-29 to 1-31). It has also been suggested that the introduction of the wheel was the factor that transformed ceramics into a commercial venture rather than a home craft. In ad-

Figure 2-2
This is a detail of the Ishtar Gate, built in the sixth century B.C. in Babylon, as it is
now reconstructed in a German museum. Tile reliefs of bulls decorate the walls that led
along the processional approach to the gate. Tin-lead glazes. Babylon, c. 580 B.C.
Courtesy Staatliche Museum zu Berlin.

dition, as the demand for votive figures grew, the use of molds to produce them in quantity became common. Finally, the development of glass-making techniques led to the use of glazes on pottery, and by the middle of the second millenium B.C., western Asia had become a center of ceramics production. Even if the original discovery of glazes was an accident, their refinement was certainly a conscious effort. This is proved by the glaze formulas, along with instructions for applying them to **greenware,** that were carefully noted on clay tablets—the first potter's glaze notebooks. At the same time, increasing urbanization and wider trade introduced new ideas and new wares, while migrating ceramics workers brought their differing techniques to the cities in western Asia. It is a complex task beyond the scope of this survey to follow the distribution of the different types of pottery and their ornamental motifs as

they spread throughout western Asia, but there is no doubt that pottery traveled with the traders as they journeyed between towns along the caravan routes of Asia Minor.

Mesopotamian Architectural Ceramics

As early as 2600 B.C. even before glazes were developed, in Sumeria and Babylonia tubular pegs of fired clay painted with red, black, and white earth pigments were pushed into the mud walls of important buildings in geometric patterns to form mosaic patterns. Later, the sun-dried brick walls of Assyrian, Babylonian, and Persian buildings were covered with glazed tiles that protected them from weather and added colorful decoration (2-2). The application of color to the sur-

Figure 2-3
Homer described a circular dance, comparing the
velocity of the whirling men and women to the
motion of the potter's wheel. These Minoan dancers—
noblewomen or priestesses of the mother goddess—
may also portray the revolutions of the turntable that
formed Minoan pottery. Palaikastro, Crete, 1400–1100
B.C.

face of these tiles and bricks, on which humans,
lions, bulls, and mythical animals were modeled
in relief, depended on a knowledge of applied lead
and alkaline glazes, as opposed to the integral
glazes of Egypt. These glazed surfaces also required the addition of tin oxides to make the
glazes opaque. By using such a glaze on a brick
or tile, it was possible to cover the reddish color
of the earthenware, and the resulting **tin-glazed**
white opaque surface formed an excellent background for painted decoration. Once the Mesopotamian potters learned to add opacity and color
to glazes, they also began to use them on tiles,
separating the areas of the design with raised lines
of slip to keep the colors from running into each
other. The knowledge of how to make and glaze
tiles was handed down from generation to generation to become a notable aspect of Mohammedan
architecture (3-34), and in later centuries, as the
Moslems pushed into Africa and Spain, the use of
glazed tiles eventually reached Europe (6-2).

THE MINOANS

Situated as it is in the Mediterranean between
Egypt and western Asia, the island of Crete naturally developed a seagoing society. With a well-
disciplined navy, the island was safe from inva-
sion, so it enjoyed the peace that made it possible
for its inhabitants to develop an elaborate and sophisticated culture based on commercial relations
with its mainland neighbors. Influenced by artistic and religious ideas from both Egypt and Mesopotamia, this culture, called Minoan after Minos, one of its kings, lasted from around 2500 to
1100 B.C.

The early Cretans worshipped a mother goddess, made images of her in clay, left offerings to
her on decorated ceramic platters, and sculpted
clay figurines of her priestesses dancing a sacred
dance (2-3). Cretan women, at least those of the
upper classes, enjoyed more freedom than women
in other Mediterranean cultures, and took part in

ritual sports as well as dances. It is possible that they were also artists, making or at least decorating some of the ritual vessels.

The nobility lived luxurious lives in large palaces, whose rooms, arranged in a complex layout, were decorated with colorful murals. They also enjoyed such comforts as baths, which were hooked up to **terra-cotta** drainage systems, some of whose pipes can still be seen under the palace of Knossus. Also under the floors of the palace lay a vast subterranean storage area, where grain, oil, and other foodstuffs for the palace were stored in large jars, or *pithoi* (2-4). Many of these *pithoi* are still in place, testifying to the permanence of clay, for they survived the fire that destroyed the palace around 1450 B.C. The maze of storerooms that held these *pithoi* may have been the basis of the Greek belief in a labyrinth where the half-bull, half-human Minotaur roamed and roared, demanding human sacrifice. According to this legend, the monstrous creature demanded a yearly tribute of young men and women from mainland Greece. Finally, the Greek hero Theseus killed the Minotaur and rescued the captives by unwinding a ball of string as he penetrated the maze and then following the string back out to lead them to safety. In a folk dance still popular in Greece, a line of dancers winds in and out, supposedly representing Theseus leading the young men and women of Athens out of the Minotaur's labyrinth.

Not only can one see the ancient *pithoi* that survived the fire still in place in the storerooms at Knossus, but not far away in the hills is a monastery that still keeps the olive oil it produces in similar, more recently made *pithoi*. These jars, taller than people, were made about fifty years ago in the nearby village of Thrapsanon, where some potters still use techniques that are the same as or similar to those in use on Crete around 1400 B.C.

Cretan Pottery-Building Techniques

Thrapsanon has been a potter's village for generations. One of the older monks in the monastery remembers that fifty years ago more than one hundred potters were building the *pithoi*

Figure 2-4

Storage jars, called *pithoi*, still in place in the storerooms of the royal palace at Knossos, Crete, once held grain, oil, and apparently honey. According to legend, the young son of King Minos died by falling into a jar of honey; he was found with only his legs sticking out. The *pithoi* were built up with coils in six bands. Note the applied coils pressed on with the potter's thumb that mark the joints. Knossos, Crete, c. 1400 B.C.

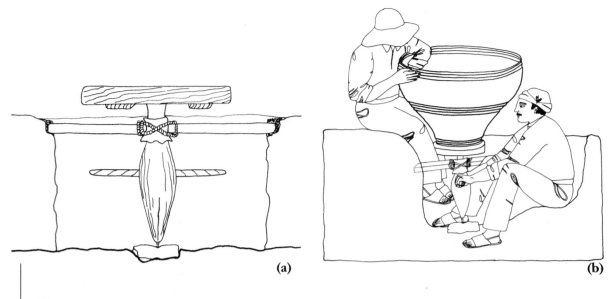

(a)

(b)

Figure 2-5
(a) Detail of the wheel and axle of a turntable used today on Crete. Braced by a cross-piece of wood resting on the sides of the trench, the axle passes through a notch in the plank. **(b)** The assistant, sitting at the bottom of the trench, turns the wheel. As the jar grows, the master potter sits higher, finally standing to shape the last band.
Drawings based on observation and on the article, "The Potters of Thrapsano," by Maria Voyatzoglou in Ceramic Review *(November-December 1973).*

there. Nowadays only a small group of potters still builds these jars on turntables and fires them in vertical kilns similar to the ancient ones. During the cool months of the year, the potters work indoors making thrown domestic ware, but in June they move out into the fields near the kiln to make smaller versions of the thick-walled ancient storage jars.

Revolved by an assistant who sits on a trench at the potter's feet, the turntable on which a modern jar is built consists of a disk of moisture-resistant plane wood that rotates on an axle of olive wood, which, after becoming smooth from the friction, revolves quite easily (2-5a). These contemporary wheels may well be modeled on the ancient ones. A Cretan potter's wheel dating from 1700–1450 B.C. in the Heraclion Museum consists of a clay disk with a socket in the underside into which a wooden axle would have been fitted, probably revolving in a stone socket just as the Thrapsanon ones do today.

Continuing Traditions

Thrapsanon potters work in teams. After a row of the pots has been started, an assistant moves along from one turntable to another, adding new coils to each pot as the first section hardens somewhat. Then the master potter progresses along the row, working on the jars in succession, sitting on the edge of the trench while an assistant turns the wheel (2-5b). These wheels do not revolve fast enough to allow the clay to be centered and the walls to be raised by centrifugal force, so the master must pull up and smooth out the coils, forming one section on a jar, then moving along the trench to another wheel. When he has completed a section on all the jars, the first ones are usually stiff enough for him to start over again to add another section. Just as the ancient *pithoi* were built in six sections, so are the present-day versions, with an extra coil added at each seam to

Figure 2-6
In Thrapsanon, potters still make large storage jars, working outdoors on turntables set in trenches. Like the earlier ones, the jars are built up in sections by an assistant, followed by the master potter who shapes and completes the pot with six bands.

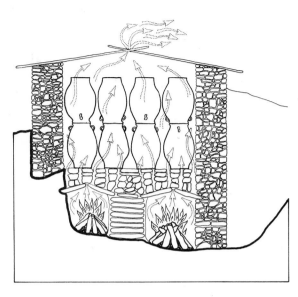

Figure 2-7
A schematic diagram of a Cretan kiln in use today shows the cylindrical form typical of the kilns of ancient Mesopotamia. Minoan potters who made the *pithoi* in the Palace at Knossos probably fired their jars in kilns like this, using shards of pottery instead of sheet metal to close the top. *Drawing based on observation and on information in the article "The Potters of Thrapsano," by Maria Voyatzoglou in* Ceramic Review *(November-December 1973).*

strengthen the wall at that vulnerable point (2-4, 2-6).

When a row of jars is completed, handles are added and designs may be scratched into the walls. The pots are then left to harden, and by the next day they are usually stiff enough to be removed from the turntables. Placed in the hot sun, they are left until they are thoroughly dry, ready for firing in the kiln (2-7).

The Cretan Firing Method

As soon as enough jars have been made to fill a kiln, they are fired in a vertical kiln that is basi-cally the same as those used in most ancient Mediterranean cultures (2-8). Made of rocks smeared with heavily tempered refractory clay, the modern kiln is sunk into the ground with a perforated clay floor above the **firebox.** Access to the firebox is down a sloping trench at the back, giving the stoker access to feed dry brushwood through an opening in the wall. The fire is started in the early afternoon and is tended carefully until the firing is completed around sunset (2-8).

This method of building and firing the large jars is the result of empirical knowledge built up over generations, possibly going back as far as 2000 B.C. The young boys helping in the work-shops today are learning the craft through expe-

Figure 2-8
The front of a kiln at Thrapsanon, Crete. Built of stones covered with clay, it is basically a vertical cylinder sunk into the ground. The opening in front that allows loading of the large jars will be closed with stones and clay after the kiln is full. The heat rises from the fire pit through holes in the floor. A stoker adds wood through a hole at the back for the firing, the duration of which depends upon the size and number of jars. Thrapsanon, Crete.

rience just as potters have always learned their craft. Hopefully, some of them will keep the tradition alive, leaving their own thumbprints in the clay to be found by future archaeologists.

Minoan Decorated Pottery

The potters in ancient Crete not only made tall storage jars, but Minoan potters in various parts of the island also created elegant utensils and containers in startling variety, forming clay into objects for purposes that ranged from "teapots" with strainers for preparing infusions of herbs, to low tables on which offerings were left for the sacred snake who protected the household, to graceful vases decorated with paintings of sea creatures or plant forms (2-9, 2-10).

The nature-loving Minoans drew inspiration from living forms, translating them into decorations that they applied to their vessels after firing. Freely drawn and painted with black, white, and earth pigments, the palm trees, octopuses, flowers, leaves, dolphins, and shells were sometimes simplified and sometimes contorted (2-10) to accentuate the curves of the vases and jars. Although at times the decoration becomes so overwhelming that it distracts the eye from the shape of the vessel, at its best it is flowing and harmonious, expressing the Minoan love of bright colors, luxury, and the rhythms of the dance.

Around 1450 B.C., the sophisticated Minoan civilization either fell to invaders or was destroyed by a natural disaster. Knossus was destroyed by fire and the huge *pithoi* in the palace were buried until they were unearthed again in the 1920s. After the disaster, Crete lost its powerful position, and Mycenae became the dominant state in the Aegean for the next two hundred or more years.

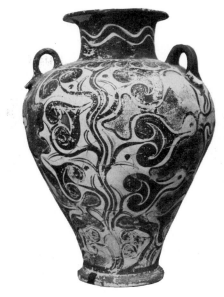

Figure 2-10

Made and painted during the later period of Minoan art, just before the disaster that destroyed the palace, this Minoan vase is almost overwhelmed by the nervously twining decoration applied over its handsome shape. 1700–1450 B.C.

Figure 2-9

The palm trees decorating this Minoan *pithos* from the palace at Knossos are outlined with red against a solid background. With their curving fronds emphasizing the swell of its body, the vessel exhibits the love of nature and the vitality so typical of Minoan pottery. Made in one of the potters' workshops at Knossos between 2000 and 1700 B.C.

MYCENAE

The Mycenaeans, named for one of their massive palace-citadels on the Greek Peloponnesus, were influenced by the art of the Minoans (2-11), but the essence of their aggressive military society is probably best illustrated by the lines of marching soldiers on the *Warrior Vase* (2-12).

The king, or overlord, of the commercial town of Mycenae lived in the fortress-palace on the top of a hill overlooking the Argive Plain. In the workshops surrounding the palace, potters, goldsmiths, and armorers produced decorated vases, rich golden cups, and beautifully inlaid bronze weapons for royal use or for burials. But, along with these luxury goods, Mycenae also de-

Figure 2-11

Octopuses encircle the curving form of a vessel either made in Crete and exported to Mycenae or made by local Mycenaean potters influenced by Cretan styles. 1450–1400 B.C. *Courtesy the National Archeological Museum, Athens.*

Figure 2-12
The Mycenaean *Warrior Vase* shows soldiers marching in full war gear with shields, spears, and plumed helmets, while the female figure on the left stands with her hands over her head in the traditional Greek pose of grief. Compared with the Minoan urns, this vessel's decoration illustrates the profound contrast between the peaceful Minoan culture and the aggressive Mycenaean society. 1300–1200 B.C.
Courtesy the National Archeological Museum, Athens.

pended on the potters to supply storage jars and their accompanying inscribed tablets for the palace storerooms or for the warehouses containing the commodities of the wealthy merchants. Since the powerful Mycenaeans held territorial and trading rights throughout what later became Greece, and even on the mainland of Asia Minor, it may well be that the Trojan War was really fought for strategic and commercial reasons rather than, as Homer tells it, to rescue Helen, the beautiful wife of Menelaus.

In about 200 B.C., the great Mycenaean citadels fell in their turn to Doric invaders, and the area that later became Greece entered a period of disruption characterized by waves of migrations. The armored men painted on the *Warrior Vase* vividly portray the type of soldiers who tried with little success to hold back these invasions. Life became unsettled, and the only record we have of this period is in its pottery. But, as often happens, the influx of new races that eventually melded with the existing inhabitants of the mainland had a stimulating effect. From the chaos a new civilization emerged, one that was to have a profound effect on the history of the Western world.

GREECE

It is apparent from Greek legends and mythology that clay held an important place in early Greek life. For instance, according to a legendary explanation of the beauty of Greek pottery shapes, the first ceramic wine cup was molded over the breast of the beautiful Helen of Troy. Mythology also tells us that the goddess Athena was the inventor of many useful articles, including the earthenware pot, and that when Prometheus, at war with the Titans, turned to her for help, she fashioned soldiers out of clay and brought them to life to help Prometheus defeat his enemies. Clearly, the early Greeks recognized clay's special qualities, and Athenian potters lived up to the reputation of their patroness, Athena, for under her patronage they created some of the world's most admired pottery.

The type of vertical kiln in which early Greek ceramists fired their wares was probably brought there by potters from Asia Minor, an area with which Greece had strong ties and whose decorative motifs Athenian potters adapted to their work. Later, the Greeks refined the kilns by adding a side tunnel to hold the fire so that the heat, but not the flames, would reach the pottery. We do not know when the kick wheel was introduced into Greece, but turntables were efficient enough there by 800 B.C. for the potters to build huge vases (2-13).

Greek Geometric Style

More than four feet tall, the Geometric-period urns are a testament to the shaping and firing skill of the early potters (2-14). Called Geometric because of their stylized painted decoration, these vessels represent a remarkable technical achievement.

It is clear that the potters now had the technical knowledge and skill to produce magnificently shaped pottery, so when Greece began to recover from the effects of the disruptions, the pottery industry expanded rapidly (2-15). Corinth, which was located near beds of white and cream-colored clay, was the first big ceramic center in early Greece, but by around 550 B.C., the potters of Athens had surpassed those of Corinth,

Figure 2-13
A large Geometric-style urn depicts warriors and chariots in a funeral procession. Tall urns decorated in this manner were placed on graves in the Athenian Diplyon Cemetery, where they served as memorials as well as ritual vessels. The decorator's brushstrokes are clearly visible, filling in the solid black, detailing the manes of the horses, and creating ornament on the chariots and bands of abstract decoration. *Courtesy the National Archeological Museum, Athens.*

Figure 2-14
On this huge Geometric krater, the figure of the deceased is shown lying in state, surrounded by followers in the characteristic mourning pose. Amidst the pomp of the funeral ritual, the seated woman and child and the domestic animals are a sad, homely touch. Eighth century B.C. *All rights reserved, the Metropolitan Museum of Art, Rogers Fund, 1914 (14.130.14).*

DECORATION

The decoration used on the Geometric urns was totally different from the flowing forms painted on Minoan ceramics. Deceptively simple and abstracted, it showed a new sense of discipline and an intellectual approach to design. It is clear that the person who painted these alternating bands of abstract decoration and human figures approached the design rationally, carefully choosing the placement that would best emphasize the impressive shape and size of the vessel. No decoration could have accomplished this better than the simple patterns and rows of severe figures that encircle them. Although the scenes of funeral processions in the areas between the bands of meanders, zigzags, and diamond patterns project a strong emotional quality, its expression is subordinated to the structure of the vessel, and does not destroy the successful relationship between shape and ornament. In this rational, carefully thought out Geometric pottery (2-13, 2-14), we can see the developing characteristics of later Greek art.

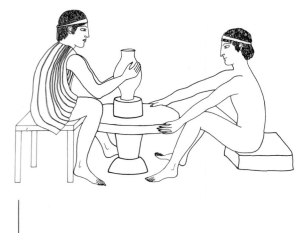

Figure 2-15
A Greek potter works on a wheel rotated by an assistant in about 600 B.C. According to legend, Talos, nephew and apprentice of the Greek craftsman Daedalus, invented the potter's wheel, whereupon Daedalus became so jealous that he pushed Talos off the rock of the Acropolis in Athens.

and Athens became the main Greek ceramics center. From that time on, through the Golden Age to the last days of the Roman Empire, the greatest vase makers in the Mediterranean world were the Greeks, and their wares would be transported throughout the Eastern world and into Europe. Greek **amphorae,** containing wine, have been found in sunken ships off Southern France, while the greatest amount of Greek pottery ever found has actually been unearthed at various sites on the mainland of Italy, where many of the most beautiful Athenian vases were sent as export items. The excavations of the port of Spina on the Adriatic coast of Italy, long hidden under a lagoon and marsh, uncovered hundreds of intact Greek vessels.

Athenian Pottery

Athenian potters worked in a quarter of Athens called the Kerameiskos, located near large deposits of clay, or **keramos,** from which our word *ceramics* is derived. Most of the master potters

who worked there were foreigners, drawn to Athens from all parts of the Mediterranean. As the ceramics center of their world, Athens offered these potters the opportunity to make a good living. Working alongside each other and exchanging knowledge and techniques, these potters who came from many cultures melded ideas and styles from many sources, thereby enriching the craft of pottery in Greece as well as influencing the art of painting there. Here, in the Kerameiskos, pottery production was organized into a factorylike situation—in some of the potters' shops, as many as seventy assistants worked under the master potter who owned the business. Working on a wheel propelled by an assistant, the master potter probably filled the most important orders for nonutilitarian vases himself (2-16). If they were to be especially large, he would make them in sections and then attach the parts with slip—a process called luting.

The celebrities of the day—political, sports, and theater figures—would visit the most famous potters' shops to order vases celebrating a ritual dance (2-17) commemorating a victory, the death of an important person, or honoring the winner

38

Figure 2-16
In this portrait of the potter at work in his shop, painted on the interior of a black-figure cup in the beginning of the fifth century B.C., he is shown sitting on a low stool, apparently adding handles to the wine cup on his turntable. *Courtesy the Trustees of the British Museum, London.*

Figure 2-17
Dionysus was the Greek god of wine, so the festival of Dionysus was a popular theme of decorations on drinking cups such as this black-figure *kylix*. Originally religious rituals, Dionysian festivals were later performed in theaters with actors portraying the god, his attendant satyrs, and maenads; from them developed the classic Greek theater. *Photo: Hannibal, Athens.*

SHAPE

The master potters of Greece in the classical period continued to create the traditional Geometric shapes, refining them and developing new vessel forms to be used for such diverse purposes as flasks to contain the oil that athletes rubbed into their skin; flaring bowls, or kylix, used for drinking wine mixed with water; and oinochoe, jugs used for pouring. As time went on, the shapes of the new vessels in turn became traditional, and the thousands of vessels produced by Greek potters rarely varied from these basic forms. This meant that the skill of the potter was concentrated on refining the vessel forms to their ultimate elegance. The potter even followed a prescribed shape when making utilitarian pots like the amphorae that carried oil and wine to the colonies, forming pots that were not only well-adapted to their use but also graceful and attractive. So successfully were the traditional shapes delineated that only rarely does one see an awkward vessel or one whose form seems inappropriate to its use. Actually, most of the Athenian decorated pottery was intended not for its original utilitarian use, but for memorial, display, or commemorative purposes. These display vases were avidly collected by the well-to-do in both Italy and Greece and were prized for their elegant forms as well as for the paintings on them. The paintings themselves, at least those by the best artists, respected the shapes of the vessels, enhancing rather than disrupting their forms.

These traditional vase shapes first formed by potters near the clay pits of Athens have become part of our Western heritage (6-18), and to this day some of the basic Greek pottery shapes are reinterpreted successfully by contemporary potters (12-2).

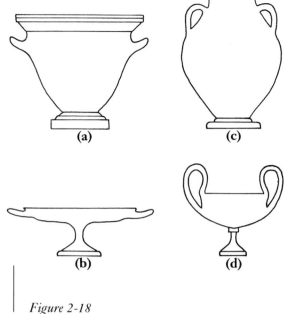

Figure 2-18

Some of the many shapes so skillfully formed by the potters of classic Greece. **(a)** The *amphora*, generally oval-shaped, with a narrow mouth and a small lid, was used for carrying liquids. *Amphorae* were used as prizes for winners of athletic and drama contests. **(b)** The *kylix*, a drinking cup, was used for wine mixed with water. **(c)** The *krater*, whose shape and handle position varied, was used for mixing wine and water. Its wide mouth made blending easy. **(d)** The *cantharus* was a globlet with high, curved, exaggerated handles.

of an Olympic contest (2-18). Now, for the first time, individual artists signed their pottery, and because many vessels bear inscriptions such as "Exekias made and painted this", (page 26) we know that some of the accomplished painters were also master potters, who often became as famous as the star athletes. It is also known that although the commemorative vases and cups were made by men, some of the painters who decorated them were women.

Black-Figure Pottery

Developed originally in Corinth, a new decorative style called **black figure** became popular by the end of the seventh century B.C. In this style, the figures were painted on the light clay body with a specially formulated slip. The artist drew in details of clothing and features by scratching lines through the slip with a sharp instrument, revealing the lighter color of the clay beneath. The new style was soon taken over by Athenian potters, who refined it and quickly captured the export market for this type of pottery.

Firing process   The firing process used to achieve the contrast between the black figures and the buff or reddish background was a complex one. The specially formulated slip with which the figures were painted contained iron oxide that turned black when fired in a **reduction** atmosphere. The black and red colors were the result of a single firing in which reducing and oxidizing atmospheres were produced alternately in the kiln (2-19). Reduction occurs when a fire is smothered and the flame does not get enough oxygen to burn freely. In an attempt to get more oxygen, the flame will draw oxygen from the metal oxides in the clay, and in so doing will release the metal and change its color. To achieve black-figure decoration, the Greek potter first fired the pottery in an oxidizing atmosphere in which the flame burned freely, firing the clay to its natural reddish color. The artist then smothered the kiln chamber to create a reduction atmosphere, which turned the painted-on slip black. If the slip had been correctly formulated, the slip-covered areas remained black when the kiln was returned to an oxidizing atmosphere while the uncovered areas came from the kiln the reddish or buff tone of fired earthenware clay. The glossy brilliance of the black that is such a feature of these Greek vessels resulted from the beginnings of vitrification in the fine slip under the action of an alkali such as wood **ash.** This method requires great care and control of the firing, since the pot can turn completely black if the kiln is not oxidized at the right time.

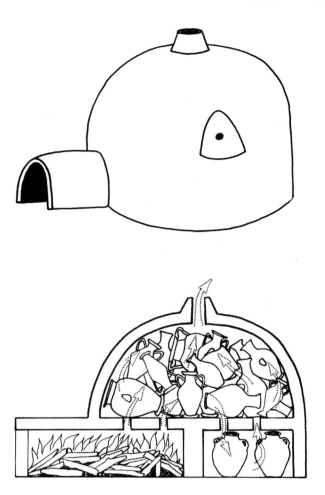

Figure 2-19
Greek kilns were built in a beehive shape with a tunnel at the side for the fire and a vent on the top to control the draft. Paintings on pottery show potters opening or closing the vent to change the kiln atmosphere in order to create the black and red decoration on the pottery.

Red-Figure Pottery

Around 525 B.C., vessels painted in a new style appeared in Athens. These were created with what is called a **reserve** (not reverse) pro-

Figure 2-20
When painting the red-figured pottery, the decorators painted around the figures, leaving them the natural red of the fired clay. Now the lines were painted with a fine brush. On this stamnos, probably a presentation piece, Odysseus is shown resisting the song of the Sirens. He first stuffed his crew's ears with wax and then bid them tie him to the mast so he would not be lured onto the rocks by the Sirens flying above the ship. Ht. 13⅞ in. (35.2 cm). Vulci, c. 490–489 B.C. *Courtesy the Trustees of the British Museum, London.*

cess. In it, the black-firing slip was painted *around* the figures, thus reserving the color of the red clay for the figures themselves (2-20). When the vessel was fired and the background slip became a lustrous black, the red figures stood out in contrast. To intensify the red tone of the figures, the artist sometimes first coated the vase with a wash of iron or a thin iron-laden slip. Within the red figures, the details of faces, bodies, clothing, and armor were painted with thin black lines, for which the painter used a single-haired brush. Once it was painted, the pottery was fired in alternating reduction and oxidation atmospheres, the same technique as that used for black figure pottery.

Early Greek Architectural Ceramics

Greek ceramicists did not limit themselves to producing elegant presentation vessels; they also used clay for more practical purposes. One of these was the protection of the wooden structure of early temples. The early builders sheathed the ends of the wooden roof beams with terra-cotta tiles vertically grooved to allow rainwater to run down off them. Between the beams and alternating with the grooved tiles, ungrooved terra-cotta tablets displayed painted designs. Both these features were later copied in marble in the sculpture-decorated metopes and grooved triglyphs of the classic temples. The gable fronts of the early temples were also decorated with sculptures modeled in clay—forerunners of later marble sculptures—and the cult images inside the temples representing the gods or goddesses to whom the temples were dedicated were also made of clay. Built up with coils and wads, these sculptures were fired, then painted in realistic colors. Not many examples of sculptured decorations from the early temples have been uncovered in Greece, but a number have been found in excavations in the Greek colonies in Sicily and southern Italy. The painted terra-cotta antefixes along the ends of the tiled courses on the sides of the roofs, the large in-the-round sculptures at the apex of the roof called acroteria, and the brilliantly painted figures in the gable ends were all features of early Greek temples that would later be copied and exaggerated by Etruscan sculptors and builders (2-24).

Terra-Cotta Figurines

Beginning with the earliest small votive offerings formed of slabs, then progressing to handformed in-the-round representations of gods, goddesses, and heroes and the mass-produced Tanagra figurines, for centuries Greek potters had been creating a profusion of small terra-cotta figurines from which we can envision a vivid picture of life in Greece. At first handformed, the Tanagra figures were later produced in quantity through the use of **press molds.** These were negative molds made by stamping an impression into damp clay using the fired original. The resulting negative was then fired to harden the mold. Next, a slab of damp clay was pressed into the mold to create a positive reproduction of the image. Sometimes as many as fourteen molds were used to make one figurine, and parts of figurines were often interchanged to vary the pose. All the figures were brightly painted after firing, and some still show traces of that color. From the fourth century B.C. on, quantities of these figures made in the mainland pottery centers of Boetia were sent to the Greek colonies in Italy and Sicily and to Asia Minor, where there was a large market for them. In fact, the molds themselves were sent abroad, where the ones made by well-known mainland potters and sculptors were sold for extremely high prices. In this way, a potter in Sicily using molds sent from Athens could produce figurines of popular actors playing in the latest comedy by Aristophanes (2-21). However, although a potter in Asia Minor could make a figure that looked exactly like a Tanagra product, experts today can determine a figure's origin by analyzing the makeup of the clay or the type of temper used.

In addition to the comedy figures, graceful figurines of women dancing, arranging their hair, gossiping, and caring for children were also in demand. These give us a glimpse into the sheltered life of Greek women. Because dance and song were important aspects of Greek life, and because religious observances frequently included dances, figurines of women, perhaps inspired by (2-22) girls dancing at dawn to honor a goddess, or a chorus singing and dancing in praise of a god at his sanctuary were favorite subjects with artists. Even in these small sculptures, we can see the grace, elegance, and dignity so characteristic of Greek classic art.

Terra-cotta reliefs that were also mass-produced in molds apparently played the same role for the Greeks as inexpensive art reproductions do in modern life, for they were used in homes as decoration, as well as in temples as votive offerings. They, too, show us how the Greeks lived—a cook in her kitchen, a housewife putting folded garments away in a chest and heroes and athletes achieving feats of bravery and skill. During the Hellenistic Period, in the final days of the Greek primacy in the Mediterranean, the small sculptures, like large marble sculptures, became more realistic. There was a growing taste for portraiture and images of deformed or crippled persons, sculpted with devastating realism.

Figure 2-21
Comic terra-cotta figures from the theater were extremely popular in Greece, where comedies were broad and earthy. Actors' figures were often distorted with padded tights and jerkins. Here two actors portray drunken old men. Middle of the fourth century B.C. *Courtesy Staatliche Museen zu Berlin.*

Figure 2-22
The freedom of action typical of later Greek sculpture is shown in this figure of a dancing woman. Called Tanagra for the town in Greece where they were made, figurines like this one were also copied in the colonies, using molds bought from master Tanagra potters. Arms and heads were often interchanged and attached with slip to vary the gestures or poses, and sometimes as many as fourteen molds were used. All were painted in lifelike colors after firing. Ht. 10½ in. (26.7 cm). Second century B.C. *Courtesy the Trustees of the British Museum, London.*

Greek Influences Abroad

As we have seen, Greece extended her colonies and trading networks all over the Mediterranean, using her famous ships to carry conquering soldiers, traders, colonists, and Athenian pottery to distant ports. Greek contact with Italy had begun early—Mycenae traded with southern Italy as early as 1400 B.C.—and Greek traders were attracted to central Italy by the metal ore of the region's mines as well as by the timber of its forests. The Greek ships carried in them the best productions of the Corinthian and Athenian potteries, and prominent local officials in far-flung colonies proudly added these works to their collections. Greek potters also sailed aboard the ships, carrying with them their knowledge of clay techniques. In southern Italy, these potters developed a flourishing industry, and the vases and sculpture they produced were traded throughout the Italian peninsula; thus, were Greek ceramics brought in quantity to the Etruscan inhabitants of central Italy.

THE ETRUSCANS

The origin of the Etruscans has long remained a mystery. Some scholars have believed they emigrated from Asia Minor; some say they came from Egypt. Other suggest that the Etruscans were Indo-Europeans who came down from the north, and still others that they were indigenous to Italy. Whatever their origin may finally prove to have been, the Etruscans adopted and profited from ideas and techniques from many different sources, including the local farming peoples of Italy who may actually have been their ancestors. These farmers—called Villanovans, for the name of the town where objects from their culture were first excavated—had used clay molds to produce metal tools and agricultural implements, had buried the ashes of their dead in clay pots with helmetlike covers, and had also used earthenware clay for domestic vessels. Like the Villanovans, the vigorous, commercially oriented Etruscans also made use of Italy's rich natural resources, developing a metal industry whose smelting furnaces polluted the air around their industrial towns. Drawing inspiration from Greek religion and mythology, they also absorbed Greek ceramics technology. Adapting the imaginary animals, sphinxes, winged bulls, and griffons of Asia Minor to their own uses (2-23) and merging these influences with their own inventive and artistic vitality, they created a characteristic art that reached its peak between 700 and 400 B.C.

Etruscan art expressed an unrestrained love of life and its pleasures along with a cheerful attitude toward death and the afterlife. Their tombs, painted with scenes of men and women whirling in ritual dances and enjoying funeral banquets, are joyous rather than sad. Suggesting a celebration of life, they contrast vividly with the solemnity of the mourning scenes on the Greek Geometric-style vases (2-14).

Etruscan Clay Sculpture

The local clay from the fertile earth of Etruria was regarded by the Etruscans as a noble material. Perhaps because clay is a medium that encourages spontaneity and immediacy, it was particularly well suited to the exuberant Etruscan temperament. When their sculptors used it for the life-sized figures that decorated hilltop temples, they manipulated the clay vigorously, expressing the intensity of feeling characteristic of the Etruscan people. Because fired clay was an excellent material on which to paint, it was also an appropriate material on which the Etruscans could exhibit their love of color and surface decoration. Always brightly painted, their sculpture was sometimes heroic, sometimes comic, sometimes tender, and at other times demonic (2-24).

Etruscan Architectural Sculpture

Etruscan architectural sculpture, like the early Greek architectural sculpture from which it developed, was used to cover the wooden structure of temples and other buildings. At the excavations of Estruscan Misa, outside present-day Bologna, excavators unearthed the terra-cotta facings of the building that had enclosed the sacred spring. These architectural components had probably been made in the potter's shop that was also excavated there. The well-organized shop had contained storage bins for clay and piping that

Figure 2-23
The animal-head pouring spout of this thick-walled, highly polished jug exhibits the characteristic Etruscan taste for fantasy. The jug's decoration also shows the influence of Greek myths on the potters of Etruria: Hercules is shown capturing the Cretan bull that the god Posieden had given to Minos. The jug was formed of the *buccero* clay from Spain that was said to give a pleasant fragrance to liquids stored in containers made of it. Sixth to fifth century B.C. Archaeological Museum, Florence. *Courtesy Superintendent of Antiquities, Florence.*

Figure 2-24
Usually Etruscan antefixes were surrounded by
brightly painted shells to increase their size. This one
is typical of those placed along the edge of temple
roofs to mask and protect the ends of the tiles. The
hideous Gorgon, Medusa, was a favorite subject for
terra-cotta temple decorations. From the Temple of
Apollo, Veii, sixth to fifth centuries B.C. Museo di
Villa Giulia, Rome. *Courtesy Alinari-Art Reference
Bureau.*

brought water into the shop from quite a distance,
indicating its importance to the community.

One suspects that the Etruscans continued to
use clay long after the Greeks had begun building
with stone rather than wood because they felt
particularly at home with clay—in fact, even
when the Etruscans occasionally built stone temples, they sometimes attached terra-cotta decorations to them.

A typical Etruscan temple would be decorated with rows of standing figures along its roof-
line (2-25), a figure on horseback or in a chariot
behind four horses at the gable peak, human or
demon faces on **antefixes** at the ends of the roof
tiles, and a sculptured group in the pediment, all
of them painted with blue, purplish black, and
liberal amounts of red. The antefixes were often
in the shape of a Gorgon's face. The Gorgons, of
whom Medusa (2-24) was the most famous, were

Figure 2-26
Found in a tomb in fragments, this famous
Sarcophagus of a Married Couple was built in two
parts. Fired and originally brightly painted, it is
shown here as it was first repaired but unrestored. 55
in. (140 cm) Cerveteri, sixth century B.C. Museo
Nazionale di Villa Giulia, Rome. *Courtesy Alinari-Art
Reference Bureau.*

◄   *Figure 2-25*
Vulca, a famous Etruscan sculptor, made this free-
standing, brightly painted figure of Apollo. Fired in
one piece, with an opening in back to allow for vapor
escape, it was part of a life-sized group that once
stood on the roof of the Temple of Apollo at Veii
depicting the conflict between Hercules and Apollo
over a stag sacred to Artemis. The decorated shape
between the legs was necessary to support the striding
figure. Ht. 68½ in. (175 cm). Veii, 510 B.C. Museo
Nazionale di Villa Giulia, Rome. *Courtesy Anderson-
Art Reference Bureau.*

capable of turning humans to stone merely by
looking at them. It is an interesting sidelight that
in Greece and Greek Italy, a Gorgon mask was
always hung over a kiln (as well as a bread oven)
to deter the inquisitive.

In addition to the temple figures, the sculptors also modeled life-sized terra-cotta figures of
the dead for the coffins of the rich. These figures
on the sarcophagi were painted realistically, while
the side panels frequently carried mold-formed
reliefs of battles and heroic deeds. Some of the
figures on the sarcophagi are obviously stock figures, personalized only by an added portrait
head, but many are individually sculpted figures,
portraying nobles on banquet couches.

For an Etruscan who could afford to have an
individually made sarcophagus, the sculptor
Vulca from Veii made one of the great works of
Etruscan art, the *Sarcophagus of the Married Couple*
(2-26, 2-27). On it a man and his wife recline together on their banquet bench in an affectionate
pose that suggests not only their close relationship, but also the equal position of men and
women in Etruscan society. In contrast, in Greece
and Rome wives never attended banquets.

Later Etruscan sculptors, influenced by Hellenistic Greek art, became increasingly interested
in portraiture, and lifelike representations of bald,
obese individuals occur frequently on the coffins.
Etruscan sculptures, dug up during the Renais-

Figure 2-27
Now restored in the Museo Nazionale di Villa Giulia Museum in Rome, the sculpture is a testimony to the permanence of fired clay and the durability of emotion expressed in it. The ability of clay to withstand centuries of neglect and damage allows us to sense the affection of the couple on their ritual banquet couch and to appreciate the technical knowledge of the Etruscan sculptor whose sensitivity and creativity made this work of art possible. *Photo taken with permission, Museo Nazionale di Villa Giulia Museum, Rome.*

sance search for antiquities, influenced such Italian sculptors as Donatello (6-8) and even today there are sculptors in Italy who, while working in their own contemporary style, still carry on the vigorous Etruscan tradition of clay portraits.

ROME

The Etruscans, who settled before the Latins in what is now Rome, were the first rulers of that area, and just as the Etruscans drew on Greek technology, so the Romans drew on the Etruscan knowledge of art, engineering, and ceramics. In fact, they called the famous Etruscan sculptor Vulca (2-25) to Rome to create the sculpture for the city's most important temple, the Temple of Jove. The Romans also continued to use clay for portrait sculptures, frequently casting them in bronze from the clay models.

Arrentine Ware

The Romans adapted much of their ceramic technique from the Etruscans or the Hellenistic Greeks, and with their characteristic organizational skill, they transformed their pottery workshops into factories. Although the most characteristic Roman ceramics—domestic red earthenware with decoration in relief—was of a type originally produced by the Hellenistic Greeks, it was the Romans who developed ways of producing it in great quantities, using **parallel-flue kilns.** Called arrentine for the town of Arezzo where it was made—a factory there had a mixing vat with a ten-thousand gallon capacity—this **ware** was made in stamped molds that were revolved on potters' wheels. When damp clay was pressed into the revolving mold, it produced a positive impression of the design (2-28). Production soared, and the ceramics factories were highly successful financially. Both the emperor Hadrian and the consul Marcus Aurelius are known to have made fortunes from the factories they owned.

This red arrentine ware was coated with the same type of extremely fine slip as that was used in Greece for the red and black pottery, but in Rome it was known as **terra sigillata** (literally, "sealed earth"). Although some potteries were noted for their all-black ware, fired in a reducing atmosphere, the most famous of the Roman ware was fired in an oxidizing atmosphere so that it came out a rich red, whose glossy finish is largely the result of a micalike material in the clay that made up the slip. This red ware, with its molded reliefs, was made not only in Italy but also in other areas of the Roman Empire—Switzerland, Gaul, and England also produced typical terra-sigillata-finished pottery.

Like the Greek potteries, the Roman factories made tiles and ceramic plaques to decorate their elaborate public buildings and luxurious homes. Clay was also used as a basic construction material, particularly in the early days of Rome, when buildings were frequently made of brick and faced with stone. In the capital city, at the height of the Roman Empire, brick and terra-cotta were no longer in fashion, and Emperor Augustus could boast, "I found Rome of brick, I leave it of marble." In the less highly developed areas of the Roman Empire, however, it was the Roman use of clay building materials—bricks, roof tiles, ceramic floor coverings, and ornamentation—that often differentiated the buildings of the well-to-do Roman conquerors from the simpler wooden

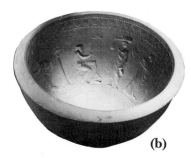

Figure 2-28

Arrentine pottery from the Roman factories was shipped throughout the empire. To make this relief-decorated ware, the potter pressed damp clay into a fired mold, smoothing it against the walls as the mold turned on the wheel. When the clay was removed from the mold, the impression appeared in relief on the exterior of the vessel. **(a)** A fired pottery stamp used to impress the decoration into a mold shows a satyr playing a double flute. *The Metropolitan Museum of Art, Purchase Funds from Various Donors, 1926 (26.81.2)* **(b)** This terra-cotta mold was used to form a bowl depicting the mysteries of Dionysus. *The Metropolitan Museum of Art, Rogers Find, 1923 (23.108).* **(c)** A fragment of a relief-decorated bowl made in a mold. Late first century B.C. to early first century A.D. *The Metropolitan Museum of Art, Gift of J. Pierpont Morgan, 1917 (17.194.1931). All rights reserved, the Metropolitan Museum of Art.*

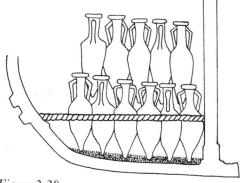

Figure 2-29

The Greeks, Etruscans, and Romans shipped millions of amphorae filled with wine, oil, and grain throughout the Mediterranean area. Fitted into the holds of merchant ships, these containers became the unit of measure by which the capacity of a vessel was calculated. The drawing shows how they were stacked.

houses of the local inhabitants. The Roman colonists also brought such luxuries as public bath houses, whose rooms were heated by hot air sent from wood-burning furnaces through terra-cotta pipes in the floors or walls. With a large population at home to feed and far-flung armies to supply, the Romans also perfected the transport of foodstuffs, oil, and wine, carrying it in terra-cotta amphorae designed to be stacked in the holds of ships (2-29). So many of these amphorae were brought to Rome filled with foodstuffs from the colonies that there is a hill in Rome, II Testaccio, that was gradually built up of the broken amphorae thrown away after their contents had been transferred to the Roman warehouses along the Tiber River.

Wherever they settled, the Romans introduced the use of the pottery wheel and the expertise of firing in vertical kilns, both techniques that had been unknown in Northern Europe before the Roman Legions arrived. When the Roman Empire crumbled and Europe settled into the Dark Ages, the knowledge of the potter's wheel and the Roman kiln were lost. In England, their use was only reintroduced around the ninth to the twelfth centuries A.D. Chapter 6 will pick up the story with the return to Northern Europe of advanced ceramic technology that made it possible for ceramics to regain its importance in the Middle Ages. Now, however, we will turn to other areas of the world where rich clay traditions also developed, some of which profoundly affected the history of ceramics in the Western world.

49

3

The Orient

Ceramics formed the background of early Chinese art, indispensable, ubiquitous, reflecting the needs and tastes of the highest and lowest.

Michael Sullivan*

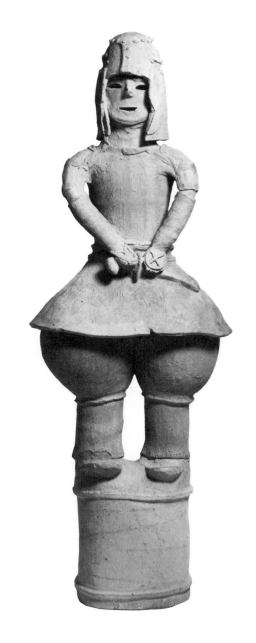

Until quite recently, the West has known much more about art in early Mediterranean societies than about the artistic developments in other parts of the world, and Westerners have tended to believe that all civilization started in the Mediterranean. This was largely due to the fact that when archaeology began as a science in the 1800s, it centered on that area because it was familiar ground, made so by the Bible and by Greek and Roman mythology, literature, and history. This attitude also reflected a cultural egocentricity that has caused us to favor the Western cultural heritage.

THE EARLIEST KNOWN POTTERY

Now, however, archaeological exploration has extended our knowledge beyond Europe, the Near East, and the Mediterranean to Africa, the

The eyes and mouth of this *haniwa* warrior are holes, giving his face expression as well as letting the vapor and gases escape in the firing. He is fully armed with helmet, sword, and arm protectors. The *haniwa* were originally simple clay cylinders sunk in the ground around the mounded royal tombs, probably to keep the soil from eroding. Later they were modeled to depict animated dancers, singers, farmers, warriors, and animals. Earthenware, Fujioka, Japan, Late Tumulus period, c. sixth century A.D. *Courtesy Asian Art Museum of San Francisco, the Avery Brundage Collection.*

*The Arts of China, Berkeley, University of California Press, 1973.

Russian steppes, eastern Asia, the Americas, and the Orient (3-1). We now know more about the early uses of fire and tools and the development of pottery making in many areas of the world, and archaeologists have found pottery that predates the ceramics from Asia Minor that were once thought to be the earliest. Excavations in Japan, Taiwan, and China have unearthed extremely early pottery, of which the Japanese is at present considered to be the oldest pottery found in the world. Fashioned by human hands between twelve thousand and nine thousand years ago, the Japanese pottery is the oldest example yet known of fired *vessels*. Small fired sculptures of a woman and animals found in Vestonice, Czechoslovakia, that date from around 26,000 B.C. are so far the oldest fired-clay artifacts found. As excavations in various parts of the world continue to unearth sites of early human habitation, our knowledge of the lives and crafts of early humans widens. Perhaps by the time you read this paragraph, experts will have dated an even earlier example of the use of fire to harden vessels made of clay.

Figure 3-1
Neolithic potters in China made urns, low bowls, and jars of red earthenware clay on turntables, burnishing them before firing. After firing, they painted the vessels with mineral oxides in geometric patterns and flowing spiral designs in red, purple, and black. Ht. 13 in. (33 cm). Found in a grave. Panshan, China, 2500–1500 B.C. *Courtesy Collection Haags Gemeentemuseum, The Hague.*

CHINA

Another archaeological site in the Orient that has given us a considerable amount of information on early ceramics technology was discovered at the village of Panpo, on the Yellow River in central China. Excavations there have shown that between six and four thousand years ago hunters settling there created a farming civilization, founded villages in which people lived in permanent houses, maintained a cemetery, and built kilns for firing vessels.

Neolithic Pottery in China

Skilled in the crafts, the Panpo villagers made tools from stone and pottery from *huang tu*, a yellow clay rich in alumina that they tempered with sand. They ornamented their pots with fingernail and tool-impressed textures and painted them with decorations, consisting mainly of geometric shapes and lines that were composed with great sensitivity to the form of each pot. In addition to the geometric decoration, some of the pots show abstract representations of animals and humans. The rims of some of them also bear carefully arranged marks that might have been examples of a method of recording events, possibly even the beginning of writing, a skill that was perfected at a very early date in China.

By about 2,000 B.C., in Kansu province, potters were shaping clay into thin-walled pottery, which they usually painted with **hematite** powder (red iron oxide) and manganese oxide in a variety of line designs—bands of circles, crosses, dots, and triangles. Other vessels were painted with elegant spiral patterns or fluid lines that suggest waves or the currents of a river. The shapes of these pots are refined, some are set on pedestals, while their painted designs are all elegantly composed to emphasize rather than detract from the form of the vessels.

At various places in central and eastern China, potters around four thousand years ago also made vessels in a tripod shape with three hollow legs, their form probably based on three pots

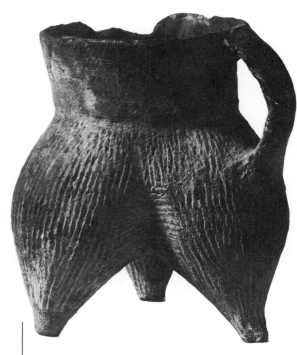

Figure 3-2
Called a *li*, this Neolithic tripod-shaped vessel may have developed from three pots joined together. Mushroom-shaped clay tools unearthed at excavations in China may have been held inside the walls of similar pots to support them while the potter paddled the outside of the walls, thinning and texturing them. Gray pottery. Ht. 6 in. (15.2 cm). China, c. 2000 B.C. *Courtesy Asian Art Museum of San Francisco, the Avery Brundage Collection.*

joined together (3-2). Called a *li*, this shape may have had fertility significance or the shape may have been derived from pots that were originally designed to boil liquids on an open fire. The example shown is decorated only with striations, its form rather squat, but some of these pitchers are well-proportioned, with graceful long spouts and swelling legs tapering down to pointed feet. Many are decorated with applied coils and pellets of clay in designs similar to the bronze urns of the Shang period.

At about the same time (2000 B.C.), another Neolithic clay culture called Lungshan, on the lower Yellow River, was making extremely thin-walled black pottery fired in reduction. From ridge marks on the vessel walls, archaeologists

have deduced that this pottery was made with a relatively advanced wheel—apparently a true potter's wheel that turned at least a hundred revolutions per minute.

The kilns in which the early Chinese potters fired their ware were somewhat different from the early kilns in the Middle East. Many of them were built into the ground and had a side tunnel in which a wood fire burned, so that the heat flowed up into the chamber where the pots were placed (3-3). These kilns were small—only able to fire three or four large pots and about ten smaller ones up to a temperature of around 1470°F/800°C.

Shang Dynasty (Sixteenth to Eleventh Centuries B.C.)

As the Neolithic villages in China grew in complexity, they developed rigid traditions, and class lines developed. Local chiefs became overlords, ruling a society in which serfs and slaves farmed the land for the landlords, while artisans produced luxuries for the upper classes.

Eventually the first true Chinese dynasty—the Shang (from about the sixteenth to the eleventh centuries B.C.)—placed a central ruler above the local landed lords, and from then on dynasty succeeded dynasty. For our purposes, there is no need to remember the intricacies of China's political history, but since certain dynasties were more significant in the history of pottery or contributed particular innovations to ceramics technique, we will emphasize their contributions to China's long history.

By now cities were built with large religious centers and palaces where the rulers and nobles lived, enjoying the luxuries produced by the artisans. These kings and nobles were buried, along with the bodies of their sacrificed slaves and horses, in elaborate tombs that contained ritual bronze urns and pottery.

It is helpful when studying the various styles of Chinese ceramics to remember that the herd-tending nomadic tribes of central Asia moved constantly through the mountains, steppes, and deserts of that vast area. Periodically these raiders appeared on their swift horses to raid the more settled Chinese communities, sometimes destroy-

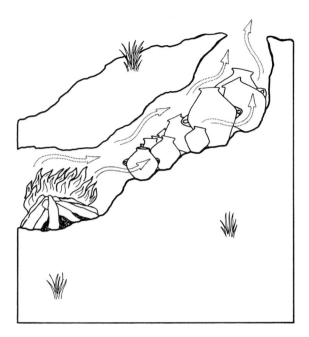

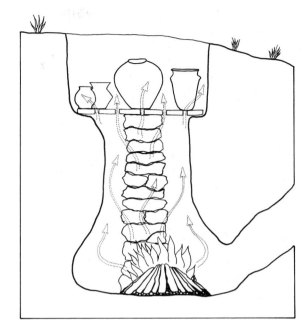

Figure 3-3
The earliest Chinese pottery was fired in kilns dug almost horizontally into the earth with side tunnels for the fires. One type had small heat vents in the projecting floor to distribute the heat more evenly around the pots.

Figure 3-4
The hearth of this type of kiln was supported on a pillar. By the end of the Shang dynasty, the firing chamber was larger, the ware was placed above the fire on a permanent grate, and the kilns may have had domed roofs built up over the opening each time they were fired.

ing them, sometimes becoming assimilated and passing on the ideas and artistic styles they had absorbed in their nomadic wanderings from one part of the continent to another. Often, the reason for these raids was to force the farming villagers to trade the products of their crafts, such as pottery, in return for the horses the nomads bred.

Influenced by the peoples who lived around them in Asia, copying the elaborate burial rituals and the knowledge of wooden construction from the northern tribes, as well as the stamped pottery designs of stylized dragons from their crocodile-worshipping southern neighbors, the Shang melded all these influences into a characteristic style that was reflected in both their pottery and their bronze vessels. These elaborate bronze food and ritual vessels, used only by the wealthy, the priests, and the nobility in their burials, were made with highly sophisticated casting techniques based partly on ceramics technology. The bronze vessels for which the Shang period is noted were cast in fired clay molds.

Shang kilns   As a thriving pottery industry developed, kiln design changed somewhat. We know what the Shang kilns looked like because at Chengchow, a Shang city, excavators discovered fourteen kilns in the potters' quarter. These kilns were vertical, about four feet in diameter, and had a central pillar or wall that supported a perforated clay floor on which the pots were placed (3-4). As kiln technology improved, potters learned to fire

Figure 3-5

Made of almost pure kaolin, this fine white urn was fired to around 1832° F/1000° C. Too fragile for ordinary use, it was probably kept for ceremonial use. Excavated potters' tools include stamps with dragons and squared spirals like the decorations on this jar. Ht. 8 in. (20.3 cm). Anyang, Honan, China, late Shang dynasty, 1300–1028 B.C. *Courtesy Asian Art Museum of San Francisco, the Avery Brundage Collection.*

at temperatures of up to 2190°F/1200°C, and by around 1400 B.C., the Chinese had made the first high-fired pottery, known as **proto-porcelain** (a form of what we call stoneware), made with **kaolin,** a white primary clay found in large deposits in China.

Shang glazes Along with the technical advances they made in kiln building and firing, the Shang potters also discovered how to cover their pots with glaze. This knowledge probably developed as Shang potters observed the accidental ash glaze that formed when ashes from the wood fire fell on the shoulders of vessels in the kiln. Wood ashes contain alkalies, such as potash and soda, as well as silica and alumina, and the high kiln temperature caused the minerals in the ash to fuse with the silica in the clay, forming a glaze. Noticing how the ashes formed a shiny coating on the shoulders of their pots, the potters undoubtedly

began to experiment with different materials, eventually succeeding in creating a deliberately applied high-fire feldspathic glaze that fused with the proto-porcelain clay body to make a coating that became an integral part of the fired pottery. One can imagine the amount of glaze testing that went on in Shang potters' shops before the first successful deliberately applied glaze was formulated. The yellowish-brown or greenish glaze marked the first step in the long search for refinement in glazes, a search that occupied potters in China for many centuries (Color plates 1, 2, and 3).

In the later days of the Shang dynasty, some very fine white vessels were made of almost pure kaolin in shapes very similar to the bronzes (3-5). Decorated with designs that show probable influences from Southeast Asia and the cultures in western Asia that used animal decorations, these rare, fragile vessels were made from a clay body that was the direct predecessor of the true porcelain of the Sung period.

Chou Dynasty (Eleventh Century to 722 B.C.)

The ceramics of the Chou dynasty continued along the lines established in the Shang dynasty, with Chou potters creating earthenware copies of the more expensive bronze vessels. These potters were also kept busy making protoporcelain into wine vessels, bells, and footed basins to serve the court. Building on Shang technical knowledge, they improved the stoneware body and learned to cover it with a smoother, more translucent, and more resistant glaze. These developments resulted partly from a more advanced kiln design that now distributed the heat around the firing chamber through quite complex duct systems. This achieved a more uniform firing temperature throughout the kiln.

Clay and Bronze Casting

As so often happened in early cultures, metallurgy and ceramics were interrelated in China. During several dynasties and the Warring States period (c. 480–21 B.C.), when the bronze industry flourished, clay played an important part in the production of the impressive bronze objects made

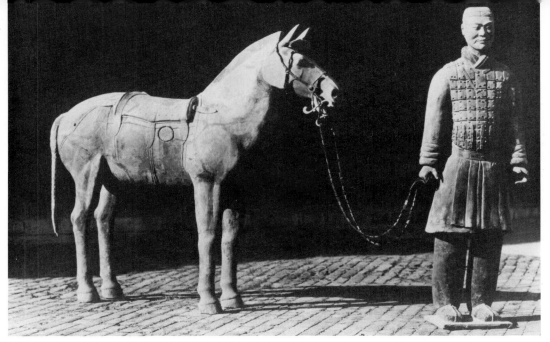

Figure 3-6
Part of a terra-cotta army, this horse and groom were placed in the tomb of the first Emperor Qin. Seven thousand strong, the hollow-built soldiers and horses were supported on solid legs and held real weapons, and each one was sculpted as an individual portrait. China, 246 to 210 B.C. From the exhibition The Great Bronze Age of China: An Exhibition from the People's Republic of China. *Photo courtesy the Metropolitan Museum of Art, all rights reserved.*

by artisans using highly developed casting techniques. For example, excavation of fifth century B.C. bronze workshops have revealed more than thirty thousand clay models and molds used for casting bronze vessels. Also found there were finished bronze objects, ranging from small delicate animals to large animal-mask reliefs, all cast in multiple-part molds.

Confucianism and Taoism

After the decline of the Chou dynasty and the Warring States period, China entered a time of chaos, but one of great intellectual ferment. At this time, two scholars propounded two quite different philosophies, initiating a moral and intellectual conflict that was reflected in China's later social, political, and artistic history. These two philosophies were known as Confucianism and Taoism. Confucius (or Kung Fu-tse, 551–479 B.C.) taught that one could be fulfilled only by following one's appointed role in a rigid social order. This idea was in direct opposition to the teaching of Lao-tze (604?–531 B.C.), who believed that discipline and authoritarianism wrongly repressed the natural instincts that would lead to

harmony with the universe. Both the scholarly orderliness of Confucianism and the mysticism of Taoism were reflected in the art of China, and Taoism also would become an important influence on certain segments of Japanese society.

Qin Dynasty (c. 221–202 B.C.)

The totalitarian Qin conquered all of China, unifying it under a powerful central government and governing through fear. Until recently, this period was considered unimportant in art history, and its rulers were seen as ruthless tyrants who made little contribution to Chinese culture. Certainly they were ruthless—their philosophy was that it should be worse for the people to fall into the hands of the regime's police than to fight an enemy state. The First Emperor Qin Shih Huang Ti used seven hundred thousand laborers to create the imperial tomb, and the Qins' greatest contributions to art in general were for their own glorification. One of these is the army of terra-cotta soldiers and horses that was buried with the First Emperor Qin Shih Huang Ti in battle formation, facing eastwards towards his enemies in the lower Yellow River valley (3-6). The incredi-

55

Figure 3-7
Peasant rebellions were frequent in the Han period, so landlords and their families took refuge in watchtowers such as this one guarded by archers and sentries. Grave model, green lead glaze. Ht. 33¼ in. (84.4 cm). Han dynasty, second century A.D. *Courtesy of the Freer Gallery of Art, Smithsonian Institution. Washington, D.C.*

ble tomb included models of the Yellow River and automatic crossbows fixed to kill any grave robbers attempting to enter it. Started when Emperor Qin came to the throne at the age of thirteen in 246 B.C., seven thousand of these life-sized figures were made in clay to represent the army that protected him from his enemies. When this remarkable army was excavated, it was discovered that although the soldiers' bodies were somewhat standardized, their faces were individual portraits—no two faces were alike. These are the earliest realistic Chinese clay sculptures yet found, revealing a highly developed ceramic sculpture tradition and an amazing mastery of firing technique. Made of the heavy clay found in the vicinity of Mount Li, their bodies are solid from the abdomen down.

Han Dynasty (c. 206 B.C.– A.D. 220)

Under the Han, China again enjoyed a period of comparative peace; however, the Han took from the Qin the concept of a powerful central government, so the life of the ordinary people probably changed very little, ruled as they were by a professional army, a bureaucracy, and local landlords. Much of what we know of their lives comes from the countless ceramic grave models made for the landed farmers and warriors (3-7). These grave models, called *ming-chi*, were buried with the dead instead of live slaves and horses for their use in the afterlife. Some of the buried objects were treasured personal possessions placed beside the dead, while others were made especially to accompany the deceased into the afterlife.

Han lead glaze   Made of earthenware, most of the grave models were unglazed and painted with unfired pigments that have largely worn off, but some were coated with lead glaze, a novelty that must have seemed quite marvelous to the rural landowners who commissioned the models (3-7). How mysterious the action of the fire on clay and glaze appeared to the potters themselves is illustrated by a legend that tells of a hard-working potter whose firing of a large and precious pot had failed. Greatly upset that his work was destroyed, the potter jumped into the kiln to die in the flames. After that sacrifice, it was said that, miraculously, all the pots always fired perfectly. Because this sacrifice helped them in their work, from then on potters worshipped him as the god Tung, "Genius of Fire and Blast" (3-8).

Lead glazes had been in use in Mesopotamia since the sixth century B.C., leading to speculation about whether knowledge of these glazes had been brought to China by traders following the Silk Route. Established in the second century B.C., this caravan route led from China through Afghanistan to Iran and on to Rome, carrying China's fine silks and lacquer ware to the West. In about 550 B.C., the Persians had conquered large areas of western Asia, extending their empire as far as the Indus River in India. These Sassanid Persians, as they are called, traded with the Chinese silk merchants, selling them Persian gold and silver vessels that were transported back with the caravans to China. There potters saw them and adapted their Western motifs and shapes to Chinese ceramics. For example, pottery flasks modeled on Persian forms show Sassanian figures in relief under a brownish glaze. We do not know whether some Sassanian potters actually came to China with the returning caravans and taught the Han potters their glaze techniques or whether Han potters traveled to western Asia and brought back the knowledge. It is true, however, that lead glazes appeared in China just at this time and that Chinese pottery was traded across large areas of Asia. Thus, each culture absorbed artistic influences from each other, and international trade came to be of vital importance to the Han potter. Speculations about the economics of trade no longer seem so abstract when we look at the ridges made by a potter's hands on a piece of Han pottery and realize the part his pottery played in trade.

Han technical improvements   Firing and glazing techniques continued to improve during these centuries and on into the following periods as potters continued to experiment with high-fire glazes (3-9). By the end of the Han dynasty, potters in southern China were making a type of high-fired-glazed stoneware called Yuëh ware, whose greenish glazes came close to the famous green celadon glaze of the later Sung period (Color plate 1). So many kilns were being fired

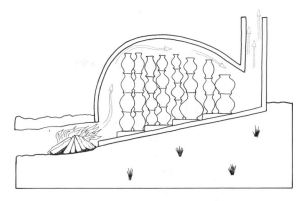

Figure 3-8
Kilns were now built with permanent domes designed to direct the heat up over the stacked ware and then downward before it went up the chimney. This construction allowed potters to fire at temperatures of 2192° F/1200° C or more.

Figure 3-9
Wood ashes fell on the shoulder of this Han stoneware jar, fused with the silica in the clay, and formed an accidental glaze. Stoneware. Han dynasty, 200 B.C.–A.D. 221. *Courtesy Royal Ontario Museum, Toronto, Canada.*

Figure 3-10
In this northern Wei dynasty (A.D. 386–534) tomb model we can see how architectural roof tiles and ornaments were used on palaces and temples. China's ceramic industry turned out quantities of molded or stamped bricks and tiles decorated with scenes of farm life, craft shops, hunters, and processions of notables. Northern Wei, A.D. 386–534. *Courtesy the Board of Trustees of the Victoria & Albert Museum.*

with wood in the ancient kingdom of Yüeh that a ninth-century poet, Lu Kuimeng, wrote:

In autumn, in the wind and dew, rises the smoke of the kilns of Yue
It robs the thousand peaks of their kingfisher blue.

Toba Wei (A.D. 386–617)

After the fall of the Han dynasty, northern China was overrun with waves of nomadic horse-men until the Toba Wei, a Turkish tribe, took control in A.D. 386. These invaders ruled through military officials who had become part of the Chinese bureaucracy, abandoning their nomadic lives and adopting Chinese language, building styles (3-10), and dress along with the Buddhist faith. We can see their Western faces reflected in the ceramic sculpture of the time (3-11). Various groups of Wei and other succeeding dynasties ruled the country until the beginning of the Tang dynasty.

Figure 3-11
The Toba Wei, a Turkish tribe, conquered northern China in A.D. 386, ruling through military officials who were realistically modeled in earthenware figures. After this one was fired, it was painted with red and white, with black for his mustache. Ht. 35 in. (88.9 cm). *Courtesy Asian Art Museum of San Francisco, the Avery Brundage Collection.*

Tang Dynasty (A.D. 617–906)

Tang ceramics reflect the cosmopolitan quality of this period in China's history. Following the trade routes across central Asia, down into India, and through the Roman Orient, outside influences arrived with the caravans, while foreign ships brought people of all races and creeds to the ports of Canton and Yangchow. Noble Turks arrived with retinues of dancers, musicians, and servants whose clothing and faces fascinated the Chinese. Along with the camels and their drivers from the silk caravans, these foreigners appear in the clay figurines that were made in quantity and glazed with polychrome lead glazes (3-12). Made by mixing copper, iron, or cobalt with lead silicate, these blue, green, brown, and yellow glazes were often applied over a white slip. They were apt to be runny because of the action of the lead flux, and the potters applied them freely so that they ran down the side of the figures, color over color. The Tang potteries also produced many unglazed sculptures of female musicians, dancers (3-13), and court ladies, reminding us that during this dynasty China was governed for fourteen years by the Empress Wu. During her reign, upper-class women were educated, wrote poetry, rode horseback, and played polo. It was a tolerant society; foreign religious groups were allowed to build their temples and churches in the capital, among them the Buddhists, whose religion eventually became dominant in China.

Western shapes continued to be popular in ceramics. These ranged from pilgrim bottles from Sassanian Persia, to pottery copies of metal drinking goblets, to Hellenistic amphorae. All were absorbed into the Tang potter's repertoire but, as is usually the case in the exchanges of art styles, they were adapted to local taste and materials.

The first true porcelain Under the Tang, the fine ware from the Yüeh kilns became more refined, until finally a true porcelain was attained and perfected in the Tang dynasty (3-14). Porcelain is a clay body composed of kaolin, feldspar, and silica, and when fired to a temperature of 2370 to 2440 F°/ 1300° to 1450°C or more, it becomes vitrified and translucent. China's fine porcelain was described by a Moslem merchant as so

Figure 3-12
Chinese potters made many models of the western
Asian camels and their drivers who traveled the Silk
Route. First they modeled the camels; then they made
their humps and packs and drivers, attaching them
before glazing the pieces with yellow, green, and
brown glazes that were allowed to run down the
sides. Buff earthenware, brown and green glazes.
China, Tang dynasty, A.D. 618–907. *Courtesy the Board
of Trustees of the Victoria & Albert Museum.*

Figure 3-13
A slender dancer from the Tang court was modeled in
earthenware and then painted. Traces of pigments can
still be seen on her clothing. Tang dynasty, A.D. 618–
907. *Courtesy the Board of Trustees of the Victoria &
Albert Museum.*

thin one could see the sparkle of water through it,
and it was this translucence that caused it to be
treasured by Chinese connoisseurs and poets.
They called it white as snow or silver, preferring
it for cups from which to drink tea. Only the fin-
est porcelain was considered good enough to be
used at court, and eventually the court established
the official Imperial Kilns in order to control the
quality of the ware. Chinese potters were able to
develop this fine porcelain because of their discovery of China's large deposits of both the white
primary clay, kaolin, and **petunze,** or *pai-t'un-*

tzu, a white feldspathic rock essential to the making of porcelain. During high firing, the petunze
(our **Cornish stone,** or **Cornwall stone**) melts
and surrounds the particles of kaolin so that they
can fuse.

Sung Dynasty (A.D. 960–1270)

The ceramics of the Sung dynasty, like those
of the Tang, reflected the taste of the court, where
every educated person studied painting and cal-

Figure 3-14
Pure white, hard, translucent, and resonant when struck, Sung porcelain became the standard against which all later porcelain was measured. Chinese potters had the necessary firing technology, and China had the kaolin and petunze needed to achieve its purity of body. Ht. 7¾ in. (19.7 cm). White porcelain ewer, Sung dynasty, eleventh to twelfth century A.D. *Courtesy the Board of Trustees of the Victoria & Albert Museum.*

ligraphy and even the emperors were painters and poets. In this atmosphere of culture and artistic accomplishment, the ceramics were elegant, formal, and exquisitely crafted (3-14). Produced in several pottery centers, some of which had as many as two hundred kilns, much of Sung porcelain was formed with carved molds that transferred their designs onto the damp clay as it was pressed over them. Other porcelain vessels were rimmed with bronze or silver to cover the band of clay that was left unglazed when the ware was fired upside down.

Sung glazes   When Westerners think of Sung ceramics, what usually comes to mind is the **celadon** glaze, called after a character in French theater who wore that shade of green. Called *ch'ing t'zu* in China, this soft green glaze was the result of centuries of experimentation in an effort to achieve the color and surface of the sacred stone jade (Color plate 1). The iron oxide in the glaze used on both stoneware and porcelain fired in a reduction atmosphere to a wide range of tones, from leafy green to watery bluish-green depending on the ingredients and the oxides present in the clay body. For example, the greenish-brown celadon ware from northern China was made of a gray porcelaneous body on which the glaze was fired first in reduction at a high temperature and then in an oxidizing atmosphere as it cooled. On the other hand, at the Lungchuan potteries the glaze was used on a grayish white stoneware body fired in reduction, and on this body the glaze became a pale olive green.

We must remember that the glazes composed at this time made use of local, natural materials as sources for the necessary ingredients. Ashes were an important part of the glazes, and rice straw was a popular ingredient. Rice straw is high in silica, which contributed to the stability and hardness of the glazes.

Chinese ceramics continued in great demand abroad, where the Arab countries bought it in great quantities—thousands of shards of both Yuëh ware and white porcelain were found in the ruins of the summer palace of the caliphs. Celadon was also popular there, because the uneasy rulers of the Arab world believed that the Chinese celadon ware would crack and change color if exposed to poison, so it was used as a way to detect assassination plots. This idea may have been a result of the **crackle glaze** deliberately exploited for its decorative effect by Chinese potters who found that the glaze would crack if it were not properly formulated to shrink along with the clay body. The porcelain exported to Persia made from the excellent clays of China was envied by the potters there, who used their white tin glazes to cover their coarse red clay in an effort to compete with Chinese imports.

Other Sung glazes   The Sung potters, in addition to making the classic white-glazed por-

Figure 3-15
The Sung potters made brownish-black glazed bowls for the popular tea ceremony. Often mottled or streaked with "oil spots" or "hare's fur," their *Tien-mu* glaze became popular in Japan, where it was known as *tenmoku*. Bowl, Chien ware, *tenmoku* glaze. Ht. 2¾ in. (7 cm). China, Sung dynasty, tenth to thirteenth century A.D. *Courtesy Asian Art Museum of San Francisco, the Avery Brundage Collection.*

celain and soft green celadon and crackle glazes, produced the brilliant Chun glaze (Color plate 2), whose purple and red splashes were created when spots of copper and manganese oxidized in the glaze during firing. Another glaze developed in the Sung period was exported to Japan, where it became popular with Japanese potters, and eventually, through them, with Western potters. This was the blackish-brown *Tien'mu* glaze, named for a mountain near Hangchow (3-15). This **slip glaze** was called **tenmoku** in Japan, the name by which we still call it. A thick, oily-looking glaze that often collects in rolls and drops at the bottom of a piece, its surface may show "oil spots" or "hare's fur," an effect that was deliberately sought. These glazes developed during the Sung dynasty represented a developing expertise and aesthetic sensibility in the formulation and use of glazes that would later cause a sensation when they became known in Europe.

Sung kilns   Chinese kilns were now much more advanced, often built into a hill in a series of stepped levels, sometimes as long as 165 feet (50 meters). The firing kilns were vividly portrayed by Chinese writers as giant dragons spitting fire. Most were fired with wood, although some smaller ones used coal, and the potters had to solve the problem of the free ashes spoiling the celadon glaze. The solution was to fire each separate piece in a fire-resistant container, a **sagger** (3-16), that would protect the ware from the wood ash; the Lungchuan kilns could fire as many as twenty thousand saggers at one time (3-17).

Underglaze   We have seen how Persia and China carried on trade across Asia. One result of this trade was that Sassanian designs were copied first by silk weavers in China and then by Chinese potters. Toward the end of the Sung dynasty, the potters had become increasingly interested in colorful, high-fire glazes and other methods of surface decoration, and had also experimented with painting floral designs in black under a transparent glaze. This type of painting under a glaze had been used in western Asia since the ninth century

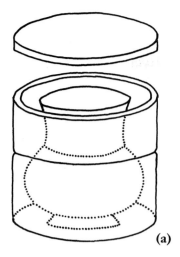

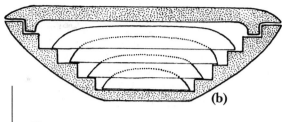

Figure 3-16
Different types of saggers were used to protect the porcelain from the flame and ash during firing. **(a)** This type held a single piece of pottery upright. **(b)** Other saggers could hold several nested bowls of different sizes resting on their rims.

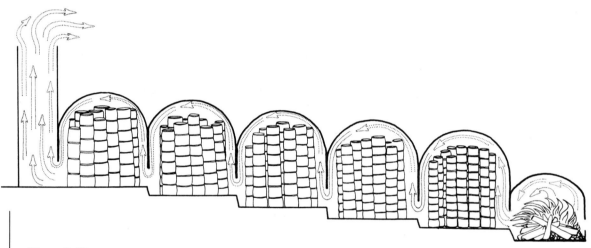

Figure 3-17
Kilns built on sloping ground were now divided into chambers. Each chamber was a separate down-draft kiln; as one chamber heated to the necessary temperature, fuel was fed through the stoking holes in the next highest chamber. Each chamber was heated in turn, and its heat transferred to the next, preheating it and thus optimizing fuel use.

(3-30), and now Chinese potters tried their hands at it, entering a new phase of pictorial decoration that would have a great effect on later Japanese and European ceramics. In the fourteenth century, they experimented with using copper oxide to paint red underglazes on their pots, but the red was difficult to control, bleeding into the white or losing its color when fired. Giving up on the copper, they began to use cobalt for underglaze decoration on porcelain. To apply underglaze, the artist first allowed the body to dry, and then applied the pigment to the unglazed body and covered the vessel with a semiopaque glaze. After a single firing, the cobalt blue became suspended in the translucent glaze between the outer surface and the body, acquiring luminosity and brilliance

Figure 3-18
Mythical beasts in a fanciful landscape decorate this white porcelain plate with underglaze decoration made in the reign of Emperor Wan Li. The underglaze was painted with cobalt oxide on the unglazed body, and the plate was then covered with a semi-opaque glaze that, when fired, allowed the blue to show through. Blue and white ware, Ming dynasty, A.D. 1575–1619. Diameter 12¼ in. (31.1 cm). *Courtesy the Board of Trustees of the Victoria & Albert Museum.*

Figure 3-19
An unusual Chinese kick wheel, rotated by an assistant who provided the power with his foot while hanging on to a rope. Such ingenious methods of speeding production turned the potters' workshops into the seventeenth-century equivalent of assembly lines.

(3-18). The Chinese cobalt, however, contained a high proportion of both manganese and iron impurities, so it fired to a dull blue; Persian cobalt, on the other hand, contained no manganese and fired to a clear blue. To satisfy the Chinese demand for brilliant color, the trading caravans brought Persian cobalt to China, where it was called *hui hui ching*, or Mohammedan blue. Eventually, the Chinese learned to refine the iron out of their own cobalt, but they could never completely eliminate the manganese, so they mixed local cobalt with the expensive imported oxide, using this mixture for most of the blue and white ware. Only the court porcelain, made in the official Imperial Kilns in Ching te chen, was painted with the pure Persian cobalt. Ching te chen had become a ceramic center in the fourteenth century, largely because there were rich deposits of kaolin nearby.

Blue and white export ware   Chinese blue and white ware became popular all over Asia; shards of it have been found on the shores of the Persian Gulf. As the demand for it grew, much of this ware came to be made for export to Persia in shapes copied from Persian metal objects and with Persian inscriptions as decorations. Near the turn of the seventeenth century, however, Chinese potteries began to export a certain type of thin, rather brittle blue and white export ware to Europe. The appearance of this pottery caused great excitement there, because European potters did not know how to make the thin, fine porcelain. Soon the Dutch were importing the ware by the shipload, and the Chinese factories had to speed up production to meet the demand (3-19). As time went on, however, the Chinese adapted their pottery shapes and decorations to Western taste, even illustrating European popular stories on the ware, showing successive episodes in the continuous manner of Sung scrolls.

Ming Dynasty (1368–1644)

Chinese potters continued to make their wares using traditional Sung forms and glazes. With the Ming dynasty, however, new, heavily decorated wares appeared. At the Ming court, whose rulers liked to consider themselves the heirs to the refinement of the Sung dynasty but who in reality were men lacking in the good taste and education of the Sung rulers, artists were honored and treated with great respect only as long as they followed the rigid rules laid down by the emperor. They could be disgraced, exiled, or even executed for a slight deviation in their work—for example, for painting an ordinary person wearing a color that was reserved for high officials. Lovers of rich, luxurious living, the Ming officials commissioned lacquer ware, embroidered silk, enameled metal objects, and highly decorated ceramics—the "three-color" and "five-color" wares painted with **china paint,** or **overglaze enamel.** These **overglazes** were colored with metallic oxides and contained a great deal of lead so that they would melt at a low temperature, around 1470°F/800°C. The overglaze enamels were painted over the body glaze and, when the pottery was given a final low-temperature firing, the overglaze melted and the lead in the main body glaze also softened it enough so that the overglaze fused into it.

This many-colored type of decoration became so popular and the demand for enamel-decorated ware so great that the potter could no longer decorate his own pieces. The potteries now became factories. We know a good deal about the Imperial Kilns, where the export porcelain and overglaze-decorated ware were produced, because a European priest who lived in China from 1698 to 1741 visited them. Some say he was a spy for the European ceramics factories. The priest described in letters sent home to Europe how the decorators were so specialized that one man would paint only one type of leaf, flower, or figure, and as many as seventy might work on one piece of ceramics in an assembly line. Obviously, the personal relationship between potter and pot had been broken.

Architectural Ceramics

From at least the Warring States period on, the making of roof tiles had been part of the ceramics industry in China (3-10). Impressed with fired-clay stamps or made in carved molds lined with cloth to keep the clay from sticking, unglazed earthenware clay tiles, decorated bricks, and architectural ornaments were an integral part of the decoration on wooden buildings, even before the knowledge of glazes made brightly colored clay tiles possible. We know from literature of the Han period that the mansions and palaces of the rich and noble classes were made of wood, the walls were covered with paintings, and the beam ends, lattice doors, and balconies were carved and painted vermilion. Once the knowledge of lead glazes reached China in the Han period, the greenish lead glaze that covered the grave models (3-7) was adapted to cover earthenware tiles as well. From then on, as more and more colors became available to the potter, ceramic tiles and roof ornaments became more brilliantly colored, and by the time of the Ming dynasty, the roof ornaments were glazed with a riot of color.

Manchu (Ching) Dynasty (1644–1912)

Tsang Ying-hsuan, the director of the Imperial Kilns for a good number of years starting in 1682, was responsible for the development of a group of glazes that became extremely popular with connoisseurs of fine porcelain, first in China and later in Europe. Along with such glazes as a clear yellow, a spotted yellow, a turquoise, and a rich black, the most famous glazes of this period were the ***sang de boeuf,*** or ox blood (Color plate 3), the subtle "peach bloom," and the *claire de lune,* or moonlight, glaze. It was the fashion at this time for affluent scholars in China to collect porcelain objects covered with rich glazes shaped into boxes to hold the red paste with which they stamped their names on their calligraphic scrolls, as pots for washing or holding their brushes, and formed into graceful vases to hold the single flower they might place on their desks. These classic pieces, whose forms revived the dignified simplicity of Sung pottery, were the envy of European collectors, who spent fortunes to buy them. Under Tsang Ying-hsuan's direction overglazes were used subtly, and the *famille verte* and *famille noire* vases and bowls on which sprays of flowing trees, birds, and butterflies were painted were also avidly collected in Europe.

To compete with the Chinese imports, European potters tried for years to copy the thin, translucent porcelain, but it was not until the eighteenth century—1710, in Germany, to be exact—that porcelain was finally produced in Europe.

CHINESE INFLUENCES ON KOREA AND JAPAN

The Korean peninsula, close as it is to China, was deeply influenced by Chinese thought and Chinese art. However, the original prehistoric people of Korea, the Yemaeks, who settled the peninsula in a time known to historians as the Plain Coarse Pottery period, apparently came from the north. Legend has it that Tan'gun, the founder of the first kingdom, was the son of a female bear and a Yamaek, who himself was a son of the divine creator. His kingdom was said to have been founded in 2333 B.C.

Korea

Documented Korean history, however, begins at the end of the second century B.C., when the Han dynasty armies from China invaded and occupied an area of the northern Korean peninsula, holding it until 313 A.D. Buddhism also arrived with the invaders, and although the local inhabitants resisted the new religion for some time, it eventually became the main religion in Korea, whence it was taken to Japan. While the Chinese invaders settled in the north, the native Koreans established a series of states further south—the Three Kingdoms—of which the Silla is the most interesting to us because of its characteristic ceramics. Along with clay figures and objects made to be placed in tombs (3-20, 3-21), the Silla potters also produced pottery, frequently made in several parts, with the bottom perforated to create a stand (3-22). By the time of the Tang dynasty in China (A.D. 617–906), the Silla rulers

had unified the three kingdoms and formed an alliance with the new imperial Chinese court. Goods were exchanged actively with China, and Korean scholars and functionaries went there to study the economic and cultural policies of the Tang court, while those at home in Korea founded a university that taught Confucian studies. Throughout the Korean peninsula, Buddhism grew in influence. Chinese art and ceramics continued to be popular. At this time, the technique of intentional glazing reached Korea and was adopted by the Korean potters and through Korea eventually reached Japan.

Japan

The early inhabitants of the isolated islands of Japan practiced an animistic religion, in which the world was given life by supernatural beings called *kami*, who were believed to have been created by the gods at the same time as human beings. The early Japanese believed that these all-pervading spirits breathed life into everything that existed—trees, rivers, ocean waves, and plants. Just as all of nature was animated by the *kami*, so too were the skillful hands of a fisher, an archer, or a potter. This vitality, which the hands of the potter passed on to the clay, was a characteristic of native Japanese ceramics, one that manifested itself through the later centuries, despite continuing influences from China and Korea.

With mountains and deep valleys separating villages from each other, Japanese society developed intense local rivalries from the very earliest days, and civil war between chieftans and clans was almost constant. During centuries of upheaval, artisans lived quietly in their villages, staying on the same land for generations, digging clay from the same bank, and firing their kilns on the same hillside. As a result, Japanese potters developed an intense personal relationship with clay and kept this characteristic attitude for centuries.

Jōmon pottery and sculpture   As mentioned earlier, the first inhabitants of the Japanese islands are among the earliest known to have learned to fire pottery. Made of a reddish earthenware, their early handbuilt pottery, produced from about 10,000 to 300 B.C., was called Jōmon, the word for "cord," because the pottery's decoration con-

▲ *Figure 3-20*
An ash-glazed stoneware tomb model of a Korean
warrior wearing leather-plated armor. The funnel on
the back of his horse and the spout on the horse's
chest suggest it was a ritual vessel for pouring
libations. The ring on the spout probably held a
"dangler" of clay links, a characteristic decoration on
such vessels. Ht. 9¼ in. (25.5 cm). North Kyongsang
province, Korea. Old Silla dynasty, fifth to sixth
century A.D. *Courtesy National Museum of Korea.*

◀ *Figure 3-21*
This stoneware chariot model from a tomb of the Old
Silla dynasty in Korea reproduces all the details of the
carts in use at that time. So far, it is the only cart
model found there with movable wheels. Old Silla
dynasty, fifth to sixth century A.D. North Kyongsang
province. *Courtesy National Museum of Korea.*

Figure 3-22
Fired to stoneware hardness, the gray clay of this jar is covered in places with a natural ash glaze. The pedestal base is typical, and the incised line drawings of deer suggest a relationship with the northern tribes, who used deer horns in shamanistic practices. Old Silla dynasty, fifth to sixth century A.D. Uljn-gun, Korea. *Courtesy National Museum of Korea.*

sisted of cord impressions along with deep carving (1-3). The clay workers of the Jōmon period also made vigorously modeled and carved male and female figures (3-23), possibly fertility figures, that were probably used for rituals associated with appeasing the nature spirits. Heavy and rough but full of vitality, the Jōmon vessels and figures reflect the Japanese response to the earthy quality of their material, and are among the most impressive of humanity's creations in clay. Although there are differences in the ceramics produced within that long span of time that has been divided by art historians into Early, Mid and Late Jōmon, the overall characteristics of the pottery and sculpture of the entire period are the same: thick-walled and built by a slab or coil method, probably without a turntable, this pottery was made of a coarse clay containing a considerable amount of impurities. Like all early pottery, it was low-fired, perhaps in open fires and possibly in simple pit kilns.

Foreign Influences

By the beginning of the third century B.C., a new people, the Yayoi, immigrated into Japan from the north by way of Korea. These Korean immigrants had been much influenced by China, and among other innovations they brought the potter's wheel to Japan. As Japanese potters learned to use the wheel, they quite naturally modified the characteristics of their indigenous pottery. Their pots became thin-walled and rather graceful in shape and were sometimes raised on perforated stands. As contact with Korea became more common, the ceramics industry in Japan expanded and crafts guilds became part of Japan's highly organized class system.

Old Tomb Period (Third to Sixth Centuries A.D.)

During this period, called the Old Tomb owing to the many tombs dating from that time, entire communities of potters came, or were brought, to Japan from Korea. The ware they made—a pottery known as Sue—was fashioned of a high-fired, dense gray body into what was undoubtedly a luxury item, obviously influenced by the pottery of Korea (3-22). At the same time, proto-porcelain was being brought to Japan from Korea, and with it arrived the technique of applying glazes.

Although the Japanese potters, like the Chinese and Koreans, now became dedicated to refining clay and glaze, some of the vitality of the earlier Jōmon period was maintained in the vigorously modeled *haniwa* sculptures made during the Old Tomb period (page 50). Legend tells us that the *haniwa*, literally "clay circles," were originally made as substitutes for the live personal attendants who had formerly been left to starve to death half-buried in the ground around the tombs of notables. In actuality, the sculptures were derived from the simple cylinders that were embedded in

Figure 3-23
Like the Late Jōmon pottery (1-3), Jōmon sculptured figures were carved with swirls and textured areas alternating with highly polished sections. Full of vitality, they may have had a fertility significance. Aomoni Prefecture, Japan, Late Jōmon, first millennium B.C. *Courtesy Seattle Art Museum, Floyd A. Naramore Memorial Purchase Fund, 76.35.*

the ground around the mounded earth of the tombs, possibly to keep the earth from sliding. These *haniwa* pictured the everyday life of Japan, portraying warriors, farmers, singers and dancers, houses, horses, and other animals. Some *haniwa*, sculpted as waterbirds, were so placed to appear to be swimming on the water of the shallow ponds next to the mounds.

Tradition tells us that a thirteenth-century Japanese Buddhist priest, Toshiro Kato Shirozaemon, went to China to learn more about ceramics techniques, and that when he returned in 1227, he carried some Chinese clay with him. When he later discovered good clay in Japan, he was said to have founded the pottery industry of Japan in the Seto area, still the largest pottery-producing area in the country.

Japanese Kilns

Whether or not this Chinese-trained potter was actually the founder of the industry, there is no doubt that much of the technique at that time originally came from China and that the workshops in Japan fired their stoneware (3-24) in kilns called *anagama* modeled on the sloping kilns of China and Korea. Sometimes known as snake kilns because of their length and form, these kilns were built up a hill in one long tunnel with no interior dividing walls (3-25). In them, the Japanese potters fired pottery whose glazes were meant to imitate the celadon and other Chinese glazes of the Sung period. But because the Japanese lacked the centuries of accumulated knowledge of the Sung potters, their ware was coarser and coated with a greenish and sometimes yellow glaze that did not attain the quality of Chinese glazes.

As Buddhism became the dominant religion in Japan, Japanese sculptors copied from the Chinese sculptures of the Buddha and heavenly beings from India associated with Buddhism. In the Nara period (A.D. 710–784), the Japanese created clay temple figures—some made of clay mixed with straw and built over wooden forms— that reflected the restrained spiritual quality of the Buddhist religion. Never fired, these figures were merely coated with fine clay and then painted; incredibly, some have survived to our day.

Figure 3-24
Comparing this ash-glazed Japanese stoneware jar with a similar Han jar (3-9), one can see how much the early stoneware of Japan owed to Chinese influences. However, the lively, almost awkward way in which the narrow neck sits on its swelling body exemplifies the direct and vital Japanese attitude toward clay. Ninth or tenth century A.D. *Courtesy the Board of Trustees of the Victoria & Albert Museum.*

Zen and the Tea Ceremony

The tea ceremonies that had become popular in China during the Tang dynasty were intimately associated with ceramics. Although many connoisseurs preferred white or celadon tea cups, others felt that the black *Tienmu* glazed tea bowls were the most effective background for the foamy green tea that was beaten to a froth before serving. During the Sung dynasty in China, the Chan sect of Buddhism had emerged; like the Taoists they emphasized self-cultivation and meditation.

Called Zen in Japan, this sect developed a highly ritualized ceremony, in which the drinking of tea and its attendant rituals became a means of acquiring nobility and purity of thought. Brought to Japan by returning Buddhist monks around A.D. 1200, Zen became an integral part of the search for enlightenment in Japan, where all aspects of the ceremony expressed the Zen ideal of simplicity and refined poverty. Chinese tea bowls were introduced, along with tea houses where the ceremony was performed. The participants in the ceremony walked through a stylized garden, approached the tea house on stepping stones, and crouched to enter through a low door in a symbolic leavetaking of the outside world and a humbling of themselves in preparation for the ceremony.

Tea Ceramics

An influential Japanese tea master, Sen no Rikyu (1521–1591) preferred to use the simple rice bowls of Korea and the brown and black iron tenmoku glaze for his tea bowls. Others followed his lead, and soon there was a demand for these *chato*, or tea ceramics, which included tea caddies, bowls, jars, and flowerpots along with the tea bowls (3-26). First made in Kyoto in the sixteenth century by a Korean who had married a Japanese woman, these roughly shaped tea bowls were made on his death by his widow. Her son Chojiro (1515–1592) carried on the tradition, as did a grandson, who was given the right to mark the character *raku* ("pleasure") on the bottom of his bowls. From then on, successive generations of the family made **raku** tea bowls in Kyoto into the twentieth century.

These Japanese *chawan* (tea bowls) were pinched from a solid lump of clay and then carved into their final shape. This method produced a bowl with no joints, and was done for practical as well as aesthetic reasons, because the bowls were subjected to great temperature changes when they were placed in and removed from the red-hot raku kiln. This firing, in a special small square kiln, generally created cracks, pits, and other variations in the glaze, further individualizing each bowl. The coarse clay body from which the tea bowls were made did not conduct heat quickly, and part of the enjoyment of the ceremony was the gentle,

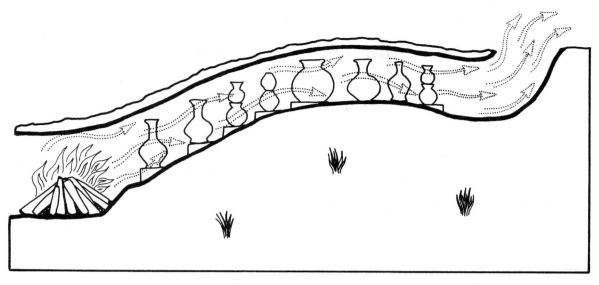

Figure 3-25
In Japanese snake kilns, modeled on similar Chinese and Korean kilns, the pots were
packed on top of one another on circular stands with slanting bases to keep them level
on the sloping floor. Sometimes the ware was placed in saggers to protect it from the
flames and ash that roared up through the kiln as the firing reached its height.

Figure 3-26
Classic Japanese raku tea bowls were carved in one
piece, not thrown or coiled. This helped them survive
the temperature changes they underwent when they
were placed in and removed from the red-hot raku
kiln. The shape of the lip, the "tea pool" in the
bottom, and the interior spiral that leads the tea to the
drinker's mouth were all regulated by strict rules.
Raku, earthenware with black-brown glaze. Japan,
seventeenth century. *Courtesy the Board of Trustees of the
Victoria & Albert Museum.*

Figure 3-27
Bizen ware was made of coarse, low-fire clay fired over a long period of time. In order to achieve the dark fire splashes and varied surface effects that appealed to the Zen masters, potters introduced straw into the kiln, causing local reduction. This jar exemplifies the rough surfaces and asymmetrical shapes of the Bizen tea ware. Earthenware. Japan, seventeenth century A.D. *Courtesy the Board of Trustees of the Victoria & Albert Museum.*

slow warming of the hands by the hot tea served in them. The experience included an appreciation of the rough surface of the bowls as they were held in the hands. Each piece of *chato* expressed the character of the master potter who made it; some famous bowls were given names and are now classified as National Treasures of Japan. Also among the treasured tea ceramics are the *cha-ire*, or tea containers, in which the finely powdered tea was kept.

Bizen

Among the most famous of the tea ceramics were those that came from the **Bizen** kilns, where a rustic type of pottery greatly valued by tea masters was fired in a deliberate effort to achieve accidental fire markings (3-27). To create a wide range of surface effects on one pot—rosy red, matt black, greenish glaze, with areas of opales-

cence—the potters packed the *cha-ire* inside the other pots lined with straw or placed bags of straw next to them in the climbing *anagama* kilns. As the straw burned, it produced areas of local reduction that were responsible for the variations on the surface.

Both the raku method of placing tea bowls in the hot fire and the Bizen use of local reduction firings have had an influence on contemporary Western pottery, especially since the resurgence of interest in Zen. Potters all over the world now use tenmoku glazes, fire in wood kilns of Japanese-derived style (16-14), and practice variations of the raku firing process, some of which the early tea masters might have trouble recognizing (16-21). But they would probably feel in accord with the aesthetic attitudes of the contemporary potters and appreciate the expressive qualities of their work.

The Japanese Porcelain Industry

Japanese potters did not limit themselves only to these deliberately rough wares produced in the Tamba, Tokoname, Bizen, and Shigaraki kilns. At the beginning of the sixteenth century, a Japanese potter visited China to study the porcelain industry there, hoping, without success, to find the necessary ingredients for porcelain on his return to Japan. In around 1605, an immigrant Korean potter, Ri Sampei, did find kaolin in the Arita district of Japan, and the porcelain industry founded there grew so rapidly that by 1664, forty-five thousand pieces of porcelain were being shipped to Holland each year. Japan quickly outpaced China in the export trade, and so many trees were cut down to fuel the kilns that the government finally restricted the building of new ones. By this time, the Japanese kilns, like those of China, were divided into chambers, and potters had also learned from China the techniques of underglazing with cobalt blue and using brightly colored overglazes. With a natural sense of design and skill with the brush, Japanese potters created some enameled ware of great beauty, but like Chinese potters, they felt the need to satisfy the Western taste for garish colors and over-elaborate forms. To speed production, each piece was worked on by many people, which meant

Figure 3-28
Ogata Kenzan, the potter, signed this square tray on the base, while Ogata Kōrin, his brother, signed it above his free brush painting of irises. The brothers often composed asymmetrically, leaving a large area undecorated for contrast and balance. Stoneware tray by Ogata Kenzan, decorated by Ogata Kōrin, Kyoto ware. 8⅝ in. square (21.7 cm). Edo period, 1615–1868. *Courtesy Freer Gallery of Art, Smithsonian Institution, Washington, D.C.*

Figure 3-29
A late Edo period plate from Shigaraki shows the nature motifs widely used in that period; waving bamboo, painted in free, sparing brushstrokes was especially popular. Shigaraki, Japan, Late Edo period, 1600–1868. *Courtesy the Harvard University Art Museums (Arthur M. Sackler Museum), gift of Charles Bain Hoyt, Esq.*

that much of the ware exported to Europe did not meet the high aesthetic standard demanded by knowledgeable collectors in Japan.

Ogata Kōrin and Ogata Kenzan

Despite the emphasis on mass production of export ware, there were potters in Japan who maintained a close personal relationship with clay, forming their pottery themselves with restraint and decorating it with graceful underglaze brush paintings. In the seventeenth century, the capital of Japan moved from Kyoto to Edo, leaving behind some impoverished noble families who had to earn their livings by teaching art, music, or po-

etry. Two brothers from a wealthy background, Ogata Kenzan (1663–1743) and Ogata Kōrin (1658–1716), were forced by circumstances to become potters and painters, applying their highly developed taste and visual awareness to ceramics. Inspired by nature, they often worked together, and both signed the pieces on which they collaborated. The decoration was brushed freely on simple shapes with masterly strokes in brown or black on a white clay body, or on a colored clay covered with a white slip (3-28). Other Edo period potters (3-29) who remained in a close relationship with clay greatly admired the Kenzan name, and throughout the years that name has been bestowed as an honor to potters considered worthy of it. In the twentieth century, one Western potter, Bernard Leach of England (8-2), was honored with the name Kenzan VII.

PERSIA AND THE ARAB WORLD

We must backtrack here and recall that around 550 B.C. the Persians had conquered large areas in western Asia, Egypt, India, and Greece, absorbing cultural and artistic influences from the past as well as from all parts of their empire, and combining these influences with their own taste for the ornate and luxurious to create a new Sassanian culture. Persian cities became the meeting place of two worlds—central Asia, India, and China to the east, and Syria and Rome to the west. Then, in the seventh century A.D., when the Moslems conquered Persia and other eastern territories, the taste of the Sassanian Persians began to influence Islamic ceramics and the Persians' knowledge of lead-tin glazes was passed on to the Arab world.

At the beginning of the fourteenth century, Abu'l Qasim, who lived in Kashan, wrote a ceramic "how-to" book that gave, among many recipes, one for a clay body that became a popular substitute for Chinese porcelain. It consisted of a glass **frit,** quartz, and white clay, and was formed on the wheel. Because the clay was not very plastic, vessels had to be made in small sections. The next section would either be thrown on the already leather-hard first section or made separately and luted to it when it too became leather hard. Then, when the entire vessel was leather hard, the potter would thin it by gradually scraping away clay from the walls as the vessel turned on the wheel. Vessels made of this clay body, if thinned enough, could become translucent like the Chinese porcelains but were never as hard. Abu'l Qasim also gave directions for heating quartz and soda ash for many hours, constantly stirring it and then throwing it into a pit full of water to form the frit, which was eventually ground into powder. He described the terrifying, thunderous roar that was produced when the water and molten glass met, saying that if anyone had not seen and heard it he would fall trembling on his knees.

Pottery and ceramic tiles became important elements in Moslem art. One factor of great importance in the development of Islamic art was the prohibition in the Koran, the Moslem religious text, against the portrayal of human figures

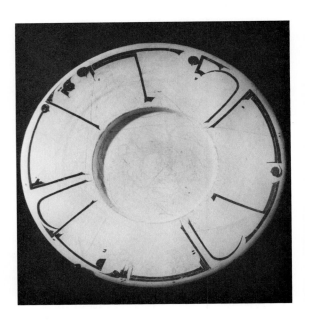

Figure 3-30
The inscription in Kufic script on this Iranian plate creates an abstract design but also preaches a lesson: "Deliberation before work protects you from regret." The potter decorated the plate with underglaze on white slip-covered earthenware in an attempt to copy the underglaze-decorated porcelain of Sung China. Diameter 14⅝ in. (37.2 cm). Iran, Samanid period, tenth century A.D. *Courtesy the St. Louis Art Museum, museum purchase.*

in the mosques. Since sculpture in the round was considered to be blasphemy, ceramic sculpture hardly existed in Islamic countries. Instead, Islamic potters were constrained to use leaves, flowers, and quotations from the Koran for decoration, painting them with colorful glazes on their plates and bowls and on the tiles decorating the domes and minarets of the mosques and the cool courtyards and fountains of luxurious palaces throughout the Moslem world. The inscriptions that appeared on both tiles and pottery were frequently pious, commendatory, or admonitory (3-30, 3-34).

Luster Ware

It was also against the teaching of Islam to use precious metals on earth, for the Koran taught

Figure 3-31
Black, white, and blue glazes were a popular combination with Persian potters. The inscriptions on such bowls might read "Sovereignty is God's" or "Blessings and beneficence." Kashan, Persian, thirteenth century A.D. *Courtesy the Metropolitan Museum of Art. Bequest of William Milne Grinnell, 1920.*

Figure 3-32
Opaque white tin glaze makes an excellent background for colored glazes and iridescent yellow luster overglaze decoration on a bowl from Kahr, near Teheran. Diameter 7½ in. (19.1 cm). Late twelfth to early thirteenth century, A.D. *Courtesy the Board of Trustees of the Victoria & Albert Museum.*

that the faithful would be rewarded in paradise with vessels of gold and silver. In addition, in Sassanian Persia there was a shortage of silver, and silver vessels became even more expensive and difficult to obtain. Potters, therefore, looked for a substitute material that would give the appearance of metal but would still allow its owners to remain good Moslems. This led them to develop a form of overglaze called **luster.** This iridescent decoration was made with metallic salts—copper or silver, for example—mixed with a paste of gum or clay and painted on top of the glaze. The piece was then given a low firing at 1112° F/600° C, in a reducing atmosphere, after which the kiln was sealed and allowed to cool. Although the Egyptians had used luster earlier, it was the Islamic potters who perfected it, using it with rich effect. As the religious climate of Islam grew less strict,

potters did begin to portray the human figure (3-32) along with animals and birds, sometimes combining them into fantasy creatures or using animal shapes for ceramic jugs or other objects (3-33). But the human figures did not appear in the tiles that enhanced the walls of the prayer niches. These continued to display pious inscriptions and arabesques of plant forms (3-34).

As the Mohammedans spread west through the Mediterranean and along the northern coasts of Africa, they carried with them pottery techniques and artistic styles from the East, changing the native art wherever local inhabitants were converted to Islam, and when the Moors crossed to Spain around A.D. 700, the influence of Islamic art reached the European continent. In Chapter 6 we will see how this influence affected the development of European ceramics (6-1, 6-2).

Figure 3-33

Luster overglaze decorates a water jug used for washing the hands. These *aquamaniles* had tubes inside them to direct the water through the mouth of the animal. Made of red earthenware, this one was first covered with white glaze and then painted with copper luster overglaze and fired at a low temperature in a reducing atmosphere. Length 11¾ in. (29.8 cm). Persia, late fifteenth or early sixteenth century. *Courtesy the Board of Trustees of the Victoria & Albert Museum.*

Figure 3-34
Earthenware tiles glazed with opaque tin glazes decorated palaces, mosques, and tombs in Persia and later throughout the Moslem world. Brilliantly colored in blues, greens, and yellows, the tiles were often cut in the shape of stars, leaves, and flowers. Vines and flowers twine in interlaced decorations called *arabesque*, while Arabic script is used as decoration. From a tomb. 21 in. square (53.4 cm). Persia, thirteenth century. *Courtesy the Board of Trustees of the Victoria & Albert Museum.*

Figure 3-35
Sensuously modeled figures of nature spirits and fertility deities covered the facades of the temples in India. Whether they were modeled in clay or carved in stone, they exemplified a sculptural tradition in which the forms of the human body imply the bounty of nature. Fragment of a relief from a temple or monastery near Allahabad, India. c. A.D. 700. *Courtesy the Board of Trustees of the Victoria & Albert Museum.*

INDIA

Despite the fact that oceans and mountains ring the vast land of India, the land has received numerous migrations of peoples in waves. These influxes have ranged from the invasions of the Aryans in about 1500 B.C. through those of the Iranians, Greeks, Arabs, and finally the British, in 1815. As a result, there has always been great diversity in the peoples of India, and the three main religions—Hinduism, Jainism, and Bud-

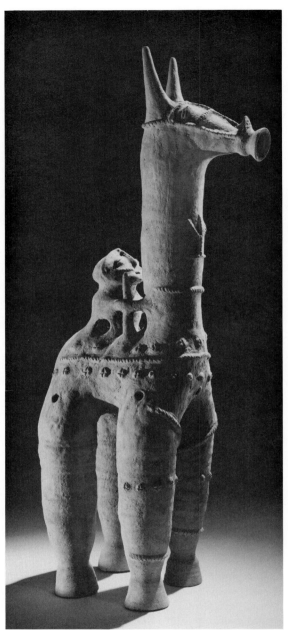

Figure 3-36
The tradition of modeling votive images from the earth is a long one in India, and the horse has been a favorite image there since the remote past, symbolizing hope and protection. It is the steed of the Spirit Riders, who are believed to guard the villages. Votive horse and rider, terra-cotta. Bhil tribe. Ht. about 3 ft. (91.4 cm). India, twentieth century. *Courtesy Philadelphia Museum of Art: Purchased (67-197-1).*

dhism—have offered the artist a rich heritage of images upon which to draw. The artist in India was a member of a guild, and worked closely with representatives of the different religions who instructed him in the complex symbolism of the cults so that he might depict the deities with their proper attributes and in the proper attitudes. One must remember when looking at Indian sculpture that no matter how sensual or erotic the images are to our eyes, to the Indian viewer they are always religious, for the religions of that land expressed spirituality through the beauty of the human form.

But even if the artists who created the sculptures decorating the temples were anonymous, their gestures have been preserved for centuries in the fired clay of the terra-cotta reliefs that remain from temples and monasteries (3-35). Clay had been an essential part of Indian life for thousands of years. Not only was the earth of the river valleys essential to the Indian people for their livelihood, but it was also a source of the material they needed for making essential vessels, buildings, toys, and religious images. Although the best-known temples in India were built of stone, in areas where stone was rare, itinerant bands of terra-cotta craftsmen made and decorated brick temples well into the nineteenth century. A symbol of the fertility of the earth, the clay they used on these temples was in itself sacred. Working under a master, the guild members made the bricks and built the temples, while the modelers made the sensuous images of fertility deities and mythological personages that decorated the temples. Generally, the sculpture was made in molds and then worked over when leather hard. It was frequently burnished and the decorative details were added with pointed instruments made of bone or bamboo. One can see, in looking at such sculpture, how the modeler used each of these processes. Finally, the reliefs were fired in kilns built at the site and installed on the temple facades.

Today, the tradition of clay sculpture in India is still alive in rural areas, where village shrines are decorated with deities and protective spirits of fired clay (Color plate 7). In addition to the figures that remain in place, large unfired-clay figures are made for local religious festivals, and when the ceremonies are over they are placed in the river to disintegrate and return to the earth. Ranging in size from small votive sculptures up to huge fired-in-place horses, these rural ritual images express the hopes and fears of an agricultural society dependent on the weather for the success of their crops and continued protection against famine. The Spirit Riders protected the village fields, riding their boundaries at night. These benevolent spirits and their horses were often depicted in clay (3-36).

4
Africa

*. . . form and content
are scarcely separable in
societies in which the
artist is an integral
member of the
community, not an
individual struggling to
express a purely private
vision.*

Frank Willet*

T he African continent is vast, encompassing many different natural environments. Wide-open grassland; hot, dry deserts; deep rainforests, and cool mountain highlands—each is part of Africa's rich natural heritage. Just as the land is infinitely varied, so are the people who have lived on it. Like all major continents, Africa has seen a procession of peoples moving across its land for thousands of years, hunting its wild animals, driving their domestic herds to new grazing lands, moving on in search of a better place to live. In the process, newcomers have pushed the original inhabitants or earlier immigrants ahead of them, resulting in a complex intermingling of peoples and racial strains. The life styles, beliefs, the ceremonies, legends, and arts of the African

African Art, An Introduction, N.Y. and London, Oxford University Press. 1971.

Naa Jato, who was active in the Cameroon in the 1930s, handbuilt this palm wine container, depicting on it scenes of village life. She applied the relief figures while the clay was damp, and once the walls were leather hard, she burnished the areas between them with a smooth stone. Earthenware. Ht. 16½ in. (42 cm). Cameroon, Northern Mfunte, Lus group, 1936. *Courtesy the Portland Art Museum, Oregon. The Paul and Clara Gebauer Collection of Cameroon Art. Photo: Bill Grand.*

peoples also vary greatly from group to group and place to place. For this reason, we cannot speak of African art or African ceramics as if they were the products of a single culture.

EARLY AFRICA

At one time, what is now the Sahara Desert was grassland, supporting herds of animals, the home of a pastoral people who covered the walls of caves with paintings and carving of elephants, rhinoceroses, horses, and camels, as well as domestic cattle. They also made pottery that has been found along with cave paintings, dating from between 4000 and 1200 B.C. Then, when years of drought hit the area and vegetation died, the people and animals moved on, leaving behind them only ceramic shards and the animals painted on the walls.

Eventually, groups of people living in different parts of the African continent settled into agricultural ways of life that allowed them to develop crafts. As in most other early cultures, clay and metal working developed here simultaneously—not a surprising development, since both pursuits are fire-related. Even today, the links persist; in Upper Nigeria, for example, the wives of the iron workers are the potters.

NOK TERRA-COTTA SCULPTURE (fourth to fifth centuries B.C.)

In northern Nigeria, near the village of Nok and at Taruga, iron-working furnaces, tin mines, and iron tools that date from around the fourth or fifth century B.C. have been found along with fragments of almost life-sized terra-cotta sculptures of humans and animals (4-1). The technical knowledge required to build and safely fire such large sculptures suggests that people must have been working with clay here for some time, and the expressive ways in which the sculptors indicated human feelings speak of a rich artistic heritage.

Whether these sculptures represented important persons or ancestor figures we do not know. We do know, however, that Nok was one of the

Figure 4-1
Ancient Nok sculptors shaped clay into images that speak to us with a sense of urgent life. The faces appear carved, suggesting that their forms may have been based on wood carving. Almost life-sized, the figures are a remarkable technical achievement in building and firing clay. Nok culture, second century B.C. *Courtesy Jos Museum, Nigeria.*

many cultures in Africa to develop a royal court art, centering around the king or chief, and that sculptor-potters in these societies were often retained by the king to create ceremonial and status objects in addition to ancestor figures. Ancestors were of the greatest importance among many peoples in Africa, who believed that if the traditions the ancestors handed down were broken, misfortunes would result. The sculptures, made of rough, heavily tempered clay and exhibiting a sophisticated simplification of form, speak to us across the centuries.

Interestingly, women today in some of the small groups living in this area make pottery similar in shape to ancient Nok pottery and also occasionally make sculptures for grave memorials

Figure 4-2
Ife sculptures are more realistic than those of the Nok, but some of the details of clothing and hair are similar. The dates of the life-sized Ife sculptures are uncertain; some date them at A.D. 600–1200 and others at 800–1400 A.D. Terra-cotta. Ife. *Nigerian Museums. Courtesy the Trustees of the British Museum, London.*

and ritual use. It is possible that they are the inheritors of the Nok culture but, like so much in the story of African ceramics, this is only conjecture. Until more archaeological exploration has been done there, our knowledge of the history of clay working in Africa will be far from complete.

IFE SCULPTURE (A.D. 800–1400)

One of the royal courts of Africa centered in the city of Ile Ife, in southwestern Nigeria, where, from around 800 to 1400 A.D., the Yoruba people produced a rich and lively art. There have been no archaeological finds yet that can fill the gaps in our knowledge about the years between the end of the Nok culture and the flowering of the Ife culture. It is possible that the two cultures were not connected, but some similarities between them suggest that the Nok sculpture may have influenced Ife sculptors (4-2). Both cultures made large terra-cotta sculptures on which the forms were simplified, and some of the detailing of beaded decorations and hair on the bodies are similar. But the Ife sculptures are more realistic than those of the Noks, and closer in many ways to Benin sculpture, in which individuals were represented in terra-cotta portraits that were models for bronze casts.

By the eleventh century A.D., the sculptors of Ife were skilled in bronze casting, a craft that relied on ceramics for the crucibles in which the metal was melted, molds in which bronze objects were cast, and the originals from which the molds were made.

BENIN SCULPTURE

In Benin as in the Nok culture, sculpture was a court art focused on the king, who, it is said, brought a talented Ife sculptor, Iqu-igha, to Benin to teach the craft of working in bronze to the local sculptors. As in other African cultures, preserving the memory of historic happenings and the images of royalty and their ancestors was one of the main assignments of sculptors. Most of the known Benin sculpture consists of portraits cast in bronze, but enough terra-cotta portraits have been found to show that clay was undoubtedly the material in which the original models were created.

RITUAL CERAMICS

What we call art has served ceremonial and ritualistic functions in many cultures throughout the world. In Africa, as elsewhere, the people often believe that ritual objects have the power to protect people from or control evil forces, or intercede with supernatural spirits. In earlier days in Africa, the ritual objects were made for use and were associated with the passage from one period of life to another, or with death. In Ashanti graveyards, terra-cotta sculptures of heads were given an honored place, probably as memorials to the deceased (4-3). Many of the ceremonial objects and ceramic vessels were used by the secret male societies that governed the initiation of youths into manhood, while others were related to the puberty rites of the women. Still other pots were used in ceremonies, festivals, and rituals dedicated to the spirits of crops and fertility or to bringing good fortune (4-4). One outstanding group of sculptured pots from the Ibo village of Osisa, on the west bank of the Niger River, was made to be placed in the village shrines dedicated to Ifijiok, the Yam spirit (4-5).

Other ceremonies, such as the initiation of the leather artisans of the Korhogu region, also required sculpture or pottery. In these ceremonies, unbaked clay figures, realistically modeled, were used to teach initiates about the guild of craftsmen they were joining. Burial rites also required ceramics: in Ghana, the Ashanti placed a type of ornamented pot called the *abusua kuruwa*, along with a cooking pot, utensils, and hearthstones, beside the grave of the recently buried. In it was placed hair that all the blood relatives of the deceased had shaved off their heads. Thus, what we call art was made for use, and the ceremonial and ritual ceramic objects all had functions, albeit not everyday ones, that were just as essential to religious ceremonies or rituals as pieces of domestic pottery were to daily life.

Figure 4-3
Terra-cotta sculptures like this one were apparently used in Ashanti funeral ceremonies or as memorials to the dead. This example was sculpted more than a hundred years ago by a craftsman of the Kwahu, an Ashanti group. Ht. 15 in. (38 cm). Kajebi, Ghana. *Courtesy the Trustees of the British Museum, London.*

Figure 4-5
The Ibo, who lived west of the Niger River, placed sculptured pots on altars dedicated to Ifijiok, the Yam spirit. This one shows images of the chiefs, their wives and children, and attendant musicians. Ht. 13¾ in. (35 cm). Ibo, Osisa, Nigeria. *Courtesy the Trustees of the British Museum, London.*

Figure 4-4
Called a *Mogyemogye*, or "jawbone" pot, this vessel displays decorations similar to those used on Ashanti gold work. It held the wine that was poured over the Golden Stool of Ashanti. According to legend, the stool fell from the heavens, bringing good fortune to the Ashanti, so it was greatly revered. Ht. 18 in. (46 cm). Abuakwa, Ghana. *Courtesy the Trustees of the British Museum, London.*

FOREIGN INFLUENCES

Just as China and Japan absorbed and modified the Buddhist art that came from India, so Africa has absorbed and modified the artistic ideas that have come to the continent through invasions, migrations, and trade with other peoples. For example, the Kabyle pottery of Algeria is decorated with white, brown, and black designs that are remarkably similar to ancient ware made in Bronze Age Cyprus, suggesting that there may have been a lingering Cypriot influence. The Cretans, Greeks, and Romans all came to northern Africa, and along with the Coptic Church in Egypt and Ethiopia, all had varying effects on local ceramic styles. In addition, the Moslems brought to Africa their religious prohibitions against representing human forms, changing the styles of ornament in the areas that were converted to Islam. From the time the Europeans came to Africa, in the 1600s, local art often reflected the new teachings of Christianity. Unfortunately for the traditional crafts, however, the exposure to twentieth-century foreign influences has been largely a destructive one.

CRAFTS IN EVERYDAY LIFE

In Africa, as in most other preindustrial societies, art has not been separated from everyday life as it has in Western societies since the Renaissance. The artist in African cultures was never divorced from the people who used his or her creations, and although some persons may have achieved the highest skill at weaving, pottery making, singing, or dancing, their work was considered to be a reflection of normal human activity. That beauty was part of everyday life is testified to by a Yoruba poet who celebrated equally the beauty of fast-running deer, children, a rainbow, and a well swept veranda, saying, "Anybody who meets beauty and does not look at it will soon be poor."

EARLY POTTERY TECHNIQUES

Our knowledge of early pottery techniques in Africa is scant, and in order to form some sense of how potters made and fired their creations we can only study traditional methods that remain in use today. Among the African ceramic treasures in the storerooms of the British Museum is a modest box labeled "African female potter's tools," collected in the 1880s. This box contains only a piece of metal for scraping, a wooden tool for making designs, smooth stones for polishing, a pointed shell for punching holes, and a corn cob and smooth seed pods for impressing designs—touching and mute reminders that potters all over the world have shaped and smoothed clay pots in very much the same fashion for thousands of years (1-24, 5-17). But despite many similarities, the methods used today may have been changed by contact with other cultures, so we cannot take them as "living archaeology," but rather we must look at them as only suggestions of some of the traditional methods that have been handed down from one generation to another. And, although we find some similarities in technique among artisans across the continent, we also see great variations in the traditions of the widely separated groups who have lived on the African continent.

One factor does remain the same throughout all cultures there; until recently, pottery in Africa has always been handbuilt. Only in Egypt were turntables on axles, kick wheels, and permanent kilns known and used. In addition, with few exceptions, in Africa pots have always been fired in open firings (4-12).

Until recently, low-fired earthenware pots were used for all domestic needs—for example, cooking; storing food, beer, or honey; carrying water (1-23); and dyeing fibers. Because there was no need for a higher fired ware, none was developed; in fact, earthenware was better adapted to the rural life than high-fired ceramics would have been. Earthenware is, for example, better for cooking over an open fire, because its coarse clay allows the pots to expand and contract, reducing the likelihood of cracking. Also, earthenware is best for storing drinking water in a hot climate, because the porosity of the clay body allows the water to cool by evaporation. Where clay was plastered over a frame of wood and straw to build the walls of houses, it was used because it was the most plentiful material and could be built up into thick walls that kept out the heat. Another traditional use for clay in certain areas of Africa was the building of storage bins that look like large pots with straw hats. These clay granaries protect the grain from weather and rats. Like many other peoples in warm countries, Africans have for centuries built storage buildings, houses, and mosques with mud and clay. After the beginning of the nineteenth century, the walls of many such buildings were decorated with sculptured clay reliefs. Before that, the mud bricks with which the walls were built were often set in decorative patterns.

Division of Labor

Traditionally, African men and women have had distinct roles and have rarely done the same work. Pottery there is still usually reserved for the women. As in the American Southwest, African mothers teach their daughters, handing down the empirical knowledge of generations. The hands of African women traditionally dig the clay, prepare

▲ *Figure 4-6*
Tobacco pipe bowls, attached to long hollow stems, were often used in male ceremonies. White chalk or ash was rubbed into the incised crosshatching typical of their decoration to emphasize it. Length of bowl 3⅛ in. (8 cm). Shilluk, Sudan. *Courtesy the Trustees of the British Museum, London.*

◄ *Figure 4-7*
Made in the shape of an elephant, this pipe bowl was highly burnished. Usually, men made such pipes or other ceremonial objects. Ht. 1¼ in. (3 cm). Batotela, Zambia. *Courtesy the Trustees of the British Museum, London.*

it for use, and shape it, often according to rules and taboos. For example, the Mongoro potters of the Ivory Coast sacrifice a goat or rooster before digging clay as a way of asking forgiveness from the gods. Until recently, among the Shai people of Ghana, every house had a potter, all of them women. In earlier centuries, the pits where the Shai dug their clay were under the control of priestesses, who presided over the rituals governing its removal—for example, only women who had passed puberty could dig the clay. Although women have been potters for centuries in Africa, only recently have the names of women potters become known. One such potter, Naa Jato, lived in a village in the Cameroon, where she made palm wine containers commissioned by the male clubs and local chiefs (see page 80). Hers were not

ordinary domestic pots, and the relief decoration she added to the clay of the handbuilt walls was lively and humorous, giving a vivid portrait of the life of the people in her village.

Where men have been involved in pottery in Africa, they have frequently made only a special type of pottery or have used techniques that differed from those of the women. In Ghana, for instance, taboos forbade men to make domestic ware. On the other hand, among some peoples the men make pottery and the women are forbidden to come near them during certain parts of the process. And in some cultures the making of ceremonial ceramics—objects traditionally associated with the men such as ritual drums, pipes, and bellows tips for smelting—were made by the men exclusively (4-6, 4-7).

Another rule forbids Ashanti women from making pots decorated with human figures. The reason given is that a woman who did this once became sterile, because she had made an image of a human instead of bearing a child. In the diversity of these rules and taboos, we can see that ceramics reflect the richness and variety of the many cultures that have flourished in Africa (4-8).

CONTEMPORARY POTTERY TECHNIQUES

Almost every type of handbuilding technique is used today in Africa. A potter might start by pressing the clay into a base mold, first leaving it to stiffen somewhat and then building the rest with coils. Conversely, sometimes potters start by forming the upper section of a pot first, letting it stiffen, and then when it is firm enough, building coils onto it to form the lower section upside down (4-9). The Ashanti women, however, use no coils at all; they make the whole pot by pulling up the sides from one lump of clay, walking around it backwards as they do so. Elsewhere, a potter may form the base of a pot by hollowing out a lump of clay with her fingers and then building the walls. Still others start the base by pressing clay into a mold lined with leaves or ashes to keep the clay from sticking; as they build the walls, they pound the clay with a wooden beater while holding a stone inside—much as the women in Fiji shape their pots (1-16). The base may be part of a dried gourd or the bottom of an old pot turned with the hands or feet as the pot is built. Sometimes a potter makes use of the hollowed-out stump of a tree or another large fired pot as a stand on which to build at a convenient working height (4-10).

Where coils are used, they are scraped, pressed, or beaten as they are added to meld the walls together. The outside is then smoothed with the fingers, a shell, or a bit of dried gourd or a piece of leather.

Finishing

There seem to be as many methods of finishing pots as there are peoples in Africa. Some potters burnish pots with stones or smooth seed

Figure 4-8
These tiny, burnished black pottery figures from Ethiopia were made by a group of Jews who settled there long ago. In scenes from daily life, a woman grinds corn while a child peers over her shoulder, and another woman carries water from the spring or river in a clay pot. *Photo by Mogens S. Koch, Denmark.*

Figure 4-9
An Ashanti woman potter, making a series of large pots, builds the upper section first. When these sections are stiff enough to support more clay, she turns them over and completes the bottom section. Ghana. *Courtesy National Museum of African Art, Washington, D.C., Eliot Elisofon Archives, Smithsonian Institution. Photo: Eliot Elisofon.*

Figure 4-10
Some African women today continue to shape pots using methods that are thousands of years old. From them, we can learn the traditional methods and hope to preserve that knowledge. Here, a potter uses both a fired pot and a broken one as a base in which to form her pot. *Courtesy Field Museum of Natural History, Chicago.*

pods, rubbing until the leather-hard surface is polished (1-24). Sometimes the clay of the pots has been tempered with mica or covered with a mica-containing slip so that the surface of the burnished pot sparkles as bits of glistening mica reflect the light.

In many villages, the potters coat fired pots with resin, palm oil, or mixtures made from boiling certain leaves in order to reduce their porosity. Applying these mixtures may change the color of the red clay body to a dark brown. Because the color of this sealing material appealed to some potters, they now sometimes apply this vegetable material only for decoration, in patterns of bands, lines, or triangles. They also sometimes splash it over the whole pot while it is hot for a marbled effect.

Decoration

Depending on the local pottery tradition, African potters use a great variety of decorative techniques to enhance the surfaces of their pots. They may scratch their designs into the damp clay with a knife or stick, press patterns into it with twisted or plaited straw or a natural object such as a corn cob (4-11), or roll repeat designs onto the clay with a carved wooden wheel, called a **roulette.** Water or milk pots from Botswana are decorated with patterns in which dark-toned graphite triangles contrast with areas of untreated clay body, while the Ibo color only the raised bands of clay that they attach around their large-bellied vases in undulating patterns.

Some of the decorative techniques may have had their origin in function. For example, impressed, carved, or raised designs on a water pot make it easier to lift a heavy, slippery pot full of water (1-23). In Uganda, some potters copy in clay the shapes of calabashes used originally as

◀ *Figure 4-11*
Demonstrating traditional methods at the Field Museum of Natural History in Chicago, Ladi Kwali of Nigeria builds and decorates a water pot. **(a)** She starts to narrow the neck as she adds coils, pressing them tightly onto the walls. **(b)** She has shaped the neck and the rim and adds decoration by pressing a textured tool into the damp clay. *Courtesy Field Museum of Natural History, Chicago (Neg. #82515).*

Figure 4-12
Ashanti women of Ghana arrange their pots for firing, alternating several layers of pots with fuel. Sometimes as many as three hundred pots are fired at one time; at other times, one large pot is fired alone. Wood, grass, millet, or straw is used for fuel. In a few places in western Africa, a low wall is built around the pots to deflect the wind and hold in the heat, making a rudimentary kiln. Ghana. *Courtesy National Museum of African Art, Washington, D.C., Eliot Elisofon Archives, Smithsonian Institution. Photo: Eliot Elisofon.*

containers or ladles, while others carve lines on their pots that duplicate the patterns originally made by the fiber or leather thongs that were laced around the gourds as handles. Whatever the method of decoration, each region or group of peoples has stayed within its own tradition, repeating its designs consistently over time.

Firing

Once the pots are finished, they are left to dry. If the weather is too hot, they are placed in a cool spot with fired pots placed over them to keep them from drying too quickly. Before firing, the potters might heat them by burning grass inside them, as in Ogbomosho, Nigeria (1-32).

Almost all pottery firing in Africa is done in an open fire. The length of firing time varies from place to place and, according to the size, number,

and thickness of the pots. It may last for several hours or only for a few minutes. Indeed, some potters fire their pots for only a short time at a low temperature, leaving it to the housewife who buys them to give them a second firing when she gets home.

Living close to the earth, the rural African potters have always adapted their firing techniques to the ecology of the countryside around them, using the most readily available fuel. Placing pots in an open fire might seem like an easy way to fire, but heating a large number of good-sized pots to maturity in an open fire is actually an intricate process, requiring skill and patience. How to place the pots, how to stack the fuel, what fuel to use, how to keep the fire burning, and even when to fire to avoid gusty winds that might create sudden flare-ups—all this accumulated knowledge results from generations of experimentation (4-12).

91

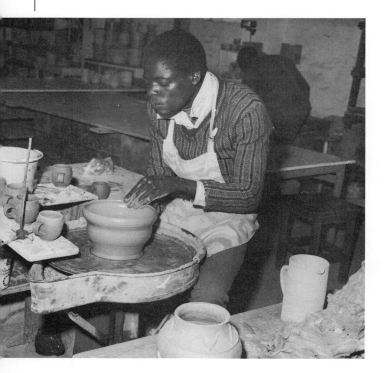

Figure 4-13
A contemporary potter in a studio in Lusaka, Zambia, uses local stoneware clay on a kick wheel. Similar workshops have been started in several African countries to meet the demand for pottery that is more durable than earthenware. These workshops also make pots in historical shapes, decorating them with traditional designs. *Courtesy Zambia Information Services, Lusaka, Zambia.*

CHANGING CRAFTS IN CHANGING TIMES

It is true that even today large numbers of pots are produced by traditional methods in Africa, and in some places women potters still carry their fired pots on their heads for ten or fifteen miles to other villages to market them. But in Africa, as all over the world, many traditional crafts have already disappeared. It is feared that the rich African heritage of ceramic technique may be lost, as is already happening in some parts of Africa as the continent becomes more urbanized. The future of traditional pottery in Africa is now uncertain as plastic and factory-produced domestic ware take over the market. Will traditional work be made mostly for tourists and collectors as is the case elsewhere? In an attempt to save some of the older African forms and decorative styles, several workshops have been established. Here traditional shapes and decorations are adapted to wheel techniques and glazed stoneware (4-13). Potters such as Ladi Kwali in Nigeria (4-11) and Abasiya Ahuwan of Nigeria are deeply committed to preserving their traditional heritage and are trying to develop an awareness and respect for old methods among the younger potters. Thus, new styles of ceramics may emerge that will combine old and new techniques and forms to create an art that is truly expressive of present-day Africa.

5
The Americas

*He who animates the clay
with penetrating eye
amasses and shapes it.
The good potter puts
effort into things,
teaches the clay to lie,
converses with his very
heart, breathes life into
objects, creates . . .*

Aztec poem*

Maya players in the ritual ball game wore protective belts, helmets, gauntlets, and knee pads; players were usually forbidden to use their hands or feet, so they kept the ball in motion with their bodies. Since reliefs on the Toltec ball court at Chichén Itzá show the decapitation of a ball player, it is possible that the losers were sacrificed—although some suggest it was the winners who had the honor of being sacrificed. Ht. 6 in. (15.2 cm). Jaina, Campeche, Mexico, A.D. 700–800. *Courtesy Museo Nacional de Antropologia, Mexico.*

Some scholars believe that both North and South America were settled by around twenty thousand years ago, but others set the date at sometime after fourteen thousand years ago.

Geologists say that at one time thousands of years ago, the American and Asian continents were connected by a land bridge. Before that bridge was flooded by the rising water of melting Ice Age glaciers, groups of Asian hunters followed their prey—mammoths, bison, and other large animals—across it and stayed on to move slowly down the continent.

Whatever the date of their arrival, some groups, we know, spread out into the North American Great Lakes area, the Plains, the Mis-

Crafts of Mexico, Chloë Sayer, Doubleday & Company, Inc., Garden City, N.Y. 1977.

93

sissippi Valley, and the East Coast. Others gradually pushed farther south into what is now Mexico, down through the Isthmus of Panama, and on into South America, eventually reaching its very tip. Recently, excavations in Chile unearthed a community of fourteen small attached structures, each with a clay-lined hearth pit. Two large community hearths and stockpiles of clay were found outside the buildings, the clay having been brought from distant bogs and rivers. These finds suggest that people had settled there for at least a season or two, and from radioactive carbon dating of the charcoal and animal bones found around the huts, the excavators concluded that the settlement was between 12,500 and 14,000 years old. For these nomadic people to have established a semipermanent community in this place by that date means that migrations across the land bridge must have occurred considerably earlier.

At any rate, some time between twenty thousand and twelve thousand years ago, as small groups of hunters stopped along the way, adapting their lives to differing local environments, they gradually developed varying racial characteristics, languages, religions, and art styles (5-1, 5-4, 5-11). The settled descendants of these early hunters became the artisans, potters, and sculptors whose skill and artistic ability created the advanced and sophisticated cultures that later flourished in Mesoamerica and South America.

MESOAMERICA

Mesoamerica is a name coined by archaeologists to embrace central and southern Mexico, Guatemala, El Salvador, and parts of Honduras. Although the cultures that developed in those areas vary, some features are common to all of them: most cultivated maize, used hieroglyphics, built large stone monuments, created calendars, and understood and used some form of mathematics. In their attempts to control the environment, improve their crops, and ensure the continuance of the race, they developed religions oriented toward fertility and centering on gods that were the personifications of animals or humans.

In the ancient civilizations of North and South America, the domestication and cultivation of maize preceded the growth of urban civilizations, and the seasonal rebirth of the maize came to have religious significance that was reflected in the art of the varying cultures. As the young maize plants pushed through the earth each year, were watered by the rain, and ripened in the sun, the promise of food and life was renewed. This yearly event led the farming villagers to express, in rituals and offerings to the fertility gods and goddesses, their hopes for good crops, fears of drought, and gratitude for sunny skies. The fact that they were able to store away the maize ensured them of the necessary leisure to engage in crafts and made it possible for them to develop rituals, art, music, and dance, to build the temples needed for the ceremonies, and to make ceremonial vessels from clay to use in the rituals (5-4).

Along with the large numbers of artisans needed to build, carve, and paint the walls of their temples, potters were needed to shape elaborate burial and offering urns. Most of the ceramics that have survived in Mesoamerica have come from tombs, where they were protected from breakage. This makes it appear as if the bulk of ceramic-vessel production was devoted to religious objects, but we know from wall paintings, sculptured reliefs, and a few codices, or illustrated books, that Mesoamerican potters also made simpler vessels for storage, cooking, drinking, and other household uses.

The early potters of the Americas used handbuilding techniques and simple turntables; the potter's wheel did not appear on the continent until it was brought by Europeans. The early artisans of the Americas shaped their vessels with coils, modeled the figurines by hand, and, in some areas, pressed clay into molds to speed up production of sculptured pots and figurines. Firing was done in an open fire or a pit surrounded by a low wall of stones and clay.

Olmec Influences
(c. 1200–500 B.C.)

Many of the common features of the Mesoamerican cultures are believed to have come originally from the Olmecs (5-1). It has been suggested that the Olmec artifacts represent an art

Figure 5-1
Olmec terra-cotta figures with the typical pouting mouth were usually coated with white or cream-colored slip. Their meaning is unknown: one Olmec stone carving shows a woman mating with the jaguar god; since the Olmec religion saw the jaguar as the source of all life, some authorities believe the sculptures represent were-jaguars, offspring of the union. Ht. 3 in. (7.6 cm). Olmec, Las Bocas, state of Puebla, Mexico. *Courtesy Museum of the American Indian, Heye Foundation.*

style rather than a separate culture. It may be that there actually was a separate Olmec people whose civilization was centered in the eastern coastal regions of what is now Mexico. It is also possible that the Olmecs were the basic group from which each of the subsequent cultures in the surrounding areas of Mesoamerica derived. Whichever is the case, the advanced agriculture and crafts, the astronomical observations, and the irrigated or drained coastal lands of Mesoamerica indicate that these people had developed sophisticated technology. The ceremonial centers, which contained courts for a ritual ball game, and the enormous stone heads that were rafted across sixty miles of water to the island of La Venta also show that the

people who made them were capable of complex community efforts. They traded jade, kaolin, turquoise, and shells with other groups, and passed along with their trade goods their religious concepts, which included the cult of a jaguar god, whom they believed controlled the rain and fertility.

Some scholars believe that the typical "Olmec mouth" is based on the shape of a jaguar's mouth. The stone sculptures at La Venta display this sullen, pouting mouth with down-turned lips that appears in the sculpture of many areas in Mesoamerica (5-1).

Tlatilco (c. 1300–900 B.C.)

One culture in which this feature is particularly prevalent is known as Tlatilco, a name that means "the place where things are hidden." The name is appropriate, because high on the Central Plateau, near present-day Mexico City, at the site of a village named Tlatilco, archaeologists have found large numbers of graves in which innumerable clay figurines (5-2) and pottery were buried. This village seems to have been the center of a culture that borrowed technology and artistic ideas from the Olmecs while creating its own characteristic style. Because the amount of clay sculpture and pottery found in the burials there was so large, it has been suggested that Tlatilco was a sizable, wealthy village surrounded by smaller, less affluent villages.

The Tlatilco potters scraped, polished, and stamped their pots, or decorated them with textures made with the edges of shells that they got in trade from the coastal areas. They also painted their pottery with red, yellow, and white geometric designs or stylized snakes or jaguar claws, another Olmec influence. One type of jar from Tlatilco had a double-necked spout—the "stirrup" shape that later appeared in Peru and the North American Southwest, probably carried to those areas through trade or migrations (5-11).

The sculptors who worked the abundant clay of the Tlatilco region modeled it into human figures—the bulk of which portray large-hipped women, the "pretty ladies" of Tlatilco (5-2). Most of these figures are naked but some are wearing short skirts, and they are usually painted with lines suggesting tatoos, clothing, or body paint.

Figure 5-2
Clay figures of two-headed or double-faced women with carefully styled hair are frequently found in burials at Tlatilco. Authorities are unsure of their significance, but it is suggested that they represent the duality of nature. This one shows traces of the color that usually decorated them. Tlatilco, Mexico, 1300–800 B.C. *Courtesy Museo Nacional de Antropologia, Mexico.*

All have elaborately styled hair, and the most unusual ones have two heads or two faces that share a third eye.

Male figures—of musicians, acrobats, and dwarfs, along with masked figures that probably represent priests or shamans—have also been found in burials. Among them is the earliest clay representation of a ball player, wearing the characteristic padding used in the ritual ball game that is depicted in paintings and sculptures throughout Mesoamerica up to the time of the Spanish conquest in 1520.

The Maya (tenth or eleventh century B.C.–A.D. 900)

The Maya worshiped the four Chacs, or rain gods, along with the gods of wind and sun—all-important elements in a society based on maize. The Maya also recorded past history in hieroglyphics on stone monuments, developed an accurate calendar, and created impressive stone pyramids and temples in the jungle area of Mexico and Guatemala, where their advanced civilization was centered. Found along with the temples were many gold, jade, and clay artifacts.

According to the *Popul Vuh*, the sacred book of the Quiche Indians in Guatemala, who still speak Mayan, the first humanlike creatures were modeled out of clay by the gods. The gods are said to have destroyed these clay people, however, because they could not think, and finally, says the sacred manuscript, "only maize was used for the flesh of our first fathers."

The ceremonial pottery of the Maya was quite simple in shape; the potters seemed more interested in producing a smooth painting ground than elaborate pottery shapes. Their cylindrical vases were often covered with plaster to give the painters a better background on which to compose figurative paintings in black, red, and white slips and oxides on an orange background. These stylized paintings show priests, warriors, and nobles wearing ornate headdresses and engaging in raids on other tribes for prisoners. They also vividly depict the rituals that followed the raids when the prisoners were brought to the temples for sacrifice.

Mayan terra-cotta figurines Although a few codices survive, one of the best sources of information about Mayan life is the large number of terra-cotta figurines buried with the dead on the island of Jaina, opposite Yucatan. Expressive, lively, and beautifully crafted, these clay sculptures show us kings and notables in huge headdresses, statuesque ladies wearing heavy jewelry, and ball players in ritual costume—all serious and intent on the ritual acts in which they are involved.

The so-called ball game in which these padded Mayan players contended was played in courtyards outside the temples, where many

Figure 5-3
The Remojadas culture in Veracruz was one of the few to depict a happy people—many of the figurines show laughing children. This sculpture of two children swinging happily in Veracruz around A.D. 500 is also a whistle. *Courtesy the Museum of the American Indian, Heye Foundation.*

spectators watched and bet on the outcome (see page 93). The rules varied from culture to culture throughout Mesoamerica, but in all of these ritual games the ball was passed from player to player from one end of the court to the other—at the Mayan center of Chichén Itzá there was a stone ring on each side, and whichever team got the ball through the ring won immediately. Recreation was not the purpose of this athletic contest, however; the ball probably symbolized the sun, and the "game" often ended in sacrifice—probably to the gods of sun and rain.

Despite the rituals requiring sacrifice or autosacrifice and the slave economy that supported the nobility and the priesthood in luxury, some of the figurines show that a gentler side existed in the Mayan culture. In these small clay sculptures, women weaving, cooking, and caring for children, the old, and the ill all come alive in clay.

The Mayan civilization eventually lost its vitality; its cities declined and the jungle grew over them, but the influence of the Mayan culture, like that of the Olmec culture, was felt in other parts of Mesoamerica.

Veracruz—Remojadas (c. 500 B.C.–A.D. 900)

On the Gulf Coast, in central Veracruz, a culture that centered in Remojadas and later in El Tajin produced a large number of clay figures, many of them joyful and smiling. Such cheerfulness is rarely represented in Mesoamerican art, and the thousands of figures found there, many of them captured in clay in the middle of a belly laugh, give the impression of a fun-loving people who faced life and death with a smile (5-3).

Some of the figures have emblems of life and movement on their headdresses, so they may have had some connection with life-giving rituals. The earliest of these lively figures were sculptured solid and modeled individually by hand, while the later ones were made in molds or built up hollow into nearly life-sized figures.

97

Teotihuacán (c. 100 B.C.–A.D. 850)

On the Central Plateau north of Mexico City loom the impressive ruins of the sacred city of Teotihuacán. Rising steeply from the flat plain, the pyramids stand as mute reminders of the bustling city that once flourished there. Teotihuacán was not only a religious center—the focus of rituals dedicated to the deities associated with water, fertility, and agriculture—it was also a residential center. During its height, the potters and sculptors lived in a special area given over to the crafts where they shaped large, three-footed ritual cylinders decorated with jaguars or human heads or coated with plaster and painted with images of the gods in brilliant color. The shape and decoration of these vessels have led some scholars to suggest a link with Chinese Bronze Age urns.

According to an anthropologist who has studied the fingerprints of the potters of Teotihuacán, the prints on earliest clay artifacts—mostly simple domestic pottery—are women's prints. Later pottery, made at a time when pottery was no longer made solely for domestic use, shows male prints, and in the final period, when the culture was declining, the prints are female again, suggesting that the craft was once more directed toward supplying the needs of the home.

The small clay figures and masklike terracotta faces that are now sold to tourists in the hundreds at the pyramids are reproductions of the many early ones found in the graves at Teotihuacán. The ancient ones were at first modeled by hand, but the demand became so great that they were later made in molds, as are the copies sold today.

The Zapotecs (c. A.D. 300–900)

Twelve hundred feet up the mountain at Monte Albán, near present-day Oaxaca, the Zapotecs built a great ceremonial center. There is some dispute about earlier settlements there—some argue that they were strongly influenced by the Olmec culture, some that the Olmec civilization itself actually began in the valley below and radiated outward from there.

Figure 5-4

Elaborate urns like this grayware Zapotec funerary urn held food, incense, or water offerings for the gods in the small containers held between the god's hands. Ht. 13½ in. (34.3 cm). State of Oaxaca, Mexico. *Courtesy Museum of the American Indian, Heye Foundation. Photo: Carmelo Guadagno.*

The most characteristic ceramics created by the Zapotecs are large sculptured urns, some as tall as thirty-three inches (eighty-four centimeters), placed with the dead in the cave tombs at Monte Albán (5-4). These ritual urns represent human or jaguar figures. The humans wear large earplugs and decorative headdresses, and hold in their hands in small containers offerings of fire, incense, food, or water destined for the gods represented on them. Figures of women also appear on the urns dressed in a style still worn by Zapotec women in Oaxaca, with a *quechquemitl* over the shoulders, necklaces and ear ornaments, and cords braided into their hair. The urns were originally hand modeled, but toward the end of the Zapotec period many were formed in molds, and by then the standard of craftsmanship was in general lower. The Zapotec culture itself declined, and Monte Albán was eventually taken over by the Mixtecs, who were noted more for their gold work than their ceramics.

The Aztecs (c. A.D. 1325–1520)

The Aztecs, whose city at Tenochtitlán astounded the Spaniards when they arrived in 1520, built their great ceremonial center on an island where Mexico City now stands. Known for their engineering skill in building aqueducts, draining marshes, and creating a network of canals, the Aztecs dominated their neighbors, demanding tribute from them. They also raided them to procure the constant stream of victims they needed for their human-sacrificial religious rites. The Aztecs believed that the sun god had to be fed blood every day in order to be strong enough to win his nightly battle with the jealous gods of the stars and moon, who wanted to keep him from returning to light the sky.

Aztec art owed much to the surrounding cultures, especially the Mixtecs of Oaxaca from whom they learned the craft of painted pottery—a delicate orange ware decorated with gray, yellow, or white. Aztec trade was extensive, as was the tribute they extracted from other people. Paintings in codices show the arrival of the tributes: feathers for ritual costumes, skins, and fabrics, often carried to the city in pottery vessels. Other paintings show babies being baptized in pottery tubs, tripod urns with food in them, and elderly people drinking their daily allotted ration of *pulque*, the Aztec liquor, out of wide, shallow pottery cups. All the usual domestic pots appear, giving us a clear idea of the importance of clay in the daily life of pre-Columbian Mesoamerica.

WESTERN MEXICO

In the western areas now covered by the states of Michoacán, Guanajuato, Jalisco, Colima, and Nayarit, the villages were isolated from other Mesoamerican cultures and show only a few traces of Olmec and Teotihuacán influences. Nor did they develop as powerful or wealthy a priesthood—no monumental religious centers were built here—for the inhabitants were apparently not as deeply involved with ritualized religion as in other areas of Mesoamerica.

What has remained of early cultures here is a

Figure 5-5
The flat heads seen on figurines from Jalisco were not a distortion but the result of the custom of binding infants' heads to a board at birth. The clothing of this mother nursing her child shows typical designs and details that were applied in color after firing. Ht. 17½ in. (44.5 cm). Magdalena, Jalisco, Mexico, A.D. 300–900. *Courtesy Museum of the American Indian, Heye Foundation.*

wealth of small clay figurines that suggest that the artists were more concerned with portraying life on earth than with pleasing the gods (5-5, 5-6). From around A.D. 300 to 900, sculptors in western Mexico modeled clay into figures that depicted nursing mothers, musicians, dancers, priests or shamans, children at play, rabbits, armadillos, mice, and parrots, along with houses, temples, and ball courts. In comparison with, say,

Figure 5-6

A group of figures from Jalisco, about seven inches tall, recreates a scene in which a man wearing a snake and feather headdress, possibly a priest or a shaman, beats time with paddles as he accompanies the dancers. Since this is not their original grouping, it may suggest relationships that never actually existed. Jalisco, Mexico, A.D. 300–900. *Courtesy Museum of the American Indian, Heye Foundation.*

the stylized, elaborated figure on a Zapotec funeary urn (5-4), the sculpture from this area is lively and human.

Although there is great similarity among these small sculptures from various parts of western Mexico, regional differences tell us about local customs. For instance, we learn that the women of Nayarit usually went naked or sometimes wore short skirts but always dressed their hair carefully and wore large earplugs and, usually, necklaces. The men are often shown wearing light armor woven from fibers, carrying clubs, and throwing spears. Many of the Nayarit figurines are almost caricatures, with the ill or deformed represented in an exaggerated manner. In Jalisco, on the other

hand, despite some exaggeration of the deliberately deformed heads (5-5), people are shown more realistically; a woman nursing her child, a young man looking into a mirror, an old man carried in a litter, and singers and dancers all bring us close to life as it was lived in this beautiful part of the central plateau of Mexico.

In Colima, highly skilled sculptors modeled a seemingly happy people at peace with their environment and apparently free of the need to propitiate frightening gods through sacrifice and ritual (1-8).

With the arrival of the Spaniards, who carried guns and rode horses, the old cultures of Mexico were destroyed. Since then, the ceramic

Figure 5-7
In the Morelos area of Mexico, this clay silo was once used to store seed corn and peanuts. No longer used as a granary, it now holds the important possessions of the family. Clay mixed with straw. Ht. 15 ft. (4.6 m). *Photo: Jens Morrison.*

Figure 5-8
The pot this Mexican potter is removing from the fire has been fired to maturity at about 700° F/371.1° C). In many parts of Mexico, potters use a pine pole to remove pots from the fire—the larger the pot, the more leverage is required to move it. Once removed, the pots are placed on three stones to cool evenly. *Photo: Jens Morrison.*

arts of Mexico have been greatly influenced by the Hispano-Moresque styles brought by the invaders. Tiles and wheel-thrown pots and bowls are colorfully decorated with motifs very similar to those brought to Spain by the Arabs. But despite these outside influences and the spread of plastic and metal for domestic use, in some areas of Mexico the local traditions persist: porous earthenware jars are still used for drinking water, and earthenware for shallow casseroles are used for cooking on charcoal fires. Much of the "folk art" may now be made more for the tourist market than for local use, but potters continue to make the beautiful polished black pottery in the Oaxaca area, to sculpt the small group scenes called *chian-*

gos in the central mountains, to coat storage bins with clay (5-7), and to shape clay into toy whistles and whirling clay *voladores*—all evidence that today's descendants of the pre-Columbian inhabitants still see life with artists' eyes and use the ancient techniques of their ancestors (5-8).

THE ISTHMUS AREA

In the narrow neck of land between the two Americas, in what is now Panama, Costa Rica, and parts of Colombia, rich gold mines yielded quantities of the shining metal. Although clay

Figure 5-9
There is a remarkable resemblance between the decoration and shape of this vessel and those made in ancient China (3-1). Some writers suggest there may have been communication between China and Mesoamerica. The stylized painting of the crocodile god is in black and red on a cream slip. Ht. 9¾ in. (24.8 cm). Veraguas, Panama, A.D. 1000–1500. *Courtesy Museum of the American Indian, Heye Foundation.*

was used to make simple pottery here as early as 2000 B.C., gold was the most important art medium in this area. But clay had a functional purpose in the fabrication of gold artifacts; the goldsmiths used two-part ceramic molds to cast their solid-gold ornaments.

Later, in the province of Veraguas in Panama, potters working during the centuries just before the arrival of the Europeans created elegantly shaped bowls, jars, and pedestaled urns (5-9). They decorated these pieces with forceful and stylized figures of animals and gods painted in red, black, and purple in a rhythmic style quite unlike other Mesoamerican or Peruvian pottery. Some historians have suggested a link between the decoration of these pots and Chinese Neolithic pottery (3-1).

After the Europeans arrived, this sophisticated ceramic craft was lost, and today in Panamanian villages the women who still make their own domestic pots form them with coils in a few simple shapes. Only a handful of the traditional potters there still make the type of three-legged pot that might be an echo of earlier days, when the potters had a large repertoire of elegant shapes.

SOUTH AMERICA

Thousands of years ago, as bands of hunters made their way along the western coast of the southern American continent, some of them found hospitable surroundings that led them to settle in the low, fertile valleys that break up the long coastline. Others hunted wild animals into the high mountain plains and valleys; still others made their way into the dense jungles on the eastern side of the towering Andes. These early peoples did not make pottery, but they formed fertility figures and representations of birds and animals out of clay, leaving them unbaked.

It is not known for certain just where in South America fired pottery was first made, although finds in Ecuador suggest that farming cultures producing pottery developed there at least as early as in Mesopotamia. Since there are still large areas in this vast continent where there has been little excavation, the picture that has emerged is somewhat uneven. Nevertheless, we do know that approximately between 1800 and 900 B.C., people in the north and south coastal areas of South America settled into large villages and that technical improvements were made in agriculture, weaving, pottery, and stone architecture. The pottery of this period was well made but simple, with only a little decoration, usually geometric.

By around 900 to 600 B.C., in the southern Paracas area of what is now Peru the potters were already forming clay into the whistling jars and stirrup-spouted pots whose basic forms would be used for centuries by the potters of the Andes region (5-10).

Chavin (c. 900–200 B.C.)

Contemporary with Paracas culture, the Chavin, inspired by a new religious cult that may have spread from the eastern rainforests, conquered a large area and built a huge stone religious center at Chavin de Huantar, in a high valley.

Sculptors there carved, among other god images, a monumental stone image of a human with a smiling fanged mouth. This sculpture influenced the art of nearby and later peoples. Much of the pottery that was to develop in the central Andes was clearly influenced by Chavin stone carvings.

Moche (c. 200 B.C.–A.D. 600)

Whether or not it was a result of Chavin influence, the Mochica ceramics certainly showed a strong sculptural sense. In around A.D. 400, at their most productive and creative, the talented sculptor/potters working in and around Moche modeled stirrup-spouted drinking vessels into realistic portrait heads (5-11), made models of houses and temples (1-9), and modeled amusing figures of daily life. Their ceramics were made not only for grave offerings but also for ceremonial use.

The potters formed the figurative models and vessels by hand modeling, or by building with coils, by pressing clay into two-part molds, or using a combination of these methods. The pots are often so well finished that it is difficult to tell where on the vessels each technique was used. The process of making and using molds first required that the sculptor shape a model in solid clay and then make a mold by pressing two slabs of damp clay onto the front and back of the model. After allowing the clay to stiffen somewhat, the sculptor removed it and fired the resulting two-part impression. After these two sections of the mold were fired, the sculptor pressed damp clay into them to form the two parts of the the pot. Finally, he would join these two parts together to make a hollow jar. To make the spouts, the potter/sculptor wrapped strips of clay around wooden rods; when the clay stiffened enough to allow removal of the rods but was still pliable, he bent the spout to shape and attached it to the pot. Once the spouts and handles were attached, he would add the details of face or body by carving into the clay or by adding additional clay forms, thus, individualizing each jar. The pots would then be slip-painted, burnished, and usually fired in an oxidizing atmosphere, although occasionally they were deliberately reduced in order to turn them gray or black. Some

Figure 5-10
A Paracas potter in Peru combined relief sculpture and incised lines to embellish this stirrup-spouted vessel. Similar bird and human-face motifs are typical of pottery from Peru, but the shape of this pot may have come through trade from Tlatilco in central Mexico. Ht. 7½ in. (19.1 cm). Paracas, South coast, Peru, 900 B.C.–A.D. 200. *Courtesy the Fine Arts Museums of San Francisco, M. H. de Young Memorial Museum.*

Figure 5-11
A stirrup-spouted jar from Peru is also a portrait,
possibly of the person with whom it was buried; the
paint or tattooing on the face may indicate his rank.
Most Mochica jars were made with a combination
technique involving both handbuilding and molds.
Ht. 12 in. (30.5 cm). Mochica culture, Trujillo, Peru,
A.D. 200–600. *Courtesy Museum of the American Indian,
Heye Foundation.*

had details drawn on them with applications of an
organic black pigment that was scorched onto the
burnished surface after firing. There is no doubt
that many of the pots were individual portraits,
and it is possible, by studying large numbers of
these pots sculpted by the Moche potters, to recognize the work of individual artists. We may
even see what the artists looked like themselves—
sculptured pots depicting potters have been
found. Most of them carry bags over their shoulders, probably holding their tools. Bags like this
have been found buried with their owners containing burnishing pebbles, pointed sticks, molds,
and stamps.

The liveliness and skill with which the
Moche potters modeled their sculptured vessels
were outstanding, and it is small wonder that later
artists, from Paul Gauguin to contemporary ones,
have been influenced by the creations of these
skillful and sensitive potters.

Nazca (200 B.C.–A.D. 600)

Another local culture to appear after the decline of the Chavin empire was that centering on
the Nazca valleys along the southern coast. The
people who lived here built shrines, adobe pyramids, plazas, and cemeteries; they wove intricate
textiles and slip-painted their pottery with symbolic decorations (Color plate 5). Less interested
in realism than the Moche, they outlined their
flat, stylized painting with black lines around
each area of colored slip; potters sometimes used
as many as nine colors on their pots. Mythological
creatures, masklike faces, and catlike images appear on their bridge-handled pots.

At this point, the story of the groups who
lived in what is now Peru becomes even more
confusing. Between A.D. 600 and 1000, centers of
power shifted frequently. Finally, after a period
in which two cities high in the mountains on Lake
Titicaca gained and then lost dominance, new regional cultures developed.

Chancay (c. A.D. 1000)

One such culture, that of the Chancay Valley
on the central coast, produced pottery with decorative geometric and stylized animal designs,

Figure 5-12
Monkeys, cats, and other animals frequently appeared on pottery in the Chancay Valley. On this pot, the animals' heads form the eyes of a human face in relief. 5 × 5 in. (12.7 × 12.7 cm). Chancay Valley, Central coast, Peru, A.D. 600–900. *Courtesy Fine Arts Museums of San Francisco, M. H. de Young Memorial Museum.*

Figure 5-13
Jars in which the liquid made a whistling sound when the jug was tilted were popular in the Chimu-Inca cultures. Polished black ware, Chancay Valley, Central coast, Peru. *Courtesy the Fine Arts Museums of San Francisco, M. H. de Young Memorial Museum.*

sometimes painted on a layer of plaster, in black or brown and white. At times, these painted decorations were combined with three-dimensional modeling, and the painted animals were reduced to squares, rectangles, and triangles (5-12).

Chimu (Mid-1300s)

The Chimu rulers, on the north coast, conquered territory far beyond the boundaries of the Moche sphere of influence, placing their court in the city of Chan Chan. The ruins of this city, laid out in an urban plan, cover more than eight square miles, and are surrounded by enormous walls of sun-dried bricks plastered with clay and carved with stylized animals and geometric designs. The Chimu were fine metal workers, cre-

ating intricate jewelry by casting it in one- and two-part ceramic molds, but they were not as gifted in ceramics. Although they tried to rival the earlier Mochica pottery, their highly polished black ware did not achieve the high level of those creative potters' ceramics (5-13).

Inca (c. A.D. 1400–1533)

The Inca empire rose in one century from a small, unimportant group of people fighting with its neighbors to an awesome power that maintained military and administrative control over a huge area from Chile to Ecuador. Rich, with treasuries full of gold, the Inca nobility used bronze and silver vessels, while the poor and the large army that policed them used clay pots. Since much of the pottery that survives was apparently government issue to military posts, it is rather standardized.

The Inca splendor and military dominance over other cultures in South America came to an abrupt end in 1533, when the Spaniard Pizarro entered Cuzco and looted the famous treasuries in order to send gold back to the rulers of Spain.

FOLK TRADITIONS TODAY

The cultural disruption that occurred with the arrival of the Spaniards broke the tradition of making decorative and ritual clay vessels in which the Moche and Nazca cultures had excelled. New technology—the true wheel and more advanced firing methods—modified the native clay traditions in South America, while changes in religion, life style, and eating and cooking habits brought new shapes to the pottery. In some villages, pottery somewhat reminiscent of the earlier cultures has persisted, and in some of the more isolated mountain villages, where transportation is still difficult, families continue to make pottery for their own use. But in general the traditional potters make their ware only when they can sell it locally more cheaply than metal or plastic containers or when they are able to sell decorative pottery to collectors or tourists.

The techniques used by village potters today are variations of those we have seen elsewhere in the world. Most of the ware is handbuilt in bases formed of old bowls or other convex objects and revolved on a flat stone, sometimes with the help of a clay disk with a protruding pivot on which it turns (1-31). In one area, the potters drape slabs over the bottom of old pots covered with burlap, much as some contemporary potters form their pots over plaster hump molds. Firing techniques vary from open firing with grass, straw, and dung to updraft, Mediterranean-style kilns modeled on those brought by the Spaniards.

Recently, in parts of Peru, a revived interest in ancient cultures has led some potters to make imitations of Nazca ware, and in Chile and Colombia some are using molds to make sculptural groups of human figures, birds, and animals for tourist and export trade. Often these are made in family workshops, where mother, father, and children do all the forming, firing, and finishing, each family developing an individual decorative style that is recognized by collectors. The same question that traditional potters face elsewhere also arises here—how to keep up the traditions of the old while avoiding slavish copying of historical styles. How this question is answered will affect the future of potters all over Mesoamerica and South America.

NORTH AMERICA

Some of the groups of nomad hunters who came down into the North American continent from Asia settled in the areas of present-day New Mexico, southern Colorado, and Arizona. Known to us as the Basketmakers, they probably received stimulus for their pottery making from Mexico; apparently, groups of people pushed up from Mexico into the Rio Grande Valley of the American Southwest, meeting and mingling with the earlier settlers there. In any case, contact with Mexico's more northerly cultures was close enough for their influences to be felt. For example, the adobe clay houses built under overhanging cliffs in New Mexico and Colorado had their exact counterparts in northern Mexico, which were built at about the same time, and the decoration on certain early pottery from Arizona shows many resemblances to motifs used on Mexican pottery.

How Pottery Came to the Southwest

Legend gives us a more colorful story of the beginnings of pottery in the American Southwest. According to Cochita legend, pottery making was learned from Clay Old Woman, who was sent to the village from *Shipap*, the underworld, the place of origin of all people. Her mission was to teach the villagers how to make pots, so Clay Old Woman mixed the clay with sand, softened it with water, and then began to coil a pot. While she was busy demonstrating her skill, her husband, Clay Old Man, danced and sang. The village people watched her carefully, but when the pot was about a foot and a half high, Clay Old Man broke it with his foot and ran off with it. She chased him around the village, retrieved it, made it into a ball of clay again, and built another pot. Each person of the pueblo took a piece of clay from this pot and started to make pottery, following the steps Clay Old Woman had taught them. Now, they say, if the people of Cochita forget how to make pottery, two masked dancers come to remind them about the day they gave clay to the pueblo.

Whether you prefer the archaeological or mythical version of the beginnings of pottery in the American Southwest, there is no doubt that the craft of pottery making has played a large part in both the sacred and domestic life of the peoples who live in this land of mesas and spacious skies.

Southwestern Ceramics

In the region where present-day New Mexico, Colorado, Utah, and Arizona meet, the descendants of the Basketmakers merged with new peoples from the south and between A.D. 700 and 1100, began to build clusters of permanent homes, some of whose ruins still stand. These were the first *pueblos*, the name the Spanish later gave to the villages. The same name, capitalized, has also been used by outsiders as a name for the inhabitants, but nowadays most village dwellers there prefer to be known by their native names, such as Tewa or Cochita. At various times, in different villages or groups of villages, pottery production reached a peak of creativity, declined, and was then renewed. The art of the Native Americans who lived in the many pueblos in this part of the country was a living art, developed to meet the needs of daily or ceremonial life, and as those needs varied from place to place, so did the pottery.

Mimbres (c. A.D. 700–1100)

One outstanding ceramic tradition that developed in the Southwest was that of the people the Spanish called Mimbres (meaning "willows"), who settled in the southwestern area of New Mexico near what are now the Arizona and Mex-

ican borders. Originally, these hunters and gatherers built their homes on the heights above the valley, perhaps for defense, but after about A.D. 550, when they became dependent on agriculture, the group moved down to the Mimbres River plain, founding small villages near their crops. It was after this move that they began the custom of burying pottery bowls along with the dead under the floors of their houses. By the classic period of Mimbres pottery (c. 1000), the bowls were carefully placed over the heads of the dead, with a small hole broken through the bottom of the bowl. Interpretations of this custom differ—some say it was made to release the spirit of the bowl.

At no time, even at its height, did the Mimbres population exceed around twenty-five hundred persons. Considering the number of skillfully made and exquisitely decorated bowls that have been found at their village sites, it would seem that a large proportion of the people had great artistic ability (5-14).

Coil-made, smoothly scraped, and thin-walled, the Mimbres pottery in the earlier years was coated with a layer of iron-rich slip, burnished, and fired to a rich red. By around A.D. 750, the pottery was fired in reduction, and the bowls, small jars, and large jars showed the characteristic black and white decoration (5-14). By about A.D. 1150, the Mimbres culture had collapsed, and by A.D. 1400, large areas of the Southwest had been abandoned by the indigenous groups of peoples, possibly owing to years of drought. At that time, the population became more concentrated in the Hopi, Zuñi, and Rio Grande areas.

From around A.D. 1600—when the Spaniards first arrived—until the present, so many new ways of life, new power structures, and new religious influences came to the area that the native peoples had to struggle to maintain their traditions. But whether these influences came from Mesoamerica, from the Spaniards, from contact with other native peoples, or from the tourists who began arriving when the railroad came in 1880, the potters in the pueblos usually took the new ideas and adapted them to fit their own way of life. The potters continued to use ancient forms and create designs that were well adapted to the forms of each pot (5-15).

Some of the potters active in the Southwest today make a special double-spouted wedding

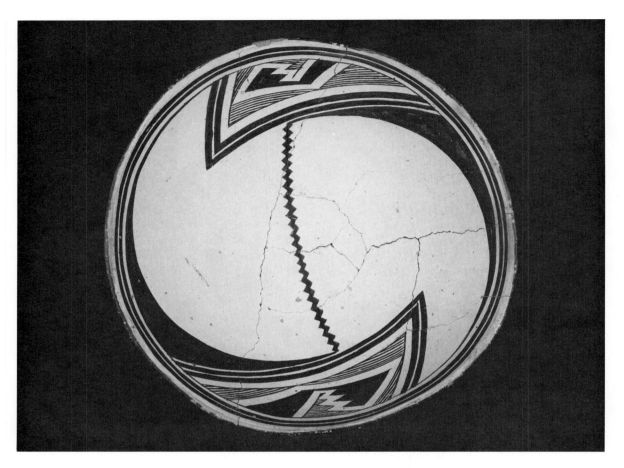

Figure 5-14
Responding to the "contemporary" appearance of such bowls from the classic Mimbres period, we tend to forget that the artists who painted them had quite different cultural and artistic motivations. This bowl, although broken and mended, has no "kill hole"—the hole usually made in the bottom of bowls to be buried in graves. Found on the Pruitt Ranch, Mimbres Valley, New Mexico. *Courtesy Arizona State Museum, University of Arizona.*

vessel with a bridged handle that is reminiscent of South American spouted jars (5-10, 5-11). Drinking jars such as these are known to have been used at wedding celebrations as recently as forty years ago; the bride and groom drank from opposite sides of the jar, and then it was handed around so that the men could drink from the groom's side and the women from the bride's. It is not known if the shape was devised at that time or if it is traditional.

The men sometimes made, or at least decorated, the ceremonial vessels needed for the religious life of the village. These were shaped in forms that were dictated by their use in the sacred

rituals. Since many of these ceremonies have remained secret, the use of certain types of vessels or the meaning of their symbolic decoration is not known. Pitchers, rectangular bowls, footed bowls (some with handles), low bowls (some with sculptured figures of frogs)—all these were used in some way in the sacred ceremonies.

Pottery Techniques

The different pueblo groups varied in the ways they dug, prepared, and finally shaped the clay. Generally, however, the women, who were the potters, dug the clay out with sticks, speaking

Figure 5-15
A Hopi potter in Arizona around the beginning of the twentieth century shaped her pot with coils, using a basket as a base. She spread her wet clay on a rock to stiffen it slightly before using it. *Courtesy Museum of the American Indian, Heye Foundation, N.Y.*

to the earth and asking its permission, for they felt that the clay had life and feelings deserving of respect. Sometimes they had to travel quite a distance to find the right clay (1-11). In Santa Clara, for example, the clay—*Na p*—was gathered at a place called *NA Pii* we, about a mile west of the pueblo, while the tempering material, *Shunya*, was found about seven miles away. Once dug, all materials had to be carried in a basket or a hide container back to the village, where a great deal of work went into its preparation. The dry lumps had to be pounded out, the stones and other impurities removed, and often the clay was ground on a stone until it was fine, in the same manner that maize was ground.

Tempering materials   Next, the gritty material, the temper, was mixed in. The villagers based their measurements on experience—so many handfuls of temper to so much clay. This temper coarsened the texture of the clay, allowing the air to escape so that the pot would not crack while drying or burst in firing. Each village or area had its own kind of temper. The Zuñi, for example, have always added ground-up broken pottery to the new clay, thereby incorporating a bit of its history into its pots in each generation. On the other hand, the potters of Taos and Picuris needed no temper, for there were abundant bits of mica already in the local clay. Other pueblos have used volcanic sand or laboriously ground

Figure 5-16
Water jar made in an Acoma village in the nineteenth century. The flowing bands that swing around the swelling shape are painted in two shades of orange. Ht. 9¾ in. (25 cm). McCartys, New Mexico, c. 1890. *Courtesy Museum of New Mexico. School of American Research. Photo: Arthur Taylor.*

Figure 5-17
Tewa potter Maria Martinez of San Ildefonso, in a photo taken around 1940, shapes and thins the walls of a pot by scraping with a piece of dried gourd. The base of the pot was started in a *puki*, in which she carefully pressed the clay outward with her left hand to shape the profile into a graceful curve. San Ildefonso, New Mexico, c. 1940. *Courtesy Collections in the Museum of New Mexico. Photo: Wyatt Davis.*

lava-rock into a powder. Mixing was done with the hands or sometimes the feet.

Potters here did not age their clay as the Chinese did. Once they had mixed it, they wrapped the clay in a damp cloth or sometimes buried it in the ground to keep it out of the sun until the potter was ready to use it.

Building with coils   Coiling was the traditional method of pot building. The bottom of a pot was first formed in some sort of base mold—a basket, a broken pot, or a *puki*, a specially made shallow bowl (5-15). Potters kept a set of base molds shaped to suit different types of pots; water jars, for instance, were started in molds that had convex areas to make the bottom of the water jar concave so it would fit the head for carrying (5-16).

The coiled walls were built up straight, carefully pushed outward to the desired shape, and scraped (5-17). Using this coiling method, potters could form pots of many shapes: flaring or nar-

row-necked storage jars to hold maize; open dough bowls that would hold a week's supply of bread dough; narrow-necked water jars; shallow, flat bowls; canteens; many types of swelling, globular vessels; and some special shapes.

Finishing the pots   After a pot was shaped, it was dried away from the sun and watched by the potter for cracks. Little cracks were mended with damp clay, but pots with large ones were discarded. The exterior was then smoothed again with a pottery fragment or a piece of dried gourd and coated with slip to cover the rough, coarse texture of the clay body. This slip coating provided a smoother base for painted decorations. The slip was usually red, white, or off-white and made of fine clay that could only be found in certain places. Those villages without adequate slip clay near them traded with others for it. The white slip was basically kaolin, while the cream slip was largely bentonite. After the slip was applied, the pot was burnished with smooth, rounded stones or pieces of leather or rags (5-18). Collections of rubbing stones in various shapes and sizes were handed down through generations of potters, and it was considered bad luck to lose one. Less often, the damp clay body was left uncoated, and was puddled, a method of stroking the clay body with a stone to float the finer clay particles to the surface to smooth it.

Decoration   After the slip had been burnished, the design was applied. Various types of pigment such as fine mineral-colored slips and vegetable pigments were used. The mineral-colored slip usually fired to shades of dark brown, black, and sometimes red, and the vegetable paint burned black during firing. Called *guaco*, this paint was made by boiling new shoots and leaves of the Rocky Mountain bee plant into a syrup. Hardened and formed into a block, the paint could be kept for years and mixed with water when needed. Traditionally, the artist applied the paint with a brush made by chewing bits of yucca leaf or other vegetation to the desired consistency. The dull, black decoration, which contrasts so handsomely with the glossy finish of contemporary Santa Clara and San Ildefonso pots, is produced by painting designs with fine slip on top of the polished surface, then firing in a reduction atmosphere which turns the pot black. The slip paint comes out of the fire with a matt surface, while the burnished part of the pot stays shiny.

Decorative motifs have varied throughout the years and in different areas from geometric and symbolic designs painted in black on white (5-14), to flowing polychrome decorations, to stylized images. Some of the images painted on early pots portrayed bird, animal, and plant forms; the sacred twin clowns; symbols of clouds, rain, and lightning; plumed serpents; and feathers. Others are decorated with what appear to be totally abstract patterns. The meanings of many of these symbols remain secret; in some cases the original meanings have been lost. For example, some of the early pottery is circled by bands of color or black lines, and these encircling lines, sometimes called the spirit path, almost always have a break in them somewhere. Some authorities say the break was put there to keep the soul of the pot from being imprisoned, while other scholars believe that its true meaning is lost.

Figure 5-18
Maria Martinez polishing a slip-painted pot with a smooth stone to give it a rich, glossy finish; there are no glazes on her pots. San Ildefonso, New Mexico, c. 1940. *Courtesy Collections in the Museum of New Mexico. Photo: Wyatt Davis.*

Firing   After a pot was decorated, it was ready for firing. The traditional methods of firing have remained very much the same to the present day, except that today's pottery—most of which is made for decorative purposes and is not intended for domestic use—is fired at a cooler temperature than in earlier times. Like the potters of Fiji, Africa (1-33,4-12), and other traditional cultures, potters in pueblos such as San Ildefonso and Santa Clara still fire in open fires, using available local fuels—cow or sheep dung, wood, or even, in the Hopi areas, soft coal. Nowadays the pottery is placed on sheet metal or a metal grill and is covered by sheet metal, but the method is still basically the same open-firing method as that

Figure 5-19
Julian Martinez removes a burnished wedding jar from the open firing, whose reducing
atmosphere turned the pots black. Maria Martinez and her husband Julian worked
together—Maria shaping and Julian decorating—to develop their famous black pottery.
Later, their son, Popovi Da, was the decorator. San Ildefonso, New Mexico, c. 1940.
Courtesy Collections in the Museum of New Mexico. Photo: Wyatt Davis.

used by potters in the Southwest for centuries (5-19). Usually the firing is done in the evening or early morning to avoid any wind that could cause the fire to burn unevenly, possibly causing breakage. The firing nowadays generally takes from around thirty minutes to an hour and a half, after which some potters leave the pottery to cool in the fire, while others rake away the coals and remove the fired pots with long sticks.

Clay Sculpture

Clay sculpture was not common in the early pueblos, although a few pots were made in the shape of birds or had sculptured animals on them. But by 1890, when the tourists began to come to buy curios, some potters began to make human figurines, and today this sculptural tradition continues in the Cochita pueblo (5-20), while some of the younger potters in San Ildefonso make black and polychrome animal figures.

Continuing Traditions

Nowadays, the pottery and sculpture are made more for sale outside the pueblos than for local use. Following the example set by the famous potters of San Ildefonso Maria and Julian Martinez, potters in several villages have revived traditional methods, and whole families—grandparents, great-grandparents, and their descendants—approach pottery making with dedication and love, respecting tradition while developing new shapes and decorations.

NORTHERN AREAS

Some of the migrants who crossed the land bridge to North America spread out over the Great Plains to the Southeast, the Mississippi Valley, and the East Coast. These people did not develop a pottery tradition as complex as that of the Southwest cultures, largely because their life styles were less settled. They did not cultivate maize, they remained hunters living nomadic lives for a much longer time, and after the arrival

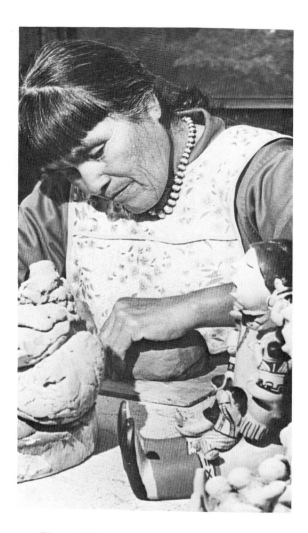

Figure 5-20
Helen Cordero, of the Cochita pueblo, continued a tradition of sculpted figures that started there in the 1880s. Her brightly painted *Storyteller* sits with eyes closed, chanting, while delighted children climb over him. *Courtesy U.S. Department of Interior, Indian Arts and Crafts Board, Washington, D.C.*

Figure 5-21
Dark, burnished pottery, usually with incised
decoration, was typical of the Mississippi Mound
Builder culture. Its swirl design is remarkably like
those on pottery from Egypt (1-27), China, (3-1), and
Colombia (5-9). *Courtesy Museum of the American
Indian, Heye Foundation, N.Y.*

of horses with the Spaniards, many went back
again to a seminomadic life.

The Mound Builders

In the Mississippi Valley, one group, possibly
influenced by weak group memories of Mesoamerican pyramids, built large earth mounds.
Called the Mound Builders, these people also
made the most skilled pottery of the more northerly regions of the continent (5-21). Other northern tribes, including some as widely separated as
the Iroquois and the Florida Cherokee, also made
black or grey pottery and sculptured animal figures as bowls for pipes they used in ceremonies.

Color Plate 1
Ceremonial jar, China. Porcelaneous stoneware, celadon glaze. Late Northern Sung
dynasty, 11th century A.D. Height 9½ in. (24 cm), diameter 5 in. (12.7 cm). *Courtesy,
Asian Art Museum of San Francisco, The Avery Brundage Collection, 62 P147.*

Color Plate 2
Chūn ware bowl, China. Sung dynasty (A.D. 960–
1279). Stoneware, lavender glaze splashed with
purple. Diameter 7½ in. (19 cm). *By courtesy of the
Board of Trustees of the Victoria & Albert Museum.*

Color Plate 3
Vase with red copper glaze, China. K'ang-hsi
period, A.D. 1662–1722. *By courtesy of the Board of
Trustees of the Victoria & Albert Museum.*

Color Plate 4
Lead-tin-glazed plate from Deruta, Italy, c. A.D. 1530. Diameter 8 in. (20.6 cm). *Courtesy, Indiana University Art Museum.*

Color Plate 5
Spouted jar from the Nasca Valley, Peru. Decorated with wild cats and fruit. Height 8 in.
(20.3 cm), diameter 6¾ in. (17 cm). *Courtesy, Museum of the American Indian, Heye Foundation, N.Y.*

Color Plate 6
Antoni Gaudí i Cornet, 1852–1926, architect, Spain. Casa Batlló,
Barcelona. Decoration on facade and ceramic disks by José Maria Jujol,
1879–1949, Spain.

Color Plate 7
Figures in a village shrine, India. Painted terra-cotta.
Photo: Alain-M. Tremblay.

Color Plate 12
Tony Hepburn, U.S.A. *Strong Support*. Stoneware, wood.
37 × 35 × 15 in. (94 × 89 × 38 cm). *Courtesy the artist.*
Photo: Brian Oglesbee.

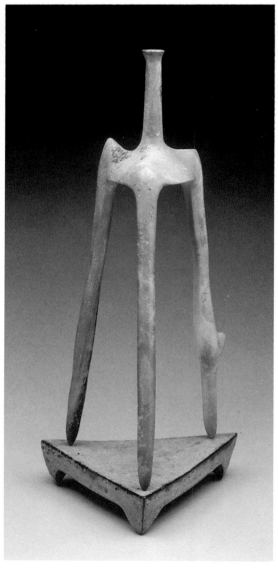

Color Plate 13
Richard Hirsch, U.S.A. *Vessel and Stand #15*. *Coper-Metti*
Series. Terra sigillata, low-fire glazes, raku. 22½ × 10½ ×
10½ in. (57 × 27 × 27 cm). *Collection Museum of*
Contemporary Ceramics, Ghent, Belgium. Courtesy the artist.
Photo: Dean Powell.

Color Plate 14
Stephen De Staebler, U.S.A. The courtyard of his studio. (Left) *Standing Figure With Yellow Aura.* 92½ in. × 21 × 19 ft. (2.3 × 6.4 × 5.7 m). (Right) *Standing Figure with Tilting Head.* 91½ in. × 15 × 21 ft. (2.3 × 4.6 × 6.4 m). 1985. *Courtesy the artist. Photo: Scott McCue.*

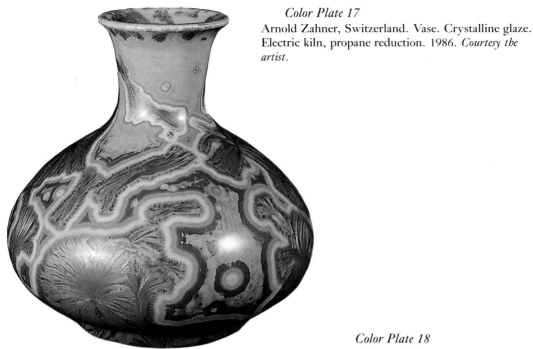

Color Plate 17
Arnold Zahner, Switzerland. Vase. Crystalline glaze. Electric kiln, propane reduction. 1986. *Courtesy the artist.*

Color Plate 18
Mayer Shacter, U.S.A. *Not Necessarily Another Million Dollar Idea.* Unglazed stoneware, luster. 14 × 10 × 4 in. (35 × 25 × 10 cm), 1987. *Courtesy the artist.*

Color Plate 19
Clayton Bailey, U.S.A. *Drop Coin, Fight Satan.* Low-fire clay, imitation fire, light, sound. 1987. *Courtesy the artist.*

Color Plate 20
Patrick Loughran, U.S.A. Plate and detail. Glazed terra-cotta. Diameter, 24 in. (61 cm), 1987. *Courtesy the artist.*

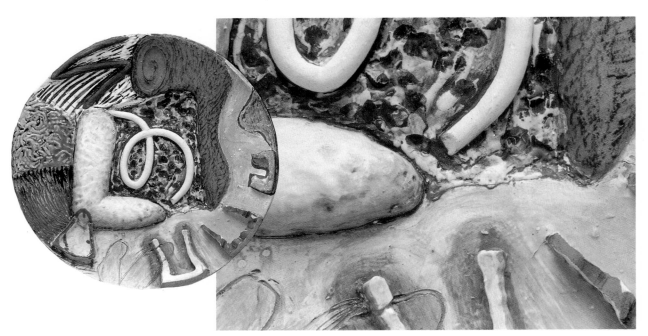

Color Plate 21
Deborah Horrell, U.S.A. *Passages: Heaven, Hell &*
The In-Between. Created at Otsuka Factory, Japan.
Glazed ceramic panels. 9 × 6 × 18 ft. (2.7 × 1.8
× 5.5 m), 1985. *Courtesy the artist. Photo: Fredrik*
Marsh.

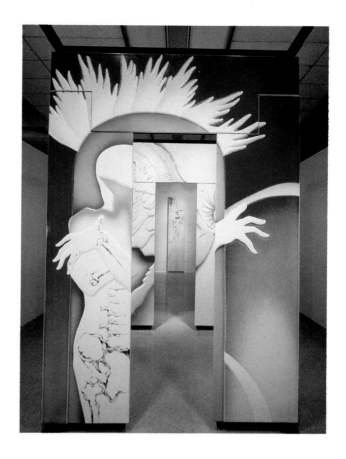

Color Plate 22
Jindra Viková, Czechoslovakia. *Attempt of*
Definition of One Moment. Porcelain, metal tubing.
43 × 26 in. (110 cm × 65 cm), 1987. *Courtesy the*
artist.

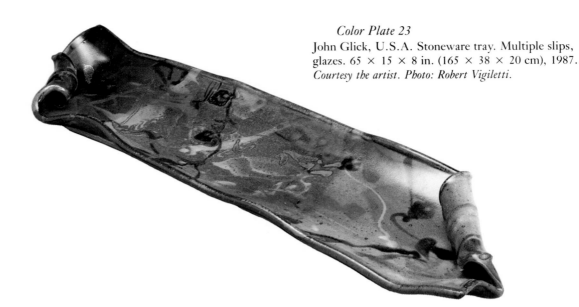

Color Plate 23
John Glick, U.S.A. Stoneware tray. Multiple slips,
glazes. 65 × 15 × 8 in. (165 × 38 × 20 cm), 1987.
Courtesy the artist. Photo: Robert Vigiletti.

Color Plate 24
Roseline Delisle, U.S.A. *Série Pneumatique 10.*
Porcelain. 10 × 5 in. (25 × 13 cm), 1987. *Courtesy
Dorothy Weiss Gallery. Photo: Susan Einstein.*

Color Plate 25
Michael Frimkess, U.S.A. *The Marriage of Auntie
Suzanna.* Low-fire clay, glaze, china paint. 34 ×
11½ in. (86 × 29 cm), 1977. *Courtesy the artist.*

Color Plate 26
Maria Bofill, Spain. Group of vessels. Porcelain, engobes. Hts. 4 to 6 in. (10 to 15 cm),
1986. *Courtesy the artist.*

Color Plate 27
Belinda Gabryl, U.S.A. *Tornado Teapot and
Creamer.* White earthenware, low-fire glaze. 13 ×
8½ × 9 in. (33 × 21.5 × 23 cm). *Courtesy the
artist. Photo: James Beards.*

Color Plate 28

Susan and Steven Kemeneffy, U.S.A. *Autumn Louise*. Raku fired wall piece. Approx. 2½ ft. × 4 × 8 in. (7.6 m. × 10 × 20 cm), 1987. *Courtesy the artists.*

Color Plate 29

Sandro Lorenzini, Italy. *Guerrieri*. Stoneware installation. Oxides, glazes. *Courtesy the artist.*

6
Europe

*Earth I am, it is
most true.
Disdain me not, for so
are you.*

Inscription on an early
English plate

Brown earthenware "Harvest" jug. To decorate such jugs, the artists trailed white slip over the surface and then scratched lines into it to create the detail. This one includes the royal coat of arms, the lion and unicorn, and an inscribed motto. England, 1775. White slip over earthenware, sgrafitto decoration. *Courtesy Royal Albert Memorial Museum, Exeter, England.*

As the unifying force of the Roman Empire waned in Europe, new ideas and influences appeared. The Christian religion, brought to Rome by missionaries from Judea, had created an art that incorporated styles and motifs from classic Greece and Rome, along with those from Byzantine art, which had in turn been influenced by art from India, Egypt, Persia, and the ancient Mesopotamian cultures. While these two cultural streams—the classical and the Oriental—merged in the art of medieval Europe, the influence of Islamic art was also spreading as the Arabs thrust westward. The potters soon followed the Moslem forces—potters were always among the first settlers to follow invading military armies, because the soldiers and the immigrants who followed them soon had to replace their fragile cooking and storage pots.

SPAIN

The Islamic Moors invaded Spain from North Africa around A.D. 700, and Islamic potters came with them, bringing their knowledge of glazes and lusters as well as the characteristic Moslem style of decoration (3-31 to 3-34).

Figure 6-1
The dark green, yellow, and gray-blue glazes on a Hispano-Moresque tin-glazed plate are separated by lines painted with a mixture of manganese and grease in a technique called *cuerda seca*, used to keep the glazes from running into each other. Tin-glazed earthenware. Diameter about 9 in. (22.9 cm). Spain, fifteenth century. *All rights reserved, the Metropolitan Museum of Art, Rogers Fund, 1930.*

Hispano-Moresque Ceramics

The Moors occupied a large part of Spain for nearly eight hundred years, developing there an art style that combined the native and imposed styles into a new one, known as **Hispano-Moresque.** This style made use of decorative ideas and ceramics techniques that would eventually spread far beyond Spain and would profoundly influence European pottery as well as pottery in Spanish America (6-1).

In Spain, the potters found ample supplies of tin to use in their glazes. To the basic lead-tin glaze, they added cobalt, copper, manganese, and iron, creating colorful glazes—blue, green, purple, brown, and yellow—with which they covered their plates, bowls, and tiles. Using these oxides, they also painted decorative motifs onto pottery or tiles that had been given a first low firing (**bisque**), and then coated with a white background glaze; then they fired them once more. In addition, to give the tiles a rich metallic sheen, they often fired lusters onto the glazed surfaces using a reducing atmosphere in the kiln. When these bowls or tiles were removed from the kiln, in the words of a fourteenth-century Islamic writer on ceramics, "everything which has had a fire of this kind glistens like red gold and shines like the light of the sun."

Tiles   The characteristic Islamic use of tile—either as solid-colored tiles that were cut into small mosaic pieces and then set in patterns or as square tiles that were patterned with plant forms and geometric designs—first appeared in Spain on the walls of Moorish palaces and mosques around A.D. 1300. The tiles were made with two techniques, called *cuerda seca* and *cuenca*, whose purpose was to keep the multicolored glazes from running into each other when they were fired. In the *cuerda seca* technique, the potter drew lines around the areas of the design using a mixture of manganese and grease, and then filled in each area with a different color of glaze. This method was also used on pottery, where it gave strong outlines to the fired designs (6-1). Later, the *cuenca* method became more popular for use on tiles. In this technique, the designs were impressed into the damp clay, forming indentations and ridges that kept each color of glaze from spilling over onto the neighboring areas (6-2).

The Spread of Tin Glazing

The region of Valencia, on the Mediterranean coast, was—and still is—one of the most important Spanish pottery centers, and even after the Moors were expelled from Spain, the potters there continued to decorate their pottery with Islamic glazes and lusters, using Moorish-influenced designs.

We should remember that even though travel on sea and land was dangerous and difficult, people and goods nevertheless moved constantly across the Mediterranean and overland throughout Europe. Italian potters, for instance, are known to have worked in Spain at a very early date. Conversely, much of the tin-glazed deco-

Figure 6-2
Tiles like this one glazed in black, yellow, and green, were decorated using the *cuenca* technique. In this method, designs were first impressed into the damp clay and then filled with glaze: The indentations kept the colors separate in the firing. Similar tiles covered palaces and mosques in Spain during the Moorish occupation. Earthenware. Spain, seventeenth century. *Courtesy the Cooper-Hewitt Museum, Smithsonian Institution/Art Resource, N.Y.*

rated pottery made in the Valencia area was exported to other parts of Europe via Mallorca in the Balearic Islands. The term **maiolica,** which is the Italian name for decorated tin-glazed pottery, is believed by some to come from a corruption of the place name Mallorca, while others say it derived from the phrase *obra de mélica,* a term used as early as 1454 to describe the pottery made at Manises, near Valencia. Whatever its derivation, the term *maiolica* (or *majolica*) is still used for this type of pottery.

ITALY

By the thirteenth century, decorated pottery from Spain was being traded to Italy, and it, along with glazed and decorated Byzantine pottery, which was imported through the port of Venice, exerted a strong influence on Italian ceramics. That the Italians treasured glazed and lustered pottery bowls from the East is clear from the place of honor they gave to those bowls by setting them into the brickwork of the towers and facades of their Romanesque churches. These lustered bowls, still to be seen in towers in Italy, were placed there, it is said, to glorify God as they reflected the first rays of the sun in the morning and the last in the evening. Lead glazes had been used in Italy since at least the ninth century A.D., and tin-glazed ware had been made in Sicily and southern Italy by the eleventh or twelfth centuries A.D., but the brilliant color and luster of the maiolica that came from Spain had a greater appeal. In addition, it arrived in northern Italy at an opportune time, when a rich ruling and mercantile class that could afford the luxury of this imported ware was growing in the Italian city-states. Popes, bankers, and princes bought the imported glazed and decorated bowls and plates to display on their walls, and Italian potters soon began to copy this ware, hoping to get a share of the luxury market for themselves.

Italian Maiolica

By the turn of the fifteenth century, as their knowledge of glazing techniques was being perfected, the potters in numerous ceramics towns in Italy were producing white and colored maiolica and learning how to apply luster as well.

The Italian cities of Faenza, Deruta, Vicenza, Siena, and Perugia all developed pottery industries that embodied the new aesthetic ideas of the Renaissance. Potters in those cities now made glazed pottery that was both colorful and practical (6-3, Color Plate 14). Because it could be easily washed, the tin-glazed ware was at first especially popular in pharmacies for jars containing herbs, medicines, oils, and ointments. The earliest Italian maiolica had been decorated with geometric designs—cross-hatching, circles, and dots—but soon other types of ornament came into use. Oriental motifs, traceable back to Persia, and designs and motifs from medieval illuminated manuscripts from northern Europe appeared along with classical and Renaissance ones (6-4). Now the

Figure 6-3
In Deruta, in northern Italy, techniques learned from Spain were used to create pottery known as maiolica (Color plate 4). This dish is decorated with mother-of-pearl luster outlined in blue. Diameter about 10 in. (25.4 cm). Deruta, 1530. *All rights reserved, the Metropolitan Museum of Art, gift of Henry Marquand, 1894.*

Figure 6-4
Called a pilgrim bottle because its shape was based on the flasks tied to the harnesses of travelers' horses, this maiolica bottle was made in Faenza, the leading Italian ceramic center in the sixteenth century. On it, Gothic and Renaissance motifs merged to create a characteristic design of dolphins entwined in tendrils of vines. Height 13⅝ in. (34.6 cm). Faenza, c. 1540. *Courtesy the Cleveland Museum of Art, gift of J. H. Wade.*

maiolica was considered elegant enough to be given as a gift to the Medici ruler, Lorenzo the Magnificent, who, acknowledging a gift of the new ware, wrote in 1490, "They please me by their perfection and rarity, being quite novelties in these parts, and are valued more than if of silver. . . ."

Improved techniques   By the time the maiolica had reached that degree of elegance, the methods of forming and firing it had improved and pottery workshops had been organized around the apprentice system, with assistants working under the supervision of the master potter. One of these master potters, a sixteenth-century Italian named Cipriano Piccolpasso, wrote *The Three Books of the Potter's Art*, describing his methods and those of other potters. By reading this early ceramics manual, potters could learn how to work more efficiently. For example, Piccolpasso tells them to make the pivot of the wheel axle from steel, to set it to revolve on a flint socket or steel plate, and to wrap the bearing near the top of the axle with oiled leather to make it turn more easily. He also describes how to mix clay (6-5), how to form pots on the wheel (6-6), how to finish them, and how to build a kiln and fire it (6-7).

According to Piccolpasso, vases and jugs were sometimes made in two parts, with the neck attached with slip while damp, or even sometimes stuck on with glaze after the first (bisque) firing.

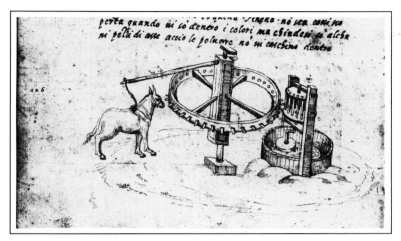

Figure 6-5
The Three Books of the Potter's Art, by Cipriano Piccolpasso, is a storehouse of information about sixteenth-century Italian pottery techniques. Here, he illustrates harnessing mule power to speed up the mixing of clay and glaze materials. Italy, c. 1556. *Courtesy of the Board of Trustees of the Victoria & Albert Museum.*

Figure 6-6
Kick wheels are shown in an Italian potter's shop of the sixteenth century. Piccolpasso states that the diligent artisan must work as carefully on the outside surface as on the inside, smoothing out the ridges of clay that appear on the walls of the vase. Cipriano Piccolpasso, *The Three Books of the Potter's Art*, Italy, c. 1556. *Courtesy of the Board of Trustees of the Victoria & Albert Museum.*

Figure 6-7
Piccolpasso captures the tension of firing as the master potter urges assistants to load in wood to keep the fire going, while he times its duration with an hourglass. This sixteenth-century kiln was built of brick with flues in the floor that allowed the heat to rise through the stacked pottery; after the arched door had been bricked in, the smoke and heat escaped from vents in the roof. Cipriano Piccolpasso, *The Three Books of the Potter's Act*, Italy, c. 1556. *Courtesy of the Board of Trustees of the Victoria & Albert Museum.*

Bowls, he said, were often finished upside down on the wheel, with their walls thinned and smoothed by a template held against the side walls while the piece was turned on the wheel. In the same way, he stated, the wheel could be used while decorating pots.

Decoration

Toward the end of the fifteenth century, presentation pieces—*piatti di pompi*—became an important part of the output of Italian potters. These consisted of souvenirs and gifts, wedding bowls displaying portraits of the betrothed, and dishes painted with portrayals of women and children and intended to be filled with appetizing food as gifts for new mothers.

The earlier maiolica has often been classified as "austere style" or "severe style," owing partly to the simplicity of its forms and partly to the style of the painted decoration that used flat areas of color, often outlined with dark lines or with the details of faces and clothing drawn in with a brush. No attempt was made to show perspective, and as a result, the figures remained on the flat plane of the plate. As time went on and the techniques of painting with glazes improved, the decorators used the white-glaze surface of the maiolica merely as a ground on which to display their knowledge of the new Renaissance method of depicting space through the use of perspective.

Now, when the pottery decorators were copying engravings of paintings by famous artists such as Raphael and using perspective and shading to create illusionary space and three-dimensional form, the biblical and mythological figures in landscapes and architectural settings appeared to be three-dimensional, with little relation to the shape of the vase or the flat plane of the plate.

Clay Sculpture

While Renaissance painters were producing the illusion of space on the walls and ceilings of palaces and religious buildings, and ceramic painters were following their lead in their own medium, sculptors were modeling the human figure in the round instead of in **bas relief.** Clay, as we have seen, had been used by the ancient Etruscans to model large free-standing figures for their temples (2-25) and tombs (2-26), and by the Romans for portraits. This tradition of using clay for sculpture had continued in some areas of Italy; for example, in the late fifteenth century in northern Italy, several sculptors in Ferrara, Modena, and Bologna created religious groups out of the abundant local earthenware clay, painting them with realistic colors after firing.

During the height of the Renaissance, however, most sculptors used clay (as well as wax) to make the originals from which bronze statues were cast. But some, such as Donatello (6-8), and Verrocchio, used terra-cotta clay to create portraits that were apparently intended not for casting but as works of art in themselves. Indeed, Verrocchio had some of his sculpture glazed in the workshop of the Della Robbia family so that its surface would be more durable than the usual paint that was normally applied to terra-cotta sculpture after firing.

Architectural Ceramics

Like the Islamic countries, Italy traditionally used ceramics in architecture. The Etruscans had covered their temples with terra-cotta decorations and sculptures (2-24, 2-25), and the Romans had called in Etruscan sculptors to decorate theirs. In some areas of northern Italy, where there was little good local stone for building, decorative bricks were molded for use around windows, doorways, and sometimes even the whole facades of buildings. With the development of maiolica, the tiles made to be used on the floors of churches and palaces could be glazed with blue, orange, green, and purple. Medieval floral motifs were often combined with Persian and classical ones, creating a colorful record of Italian Renaissance life. Coats of arms of prominent families, drawings of animals, representations of tools of various trades, portraits, and symbolic references to well-known figures of the day were all painted on the tiles.

In the mid-fifteenth century, Luca della Robbia (1389–1482), impressed with the colors that could be obtained with opaque tin glazes, saw the possibility of applying them to sculpture. After much experimentation, he succeeded in develop-

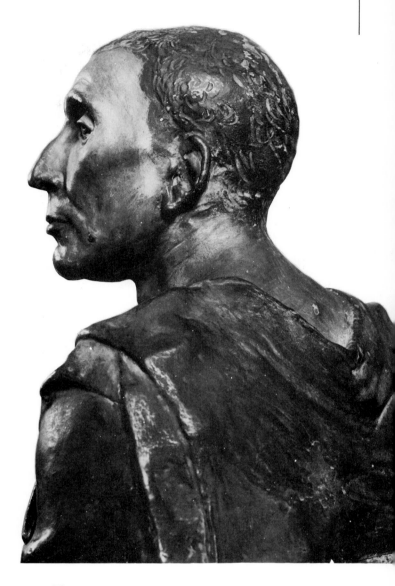

Figure 6-8
This terra-cotta bust attributed to Renaissance sculptor Donatello (1385–1466) probably represents Niccolo da Uzzano, leader of a group of merchants who tried to resist the rising power of the Medici in Florence. Portrait sculptures like this one, which may have been made from a death mask, continued the portrait tradition of the Etruscans and represented a break with medieval religious sculpture. *Courtesy Alinari.*

Figure 6-9
The Virgin Worshipping the Child by Luca della Robbia (1399–1482). Della Robbia was
the first to apply brightly colored tin glazes to large terra-cotta reliefs. Three
generations of his family carried on the tradition into the sixteenth century; his
nephew, Andrea della Robbia (1455–1525), made the frame for this medallion,
decorating it with fruit and flowers in the typical family style. Luca della Robbia, wall
plaque, fifteenth century. *Courtesy the Philadelphia Museum of Art, purchased by the W. P.
Wilstach Collection (#30.1.1).*

ing rich glazes, which he used on terra-cotta panels and medallions modeled in relief, many of which can still be seen on buildings in Florence. His depictions of the Madonna are usually surrounded by wreaths of flowers and fruit that display the colorful glazes to great advantage (6-9). The composition of the glazes remained a family secret that was handed on to his nephews but was eventually lost.

NORTHERN EUROPE

The wealthy city-states of Italy and the mercantile cities of northern Europe both traded with and periodically waged war against each other. Considering the barrier imposed by the Alps, travelers and armies moved between the areas with remarkable ease. Northern artists came to Italy to study the classical remains being unearthed there, and Italian artisans went north to work. For example, potters from the Italian ceramics town of Faenza went to France, and it was from the French spelling of the name of their town that the word **faience** came to be applied to tin-glazed earthenware.

The very early history of ceramics in northern Europe is somewhat similar to the story in the southern countries, but it differs in certain ways. Neolithic and Bronze Age potters in northern areas had made urns and vessels by hand, decorating them with patterns of incised lines and textures. Handbuilt black vessels with incised lines often emphasized by white chalk, funerary urns painted with swirls, rough pots with fingernail textures—all these had been made in early periods from Scotland (1-13) to Denmark, from Switzerland to Hungary. Many of them, especially the pots of the La Tène and Halstatt cultures, were shaped with a fine sense of form and decorated with sensitivity to the relationship between form and decoration. But a continuing and developing tradition of pottery making had not blossomed in northern Europe into anything approaching Greek or Roman ceramics, probably because urban centers such as those in the Mediterranean had not developed there.

The Romans took their ceramics techniques to northern Europe, where the local potters learned from them to use the true wheel and to build more advanced kilns such as the parallel-flue kiln. But after the Romans left, most of northern Europe forgot these techniques, and it was not until sometime between the midninth to the twelfth centuries that potters there again learned to use the kick wheel and to fire in more efficient kilns.

Some medieval kilns were basically the same as the simple Mediterranean updraft types—circular, vertical, having some sort of perforated floor resting on a central pillar, one fire underneath, and a vent at the top. However, by the thirteenth century, double-flue kilns were used in which the pots were stacked on the floor of the firing chamber and a temporary vault of turf or of clay smeared on a wicker support was built over them. Eventually, in the fifteenth and sixteenth centuries, circular, multiflue updraft kilns were used with fires built in each of five or six radiating flues, and simple versions of the Roman parallel-flue kilns were also reintroduced. The kiln designs varied in detail from area to area, however, and pit firing was used continuously in rural areas. In pit or open firing, the ware was usually placed in saggers and covered with shards with holes left around the sides for adding wood to the fire.

Architectural Ceramics

By the time the Roman Empire had declined and the legions had returned home, the large-scale production of bricks and roof tiles that the Romans had developed to build their military posts and urban centers had died out. Later, when the parallel-flue kiln returned, potters in northern Europe began to make bricks again along with tiles, chimney pots, drains, water pipes, and decorations to be placed atop gabled roofs.

A characteristic use of clay for architecture during the medieval period in England was that of tiles for the floors of churches and large homes. These tiles were made by *tyghlers*, men who traveled around making tiles near the site at which they were to be installed. The tiles were made of earthenware, and white clay lines were inlaid in the red clay to make line drawings of floral motifs, animals, saints, bishops, and nobles pictured in elaborate architectural settings.

Another use of clay at this time was for stoves

(a)

(b)

Figure 6-10

For the castle museum in Lenzburg, Switzerland, Ernst Häusermann and Peter Schmid researched and built a reconstruction of an early medieval heating stove. **(a)** They built the firebox of brick, coated it with layers of local low-fire clay mixed with straw, sand, and weed seeds, and then painted the unfired exterior with whitewash. Wood-fired pots were set into the rounded top to radiate the heat. With even a small fire, the pots send out a remarkable amount of warmth. Steps at the side provide a cozy sitting space. **(b)** The completed stove. Lenzburg, Switzerland. 1986. Ht. 71 in. (180 cm). *Courtesy, Ernst Häusermann. Photos, Hans Weber.*

to heat the cold homes of northern Europe. Early medieval stoves had been built of ordinary bricks and then coated with layer upon layer of coarse, wet clay mixed with straw and sand as temper (6-10). In many of the early stoves, earthenware pots were set into the sides or top to conduct the heat outward. Later, the stoves were constructed with specially designed glazed tiles that radiated the heat while serving as colorful decoration (6-11).

Medieval Jugs

Probably the largest part of the medieval potter's output took the form of jugs. Ordinary people at this time ate off wooden plates and drank from horn or wooden cups, and the nobility used metal plates, goblets, and bowls. Everyone, however, needed jugs for carrying water, wine, or beer, and jugs remained part of the potter's staple output for at least two hundred years (6-12).

Figure 6-12
A medieval potter makes a characteristic cylindrical jug using a kick wheel. Rotating the wheel with her foot, she uses a notched tool to decorate the jug as the wheel turns. The wheel head was supported and attached to the base with several wooden posts. Redrawn from a fifteenth century playing card.

The early medieval jugs were rough and crude but strong and bold in shape, with varied decoration—stamped and combed designs (6-13), trailed slip decoration, and human and animal figures and faces in relief were all used. Others were coated with a lead glaze that fired a yellowish-brown. The main glaze used in northern Europe at this time was made from a lead powder called **galena**; it was dusted onto the ware, where it adhered to the surface to create a yellowish transparent glaze. This lead glaze could be colored with oxides—copper to make it green and iron to make it reddish—but the addition of these oxides did not make the glaze opaque, so it did not cover the body color completely.

By the end of the thirteenth century, pottery as tableware had become widespread in northern Europe, and the amount of this ware produced was very large. Now the domestic objects made of ceramics included the ever-present jugs along with cooking pots, bowls, skillets, lamps, cups, weights for spinning wood, mortars, and numer-

Figure 6-11
By the sixteenth-century, heating stoves in Europe were covered with glazed tiles molded in relief that both served to radiate heat from the wood fire and provided a decorative surface. The repeat-pattern tiles are green, while the middle border of figures and the top decorations are multicolored. Austria, 1589. *Courtesy Philadelphia Museum of Art, gift of Henry Dolfinger (#29.56.1).*

Figure 6-13

The jugs made in medieval England were glazed with a lead powder, galena, that was sprinkled onto the surface of the clay. During firing the lead combined with the silica in the clay, forming a glaze. The incised lines on this jug, made with a notched tool, were typical decorations, as were designs made with stamps and small wheels called roulettes. Ht. 14⅝ in. (37 cm). Lead glazed, England, c. 1300. *Courtesy the Syndics of the Fitzwilliam Museum, Cambridge.*

ous others. Potters settled near available clay sources and dug their clay from pits near their cottages. As the pits were dug deeper and rains filled them with water, they became so dangerous to travelers that in England in the fifteenth and sixteenth centuries the courts ordered potters not to dig clay within eight yards of the highway.

German Stoneware

While the potters of Britain and France were making lead-glazed jugs from local earthenware, the potters working along the Rhine Valley in Germany were discovering that the abundant local clay could be fired to a high temperature 2218°F/1250°C, making it dense, impervious to liquid, and resistant to acids. The Rhine Valley was a logical area for the development of high-fire pottery in Europe, for in addition to the large supplies of stoneware clay, the forests of northern Europe provided ample wood for the kilns and the river served as a water highway for shipping the pottery easily. The first stoneware was made near Bonn in the middle of the twelfth century, and from then on the potters along the Rhine made jugs. The basic form of these remained the same for several centuries, but the styles of decoration changed as new fashions and techniques developed. From about A.D. 1300 on, the use of stamped, applied decoration was particularly characteristic of the Rhenish jugs. Many of the jugs were decorated with medallions in bas relief. To create these medallions, the potter first carved an original in stone and then the stone carving was pressed into clay to create a positive that was fired at a low temperature. From this clay positive, any desired number of negative clay molds could be made, and it was from these that the relief medallions were created. Apparently, carving the stone original allowed more precise details, and the low-fired clay molds were porous so that the medallions could be removed easily when the mold had absorbed water from the damp clay. Once the medallions were made, they were luted to the jug. The clay body of the stoneware jugs fired to a dull gray color, so the jugs were often coated with an iron wash to give more color to the body.

Salt Glazing

The lead glaze used on earthenware was useless for glazing stoneware, for it would melt and run off at the high temperature needed to fire that heat-resistant ware. We do not know if the potters deliberately attempted to discover a glaze that could be fired at the high temperature stoneware required or if the discovery of salt glazing was accidental. At any rate, it was found at some point that if salt were introduced into the kiln, it would vaporize in the heat, and as the sodium in the vapor settled on the stoneware, it would combine with the silica in the clay body to create a shiny, transparent coating on the pottery (6-14).

Salt-glazed ware became extremely popular, and the Rhine Valley potteries were organized to produce it in large quantities. Large quantities of jugs were exported down the river to the Netherlands, France, the whole of western Europe, and on to England, even reaching the early American colonies. Because the industry was important economically, the stoneware potters kept their techniques secret, creating ill feeling and envy among the earthenware potters. As a result, the stoneware potters were actually expelled from one city, ostensibly because of the danger of fire posed by the kilns, but probably because political pressure was exerted by the earthenware potters.

The potters in Germany continued to guard the secret of the salt glazing zealously, and it was not until the midsixteenth century that French potters began to make salt-glazed stoneware, and not until 1671 was a patent taken out in England for the manufacture of this product. Even then, country potters continued to make slip-decorated earthenware jugs (page 115) into the nineteenth century.

The Spread of Faience

In the fourteenth century, potters from Spain had brought the technique of opaque tin glazing to France, but it was not until the sixteenth century, when Italian potters came to work in France, that the French potters learned their methods of glazing, painting, and firing. Even-

Figure 6-14

Salt-glazed Bellarmine stoneware jug with face. The potters along the Rhine River in Germany found that their local clay became vitreous and impervious to liquid when fired to high temperatures. This gave them an advantage over potters who had to depend on porous earthenware clay for their pots, and the further development of salt glazing gave them an even greater superiority. The faces on these jugs were generally press-formed in molds and then applied to the jugs. *Courtesy National Museum of American History, Smithsonian Institution, Division of Ceramics and Glass.*

Figure 6-15
Relief-decorated plate by Bernard Palissy (or in his style). Palissy (1510–1590), a French glass painter, became interested in pottery glazes and used them in rich colors to enhance the realism of the modeled objects on his plates. France, sixteenth century. *All rights reserved, the Metropolitan Museum of Art, gift of J. Pierpont Morgan, 1917.*

tually they created their own style of multicolored ware, decorating it with the Renaissance motifs that were popular all over Europe. With this colorful faience, the French took over a large part of the European market.

One individualistic artist in France whose work was quite different from the usual decorated tin-glazed pottery was Bernard Palissy (1510–1590). Originally a glass painter whose work led him to an interest in glazes, Palissy created sculptural work—figurines colored with lead glazes—and a distinctive series of sculptural display plates modeled in brightly colored relief with faces, fish,

eels, and fruit (6-15), which became popular with the aristocracy. Palissy was so fascinated by glaze experimentation and so determined to develop new glazes, that at one time he sat up for six days and six nights tending his kiln. Palissy wrote that after ten years of this intensive work, "I became so thin that my legs had no roundness of shape left about them. . . . as soon as I began to walk, the garters with which I fastened my stockings used to slip down." Palissy used molds for his forms, often making them from life, and when he died his followers continued to use his molds producing copies of his work.

European Blue and White Ware

When the first shipments of blue and white Chinese porcelain arrived in Europe around 1600, Europeans were accustomed to the Italian maiolica, French faience, and Dutch delftware (all these terms mean essentially the same thing—that is, earthenware covered with an opaque white tin glaze and decorated with a variety of colors). Such pottery was thick, not translucent like porcelain, and despite the glaze coating not totally impervious to liquids or resistant to acid. The new fine porcelain caused a sensation; people had seen nothing like it before. In order to compete with the imported porcelain, the potteries in Italy and elsewhere, especially in the Low Countries, immediately began to make cheap imitations of it. Since they did not know the secret of making porcelain; they made their imitations in earthenware. Still, the opaque white glaze on earthenware did provide a good background for cobalt blue decoration, so the European potters were able to produce a relatively inexpensive copy that had the general appearance of the fine white Oriental ware even if it lacked its delicacy and translucence.

Delftware   Although blue and white ware was produced throughout Europe, the town of Delft in Holland became especially noted for it, and as with Faenza, its name became synonymous with its product. This Dutch town became a major pottery center as a result of events that had little to do with ceramics: the breweries of Delft at this time were having economic difficulties, and it was decided to turn them into potteries and teach the unemployed brewers to be potters. A great variety of tin-glazed earthenware objects was made there; apothecary jars, tiles, mugs, barbers' dishes, bowls for the bleedings so popular in medical practice, and wig stands were all decorated with cobalt blue, reflecting the rage for Chinese-inspired decoration called **Chinoiserie** (6-16). The Dutch became expert in making tiles, and the blue and white glazing became especially popular in Holland, where the shining tiled walls of kitchens, dairies, and hallways reflected the Dutch housewives' industrious housecleaning.

Figure 6-16
Made in Holland in the town of Delft, this wig stand of white glazed earthenware decorated with cobalt blue shows the influence of Chinese exported ceramics in its Oriental-style painted flowers and birds. Delft, Holland, seventeenth century. *Courtesy the Board of Trustees of the Victoria & Albert Museum.*

European Porcelain

Although the use of stoneware had become widespread throughout Europe and was made in great quantities, potters there continued to search for the secret of porcelain. As early as the late sixteenth century, Italian potters had made what is known as **soft-paste** porcelain; unlike true porcelain, soft-paste porcelain can be scratched with a sharp steel instrument. Finally, around 1710, Johann Friedrich Böttger, a chemist and alchemist in Germany, discovered how to make the true high-fired, translucent material known as **hard paste.** On the order of the king of Saxony, Böttger had been trying to making gold from less expensive materials to fill the depleted royal treasuries. It was during his search for such materials that he experimented with clays, and in the process of his experiments he discovered how to make a fine stoneware that was so hard it could be cut on a lathe. This discovery led to the founding of the Meissen ceramics factory. Then, when Böttger discovered kaolin in Saxony, he succeeded in making true porcelain. Thus, his unsuccessful attempts to make gold led to a discovery that turned out to be a commercial goldmine.

Different factors affected the way the expanding ceramics industry developed in each country. In France, for example, two quite different motives gave impetus to the industry: royal pride and French taste in food. In 1709, King Louis XIV was in need of money, so he had the royal gold and silver bowls, cups, and plates melted down, leaving himself with no appropriately elegant tableware. He then commissioned the potters of Limoges to make faience of the Italian type to replace it, thereby giving royal patronage to the industry. Meanwhile, expanded mustard manufacturing in Dijon kept the potters there busy making the faience jars in which the mustard was shipped.

After production of porcelain began in Germany, intense competition developed among other countries, and a race was on to discover its secret so they could compete with the flood of imports from China and the output of the German factories. Eventually, other European countries did learn how to make porcelain, and many of them found the kaolin supplies needed to make the fine, translucent ware.

In Denmark, the ceramics industry was at first supervised by French and German technicians who brought their techniques and even their clay with them because the local clay did not fire well. In 1779, a factory was established that became the Royal Copenhagen Porcelain Factory, and a French potter who had come to work for the Danish king was ordered to teach two of the local technicians his porcelain making secrets before he was allowed to return to France, another example of the competitiveness that was typical of the ceramics industry in Europe after the arrival of Chinese porcelain.

ENGLAND

It was partly as a result of a political event that the production of blue and white ware spread to England. In 1689, William of Orange became king of England as well as king of the Low Countries, and at this time potters from Delft went to England, taking their knowledge and techniques with them.

Along with the blue and white porcelain, tea was also being imported from China, and Chinese tea and Arabian coffee became the fashionable drinks in English drawing rooms and coffee houses. Like the Japanese potters who had had to adapt their products to the imported tea ceremony (3-26), the English potters were affected by this new social habit and had to develop new shapes for pouring out the popular new beverages.

Slip-Decorated Earthenware

While the blue and white tin-glazed ware gained popularity among the wealthy and fashionable, simple earthenware vessels were still used in most rural areas. In England, for example, potters continued to make large quantities of lead-glazed earthenware decorated with slip, and traveling pot sellers marketed the ware from village to village, selling it directly from their carts. The slip-decorated pottery was made with techniques that remained very much the same in country areas well into the eighteenth and nineteenth centuries—and these techniques are still used by some studio potters today. In one technique, the decorative slip was **trailed** onto wet slip of a contrasting color, and then a comb or another tool was dragged across it in a technique called **feathering**, which created a marbled effect (7-1). In another technique, **sgraffito**, the ware was covered with a coating of light-colored slip; then, when the slip was dry, the lines were drawn through it with a sharp instrument, revealing the darker body clay below it (page 115).

Earthenware plates, often formed by draping a slab of clay over a hump mold, were now in use on the tables of most homes. The potters also made plates for display or as wedding and christening gifts, decorating them with impressed designs filled with black and brown slips.

Kilns remained basically the same, except that now the ware to be fired was often stacked on thin slabs of stone used for shelves, and in order to keep the pots from sticking to the saggers when the glaze melted—a problem that had resulted in many ruined pots and saggers in the past—small pellets of clay were placed under each pot. Although the potteries were still basically small, family-run workshops, the basis for a much expanded ceramics industry was gradually being built up.

Figure 6-17
In the early eighteenth century, potteries in Staffordshire, England, adapted German salt-glazing techniques to small sculptured groups made of a dense, white stoneware body. The details of faces and clothing were accentuated with dark brown clay slip. Ht. 6 in. (15.2 cm). Pew group, Staffordshire, c. 1730. *Courtesy the Syndics of the Fitzwilliam Museum, Cambridge, England.*

Staffordshire Figures

In the seventeenth century, some English potters had learned to make high-fired, nonporous, acid-resisting stoneware—a big improvement over earthenware pottery. Potters experimented with different types of stoneware bodies—dark red and dark brown were usually used for teapots, coffeepots, and jugs. In 1671, a Fulham potter, John Dwight, applied for a patent to make porcelain and stoneware. Actually, his efforts to make porcelain had not quite succeeded, but he had developed a fine, white stoneware body that was especially successful for small figure sculptures, on which he used salt glaze. The salt glaze fitted the clay body well and did not obscure sculptural details by filling up indented areas. By the eighteenth century, in Staffordshire, where large numbers of potters had settled because good clay was available there, white stoneware was used in a combination of mold and

handbuilding techniques to make small sculptures (6-17). These were built with thin rolls of clay that acted rather like the skeletons of the figures; over these thin slabs of clay were draped to form the clothing.

English Ceramics Industry

England took longer to learn to make true porcelain, but in the process of experimenting with clay bodies, the potters there developed a type of soft paste that fused at a lower temperature than porcelain because it contained bone ash that acted as a flux. Still in use in England for making **bone china,** this soft-paste clay body was to have a profound effect on the world's tableware.

One potter, Josiah Wedgwood (1730–1795) probably had more responsibility than any other person for transforming the English potter-

Figure 6-18
Influenced by Greek rather than Chinese ceramics, the black "Basalt" ware of the Wedgwood pottery was made of a stoneware body colored with manganese that was so hard it could be cut and polished on a lapidary wheel. The handles are decorated with satyr masks and horns. Wedgwood Basalt ware, c. 1775, marked "Wedgwood and Bentley." *Courtesy Trustees of the Wedgwood Museum, Barlaston, Stoke-on-Trent, Staffordshire, England.*

ies from small family workshops into a mass-production industry that used steam power and large-scale distribution methods. This transformation made it possible for ordinary people to afford attractive, easily washed tableware. In addition, Wedgwood experimented with a variety of clay bodies and developed a speciality called **Basalt ware**, which was formed into classically inspired vase shapes (6-18).

Some of the social changes occurring in England during the eighteenth and nineteenth centuries had a bearing on the ceramics industry in England. The development of transportation, for example, played an important role in the industry, and by 1777 a new canal was bringing cheap water transport to the door of Wedgwood's new factory branch. Wedgwood also urged other pottery owners to join him in improving roads so that wagons could carry their ware easily. On the negative side, in the process of manufacturing large amounts of tableware, the pottery-producing areas of England became polluted with the fumes and smoke that poured from the kilns; one pottery alone might have had two dozen bottle kilns in operation at a time. Bottle kilns were the type most widely used in the industrialized pottery towns during the eighteenth and nineteenth centuries. Basically these kilns were of an up-draft design; the bottle-shaped outer structure both increased the draft to the inner kiln and protected the men carrying the saggers from the weather.

As Europe moved into the Industrial Revolution, the goal in the potteries was to make more and sell it cheaper. Steam power was harnessed to turn the mixing machinery, improved potter's wheels were sped by mechanical means, molds were used where necessary in order to form the ware faster, and workers were organized into assembly lines. Although expert potters were absorbed into the factory system, these developments kept individuals from participating in all aspects of the ceramic process. Thus, a separation developed between the individual potter and the product.

Before these mass-production methods separated the maker from the product, the artisan potter had been part of the mainstream of life; the men and women who worked with clay had filled basic needs of the community, whether for vessels

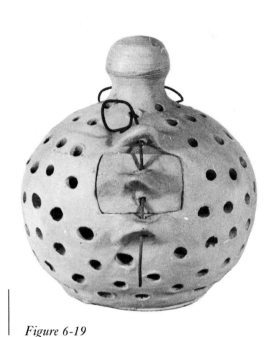

Figure 6-19
Throughout rural Europe, potters continued to make utilitarian objects of earthenware: clay provided the material for ovens, chamber pots, jugs, models of cradles for christening gifts, money jars, perforated jars to hold snails while they were prepared for human consumption, and cages, such as this one, made to hold crickets to amuse children. *Courtesy Museo Nacional del Pueblo Español, Madrid.*

Figure 6-20
The French potter Ernest Chaplet developed an interest in Oriental glazes, which he used on simple shapes reminiscent of those of Chinese porcelain (Color plate 3). His glazes influenced many other European potters to experiment with colorful glazes. Ernest Chaplet, France, porcelain, 1906. *Courtesy the Museum of Decorative Art, Copenhagen.*

to be placed on religious altars, simple cooking pots, or even rabbit hutches or cricket cages (6–19). The potters were not concerned with the place of the artisan in society, for their place in it was secure. But in an industry that was rapidly becoming machine-oriented, there seemed to be little place for the clay worker who took pride in his or her own work—who was an artist as well as an artisan.

STUDIO POTTERY

In some situations, however, an individual artist or potter could still exercise direct control over at least part of the process—either in the forming of the work or in its design or decoration. For example, in rural areas, where village craftspeople continued to work in small shops, pottery making remained very much the same as in earlier centuries. These potters supplied the local needs for a variety of domestic objects made from earthenware—and still do so in parts of Europe.

Nor did the studio potter come under the control of the factory system. The studio potter was a comparatively new phenomenon. The term *studio potter* can cover a variety of situations; for example, Ernest Chaplet (1835–1909) in France worked for two large pottery companies, but he also maintained his own workshop, and in it he worked in both stoneware and porcelain, covering his creations with glazes that rivaled those from

Figure 6-21

In the 1880s, the painter Paul Gauguin worked in Ernest Chaplet's studio handbuilding stoneware sculptural vases and figures and glazing them with Chaplet's brilliant glazes. This one, however, was made of coarse, low-fire clay, probably in a rural potter's shop in Brittany. It depicts Tahitian gods and goddesses. France, c. 1893–1895. *Courtesy the Museum of Decorative Art, Copenhagen.*

Figure 6-22

Danish artist Thorvald Bindesbøll stimulated an interest in painting on ceramics among European artists. Using professionally thrown earthenware as a ground, he painted strong abstract designs in black and white glazes, outlining them with sgraffito lines. Ht. 22¾ in. (58 cm). Copenhagen Earthenware Factory, Valby, Denmark, 1893. *Courtesy the Museum of Decorative Art, Copenhagen. Photo: Ole Woldbye.*

the Orient (6-20). It was in this shop that painter Paul Gauguin (1848–1903) first made ceramics—coil-built pots and sculptures that he considered to be an important part of his artistic output (6-21). Gauguin glazed his work with some of Chaplet's glazes, but he applied them in his own distinctive, painterly manner, creating pieces that were expressive of his own sense of form and surface. On the other hand, some artists both in Europe and the United States at this time did not form the ware themselves, but created paintings or decorations on pieces made by professional potters (6-22). They saw a piece of pottery almost as a dimensional canvas on which to paint rather than as an expressive composition.

The Arts and Crafts Movement

In the 1880s, a number of artists and art critics, in rebellion against the spread of machine-made objects and the pompous ugliness of Victorian taste, preached a return to the handcrafts. Led in England by William Morris (1834–1896) and John Ruskin (1819–1900), this group urged craftspeople to respect the materials in which they worked, and join in a revival of handcrafts that would beautify the surroundings and help the human spirit survive in a materialistic world. Morris and his followers rejected the factory situation and became influential in leading many craftspeople back to the small workshop situation of preindustrial days.

The Romantic movement in literature and art had influenced many of these artists to take their inspiration from the Middle Ages, Persia, and the art of the early Italian Renaissance. William Morris and other artists of his circle, such as William Frend De Morgan (1839–1917), designed wallpapers, tiles, stained glass, fabrics, and panels of maiolica tiles (6–23), using flowing floral forms and the greens and blues of Persian pottery.

In Spain, another believer in the medieval craft guild system, the Catalonian architect Antoni Gaudí (1852–1926), called on wood carvers, blacksmiths, stone cutters, and potters to help him realize his unusual buildings. Architecturally fascinating, his work is of particular interest to ceramists because of his manner of using glazed pottery shards to surface many of his buildings (Color plate 6). Gaudí's plans called for mosaics that, by the very nature of their collage process, had to be designed as they were created, so he entrusted the actual execution of the mosaics to a young architect, Josep Maria Jujol (1879–1949). Jujol worked along with Gaudí on the overall planning of the decoration and was responsible for supervising the tile setters at the sites as they covered the facades of buildings, roofs, fountains, benches, and ceilings with pottery rejects, broken tiles, and other found objects.

Although the members of the Arts and Crafts

Figure 6-23

William Frend De Morgan, a member of the Arts and Crafts Movement in England, started his own ceramic factory in London to produce vessels and tiles designed by himself and other artists. His tiles, their designs frequently based on plant forms, were generally glazed in blue and green, sometimes with luster overglazes. Blue, green, and turquoise-glazed earthenware tile. Sand's End Pottery, 1898–1907. *Courtesy the Cooper-Hewitt Museum, Smithsonian Institution/Art Resource, N.Y.*

Movement might yearn for lost craft traditions and attempt to restore the past by returning to earlier styles of art, it was clearly impossible for art-school-graduate studio-potters to return to the role of unsophisticated village potter responding to a neighbors' need for cooking pots. Too much had happened to change the world, and the studio potter was now faced with questions that would never have occurred to a Minoan, Islamic, Japanese, or African village potter: how to resolve the conflict between the machine and human hands, and how to choose between the desire to form

Figure 6-24
Axel Salto, who designed ceramics for Bing and Grøndahl Porcelain factory in Denmark, was a studio potter who also made one-of-a-kind pots covered with rich glazes over organic sculptural forms. Modeled and carved vase, warm brown glaze, c. 1931. *Courtesy the Museum of Decorative Art, Copenhagen.*

clay with honesty and integrity and the need to compete with cheap, machine-produced goods. Some studio potters—for example, Axel Salto of Denmark—resolved the conflict successfully by designing handsome ceramics for industrial production while at the same time creating their own individual pieces in their studios. A number of Scandinavian factories gave ceramic artists the opportunity to work in this way (6-24). The manner in which others resolved or avoided some of these questions is part of the story of the more recent past, and is covered in chapter 8.

7
The United States

. . . American ceramics, a diverse art form that has evolved along with an equally diverse society. . . .

Elaine Levin*

Historical records show that potters were aboard the ships that brought settlers to the North American wilderness. Many of these were coming as settlers to try to search for better lives in a free land, some were coming as indentured servants, while others came as slaves. Written records indicate that in New England and parts of the South, potters were at work in the colonies by the midseventeenth century, and once settlements had been established, all the villages and many plantations had potters who made their domestic ware. These potters, who came from many different backgrounds, brought with them the national or local ceramics designs, styles, and techniques of their homelands, and very soon after their arrival in the New World they began to make pottery from the local clay to supply the new colonies with functional ware.

*The History of American Ceramics, Harry N. Abrams, New York, 1988.

The Bayard Building in New York was designed by architect Louis Sullivan and built in 1897–1898. In 1896, Sullivan wrote about the "modern office building": "*How shall we impart to this sterile pile, this crude, harsh, brutal agglomeraton, this stark, staring exclamation of eternal strife, the graciousness of those higher forms of sensibility and culture that rest on the lower and fiercer passions?*" To accomplish his noble purpose, Sullivan often used ceramics to clad his metal-framed buildings, working with his designers to create the ornament that became characteristic of his architecture. Now cleaned and restored, the Bayard Building is an example of the best nineteenth-century American architectural ceramics.

137

Figure 7-1
This slip-decorated platter is an example of how the potters who came to the northeastern colonies from England reflected the types of ceramics they had made at home. These potters were also usually farmers, so their pottery was made for everyday use. Earthenware, slip-decorated. *Courtesy the Shelbourne Museum, Vermont.*

COLONIAL CERAMICS

In the seventeenth century, low-fire earthenware covered with opaque tin glazes was popular throughout Europe as dinnerware for the more affluent and as display and gift ware. The European country folk, however, continued into the nineteenth century to use local earthenware clay for many of their utilitarian objects. They either gave these objects an overall glaze of lead or first slip-decorated them with contrasting light-colored slip and then lead glazed them (6-13).

New England

Since most of the early potters who settled in New England came from Old England, the pottery they made reflected that background, and since it was produced for utilitarian use, they made it as they had made earthenware at home—slip decorated and lead glazed (7-1). Although little of the earliest New England–made pottery has survived, enough shards have been found at excavated kiln sites and enough town records have been found referring to potters' activities for us to know that potters were well established there very early. The wealthier colonists could afford to import their tin-glazed tableware and other ceramics from Europe, so the local potters concentrated on making simple earthenware utensils. For this reason, ceramics in North America was not greatly influenced by European maiolica wares, and it was some time before any decorative ceramics that could compete with more sophisticated European ware were produced in the colonies.

The colonial potter in New England was usually a farmer or fisherman who dug his clay in the fall, dried it in the winter, reconstituted it in the spring, and made pottery whenever he could spare the time. The master potter—the father of the potting family—would usually do the throwing, and a couple of his assistants—often his sons—would do the rest of the work.

The earthenware was thrown on a kick wheel and then glazed with red lead, which was ground with sand and water in a glaze mill that consisted of two millstones. To the transparent glazes, the potter added cobalt, manganese, or iron, depending upon which oxides were locally available, and he frequently applied the glaze in spots, streaks, or splatters. Slip decoration was popular; the jars, tubs, wash basins, pie plates, crocks, and porringers were trailed or painted. None of the decoration was elaborate, probably because of the Puritan attitude that condemned frivolity. But despite the strictures of the Pilgrim Fathers, the potters in New England tried to make their products as attractive as the material and the social and religious mores allowed.

Although pottery making was generally a male occupation, a good deal of the decorating and glazing was done by women, and apparently some women were potters as well. In 1716, for example, an advertisement offered the services of women potters who had arrived as indentured servants and who were available for hire, and there are records of widows who ran potteries after their husbands' deaths.

Pennsylvania

The distinctive pottery made by the Germans who settled to farm in Pennsylvania reflected the decorative traditions of German country pottery. In the midseventeenth century in Northern Europe, decorated plates commemorating important events were placed on shelves or hung on walls. The more prosperous colonial

Figure 7-2
First covered with a white, overall slip, this earthenware plate made by George Hübner in Pennsylvania was then decorated with slip-trailed tulips and Hapsburg eagles. These, as well as figures on horseback, dates, names, and inscriptions, were typical decorations on this ware. George Hübner, Pennsylvania, 1786. *Courtesy Philadelphia Museum of Art, gift of John T. Morris (#00-21).*

farmers also wanted to preserve the memories of births, weddings, or other events on plates, so dates, names, proverbs, and other inscriptions circled the edges of display plates (7-2). The plates were made of earthenware covered with slip or a glaze, with many of the design motifs—such as the Hapsburg double-headed eagle—taken directly from the decorative motifs used in the German homeland. These designs were trailed, painted, or scratched on in the style of northern European peasant art.

Afro-American Pottery

Recent discoveries and reevaluations have shown that in the earliest colonial days in Virginia and Maryland the few blacks there worked as indentured servants and craftspeople rather than as slaves. Not until later—at the end of the seventeenth century as slavery became general—did they become primarily field workers.

Decorated clay tobacco pipes, once believed to be Native American, have recently been recognized by anthropologists as having been made by these Afro-American craftspeople. The designs on hundreds of these pipes bear a striking resemblance to those on the pottery and pipes of West Africa (page 80 and 4-6). Apparently the pipes—made between 1650 and the end of the century—were made on European molds, but the incised and applied designs were African. For example, one such design included tiny circlets of applied clay that can be seen on Ife sculpture (4-2), whilte others were scratched into the clay and then emphasized with white clay rubbed into the lines (4-6). Later, a number of slaves used their pottery skills to make pots that sometimes combined European vessel forms with African imagery, including sculptured three dimensional "face pots." A few of these black potters were well known, and their work was sold at nearby market towns, earning income for their masters.

Stoneware

The perfecting of stoneware was the most important development in eighteenth-century European ceramics with respect to useful objects, because containers made of this clay body were impervious to liquids and acids. As soon as potters in Germany had begun to make stoneware jugs, those in other European countries tried to copy it, eventually learning how to fire it and coat it with a salt glaze. When, as early as 1730, English and European potters who knew the technique of firing stoneware arrived as settlers in the mid-Atlantic states and found local stoneware clay, they began to use it to make a wide variety of utilitarian ware. By the end of the eighteenth century, stoneware had for the most part replaced earthenware in domestic ceramics in the new country. Because the English potteries shipped the products of their china factories to the colonies to grace the tables of the wealthier colonists, and the clipper ships brought the treasured blue and white ware from China to New England, rural potters in the colonies concentrated primarily on producing utilitarian stoneware to satisfy the needs of simpler households. These needs were many and various: in the days before home canning or refrigeration, housewives required large numbers of containers in which to store pickled vegetables, salted pork, vinegar, and homemade

Figure 7-3

New York state and Vermont potters specialized in simple jugs, stoneware crocks, and pots decorated with chickens, eagles, and shorebirds as well as patriotic images. Sometimes stacked six feet high in the kilns, the cylindrical crocks were thick-walled enough to support the weight of those placed on them. Firing and salt glazing the utilitarian stoneware in wood kilns required from six to eight days. Ht. 11½ in. (29.2 cm). *Courtesy New York State Historical Association, Cooperstown, N.Y.*

beer. Stoneware was perfect for these uses, as it was impervious to acid as well as water and its salt glaze contained no lead (7-3).

Stoneware clay did not exist in New England and upper New York state, and the potters who made the ware in lower New York, New Jersey, Pennsylvania, and Virginia guarded the secret of its manufacture jealously and exported the finished ware to the northern areas. As the market grew larger, however, and potters in other parts of the colonies finally learned how to salt glaze stoneware, raw stoneware clay from New Jersey was shipped via waterways to northern potteries so that they could make their own stoneware. After 1820, when the Erie Canal and a network of waterways made raw materials and markets even more accessible to these potteries, a flourishing ceramics industry developed in Vermont and upstate New York.

These early stoneware potteries began as simple workshops. For example, one pottery in upper New York state that was referred to as a pottery factory in the 1850 census was described as making a hundred thousand pieces of earthenware a year with a staff of only three men, a woman, and a horse. The horse was undoubtedly used to turn the **pug mill** that mixed the clay and to carry the ware to market. The mixing mill usually consisted of a wooden tank with iron spikes set on its inside walls. The tank was filled with dry or damp clay, sand, and water, and a central shaft with spikes was turned by horse or water power, agitating and mixing the clay and water slurry. After the ingredients were thoroughly mixed, the semiliquid clay was screened to remove impurities and larger particles, then set aside to stiffen and age.

As time went on, the workshops actually did become small factories, and the work of the potter became more specialized. The master potter, using a kick wheel, would throw the basic shapes. He made tall, wide-mouthed cylinders for meat tubs; low tubs for butter pots; tall, narrow cylinders for butter churns; medium-sized cylinders as water dispensers for poultry; and smaller cylinders with an added neck and spout as jugs. Next, a finisher carefully smoothed the inside and outside and sometimes impressed decorations in the damp clay using a roulette. A third person would add the handles, and yet another worker would decorate the crock with slip of a contrasting color. The inside of the stoneware was generally coated with **Albany slip**, made from a fine clay mined near Albany, New York, that fired to a dark brown or black slip glaze. The stoneware was lined with slip glaze because it was stacked in the kiln rim to rim and base to base, so the vaporized salt did not penetrate to glaze the interiors of the crocks and pots.

Decoration

Much of the decoration was done with slip, and some decorators developed great facility in wielding the slip cup, using it to draw designs directly on the damp clay. This cup was a small pottery flask with a thin neck into which a quill was inserted; the slip ran out the hollow quill onto the

Figure 7-4
Stoneware figure of a poodle. The deep brown glaze colored with manganese that was used on pottery figurines like this poodle originated at the Rockingham China Works in Swinton, England. When nineteenth-century American pottery and animal figurines were coated with a similar glaze in America, it was usually deliberately mottled and runny. Stoneware, 1849–1858. Ht. 8¼ in. (21 cm). *Courtesy the Brooklyn Museum, H. Randolph Lever Fund. Acc. #74.19.3.*

unfired ware. Laid down in separate lines and dots, the slip flowed together in some places to form solid areas and formed lines that stood out in relief in others. The same type of cup was used to flow on oxides such as the cobalt that produced the characteristic blue decoration on many country crocks. The designs drawn on the stoneware—patriotic themes such as the American eagle or flower designs, birds, or grazing deer—reflected the interests of the people for whom the pottery was intended.

Figurines

Once the colonists settled into small-town or urban life, a market developed for small figurines that could be displayed in middle-class parlors or placed on the kitchen dressers of humbler homes. Many of these earthenware figures, like the Rockingham-glazed animals, were lively and humorous (7-4).

For the wealthier, there were more self consciously elegant figures, made of a white material called Parian Marble—actually porcelain. This material was modeled or cast into sentimental statues of children or miniature sculptures of draped ladies in classical poses that imitated in small scale the work of noted nineteenth-century sculptors.

Salt Glazing

The technique of salt glazing used in the colonies was basically the same as that used in Europe. The ware was fired in a single firing; the usual low-temperature preliminary (bisque) firing that would have driven the moisture out of the clay was eliminated. For this reason, the kiln operator had to regulate the wood fire carefully, increasing the temperature slowly to be sure that the pots would not burst as the water left the clay. When the kiln was firing at 2300°F/1260°C, the worker shoveled ordinary rock salt down into the kiln and closed the opening again. The salt vaporized almost instantly, and the sodium vapor covered the ware (as well as the kiln interior), forming a glaze as it combined with the silica in the clay body. In the words of a local potter's instruction manual, "When fit to glaze, have your salt dry. Scatter it well in every part of your kiln, during this act you must keep a full and clear blaze so as to accelerate the glazing and give the ware a bright gloss. Stop it perfectly tight and in six days you may draw a good kiln of ware."

After the introduction of the salt, the kiln would be kept at high heat for about three days, and then the temperature would be reduced so that the kiln would cool slowly to avoid damaging the ware. Finally, after about six or eight days, the door would be unbricked and, with luck, a kiln full of perfectly glazed ware would be revealed. But mishaps did occur, and many wasters—pieces of pottery that had buckled or cracked in the kiln—have been found at the pottery sites. Wastage was not the only problem facing the potters. When salt vaporizes it gives off a dangerous chlorine gas, and some citizens living near the salt kilns complained about gases released as the salt vaporized.

Potters followed the westward movement as the settlers penetrated into Ohio and beyond, setting up potteries in the new territories to provide the utensils needed in the farming communities.

Eventually, as in Europe, the potteries in the colonies became industrialized in order to supply the growing market, and small workshops could not compete with the low prices of the factory-produced goods. After the middle of the nineteenth century, many factories used molds and other industrial techniques to increase production, making it even more difficult for the small workshops to compete.

CONTINUING TRADITIONS

It was only in isolated rural areas or in mountain areas such as Appalachia, where factory-made products were hard to come by, that the tradition of the small, family-run pottery continued into the nineteenth century—and even to the present day in some places. In the Carolinas, Kentucky, the Virginias, and other southern states, a few family potteries using local clays have continued an almost unbroken tradition, producing the functional ware needed in a rural community—milk pans, bread pans, jugs, butter churns, and the usual storage crocks. At first, as in New England, such potteries produced earthenware, but by the nineteenth century most of the ware they made was salt-glazed stoneware like that made in New York (7-3). The potters in these potteries always used kick wheels, but here the potter stood, rather than sat, at the wheel to throw the pots. Kilns were built of bricks made of the local earthenware clay and were partially dug into the ground with the earth piled up around the sides of the arch to brace it. These kilns were called groundhog kilns, and kilns of this type are still used today by some country potters in that area.

Other traditional methods survive today in small potteries there although the potters' wheels may be mechanized with jury-rigged motors made from old car parts, and the mixing mills may now be run by electricity rather than turned by the family mule. However, the jugs, churns, and crocks the potters make are now more likely to be bought by collectors or tourists than by local farmers. Despite these changes, the potters there are carrying on some of the traditions of earlier American ceramics.

Art Pottery

By the end of the nineteenth century, life had become more urban in the New World, and a growing leisure class had become interested in the arts. With increasing urbanization and the competition from large pottery factories, it no longer made economic sense for the small potteries to make utilitarian ware. These factors led many potteries to hire artists to design vases, lamps, and decorative tiles to beautify the homes of the newly wealthy. Many of the old pottery companies that were scattered across the country from Ohio to California, Colorado to New York, began to produce "art pottery" in styles influenced by contemporary art movements in both the United States and France. The designs often reflected European pottery the owner or artist had seen at the international or national expositions, where large exhibitions of this new pottery were extremely popular.

As examples, the Grueby Faience and Tile Company of Boston and the Rookwood Pottery in Cincinnati were in many ways representative of these art pottery companies, each of which produced distinctive wares for which they quickly became famous. These companies hand formed their pottery, tended to follow the art styles of Europe, and appealed to middle-class housewives who wanted their homes to reflect the newest styles.

Grueby Faience and Tile Company Inspired by the French pottery shown at the Columbian Exposition of 1893, the Boston pottery run by William Grueby (1867–1925) made handmade semiporcelain decorated with reliefs and coated with distinctive **matt glazes.** Like most of the art potteries, Grueby's depended on young women to do the decorating, in this case young female graduates of art schools in the Boston area. The designs were usually based on natural forms—flowers and leaves. They were formed separately, applied to the ware, and then hand detailed.

Rookwood Pottery Started by Mrs. Maria Longworth Nichols Storer "as," she said, "an expensive luxury, for which I, luckily, could afford to pay," the Rookwood Pottery grew out of its owner's interest in china painting—a popular activity considered acceptable for the well-bred

Figure 7-5
Indian Vase, by Adelaide Alsop Robineau. Carving, characteristic of her work and often more elaborate than the swirling lines on this vase, was accomplished before firing when the piece was dry. Here, Robineau pays homage to the ceramics of the American Southwest. Ht. 14½ in. (36.8 cm). *Courtesy the Detroit Institute of Arts, gift of George G. Booth.*

woman. The earliest Rookwood output was largely the work of Mrs. Storer and her "lady amateurs," but once the company was put on a business basis, artists, some of whom came from Japan, were hired to design its ware. The Rookwood artists never worked from imposed designs but were allowed to choose their glazes or develop their own. The Standard Ware of Rookwood, frequently decorated by women students from the Art Academy of Cincinnati, was painted with colored slips and then coated with glazes. The use of colored slip under the glazes created a depth and richness that made the ware famous.

Figure 7-6
Six O'clock in the Evening and *Three O'clock in the Morning*, by George Ohr, U.S.A.
Much of Ohr's work was outside the decorative studio-pottery tradition of turn-of-the-
century America, almost foretelling the attitudes of some convention-breaking potters
of the 1950s and 1960s. Glazed earthenware. c. 1900. *Courtesy the National Museum of
American History, Smithsonian Institution, Division of Ceramics and Glass.*

Adelaide Alsop Robineau   Like numerous other women art potters in this period, Adelaide Alsop Robineau (1865–1929) came to pottery through china painting. Frustrated with decorating other people's work, however, she began to cast her own ware and then learned to throw her forms on the wheel. With the help of her husband, who did the firing, and greatly influenced by the glazes of Taxile Doat of the Sèvres Porcelain Factory in France, Robineau began to experiment with high-fire glazes, many of them **crystalline glazes**. But Robineau herself was particularly proud of her carved pieces, on which she often worked for hundreds of hours. These were either incised (7-5) or excised—in the latter method she cut out the background, leaving raised patterns and, in at least one case, a lacy openwork.

George E. Ohr   In contrast to the pottery studios dedicated to creating beautifully deco-

rated vases and bowls, George E. Ohr (1857–1918) an unusual but widely known figure in the ceramics scene, made vases and pots that expressed his unique personality. He made his ware at his Biloxi Art Pottery in Mississippi and advertised himself on signs outside as "the greatest potter on earth." George Ohr saw himself as a genius and emphasized his similarity to Bernard Palissy (6-15). Ohr was certainly the most innovative potter of his time, anticipating in his work an attitude toward clay that would not surface again until the 1950s (7-6).

Tiles

Many of the art potteries—the Grueby Company and Rookwood among them—made decorative tiles. A tile factory particularly famous at the turn of the century that is still producing tiles today, the Moravian Pottery and Tile Works of

Figure 7-7
Tile, entitled *Persian Antelope*, made at the Moravian
Pottery and Tiles Works in Pennsylvania in 1937.
Founded by Henry Chapman Mercer in 1898, this tile
factory reflected its founder's interest in historical
ceramics, using designs such as this one, influenced
by Middle Eastern as well as medieval and early
Pennsylvania-German pottery. Glazed earthenware.
*Courtesy the Cooper-Hewitt Museum, Smithsonian
Institution/Art Resource, N.Y.*

Doylestown, Pennsylvania, was founded by an
archaeologist, Henry Chapman Mercer. Many of
his tile designs were influenced by the Arts and
Crafts Movement in England (6-23), while additional inspiration came from Persia (7-7), from
Moravian iron stove decorations, from Pennsylvania earthenware pottery, and from the decorations on French, Italian, and English pottery and
tiles.

ARCHITECTURAL CERAMICS

In the midnineteenth century, builders in the
rapidly expanding American cities began to dec-

orate their buildings with details made from terra-
cotta. This material was easier and cheaper to
model than stone and was appropriate when used
along with the brick of which so many U.S.
buildings were constructed. Although terra-cotta
was often made to resemble the more expensive
stone facing, it was also used for construction details—for example, as fireproof tiles for ceilings.
But the use of terra-cotta in building did not become widespread until after the devastating Chicago fire of 1871, which destroyed many iron and
stone buildings. After that disaster, builders realized that these materials were not as fireproof as
was once believed. Many of these buildings, pre-
sumed to be fireproof, had actually collapsed in
the heat of the Chicago fire, while older ones with
terra-cotta or brick exterior facing survived. To
avoid a repetition of the Chicago fire's destruction, builders now constructed many of the new
metal-frame buildings in Chicago and across the
nation with ceramic facing. The walls of these
buildings became "curtain walls" rather than load-
bearing walls, and the use of malleable clay to
form the terra-cotta components made it easy to
apply richly detailed ornamental areas to their
facades.

Louis Sullivan

The innovative American architect, Louis
Sullivan (1818–1924) exploited the aesthetic possibilities of this new structural system by using
terra-cotta to face the metal frames of his buildings and planning areas of elaborate terra-cotta
decoration to contrast with the thin piers and columns. This ornamentation combined natural
forms with a mixture of Gothic and Renaissance
decorative motifs, and the whole was marked
with Sullivan's highly individualistic style. For
many years, designer George G. Emslie and
sculptor Kristian Schneider worked with Sullivan, designing and modeling the plaster originals
from which the molds for the distinctive terra-
cotta decoration were made. On the facade of
the Bayard Building, in New York, erected in
1897–1898, Sullivan used a combination of plain
terra-cotta sheathing and columns along with cast
ceramic ornament in such a way that the rich decoration at the top of the building seems to grow

Figure 7-8
The Art Deco period was a busy one for American ceramics factories, for architects
specified panels and tiles to clad many of their metal-framed buildings, taking advantage
of the colored surfaces that glazed ceramics created. This Oakland, California, building
for a local furniture company still displays pale green curtain walls decorated with typical
Art Deco designs and reliefs of workmen making furniture.

almost like foliage out of the upward-thrusting verticals (see page 137).

Art Deco Ceramics in Architecture

Just as art styles of the nineteenth century influenced the potteries of that time, so did new styles in the twentieth-century decorative arts have an impact on the architects who commissioned ornamental details from tile and ceramic architectural component manufacturers. In the late teens and early twenties of the new century, an interest in color in architecture developed. At first, color was used only on small areas of orna-ment that contrasted with the solid beige or white of a building, but as time went on the color was used on larger areas until finally entire building facades were faced with monochromatic glazed terra-cotta (7-8). Cast or extruded ceramics lent itself particularly well to the low-relief decoration characteristic of Art Deco ornament, and design-ers soon realized its color potential. They competed to create innovative decoration, often de-signing fantasies of color and brilliant glaze.

SCULPTURE

In the late twenties and early thirties, a num-ber of ceramic sculptors from Europe emigrated to England and to the United States to work and teach. Among those who came to the United States were the Viennese Vally Wieselthier, who brought a sophisticated style and interest in color to American ceramics. A number of Americans became interested in ceramic sculpture through the influence of these Europeans, and some of them went to Europe to study. One of these was Viktor Schreckengost, who had been raised in an American pottery-making family. Schreckengost was impressed with the Austrians' respect for clay, and felt more at home with this attitude than with that usually accepted by U.S. artists who were more likely to use the ceramic process to transform the clay in order to make it look like another material. Schreckengost created sculpture that frankly displayed the clay from which it was made, using images that were often humorous and sometimes bitingly so (7-9). Speaking of his 1940 work, *The Dictator*, he says,

> *The Dictator was an attempt to comment on what I saw in Europe, about which few people seemed to be aware. . . . I did receive some criticism at the time for mixing politics with art.*

A number of other ceramic artists active in the United States in the 1930s and 1940s also believed that clay was a material that deserved respect. Among them were Weylande Gregory, whose large-scale ceramic figures on the *Fountain of the Atoms* were a feature of the 1940 World's Fair; Carl Walters, noted for his sculptures of animals; and Thelma Winter Frazier, who expressed the feeling among these artists that they should try to make clay sculpture grow up as a fine art. Also during this time, other artists—painters and sculptors such as Elie Nadelman, Reuben Nakian, Isamu Noguchi, and Louise Nevelson—used clay on occasion, in the same way that they might use any other medium to express their concepts. One wonders what course American ceramic sculpture might have taken if World War II had not disrupted what was promising to develop into a vigorous American use of clay. But the war did disrupt it, and although some artists continued to work in the material after the war, clay did not reemerge as a widely used sculpture medium until the 1950s.

Figure 7-9
The Dictator, by Viktor Schreckengost. Of this 1940 piece the artist says, *Hitler, Mussolini, Stalin and Hirobito seemed to be following the old pattern of Nero, who fiddled while Rome burned. They are represented by little cupids trying to crawl up into the throne while the British Lion lies sound asleep at his feet.* Red clay, black engobe, white, turquoise, yellow, and black glazes. In the permanent collection of the Everson Museum, Syracuse, 1940. *Courtesy the artist and The Everson Museum. Photo: the Cleveland Museum.*

Figure 7-10
Vase, by Maija Grotell. She was noted for her imaginative use of glazes and textures. A gifted potter, Grotell emigrated from Finland in the 1920s, to become an important influence, through both her work and her teaching, in the development of ceramics in the United States. Stoneware, superimposed and inlaid glaze in turquoise and blue-grey. Ht. 12⅝ in. (32 cm), 1949. *Courtesy Everson Museum of Art. Photo: Courtney Frisse.*

Figure 7-11
Earth Crater Bowl. Gertrud and Otto Natzler, U.S.A. came to this country from Austria in 1938. They worked together, Gertrud throwing the pots and Otto formulating the glazes for use on her simple forms. The Natzlers were also influential teachers, handing on their aesthetic philosophy as well as their interest in glazes. 1956. Earthenware, green-grey glaze. Ht. 8¾ in. (22 cm), diameter 12¼ in. (31 cm). *Courtesy the Everson Museum of Art. Photo: Courtney Frisse.*

POTTERY FROM THE 1920s THROUGH THE 1940s

Like the ceramic sculptors, potters also came from Europe to the United States, bringing with them new perspectives and technical expertise. Among them were Marguerite Wildenhain, from Germany; Maija Grotell (1899–1973), from Finland (7-10); and Gertrud Natzler (1908–1971) and her husband Otto Natzler, from Vienna (7-11). Maija Grotell, who came to this country in 1927, became head of the ceramics department at Cranbrook Academy of Art, a school that was ahead of the times in teaching the crafts on an equal footing with painting, sculpture, and architecture. At Cranbrook, Grotell's dedication to ce-

ramics as an art, her disciplined craft, and her years of research into glazes that resulted in rugged surfaces and brilliant color inspired several generations of ceramics students.

Considering how widespread ceramics instruction is today, it is hard to believe that in 1938 nobody knew how to use the one potter's wheel at the University of California in Los Angeles, where Laura Andreson taught coil building and casting. Andreson had to wait until Gertrud and Otto Natzler arrived from Vienna a year later and taught her how to use it.

As has happened so often throughout history in other countries, the arrival of foreign potters and sculptors enriched American ceramics, but the war years interrupted the process by which new influences were melded into a new American style. It was not until the postwar years, with the added influence of potters such as Bernard Leach (8-2) and Shōji Hamada (8-1), who helped to bring Japanese ceramics to the attention of Western potters, that large numbers of young people were drawn to work in clay, and the stage was set for the "clay explosion" of the 1950s.

8
Worldwide Innovations

As potters, they mastered the technical processes of creating functional objects within the craft tradition; pushing forward, they took the option of relating these processes to ideas outside the craft world.

Suzanne Foley*

As we have seen, throughout history, potters have traveled from one part of the world to another, crossing cultural or national boundaries, bringing their own ways of working in clay, and exchanging ideas, techniques, and styles with local potters wherever they have settled. But in the twentieth century, exchanges of ideas or techniques that in the past might have taken decades to spread from one area to another were speeded by accelerated communications. Now, as we near the end of the twentieth century, the diversity of influences on all potters and sculptors is one of the most notable aspects of ceramics, and our sphere of interest must now include the entire globe.

Ceramic Sculpture in California: An Overview, Catalog, Whitney Museum of American Art, New York, 1981.

Little Big Horn, by Peter Voulkos, U.S.A., was composed of combined thrown forms and slabs that were paddled to alter them and then colored with black, white, and cobalt slips and glazes. Ht. 60 in. (152.4 cm), 1959. *Courtesy Collection of the Oakland Museum, gift of the Art Guild of the Oakland Museum Association.*

149

Figure 8-1
Shōji Hamada, of Japan, dedicated himself to the production of useful, folk-inspired pottery. Along with the English potter Bernard Leach, Hamada was influential in creating a bridge between Eastern and Western ceramics. Stoneware, wax-resist decoration. c. 1931. *Courtesy The Board of Trustees of the Victoria & Albert Museum. Crown Copyright.*

EAST MEETS WEST

One important interchange of ideas that came about in the early part of the century, was largely due to the friendship of two potters—Shōji Hamada (1894–1978), from Japan (8-1) and Bernard Leach (1887–1979), from England (8-2). Their life-long association demonstrated how potters from totally different cultures could come to understand each other through a shared love of the material in which they worked.

In 1909, art-school-trained Bernard Leach went to live in Japan, where he studied with the sixth Kenzan, Miura Kenya. He said that what led him to ceramics was participating in a raku party at which each of the artists and poets present decorated and fired a plate. Seeing the pots put into a red-hot raku kiln and, one of them plunged into water, on its withdrawal, Leach decided on the spot to be a potter. He stayed in Japan until 1920, and while he was there he came to know Shōji Hamada, who worked in the pottery town of Mashiko. Hamada formed his pots with local clay and glazed them with ash from nearby woods, creating pottery that reflected Japan's rich rural pottery tradition. For his outstanding pottery, Shōji Hamada was later honored by the Japanese government with the title of Living National Treasure. But when Leach returned to England in the 1920s to start a pottery in Cornwall, neither potter was as yet famous. Hamada helped Leach set up his kiln and was his partner for three years. Later, the two traveled widely together and lectured around the world, meeting with potters and students. On a trip they took together in 1952, Leach and Hamada met two people who would also become influential—Maria Martinez of San Iledefonso in the American Southwest (5-18), and Peter Voulkos (8-11, page 149), then at the Archie Bray Foundation in Montana.

Bernard Leach believed that pottery should be made for use, and although some felt that he became more interested as time went on in making exhibition pottery than in functional ware, Leach said he hoped his pots would express his philosophy of "the straightforward, the natural, the innocent, the humble, the modest." Like Hamada, who worked within the traditions of mingei, or Japanese folk art, Leach drew on the tra-

Figure 8-2
After living in Japan, English potter Bernard Leach returned to England, where his work reflected Japanese folk pottery as well as the slip-decorated earthenware made by English country potters. Leach said that through working with clay and kiln he wanted to share that "primitive energy that created the world." Stoneware, gray-green glaze. St. Ives Cornwall, c. 1931. *Courtesy The Board of Trustees of the Victoria & Albert Museum.*

Figure 8-3
Michael Cardew, a former assistant of Leach's, also slip-decorated his domestic ware and considered himself a country potter, one of the "earthenware people." This plate, however, is gray-glazed stoneware. c. 1949. *Courtesy Crafts Advisory Committee, London, and Seth Cardew.*

ditions of English folk pottery, combining its traditions with those he had absorbed during his stay in the Orient, creating decorated stoneware in which elements of both can be seen (8-2). Leach's work was greatly admired in Japan, where he was eventually honored as the seventh Kenzan. His book, *A Potter's Book*, originally published in 1940, inspired potters around the globe, and his Cornwall workshop became a place of pilgrimage for young potters. First under his supervision and later under that of his wife, potter Janet Leach, numerous pupils and assistants have been trained there in production pottery.

One of Leach's assistants in Cornwall was Michael Cardew (1901–1983), who opened his own country workshop where he made slip-decorated

stoneware whose forms expressed the honesty and integrity of their maker (8-3). Like Leach, Cardew was an important influence in ceramics in the 1960s and 1970s; he lectured and traveled widely, articulating his philosophy with wit, warmth, and humanity. His years in Ghana and Nigeria, where he set up pottery training centers to teach local potters to make stoneware, resulted in international interchanges of ideas when African potters traveled with him to demonstrate their traditional methods (4-11). His intuitive response to African pottery and his devotion to his students there inspired them to name him Baban Shaku, "father pot."

Another potter active in the global interchange in the 1950s was Kitaoji Rosanjin (1883–

Figure 8-4
Chop Dish with Moon and Grasses, by Kitaoji Rosanjin of Japan, was made from a slab and fired in the Bizen method, in which straw or other organic material is introduced into the kiln to produce local reduction in order to create surface markings. © 1988 *Courtesy The Art Institute of Chicago*. All rights reserved.

1959), of Japan (8-4), who also lectured and gave workshops demonstrating Oriental ceramic techniques in the United States. Commenting on what he saw on his trip, he was more enthusiastic and less condescending toward American pottery than some overseas visitors, and he predicted an exciting future for ceramics in the United States.

EUROPEAN INFLUENCES

An important influence in Europe emanated from the Bauhaus School, founded in Germany in 1919 and influential there until it closed during the Hitler regime. After an early interest in craft, the school rejected this approach and in the 1930s taught a doctrine of "form follows function," stating that applied decoration had no place on any contemporary product. Bauhaus ideas influenced the design of many factory-produced objects in the late 1920s and 1930s and was instrumental in effecting a change in public taste. Individual potters as well as such factories as Arabia in Finland and Wedgwood in England reflected these changing attitudes and introduced simple, cleanly designed functional tableware.

Other potters in various countries were more concerned at this time with developing their own forms than with reflecting the traditional forms of their native folk pottery. Some of these—such as Lucie Rie (8-5), Hans Coper (8-6), Ruth Duckworth, Maija Grotell (7-10), and Gertrude and Otto Natzler (7-11)—emigrated to England and the United States from Austria, Germany, and Scandinavia in the 1930s.

Lucie Rie had studied and maintained a studio in Vienna in the 1920s, winning recognition there before she went to England, where she set up a studio in 1939. Hans Coper (1920–1981) had studied to be an engineer, but left engineering for art studies and came to ceramics through an assistantship with Lucie Rie in postwar London. Rie made tableware for many years before concentrating on vases and bowls. She continued to experiment, developing special glazes and perfecting her characteristic method of producing contrasting bands of colored clay on her forms by throwing the colors of clay together on the wheel. Coper frequently made his work in two parts, assembling it after throwing and usually surfacing it with white slip and coloring oxides. Like Rie's, his work exhibited an intense interest in the formal, as opposed to the decorative, aspects of ceramics, and although they used quite different forms, both Rie and Coper created pottery that combined the classic and the innovative, justly meriting the international reputations it gained.

In the 1950s, the German potters Margarete Schott and Karl Scheid (15-5) went to England to apprentice with the potter Harry Davis in Cornwall. This was just one example of the international interchange that was becoming more common in the ceramics world at this time.

Figure 8-5
Austrian-born Lucie Rie emigrated to England
in the 1930s. Her porcelain vases feature
spiraling bands of color formed by throwing
two colors of clay together—in this case,
white and pale green porcelain colored with
copper carbonate. Once-fired porcelain. Hts.
6 in. (15.2 cm) and 11 in. (27.9 cm). *Courtesy
Alphabet and Image.*

Figure 8-6
Composite pots made in two parts from altered wheel shapes by German-born English
potter Hans Coper. The flattened upper sections are attached to cylindrical bases; the pots
are colored with manganese and white slip. Stoneware. *Courtesy Alphabet and Image.*

Figure 8-7
Picasso, who worked for several years with Georges and Susan Ramié at their pottery in Vallauris, designed *Cavalier* by imaginatively combining thrown forms. Earthenware, c. 1951. Ht. 15½ in. (39.4 cm). *Courtesy The Board of Trustees of the Victoria & Albert Museum.*

Figure 8-8
Henri Matisse made this portrait plate at the Ramié pottery in Vallauris. The drawing is black with some sgraffito, and the face is reserved in the clay body color against blue. *Courtesy Museo Internazionale delle Ceramiche, Faenza.*

Such exchanges were encouraged by the founding of the International Academy of Ceramics, a UNESCO organization.

FACTORY DESIGN

After World War II, some ceramic factories, such as De Porcelyne Fles in Holland and Bing and Grøndahl in Denmark, set up experimental studios where artists have a working relationship with the factory and at the same time are given the freedom to create their own work. There is no doubt that the establishment of these programs was of great assistance to studio ceramics during the difficult postwar recuperative period in Europe, and they have continued to play a supportive role to the present.

Another influence on twentieth-century ceramics came from contemporary painters and sculptors who on occasion turned to the medium of clay. A number of artists in Europe created numerous works in clay, either painting on professionally made pottery or designing the forms and then painting or glazing their works in close collaboration with trained potters. These artists included, among others, Pablo Picasso (1881–1973, 8-7); Henri Matisse (1869–1954, 8-8); Joan Miró (1893–1983, 8-9); Lucio Fontana (1889–1968, 8-10); and Fernand Léger (1881–1955). Picasso for example, showed a true Mediterranean's understanding of clay. He worked closely with French potters Georges and Susan Ramié to construct animals, fantasy creatures, small figurines from imaginatively altered and combined vessel forms. Henri Matisse, on the other hand, viewed pottery as a painting ground rather than a three-dimensional medium.

Of these artists, the painter-sculptor Joan Miró was perhaps the most finely attuned to the

154

Figure 8-9

Déesse was created in 1963 by Joan Miró of Spain, working with his friend, Josep Lorens Artigas, using an assemblage of forms, including that of a tortoise shell. Miró and Artigas collaborated over a number of years, creating ceramics that included plates, large and small sculptures, and a number of murals. This sculpture is part of the Labyrinth at Foundation Maeght, France. © ADAGP. ARS 1987.

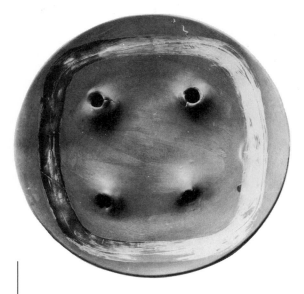

Figure 8-10

Italian painter-sculptor Lucio Fontana, after experimenting with punctured and slashed paper and canvas, did the same with clay. Fontana's innovative ceramics influenced other Europeans to approach clay with greater freedom. Maiolica fired at 1650°F/900° C. Black background with blue and gold metallic luster, fired in reduction. Diameter 16½ in. (42 cm). *Collection Carlo Zauli.*

clay medium. Miró, who made use of accident and chance in much of his work, once commented that in ceramics it is the fire that is master, and this aspect of ceramics was important to him. Over a number of years, Miró created a large body of ceramic work in close collaboration with his Catalan friend master potter Josep Llorens Artigas (1892–1980). Miró related that when he was an art student in Barcelona, his teacher, Francesc Galí, taught him about form by having him handle objects blindfolded, then draw them. Miró attributes his interest in sculpture to this exercise, which provided an excellent background for un-

derstanding sculptural form whether in marble, bronze, or clay. Miró's nonceramic sculpture and painting had been based largely on combinations of found objects, and when he turned to clay, he often used the same approach, combining disparate forms, enlarging the scale of others, and reusing forms from earlier sculptures. For instance, his 1963 sculpture *La Déesse*, made for the Labyrinth at Foundation Maeght in the south of France (8-9), reflects the forms of some of his earlier ceramic vessel-like figures, and it also incorporates a tortoise shell form that he later used as the whole body in a bronze figure.

Figure 8-11
One of many plates made by Peter Voulkos, U.S.A. This one was wheel thrown, altered, colored with cobalt and chrome, and then covered with a clear glaze. Stoneware. 1962. *Courtesy Collection of the Oakland Museum, gift of the Art Guild of the Oakland Museum Association.*

CONVERGING INFLUENCES

In the 1950s, many influences came together. These included Leach and Hamada's writing and lecturing—which introduced potters everywhere to Oriental and British country pottery—the growing interest in Zen Buddhism, the ceramics of contemporary European artists such as Miró, and New York's Abstract Expressionist painting and constructive sculpture. All these currents were destined to affect the work of a number of young potters, sculptors, and painters working in southern California in the 1950s.

From Pottery to Sculpture

The central figure of this group was Peter Voulkos (8-11 and page 149), originally a painter, who had taken a graduate degree in ceramics at California College of Arts and Crafts in 1952. After working with Rudy Autio (Color plate 30) at the Archie Bray Foundation in Montana (where he met Hamada and Leach when they stopped there on a lecture tour), in 1954 he was asked to set up the ceramics department at the Otis Art

Institute in Los Angeles. Already known for his remarkable ability in throwing on the wheel, Voulkos had also been exposed to the contemporary art movements then centered in New York. At Otis, he began to use his facility in throwing to make vessel forms that he paddled, slashed, and scratched, altering and combining them as the malleable clay responded to the gestures of his hands and tools. In his hands, the clay came to resemble the landscape forms of his native state, Montana, a resemblance reflected in some of the titles of his sculptures—*Little Big Horn, Camelback Mountain,* and *Gallas Rock.* Voulkos soon left the subdued tones of high-fire glazes behind and began to use brighter, low-fire glazes on his stoneware forms, finally supplementing these with nonceramic paint. He said that by painting on his sculpture he was using color not to enhance the form, but rather to violate it in order to add to the excitement of the piece. Despite his constant involvement with sculpture in both clay and bronze, Voulkos has never totally given up the vessel form, and he has continued to throw large vessels and plates on the wheel, treating them as he did his sculpture, slashing and puncturing the walls of the cylinders or the flat plane of the plate. Voulkos's innovative ceramics and his vital personality gathered other artists and students around him at Otis. Among these were John Mason, Paul Soldner (16-27), Jerry Rothman, Kenneth Price, and Billy Al Bengston, all of whom went on to become influential in the "clay movement" of the 1960s and 1970s.

John Mason had been a potter before going to work at Otis, but while there he began to alter his vessels, and by 1957 he was building sculptures and walls of clay with chunks and strips, using the medium of clay to record his spontaneous gestures. By the 1960s, Mason's forms became simplified into large single sculptures, many of them variations of the cross, monochromatic, and at times seemingly closer to Color Field painting than sculpture (8-12). In the 1970s, Mason's interest changed again to center on Minimalist installations in which he used firebricks rather than handformed clay forms. In the 1980s, however, he returned to the vessel form, and at this writing he is creating sharp-edged geometric vessels with striped glazed surfaces (Color plate 37).

Kenneth Price, another of the group centered at Otis, went on from there to study at the New York School of Ceramics at Alfred University, and when he returned to the West, his egglike forms and sexual imagery showed more affinity with the work of Miró than that of Voulkos and Mason. By 1970, Price was working with the cup form, first in association with biological references, then with geometrical abstractions. After Price settled in New Mexico, he created installations containing curios inspired by Mexican folk pottery, as well as making a shrine based on the roadside memorials placed along Mexico's highways. Later, he returned to explorations of form, color, and surface in brilliantly glazed geometric constructions, and then began to make organic miniatures with pitted and encrusted surfaces.

By 1958, when Stephen De Staebler entered the University of California, Berkeley graduate school, Voulkos was teaching there. De Staebler recounts that Voulkos provided quantities of clay, worked there with it himself (as well as with bronze), and said very little to his students. For De Staebler, who found that he learned about clay best by working with it, this proved to be a perfect environment. His early clay sculptures were largely based on landscape-inspired forms, and this sense of landscape continues to pervade his clay work, whether he is creating a figure, a

Figure 8-12
Geometric Form—Red X, by John Mason, U.S.A. In the 1960s, Mason simplified his earlier roughly textured cross forms and coated them with monochromatic glazes that created fields of color. Stoneware. 58½ × 59½ × 17 in. (148.5 × 151.1 × 43.2 cm), 1966. *Courtesy Los Angeles County Museum of Art. Gift of the Kleiner Foundation.*

Figure 8-13
To create *Standing Man and Woman*, American sculptor
Stephen De Staebler joined slabs on the inside in
order to maintain the fresh surface of the clay. His
towering, fragmented figures recall the forms of the
eroded sandstone banks on which he played as a boy.
Courtesy of the artist. Photo: Susan Felter.

throne, or a vessel or executing an architectural
commission (8-13, 8-27; see also page 172 and 14-
9).

In the 1930s, the Italian painter Lucio Fontana had made three-dimensional still lifes in clay,
compositions that prefigured the gestural quality
of Abstract Expressionist paintings. Later, Fontana began to slash and puncture his paintings on
paper and canvas, calling the results Spatial Concepts. He then returned to clay, making what he
called Spatial Ceramics, punching holes through
from the back of plates, creating craters in the flat
surface (8-10). Given Italy's ceramic tradition, it
is not surprising that others there—among them
Leoncillo Leonardi, Franco Garelli, and Antonia
Campi—also brought twentieth-century painting
and sculpture influences to clay, modeling the
plastic material freely and using bright, low-fire
glazes to create works influenced by Cubist and
Futurist painting. Their postwar work in clay influenced others there to discard the tradition of
decorative European ceramics and to approach ceramics in a new way.

Carlo Zauli, who started as a potter in the
ancient ceramic town of Faenza, tells how almost
any building excavation there turned up pottery
shards or slumped, over-fired **wasters** (discards),
from the kilns that had once made the town's famous maiolica (6-4). With these twisted discards
fresh in his mind, and impressed by the innovative work of Lucio Fontana and Leonardi Leoncillo, Zauli began to smash and alter his vessels,
allowing the clay to take on its own form as it
tilted and collapsed. In the 1970s, Zauli moved
on from making vessel-oriented forms to creating
large sculptures and murals (8-14, 14-7).

Some of the best known metal sculptors in
the 1960s who normally used a constructive
method, welding pieces of metal together also, on
occasion, worked in clay. Among these was
American David Smith (1906–1965), who was influential in bringing color back to sculpture. He
frequently painted his welded steel constructions
with brilliantly colored enamels, and this return
to polychrome sculpture also influenced sculptors
working in clay to utilize the full potential of
glaze.

On the East Coast of the United States, Ka
Kwong Hui, who had come to the United States
to study ceramics from China and had stayed on

Figure 8-14
Italian sculptor Carlo Zauli contrasted sharp-edged slab forms with rough areas of clay,
developing a series of visual and tactile relationships that carry the viewer's eyes along the
wall. Stoneware with "Zauli white" glaze. Ht. 59 in. (1.5 m), Length 29½ ft. (9 m.) 1974.
Courtesy of the artist. Photo: Antonio Masotti.

to become an influential teacher, was at first disturbed by the liberties that such artists as Voulkos were taking with the traditional material. Later, he recognized the importance of this approach in opening the doors to new attitudes, and in his own work turned to polychrome sculpture, using brilliant color in his sculptures based on traditional Chinese and Tibetan forms.

Another influence in midcentury ceramics surfaced on the West Coast of the United States during the 1950s and 1960s. The term *Funk* has been applied loosely to the work of several artists whose only real similarity was their irreverence with respect to established art concepts. One such artist, Robert Arneson, worked in the vessel form for some time before turning to figurative sculpture. Although influenced by the vigor and ex-

citement of Voulkos's work, Arneson nevertheless took a totally different approach to ceramics, using processes that were much closer to those of conventional ceramics, although not to its imagery. The vessels Arneson made in the 1960s depicted toilets and sexual organs, images that were startling, even shocking, when seen in the context of the glazed ceramic vessel, a form more closely associated with display, refinement, and luxury than with scatology. Like many other West Coast ceramic artists at this time, Arneson switched from using high-fired stoneware to low-fired earthenware, and as a result he could use bright colors. When, in the 1970s, he began a series of self-portraits—an image he has continued to use to the present—he utilized low-fire glazes in the manner of a realistic painter, creating naturalistic

Figure 8-15
In his installation *Fragment of Western Civilization*, American Robert Arneson, combined bricks and a crumbling self-portrait. He said, "I try not to take myself too seriously, and when I think I might be, it is time to knock over a big piece." This one is a continuing installation that changes according to the time and place of exhibition. Terra-cotta. 60 × 260 in. (152.4 × 660.4 cm). *Courtesy Fuller-Gross Gallery, San Francisco. Photo: Bayens Photo Co. Quotation courtesy John Michael Kohler Arts Center.*

renderings of the human face. Arneson used both his own and others' portraits to express his satirical ideas—political, artistic, and psychological—and some of his works of the 1970s, such as the installation Fragment of Western Civilization (8-15), point towards his later work, in which he commented on the nuclear arms threat and militarism in general (see page 210). Like other California artists of the period, such as Jeremy Anderson and William Wiley, Arneson made liberal use of the written word, scratching or stamping phrases onto the surface of his works.

Others on the West Coast also expressed their

irreverence in sculpture that tended to startle. The work of Clayton Bailey is an example. At times, Bailey's juxtaposition of clay images with everyday objects was amusing, as when he surrounded a banal electric lamp with ceramic noses (8-16), sometimes his work was disturbing, as when it depicted the image of larger-than-life insects, and at other times, it was downright gory, as when Bailey developed the character of the imaginary Dr. Gladstone. Bailey's work continues today to reflect his personal perceptions and the connections he makes between everyday or unusual objects (13-18 to 13-30).

Figure 8-16
Clayton Bailey's *Nose Lamp* combines a functioning electric lamp with glazed ceramic noses. Earthenware, low-fire glazes. 1968. Ht. 11½ in. (29.2 cm). *Courtesy M. H. de Young Museum Art School. Photo: Robert Hsiang.*

Figure 8-17
American David Gilhooly created a mythological Frog Land, in which the shiny green inhabitants engaged in behavior just as outrageous as that of humans. The base of this portrait of *Mao Tse Toad* displays biographical drawings, including one of his famous swim. 1976. 31 × 19 in. (78.7 × 48.3 cm). *Courtesy Fuller-Gross Gallery.*

Fantasy

As more and more potters and sculptors began to use clay as an expressive medium, some of them turned to narrative while others turned to fantasy or the creation of personal mythologies. For example, in the late 1960s, David Gilhooly brought to life an imaginary world in which frogs worshipped a frog god and goddess of fertility, produced a glut of food (whose color and texture low-fire glazes were ideally suited to imitate), and participated in politics (8-17), in consumerism, in erotic activities, and in religious rites. The mul-

titude of shiny green frogs that emerged from Gilhooly's hands served, under the guise of humor, as a serious commentary on human society. Another Californian, Louise McGinley, also used fantasy to comment on the human condition. Her half-human, half-bird figures often warn us of lurking dangers waiting to destroy us if we ignore them for too long (8-18).

Fantasy was not confined to California, however. In Holland, Nicholas Van Os and Jan Snoeck (14-17) along with Alan Barret-Danes in England also expressed their personal fantasies in clay. Inhabiting a world that appears far removed

Figure 8-18
In *Summit Conference* by American sculptor Louise McGinley, the artist joins her sinister
group of traders as they bargain for spoils over a campfire. McGinley fires her work at a very
low temperature and paints the surface with acrylics after firing. Life size. *Courtesy the artist.*

from the tidy landscape of Holland, Van Os's life-sized creatures are part human, part animal, part pure Van Os. One of them (8-19) was commissioned for the garden of the provincial government building of Utrecht (the equivalent of American bureaucracy commissioning a David Gilhooly for a State House). Other ceramists were intrigued with images of human habitation—for example, Bryan Newman in England, Jacques Bucholtz in France, and American sculptor Charles Simonds, who built miniature unfired buildings in unexpected places around the world.

Objects that might have been found in archaeological digs demonstrated a growing interest in prehistory among contemporary ceramists. Examples are the carefully crafted tools/bones/weapons made by Swiss artist Ernst Haüsermann, who used clay in conjunction with other materials; sculptures by Jim Adamson, who placed goose heads on scepters and enveloped a cooper's hawk in mummy wrappings and placed it in a ritual burial; and Ian Godfrey's houses and animals, reminiscent of Moche or Han burial objects. Perhaps this archaeological interest developed as those who worked in clay became more aware of their links with those who used the material in the distant past.

Still other contemporary ceramicists displayed an interest in narrative. For example, in addition to painting images of Texas musicians on cut-outs of porcelain (8-20), Chris Untersher chose to recreate miniature Americana so compellingly real that to peer down into their bedrooms, shops, or hotel lobbies makes one feel like a giant voyeur.

Figures

Although many of his earlier works had echoes of the Surreal, by the 1970s, Richard Shaw was using his skill at mold making and photo decals to create still lifes that were reminiscent of nineteenth-century American trompe l'oeil painting (8-21). Since then, Shaw has concentrated on creating figures that he constructs from such components as funnels, baseballs, paint cans, and sticks of wood, all made of clay cast in molds that he cast from found objects. His work makes use of the fact that a skilled craftsman can press or pour clay into almost any shape and can finish it to replicate almost any surface. However,

Figure 8-19
One of Nicholas Van Os's fantasy creatures graces the grounds of the Provincial Government Building in Utrecht, Holland. Built in sections and fired in a small electric kiln, it was assembled on site. Stoneware. 1978. *Courtesy the artist.*

▼ *Figure 8-20*
In *Billy Bowman*, Chris Untersher, U.S.A., painted porcelain cut-outs with underglaze colors to create a slice of American life. 1954. Ht. 15 in. (38.1 cm).

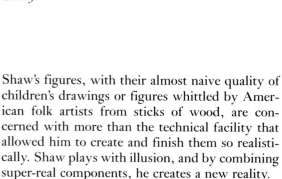

Figure 8-21
Stack of Cards on Brown Book, by Richard Shaw, U.S.A. Shaw used molds to form the decal-decorated porcelain components of his sculptures and then assembled them into constructions that create a new reality. Ht. 14 in. (35.6 cm). *Courtesy Braunstein Gallery.*

Figure 8-22
You Captured My Heart, by Patti Warashina, U.S.A., is a combination of two-dimensional painting and sculptured forms painted with underglaze colors. The figure is painted on a flat background, with nose, arms, and hands in relief, while the mouth is recessed. Low-fire clay, wooden arrows, oxidation firing. Height 30 in. (76.2 cm), width 18 in. (45.7 cm), depth 15 in. (38.1 cm). *Courtesy of the artist.*

Shaw's figures, with their almost naive quality of children's drawings or figures whittled by American folk artists from sticks of wood, are concerned with more than the technical facility that allowed him to create and finish them so realistically. Shaw plays with illusion, and by combining super-real components, he creates a new reality.

Using molds to form figurative sculptures became popular in the 1970s with a number of other artists, who used the method with quite diverse results. And it is not surprising that as more potters, sculptors, painters, and printmakers explored the almost limitless possibilities of ceramics, they found rich opportunities for expression in the human figure and face. Patti Warashina made social statements with her feminine images (8-22), Jack Earl interpreted life in a small American town (8-23), while Italian sculptor Aldo Rontini created sculptures that reflected both the Etruscan use of clay and modern photoscreening techniques. In Belgium, Carmen Dionyse developed surfaces based on multiple firing to give her haunting sculpture an ancient patina, while in England two widely different outlooks on humanity were reflected in the work of Jill Crowley and Glenys Barton. Crowley both

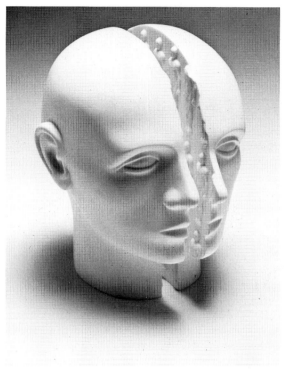

Figure 8-23

Ohio Boy, by Jack Earl, U.S.A., is a slice of home-town America formed in molds from the cast vitreous china used for bathroom fixtures. In 1976, Earl was part of an innovative program at the Kohler Company, which, along with the John Michael Kohler Arts Center and the National Endowment for the Arts, made it possible for several artists to work with industrial materials and techniques. 15⅞ × 17¾ × 11⅞ in. (40.3 × 45.1 × 30.2 cm). Slip cast and handbuilt, glazes and underglaze pencil. 1976. *Courtesy the collection of the John Michael Kohler Arts Center. Photo: Bayens Photo Co.*

Figure 8-24

In 1977, English artist Glenys Barton worked at the Wedgwood Factory, where she made a series of slip-cast works in bone china. Barton sees her work as an optimistic expression of faith in human reason and intelligence. *Courtesy the Crafts Advisory Committee, London, and the artist.*

laughed at and sympathized with men and women whose faces showed the wear and tear of lives lived out in less than luxurious surroundings, while Barton's cool, white images spoke of alienation (8-24).

By the late 1970s, figurative sculpture in clay was well reestablished and had become more concerned with form than surface. Stephen De Staebler was building towering figures in which he used both negative and positive human forms, while Mary Frank was developing an individual style of figurative sculpture (9-4) using constructed slab forms.

The Vessel

But what had been happening to pottery in these years of change? Faced with potters such as Voulkos and Zauli manhandling their vessels into contorted forms that became sculptural, and the factory production of well-designed ware that could be made much more cheaply than hand-made ceramics, potters were frequently unsure of their future role.

Some, following in the tradition of nine-teenth-century studio potters, turned to creating one-of-a-kind pottery rather than production ware. Much of this was nonfunctional, such as Erik Gronborg's *American Vase: The Winning of The West* (8-25), decorated with photo decals. In *Cabbage Cup with Soil Saucer* (8-26), Jill Crowley used clay to which crushed brick had been added, giving her tea cup a pitted and lumpy surface and perhaps poking fun at the rage for raku firing and British tea table conventions. Toshiko Takaezu, on the other hand, made enclosed vessel forms with painterly glazed surfaces.

Others responded to the challenge of creating vessels that were both aesthetically pleasing and functional as containers. The range in vessel forms was wide, from Stephen De Staebler's slab-built urns (8-27), with walls even thicker than an Etruscan sarcophagus or a Greek *pithos*, to the thin walls of Denmark's Alev Siesbye's coil-built bowl (8-28) or British Michael Casson's elegant reinterpretations of the traditional jug (12-57). Karen Karnes's work in the 1970s reflected the cylindrical forms of early American salt-glazed ware, but with seemingly simple variations Karnes made them into vases and storage containers that delight the eye and hand (8-29).

During this period, several magazines devoted to ceramics appeared in various countries. These often started out as parochial journals, but they gradually expanded their coverage to deal with international currents and methods and styles of pottery from cultures distant in time or space. As ceramists around the world became more knowledgeable about the techniques used in cultures outside their own, they researched and tested other methods of achieving surface effects through alternative firing techniques, unusual glaze and coloring effects, new combinations of materials, and concepts that had never before appeared in ceramics. Today, we may take this wide range of methods for granted, but it was not very long ago that many of them were almost unknown to most production or studio potters.

Figure 8-25

Although American artist Erik Gronborg's photo decal-decorated urn, *American Vase: The Winning of the West*, is nonfunctional, Gronborg feels that his work at this time followed the tradition of decorated pottery. Porcelain, with photo decals and luster. *Courtesy of the artist.*

Figure 8-26
To create the rough texture of *Cabbage Cup with Soil Saucer,* Jill Crowley, England, used clay heavily tempered with crushed brick, then fired it in a raku firing. *Courtesy Crafts Advisory Committee, London, and the artist.*

Figure 8-27
Although this massive urn by Stephen De Staebler, U.S.A., is functional, its ritualistic presence takes it beyond the utilitarian. Formed of four slabs joined at the legs. 1977.

◀ *Figure 8-28*
An elegant, thin-walled bowl by Alev Siesbye, Denmark, exemplifies the continuing studio pottery tradition in Europe. 1970s. *Photo: Mogens S. Koch.*

Figure 8-29
The pitted and mottled surface of salt-glaze was
characteristic of the functional salt-glazed studio
pottery Karen Karnes, U.S.A., made in the 1970s.
Now Karnes fires in a large wood kiln (Figure 9-11).
Stoneware. Ht. 16 in. (40.6 cm). *Courtesy of the artist.*

Installations and Performance

One way in which the ceramic sculptor found
acceptance in the art scene was by becoming involved in happenings or performances. For a
while, almost any unusual use of clay—for example, dancers wallowing in slithery slip or
sculptures made by shooting bullets into clay
forms—was welcomed for its new and exciting
use of clay. As ceramists responded to events and
trends in the art world, they also explored their
material in ways other than building constructive
sculptures or smashing and slashing pots: they literally immersed themselves in the clay or slith-
ered over slip-coated sheets of plastic. These activities were responses to what was current in the
art world, and they represented a new attitude toward exploring the limits of the material. James
Melchert, whose explorations of polychrome
sculpture using low-fire glazes were influential in
the development of that aspect of ceramics, was
also involved with performance and video, making such tapes as one of himself in Amsterdam
showing him with other slip-dipped performers.

In installations related to the concept rather
than the form of ceramics, William Maxwell
(8-30), John Mason, and John Goodheart (8-31),
and others expanded the idea of what clay sculpture might be. George Geyer's extrusions of clay
dissolving in water (8-32) were designed, Geyer
said, to

*obliterate even the material possibility of ceramic
sculpture once and for all.*

ART OR CRAFT?

Hundreds of pages have been written about
the place of ceramics in relation to the so-called
fine arts. For some time, twentieth-century ceramic sculptors who wanted to exhibit in museums and art galleries found that if a work was
made of clay it was automatically consigned to a
separate category. But gradually clay was ac-

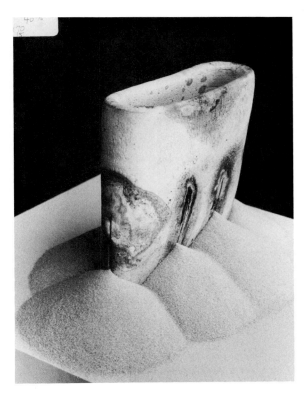

Figure 8-30
William G. Maxwell, U.S.A. allowed sand to build its own shapes as it poured from the vessel form—a combination of materials that extends our concept of ceramics. Ht. 18 in. (45.7 cm). *Courtesy of the artist.*

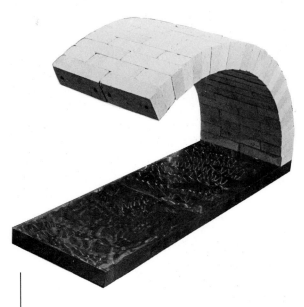

Figure 8-31
Rethinking his relationship with clay to create *Arch #1*, John Goodheart, U.S.A., used products derived from clay rather than shaping the material in its malleable state. 1976. Firebrick and steel. 20 × 50 × 36 in. (50.8 × 127 × 91.4 cm), 1976. *Courtesy Grinstead Gallery, Central Missouri State University.*

cepted as a valid art medium, and galleries and museums began to hold exhibits of ceramic sculpture—although it is true that these were generally separated from bronze or other materials usually associated with "art," rather as if acrylic or mixed media paintings were exhibited separately from those painted with oils.

Once galleries had accepted ceramic sculpture, many potters felt their work was being passed over in favor of sculptural work. It is true that the West, unlike Japan, which has always honored fine pottery, has only recently accepted pottery for exhibit in museums outside of the "decorative art" departments and along with "fine art." Pottery's arrival in the commercial art gallery is even more recent, and gallery owners have been pleasantly surprised to find how well the work of an important studio potter might sell.

Now, however, as we near the end of the century, potters and sculptors are more likely to use the methods and processes available to them as they would use any other technique in art and are more concerned with expressing their ideas, feelings, and fantasies than with exploring new techniques merely for the sake of novelty (Color plates 19, 32, and 40).

Let us hope that as we enter the 1990s, there will be less concentration within the art world on divisions, and more concern with the basic unity of all forms of art, as potters and sculptors everywhere use the elements of earth, water, and fire to create contemporary works that build on our worldwide ceramics inheritance.

◀ *Figure 8-32*
In this 1976 installation of clay and water, George Geyer, U.S.A., was concerned with communicating information about ceramic materials. "The ceramic process," he said, "is in itself the art." Clay, glass, sand, and water. 52 × 52 × 53 in. (132.1 × 208.3 × 134.6 cm). *Courtesy Santa Ana College Gallery.*

Nicholas Van Os of the Netherlands hand forms his ▶ fantasy figures with coils and chunks of clay, building in a network of supports as the work progresses. *Courtesy the artist. Photo: Fritz Van Os.*

PART TWO

SHAPING THE PRESENT

9
The Artist's Vision

In reverie, usually near dawn, I often make great pots. I usually can't remember them clearly, but I know how they feel. They are large, mysterious, yet familiar. . . .

William Daley, U.S.A.

Although William Daley may not remember his great pots clearly, surely many of the forms he later incorporates into his expressive vessels are born in those predawn moments when his imagination is released. These dreamlike reveries so easily unite physical perceptions, intuitions, and intellectual concepts, allowing the creation of mysterious pots, moving poetry, or wondrous paintings. Carl Jung called these dreams "the almost invisible roots of our conscious thoughts." Perhaps it is these invisible roots we are sensing when we respond to the expressive quality of such creations as Robert Turner's *Ife* (9-1), William Daley's sculptural vessels (9-2, 9-3), Mary Frank's *Chimera* (9-4, 9-5), Tony Hepburn's *Strong Support* (Color plate 12), Stephen De Staebler's *Double Torso on One Leg* (see page 172), and other works in clay that move us. The creators of these works

The tall, attenuated forms of *Double Torso on One Leg*, by Stephen De Staebler, U.S.A., challenge the clay to respond to the force of gravity and collapse, but they also challenge our perceptions of reality, and our imaginations. White clay, stains, and powdered pigments. Ht. 89 in. (226 cm). (See also Color plate 14.) *Courtesy, the artist.*

172

Figure 9-1
Ife, Robert Turner, U.S.A. The title of this work derives from Turner's exploration of African tribal art. *To me*, he says, *it is significant that in its power African sculpture comes from a belief in the primacy of energy in all things, an energy open to influence by humans.* Thrown and altered vessel. Stoneware with rough outcroppings; glaze sandblasted after firing to cone 9. Ht. 15½ in. (39 cm). *Courtesy Exhibit A, Chicago. Photo: Brian Oglesbee.*

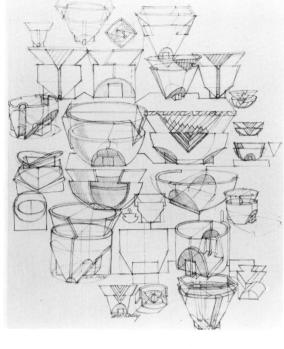

Figure 9-2
William Daley, U.S.A., says that sketches like this one represent a continuous flow of possibilities. He draws them constantly; then, if he feels one might work for a vessel, he redraws it full scale on the wall of his studio and uses it as a working drawing from which to construct the form. *Courtesy the artist.*

all share a common love of clay. But more importantly, they share the fact that they have an inner vision—whether of a pot, a chimera, a farmer, or a human torso—and they have a deep, insistent need to express that inner vision. They also have the necessary fortitude to bring the vision to fruition.

Psychologists and neurologists have often puzzled over creativity, over the reason why one person and not another may have the vision, the need to express it, and the ability to do so. Richard L. Gregory, Professor of Neuropsychology at Bristol University in England, has written at length about the eye, the brain, and our sense perceptions,* but when it comes to the subject of creativity, he has commented that we understand almost nothing of how artists can turn their perceptions around to generate "wonderful drawings, paintings, music, and buildings."

Perceptions, the basic components from which we form our concepts, can refer to any insight, intuition, or knowledge gained by perceiving through any of the senses. What the brain makes of visual or tactile perceptions depends upon each

*Richard L. Gregory. *Odd Perceptions* (London and New York: Methuen, 1986).

(a)

Figure 9-3
(a) William Daley in his studio, refining one of his vessels. Built over cardboard or polystyrene supports, these sculptural vessels are the result of a long creative process that moves from reverie to drawing to the final appearance of the imagined object. *Photo: Charlotte Daley.* (b) *Pentagonal Destination*, William Daley, U.S.A. Daley refers to the Shang Bronze Makers and the Anasazi Native Americans as *my keepers of the perfect. As master messengers of essence over vast time they will always elude final answers. I study their turns and take everything apart and never really understand why the work is so confirming and so potent.* Unglazed stoneware, cone 6. Ht. 15¼ in. (39 cm). *Courtesy Helen Drutt Gallery.*

(b)

Figure 9-4
Chimera, Mary Frank, U.S.A. As a child, Frank saw a photo of the famous Etruscan bronze chimera, and years later she returned to its image as inspiration for sculptures and drawings. This is a clay version of a sculpture that she originally created in wire and papier-mache, using some of her own monoprints for its outer skin. Terra-cotta. 18½ × 30 × 13 in. (47 × 76 × 33 cm). *Courtesy Zabriskie Gallery.*

Figure 9-5
Drawing of *Chimera*, Mary Frank, U.S.A. *After I had finished the sculpture,* Frank says, *I made many drawings of it. I saw that I had made a creature destroying itself. Had the chimera now become a metaphor for our destruction of the earth?* Charcoal on paper. 29 × 42 in. (74 × 107 cm). *Courtesy Zabriskie Gallery and the artist.*

person's accumulated experiences and background, and since each person perceives objects and experiences somewhat differently, what each one makes of those perceptions will, of course, be different. Creativity and the individuality that fosters it seem to develop in part from an acute sensitivity to one's individual perceptions and an honest effort to express the concepts or feelings that those perceptions generate.

Scientific methods may never discover just *how* a creative person is able to translate his or her perceptions into an expressive sculpture or a pleasing pot, but by listening to what some artists say about the workings of their creative processes, we may be able to learn more about our own creative potential.

STEPS IN THE CREATIVE PROCESS

In retracing the creative journey that brings him to the final form of his vessels (9-2, 9-3), Daley says that one type, the bowl, suggests to him habitation, place, and location. In exploring his concept of a bowl as a place, he asks himself,

How does the volume want to invite the mind to enter? Is the opening expansive or constricted? At what rate do I move when I come in? Is it slow or rapid? How do I move inside, all around lazily or more tightly as I go down? How do I feel inside and am I stacked ice cubes or melting ice cream, or its like taking a hot bath in a tub or sleeping in a tight toilet paper tube?

As Daley continues the exploration, he tells us that he also must consider

very practical thoughts that must lay over my dreamier ones. Will the wall structure hold up the volume, how much of the volume has to be floor, what shall I like about it, how should the pot sit— antsy or calm? What should the axis do—should they be stable or tipped? How do the ribs carry the load to the ground? Will it warp ugly in the fire? How does the pot mass as a silhouette? How does it leave the ground? How does the rim meet the air and stay inside? And is gravity on my side?

Thus, Daley vividly describes some of the steps of conception and realization through which an artist may move as he creates. First, he experiences a reverie in a moment of receptiveness to familiar yet mysterious images. Then he uses his aesthetic and kinetic imagination to project how the final product will appear and will be experienced by the viewer, and finally, and perhaps most difficult of all, he focuses a critical eye on his own creation to see if it will live up to his original vision.

Perceptions as Openings

Robert Turner (9-1, Color plate 10), speaking about his life as a potter, had this to say about the process of creating.

In art, mine has been a participatory experience in the way things seem to be and to happen in a perceived world. Indeed my pottery in retrospect is about perception, our connection-making, metaphor-making and a process of possibilities. Perceptions I see as openings toward knowing the universe we observe and toward an identity as a human being who is of the particles and workings of that universe.

Turner also believes that

in using our capacity to perceive connections—thus we alter the sense of our world, our reality.

Perceptions and Experience

Many artists refer to the importance of intuition, improvisation, and the "unforeseen openings" that lead them toward their creative solutions. Although they may intellectualize about this process later, when it occurs it is, as Turner says, a kind of "knowing that includes feeling."

Mary Frank, whose creative works include clay sculptures, drawings, paintings, and prints, sometimes explores the same image in all these media (9-4, 9-5, 11-54). Speaking of how a childhood experience is related to the images that appear in her *Chimera* drawings and sculptures, she says,

What happens to experience? Many images and ideas are fugitive. Others, over the years, slowly make their way toward me. Imagine! I first saw the chimera when I was a child. It appeared in a

Figure 9-6
For It Is Begun in This Life, Christina Bertoni, U.S.A. Bertoni says that her recent work is *drawn almost entirely from instinct/intuition. . . . After I make pieces I often find the piece confirmed by someone's writing about similar philosophic ideas.* Earthenware bisque fired, then painted with acrylic. 24 × 24 in. (61 × 61 cm). *Courtesy Victoria Munroe Gallery.*

book of Etruscan art which belonged to my mother. I took the book to bed with me even though the image frightened me. Forty years later, in Florence, I saw the bronze chimera. It was more terrifying but it was even more amazing.

Perceptions of the Environment

Frequently, an artist's visual perceptions of his or her surroundings will lead to a deeper understanding of that environment and the lives of people who live in it. In *Rural Sculptural Allegory*, Tony Hepburn created a series of sculptures about the lives of the people who live near his home in rural New York state that included one he entitled *Strong Support* (Color plate 12). Hepburn says,

I have often responded to the environment that I have lived in but only after an absorption period.

While living in upstate New York where,

severe, hard winters are followed by boot-clinging muddy spring, bright sparkling summers, and orange brown falls,

the life there became Hepburn's own. He came to understand that

working the land is an unpredictable battle which forges the body and the soul. Knarled trees and frost-turned rocks reflect the faces of those who accept the difficulties of maintaining lives and plants through a 100 degree difference in temperature. . . . One talks of artistic integrity, which has something to do with honesty of intent and execution. In these pieces I have to contend with the integrity of the people I am working from. The work has to maintain their integrity and, hopefully, live up to their stature as good, hard-working people. This aspect has, on occasion, required some adjustments to my formal instincts.

Integrity and understanding are important aspects of creativity, whether the creativity manifests itself in sculpture or pottery. Another artist, Christina Bertoni (9-6), says that art for her has

Figure 9-7
Nyama Vessel, David MacDonald, U.S.A. He draws on African face painting, costumes, jewelry, masks, scarification, and architectural details as sources for his thrown and coiled vessels. *Nyama* refers to the "essential force." Earthenware, paint, bone, raffia, and beads. Ht. 23 in. (58 cm). *Courtesy Hanover Gallery, Syracuse, and the artist. Photo: Clifford Oliver.*

become the means of working out her deepest musing on the nature of existence and nonexistence. Speaking of studying under Richard De Vore at Cranbrook, she says,

> *He kept asking me, 'What is it that you MUST do?' This baffled me at first, but then I realized that art is not recreation, and my work became very serious. . . . I have come to believe very strongly that art is not about art, it is about life and all the countless ramifications. It serves its culture by presenting basics truths in visual form so that we can see them and think about them and perhaps understand better why we are here or how things are. That is why we need artists, why we allow them to be different so that they can see for us, or interpret for us, not just entertain us.*

The experience of learning about or understanding oneself while creating appears to be quite common. Jack Sures (14-19, 15-31), referring to the sheer joy of touching and squeezing clay, says that his work is a search for his identity,

> *As I expand my abilities with clay,*

he says,

> *I expand my identity as well.*

David MacDonald (9-7) also feels that one aim and purpose of his art is

> *self-discovery and communication. In one sense, it is a very private and personal journey in search of order, reason, reality and beauty. In another sense it is an attempt to express and share with others my realizations and discoveries.*

Similarly, John Toki (14-2 and Color plate 33) feels that

> *when we create new statements through our work, we are reflecting our world, our reality.*

SOURCES OF IMAGERY

For some artists, the sources from which they draw their imagery are quite obvious, but to others, the origins of these images may not be clear, even if they appear so to the viewer. For example, Borghildur Oskarsdóttir says of her clay and glass sculptures (11-59),

> *I don't always understand completely why I make my sculptures like I do, but while working and afterwards, I learn.*

She goes on to say,

Maybe my work has something to do with Icelandic landscape, at least, that is what people say. But my sculptures are abstract and I don't think about landscape while I am working. I travel a lot in the desert of my country, and maybe I use forms and colours I have seen in my surrounding to interpret my feelings.

The Artist's Environment

Visual perceptions of the landscape, seascape, or cityscape in which an artist lives are frequent sources of imagery for those who work with clay. Eileen Lewenstein (15-15), speaking of the sea just outside the door of her studio, says,

Since setting up my studio on the beach . . . I have more and more drawn inspiration from the sea. It is there, constant, but continually changing. There are also concrete and wooden groynes and breakwaters—worn away by the sea, but built up with encrustations of barnacles, mussels, and seaweeds— changing shape slowly but inevitably.

Eduardo Andaluz, who lives in the Canary Islands, not only draws much of his visual imagery from the landscape around him, but in his lava/ clay pieces he incorporates part of his actual physical surroundings into his work (11-58). A potter whose work interprets the ice and stone of the Canadian Rockies, Les Manning (15-34), says of his landscape images that his

works take on an abstract relationship of all elements of the mountain environment. Hence, the laminated characteristics provide the duality required to describe both structural and atmospheric elements simultaneously. . . . Each work captures not only a visual interpretation of landscape but includes the spiritual nature of a moment in time.

Speaking of her sources of imagery and the way she transforms her experiences into clay and glass sculptures depicting her impressions of Holland's polderland—areas of farmland that have been reclaimed from the sea by dykes built around them—Helly Oestreicher says,

my works are approximations, insofar as they try to realize the complicated image that is woven in the mind by the impressions, reactions and emotions of experiences. . . . (11-61).

Describing how she searches for and collects the old wood, leather, and other materials that suggest her images, Chantal Talbot (Figure 11-63) says,

Walk is the beginning of it all, and watching eyes, then comes the collection.

She speaks of that moment of intuition when it all comes together:

Then, after an endless night, an instant illumination is enough to turn the narrating panels into earth.
I impregnate the slabs of earth with signs, marks, scratches
and they so impose themselves with their sweat, powerful strain, relentless stir.

Frank Boyden creates vessels on which he incises with sure, strong gestures images selected from his environment in the Pacific Northwest— images that are also important in the mythology of the earliest inhabitants of the region (9-8 and 9-9). Speaking of traveling in Peru, where he immersed himself in the work of pre-Columbian Mochica and Nazca potters (5-11, Color plate 15), Boyden says of the pots he saw there,

These are things that are so exquisite and so mysterious and so powerful that they literally changed my life and the way I think about my environment and the way I felt about myself. . . . These things are really about the people's lives, where they live, a total reflection of their environment. Really nothing was passed up. Every aspect of their culture was dealt with, somehow or other, and it's all right here. I really felt akin to that in many ways because of the microcosm of the material that I deal with in my own backyard.

Referring to her salt-glazed vessels, on which she captures momentary glimpses of her natural surroundings (15-17), Eileen Murphy says she is not interested in

just the beauty of the natural world but the moments before a hawk descends on a mouse or an alert turn of a bobcat's head. It's like a moment when these things really happen. I live on sixty acres, no visible neighbor. I do share with the fox and coyote and deer and I feel these creatures enrich my life and folks should be reminded of those who share the planet with us.

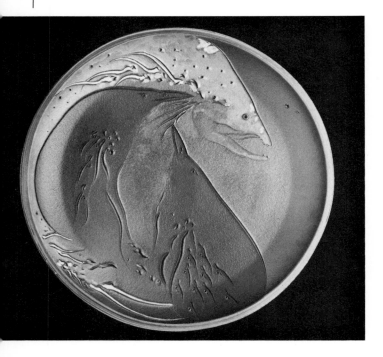

Figure 9-8
Dead Salmon and Raven Plate, Frank Boyden, U.S.A.
Boyden prefers to use incised rather than applied lines
because they are direct and interact with the light,
catching it on their edges and losing it in their
hollows. Stoneware, cone 5. Diameter 25 in. (63 cm).
Courtesy the artist. Photo: Jim Piper.

Figure 9-9
In his lithograph *Tale*, Frank Boyden explores the
images that he frequently incises on his three-
dimensional clay forms—this time on the surface of a
lithograph stone, drawing *on* the surface rather than
scratching *into* it, creating a different type of line.
Courtesy the artist. Photo: Jim Piper.

Historical Sources

There are those to whom the long tradition of
pottery is in itself a source. Janet Mansfield of
Australia, for example, is a potter who sets herself
the challenge of creating new and fresh pots
within the craft's ancient traditions (9-10). Speaking of her sources she says,

> *Looking at Cypriot pottery in museums, the forms,*
> *the mellowness of the decoration, the aptness of the*
> *decoration to the form, the purpose for which the*
> *pot was made, the mystery of the unknown people*
> *that needed those wares, one can only hope for sim-*
> *ilar relevance for the pot we make today.*

Paul Chaleff (16-16 and Color plate 8) says
that he feels that one of the reasons that

> *wood firing has such allure for potters besides the*
> *obvious excitement of the firing process is that the*
> *finished work imparts a sense of history, a contin-*

> *uum of human emotion. Indeed, I try to preserve*
> *that respect for history throughout my work in con-*
> *cept, process and in form.*

Karen Karnes, who now fires her pots in a
wood kiln after many years of firing in a salt kiln,
shows that same respect for historical forms while
creating pots that are immediately recognizable as
hers, (9-11).

There are those whose interest in history
comes from childhood experiences of unearthing
shards of pottery. Carlo Zauli, for example,
speaks of finding slumped and deformed kiln rejects in the earth of his native Faenza; their distorted forms directly influenced his later altered
pots and sculpture (8-14). Walter Keeler (16-20),
says that many of his forms

> *spring from a boyhood obsession with collecting*
> *fragments of ancient pots on the shores of the*
> *Thames in London.*

Figure 9-10
Jar, Janet Mansfield, Australia. Mansfield says she was first drawn to clay for practical reasons, to make things that would be useful and would add quality to everyday living. "Even more," she says, "I needed to create a personal expression that had meaning, that I hoped would have integrity and could aspire to some beauty." Stoneware, salt glazed, cone 10. Ht. 20 in. (50 cm). *Courtesy the artist. Photo: Jutta Malnic.*

Figure 9-11
Karen Karnes, U.S.A., referring to her slit-footed vessel says, *The cut slit adds a mystery to the piece. When you remove the cover you see that the bottom of the piece is above the slit, and that only reveals itself from a particular view.* Stoneware, wood fired. Ht. 10½ in. (27 cm). *Courtesy the artist.*

Michael Casson also says,

History is for me the great teacher, but I hope to interpret the forms for today's function.

Casson has taken a traditional form—the jug (6-13, 6-14)—and, like Mansfield and Keeler, sees the form's long history not as a limiting restriction, but as a source from which to draw inspiration (12-57).

My sources? Well, mainly European, from Cretan (great jugs), Cypriot (even better), and Medieval (best?) times.

Whether or not they are responding to the fact that ceramics is an ancient media, and that any study of its history leads one back to the beginnings of humanity, many clay artists sense

deep roots in the past and are drawn to the myths and legends by which humankind has attempted to understand and explain the world. For example, the architectural installations that Paula Winokur creates are often detailed with drawn images from a wide variety of sources, among them modern poets and writers, and a passion for prehistoric ruins and archaeological sites (14-16).

Although Richard Hirch's tripod vessels are nonfunctional (15-21, Color plate 13), he says they,

like their ancient predecessors, are celebrations of containers, with their fundamental characteristics and cultural manifestations. . . . While these vessels continue to retain the fundamental anatomy of pottery they are devised as abstractions. It is my intention that they be perceived as functionally in-

Cube Skull Teapot (Variation #6)—Yixing Series, Richard T. Notkin, U.S.A. Notkin's teapots borrow certain aspects—miniature size, color, tightly finished surface—from the Yixing teapots, but they are completely contemporary in imagery, commenting tellingly on our society. Stoneware, fired in electric kiln in oxidation, cone 5 to 6. Ht. 5¼ in. (13 cm). Courtesy Esther Saks Gallery. Photo: Richard Notkin.

accessible and formally sculptural, yet purposely contained in vessel architecture. . . .

At the same time that Patrick Siler admires traditional Chinese and Japanese brush painting and the drawings of the German Expressionists, he is also attracted to the strength and simplicity of contemporary comic strips such as Dick Tracy and Krazy Kat. These possess, he says,

a kind of uncomplicated, economical shorthand drawing that is concise, blunt and unromantic.

Siler, speaking of his series *Clayworks* (see page 189 and 16-1) says,

I believe that the subjects and images find me rather than my looking for them.

Social Concerns

Although political action and social concern are not among the most frequent sources of im-

agery in contemporary ceramics, there are those, like Richard Notkin, who use clay to comment on pressing social or political issues. Notkin believes that humanity has a choice between using its abilities for destruction or toward the betterment of our world. It is the artists, he believes, who

provide and nurture the warm spark of our creative human spirit that keeps hope alive.

Notkin's own work often addresses vital contemporary issues—as in his *Cube Skull Teapot (Variation #6)*, from his *Yixing Series* (9-12).

These ideas and images of Yixing teapots percolated through my mind for several years. . . . Although I closely imitate the scale, formats, colors and textures of the unglazed Yixing wares, my intention is to borrow from these formal qualities with honesty and a sense of homage.

Notkin feels strongly, however, that his works should reflect contemporary imagery and express our society's situation as it enters the twenty-first century. He says that by defending the artist who chooses social criticism and commentary, he does not

intend to understate the role of the abstract sculptor, or dedicated potter. Every act of creativity is a positive statement in itself, benefiting the creator and those around him. The ripple effect of many creative acts—our collective creativity—eventually reaches, touches and benefits the whole of humanity. In this lies our power as artists.

The silhouetted hands on Dennis Parks's plates (9-13) recall one of the most ancient images depicted by human beings on the walls of caves, one that may have had a magical meaning to its makers. But they were also inspired by an image from more recent history: Parks speaks of seeing a book of photographs from Japan showing a street in Hiroshima with broken buildings in the background, a scorched roadway leading into the picture, and here and there on the pavement flat, gray areas in the shape of people—adults and children. These silhouetted shadows were formed by human bodies that for a few seconds shadowed and protected the area under them from the intense heat of the atom bomb before they themselves were incinerated. Responding to the same concern for our future. Robert Arneson created a series of works that turned all his irony onto the

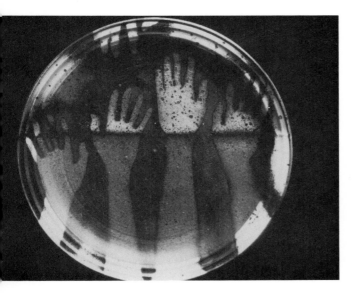

Figure 9-13
The Wish to Be a Red Indian. To make his images of hands, Dennis Parks, U.S.A., scatters mine tailings around a model's hand, creating silhouetted hands reminiscent of early cave drawings. Parks says his works also are derived from photographs he saw of the shadows of human victims of the atom bomb that destroyed Hiroshima. Stoneware. Diameter 22 in. (56 cm). *Courtesy the artist. Photo: Julie Parks.*

military establishment, and expressed his horror of nuclear war (see page 210).

Marilyn Lysohir says that the

initial impetus for my work always comes out of personal experiences and feelings. The end result however is an accumulation of fact and fancy and form and function, never a simple historical account. To explain the complete creative process is difficult and I feel most comfortable when my work can be enjoyed on several levels and especially when those levels can be experienced simultaneously.

Her installation *Bad Manners* (15-21, Color plate 15) can indeed be experienced on several levels, from the purely sensual one of color and texture to that of biting comment on our social mores. Of this work she says,

Bad Manners is about confusing luxuries with necessities.
Bad Manners is about conspicuous consumption.
Bad Manners is also about greed.
Bad Manners is about revenge and the

accumulation of securities for the insecure.
Bad Manners is about world hunger being ignored while world armaments aren't.
Bad Manners are often never honestly recognized or understood for what they are.

Autobiographical Sources

One could say that all art is in some manner autobiographical, but the work of certain artists seems to deal more directly with their personal experiences than that of others. For example, Deborah Horrell, bemused by the magic of art that allows the artist to create an object or entity that speaks of his or her interior world, wonders if there is any other realm of human activity in which an individual can express such personal feelings. Horrell's work is often based directly on her life experiences, as in her installation *Pappa can you hear me?* (9-14). This, she says is

a piece that developed, unconsciously, as a memorium to my father during the tenth anniversary of his death.

Of another work, *Flesh and Bones* (see page 276), Horrell says it was

conceived in a much more self-conscious context— struggle with 'I' and desire for a home from which to evolve, transcend.

Although many artists willingly discuss their work and their creative sources, others understandably feel that their creations speak for themselves. Elke Blodgett (16-22) expresses this feeling, shared by many visual artists, when she says,

What need is there to translate into words what I am and what I do when it is all standing there, right in front of you, to touch with your eyes, see with your hands and feel with your heart. . . .

Judy Moonellis (9-15) prefers to let her work stand for itself rather than comment on it in words. Although it is up to each viewer to interpret any art work or to see in it whatever he or she wishes to see, Moonellis's powerful visual statements appear, to this viewer at least, to be deeply concerned with autobiographical events or emotions—with the relationships of one human to another, of the individual to her inner world, and with the shared human experiences of love and hate, birth and death.

Figure 9-14
Pappa Can You Hear Me? Deborah Horrell, U.S. A. *This piece, Horrell says, is particularly poignant for me . . . simultaneously it addresses the human/archetypal desire for transcendence, loss of body concurrent with the awareness of spirit.* Porcelain, wood, etched glass, paper, acrylic, graphite; fired at cone 10. 10 × 15 × 20 ft. (3 × 5 × 6 m). *Courtesy the Wida Gardiner Gallery and the artist. Photo: Stephen Sartori.*

DRAWING AS A CREATIVE TOOL

Drawing plays an important role in the creative process of such artists as William Daley (9-2) and Mary Frank (9-4, 9-5). William Daley begins his sculptural pots with drawings that he makes in a state of reverie, and at this stage he uses the images in his drawings to nurture creative thought. He says,

I work, by making sketches, all the time, like this one, (9-2). They represent for me a continuous flow of possibilities.

Daley then continues the creative process by making more detailed drawings:

When something merits further play it is drawn on my studio walls in full scale, most often in plan and elevation. When this works, I make forms and build.

Daley uses these large-scale plans and elevations as working drawings from which to make the supports on which he builds his forms, and they allow him to explore the way in which the clay form will develop without having to contend with gravity. Through drawing, he says, he can also explore the inside and outside of a planned vessel simultaneously. Once his sketch is drawn at full scale, Daley measures the lines of the working drawings to calculate the size of the piece, allowing for shrinkage. In this way, he plans his work ahead; nevertheless, he says, he always makes his final decisions while working in the clay.

At first, it may seem that skill in drawing is not essential for making pottery or even sculpture. But being able to note down your observations, to study forms through drawing them, or to plan your work on paper is extremely useful for *anyone* in the visual arts. In addition, your eye will be sharpened as a result of constant sketching, and your sketchbook can become a source of ideas for your pottery forms or sculptures. Sketches may stay in the book unused for some time, then suddenly, when you leaf through it, they may combine in your mind with other images and memories to emerge as an idea for a pot or a piece of sculpture.

Through drawing, it is possible to capture and distill a perception, to see it more clearly, and to fix it in your mind. And through drawing, you

Figure 9-15
By presenting two totally disparate compositions on the front and back of her sculptures, Judy Moonellis, U.S.A., shows the facade that an individual presents to the world, and the frightening figures that lurk behind us all. A difficult assignment to carry out successfully, nevertheless it can create powerful images of duality: life and death, love and hate. Earthenware, terra sigillata, low-fired. 55 × 33 × 30 in. (140 × 84 × 76 cm). *Made possible by support from Cranbrook Academy of Art. Courtesy the artist. Photo: Doug Long.*

can explore the world around you, using a pencil as if it were an extension of your eyes, probing to see how one form relates to another, how the profile of an object delineates its complexity, and how light and shade define the contours of a figure, sharpening or diffusing them.

Drawing can also help you clarify concepts and work out ideas before trying them in clay. For example, Paul Astbury used ink and gouache in this way to organize his thinking about a piece of

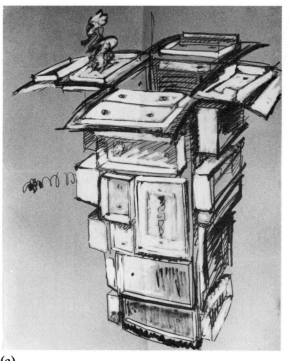

(a)

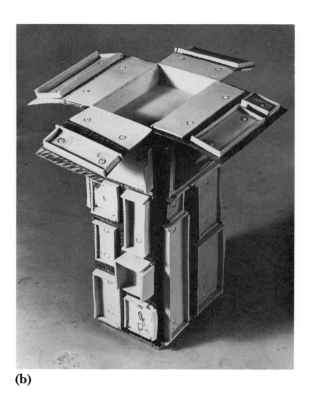

(b)

Figure 9-16

(a) *Study for Evacuated Boxes,* Paul Astbury, England. Astbury is intrigued by the combination of a permanent material—clay—with destructible substances that are vulnerable to time. (b) He used ink and gouache to work out the concept of a mixed media sculpture that he constructed of fired-clay sections, a cardboard box, and ink drawings on paper. 27 × 20 × 20 in. (69 × 51 × 51 cm). *Collection, Aberystwyth Arts Center, University College, Wales. Courtesy the artist. Photo: Keith Morris.*

sculpture (9-16). A comparison of his drawing with the final piece shows some of the changes he made when he came to construct *Evacuated Boxes* out of fired clay sections, a cardboard box, and ink drawings.

Pierre Bayle also uses drawing to make decisions before touching the clay (12-2, Color plate 9). He says,

> It is not the clay which decides the forms I make. When I settle down at my wheel, I already have a form in my head which I have drawn hours, days, weeks ago.

Borghildur Oskarsdóttir develops her forms in drawings, but she leaves herself options for change (11-59).

> For directing my ideas into suitable forms, I do lots of sketches, but even though I have come to a con-

clusion in my sketches, the forms often change when I am modeling.

Peter Agostini, who looks on his small clay sketches as drawings in clay (11-11), says that when things are happening to you it is a blur, that you cannot see things instantly, so you record ideas.

> The things of the present are seeds for possibilities. . . . keep absorbing. We all do that. We're sponges.

Drawing on Clay

Drawing has another function in relation to ceramics: the potter can use skillful drawing to enhance the surface of a pot, using the three-

Figure 9-17
Cup and Saucers by Patrick Loughran, U.S.A. Loughran considers his limited edition domestic ware to be in the long tradition of decorated pottery—maiolica, Japanese and Mexican folk pottery, and Mimbres earthenware. His decoration, however, is contemporary in both its style and its cooling tower imagery. Glazed earthenware. Cup ht. 3 in. (8 cm). (See also Color plate 20.) *In Collections of Museum Het Kruithuis, 's-Hertogenbosch, The Netherlands and Provinciaal Museum voor Moderne Kunst, Ostende, Belgium. Photo: the artist.*

dimensional form as a ground on which to incise or paint expressive or decorative images. Throughout history, from the spiraling decorations on early Chinese or Egyptian urns (3-1, 1-27), to the funeral scene on an early Greek vase (2-14), through the brush-decorated platters by Japanese potter-painters (3-28) and the images on Nazca pots (Color plate 5), from Picasso's decorated vessels (8-7) to the incised drawings that flow around Frank Boyden's vessels (12-1), artists have used the surface of pottery as a ground on which to delineate images.

But Paul Astbury, taking a different approach, made drawings of his mixed-media sculpture (9-16) before constructing it and then included ink drawings on paper as part of the sculpture, contrasting the impermanence of these materials with the permanence of fired clay.

Drawing on Three Dimensions

Drawing, says Frank Boyden,

is a joyous way of exploring my world.

Originally a painter, accustomed to drawing on flat surfaces, Boyden says that when he started to make pots he quite naturally drew on them, and that this opened up an entirely new graphic world, a world that involved three dimensions as well as movement and time (9-9). Since his drawings often move around the vessel, they force *him* to move in order to make them, and they also force the viewer to move around to see the whole composition. Boyden feels that this way of drawing is both a choreographic and narrative act, because the drawing must be followed through time in order to be experienced, just as a dance or a story proceeds through time.

Patrick Siler, also originally a painter, says that from the very start of his experience with clay, he

> scratched the surface, *put patterns in the clay itself, and painted symbols and shapes on it. Whether it is a painting or ceramic piece, drawing is a big thing with me, I initiate the whole process by drawing a picture of the piece and I finish it off by putting a picture on the piece.*

(15-18 to 15-20).

The recording of a perceived image by the artist may not be the only way in which he or she develops a drawn image. Patrick Loughran (9-17, Color plate 20) says that his images come directly from the way he works on the surface. He says,

> *The way I work has to do with responding. . . . You put a mark down and respond to it. You make another one and respond to that. . . .* *

Loughran sees his work as having antecedents in the long tradition of decorated ceramics that include Italian maiolica (6-3, Color plate 4) and the work of Palissy (6-15).

The act of drawing or painting on three-dimensional forms naturally leads the artist to consider how to relate the drawn image to the three-dimensional form of the pottery or, alternatively, how to plan the shape of the vessel to fit the drawing that will become part of its surface. Eileen Murphy is especially aware of this aspect of her thrown forms, saying that when she forms pots,

> *the rounded shoulders, or the elongated narrow form, I like to reflect what is drawn on them. A heron or a bobcat—such different life forms, such different clay forms (15-17).*

In some cases, expression is best served if the vessel is formed to show the drawn or painted image in a close compositional relationship with it.

*Functional Glamour, catalog, Museum for Contemporary Art Het Kruithuis, 's-Hertogenbosch, The Netherlands, 1987.

On the other hand, the tensions that are set up when there is a strong contrast between the drawn or painted image and its shape may better express the artist's concept. As an example, the contrast between the surface spirals and angular forms of James Caswell's vase, *The Arcade*, exploits this tension to bring vitality to the vessel (15-26). Caswell, who worked for two years as artist-in-residence at the Sèvres Porcelain Factory in France, says his time there instilled in him a great love of the eighteenth- and nineteenth-century European porcelain tradition, but he wants, he says,

> *in some way to make ceramic pieces which bear witness, are a testament, to the time in which we live. Understanding the past aids this process.*

Clearly, drawing can perform a number of important functions in relation to the ceramic process, and an aspiring potter or sculptor would do well to foster the skill, continually using and perfecting it.

AESTHETICS AND TECHNIQUE

The manner in which creative people turn perceptions around to generate pottery or sculpture varies from person to person, but in all true creation, there was originally a vision, an idea, or a concept, which, through skillful use of technique, has been translated into an actual object that we can perceive in space, can look at, touch, or use.

As you read the following chapters on ceramic techniques, it is important to keep in mind your own inner visions, whether they originate in visual or tactile perceptions, intuitions, or your emotions. As an art material, clay is quite forgiving, allowing you to change and add to it within reason. However, since fired clay will permanently preserve not only the imprint of your fingers but also the imprint of your ideas, the clarity or confusion of those ideas will also become apparent in your creations, forever recorded in the clay.

10 Getting Started

It's the person working with clay that matters to me; the connection each of us makes to it. It's awesome, this clay; as if it were the "stuff" of imagination.

———Paulus Berensohn, U.S.A.

Hands—pinching, pulling, poking, and patting clay—have formed useful and beautiful objects for thousands of years and are still leaving their imprints on clay today.

Today's ceramic artist is exposed to a flood of information and stimuli from history, from other cultures, and from other craftspeople—no clay worker in the past ever had access to so much information. Museums, galleries, and books show us a multitude of techniques, and every month the ceramics magazines publish the new work of contemporary potters and sculptors almost as soon as they open their kilns. So much information can be confusing, but as you look at illustrations of pottery and sculpture and of people working in clay (see above). Remember that others can do only just so much to help you find your way of working. What you decide to do with this malleable, marvelous, and sometimes aggravating material depends on what feels right for *you*.

Wedging the Clay, a wall panel by Patrick Siler, U.S.A., part of a series of panels entitled *Clayworks*. 22 × 26 × 2½ in. (56 × 66 × 6 cm). *Courtesy the artist.*

EXPLORING CLAY

There are many ways to explore clay. Swiss potter-sculptor-teacher Ernst Häusermann, for example, sometimes takes his students camping for a few days near a clay pit to live with clay and build caves, houses, and slides in it (10-1). Some potters, sculptors, and dancers have covered themselves with clay, dipped their heads into it, or danced in creamy colored slips to celebrate the earth material, while other artists have poured slip out to let it dry and crack in the sun (10-2). You may not care to explore clay in quite such an intense or engulfing manner, but you can squeeze

Figure 10-1
Ernst Häusermann, Switzerland, took his students camping near a clay deposit for a few days to get to know the material by living with it, digging in it, building with it, and learning what they can do with it. *Courtesy the artist.*

▼ *Figure 10-2*
Clay in Change, an environmental installation by Valerie Otani, Elizabeth Stanek, and Andrée Thompson, U.S.A. Sand, stabilized adobe, and fired clay blocks were surrounded by slip poured from a mixer. Allowed to dry in the sun and to become liquified again in the rain, the installation exhibited many aspects of clay. The artists said they were *fascinated with this material and the powerful metaphor of time and change it implies.* Installation at the Walnut Creek Civic Arts Center Gallery, California. Photo taken after one week. *Courtesy the artists.*

Figure 10-3
To create beautiful pottery, Maria Martinez needed nothing more than a level spot in the sun. In this photograph taken around 1940, she showed how she moistened her clay, kneaded tempering material into it, and worked it until she had eliminated the lumps. *Courtesy Collections in the Museum of New Mexico.*

lumps of it in your hands and feel how it responds, see what it does when you add more water to it, learn how far you can push it before it collapses, and discover what you can make of it when it does collapse.

The technical information offered in the remainder of the book is intended to help you discover your own way of working, not to dictate absolute rules. *For an artist*, says U.S. sculptor Stephen De Staebler, *the most valuable motto would be 'No rules.'*

THE WORK SPACE

You may be starting your work in a school studio, a potter's workshop, or even on your back steps. In the chapters that follow, you will see that considerable equipment is available that will make things easier for you, but you can also choose to work in the way that potters have for centuries—using whatever clay is available, forming it by the simplest methods with nothing more than the ground as your work space. Maria Martinez, for example, needed little equipment and only a few homemade tools to make her beautiful pots (10-3). In contrast, a potter may work in a studio that he or she has designed for production and teaching (10-4). Californian Eric Norstad, on the other hand, employs several people in an operation that makes use of mechanical aids, yet also relies on the handwork of experienced potters and on the careful attention he himself gives the process (12-60). A sculptor may have to deal with completely different problems and of necessity be ready to adapt any available space to his or her needs (10-5). If you are lucky, you may be able to set up your own work space. If so, there are some aspects of ceramics that you should take into con-

Figure 10-4
The Potter's Shop, run by Steven Branfman and Carol Temkin. Both are production potters, but, like many such workshops, their studio is also a teaching studio, where students, hobby ceramists, and children can learn about working in clay. *Courtesy The Potter's Shop.*

sideration when you arrange your space. But even if you are a student working in a studio over whose arrangements you have no control, you should become aware of these health and safety considerations.

HEALTH AND SAFETY

Before you start to work in ceramics, it is important that you realize that many ceramic materials are toxic in varying degrees and that they present hazards to those who work with them. There are, however, basic safety and health precautions that you should follow in order to mini-

mize the dangers of working with ceramic materials. And there are steps that you should always take to protect yourself. In the past, when the hazards of ingesting or inhaling clay and glaze materials were unknown, many workers fell ill with silicosis or chemical poisoning because of their continuous exposure to dangerous substances when they worked without proper ventilation or in unsafe working conditions.

It goes without saying that the work space should be efficient and safe. For example, all electric equipment should be properly wired and grounded to prevent possible electrical shock. Heavy materials should be placed so that they can be reached and lifted without strain on the muscles. If you have to lift heavy sacks of clay, bend your knees and lift with your entire body so that the weight is distributed and the force comes from your knees, not your back. Proper seating should be available for those working on the wheel to avoid strain on the back as much as possible.

In addition to using common sense in setting up the work space, you can now find many safety aids and considerable information that will help you avoid problems (Appendix 5A). It is important, for instance, that you inform yourself about the materials with which you work and that you do not use any of whose composition and degree of toxicity you are not aware. Appendix 1E lists the ceramic materials you are likely to use along with their toxicity. Become familiar with this list, and whenever possible, substitute less hazardous materials. For example, you can eliminate a lot of clay dust by using damp, premixed clay, but if you do wish to mix dry clay, try to choose clays that contain only small amounts of free silica and use a talc whose asbestos content is the lowest possible.

Not only should you be aware of the need for protection against immediate toxic substance exposure, but you should also take into account the fact that nowadays we are all exposed to many other pollutants in our daily lives, so the total burden of toxic substances to which our bodies are exposed must also be considered. That burden is increased substantially if you are a smoker.

Schools and public art centers can call on various government agencies and private organizations that will make health-hazard surveys of studios or offer short courses for teachers and

Figure 10-5
An artist's work space reflects the type of work done there, the personality of the artist, and
the methods he or she uses to create that work. Here Marilyn Lysohir, works on *Bad Manners*
surrounded by partially finished figures for the installation (Color plate 15). *Courtesy the
artist. Photo: Arthur Okazaki.*

professionals in safe studio design and management. As an individual, you can call on the same agencies for advice or information, and you can subscribe to newsletters that will keep you up-to-date. Some of these agencies are listed in appendix 5A, and some books that deal with safety and health are listed in "Further Reading." However, since new research is constantly being done, do not rely completely on these; keep up with the available *current* material. Also be sure that your protective equipment meets government standards.

Precautions and Safety Equipment

The composite safety chart (10-6) has drawings of the safety and health equipment that can be used at different times to protect you as you work with ceramic materials or equipment. Throughout the book, you will see a symbol in the margin that will alert you to the fact that a hazard exists. To learn which protective equipment you can use, refer to Figure 10-6.

Right now, at the very beginning of your experience in the ceramics studio, learn and follow these basic precautions:

- Do not smoke, eat, or drink in the ceramics studio. Keep your hands away from your mouth.

- Before starting to work, and periodically thereafter, make sure the ventilation systems are working properly, and that the filters within the systems are clean. Be sure that they are cleaned or changed on a regular basis.

- Use all required and recommended protective equipment.

- When respirators are not in use, store them in a plastic bag in a clean area. Do not hang them in the open where dust and pollutants can collect inside the face piece.

- Respirators will not function properly without a good seal between face and the face piece. Beards and sideburns interfere with the seal.

- Clean up tables and floors with special vacuums that filter out the microscopic ceramic material particles, or if not available use a damp mop and damp sponges for cleanup. Sweeping with brooms and brushes merely sends the particles into the air. Wear a respirator while cleaning.

- When you have finished working, clean off dusty or dirty clothing while still wearing the respirator. Following any extensive use of clay or glaze materials, it is wise to shower and shampoo dust particles from your hair.

By following the proper precautions that are discussed throughout Part II in relation to specific processes, you can ensure that your experience with clay will be both healthful and satisfying.

STARTING TO WORK

This chapter introduces you to different types of clays and explains how to mix and test clay bodies for your own use. If you are a beginner, we suggest that you study this material in conjunction with later chapters so you will be doing the clay tests at the same time that you start to work with hand building methods or on the wheel. In this way, your testing will have more meaning than if you approach it as an abstract exercise before you have any direct experience with the material.

▶ *Figure 10-6*
You can avoid using the most obviously toxic ceramic materials, but exposure to others is unavoidable. This diagram shows you some of the devices that will protect you against hazards while working in ceramics. Many variations of these are available commercially, or frequently you may make your own systems. Precautions that you should take include careful monitoring of studio cleanliness, the use of exhaust fans and hoods close to the source of contamination (with strong enough suction to remove the contaminants before you become exposed), protection against injury and eye damage, and care in handling the kiln. These are discussed in greater detail in the appropriate process sections, and throughout the book the alert symbol will warn you when safety or health hazards exist.

Take care!

Symbol will alert you to take precautions.

Exhaust systems

Fans and hoods for venting toxic fumes, mists, heat, and fumes from kiln.

Air purification

Room sized air cleaner collects fine airborne dust particles.

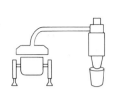

Dust collector

Collector close to source picks up heavy dust particles; for mixing, grinding, sanding, carving clay, and sandblasting.

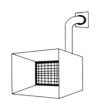

Spray booths

Vented booth with exhaust fan for spraying glazes, lusters, china paint, or booth with water curtain.

Supplied air

Mixing large amounts of clay, toxic materials, chemical powders, grinding clay, sandblasting. Requires supplied air.

Respirators

Use correct filters rated for: dusts, mists, and toxic vapors. Use when no adequate local exhaust venting present, and for salt firing.

Special vacuum

Vacuum with special filters for microscopic particles for dust pick-up. Or wet mop.

Goggles

SHADED for looking into kiln. CLEAR for grinding clay, keeping dust from eyes and contact lenses.

Face shields

CLEAR for grinding, hazardous liquids, clay mixing. SHADED for looking into kiln.

Heat resistant gloves

Aramid fiber gloves for unloading kiln, and protecting hands and arms from heat of raku kiln.

Protective gloves

For handling glaze chemicals, rubber molding compounds, and toxic adhesives.

Ear protection

Ear muffs and ear plugs for use when grinding or using noisy machinery.

Fire extinguisher

Keep near all fire and heat sources and combustibles.

First aid kit

Complete kit with eye wash, burn treatment, and first aid instruction.

TYPES OF NATURAL CLAY

You learned in chapter 1 how clay was formed through the action of geological forces and the weathering of the rocks that make up a large part of the earth's crust. Figure 1-10 shows how some clays remain in place as the feldspathic rocks of which they are largely formed decompose and how other clay components are moved by the action of rain, streams, and rivers and deposited in beds of different types of clay. Some clays can be dug up and used as they come from the ground, because they are naturally plastic and can be worked without additional chemicals. However, contemporary ceramists who mine their own clays often find it necessary to add other ingredients to the body. For example, they may add **fire clay**, a refractory material that increases the clay body's resistance to heat and, depending on the type of fire clay, may also add plasticity to the body. A ceramist may also modify the natural clay by adding grog for body strength or oxides such as iron, chrome, or cobalt for color.

Primary Clays

The clays that remain at their original site of decomposition are known as **primary clays.** These deposits supply the white china clay or kaolin that is used in porcelain, bone china, and glazes. The chemical formulas of kaolin is the closest to "theoretical clay"—a completely unadulterated clay never actually found in nature. Kaolin's formula includes mineral oxides in the following proportion:

$$Al_2O_3 \cdot 2SiO_2 \cdot 2H_2O$$

Secondary Clays

Secondary clays are clays that have washed away from the feldspathic rocks and deposited in beds that may be far from their origin. Over millions of years, as the rocks of the earth's crust broke down, the particles were weathered into increasingly smaller sizes and were continually moved down the mountains by rain and streams. As the movement continued, larger particles were dropped first, and increasingly smaller particles were carried on farther by the water to become mixed with other minerals and organic matter. These particles were finally deposited in river bottoms, on plains, or below the ocean. Similar-sized particles were deposited together; each deposit with a particular mineral and physical composition that determined the type of clay and its individual properties. Among the secondary clays are the fire clays—made up of coarse and heavy fragments that were usually dropped ahead of the smaller particles—and the common earthenware clays, and stoneware clays.

Earthenware clay   Earthenware clay, a secondary clay commonly found in deposits around the world, was the first type of clay to be widely used by humans to create ceramic objects through hardening in fire. The considerable amount of iron this natural clay contains meant that it could reach maturity at the comparatively low temperatures achievable with early firing methods. Made up of decomposed rocks along with organic material and iron, earthenware clays remain porous when they are fired to mature temperatures that range from cone 010 to cone 1 (1641° to 2109° F/ 900° to 1080°C). (**Pyrometric cones,** which are explained more fully in chapter 15, are devices that indicate when a particular clay is reaching maturity. Here, and throughout the book, when cones are referred to, the temperature reference is to large Orton cones. The small cones used in electric kiln sitters fire to maturity at a different rate. You will find a chart of cone temperatures of both American Orton cones and English Seger cones in Appendix 2A).

Natural low-fire earthenware varies in color from reddish to yellowish, depending upon the amount of iron or lime it contains. The most likely place that you will see it used is in the reddish-brown flowerpot that holds your philodendron or fern. Some earthenware clays can be dug up and used just as they come from the ground, with very little more preparation than cleaning out large impurities. Such clays were used by our Neolithic ancestors to make pots and ritual objects and are still used by traditional village potters today. But nowadays many specialized low-fire earthenwares have been developed—including white earthenware containing only small quantities of iron—and these are commercially mixed for use by potters and sculptors.

High-fire clays   The natural high-fire clays were first used in China (3-5, 3-9), then, after boat loads of Chinese stoneware and porcelain objects arrived in Europe, potters there searched for and eventually found the necessary materials with which to make their own high-fired ceramics (6-14). Used for domestic ware as well as sculpture, these clays are still popular with many contemporary potters and sculptors.

Fire clays   Because fire clays are heat resistant, they are used to make bricks for lining furnaces or fireplaces, or to build kilns. They are also used as ingredients in stoneware clay bodies. Fire clays can be used pretty much as they come from the ground.

Stoneware clays   Stoneware clay is a secondary clay made up of finer particles than those of fire clay. This clay is formed when the rock particles became mixed with small particles of iron and with decayed plants containing potassium, a mineral that acts as a flux. Large deposits of stoneware along the Rhine Valley made it possible for German potters to develop the salt-glazing techniques that gave them a competitive edge over potters in other areas (6-14). When stoneware clay is fired to maturity—depending upon its composition, anywhere from cone 1 to cone 10 (2109° to 2381°F/1154° to 1305°C)—it becomes dense, vitreous, and resistant to water and acid. It generally fires to a buff or brown color, although it is possible to mix white stoneware. Your coffee mug or the plate from which you eat your dinner is probably made of stoneware.

Ball clay   Ball clay is a secondary clay that contains little iron, which means that it fires to a gray color. This clay is used in both low-fire and high-fire clay bodies that require plasticity.

FORMULATED CLAY BODIES

A clay that is mixed for a particular use is known as a clay body. This mixture may be made up at a factory and packaged either in dry bulk or damp in plastic bags, or mixed from dry ingredients at the studio or workshop. In either case, it will contain a variety of components that have specific functions in the clay body. An example of a clay body might be a white earthenware mixed without iron in order to produce a low-fire body that can take color well. Another example, porcelain, is a mixed body made up of high-firing components that will fire to the pure white, translucent ware so esteemed in China and envied in Europe. When fired to maturity at a range of from cone 8 to cone 13, porcelain is impervious to liquids. Because of its density and imperviousness, porcelain is also used for sinks, toilets, and electrical insulators.

Components of Blended Clay Bodies

Ball Clay   Ball clay has highly plastic qualities, and for that reason it is used in both low-fire and high-fire clays bodies that require plasticity— for example, those to be thrown on the wheel. It is also used in low-fire slip for casting bodies.

Fire Clay   Maturing at a high temperature and readily available and inexpensive, fire clay is used in stoneware bodies to provide silica and alumina, a refractory material, and to increase the heat-resistant quality of the clay. Fire clays are relatively plastic.

Talc   Talc is a magnesium-bearing rock that sometimes contains impurities of iron and alumina as well as alkalis and lime. Because of its magnesium content, it acts as a flux for low-fire clays and casting slips.

Feldspars   Feldspathic rocks are among the most common rocks in the earth's crust, and the feldspars used in ceramics come from those rocks as they are broken down by geological forces. Feldspars contain alumina, silica, and, depending on the composition of the particular feldspar, varying amounts of sodium, potassium, or calcium. Feldspars are heat resistant and can be used as the principle flux in stoneware clays, because stoneware is heated to temperatures high enough to melt the feldspar (above 2192°F/1200°C). Since feldspars mined in different places vary in composition, it is important to know the chemical formula of the feldspar used.

Flint   A variety of quartz, flint acts as a glass former in glazes, but in clay bodies it remains a solid crystal during firing and does not expand or contract during quartz inversion (see chapter 15). Flint adds body and improves the workability of clay bodies.

Nepheline Syenite   Nepheline syenite is a feldspar with a lower melting point than most feldspars, making it useful in clay bodies to be fired in the medium range (cone 5). Its lower melting point is the result of its high soda and potassium content.

Grog   Grog is an additive that is now commercially made from clay that has been fired and crushed to a variety of particle sizes—usually those that will pass through a screen with 10 to 70 size meshes. The coarsest meshes (10 to 20) are commonly used in sculpture clays, while the finer grains (30 to 70 mesh) are generally used in bodies for throwing or to be carved. Grog adds porosity to clay bodies, allowing greater movement of the clay particles when the clay dries or is fired. For that reason, it cuts down on shrinkage and warping, thus making it more likely that your work will survive drying and firing successfully. More tempering material such as grog or sand means less shrinkage, an especially important consideration in clays used for handbuilding and large sculptures.

Sand   Sand is another temper (or filler) that is added in varying proportions (generally 5 to 15 percent) to either low-fire or high-fire clay bodies to be used for handbuilding or wheel throwing. It adds structure to the clay body, acting much like the rock aggregate in concrete. Its particle size is measured by mesh size—usually 30 mesh (coarse) and 60 mesh (fine). In combination with grog, the variation in particle size helps to make the clay body stronger. At high temperatures, sand may flux and form a rough texture on the surface of a clay body.

CHOOSING A CLAY BODY

As a beginner, digging your own clay or mixing your own clay body from dry ingredients may seem rather overwhelming, so it is likely that you will start working with a premixed clay body that has been developed commercially or by your school for a particular use and labeled as to its firing range. But even if you use a premixed body, you will have to choose *which* clay body to buy for your purpose. For example, if you were planning to make coiled pots and to fire them at a low temperature, you would probably use a somewhat porous earthenware, not a high-fire porcelain clay, whereas if you were planning to throw on the wheel, you would prefer a plastic clay. Very fine clays shrink more when they dry than those that are coarser or contain more temper or filler, so you would probably not use a fine body such as porcelain for building large, thick sculptural forms. (This does not mean this cannot be or has not been done, however. There are always exceptions). If you wanted to fire a large piece of sculpture to a higher temperature than earthenware will stand, you would be likely to use a stoneware body containing a lot of temper or grog, which would make it less likely to crack. Clays to be thrown on the wheel, however, must be more plastic than sculpture clays, so they are made with as little nonplastic material—flint or feldspar—as possible, and with additional plastic materials such as ball clay or small quantities (1 to 3 percent) of bentonite or macaloid.

In addition, the formulation of a clay body to fire at a particular temperature will affect its plasticity when damp. For example, fluxing materials such as feldspar and magnesium-rich talc make clay less plastic and harder to throw, but you might need to include one of these materials in order to reach the desired firing temperature, so you would have to accept less plasticity. As another example, if you wanted to throw porcelain on the wheel, you might want to increase the amount of ball clay to make it workable, but since ball clay fires to gray tones, in so doing you might have to sacrifice some of the whiteness of the porcelain. Also, since the shrinkage rates of clays vary—from around 10 to 15 percent—in mixing a clay body this is an important consideration. Ball clays shrink a great deal and cannot be used alone, but they are an important additive to less plastic clays such as kaolin, which they make more workable.

Thus, you can see from these examples that there is usually a trade-off to be made in choosing what materials to use for a clay body. On the other hand, it is possible to push the limits of a particular clay in a remarkable way. For example, one would not expect to use porcelain for a large sculpture, yet Carlo Zauli used it to create a thick wall relief about thirty feet long. Asked why he used porcelain for such a large piece, he replied that it was partly to see if he could do it and partly because he wanted the porcelain's whiteness on which to use color. In an unusual contemporary use of a material, Paula Winokur makes her fireplace surrounds of porcelain, adding detail by drawing in the clay and using color. This is not the first time porcelain has been used for interior architectural components—in the 1750s, the walls of an entire room in a royal villa were covered with nearly three thousand relief-decorated porcelain panels, made at the Capodimonte factory in Naples, Italy.

CLAY TYPES AND APPLICATIONS

Exterior Sculpture

Despite the fact that clay can sometimes be pushed beyond the limits one would expect, there are certain considerations to bear in mind in choosing a clay for specific applications. For example, in a severe climate, clay type is critical because of weather fluctuations. In such conditions, moisture collecting in the open pores of low-fired clay will alternately contract and expand as it freezes and thaws, and this will eventually crack the piece. For that reason, a dense, vitrified clay such as stoneware is essential in exterior applications where there is danger of subfreezing weather. A low-fire clay body, on the other hand, although not as strong as stoneware, can accept outdoor conditions in areas where freezing does not take place. You could safely use it in a mild climate in a spot where it would not be easily broken.

Dinnerware

Low-fire, stoneware, and porcelain clays can all be used in the production of utilitarian ware. Each, however, possesses unique characteristics that will affect how it is used.

Low-fire clay tends to be either reddish or buff (although white is also available) in color, and because it is not watertight, it usually requires glaze to form a waterproof surface. To make a piece watertight, the ceramist will often glaze the whole piece, including the **foot**, so it is necessary to place the ware on **stilts** during firing. Low-fire dinnerware does not take stove-top or over temperatures well, because the ware may crack and the glaze can **craze**.

Stoneware clay is the body usually chosen by potters for dinnerware because it is strong, durable, and takes handling well. It is also water- and acid-proof. Depending upon the composition of the body, some stoneware clays can accept oven temperatures or even low stove-top temperatures. Stoneware colors range from white to brown.

Porcelain is also especially popular for dinnerware because of its smooth white surface. On it, glaze colors can achieve a quality of depth, and when it is fired to maturity (in a range from cone 8 to cone 13, or 2305°F to 2455°F/1263°C to 1346°C), porcelain is waterproof without glaze. Cherished by the aristocracy of China, where the most precious creations of the official potteries were reserved for the emperor's household, porcelain has always had an aura of elegance surrounding it.

Firing each clay to its maturity is critical in the production of dinnerware. Equally critical is the proper **fit** of the glaze to the clay body. As we will see in chapter 15, each glaze must be carefully chosen to match the shrinkage rate of the particular clay body on which it is used, or the glaze may craze, or crawl and separate from the ware. Crazing is not acceptable in cooking or tableware, because food can be difficult to remove from the cracks, creating health hazards.

Specialized Applications

Some high-fire ceramic applications have been developed for special purposes. An example is the heat-resistant silica bricks that reflect the intense heat during reentry of NASA's space shuttle into the earth's atmosphere, becoming white hot. And at this writing, experiments are being carried on in Japan, in an attempt to create an automobile engine from specially formulated high-fired ceramics.

Figure 10-7
After digging, drying, pulverizing, and soaking the local clay, potters in Thrapsanon, Greece, spread it in the sun to stiffen. When it reaches working consistency, they will wedge and store it.

◀ *Figure 10-8*
Jens Morrison, U.S.A., searches for and digs local clay that he finds by roadsides or streams, dries it in the sun, crushes it with a rolling pin, and then uses it to develop surface texture and color on his sculptures (11-54). *Courtesy the artist.*

200

SUITING THE CLAY BODY TO YOUR NEEDS

When it comes to deciding what clay body is best for your purposes, the choices may sound confusing at first, but as you become familiar with the material, it will gradually make sense.

Sometimes finding the right clay body can take considerable effort. The potters on Crete (2-6) gather their clay, crush it, saturate it with water, and leave it in the sun to let the water evaporate (10-7). In the days when the early potters in the American Southwest dug their clay, they sometimes had to walk miles to find it. Now, at least, when a ceramist like Jens Morrison collects local clays he does not have to go on foot (10-8). Helly Oestreicher, who says there is no good stoneware clay in the Netherlands, gets hers from a friend who travels to France by truck to pick up a load, while Etsuko Tashima, who uses some of the best clay in Japan, from Shigaraki, reports,

When I go over there in a truck, I buy two tons!

Why Mix Clay Bodies?

Since a natural clay body, or a commercially mixed body may not always meet an individual's need, many potters and sculptors prefer to mix their own bodies or have them mixed to their recipes.

For example, American sculpture Richard Notkin (9-12) says,

Although porcelain is one of my favorite clays, as it accepts the greatest amount of detail, I believe in using whatever materials and techniques are the most appropriate to achieve the intended results of each new series of work. . . . For the Yixing Series, I have developed a range of fine-particled cone 5–6 stoneware bodies from a combination of ingredients available commercially: stoneware and earthenware casting slips, various dry clays, Mason stains, etc.

On the other hand, Janet Mansfield (9-10), who has a studio in an area of Australia rich in clays and other minerals useful to a potter, says,

In my pots I use all these materials, hoping to discover the qualities in them that will direct my work and give it distinctiveness. Wanting to work in this way means that I need to do much experimenting with the clay bodies, and also with how the clay will serve the forms.

American Patrick Siler likes the process of blending his clay body:

One of the things I enjoy most about starting a group of pieces is the process of making my batch of clay. Although really I haven't varied the kind of clay I use for years, I enjoy the initiation rites of the process. A little more grog (home ground possibly), a little less red clay, no feldspar this time. . . . (page 189)

Jill Crowley, in England, prepares her own clay in order to be able to mix crushed bricks into it to give the lumpy texture she wants for the surface of her sculpture (11-14), while American potter Eileen Murphy (15-16) had to develop a clay body that would be strong in the green state (dried, but not fired), because her method of drawing and painting on the **greenware** means it must stand up to a lot of handling. Spanish sculptor Eduardo Andaluz (11-59) has a unique problem in mixing the clay he uses with his sculptures that combine clay and lava:

The big problem is to join these two materials because of the different dilation and contraction coefficients. I use a refractory clay, and I add to it some powdered lava, silicon carbide and fluxes. . . . Not always the results are good enough, and lots of times it has to be fired twice or more. . . . I am guided by science a bit, and by intuition a bit.

One reason for learning to mix at least a few basic clay bodies is to become familiar with the ingredients and how they act in the clay. Even if you do not plan to make your own clay bodies in bulk, some knowledge of formulating, mixing, and testing clay bodies will add to your understanding of how the different ingredients affect the body and how a particular clay will respond to your hands, to drying, or to firing. By learning to blend clay bodies, you can learn to develop superior ones specially formulated for your own sculpting or wheel throwing. You can make a body with the particular color or texture you want, formulate it to fit the nuances of your own kiln's firing, and perhaps mix a casting slip with an especially fluid property to fit the intricacies of your plaster mold. By learning to mix your own clay, you gain control over its water content, its consistency, and its quality. You also learn how to make subtle changes in a body, and—a vitally important consideration when glazing your work— your knowledge of clay body formulas can directly affect the quality of the results you get from glazes.

Early potters had no knowledge of the chemical components of clay, of *why* different clays responded to the heat or atmosphere of the kiln in different ways, or *what* made one clay more plastic than another. They simply saw what happened when they used certain materials. But even without knowledge of the chemical structure of clay, the early potters experimented with different types of clay, and throughout history, it was this experimentation that led to the successful development of new ceramics techniques or materials—or to disasters in the kiln! By learning to mix and test clay bodies, you will be approaching ceramics with the same attitude, applying the try-it-and-see approach. This attitude, combined with some knowledge of the chemical properties of various ceramic materials, will help you carry out controlled experiments that can greatly expand your experience in ceramics.

For these reasons, we suggest that you try mixing and testing at least some of the clay bodies that have been formulated for you using only a few components; as you test them you will not have to deal with too many variables. These are part of a complete section devoted to clay and glaze testing in Appendix 1. In the same appendix, you will also find other recipes for somewhat more complex clay bodies shared by some potters and sculptors, and as you gain experience in mixing and testing clays you can try some of these.

PROTECTION AGAINST CLAY DUST

Throughout history, people have used a variety of methods for mixing dry clay ingredients, using their feet or hands (10-3), water power, or mule power (6-5) to blend the components. In the past, the hazards of breathing clay dust were not recognized, so potters who were constantly exposed to the dust, those who mined dry clay ingredients, and those who worked in dusty pottery factories, often developed silicosis, a lethal disease of the lungs.

It is not the particles you can see floating in the air that are most dangerous; rather, it is the microscopic particles that can penetrate an ordinary paper mask that do the damage. Clay dust can also be spread through a studio from the bits and pieces of clay that dry on tables or on wheels, and on the floor; sponging these off at the end of work is important.

Breathing clay dust is harmful to your respiratory system, so proper protection is essential. There are ways you can protect yourself against breathing clay dust. One of these is to keep the studio as clean as possible. Cleaning with the proper type of vacuum cleaner or damp mopping or hosing the work space at the end of work will help to keep clay from being tracked around the studio and its dust from entering the air (10-6).

Active Local Ventilation

In addition to keeping the studio clean, you should provide yourself with proper ventilation. Do not rely only on general studio ventilation. It is recommended that a studio be provided with local exhaust systems that capture the dust at its source—that is, where dry clay is mixed, carving is done, or dry clay objects are sanded. Although most studios are now provided with such active local ventilation systems that vent the dust from near to the source, if you find that you have to mix clay in a situation were such a system has not been installed, wear a respirator rated by OSHA to protect yourself against the microscopic clay particles. You should wear protective goggles as well. If you are going to be mixing large quantities of dry clay materials, the ultimate protection is a supplied-air system in which your head is completely enclosed and filtered air is supplied through a hose (10-6).

MIXING CLAY BODIES

Once you are properly protected against the clay dust, short of harnessing a mule to a mixer or contriving a water wheel, you have several choices of how to mix your clay (10-9 to 10-11). Testing is the best way to learn about clay materials and to expand your understanding of how different clays respond to the heat and the atmosphere of the kiln. Your first experience with mixing clay bodies will probably be through mixing relatively small batches in order to make test tiles which you will then fire at varying temperatures and in different atmospheres.

Mixing Test Batches By Hand

The method you will probably use first in order to mix one- to five-pound batches for making tests requires little equipment. Mix the dry ingredients, first making sure you are protected either by active local ventilation or a respirator. Use a half- to two-gallon container with a lid. A clear plastic container is especially useful because you can see if the components are well blended without opening the jar and exposing yourself to dust. Add the dry ingredients, shake the container well, and then add water until a soupy mixture, called slurry, results. The optimum water content in most damp clay bodies is roughly 25 percent. Once the dry ingredients are mixed with water to become a creamy slip, pour the mixture onto a flat plaster of Paris slab, called a **bat,** which will soak up the water quickly. Some people prefer a wooden surface; alternatively, you can pour the mixture directly onto the plaster wedging table. When most of the moisture has been absorbed or has evaporated into the air, you can lift or scrape the clay from the surface and then **wedge** (or knead) it to a uniform consistency.

Larger amounts of clay can be dry-blended in the type of mortar trough used for mixing plaster or stucco provided that some sort of dust collector or active ventilation is used over it as you blend or that you wear a respirator. Add the water until a slip or slurry is produced; then leave the mixture in the container to air dry until it is sufficiently stiffened to wedge—a process that may take days or weeks. The clay will stiffen faster if you transfer the mixture to a concrete moisture absorbing container or to a plaster surface.

Mechanical Mixers

Commercial clay mixers are basically the same as dough mixers, but are larger and are made

Figure 10-9
Carlo Zauli, Italy, jokingly demonstrates a spectacular way of mixing clay. Normally, he uses a mechanical mixer, sometimes removing chunks directly from the mixer that he feels will work well in his sculpture. If you do the same, be sure to stop the machine before reaching into it! *Courtesy the artist. Photo: Antonio Masotti.*

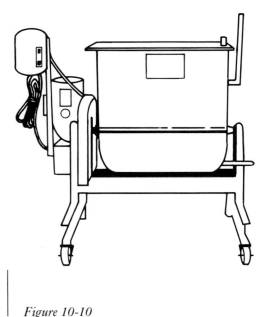

Figure 10-10
Mechanical clay mixers have revolving blades or paddles that mix large quantities of clay. The clay is dry blended first; then the water is added.

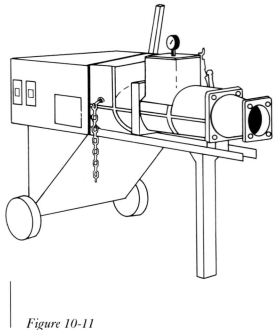

Figure 10-11
A pug mill has an auger blade and will mix, homogenize, and recycle clay. Some mills will also de-air the clay

specifically for clay. This is the type of mechanical mixer you are most likely to find in a school studio (10-10). Recommended mixers have blade guards and safety electrical shut-off switches. Never put your hands in a mixer, but if an accident should occur, reach first for the switch to turn it off.

Used in the same way as a dough mixer, a clay mixer is probably the most useful piece of equipment in a studio, because in addition to mixing clay it can also be used to recycle clay that has been discarded in the process of making pots or sculpture. Putting dry scraps directly into the mixer is not recommended, because hard chunks usually find their way into the processed clay. Rather, the dry scraps should be moistened first in a bucket; then fresh, dry clay ingredients and additional water should be added and the mixture blended. The recycled clay can then be wedged

to eliminate air bubbles and make it more homogeneous.

Dough mixers can be used to mix clay—in fact, many aspects of clay or glaze mixing remind one of kitchen procedures. To use a dough mixer, simply weigh out the dry materials, usually just over half the capacity of the dough mixer; then turn the mixer on, blend the ingredients dry, and slowly add the water.

Commercial mixers have tops that totally close up the mixing area. They eliminate the danger of any dust escaping into the air. They also have an opening for a hose or a valve to allow you to add water without lifting the lid.

Pug Mills

Pug mills are machines that are used for mixing, and sometimes for de-airing clay (10-11). The process of pugging (putting the clay through a pug mill), can eliminate the need for wedging, although many potters and sculptors still prefer to wedge the clay even after it goes through a pug mill. Since pug mills will also accept and process dry scraps, they can be used for recycling clay as well. However, if you use a pug mill to reprocess clay scraps, make sure the scraps are not so large that they bind in the blades, possibly damaging the machine. Producing a high-quality recycled clay from dry chunks usually requires that the clay be pugged two or three times. As a rule it is better to dampen any scraps before reprocessing them; this is easier on the machine and cuts down on processing time.

Some pug mills are equipped with a de-airing system that produces a clay body that is free of air, is well compacted, and with the particles pressed close together. The clays that you can buy premixed in plastic bags in ceramic supply stores have been processed in this way.

To blend porcelain clay, you should use a pug mill with stainless steel blades and hopper (mixing container). With a stainless steel pug mill there is no rust which might contaminate the pure white porcelain body, and a stainless steel pug mill is also much easier to clean.

Commercially Mixed Clay

Many ceramists use commercially mixed clay with great success, including prize-winning Canadian potter Susanne Ashmore (15-33), who makes her teapots from a premixed porcelain, P-300, used by many Canadian potters. American sculptor Richard Notkin (9-12), says,

I generally use a good commercial cone 6 vitrified porcelain (which porcelain 'purists' may scoff at), but it works quite well for my purposes, in compatible plastic clay and slip-casting batches.

Mixing for Tests

Learning to mix and test—whether clay bodies or glazes—is one of the most important skills a beginner in ceramics can learn. Not only will testing show you how to vary a clay body (and, later, a glaze), but it will introduce you to the many variables in the materials you buy and to the varying conditions that can exist in a kiln. Testing can also teach you how to use coloring materials.

Clay recipes to mix and test   The simple clay body recipes given in Appendix 1A will start you out in the testing process. Since a clay body affects the glaze you put over it, these clay bodies, formulated for *Hands in Clay*, will also be used to make the tiles on which you will test the glazes that were also specially formulated for your experiments. So you might want to make and fire extra tiles to set aside for later use.

Making test tiles   To test the clay recipes given in Appendix 1A, you will need to make a series of tiles. These can be made from slabs, rolled out to about ¼ inch thick. Cut the slabs to about 2 × 2 inches square (5 cm × 5 cm), and using a potter's needle or other pointed instrument, scratch identifying marks onto the surface of the tiles. Devise a marking system that will key into your notebook so that you can keep track of each type of clay, its firing range, any changes in ingredients you may make, and other information you wish to record. It is also a good idea to measure and mark a line 1-inch long on each tile, so that when they are fired you can measure the line and see how much the tiles shrank. Fire these tiles (see Chapter 16) according to the required temperature range, cone number, and kiln atmosphere for each clay, and record the results. Making these test tiles will start you out on your exploration of clay bodies, their qualities, and their uses.

Changing ingredients   The experienced potter formulates and tests a clay body largely by changing ingredients in small batches of the clay, testing it in the kiln, and observing the results. If you decide to do a series of tests, change the ingredients only slightly (between 5 and 10 percent), carefully noting all the materials, and in what proportion, each test batch contains so you can compare them after firing.

Once you make the first tests, you may find you need to test the clay body further, changing ingredients in increments of 1 to 5 percent for the purpose of refining it. Remember, however, that a test is only a test—the results you get with a small test tile may differ considerably from those you get when you use the clay body in a pot or sculpture. The reason is that the pot or sculpture to be fired may be more massive or may require longer firing than the tile. Also, if you fire tests in a small test kiln and the finished work in a larger kiln, the atmosphere and heat distribution in the kilns may differ. So use the results only as a guide as you narrow the possibilities.

In order to make record keeping simpler and tests more accurate, it makes sense to change just one component at a time, testing the effect of each ingredient of the clay body. As you form the test tiles, watch for any changes in clay quality that might affect the clay's workability for wheel throwing, casting, or sculpture. Even those who know a good deal about what clay ingredients do are not able to visualize exactly what will happen when the clay goes through the fire. And when glazes are formulated to fit a particular clay body, you can expect even more variables. American sculptor John Toki, says,

> Ceramics is all variables. In dealing with clay and glazes one can be specific only to a point. The sooner you recognize and accept this, the sooner you will feel at home with the process.

Each time you change the type of work you are doing, you may have to do more clay body tests. In fact, in some cases you may have to continue testing for many months to get the clay body that suits your particular needs exactly.

Color in Clay Bodies

You will want to consider the color of the clay body in relation to whatever you are planning to make with it. If you were using stoneware or earthenware for unglazed sculpture, for instance, or if you wanted to leave sections of a pot unglazed, you would probably want to use a clay body with a rich color. If you wanted to make a dark brown or black clay to use unglazed in a sculpture, as do Carlo Zauli in Italy and John Toki in the United States, you would add iron and manganese and possibly other **oxides** or stains to the clay body (14-2). It is the amount of iron and/or other coloring oxides in natural earth-

enware and stoneware that gives them their earthy tones. Because the iron acts as a flux, earthenware containing a lot of iron can be fired at the low temperatures commonly achieved with an open or a pit firing. This is what made it possible for early cultures to develop pottery. Since the clay contains a lot of iron, it will fire to buff, brown, or reddish brown. We saw how potters, first in the Middle East and then in Spain, Italy, and the rest of Europe, used opaque tin glazes to cover the reddish-brown tones of earthenware. They wanted to provide a white background on which they could paint with cobalt in imitation of the Chinese blue and white ware, or to achieve brightly colored glazes.

In order to have a pure white surface on which to paint with underglazes, you would not want to use reddish earthenware, so you would either need to mix a white earthenware or use porcelain. Once the technology of firing clay to a high temperature was developed in China (chapter 3), the clay bodies high in feldspar could be brought to maturity, and feldspar became a valuable flux. Feldspar sources, such as Cornwall stone (*petunze*, in China), or a medium-firing flux such as nepheline syenite, have a higher maturing range than iron and can be used as fluxes in porcelain. By this method, one can avoid the color imparted by the iron.

Because maturity is related to the type and amount of fluxes in the clay body and since some coloring oxides also act as fluxes, the temperature and time needed in the kiln to bring the clay to maturity are considerations in mixing colored clay bodies. Maturity, or immaturity will also affect the color and surface of the fired clay (sheen or matt), as well as the body texture (porous or vitrified).

Suppose that for some reason you wanted to fire a white, high-firing stoneware clay at a slightly lower temperature than usual; you could add some extra flux to fuse it at the lower temperature. But if you wanted to lower the maturing temperature a great deal, you would use not stoneware but a low-fire body such as earthenware. However, if you wanted to keep the clay body white, you could not use a color-imparting flux, so you would need to know how the different fluxes affected the color of the clay. You can see from this that the maturing temperature of the clay can also affect its fired color, and that a change in just one of a clay body's components can alter your clay body considerably.

Variations in Materials

Clay materials themselves can vary a good deal, thus affecting the results you may get with different batches of the same clay body. When the availability of materials changes or a specific vein of material is exhausted, a supplier might substitute a similar material but one that produces somewhat different effects. For example, when miners of Kingman feldspar hit a new vein that had considerably more iron in it, stoneware potters all over the country had to adjust their firing and glazes. Eventually, when Kingman was mined out, they shifted to Custer feldspar, similar in chemical composition yet differing subtly in color and texture.

American potter Eileen Murphy (15-17) says that she uses her own mixture of clay, because after years of trying different prepared clay bodies, she became tired of finding

> some dunted some with too little silica, some very dry, some with too much iron, some too brown, some with too much shrinkage and on and on.

But even now, using her own recipe, she says,

> the clay still varies year to year due to changes in the natural materials. The clay I just had mixed according to my recipe has more iron it it than two years previous. This strongly affects my work, because in salt firing the body is exposed, not glazed over. So, with too much iron, I have a kiln load of darker-than-hoped-for pieces, which also affects the slips I use: some rutile slips actually matched the clay body, so the detail was lost.

Using Local Clays

Instead of using commercially produced dry ingredients to mix your clay body, you can search for local clays, dig them, clean them, and test them for color and other qualities. Sometimes you can use such a clay just as it comes from the earth, or with twigs or large pebbles removed by hand

and some form of temper (probably grog) added, but if there are too many large impurities in it, you will have to screen them out. In a village in Greece, the local clay is dried into lumps, pulverized, and soaked in water until it can be poured through a screen. After this, it is spread in troughs to dry to working consistency in the sun. Using another method, Maria Martinex of San Ildefonso, New Mexico, mixed her pulverized local clay and temper together by hand, added water to it, and continued kneading it by hand to proper working consistency (10-3).

The Availability of Materials

Because clay is such a common material in our earth, we tend to think of ceramic materials as inexhaustible. This is not true; certain feldspars—such as Kingman feldspar—have already been mined out and substitutions made. Albany slip is no longer being mined in up-state New York, and as time goes on, there will probably have to be other substitutes made for depleted materials.

People who live close to the earth have a reverence for it, and do not waste the bounty it provides. Some of the materials we may need for ceramics are finite, so our attitude should be one of respect for those that the earth now provides us.

Aging Clay

Once you have mixed a batch of clay, you can set it aside like bread dough, not to rise but to age. Clay, like bread, is improved by the action of bacteria. These bacteria develop acids and gels and secrete enzymes that help break down the clay into smaller particles, increasing its plasticity. Some potters add organic materials such as vinegar, red wine, or stale beer to their clay to help in this process. Two weeks is considered by some potters and sculptors to be adequate time to ripen the clay, but other potters say the longer the clay ages, the better it becomes. Legends say that ancient Chinese potters prepared clay to be put aside for use by their grandsons. In this same vein, Michael Cardew told of some clay he buried in a hole because it did not throw well. He left it

(a)

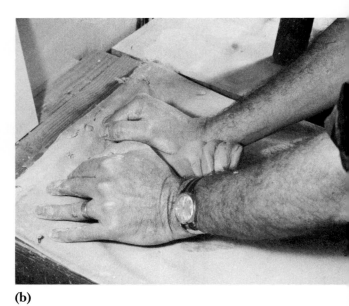

(b)

Figure 10-12
(a) Larry Murphy, U.S.A., pushing and lifting the clay on a canvas-covered wedging table using the "ram's head" method. **(b)** Pushing the clay down and out releases trapped air, eliminates lumps, and makes the clay homogeneous.

there while he traveled for ten years, tried it again without success, and then forgot it for another ten or fifteen years. An apprentice found it, and, Cardew said, used it to make fabulous unglazed terracotta garden pots.

Wedging

To carry the kitchen parallel further, the action of wedging is like the kneading of bread. It eliminates the lumps and drives out air that may be trapped in pockets or bubbles in the clay. But most importantly, wedging homogenizes the clay. You *can* eliminate small air bubbles on the wheel or slab by puncturing them with a pin, but if you are trying to throw a pot and find a moist area on one side and a stiff, hard lump in the clay on the other you have encountered an insurmountable difficulty. Even if a commercial body has been premixed, it may not be thoroughly homogenized; perhaps the bag it came in had been sitting on a shelf for a long time, or there may have been a small, undetectable puncture in the bag. Or the clay may have been left exposed to the air for a

while, so that although the interior is moist enough, the exterior has stiffened. Therefore, it is wise to wedge any clay prior to use, especially for use on the wheel.

You can see if there are air bubbles in a chunk of clay by cutting through it with a wire and looking at the exposed areas, but that will not tell you about the clay's consistency. One way to understand how wedging blends clay, is to wedge chunks of two different colors of clay until they are completely blended (10-12).

Like most of the processes you will use when working with clay, wedging does not have to be complex or mysterious. Any method—even one as unusual as that Carlo Zauli jokingly demonstrated (10-9)—is satisfactory as long as it accomplishes the objective. For some handbuilding methods, it is enough to cut the clay in half and slam one section down on a solid surface and the other on top of it, but since this separates rather than tightens the clay particles, it does not make the clay cohesive enough for wheel throwing.

Spiral and ram's head wedging   Two traditional wedging methods are shown in Figures

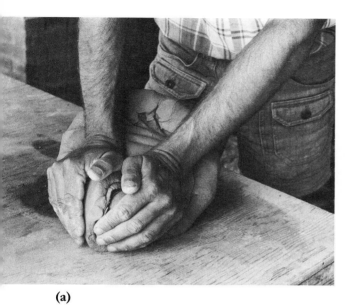

(a)

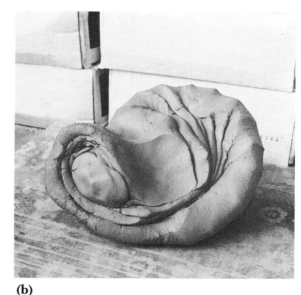

(b)

Figure 10-13
(a) Ron Judd, U.S.A., demonstrates wedging clay in the spiral method, using a slight twist of the hands. This opens up all parts of the clay ball, allowing any air bubbles to escape. **(b)** Spiral wedging also lines up the clay particles in the direction in which the pot will be thrown on the wheel.

10-13 and 10-14. They should be done on as low a surface as is comfortable. Your body should be higher than the table for good body leverage, so that you can use your body as well as your wrists and arms. Your body should be involved in the rolling action or you will tire yourself at the wedging board before you even sit down to throw.

The wedging board should be firm and well anchored, to keep it from moving too much as you push down and out on the clay. The surface can be plaster, which will soak up a lot of moisture from the clay. Some potters, however, cover the plaster with a light cloth or use a canvas-covered board as a surface to avoid the possibility of picking up bits of plaster from the table and mixing them into the clay. Tiny bits of plaster in the clay will expand as they moisten and will eventually pop the glaze from the surface of the object.

Either of these two frequently taught methods of wedging, the "ram's head" and "spiral" methods, will prepare the clay for throwing. Some potters feel that the spiral method does a better job, because it lines up all the particles of clay in one direction. Both methods not only de-air the clay and take out lumps and bubbles, but also tighten the clay into a firm, compact ball ready to throw.

Whatever method you use, wedging serves another purpose. It brings you into contact with the clay you are going to use, and to some potters and sculptors this is a very important part of the process. They feel that the rhythmic action of the body and the time spent wedging the clay give them a chance to think about how they will work the clay. They also feel that the intimate contact that this process sets up between their hands and the clay establishes the mood for working. Mary Rogers, in her excellent book *Mary Rogers on Pottery and Porcelain*, (see "Further Reading,") says that while she is wedging a lump of clay she begins to feel what type of form the clay will happily take, while Stephen De Staebler, who once tried having someone assist with wedging and preparing his slabs, said,

> *I discovered that it was helping me in terms of time, but hindering me in terms of thinking.*

11
Handbuilding

*A life without making
things that tell you who
you are and what you
feel is not enough. So I
make things.*

————Stephen De Staebler, U.S.A.

O ur hands are remarkable tools; strong
yet sensitive, they can pitch out a thin, delicate
pot or build a massive sculpture. Every day of our
lives we touch things, but how often do we really
feel them? Our hands—holding the smooth, mechanical surface of a steering wheel; feeling the
pitted texture of an orange; lifting a mass of wet
laundry; holding a baby—touch and experience
so many surfaces, masses, and forms in a day, yet
how often do we differentiate between them and
remember what our fingertips felt? Unfortunately, few of us use the full potential of these
human tools. As children we are frequently cau-
tioned to keep "hands off," but in order to work
freely in clay we must change that message to
"hands on." To bring vitality to clay forms, it is
important to rediscover our tactile imagination
and memory so that we can make full use of the
sensations we experience throughout our lives.

SHAPING CLAY EXPRESSIVELY

Perhaps much of the appeal of clay is the intimate and direct relationship the potter or sculp-

Global D and D, by Robert Arneson, U.S.A. 1982–
1983. 75 × 26 × 25 in. (190 × 66 × 64 cm). *Courtesy
Struve Gallery, Chicago.*

210

tor can develop with it. Unlike stone or metal, clay can be modeled with few tools or intermediate processes to separate you from your work (11-1). You can use your hands alone to pinch, to coil, or to make slabs into a pot or sculpture of almost any size. Sculptor Stephen De Staebler (page 172) sees his whole body as a tool, and he uses it to press the clay into the forms of his figures. Speaking of clay's malleability, he says,

I can't think of another sculptural medium that has such a vulnerability to force.

Before you start to handbuild a pot or a sculpture by pinching, coiling, or building with slabs, press your thumb and fingers together and see how much force you can exert on the clay. Visualize what you can do to the clay by pressing it with your open or cupped palm. Then, with your hands flat, push down on a table with your upper body and feel the strength you could use from your arms and shoulders. Your hands are an extension not only of your arms, but of your whole body—indeed, of your entire being. It is that being, that individuality, that will give *your* pot or *your* sculpture its expressive quality. Joy, anxiety, confidence, despair, love, conflict, or integration—whatever you are, whatever you feel, can be impressed in the clay, for clay captures and holds not only the imprint of your fingers, but also the imprint of your creativity.

WORKING IN THREE DIMENSIONS

Whatever method you use to work in clay, you have to think in three dimensions. As you make your first pot or piece of sculpture, you may have the exasperating but challenging experience of working happily on one part, feeling quite pleased at expressing your ideas so clearly, only to discover when you turn the sculpture or pot or see it from a different angle that the forms and their relationships are unresolved. Most of us tend to see space as framed in two dimensions, perhaps because we are used to looking at photos, paintings, or television screens. When you make even the simplest pot or sculpture, however, you are creating an actual form in real space rather than depicting it in illusionistic space. Most people

Figure 11-1
Nicholas Van Os, the Netherlands, handbuilding his large stoneware fantasy figures, adding coils and wads of clay to construct the walls. As he builds, he incorporates an interior network of clay supports that helps to keep the damp clay from collapsing and strengthens the piece while drying and firing. *Courtesy the artist. Photo: Frits Van Os.*

have to make a conscious effort at first to consider their work from all angles. It helps to place your work on a **banding wheel** (11-23) or a revolving sculpture stand, but if the work is too large for these aids, simply walking around it often will help you gain a fresh perspective and ensure that what you do to one part will not totally change all the relationships. Also, proper lighting is as important while you are working on a three-dimensional piece of sculpture as it is to a painter working on a two-dimensional surface. Be sure you have adequate light so you can see your work properly.

As you proceed, you will want to consider how the forms of a pot or sculpture relate to each other and to the space around them, as well as how you treat the surface of the clay itself in relation to these forms. It may help to start out with a few exercises in which you shape the clay into cubes, spheres, and cylinders and combine them into simple compositions. This will force you to think about the relationships of masses in space. Doing some pencil sketches will also help you learn to observe forms in space. Notice, for example, how tensions develop between flat and curved forms, how jagged forms suggest one type of emotion while swelling soft ones project an entirely different feeling. Be alert as well to what the negative space between the forms contributes to the expression of your idea or emotion. To develop a knowledgeable eye, go to galleries and museums to look at a variety of sculpture and pots, analyze their forms, and decide whether you feel they help to express the artist's concept.

Figure 11-2
Arch, Arnold Zimmerman, U.S.A. The process of handbuilding is so adaptable that it can be used to make the most delicate pinched pots or to build towering forms such as Zimmerman's arches and vessels (11-22). The thick walls that allow for his characteristic deep carving (15-6) must be dried and fired extremely slowly. *Courtesy the artist.*

Drawing

Drawing (see chapter 9) can help you learn to observe, to see how forms relate to one another and to the space and objects around them. Drawing objects at the same scale at which you perceive them is an exercise that can sharpen your vision, and sometimes making a drawing of your sculpture at the same scale will help you plan how to proceed. In doing so, you will learn a considerable amount about the work itself.

HANDBUILDING METHODS

Handbuilding methods include pinching, modeling, coiling, and slab building, and any or all of these methods can be used in combination to build towering sculptures (11-2) or form delicate pots (11-23).

This chapter demonstrates several of these methods. Remember, however, that the particular methods shown here represent only a few of the many ways of working. There is no one "right" way to work in clay. You will develop your own way as you gain experience, and it may vary considerably from these. Because clay has a will of its own that at times will challenge you, you will have to learn how much you can impose on the clay. Clay requires a give and take, and eventually you will come to terms with the material, discovering what it can do, what you can do with it, as well as what you can best express with clay.

Pinching

Pinching a ball of clay into a simple pot is a good way to start, because it is such a direct way to work, allowing you to see how the clay responds to your hands (11-3 to 11-19). By working in this way, you will discover just how stiff the clay needs to be to hold its shape as you pinch it, how the walls feel as they develop between your fingers, how moist the edge of a pot must be to keep it from cracking, and at what point the clay will collapse as you push it beyond its limits. You will also learn to judge the thickness of the walls as you pinch them between your thumbs and fingers. Most importantly, perhaps, pinching a pot will accustom you to making a hollow form—the basis of all pots and most sculpture—so that what you learn from making a pinched pot can be applied to many other handbuilding situations.

Building Hollow

By definition, a vessel must be hollow in order to be capable of containing something. Generally a clay sculpture is also built hollow, not to contain, but to make it structurally sound and to ensure greater firing success. Small sculptures, such as the sketches an artist may do as maquettes (sketches or models) for a larger work, can be fired solid if they are not too thick (11-12). They can also be split down the middle when they are leather hard, hollowed out, and put together again with scoring and slip. It is also possible, using great care and long, slow firing, to fire thick-walled sculptures or parts of sculptures solid. But in general the easiest way to ensure success in drying and firing a sculpture is to build it hollow from the beginning, making its walls of reason-

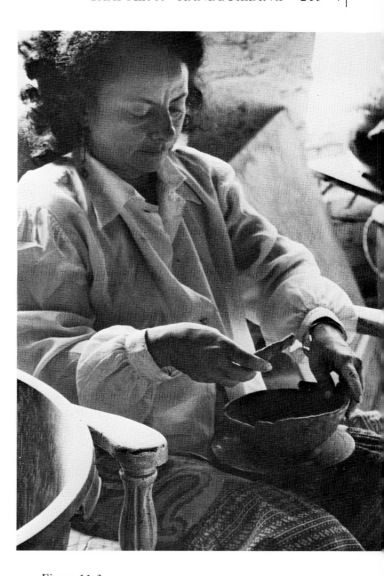

Figure 11-3
Pinching can be done almost anywhere with little equipment. In a quiet spot, the process can be a contemplative activity. Magdalena Suarez Frimkess. U.S.A. *Courtesy the artist.*

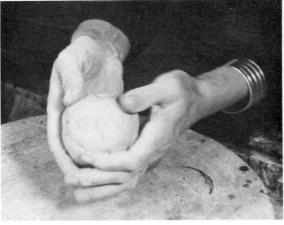

Figure 11-4
Louise McGinley, U.S.A., pats a ball of clay into shape for pinching a pot. The consistency of the clay is important—too moist and the pot will collapse, too dry and it will crack.

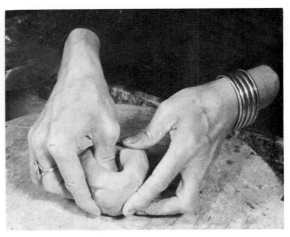

Figure 11-5
While opening the ball, McGinley holds her thumb straight and rotates the ball, leaving enough clay in the base for later shaping.

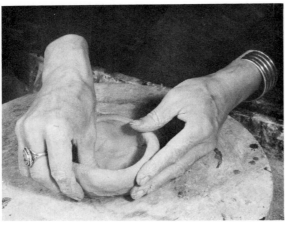

Figure 11-6
Resting the ball on a flat surface, she continues to open it while turning it, pinching the walls up between her thumb and fingers.

Figure 11-7
Adding wads of clay, she builds up the walls, constantly rotating the pot to keep it symmetrical.

Figure 11-8
As the walls grow, she checks them for thickness, shaping the pot as she goes along.

Figure 11-9
She scrapes the walls, thinning and smoothing them. Later, she will narrow in the neck of the pot.

Figure 11-10
Lawrence Jordan, U.S.A., begins one of his large pots with a solid cylinder of clay. Then, moving around the pot, he pulls the clay up from the inside, adding the gouged-out clay to the rim and pushing out from the inside as he shapes the walls. Stoneware and porcelain clay. *Courtesy the artist. Photo: Louie LaFonde.*

Figure 11-11
Sculptor Robert Brady, U.S.A., building a large pinched vessel. The fingerprints will add texture to the painterly quality that he will achieve on the surface using multiple glaze firings.

◀ *Figure 11-12*
Pucker Up Kiss, Peter Agostini, U.S.A. Small, handmodeled sketches can catch the spontaneity of the artist's gesture, preserving it permanently in clay. Many artists throughout history have used clay sketches as a way of observing and noting down what they saw. Agostini says that when he is doing a clay sketch of a model he is in reality drawing. Terra-cotta. *Courtesy Bernice Steinbaum Galley, Ltd.*

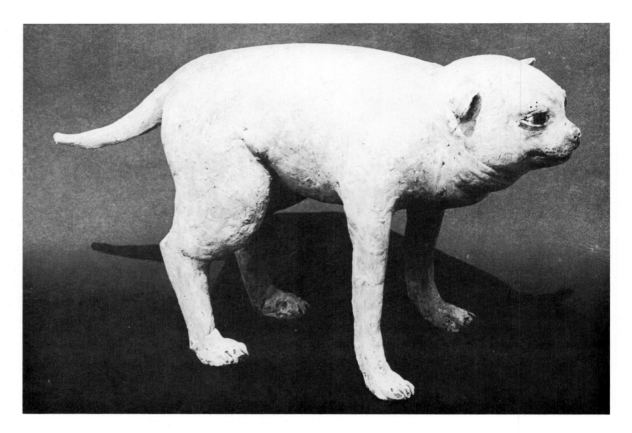

Figure 11-13
Dog, Jose Vermeersch, Belgium. Vermeersch's fat dogs stand, sprawl, or sit in human poses. Their hairless hides are speckled with engobes and their penetrating eyes are glazed. Low-fire clay. About 19 in. (48 cm) long. *Courtesy the artist and Galerie Schneider, Frieburg.*

ably even thickness. If the walls are uneven, the thick sections will dry at a different rate from the thin ones, and tensions will develop that could cause warping or cracking during drying or firing.

By working with no tools but your fingers, using the same gestures of thumb and fingers used in pinching a pot, adding more clay and melding it to previously formed sections, and shaping it into your desired form, you will discover both the exciting potential as well as some of the limitations of the material (11-10 to 11-14). The plasticity of clay can bring you joy, can challenge you, and can also drive you nearly wild with frustration; it may even force you to alter—or abandon—your original concept. You may also find that clay that lets you build rugged constructions does not take easily to thin, extended forms; it is

a material of the earth, seemingly reluctant to leave the ground and soar into flying shapes. If you decide to try to push the clay further, you should know just what you are challenging.

Supporting and Strengthening the Clay

It is difficult, especially for a beginner, to build a vertical form of damp clay without some sort of support. When the early Greeks and the Etruscans used clay for large, free-standing figures, they strengthened them by building supports of clay between the legs, either as decorative motifs—as in the Apollo from Veii (2-25)—or as

Figure 11-14
Tom, Jill Crowley, England. Coiled, pinched, and
handmodeled, Crowley's portrait was made of clay
mixed with crushed red brick. After bisque firing, she
painted it with colored slips and underglazes before a
second firing. Stoneware. *Courtesy the artist.*

Figure 11-15
Marilyn Lysohir, U.S.A., builds her figures with
interior networks of clay, including holes for inserting
supports. Here, she is burnishing the last layer of
terra sigillata with which she surfaces her figures.
Figure from her installation *Bad Manners* (Color plate
15). *Courtesy the artist and Asher/Faure Gallery, Los
Angeles. Photo: Arthur Okazaki.*

rocks, tree trunks, or other natural supports. To
be sure that any large sculpture has sufficient support both as you build it and later during drying
and firing, you can build in a grid of clay supports
as part of its construction as you build up the
walls. The American sculptor Waylande Gregory, who was making large clay sculptures in the
1940s, first built up his sculpture with a honey-
comb or wasp's nest structure and then applied
the outer walls on top of it. Marilyn Lysohir
(11-15) builds in clay reinforcing supports for her
figures, and for his large architectural pieces,
Stephen De Staebler uses an interior clay construction that both supports the piece as it is built
and fired and also incorporates spaces for the
metal reinforcing structure that will be inserted
during installation.

Armatures

From the Renaissance period until quite recently, clay was generally used by a sculptor to build a figure up on an **armature**—a support—to provide a model from which to make a cast metal sculpture. A sectioned mold was made from the model, and the casting of the bronze figure proceeded. The exceptions were usually portrait busts such as Donatello's (6-8) or the wall reliefs made by the Della Robbia family (6-9).

In these never-to-be-fired clay sculptures, the sculptor built up the clay on a framework of wood, metal, or other stiff substance, thus defeating its tendency to collapse. This type of armature also made it possible to create shapes that were liberated from gravity—perhaps a human figure in movement such as a general on a rearing horse. The clay that has been pressed onto such an armature must be kept damp, however; otherwise, it will shrink as it dries and, since the armature itself cannot shrink, the clay will crack and fall off the framework. Except in rare exceptions, this type of permanent armature is not used for clay sculpture that will be fired.

Removable Supports

It is possible, however, to use removable or burnable armatures to support the clay as you build. Wooden sticks and dowels or metal pipes (11-16,11-17) can be removed or pulled out of the clay when it has stiffened enough to hold its shape. If you use a solid support that has little give, such as wood, you may need to pad it with something that will compress as the clay shrinks as it dries; newspaper, cellulose sponges, and cotton batting are all possibilities.

Any kind of removable support you can think of that will help you defeat your enemy—gravity—is worth a try. The support may consist simply of wads of clay that hold up an extended form while it stiffens enough to support itself. Or it may be made of crumpled newspapers, cardboard boxes, towel rolls, a brick or a stone, straw, tin cans, sticks of wood, a pillow, pieces of wire, bundles of cloth, foam—anything that works and that can be removed as the clay stiffens. Wadded or rolled paper tied with string to hold the approxi-

Figure 11-16
Penelope Jenks, U.S.A., uses anything that works to support the clay as she builds. Sticks and metal pipes can be pulled out after the clay stiffens enough to hold up by itself, leaving hollow passages through which the moisture can escape as the sculpture dries and is fired.

mate form you wish has the advantage that the paper will compress somewhat, allowing the clay to shrink without cracking. The paper can be pulled out before firing or, if it is impossible to pull the paper out in places without damaging the piece, it can be left in to burn out in the fire in a gas kiln.

You can make another type of removable support by filling a plastic bag with polystyrene beads, vermiculite, or sand. This will give you a rounded support, useful if you want to shape a pot or a sculptured head or similar form. But do not pack the bag too tightly. It should be able to give a little as the clay shrinks. Also, make sure you can get to the opening of the bag easily, because as the clay stiffens, you will want to pour

Figure 11-17
Temporary supports also hold up the clay walls of artist David Van der Kop's architectural sculpture as it is being built at the Struktuur '68 workshop, in Holland. The section being built here following Van der Kop's design is only about half the height of the final piece. When finished, it will be cut into blocks, each of which will be hollowed out, fired, glazed, then permanently reassembled with steel and cement. A section of Van der Kop's plaza installation in Utrecht. *Courtesy Struktuur '68, The Hague.*

Figure 11-18
To build his large coil-formed sculptures, Graham Marks, U.S.A., first forms his coils with an extruder, then rolls them out on a table, readying them for applying over a polystyrene form. *Courtesy the artist and Helen Drutt Gallery.*

out the contents, leaving the clay to support itself. A balloon will also work as a removable support, because it can be deflated and pulled out after the clay stiffens.

Some sculptors build the clay on a polystyrene armature that has been carved to an approximation of the shape they wish to build. This is convenient, but there are disadvantages in using polystyrene unless it is a simple hump mold from which the clay can be removed *before* firing (11-18). This foam releases toxic gases when it is burned out; even if your kiln were well vented to protect you, the gases would pollute the general atmosphere, possibly even affecting the ozone layer. Some sculptors have poured solvent through a hole in the clay to dissolve the polystyrene which then runs out before firing, but solvents are also toxic, polluting, and flammable.

Therefore, using this foam as a burnable or soluable support is not recommended. And if you plan to use any other plastic material as a burnable armature, be sure that you keep up to date on its hazards and pollution potential.

Reinforcing Materials

For thousands of years, people have been reinforcing clay by adding natural fibers to it. For example, in many cultures they constructed buildings out of mud applied to a framework of reeds or twigs; others mixed straw into the clay to strengthen the sun-dried bricks they used to build palaces and ziggurats. The straw additive strengthened the clay during both building and drying, but if the brick was fired, the straw burned out in the kiln, and a porous brick was the result.

Although you can still use similar natural materials, there is now a variety of more modern ones—fiber glass screening, fiber glass fibers, woven fiber glass, and nylon fiber, for example—that you can add to the clay to strengthen it and which will melt into it on firing. Nicole Giroud in France and Joan Marmorellis in the United States, have both successfully experimented with dipping various fabrics in slip, then drying and firing the draped forms. Marmorellis used fiber glass, while Giroud, who says she took her idea from the lace collars on eighteenth-century Sèvres figurines, has tried many types of fabric, from lace to terrycloth. The fabrics she uses burn out in the firing, leaving small spaces in the walls, but the fiber glass Marmorellis uses actually melts into the surrounding clay, becoming a permanent part of it. (Use protective measures, including goggles, gloves, and a respirator, when you work with fiber glass, since the floating fibers can be inhaled, irritate the skin, or may damage the eyes).

Coiling

Coiling has been used to shape clay into useful and beautiful vessels for thousands of years. From Africa to Greece, from China to New Mexico, potters have used this method in a variety of ways (1-14, 2-5, 5-15; see also Part I opening

Figure 11-19
Marks applies the coils to his sculpture, then scrapes them to smooth and thin the walls.
Courtesy the artist and Helen Drutt Gallery.

photo). Coiling is still a popular way of making vessels and sculpture, and it is often combined with pinching. With coils, it is possible to build thick-walled vessels that might have come from an earlier age (11-21) or tall sculptural vessels (11-22). On the other hand, it is possible to scrape the walls of a coiled pot quite thin to create a delicate, elegant bowl. Coiling allows you greater control of the walls as you build them up, and as you carefully place each coil above the earlier ones you can make the vessel or sculpture slowly bulge outward or narrow inward with less danger of col-

lapsing. On the other hand, coiling is a less direct way of working than pinching, and for this reason it does not appeal to some artists.

As you plan how you will use this method, be aware of its possibilities. Consider using it in combination with pinched or thrown forms or with slabs. You might want to build a pot that reflects quite clearly the coiling process with which it was built (11-36) or you may decide to use the coiling method to build up a large sculpture that, when finished, shows no indication of the method used to form it (11-19, 11-20).

Figure 11-20
Some of Graham Marks's completed sculptures in his studio. The elaborated surfaces are
often sandblasted. *Courtesy the artist and Helen Drutt Gallery.*

Preparing to Coil   As we saw in chapter 10, the clay and temper you choose depend upon the type of work you are going to build, how thick its walls will be, and the temperature at which it will be fired. If your clay has already been put through a pug mill (10-11), wedging will not be as necessary for coiling, but it is still important to make sure the clay contains no lumps or air bubbles. If you will be melding the clay together as you work either by pressing the coils together with your fingers, by smoothing with a rib, or by padding the walls, wedging the clay before use is not as vital as it would be if you were planning to leave your coils unmelded.

Making the coils   With your idea clearly in mind or with a sketch before you, decide on the thickness of the coils you will use. At this point, it might be a good idea to experiment with making

various sizes of coils to find the way that is most comfortable for you to work. Nicholas Van Os, for instance (11-1), squeezes the clay into rough rolls in his hands; Graham Marks makes his coils in an extruder and then rolls them out on a flat surface (11-18). If you use extruded coils, **dies** of different diameters will allow you to control the thickness of the coil. Artists use any of these methods to form coils of the appropriate thickness for their work (11-21 to 11-26). Jamie Walker uses the coils straight from the extruder, which forces the clay through plexiglas dies that he cuts himself. With their solid porcelain coils and their large size, Walker's teapots are heavy and largely intended as sculptural vessels, but they are actually functional and pour well, and some people do use them (11-26 to 11-35).

If you are rolling out coils on a table, practice making some of different thicknesses. It helps to roll with the base of the hand rather than with the

Figure 11-21
Paul Chaleff, U.S.A., attaching a thick coil to one of his tall vessels. Later he will smooth the walls as the vessel revolves on an electric wheel. *Courtesy the artist.*

Figure 11-23
Alev Siesbye, Denmark, uses a banding wheel to turn her pot as she applies flattened coils, melding the joints well with her fingers as she builds the walls. *Photo: Mogens S. Koch, Copenhagen.*

Figure 11-22
When Arnold Zimmerman builds one of his towering coiled works (11-2, 15-6), he uses thick, damp coils, melding them well and waiting for the clay below to stiffen enough to carry the added weight. *Courtesy the artist.*

Figure 11-24
Shaped, the walls smoothed, thinned, decorated, and glazed, Siesbye's bowl shows no record of its forming method (8-28). *Photo: Mogens S. Koch, Copenhagen.*

Figure 11-25
In *My World*, Moira Mathew, England, allows the pattern of the coils to become an important component of her work, giving detail to the exterior surface of her bowls. The interior additions echo the coiled forms of the walls. 7 × 7 in. (18 × 18 cm). *Courtesy the artist. Photo: Peter Allan.*

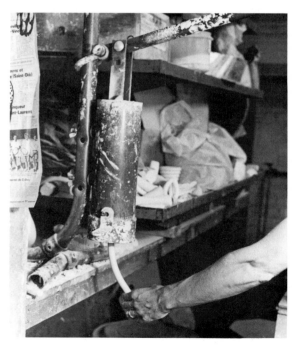

Figure 11-26
Jamie Walker, U.S.A., uses an extruder to form the solid porcelain coils for his teapots. He cuts plexiglas dies to the exact size of the coils he wants.

Figure 11-27
Walker keeps a sketchbook in which he draws notes and plans for future pots. Compare this drawing with the fired and glazed teapot in Figure 11-36 to see its development from concept to finished work.

224

Figure 11-28
Although Walker says that this part *is really mindless* for him, he realizes that for the novice, lack of care in starting the pot can cause disasters. The base has been rolled out and cut to size and is awaiting the first coil. Walker prefers porcelain for its whiteness to intensify the color of the glazes, so he has grog added to the porcelain body. *With the grog,* he says, *it is stronger than many stonewares I've used.*

Figure 11-29
Scoring the base for the first coil. Walker prefers to use only water applied with a sponge along with scoring to prepare the area where the first coil will be placed. Water is faster than slip, he says, and excess slip is difficult to clean off.

Figure 11-30
Walker places the first coil on the scored area. Before joining it, he cuts the end cleanly; then he carefully melds the joint. *This may be a little bit of overkill,* he says, *but when I put the first coil on the slab I usually smooth it in where it joins the slab.*

Figure 11-31
Before building any further, Walker places a small coil at the crucial joint between the base and the first coil; then he melds it in well, reinforcing the joint.

fingers, and to roll the coils from the middle out. The length of coils to make depends on what you find easiest to handle. Some people prefer to use coils long enough for only one ring at a time, while others build by spiraling a long coil up several times around the diameter of the form.

Coiling up the walls If you are building a pot, it will need a base. You will have to decide whether to make this flat, convex, or possibly

even concave, as with the water pots in the Southwest whose indented bases allowed them to fit on the water carrier's head (5-16). To make a convex base, press lumps of clay into the bottom of an old broken pot, a plastic kitchen bowl lined with cloth or plastic wrap, or into a specially made plaster base mold. On the other hand, to make a flat base, you can pound or roll the clay out on a board or table sprinkled with grog or sand or covered with cloth or plastic, then cut the base to the shape you want (11-28). Another alternative is to

225

Figure 11-32
As he begins to coil up the walls, Walker says, *It is mainly in the fingers, in getting the feeling when everything is right and it's going to build up—having the confidence that it is not going to fall down.* As he completes each ring, Walker dampens and scores the coil to ready it to receive the next one.

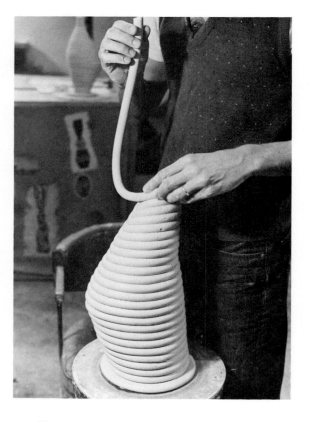

Figure 11-33
As he builds up, adding coils to the asymmetric teapot, Walker continues a rhythm of *water, score and place. When you place it the coil will stick on a little bit. The real adhesion and strength comes from using some pressure when you use the sponge between coils.*

shape the base by rolling a coil into a flat spiral and then smoothing it or allowing the coils to show. If you are building a piece of sculpture, however, there is no particular need for a base; in fact, it is generally best to leave the bottom open so you can reach in later and remove excess clay from the interior if the walls become too thick in places.

Placing the coils   One advantage of coiling is that it gives you considerable control over the shape of the pot or sculpture as you go along. Some potters shape their pots as they place the coils, while others build a basic cylinder first,

then gently push out the walls to the desired curve. To start a piece of sculpture, you can either lay out the first coils in an approximation of the form of its base and develop it as you build it up, or start with a cylinder that you push or paddle into shape as you go along. Whether you are building a pot or a sculpture, it is important to revolve it on a turntable or move around it yourself to see how it is progressing on all sides. You'll need to do this to make a symmetrical pot, but even if you are working asymmetrically, as Jamie Walker does, it is helpful to use a turntable so you can view your work frequently from all sides as you develop the forms (11-28 to 11-36).

Figure 11-34
After dampening and scoring the joint areas, Walker adds the spout to his completed teapot.

Figure 11-35
With extruded handle and knob in place on the top, the teapot is completed. The top has short interior legs that fit inside the pot to keep it from falling off. The coils match so well that it is impossible to see where the top rests.

Joining the coils Because a coiled pot or coiled sculpture, unlike a pinched one, in which the clay is actually melded together, is made up of many separate pieces, the joints must be properly made. If they are not, the coils may pull away from each other as they dry, and cracks or breaks may develop at those points when the piece is fired. Whether you add coils while the clay is quite wet or let it stiffen somewhat between rings, you must be sure that each coil is firmly attached to the one below it. If you plan to smooth the coils with a **rib** or to paddle the outside while you hold your hand or a smooth rock inside to support the walls, you may not need to do more than push them together with your thumb, because the smoothing or paddling will also meld them together, constricting the clay and strengthening the walls. Many potters or sculptors meld their coils completely as they go along in order to be sure the joints are strong or to achieve a smooth surface, while others may keep the coils distinct in order to create a surface that emphasizes or contrasts with the form of the piece. If you want the coils to retain their separate identity, as in Jamie Walker's work, you will need to score each one with a fork or a serrated rib, wet it with water or slip, and press it carefully into place. In Walker's case, the porcelain clay he uses

Figure 11-36
Fired and glazed, the completed teapot shows its genesis in the drawings in Walker's sketchbook (11-27), but also displays the changes he made as he built the piece.

is wet enough to adhere with scoring and water alone.

If you are building a small pot or sculpture, you can keep the walls pretty much the same thickness throughout, but if the piece is to be large, with a quantity of clay built on top of the bottom coils, it is a good idea to use somewhat thicker coils toward the bottom and then gradually make the coils a bit thinner as you continue so the walls will be thinner. The difference in coil thickness might not be more than a fraction of an inch, but even that can lessen the weight considerably. You will learn by experience just how much you can vary the walls and how thick they need to be at the bottom to support the upper section adequately.

Be patient when you are handbuilding a pot

or sculpture. If the clay starts to sag, it is a sign that too much weight has been applied to too moist clay and the structure is about to collapse. It is often necessary to let the clay stiffen for a few hours or even overnight before proceeding with building.

Each artist who works with this method develops his or her own variations of the basic coil method, combining it with other methods and using it merely as a tool to develop forms and create expressive vessels or sculptures. Although a book such as this one has to be separated into chapters and sections that may discuss coiling, pinching, slabs, or mold forming separately, such distinctions need not be clearly defined when it comes to working in clay. There is nothing to keep you from using a method that is a melding of all these techniques. Mainly, developing a way of working with coils becomes a matter of finding out what works for you.

Slabs

The constructive method of building pots and sculptures from slabs of clay is a relatively new development in ceramics. It is true that small, flat slabs of clay were used in the past to build pots (1-15, 1-16) or pressed into molds to make figurines, but the method of building up forms from slabs as it is often done today grew out of the changes that took place in twentieth-century sculpture when constructive, as opposed to cast-metal, methods became popular (page 149).

Making slabs   You can make the slabs with which to construct, drape, or press-mold pots and sculptures by slamming the clay on alternate sides on a table or floor until it flattens, by rolling it out flat with a rolling pin (11-37), by combining small slabs to make large ones (11-38), by putting the clay through a mechanical roller that will give you a slab of even thickness (11-39), or even by casting slabs by pouring slip onto a flat plaster bat or into a two-part mold. Owing to the pressure one needs to exert on the clay to make slabs, slapped, rolled, or pressed slabs generally provide a structurally strong and dense building material.

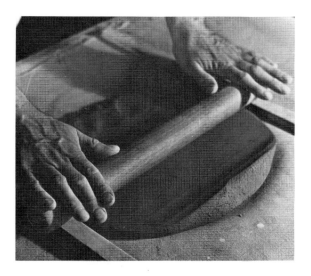

Figure 11-37
Using a kitchen rolling pin or a dowel and two strips of wood as guides is an easy way to make slabs of even thickness for pots or small sculptures. Michael Woods, England. *Courtesy Alphabet and Image.*

Figure 11-38
Stephen De Staebler, U.S.A., presses and joins smaller slabs together to form large, thick sheets, which he uses to form his figures, (see page 172 and Color plate 14), his large pots (8-27), and his thrones (11-38). De Staebler does not use a slab roller, preferring to maintain the involvement with the clay that handforming his slabs allows. *Courtesy the artist. Photo: Susan Felter.*

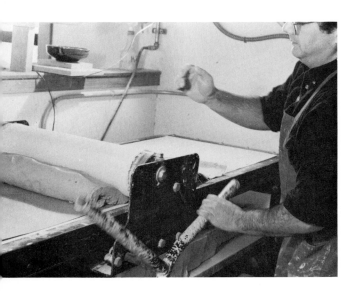

Figure 11-39
Brian Fallon, working at the Norstad Pottery in California, rolls out a slab with a mechanical slab roller before forming the base of a sink (Figure 12-6). Slab rollers speed the process and allow control over the thickness of the slab.

Figure 11-40
After rolling out a slab with a mechanical slab roller, Gary Holt, U.S.A., cuts the leather-hard clay, using one of the beveled straight-edges he has made for cutting different angles.

Figure 11-41
Here he scores the beveled edge of one of the wall sections.

Figure 11-42
Holt applies slip over the scorings along the edge of a wall section.

Figure 11-43
Gary Holt carefully presses together the first two slip-painted beveled edges of a tall slab construction.

230

Figure 11-44
Holt dips a thin, hand-formed coil in water in preparation for using it to reinforce the joint.

Figure 11-45
He places the thin coil inside the corner to strengthen the vulnerable joint.

Constructing with slabs You can use the slabs while the clay is soft, coaxing them to take the desired form and possibly using some of the supports mentioned above. Or you can roll them out, cut them to the desired shape, and then allow them to stiffen to leather-hard consistency and attach them to each other to create hard-edge forms. This method requires advance planning, since you will need to measure and cut the slabs carefully so that they fit cleanly and tightly. Gary Holt, for example (11-40 to 11-50), cuts his slabs with a straight edge that has been shaped to give the correct angle of beveled edge that will allow his slabs to fit tightly. Once cut, the edge of the leather-hard slabs should be scored and painted with water or slip; some people swear by slip, others prefer water alone. The slab edges are then pressed together tightly, and sometimes a small roll of clay is inserted along the joints to make them firmer. This method of building with slabs in a precise manner, cutting out and assembling the leather-hard shapes, allows you to keep a great deal of control over the form as you build it.

There are a number of other ways in which you can manipulate slabs in a more direct manner by allowing them to drape over a hump mold or

Figure 11-46
He then carefully melds the coil into the joint.

231

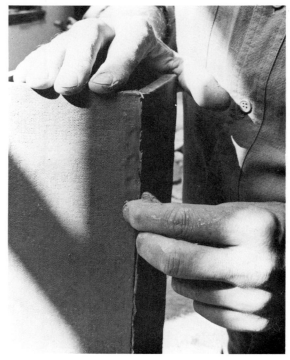

Figure 11-47
To give the joints additional strength, he pinches the edges.

Figure 11-48
The third wall goes on neatly, ready for the final section to be attached.

Figure 11-49
Because the clay slabs had become quite stiff and the slip rather thick during the photo session, Holt gives the base an extra-heavy application of slip.

Figure 11-50
With the base attached and all walls in place, Holt paints the joints of his form with wax-resist compound to keep them from drying too fast.

232

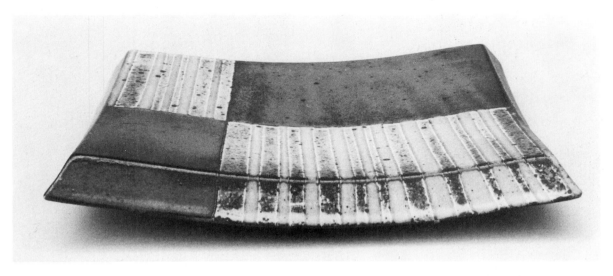

Figure 11-51
Ursula Scheid, Federal Republic of Germany, used a slab of clay to create a platter.
1 × 9 × 8 in. (3 × 23 × 20.5 cm). *Courtesy the artist. Photo: Jochen Schade.*

in a canvas sling while they stiffen. And once you learn just how stiff the clay has to be to stand up, you can build vertical forms or even take advantage of gravity and allow the clay to find its own place of rest. Whether you want to make rough-textured and freely shaped pots or sculptures, or to build hard-edged, meticulously finished forms, the range of possibilities for working with slabs is almost endless (11-51 to 11-56).

KEEPING YOUR WORK DAMP

On seeing a room full of mysterious forms shrouded in plastic, a visitor at a school ceramic studio once asked, "Why do the students always hide their work?" The "hidden" forms, of course, were unfinished pieces either being kept damp while waiting for additional work or being dried slowly before firing.

To keep your work damp, first wrap it in cotton rags, blankets, towels, or sheets that have been saturated in water—but that are *not* dripping wet—then cover it completely with plastic. Even a construction as huge as Van der Kop's plaza sculpture (11-17) was kept wrapped in plastic

Figure 11-52
Folding Box Form, Karl Fulle, German Democratic Republic, says his forms were inspired by Japanese origami shapes, which he made into enclosed forms. Built with triangular slabs of clay, Fulle's boxes make the most of the play of light and shade that develops on the fingerpainted engobe surface. *Courtesy the artist.*

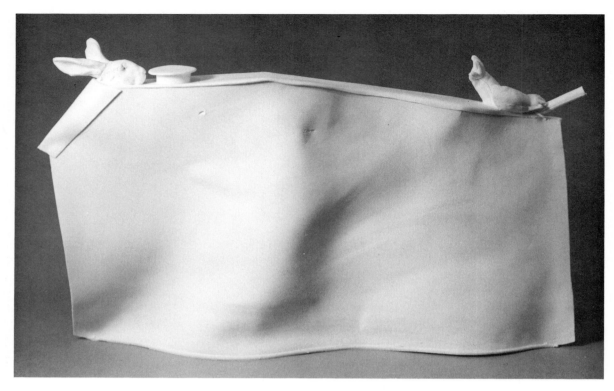

Figure 11-53
Rabbit Speaks, by Phillip Cornelius, U.S.A., was made at the Sèvres Porcelain Manufactury in France, where Cornelius worked while on a French government grant. His sculptural containers are made of exceptionally thin porcelain slabs—1/20 to 1/25th of an inch thick. This one was fired at the factory at cone 15. Normally, he fires his work at cone 10 to 12 in a gas kiln to which he adds about 120 pounds of charcoal to produce a wood-fired effect. Porcelain. *Courtesy Dorothy Weiss Gallery and the artist. Photo: Philip Staratt.*

◀ *Figure 11-54*
Casa de Yolotepec, Jens Morrison, U.S.A. Morrison's slab-built houses represent a homage to the people and places of Mexico, where he often travels studying its architecture and folk art. Earthenware, fired at cone 05–04; underglazes, clear glaze, lusters, and metallics fired at cone 019. Ht. 22 in. (56 cm). *Courtesy the artist. Photo: Bob Nishihira.*

Figure 11-55
Chant, Mary Frank, U.S.A. To create her expressive figure, Frank used damp clay slabs almost as sheets of moistened drawing paper, incising them, then forming sculpture by folding and draping them. Unglazed clay. 44 × 38 × 60 in. (1 m × 96 cm × 1.5 m). *Courtesy Zabriskie Gallery and Virginia Museum of Fine Art, Richmond.*

Figure 11-56
De Staebler's thrones are made from slabs draped over slab-built pedestals and formed by body pressure—by sitting in them. *I am tempted*, he says, *to work even bigger than my body can relate to, but if I insisted on going much past the optimum scale that permits my body to be involved, I'd have to change my idea of form—that form that can be arrived at through forces imposed on the clay.*

while it was in process. For sculpture on whose surface you do not mind a certain measure of coarse texture, you can add 1 to 5 percent pearlite to the clay before you start work. This will help keep the work at a consistent moisture level for a longer period of time.

A misting spray bottle is a useful aid in keeping your work from drying out too fast; use it to spray the wrapping cloths to keep them moist but not too wet. Be careful, however, not to overspray a piece or to redampen a too-dry one. Just how damp you will want to keep your work depends partly upon how you work. For instance, if you will be attaching new wads of clay to a pinched sculpture, you will need to keep it quite damp in order to meld in the new parts. Or if you are adding soft clay coils, you will also want to keep your work quite damp. If, however, you are working with stiffer clay, scoring and painting with slip to attach new coils, then you can allow the piece to

stiffen until it is firm to the touch. For slabs, leave them to stiffen to leather hardness before proceeding.

Some studios have damp rooms where the humidity is carefully controlled to maintain the dampness of objects or to dry them very slowly. If such a facility is not available, you can use a covered canister or tin for small work, an old camping refrigerator or an inexpensive polystyrene cooler for somewhat larger pieces to keep your work damp between sessions. But the best method for large sculptures or thick-walled pots is to wrap them tightly in plastic between sessions. On the other hand, if you want to let a sculpture stiffen enough to be able to carve details in it (15-6), wrapping it loosely will allow it to set up slowly and safely. Others have stiffened their work by placing a few sheets of crumpled newspaper inside, lighting them, and allowing them to burn out to let the heat stiffen the clay. (If you do

235

this, do it outside in a well-ventilated area with no combustible materials nearby.)

DRYING YOUR WORK BEFORE FIRING

The thoroughness and care with which you dry your pot or sculpture are as important to the total process as the forming, because hours of work can be destroyed by careless drying. The thicker the walls, the more slowly a piece must be dried before it is safe to expose it to the warm air of a studio. As clay dries and the moisture leaves its pores, the particles move together. Shrinkage (generally 5 to 10 percent and sometimes as much as 20 percent) occurs during this process. If this occurs too fast it can warp or cause cracks or even breaks in the walls or joints. This is another reason for making sure the walls are reasonably even throughout a piece, for a very thin section will dry much more rapidly than a thick area. Painting small appendages or edges with wax resist will also help to keep them from drying too fast. If this happens, you may face discouragement as the work of hours or days warps or pulls apart. Once your work seems dry to the touch, it can safely be exposed to the air to continue drying, but it must be completely dry before it is fired.

The key to successful drying is to let it dry slowly until the surface changes from a damp to a dry, matt look. When you see that the surface has changed in this way, you will know that it has shrunk about as much as it will until it is fired. Up to this point, any heat to which you subject the work to accelerate the drying must be used only with great care. It is best to dry your work slowly and evenly in circulating air. It *is* possible to use a hair dryer or heat lamp to help stiffen the clay, or to place the work near a warm kiln to speed up the stiffening. If you place your work near a heat source, however, don't forget to turn it often to keep one side from drying faster than another. One ceramist sets his work on a slowly revolving electric wheel with a hair dryer directed at it.

One way to judge if a piece is dry enough to place in the kiln is to hold it next to your face. If it still feels cool, the chances are that it still contains moisture and needs additional drying time.

Another test is to put the piece near a kiln or other heat source and hold a mirror or piece of glass next to it—if the glass fogs, some moisture is still coming from the clay and it needs to be left to dry longer.

Once a large piece of sculpture (or sections of a large work) is dry, you can place it in a gas kiln to preheat, leaving one burner on low and the kiln door slightly open (3 to 10 inches) for 24 to 48 hours until you are *sure* that all moisture has been driven out of the clay. For an electric kiln, leave it overnight with the lid propped open 3 to 5 inches, all the spyhole plugs open, and the heat on low. There is no way you can *overdry* your work before firing it, so give it some extra time and slow warmth rather than risk having your piece blow up in the kiln.

Now the pot or sculpture is ready for firing, an exciting, challenging, and sometimes frustrating process covered in chapter 16.

REPAIRING DRY WORK

Sometimes, an arm or a finger may break off a totally dry figure or the handle may come off a pitcher. Do you have to throw the whole thing away? No, with care you can dampen the dry sections enough to reassemble them. Wrap the dry sections with moist (not wet) rags overnight. On the next day, remoisten the rags and rewrap, repeating the process until both parts become damp enough to be scored, painted with slip, and reattached. To prevent the sections from crumbling, don't rush the redampening; for a large piece of sculpture, redampening both parts equally may take two or three days.

Sometimes you may have to decide that redampening a broken pot or piece of sculpture would not be worth the effort. In such cases, go ahead and fire the main section along with the broken-off part and use an adhesive to glue them together after preliminary (bisque) and glaze firing. To do this, you can make use of a method employed by industrial ceramic companies: mix epoxy with ceramic stains to match the glaze. If your clay body is coarse, you may want to mix a little grog into the epoxy to give it texture. (For additional information on adhesives, see appendix 4B).

COMBINING MATERIALS

Mixed media is a modern name for an old way of working. Clay, one of the earliest sculptural media, has always lent itself easily to adding materials—holes poked into the damp clay could hold feathers or grasses after firing or allow objects to be tied onto the sculpture. For instance, an ancient Egyptian terra-cotta sculpture of a hippo had holes poked into the clay around it in which reeds were probably stuck to suggest the rushes along the Nile. In New Guinea, clay, straw, and hair were combined in a fertility object (11-57), and in Africa, many materials were commonly used along with clay. There were no divisions there between art materials such as later developed in Europe when clay came to be considered a craft rather than an art material. There, the artist chose whatever material best suited his or her idea. This attitude toward materials and clay was continued in the work of some Afro-American artists. This is seen, for example, in the work of the anonymous artists who made the "mixed media" grave markers in nineteenth-century cemeteries in the American South, and in the contemporary *Nyama* vessels of David MacDonald (9-7). At the turn of the century in Europe, influenced by African art, Picasso and the Surrealists startled the art world by rejecting the old view of sculpture as cast bronze or carved marble figures or portrait busts. They began to construct their sculptures out of found objects.

Present-day sculptors combine almost any conceivable material with clay to create sculptures that are not conventional ceramic works but that make use of clay for at least part of the work. For example, Ronnie Barron combines already fired found ceramic objects and refires them in blocks of clay (11-58); Eduardo Andaluz fires clay onto lava rock (11-59); Borhildur Oskarsdóttir shapes both clay and glass into evocations of mountains and ice (11-60); Elisenda Salá uses iron, clay, and fiber in her columns (11-61); and Helly Oestreicher (11-62) combines clay with sheets of glass to create evocations of landscape. Jo-Anne Caron makes use of contemporary plastic materials and lighting (11-63), while Chantal Talbot combines old feathers, clay, weathered wood, and rope in her mixed media sculpture (11-64).

Figure 11-57
Mixed media is not a new concept; a nineteenth-century roof ornament from the Sepik River Valley in New Guinea combines fired clay, straw, and hair into a fertility figure. *Courtesy Staatliche Museum für Völkerkunde, Munich.*

Figure 11-58

Quacking. Ronnie Baron, U.S.A. Baron searches in second-hand stores for ready-made ceramic figurines that he embeds in solid blocks of clay, then refires. He sees his pieces as extensions of archaeology. *Perhaps, like Pompei, I am freezing our particular moment in history and thus making the artifacts of tomorrow.* Earthenware, found ceramics, decals, underglaze, glaze. 24 × 24 × 62 in. (61 × 61 × 157 cm). *Courtesy the artist and Bluxome Gallery. Photo: Tony Novelozo.*

Figure 11-59

Volcanic 11, Eduardo Andaluz, Spain, made use of the lava of the volcanic Canary Islands, where he lives, as a component of this sculpture. He combined it with clay to extend and alter its natural forms. He mixes the clay so it will have the same contraction coefficient in the kiln as the lava, changing the proportions of materials in the clay body each time, because the chemical composition of the lava varies from place to place. Lava and clay. 12 × 11 × 8 in. (31 × 27 × 21 cm). *Courtesy the artist.*

UNFIRED CLAY WORKS

Ever since an Ice Age artist sculpted the unfired clay figures of bison that were found in a cave in France, people have made clay images that have never been fired. In China, for example, sculptors incorporated straw into damp clay to form religious images and painted them when they dried. Some of these survived a surprisingly long time—since the seventh century A.D. A number of artists today have also explored ways of using clay and earth materials in their unfired state. George Geyer (8-32) exposed damp clay to the disintegrating action of water on clay placed either in tanks or exposed to the waves of the ocean, while William Maxwell not only used a clay component—sand—to create an installation (8-30), but also made excavation pieces in which he sculpted the land into forms that he left to weather or to be grown over with grass. Daniel Pontereau, in France, has used powdered clay mixed with cement, sand, gravel, and unfired clay to create indoor and outdoor installations. Other artists, including Joyce Kohl, Robert Lyon, and Nicholas Kripal in the United States, have also combined damp clay with a variety of materials—asphalt, glue, and similar additives—to create unfired pieces in which the additive stabilized the clay to varying degrees.

POSTFIRING CONSTRUCTION

With expanding concepts of what constitutes ceramic sculpture or sculptural vessels, numerous artists have turned to postfiring construction methods that allow a pot or a piece of sculpture to be made in sections, then assembled after firing (11-61 to 11-64). This gives the maker greater freedom to put together forms that would be unlikely to survive the fire intact, to make larger pieces, or to combine several materials in mixed media constructions. The sections can be assembled permanently after they have been fired, or they can be designed to be demountable, making a large piece easier to move or ship. These methods depend on the use of modern adhesives that can make the joinings either strong and permanent or capable of being taken apart when needed.

Figure 11-60
A Shaded Shelter. Borghildur Oskarsdóttir, Iceland, says she does not consciously think of the mountains and ice of her native landscape when she creates her sculpture. Oskarsdóttir's clay forms are built of stoneware and colored with oxides and stains. She makes bisque-fired clay molds in which she casts the glass, which she then sandblasts. Stoneware and glass. Electric kiln, 2233 °F/1280 °C. 20 × 10 × 12 in. (52 × 25 × 30 cm). *Courtesy the artist.*

Figure 11-61
In her mixed media installation *The Roots*, Elisenda Salá, of Barcelona, Spain, attached handmade slabs of stoneware clay and natural fibers to iron columns and set them up on a beach. In *Roots*, Salá says, *I express the feelings of my native country, Catalonia, that has been oppressed so long.* Stoneware, colored with glazes and stains; electric kiln, oxidation. Ht. 79 in. (200 cm). *Courtesy the artist. Photo: Jordi Gumi.*

Figure 11-62
Polderland, by Helly Oestreicher, Holland.
Oestreicher works with two related materials—clay
and glass—to create an evocation of land reclaimed
from the sea in Holland. She combines handbuilt
slabs of lightly glazed stoneware with two sheets of
glass, one of which is cut with an uneven line.
Oestreicher says that as one walks around the
sculptures, *The landscape unfolds itself through the
changing perspective seen in the glass, which, having its own
form, is part of the sculpture and frame at the same time.*
Aluminum base, 2 ft. 4 in. × 3 ft. (71 cm × 92 cm).
Courtesy the artist.

Louise McGinley, for example, fires her large
pieces in sections, fills in the joints with a non-
permanent putty and then colors it to match the
painted surface. Later, if she wants to move the
piece, the putty can be broken apart and the sections disassembled. Helly Oestreicher, who
makes mixed media works that combine glass
with clay, uses a transparent adhesive to attach
the colored and plain glass invisibly (11-62).

Given the popularity of mixed media and of
constructive methods of forming sculpture, it is
helpful to become familiar with adhesives (see
Appendix 4B).

ADHESIVES

Silicon

This type of adhesive can be used for the
temporary and, in some cases, permanent gluing
together of ceramic sections. Its value here is that
it is flexible, and can also fill relatively large gaps
between sections. When used in small amounts,
the adhesive can be pried loose or cut apart with
a knife, so it can also be used for gluing ceramic
to concrete, to wood, or even to tile floors for temporary installations. Silicon can also be used to
glue glazed sections or to repair functional pottery
for use in the oven or on top of the stove: it can
take some oven heat without disintegrating, but it
must not come in direct contact with the flame if
used on top of the stove.

Epoxy

Two types of epoxy are used by ceramists.
The five-minute-setting epoxy is valuable for
quick repairs that will set while you hold the
parts together, but it does not usually hold up
when exposed to excessive moisture or direct
water contact. Overnight-setting epoxy is generally stronger and more resistant to weather. Neither of these types of epoxy can take direct flame,
oven, or kiln heat.

Both types of epoxy can be colored with ceramics stains, clays, or even tempera paints to
achieve colors for patching, to match the glaze, or
fill in cracks. In Appendix 4B, you will find a list
of color additives that can be used to color epoxy
for repairing fired work along with other information on adhesives.

POSTFIRING
REINFORCEMENT

Frequently, a piece of sculpture or large pot
comes through the fire successfully, but the ceramist is concerned about whether it will take the
stresses and strains of shipping, hanging, or other
installation procedures. In this case, it is wise to
reinforce. For example, Marylyn Dintenfass rein-

Figure 11-63
In *Carnival at Gizeh*, Jo-Anne Caron, Belgium, uses slip-cast unglazed porcelain that she combines with fluorplexiglas. She lights her constructions with halogen light to achieve colored, sharp shadows and edges. In this way, she says, *I can play around with the forms of the shadows and even project them on the wall or ceiling, which give me some sort of fourth dimension.* Slip-cast porcelain with fluorescent plexiglas and feather. *Courtesy the artist.*

Figure 11-64
The Burned Triangles, Chantal Talbot, Belgium. Talbot's fired clay, old wood, leather, canvas, ropes, bones, and tarred feathers combine to echo lines of her poem: *Immortalized through the diabolical action of fire,/the marks, sharp scratches, raised sand and enamel, the vibrations of lived/moments are forever set as the lava from the volcano.* Mixed media, stoneware, glazes, single-fired in oxidation in electric kiln. 94 × 79 in. (240 × 200 cm). *In the Collection of the Town of Mino, Japan. Courtesy the artist. Photo: Luc Schrobiltgen.*

forced all the thin porcelain slabs of her work for the Connecticut State Court Building before installing them (14-12), and John Toki reinforces his large wall pieces with fiber glass on the back before hanging them (Color plate 33). In areas where earthquakes are prevalent, strengthening with epoxy and fiber glass and inserting neoprene pads between the sections will help a piece survive a quake. This epoxy and fiber glass combination can also be used to glue wires or metal brackets to pottery or sculpture for hanging it on a wall. For extremely heavy works, however, it is advisable to consult with a structural engineer about con-

structing stronger supports. With these modern developments in adhesives, it is no longer necessary to be quite as concerned about breakage in the kiln or to be limited in your design of sectional sculptures.

This chapter on handbuilding has introduced you to a wide variety of working methods, some traditional, but some that you may never have connected with ceramics. By using these methods singly, in combination, or along with wheel-thrown, press-molded, or slip-cast forms, you will greatly expand the number of ways you can work with clay.

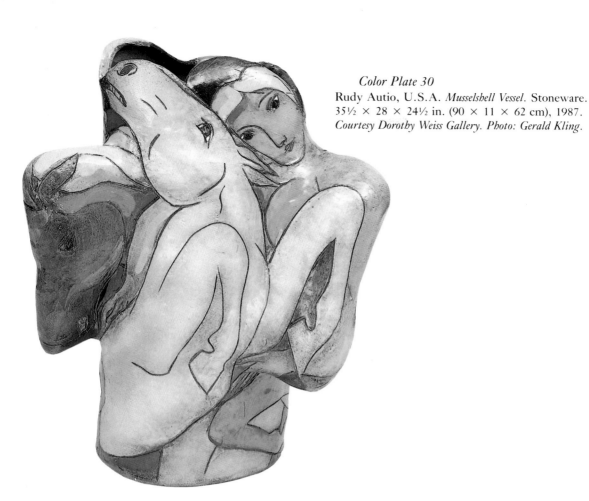

Color Plate 30
Rudy Autio, U.S.A. *Musselshell Vessel.* Stoneware.
35½ × 28 × 24½ in. (90 × 11 × 62 cm), 1987.
Courtesy Dorothy Weiss Gallery. Photo: Gerald Kling.

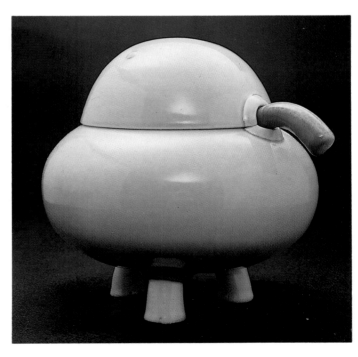

Color Plate 31
Harris Deller, U.S.A. Soup tureen.
Porcelain. Celadon and copper red glazes.
Ht. 11 in. (28 cm). *Courtesy the artist.*

Color Plate 32
Bernard De Jonghe, France. Mountaintop Installation. Wood fired, cobalt glaze. 1986.
Courtesy the artist.

Color Plate 33
John Toki, U.S.A. *Blue Moments.* Stoneware,
porcelain, assorted glaze stains. 57 × 50 × 11 in.
(145 × 127 × 28 cm). *Courtesy the artist. Photo:
Scott McCue.*

Color Plate 34
Marylyn Dintenfass, U.S.A. *Imprint Fresco,*
installation, Port Authority, N.Y. *Courtesy the artist.*

Color Plate 35
Barbara Grygutis, U.S.A. Model, proposal for
Arizona Peace Officers' Memorial. Exterior, buff
stoneware tile; interior, cobalt blue tile. Granite
pillars. *Courtesy the artist. Photo: Tim Fuller.*

Color Plate 36
John Donoghue, U.S.A. Plate. Earthenware, relief. Diameter 20 in. (51 cm), 1987.
Courtesy the artist.

Color Plate 37
John Mason, U.S.A. Untitled, 1987. *Courtesy Rena
Bransten Gallery and Wanda Hansen.*

Color Plate 38
Benet Ferrer, Spain. *Construction #3*. Glazed terra-
cotta. 23 × 12.5 × 12.5 in. (59 × 32 × 32 cm),
1986. *Courtesy the artist*.

Color Plate 39
James Melchert, U.S.A. *Night Sounds In Camoglie*.
Ceramic tile, china paint. 14 × 14 in. (35 × 35 cm),
1986. *Courtesy Fuller Gross Gallery*.

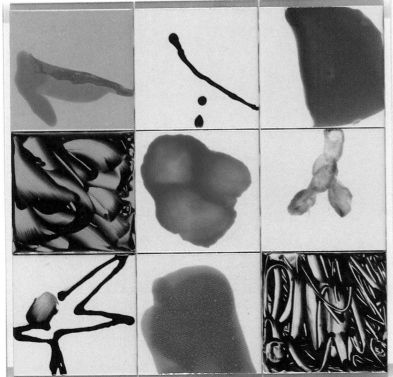

Color Plate 40
Anthony Natsoulas, U.S.A. *Facing It*. Ceramic, glaze, canvas. Painting by Martin Camarata.
70 × 32 × 40 in. (178 × 81 × 101 cm), 1986. *Courtesy Rena Bransten Gallery.*

Color Plate 41
Arnold Zimmerman, U.S.A. Installation, sculptural vessels, Everson Museum, Syracuse.
Stoneware, 1987. *Courtesy the artist.*

Color Plate 42
Kimpei Nakamura, Japan. Waterfall, Toshiba Building. Ceramic on cement. 16 ×
49 ft. (5 × 15 m). *Courtesy the artist.*

Color Plate 43
Jun Kaneko, U.S.A. *Tall Dangos*. Stoneware,
70 × 22 × 30 in. (178 × 56 × 76 cm).
Courtesy Dorothy Weiss Gallery.

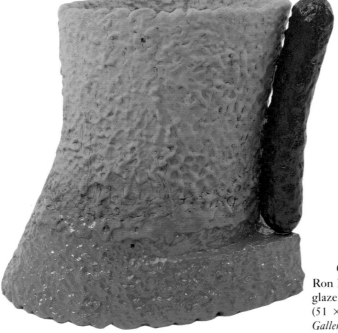

Color Plate 44
Ron Nagle, U.S.A. Untitled. Earthenware,
glaze, and acrylic enamel. 20 × 14 × 18½ in.
(51 × 36 × 47 cm). *Courtesy Rena Bransten
Gallery.*

12
Throwing on the Wheel

As I looked down at this pot spinning on the wheel, suddenly I thought of how everything in the universe is spinning and of how the quality of spinning can't be destroyed.*

————Robert Sperry, U.S.A.*

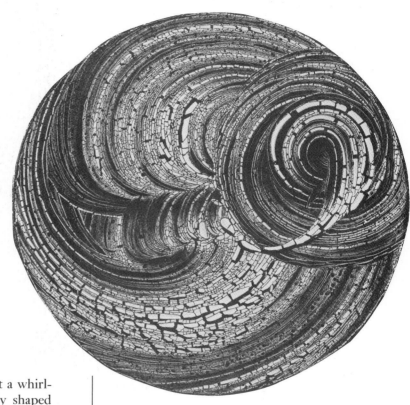

Plate, Robert Sperry, U.S.A. Stoneware, white slip over black glaze. Diameter 28½ in. (72 cm). *Courtesy the artist. Photo: Jim Ball.*

The image of a potter sitting at a whirling wheel, bringing to life a beautifully shaped vessel from a lump of inert clay, has great fascination. Watching the fast-rotating wheel can lead to fantasies of the marvelous pots you might make on it. Like any skill, working on the wheel may appear easy when experts do it, but when you try it yourself, fantasy, as well as the pot, often collapses in the face of reality.

The potter's wheel developed over centuries from the turntables that potters used to rotate their handbuilt pots so that they could form and smooth them evenly (1-29 to 1-31). The true potter's wheel must rotate at a speed of at least 100 rotations per minute; below that speed the potter

*From a conversation with LaMar Harrington, quoted in *Robert Sperry: A Retrospective*. Bellevue Art Museum, Bellevue, WA, 1986.

is unable to make use of **centrifugal force** in **throwing.** The development of this faster wheel made it quicker and easier to make thin-walled pots of a consistent size.

A book can give you only basic information to study along with the instruction and guidance of an experienced potter, the rest is up to you. Even if it is easier to produce a series of pots quickly once one has learned to throw them on the wheel, only after you have had much practice will your body become so trained in the movement of throwing that you can concentrate your attention on the form of the piece you are making.

FORM

Even before you start to learn to use the wheel, give some thought to what you hope to make on it and to the formal aspects of pottery in general. In this chapter, and throughout the book, you will see examples of thrown pottery made by ceramists who use the wheel with such skill that their concern and thought now go into the design of their forms. Study their work with a critical eye, not to copy it but rather to see how they used the wheel to bring vitality to a vase shape on which to incise drawings (12-1), or to create a classic form to which handles bring an element of surprise and lightness (12-2). Look at how they used the wheel to form the sharp profile of a double vessel (12-3), or to develop subtle relationships by contrasting the narrow neck of a heart-shaped vase with the curves of its body (12-4). Or see what can be created by refining the basic cylinder form to its ultimate perfection and then glazing it with sensitivity (12-5). These experienced artists, along with others, use the wheel creatively. To them, throwing is not an end in itself, but only a tool they can utilize in order to realize their creations (12-6). They have spent years mastering the skill of throwing, and they continue to practice it with joy. French potter Pierre Bayle, for example, has been working on the wheel since the age of fourteen, when he learned it in a flowerpot factory. Now in his forties, he still spends ten days twice a year working in a pottery factory in order to recover and refine his throwing skill. Bayle, master of form, says he knows when one of his pots is beautiful, but that its appearance on his

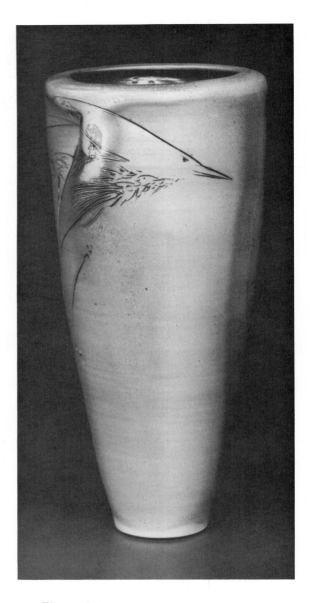

Figure 12-1
Intent on the way a drawing must be distorted to fit the contours of a three-dimensional vessel, Frank Boyden, U.S.A., sees his work as narrative or choreographic, involving movement and time. Wood-fired, Limoges porcelain. Ht. 13½ in. (34 cm). *Courtesy the artist. Photo: Jim Piper.*

Figure 12-2
Bowl, Pierre Bayle, France. Bayle stresses that technique is only one aspect of a work of art; the spiritual is equally important, and the two must remain in balance. White earthenware, coated with fine, local red clay slip. Oxidation and reduction firings. *Courtesy the artist. Photo: J. P. LeFevre.*

Figure 12-3
Olaf Stevens, the Netherlands, wheel-formed this double form in separate sections, then assembled them. The decorations were made by applying adhesive paper stencils and sandblasting the exposed surface. Porcelain, black glaze fired in reduction at 2336 °F/1280 °C in a gas kiln. *Courtesy the artist.*

Figure 12-5
Ursula Scheid, West Germany, adroitly balances form, color, and texture to create a miniature box. Porcelain, reduction firing. Ht. 3 in. (8 cm). *Courtesy the artist. Photo: Bernd P. Göbbels.*

Figure 12-4
Porcelain vase, Catherine Hiersoux, U.S.A. The relationships between the delicate rim, the narrowing of the neck as it moves from neck to swelling body, and the almost imperceptible curve as the base swells into the body proclaim the skill of the potter's hands and her sensitivity to three-dimensional form. Ht. 12½ in. (32 cm). *Courtesy the artist.*

wheel does not come as a free gift—there are years of work behind it (12-2). But, Bayle stresses, technique is only one aspect of a work of art; the spiritual aspect is equally important, and the two must remain in balance.

As well as training your hands and fingers to follow your creative impulses, and learning to observe and transfer to the clay the forms you have observed and come to know through your senses, there is that further dimension to consider in your development: the spiritual one that will give your pots soul.

LEARNING TO USE THE WHEEL

Before you can even begin to think in terms of making a pot, you will need to learn to control the wheel, center the clay, and throw a basic cylinder. It may be difficult to curb your enthusiasm and put off trying to make a pot while you practice making basic cylinders, but if you master this part of the process, your persistence will pay off in the end, and the day will come when, with sensitive, skillful fingers you will throw a vase (12-7).

There may be both electric and kick wheels in the school or studio where you learn to throw. The electric wheel looks easy, while the kick wheel seems difficult to manage. Some beginners do, however, learn more quickly and feel more in control of the wheel's speed by learning on a kick wheel. Others are more comfortable working on an electric wheel. The type you use will be a matter of personal preference or availability.

Figure 12-6
Maria Bofill, Spain, combined wheel-thrown porcelain forms and slabs, uniting the entire composition with a monochromatic black glaze that calls attention to the refinement of the vessel's profile. Porcelain, reduction firing, constructed after firing. Ht. 5 in. (12 cm). *Courtesy the artist.*

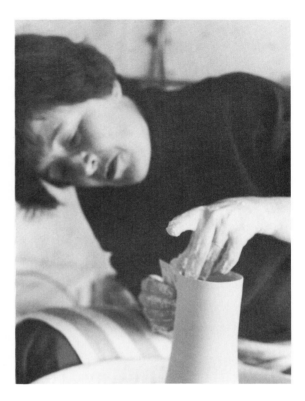

Figure 12-7
Eileen Lewenstein, England, working on the wheel. A potter's hands must be strong and sure in order to wedge and center the clay before starting to throw, but her fingers must also be sensitive in order to feel the thickness of the walls and to give the finishing touches to a simple yet elegant vase.

Using a Kick Wheel

The photos of the basic wheel processes in this chapter were made of a potter working on a kick wheel. One advantage of this type of wheel is that it can be used by both right- and left-handed individuals. In general, the methods of working on both types of wheels are the same, but there are a few extra factors to consider in using a kick wheel.

First, put on rubber-soled shoes; then prac-tice getting the wheel in motion. Kick from the inside near the shaft, thrusting out with a rolling motion, making use of the favorable gear ratio close to the shaft (12-8). You will find that you can get the wheel moving and keep it going with less effort by working in this way than by trying to keep up with the faster-moving outside rim. The action of kicking the wheel results in the transfer of movements to the rest of your body: notice how your hair falls into your eyes or your sleeves roll down as you kick. These movements

Figure 12-8
Larry Murphy, U.S.A., demonstrates the easiest way to rotate a kick wheel—kicking from near the shaft outward to take advantage of the favorable gear ratio.

transferred through your arms to the clay could cause it to move off center, so don't kick while your hands are on the clay.

A beginner tends to get the wheel up to working speed, let it slow down almost to a stop, kick it back to speed, then let it slow down, over and over. It is better to get a rhythm going, take a breath every couple of seconds, remove your hands from the clay, and give the wheel a couple of kicks to keep the wheel head moving.

During the first step on the wheel—centering—the wheel should be turning rapidly. The centrifugal force created by the speed will help you center the uneven lump of clay. Then, with each succeeding step, you will slow down a little, until at the end of the process of finishing the lip, the wheel will be barely moving. Once you feel you can control the wheel reasonably well, you are ready to learn to center the ball of clay that you have wedged.

Although throwing on the wheel does not expose the worker to the same hazards as mixing clay, it is important to remember to clean up the wheel and the floor daily at the end of the work period, using damp sponges and mop and wearing a mask. This is to avoid spreading dust around the studio. Another consideration when throwing is the physical strain of leaning over the wheel for long hours. Those who will be working for lengthy periods in that position should do exercises that will strengthen the back, and should give thought to the position and type of seat they use. A proper position can eliminate a lot of strain. The traditional potter in our southern states used, and many still do, wheels at which the operator stands. Adaptations of these have been developed to lessen back strain. Another physical condition that can cause the full-time potter pain over time is one known as the carpal tunnel syndrome; it is caused by a pinched nerve in the wrist. This usually develops as a result of repeated actions involving the hands and wrists held in a strained position—for example, while wedging or throwing. If, however, you are aware of these physical problems and learn to minimize them from the beginning you should be able to avoid them even if you do become a full-time potter.

Centering

One dictionary defines *center* as "the point around which something revolves; an axis," while another includes an alternate definition, "the point toward which any force, feeling or action tends, or from which any force or influence takes its origin." Both definitions have meaning in relation to centering clay. Although **centering** is a physical process involving placement of your hands, where you press the clay, and how fast you kick the wheel, it also has other dimensions. We think of a centered person as being steady, in balance. It is this inner steadiness that you will want to draw on as you start to center the clay on the wheel.

The principle behind centering is that if an uneven lump of soft clay turning around the fixed point in the middle of the wheel comes in contact with a steady force pressing against it—your hands—it will become evenly centered and perfectly round. The importance of centering cannot be overemphasized, for if the clay is not perfectly centered, there is no way you can throw an even pot (12-9 to 12-18).

Figure 12-9
Larry Murphy, U.S.A., demonstrates centering. He has rolled the wedged ball of clay back and forth on the wedging table or wheel head to form a cone.

Figure 12-10
He slams the coned end on the wheel, driving the cone up into the lump to compress the clay. This gives the base added strength and helps it resist cracking.

Figure 12-11
He pushes and pats the clay on the wheel into a beehive shape before centering it.

Figure 12-12
Dripping water on the clay, he takes care to avoid weakening it by getting it too wet.

Figure 12-13

To center the clay, Murphy links his hands by holding the thumb of one hand with the other, pressing down with the heel of one hand and pressing in with the other.

Figure 12-14

Eileen Lewenstein crosses her thumbs while pulling up the cone during the centering process.

Figure 12-15

Murphy cones up, squeezing the clay into a cone. He advises against coning up one ball of clay too often, as it can bring water into the clay and weaken it.

Figure 12-16

Once the cone has reached full height, he presses it back down with one hand on the side, bending it off center a little as he presses.

Figure 12-17
Experienced potters may only cone up when centering large amounts, but beginners will find it helpful to do it each time they start to center a pot.

Figure 12-18
Centered clay. If you hold your hand against the clay as it revolves, you can feel if it is centered properly.

In order to center, you should keep your hands and forearms perfectly still, so you need to anchor your arms in some way. One way to do this is to press your elbows inward tightly against your body. Or you can press them against your upper legs, your sides, or even the wheel frame—whichever is most comfortable and gives them the best support. Your hands should be joined in some way to keep them steady; whatever method of joining them you use, be sure that they are not working independently, but rather that they are functioning together as one tool. One hint to beginners is to be sure the clay you use is soft enough when you practice centering. You don't want to have to fight the clay, and clay that is too hard can exhaust you. Now you are ready to practice centering a not-too-large ball of clay.

Opening

The next step to learn after centering is opening the clay mass (12-19 to 12-24). This is not difficult, but it takes concentrated force. In order to open the centered clay evenly, you will need to continue bracing your arms, keeping your hands

working together. As you press your finger or thumb down into the clay, you will be forming a centered lump of clay with a hole in it. Beginners often make the mistake of trying to throw from this doughnutlike lump rather than from a fully opened shape. Remember that the clay is not fully opened until you have formed the bottom of a cylinder and straightened the walls. To do this, you will need to move your finger or fingers across the bottom of the clay parallel to the wheel head in accord with the speed of the wheel, leaving enough clay on the bottom to form the base of the cylinder. Only now are you ready to pull up the walls.

Pulling Up the Walls

If the clay has been centered and opened properly, this last step is not as difficult as it may appear. However, if these steps have not been performed with care, then pulling up the walls evenly is almost impossible. When you are pulling up the walls, you will find that they rise more easily if you pull them at the same speed as the wheel is revolving—don't try to pull faster.

To pull up the walls, place the fingers of both

Figure 12-19
Opening with his index finger, Murphy presses straight in without letting the hinging motion of his finger pull the clay off center.

Figure 12-20
A cross-section shows the action of his index finger as it presses straight down into the clay.

Figure 12-21
Opening with the middle finger gives added depth, useful for throwing a large pot.

Figure 12-22
Whether he uses one finger, two fingers, or his thumb, Murphy makes sure that the tip presses straight down the clay mass toward the wheel shaft.

Figure 12-23
He carefully moves the index finger across the bottom of the opened clay, about ½ inch above the wheel head, to form the base of a cylinder.

Figure 12-24
The cross-section shows the position of his index finger inside the pot as he completes the bottom.

hands opposite each other on the inside and out-side walls of the low, opened cylinder. It is the even pressure you exert on the clay between your fingers that makes the walls rise (12-25 to 12-33). If you place your hands so that they force less clay to pass between them than the thickness of the opened walls, the extra clay will respond by moving, and it has nowhere to go but up.

Remember that the opened clay is revolving on the wheel and that it is being subjected to a centrifugal force that tends to make its walls flare out. To counteract that thrust and make the walls grow straight up, press your hands slightly inward. Visualize a line that goes up the shaft of the wheel and straight up through your clay; then lightly move the walls in toward it.

While you are counteracting the centrifugal force, it is a good idea to counteract any desire you may feel to start making a pot. Continue practicing with the cylinder even longer than you think is necessary. If you can throw the three basic types of cylinders (12-34), there is no shape you cannot throw, and as you become more proficient and begin to think about design, you can start with one of the cylinder forms and go on from there (12-35, 12-36). In this way, your pots

will be properly engineered before you even start to shape them and when you come to cut the pot off the wheel you will feel the satisfaction of having created a clean, fresh form.

SHAPING

Once you have mastered the basic cylinder shape, you can begin to think about throwing the pot of your dreams. An experienced potter, one who knows what technical problems he or she must contend with, can give attention to both the throwing of the cylinder and the shaping at the same time, but a beginner usually has to separate the two, dealing with them as two distinct processes.

A basic cylinder is rather like a painter's clean, stretched canvas waiting for the first brushstroke. Just as a painter uses a sketchbook to work out ideas or keep notes for possible paintings, so you can use yours to note possible forms as you see them. A rock, a tree trunk, a human figure, parts of machinery or even smokestacks—almost any form in nature or your daily surround-

Figure 12-25
He straightens the wall to a 90-degree angle in preparation for pulling it up into a cylinder.

Figure 12-26
Another cross-section shows the position of his finger while he straightens the walls.

Figure 12-27
In still another cross-section, Murphy demonstrates smoothing the bottom with a rib.

Figure 12-28
Picking up a bead of clay between two fingers is an easy way to learn the proper finger position and spacing for forming the walls.

Figure 12-29
He starts to pull up the walls with the knuckle of one hand on the outside and fingers of the other hand inside.

Figure 12-30
The clay is forced upward through the space between the fingers, causing the walls to rise as he pulls them up with the outside fingers holding a sponge.

Figure 12-31
This cross-section shows his finger position as he thins the walls. *You may use your knuckle on the outside, but fingertips are more sensitive.*

Figure 12-32
Always leave a little extra clay at the top, he advises. *Its weight helps to keep the cylinder centered and the extra clay provides you with material for a rim.*

Figure 12-33
A completed cylinder seen in cross-section. *Technical skill takes you this far,* says Murphy, *now the artist in you must take over to shape the cylinder.*

Figure 12-34
You can make almost any shape you wish from the three cylinders outlined with heavy lines.

Figure 12-35
Murphy smooths the walls with a rib. *Clay particles become separated as you throw, and pressure from your fingers or a rib will tighten them.*

Figure 12-36
Clean out excess water as you throw with a sponge attached to a long stick. This will keep the water from penetrating and weakening the clay.

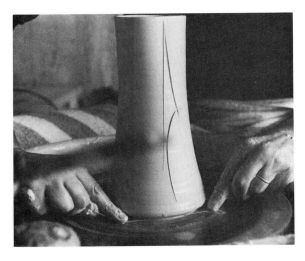

Figure 12-37
Eileen Lewenstein, England, holds a wire taut as she draws it under the base of her completed vase, cutting it from the wheel.

ings may suggest a pot form. Now your creativity comes into play.

And just as a painter or sculptor needs to stand back from the easel or sculpture stand occasionally to gain a new perspective, so you should move back from your pot on the wheel occasionally to see how it is progressing.

Keep the clay alive as you work and do not weaken it by adding too much water or by stretching it. Remember that clay loses its plasticity if it is overworked, so if your desired shape does not appear after a reasonable amount of time, discard that clay and start over with a fresh ball. Do not count on correcting a badly designed or clumsily thrown pot by trimming it later. When you have completed a good cylinder, remove it from the wheel with a wire (12-37) and set it aside until it is leather hard so you can practice trimming it.

MAKING A TEAPOT

Although making a teapot is a project beyond the skill of most beginners, it is shown here because it illustrates most of the skills a production potter needs. First, you must be able to develop the basic cylinder into a shape that will be both pleasing and functional. You must learn to balance the handle and the spout; the handle should be large enough to fit the hand but not so large as to be out of scale in relation to the spout. You must design a spout that pours well, attach it so that it stays bonded to the pot, and learn to make a lid that fits and doesn't fall in the cup when you pour. Learning to control the thickness of the walls is also important, for walls that are too thin don't have the insulating qualities that are characteristic of a ceramic teapot, and walls that are too thick will make the pot too heavy to lift comfortably. Finally, you must learn to trim the finished piece. When you are able to deal with these considerations satisfactorily, you are ready to make just about anything.

Trimming

The shape of your pot will be fresher if it grows organically from the action of your hands on the clay as it spins on the wheel, rather than if you depend on a great deal of trimming to reshape it. But trimming is useful to refine your good pieces, to thin areas that are too thick, and to give sharp definition to an edge. For these purposes, it is an important skill to learn. There are two examples of trimmings in this chapter: trimming a teapot and lid are illustrated (12-38 to 12-41) and, on pages 267–269 Catherine Hiersoux demonstrates trimming a plate (12-70 and 12-72).

Working Off the Hump

Although throwing off the hump is not an essential skill, it is a good technique to learn, especially if you want to throw a series of similar pieces quickly. It saves time, because instead of wedging and centering new lumps for each piece, you merely center the top section of the hump, throw the piece, cut it off, and continue throwing (12-42 to 12-45). Also, some potters feel that it is best to throw a teapot, spout, and lid from the same piece of wedged clay. Whether or not there is an actual physical advantage to this method, they find it satisfying to make all the parts from the same cohesive lump of clay.

Figure 12-38
Murphy measures a teapot rim using **calipers** in order to make a lid to fit.

Figure 12-39
Once the teapot and lid are leather hard, he places the lid in the opening of the teapot to keep it in place while trimming it.

Figure 12-40
With a chuck holding the teapot steady upside-down on the wheel, he holds a metal jar lid on its base to distribute the pressure of his fingers while he trims.

Figure 12-41
As he trims, he judges the thickness of the bottom by tapping it. Experience tells him by the sound when it is just right.

Figure 12-42
Here the centered clay is ready for throwing the lid and spout off the hump. *Throwing off the hump saves time, because you only need to center the top of the clay each time.*

Figure 12-43
By opening a small cylinder on the upside-down lid, he makes an extension to hold the lid secure in the teapot while pouring.

Figure 12-44
He checks the measurement with calipers to be sure it will fit.

Figure 12-45
After he finishes the lid, he removes it with a wire and sets it aside to stiffen.

Figure 12-46
Collaring in the spout, he shapes it with a metal rib.

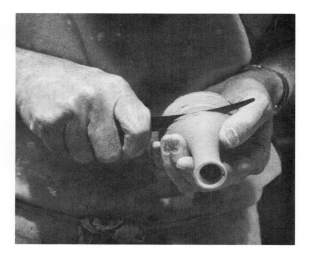

Figure 12-47
Slicing the spout to fit the curve of the teapot, he uses a curved **fettling knife.**

Spouts and Handles

The form of a spout or handle can affect the whole appearance of a coffeepot or teapot. A spout can be elegant and formal (3-14), simple and functional (12-55), or perky and cheerful. A handle may be purely decorative (6-18), or it may be both functional and beautiful. It can even be pretentious or suggest parts of the body (8-7, 12-83). Not only does the design of the spout or handle affect the appearance of a pot, but the skill, or lack of it, with which either spout or handle is shaped can make pouring a liquid from a teapot or jug either a satisfying or a frustrating experience.

A thrown spout (12-46) or any other part that is thrown separately and attached to another shape, will twist slightly as it is fired. With the spout attached firmly at one end, the free, or pouring end, will make about a 10 to 15 degree turn in the firing. So if you want your pot to pour tea directly into the cup instead of onto the tablecloth, you must take this into consideration. You will have to learn by trial and error the proper angle at which to cut the lip of a spout in order to counteract the twist.

Of course, it is essential to attach the spout and handle firmly to a teapot (12-47 to 12-50). Nothing could be more embarrassing to a potter than having a handle fall off a pot as the liquid is

Figure 12-48
He scores the teapot and the end of the spout before painting it with slip and joining them.

Figure 12-49
An old pen nib makes an excellent tool for cutting strainer holes in the wall of the teapot where the spout will fit.

Figure 12-50
To compensate for the slight unwinding that will occur during firing, cut the end of the spout at an angle.

poured. When you attach a handle with slip, you must be sure that both leather-hard parts are ready to absorb the moisture of the slip, and that the scored clay on both parts blends together into a complete bond.

Graceful, pleasing handles that complete the design of a cup, teapot, or pitcher can become important accents, as can the spouts on pitchers. An appropriate handle can carry the eye down toward the base of a pot, completing the composition, and the negative space between the handle and body of the pot is as visually important as the handle itself. It takes thought and care to design a handle that will be both decorative and functional. How the handle fits the user's hand and fingers and whether it helps one tilt the pitcher or pot to a proper pouring angle are equally important considerations. On the other hand, if function is not important to you, a handle can be treated as part of a sculptural whole, and it may work in contrast or in countertension to the pot. Numerous artists use the shape of a teapot or other functional pottery as a springboard to the creation of sculptural vessels (11-35, 15-39, and Color plate 27).

Handles may be made by pulling, as illustrated (12-51 to 12-54), or by using an extruder as Carol Temkin did when she made the arching handle of her teapot (12-55).

Figure 12-51
To make a handle, attach the moist clay to the scored teapot with a small amount of water.

Figure 12-52
After attaching the handle, he pulls out the clay, using a wiping motion.

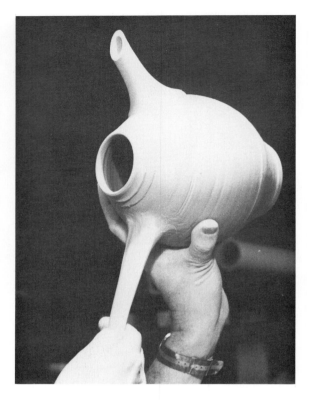

Figure 12-53
Gently stroking the handle, he brings it to the desired length and thickness.

Figure 12-54
With a final gesture that leaves his fingerprint in the clay, Murphy completes the teapot, attaching the handle at the bottom.

Pitcher Lips

Making an attractive and functional pouring lip on a pitcher is another skill you must learn if you wish to make a wide range of domestic ware. Once you have shaped the body of the pitcher—whether it is a delicate porcelain creamer or a robust stoneware jug that evokes images of warm milk right from the cow—you will want to make a lip that says "pour me." Most beginners are so delighted when they produce a nice round rim that they cannot bear to change its line with a lip; as a result, they make timid little indentations that would hardly pour satisfying streams of water, wine, or milk. You must learn to be bold about lips and to expect to spoil a good many before you can develop a personal signature that gives character to a pitcher's rim (12-56, 12-57).

Figure 12-55
Teapot, Carol Temkin, U.S.A. Details of spout and handle can totally change the personality of a teapot—a self-assured handle and no-nonsense spout give this thirty-six-ounce porcelain teapot a friendly look. Porcelain; turquoise satin-matt magnesia glaze; oxidation, cone 10. *Courtesy the artist. Photo: Robert Arruda.*

Figure 12-56
With a bold motion of his finger and thumb, Murphy presses the lip into shape to form a functional and attractive pitcher spout.

▶ *Figure 12-57*
Michael Casson, England, threw his jug with sensitive fingers, imbuing it with life. He rewords a comment by composer Igor Stravinsky: *Don't despise the fingers; they can release the imagination.* Casson dipped the jug in blue slip and wiped it very quickly with his fingers and a sponge, creating a decoration that emphasizes its curves. Stoneware; salt glazed, wood fired, cone 10. Ht. 17 in. (43 cm). *Courtesy the artist. Photo: John Coles.*

MAKING DOMESTIC WARE

After you have learned to make a basic cylinder, you can begin to think about designing pottery to use in your home—cups, teapots, coffeepots, casseroles, or any of the many useful objects you can make out of clay. Making domestic ware calls on all your skills, presents you with aesthetic decisions to make, and challenges you to learn about using color, texture, and glazes as well as about firing a kiln. The term *production potter* usually refers to a potter who makes a full range of domestic ware and often what is generally called studio pottery as well. This second term covers vases, bowls, and any other pieces that are made "one off," more for display than for everyday use. The production potter/studio potter may work alone in a studio (12-58, 12-59), may work with one or two colleagues or helpers, or may set up a large workshop that employs several people.

Production potters must deal with numerous problems beyond those posed by the clay, glaze, and fire. Of course, they must be capable of making domestic ware of a high standard, but in addition they also face the considerations of marketing, building up a clientele, producing items to order, repeating these items to a certain standard, formulating glazes, procuring materials, living on an uncertain income, constructing kilns, maintaining a studio, managing the business, controlling overhead, and paying taxes. At the same time, they must continue to grow as artists, improving their forms and glazes and exploring new ones. It is a life with compensations, but if you are considering becoming a full-time potter, it is a good idea to become aware of all its aspects. Ceramics magazines frequently publish profiles of potters who have made this choice, and from reading these you can form a quite realistic idea of what might lie ahead. Or you may be able to talk with some production potters in your area to get a first-hand view of their lives.

Jiggering

Making use of a mold on the wheel to form a piece of pottery is an ancient process that is now

Figure 12-58
Ron Judd, U.S.A. An expert production potter can throw a series like this set of goblets, repeating size and form but leaving the subtle imprint of his fingers on his work, differentiating it from machine-made pottery.

called **jiggering**. In its simplest form, it consists of placing a bisque-fired or plaster mold on the wheel, pressing clay into it, and proceeding to form the walls against the mold as it turns, often using a curved template—pattern—to shape the inner curve. It is an ancient method: the Etruscans used it; and Romans used carved molds in which they produced the red relief-decorated Arrentine ware (2-28) that was exported all over Europe. Using the same basic method, assistants in Eric Norstad's workshop (12-60, 12-61) use molds

(a)

Figure 12-59
Janet Mansfield, Australia, works at her wheel, creating objects that give pleasure to those who hold and use them. Mansfield says, *I was first drawn to clay for practical reasons. I wanted to make things and I wanted these objects to be useful and add quality to every day living. Even more I needed to create a personal expression that had meaning, that I hoped would have integrity and could aspire to some beauty.* Courtesy the artist. Photo: Jutta Malnic.

(b)

Figure 12-60
(a) Brian Fallon, assistant in Eric Norstad's production pottery, measures the thrown, bottomless cylinder from which he will throw a large stoneware sink. In a traditional method called jiggering, he uses a mold in which to shape the sink. He first cuts out a circle from a slab to form the sink bottom then places it in a large plaster mold. He then cuts out a hole for the drain. **(b)** He places a cylinder upside down in the mold on a wheel, and removes the bat using a wire.

Figure 12-61
Fallon opens the cylinder, pressing it against the sides of the mold, shaping and smoothing it as the wheel turns. Here, he finishes the edge. With the use of the mold, he can throw a large sink in about fifteen minutes. The Romans used a variation of this method to make their decorated Arrentine ware (2-28).

to make domestic sinks. Large factories, however, employ machines that perform the process at great speed and produce identical dinnerware and other objects.

Throwing Plates

Throwing and finishing a plate on a wheel are demanding processes but rewarding ones to master (12-62 to 12-65). One of the most important requirements is confidence, and that is something that comes only with practice. It is best to try throwing plates only when you feel you have mastered the other basic skills on the wheel. In throwing plates, keeping the clay alive and fresh is vital, perhaps even more so than with other objects, because the flat bottom of a plate is subject to so many stresses and strains as it is formed, dried, and fired.

Assured and practiced hands are doubly important in throwing plates because you cannot go back and make corrections. For this reason, it is a good idea to have the form of the plate in mind before you start and to think ahead to the motions and actions you will have to perform to make it. Design considerations include the relationship of the curve of the plate to the base, the design of the rim and foot in relation to the whole, as well as the design of the rim detail. You might, for example, want a rim that has precise tooling on it to create a frame around the plate, or you might prefer to leave it neutral, rather like an unframed canvas. If, while you design the plate, you also keep in mind the type of decoration you intend to use on it, your final product will be better integrated. But, like everything else in ceramics, your plates may not always come out as you planned. Catherine Hiersoux says that sometimes

the elegance I want makes it difficult for the plate to hold up through a firing. Working with clay you have to be flexible, and this applies equally to plates. You may prethink what you are going to do, but along the way if it is starting to take on another look, you have to be ready to change your ideas and go with whatever is happening.

Throwing a plate entails using the basic wheel skills, but there are also special factors to take into account. For example, you must be sure to compress the clay thoroughly in the horizontal area of the plate; otherwise it may warp or crack on drying or firing. Another area that requires special care is the curve between the base and the sides. It is important to maintain a smooth, concave curve, and as you pull out the walls at the side, you should gradually decrease their thickness. However, take care that they do not become too thin or too extended, or they may crack or collapse (12-66 to 12-69).

Figure 12-62
Catherine Hiersoux, U.S.A., centers a fifteen-pound lump of clay. As she brings it down, she takes care not to trap air under the extended edge.

Figure 12-63
Using her forearm with a tight fist for added force, she flattens the clay. This also helps her avoid muscle cramps.

Figure 12-64
Once the clay is flat, she starts to open it, using both hands.

Figure 12-65
She begins to pull up the sides, with the clay opened as far out to the edge as possible but still supported by the bat.

Figure 12-66

It is extremely important at this point to compress the clay with a wooden or hard rubber rib for strength and to prevent cracks. Because the flat area can't take a lot of handling, Hiersoux prefers to finish the bottom completely before thinning the walls.

Figure 12-67

Now Hiersoux can begin to work on the walls before extending them to develop the form of the large plate.

Figure 12-68

She gradually decreases the thickness of the walls, paying attention to the visual impact of the curve and maintaining its profile while supporting the rim with one hand as she works.

Figure 12-69

She makes sure she maintains the curve as she gives the rim its finishing touches.

Hiersoux throws her plates on a plaster bat that fits the size of her planned plate. She prefers a plaster bat to a wooden bat, because plaster helps the base to dry by absorbing moisture and because the plate will lift right off without the use of a wire. She has found that removing one of her plates with a wire can increase the chances of the porcelain warping or distorting.

Drying and Trimming Plates

Drying a plate can be tricky. It must dry from the inside outward, but in the process the curve and rim must not dry too quickly. For this reason, depending on how humid or dry your studio atmosphere is, you may need to wrap the rim. Hiersoux dries a plate like the one illustrated for

Figure 12-70
With a leather-hard plate centered on the wheel,
Hiersoux starts to trim the bottom, removing the
excess clay and forming the foot.

Figure 12-71
Tapping the bottom to be sure it is not becoming too
thin, she completes the double foot needed to support
the plate's diameter.

Figure 12-72
Hiersoux finds that old bleach bottles cut into a
variety of profiles work well for finishing her
porcelain plates.

about an hour right-side-up until it is stiff; then
she removes it from the bat and turns it upside-
down to continue drying. Once the base is leather
hard, she will trim it, turn it right-side-up again,
and let it finish drying.

Trimming is especially important in the base
area, because that is where the weight is (12-70 to
12-72). An excessively thick base not only makes

a plate heavy but also it is visually clumsy. On the
other hand, if the base becomes too thin, it will
warp. According to Hiersoux,

> *It is largely a matter of trial and error and feel. I
> have done enough plates, so I know. You can keep
> taking it off the wheel to test the thickness, but if
> you do that, the extra handling makes it more likely
> to warp. Tapping it to see how it sounds will help
> you know if it is getting too thin, and if you begin
> to feel a vibration as you trim, then the next cut
> may be too much.*

The placement of the foot determines the size
of the ring of clay she will attach. The best size
to choose is related to the curve of the sides; the
greater the curve, the narrower the foot can be.
Says Hiersoux,

> *On a large plate like this, I use a double foot. I
> make the middle ring slightly lower than the outer,
> because when the plate is turned right side up, the
> base will sink a little, and the inner ring will get
> lower.*

Hiersoux says she used to make and bisque
fire her plates; then she would look at the blank,
bisqued plates and decide on the decoration. She
says,

Figure 12-73
Using a mallet made from a four-by-four covered with an old sock, David MacDonald, U.S.A., pounds the clay mound flat, then opens the mass using the tip of the mallet. *Courtesy the artist.*

Now I have the decoration in mind before I start to throw. That way, I can do things in the throwing that will make the decorating easier.

David MacDonald uses a different method to open his large plates (12-73, 12-74). He first centers the clay, then uses a mallet to hammer out the sides, roughly opening the mass. From this rough opening, he goes on to pull up the sides, level them out, form the curve, compress the bottom, and complete the plate before he decorates it with carving, slip trailing, or glaze (15-4 and 15-13).

Figure 12-74
He opens the mound wider before starting to flatten out the plate. Until the plate is completely opened, he uses no water. After it is opened, he continues spreading and flattening it to create one of his large carved or slip-decorated plates (15-13). *Courtesy the artist.*

ALTERED WHEEL-THROWN FORMS

Basic wheel-thrown shapes luted together, altered, or combined with other components made from slabs, coils or with the extruder can bring new and unexpected relationships of volume and profile to vessels. English potter Walter Keeler, who has moved back and forth between making useful pots and making nonfunctional ones, says,

The idea of assembling components was particularly rewarding, and has led on to many of my current

forms. Function, though, has remained a vital catalyst for me in creating new pots. I like my pots to be animated and if possible a little impatient. I am pleased if they make people smile (12-75).

When you stop to think about it, whenever you pinch a lip into a pitcher rim, you are altering a wheel-thrown vessel. Until comparatively recently, most altered vessels stayed within the general category of containers even if, like Palissy's plates (6-15), they were unlikely to be used for anything but display. Hans Coper, for instance (8-6), who altered and recombined wheel-thrown

Figure 12-76
Catherine Hiersoux, U.S.A. Translucent and delicate, Hiersoux's thrown and altered porcelain bowl is in the tradition of precious display ceramics. Porcelain. Diameter 17 in. (43 cm). *Courtesy the artist. Photo: Richard Sargent.*

Figure 12-75
Angular Teapot. Walter Keeler, England, threw his teapot upside-down, added a slab base, struck the pot and spout with a metal file to make the score lines, extruded a handle, and assembled the parts when leather hard. Keeler has a collection of tinware utensils that influenced his choice of forms. Stoneware, cone 10; oxides and stains mixed with engobe, salt glazed. Ht. 8 in. (20 cm). *Courtesy the Aberysthwyth Arts Center and the artist. Photo: Keith Morris.*

forms, made vessels that *could* contain, although his work is usually treasured for its appearance rather than its usefulness. Many other ceramists continue this tradition of maintaining the basic vessel form while altering it enough to impose on it a new quality or individual style (12-76, and Color plate 36).

Pablo Picasso, however, working with potter Georges Ramié (8-7), was not interested in making containers, so when he constructed images out of wheel-thrown components, they emerged as sculptures that did not serve the traditional functions of pottery. Starting in the 1950s, such artists as Lucio Fontana (8-10), Peter Voulkos (8-11), and

Carlo Zauli (8-14), among many others, altered, deformed, combined, slashed, crushed, and paddled their pots, transforming them from containers into nonfunctional objects. This move toward the sculptural on the part of many ceramists not only altered the appearance of the pots but altered the directions taken by ceramics in the last two or three decades.

William Daley (9-3), who has dedicated his life to making vessels from clay, has this to say about his use of the sculptural vessel form:

> *For me the expressive quality of a vessel is of first importance. . . . The function of a vessel need not be specific. Work created to be held, touched, and seen is valid to the degree that a person responds to its form. Its presence is the vessel's reason for being.*

Robert Turner (9-1) alters his vessels with just a few—but such telling—gestures that transform a pot into an expression of our relationship to the universe. This approach, in which the container becomes an expressive object created to be seen, held, or touched rather than to be used for a containing function, led to a continuing debate about whether the resulting creations were pot-

Figure 12-77
Eye Pot, Minako Dohkan, Japan, adds colored glass cut-outs to a "functional" teapot form, thereby making its use highly unlikely. Porcelain with low-fire glazes. *Courtesy the artist.*

tery or sculpture, art or craft, and where they should "fit" in ceramics (12-77). Purists have continued to see the true function of ceramics as providing either useful domestic containers or beautiful ones for display. Probably more has been written about this than about any other subject in contemporary ceramics. Categories aside, there would seem to be room for all—art, craft, sculpture, pottery—on this earth in whatever combination the imagination may place them. If, however, you are interested in seeing just how much emotion this controversy has stirred up, the back copies of ceramic magazines and some of the books listed in "Further Reading" will provide you with plenty of reading material.

COMPOSITE POTS

What do you do if you want to throw a pot that is taller than your arms? Eileen Murphy, who is not very tall and whose arms are short, has this problem. It is impossible for her to reach in to throw as large a pot as she wants, so she solves the problem by throwing a series of rings on the wheel and then luting the sections together. In this way it is possible to combine several wheel-thrown sections in order to make a form that is larger than you can make on the wheel, or to build up a large jar with coils while using a revolving wheel to help you smooth the walls. There is nothing new about combining forms or methods. Traditional potters frequently made pots in sections; many of the jugs that were the mainstay of a medieval European potter's livelihood were made in two parts, and in his "how-to" book published in 1556, Italian potter Piccolpasso explained both how to attach separately thrown forms while they were damp and how to "glue" parts after the bisque firing by using glaze that would melt and fuse the parts together in the second firing. One method of making the large pieces that are traditional on Crete, quite probably used since the days of the Minoan potters (2-4), has been given a modern touch by Paul Chaleff, who built up and smoothed his six-foot-high jars outside his studio using coils and an electric wheel (12-78,12-79). Catherine Hiersoux makes all the sections of her tall jars on the wheel and then lutes them together with slip before firing (12-80,12-81). Other potters alter and combine in a variety of ways, even creating double vessels that can be taken apart and displayed separately (12-82).

POSTFIRING CONSTRUCTION

The trend toward constructed objects built up of a number of parts has been speeded by the development of modern adhesives. At one time, constructing after firing would have been considered "cheating" in most ceramics circles, but now, whether they want to combine wheel forms into a vase that suggests a human figure (12-83), or attach the components of a wall piece to a plywood

◀ *Figure 12-78*
Paul Chaleff, U.S.A., uses coils to construct jars that are more than six feet in height. He works outside his studio, using an electric wheel to turn the jar as he builds. *Courtesy the artist.*

▼ *Figure 12-79*
The wheel rotates the jar as Chaleff smooths the walls. His wheel and coil method is a modernization of traditional techniques used around the Mediterranean and in Korea and Japan. Chaleff says that he tries *to preserve that respect for history throughout my work in concept, process and in form. Courtesy the artist.*

(a)

(b)

Figure 12-80
(a) Catherine Hiersoux, U.S.A., makes a large jar in sections. She prepares to add the second leather-hard section. Note the flange on the inside, made to fit securely over the scored and slip-painted lower section. **(b)** She lowers the upper section, still attached to its bat, onto the lower section.

◀ *Figure 12-81*
After melding the joint with her thumb and cleaning off the excess slip, Hiersoux uses a rib to smooth and shape the tall jar. The third section will provide the neck and lip.

Figure 12-82

Barbara Reisinger, Austria, made this double vessel from one plate and one bowl, cut and assembled. *My double vessels,* Reisinger says, *can be put together or used one by one. While watching you can associate them with planets, their circles or moonways.* This one was fired upside-down in a gas kiln in reduction at 2300°F/ 1260°C. Porcelain. Ht. 4 in. (11 cm). Diameter 12 in. (30 cm). *Courtesy the artist.*

Figure 12-83

Composite pot with wheel-thrown and coiled sections by Jamie Walker, U.S.A. Walker says that while traveling in Mediterranean countries he made sketches for pots, but it was not until he was back in his studio working on them that he realized that his inspirations were the "earth mother" types he had seen on his travels. Porcelain; slip glaze with glass from Kügler rods. Ht. 26 in. (66 cm). *Courtesy Dorothy Weiss Gallery. Photo: Marshall Boman.*

base, contemporary ceramists use adhesives freely (see Appendix 4-C).

Now that the smoke has settled over the battlefields of the "clay revolution," you will probably not be as concerned with developing new techniques or methods, for so many have already been explored and perfected. This means that you are freed of many restraints and have available a wider range of methods or combination of methods with which to work than at any time in ceramics. But it is still of vital importance to master the basic skills so you can develop your *own* way of working. In looking at examples of wheel-thrown, altered, or combined forms, try to view them critically to determine which method would be most appropriate to your concept or with which you can best express your feeling. Then adapt and use that one in your own way as honestly as you can.

13
Working with Molds

*With clay you can make
all of the incredible
wondrous things that you
can imagine.*

——Clayton Bailey, U.S.A.

For several thousand years, potters and sculptors have been making wondrous things with clay in molds. Archaeologists have found mold-formed clay figures at ancient temple sites—replicas of gods and goddesses made for pilgrims to give as offerings—some of which date from about 2000 B.C. They have also found some of the clay molds in which the figures were made. And ever since Greek and Roman potters formed pots and small sculptures using molds, molds have also been continuously used in ceramics factories to mass-produce a variety of objects such as dinnerware, decorative figurines, plumbing fixtures, and insulators.

Thus, like so many contemporary ceramics processes, the technique of pressing, pounding, or pouring clay into a mold is an ancient one. What *is* new is that using molds to create images is no longer considered a mass-production method alone. Contemporary ceramics artists now regularly use molds to assist them in making one-of-a-kind vessels or sculptures (see right) as well as using them in a more traditional manner to make tiles and other types of modules.

Flesh and Bones, Deborah Horrell, U.S.A. Kohler porcelain, acrylic, graphite, 72 × 53 × 60 in. (183 × 135 × 152 cm). *Courtesy the Kohler Collection and Wila Gardiner Gallery. Photo: P. Richard Eells.*

HUMP MOLDS

The first mold may have been a rounded stone over which someone pressed clay to make a simple container. Called a **hump mold,** such a mold can be made of any material over which you can drape or press clay. Many objects—a rounded rock from a riverbed, an inflated plastic bag, a balloon, a bag of sand or vermiculite, a polystyrene form, a cardboard shape, or a specially made plaster or terra-cotta hump mold—will allow you to support the clay as it stiffens and takes on the shape of the mold. Low-fire clay and plaster are, however, particularly useful as mold materials, because their porosity allows them to absorb moisture from the clay, causing it to stiffen quickly (13-1).

You can place the clay over a hump mold in the form of slabs, wads, or coils, patting it on with your hand, paddling it, or scraping to make it smooth. Whatever method you use to apply the clay, by working on a hump mold you can easily make a wide-mouthed form (13-2), as long as the mold is not shaped to curve inwards, causing an **undercut.** If the mold did curve in, the stiffened clay would be tightly held around the inward-curving area, like a clasped fist, and the formed clay would have to be cut in order to be released from the mold.

It is also necessary to watch the clay carefully as it stiffens on a hump mold and to remove it before it dries too much because if the clay shrinks while on the rigid hump mold, it cannot contract against the mold, and the result will be cracks or even breaks in the walls.

Hump molds can be used in a variety of ways—for example, to support the wide, flaring form of a bowl that might be difficult to keep from collapsing while being handbuilt right side up (13-3). Clay coils can be stiffened over a mold, creating a vessel with coil patterns (13-4), or they can be formed over a large mold and scraped smooth (13-5). There is sometimes little to differentiate hump molds and the type of sculpture supports illustrated in chapter 11. William Daley, for example, uses polystyrene foam or cardboard shapes (fabricated with a glue gun) to support the clay as he shapes his vessels either in or over the forms (9-3); in effect, he is using both hump and press molds.

Figure 13-1
Ernst Häusermann, Switzerland, shapes a bowl on a porous, bisque-fired hump mold. As the mold absorbs moisture from the clay, the bowl will stiffen enough to be removed. Notice that the mold does not curve inward, for that would cause an undercut that would make it impossible to lift the stiffened bowl off the mold. *Courtesy the artist.*

Figure 13-2
Slapping the stoneware clay, Häusermann thins the walls, at the same time extending them farther down the mold. Once he has thinned the walls, he will attach the foot; then, when the clay has stiffened enough, he will be able to remove the bowl and finish the shaping process. *Courtesy the artist.*

Figure 13-3
Here is one of a series of Häusermann's hump-molded bowls. Altered and fired in oxidation in an electric kiln, the bowl is partially coated with a glaze made from beechwood ash from his wood stove. He also adds local earth materials to the clay to give it a rich, roughened surface. Ht. 9½ in. (24 cm). L. 21 in. (53 cm). *Courtesy the artist.*

Figure 13-4
Moira Mathew, England, constructs her bowls (11-24) over plaster hump molds. She allows the coiled construction to remain visible as an important feature of the completed design. Earthenware. *Courtesy the artist. Photo: Peter Allan.*

Figure 13-5
Graham Marks, U.S.A., uses coils to build his sculpture upside-down over polystyrene foam hump molds. He melds the coils together by scraping the surface. *Courtesy Helen Drutt Gallery.*

Figure 13-6
Gunhild Aberg, pressing a slab into a plaster mold, uses a smooth, rounded stone to pound the clay gently into the one-part mold. *Photo: Mogens S. Koch.*

Figure 13-7
Carlo Zauli, Italy, frequently uses press molds made from plaster to build sections of his sculpture. This small press-molded section shows the network of clay supports that give added support to the section without too much added weight.

PRESS MOLDS

A press mold does not have to be elaborate; you can use a kitchen mixing bowl lined with a piece of plastic wrap or cloth or even a milk carton or cardboard box, and press slabs, wads, or coils of clay into it.

Plaster Press Molds

A press mold made from plaster is, however, especially convenient, because it draws the moisture out of the clay, and with proper care the stiffened clay can be removed from it in one piece (13-6). Using a plaster mold also has the advantage of allowing you to reproduce your own original (13-32), as Carlo Zauli frequently does for sections of his wall reliefs. Christina Bertoni, on the other hand, makes a pinched bowl and casts it in plaster, replicating its exterior fingerprinted texture. She then presses clay into the mold with her fingers and in this way creates bowls that carry the impressions of her fingers on both the inside and outside (9-6). Eileen Lewenstein in England (15-15) and Patrick Loughran (Color plate 20) also use press molds to form their plates. Another advantage of a plaster or bisque fired mold is that you can reuse it if you store it in a dry place. A plaster mold used as a press or hump mold can last for hundreds of reproductions, so you can make many copies from the mold and then alter the copies, creating one-of-a kind pieces from the same mold. Slip molds do not last as long because the sodium silicate and soda ash in the slip accelerate the deterioration of the plaster.

To make a one-part press mold you must choose an object to cast that has no undercutting—for example, the simple mold into which Gunhild Aberg pounds clay with a stone will pose no problem in removing the stiffened clay cast (13-6). Pressing clay into this type of mold will result in a simple, open, concave form. To create a closed, hollow form you could make two concave press molds, press clay into each part, let it stiffen, and then remove it and join the two clay sections while they are damp. Many of the face pots from Moche were made in this way (5-11).

Press molds can be used for more complex projects. Robert Arneson, for example, forms much of his sculpture in plaster molds into which terra-cotta clay is pressed to form one-half of a portrait head; then both parts are joined. Carlo Zauli often uses plaster or wooden molds to make large wall reliefs, pressing clay into them and then firing the sections separately to be assembled later. He builds a network of supports into the sections while the clay is being pressed into the mold in order to strengthen the piece without adding too much weight (13-7,13-32). Then, after the clay is removed from the mold, he can work on the still-damp outer surface, tooling it to refine it as he wishes.

ALTERING MULTIPLES

Some of the advantages of working with press molds are the facts that one can make hollow forms so easily and can work back into the damp sections when they come out of the mold. By adding clay, by carving or tooling the surface, or by altering the vessel or sculpture's shape, you can use a press-molded form as the basis from which to develop a wholly new work. You can also combine a group of mold-formed sections from your collection of hump or press molds, combining them into new, composite pieces.

MAKING PLASTER MOLDS

If you have not used plaster before, you will find it a fascinating and versatile material. The type of plaster used for molds is plaster of Paris, made from one of a group of gypsum cements, essentially calcium sulfate, a white powder that forms a viscous solution when mixed with water and hardens into a solid mass. For the mold used in the demonstration, John Toki used Pottery Plaster #1.

There are a few cautions to note before you begin to work with plaster. Although not hazardous, as is clay dust, it can be irritating to your respiratory system if breathed, so be careful when you use it in the dry form. Never pour plaster

down a sink! Your plumbing will be totally blocked if you do, because plaster sets up into a solid mass that cannot be washed out of the pipes.

Store plaster of Paris in the bag in a dry place, preferably on wooden slats that let air circulate around the bag, for if it becomes damp in the bag the plaster will be useless when you come to use it.

It is possible to smear an object (with no undercutting) very lightly with oil or soap, pour a couple of inches of plaster in a cardboard box, place the original on this layer, pour more plaster around the original up to but not over its top, and end up with a one-part mold that will work reasonably well for a few casts. If, however, you follow the directions provided by John Toki, who has made molds professionally, you will learn how to make an even-walled mold that can be used for slip casting as well as for press molding. A slip mold made of pottery plaster will last for at least twice as many casts as one made of ordinary casting plaster. Slip molds do not last as long as press molds, because the sodium silicate and soda ash in the slip are absorbed into the plaster and accelerate its deterioration. In industry, where the highest quality casting and high-speed production is called for, a plaster slip mold is used only between 50 to 150 times owing to the need for perfect replicas and the established production schedule per eight-hour working shift. But a studio potter could probably use such a mold for a couple of hundred casts. Once you have learned how to make a good one-part plaster mold, you will have mastered the basics of mold making. To go on to make more complex molds, we suggest you study one of the specialized books listed in "Further Reading."

Making a Mold for Slip Casting

To make a demonstration one-part mold, John Toki chose a simple stoneware bowl with no undercutting or details. When you choose or make the original from which you will make a mold for slip casting, remember that your final cast will turn out to be considerably smaller than the original as a result of shrinkage during drying and firing. One of the refinements to learn in making a mold for slip casting is the slip reservoir.

Figure 13-8
In preparation for making a mold from a bowl, soaping the original to make it release easily from the plaster mold is essential. Any soap bubbles should be carefully brushed out. The clay reservoir mass has already been formed at the base of the bowl, and both are set on a plywood base.

The purpose of this reservoir is to form a chamber that will hold extra casting slip in order to create pressure on the slip in the mold during casting, thus ensuring that the slip will be pressed against the plaster walls, assuring the formation of even clay walls that replicate the mold exactly. This can be especially important in the casting of a thick slab. The reservoir is made by attaching an extra clay mass to the object from which you make the mold, forming it to follow the contour of the object. The reservoir and object to be cast must have a slope of at least one degree to make it possible to remove the mold.

After the clay for the reservoir has been shaped, the object should be set on a base. Plywood will do. Attach the object to the base with silicon glue or sticky clay to keep it from lifting as the plaster is poured around it. Next, soap the original to keep the plaster from sticking to it (13-8). The clay reservoir mass does not need to be soaped (if the original you are going to cast is made of damp clay, you do not need to soap that either), because you can remove it and wash the damp clay out of the mold. The best thing to use for soaping is a water-base mold soap, diluted two to one with water. The drawings in Figure 13-9

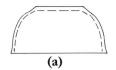
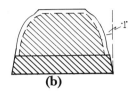
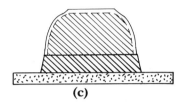
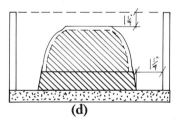

Figure 13-9
Drawings show steps in preparation for making a mold. **(a)** The empty bowl from which the mold will be made. **(b)** The bowl filled with clay, with the reservoir mass extending below it. This will make a chamber to hold extra slip that will exert pressure to produce an evenly walled cast. The reservoir must have a minimum slope of 1 degree in order to release the mold easily. **(c)** Soaped bowl and reservoir set upside-down on a plywood base. **(d)** Walls made from flexible linoleum, metal, clay, or plastic should be placed about 1 to 1¼ inches away from the original, and they should also extend high enough to allow for a solid plaster base of 1 to 1¼ inches. It is wise to seal any cracks with wads of clay where plaster might run out. The dimensions on the drawing are only those used for the mold shown in the accompanying photos.

show the preparations for making a mold. Surround the original and the reservoir with a wall made from linoleum, tar paper, sheet metal, clay, or plastic. For the demonstration, Toki used a strip of floor linoleum bent into a circle and secured with a mold-form clamp, but you could also use duct tape, a metal strip with a turn buckle, a strip of tire inner tube, or a large rubber band to secure the wall. The wall should be placed so that it is about 1 to 1¼ inches (2.5 to 3 cm) away from the original and extends to 1 to 1¼ inches above it. This spacing will create a plaster mold of optimum thickness. Thicker walls would not be any more absorbent, although if the mold is a large one, thicker walls *would* add to its structural strength. On the other hand, too-thin walls will become saturated with moisture too quickly and the casting slip will not set up. To be sure that the wet plaster does not leak out around the walls or at the seam, plug these areas with damp clay pressed firmly into the cracks. Before mixing and pouring the plaster, be sure to soap the walls and the plywood base to keep the plaster from sticking to them, using the same solution of soap you used on the original. Coat the walls first; then sponge the absorbent plywood with water and soap it as well.

Mixing Plaster With a Scale

Although it is possible to measure out and mix plaster by eye, it is more satisfactory to measure the ingredients with a scale. To do this, measure powder and the water in a ratio of 2½ to 2¾ pounds of plaster to 2 pounds water; that is 2 parts water to 2½ parts plaster by weight. This ratio is based on the water-absorbtion ability of the plaster. For the illustrated mold, Toki used:

2¾ pounds plaster
2 pounds water = 81 cubic inches of plaster

These measurements yielded a mold weighing 4 pounds, 12 ounces wet. If you want to make a larger mold, keep the same ratio of water to plaster when you measure the larger amounts.

Water temperature makes a difference in the setting-up time of plaster; cold water will set up at a slower rate than hot water. This setting-up was based on using water at about 72°F/22.2°C.

Learning just how long it will take to pour the plaster and how soon it will set up is a matter of experience. About 20 to 40 minutes is an average time, depending on the type of plaster used, the presence or absence of retardant, and the atmospheric conditions in the work area. It is possible to add **sodate retarder** to the plaster if you feel the mixture will set up too quickly for you to use it comfortably. This chemical slows the setting time; adding ¼ to 2 tablespoons of retardant can delay the setting-up time from 10 to 60 minutes. Vinegar also works as a retardant.

Use a pliable plastic bucket or basin for mixing plaster so that when the residue hardens you will be able to squeeze the bucket walls and shatter the plaster into fragments to remove it.

For precise control, measure the mixing time with a timer—a kitchen timer or a photographic lab clock will work. Using a timer will help you avoid overmixing, which can result in a plaster that is too dense, or undermixing, which can result in a mold with walls of unequal density. If different sections of a multi-part mold are unequal in density, they will absorb water unequally, possibly causing the slip-cast object to crack at the mold seam while it is still in the mold after the slip has been drained. Clearly, for a one-part or a press mold this factor is not as critical.

Measuring and Mixing Plaster Without a Scale

It is possible to measure plaster without a scale and mix it by hand, but this method is not as satisfactory as using a scale to measure the ingredients. It can work for making hump or press molds, but for slip casting it is important to weigh the plaster carefully and mix it with the right amount of water in order to produce consistency in the absorptive properties of the mold. If you have trouble making a satisfactory mold using the hand method, switch to the scale method.

Fill a pliable container about one-half full of water. This amount of water will yield about two-thirds of a bucket of mixed plaster. Instead of weighing the plaster, add it slowly by sifting it in handfuls into the water through your fingers until it mounds above the water line like a steep, mountainous island rising above the ocean. This pro-

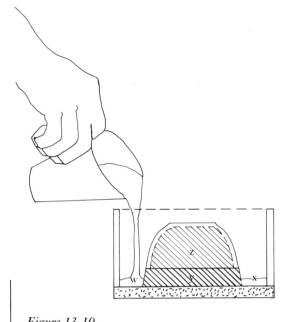

Figure 13-10
Pour plaster starting at the lowest point (*w* or *x*) around the reservoir (*y*). Let plaster rise up from the bottom up over the original (*z*).

cess, in which the plaster powder becomes chemically combined with the water, is called *slaking*. When the last bit of plaster that shows above the water line becomes moist, let the batch sit *untouched* for 2 minutes. This will help to eliminate air bubbles and to keep the mixture from setting up too quickly. After two minutes, begin mixing slowly with your hand submerged to avoid creating air bubbles in the plaster. Rocking the bucket gently on the floor will also help to make the air bubbles rise to the top. Continue mixing for 2 minutes; then pour.

To mix the same formula of plaster with an electric mixer, measure as above, add the plaster to the water, and when the last bit of plaster becomes moist, wait 2 minutes without touching it. Then mix with the mixer for 1 minute and pour.

Pouring Plaster

Pour the plaster carefully around the reservoir into the space between the original and the walls, always starting at the lowest point (13-10, 13-11). Let the plaster rise up and over the original to the top of the walls or to the point at which it will rise 1¼ inches (3 cm) above the bowl. Avoid splashing or dripping plaster on the original as you pour around it, because splashes

Figure 13-11
Roslyn Myers pours the plaster carefully into the space around the reservoir mass, taking care not to spatter or drip any onto the original.

or drips will cause hard spots in the mold that could create unequal density in the walls. If the walls of the mold are uneven in density, different parts of the mold will absorb water from the slip unequally, creating unequal walls in the final cast. Some casters stir the plaster with their fingers after pouring it into the mold to make the air bubbles rise to the top and disappear.

Before you try to remove the original from the mold, let the plaster stand for between 15 and 20 minutes, or until the mold begins to get hot (13-12). Removing the original from the mold before the plaster has set properly can damage the mold severely, possibly creating a distorted mold or causing cracks or fractures. Once the plaster starts to get hot, it has expanded to its farthest point and will separate more easily from the original. If the plaster has cooled down, a slight

Figure 13-12
Before removing the original, leave it and the completed mold untouched until the plaster starts to get hot—usually between twenty and forty minutes. With the clay reservoir removed, you can see the space for the extra slip in the mold above the rim of the bowl.

amount of moisture may develop between the plaster and object, causing the plaster to bond to the original through condensation suction. If this happens, the two should be easier to separate if you place the mold and the original in hot water.

SLIP CASTING

When you are ready to start casting with slip, you will have to decide whether to mix your own slip from the particular type of clay you wish to use or whether you will use commercial slips. For clay that will be used for handbuilding, it is important that the clay particles flock together, but for a clay to be used for slip casting, you will want the particles in the water to stay separate and in suspension. For this reason, casting slips contain **deflocculants.**

Deflocculants

A deflocculant, such as soda ash, sodium sil-icate, or Darvan #7, is added to slip to keep the

clay particles in suspension and to reduce the amount of water needed to make the slip. It is important to keep the proportion of water as low as you can in casting slip, because if it contains too much water the clay and fluxes will settle in the bottom of the container. But if you add too much deflocculant, you will get settling! It is not easy for a beginner to make successful casting slips, because the proportion of deflocculant added to the clay and water must be exact, and the type of clay used also makes a difference—for example, plastic clay that throws well does not work well for casting. Variations in the water quality can also affect the composition of the slip, and water evaporation can cause the slip's consistency to change. You should also remember that some water and deflocculant will have been drawn into the mold during casting, so if you pour the extra slip drained from the mold back into the container, you will change the proportion of water and deflocculant in the remaining slip. To compensate for this loss, you may add very small amounts of water plus a few drops of sodium silicate.

Since commercial slips are formulated to avoid most of these problems, we suggest you use them, at least at the start. In this way, you will learn the correct viscosity of slip. However, if you want to try making your own slip, there is a formula for a low-fire slip in appendix 1A.

The type of slip you will choose and its firing range depends on what it is that you plan to cast. For your first attempts at slip casting, Toki suggests you use low-fire slip because of its greater flexibility and the fact that warping problems are not as great with this type of slip as they might be with a high-fire slip.

Drying the Mold

After you have made the mold, dry it slowly in a warm atmosphere or place it near a heat source that will not rise above 120°F/48.8°C, because excessive heat may cause the mold to crack and deteriorate and thus lose its moisture-absorbing properties. Circulating heat is best. The mold must be thoroughly dry before you use it for slip casting, because it must absorb a considerable amount of water.

(a)

(b)

Pouring Slip

Before pouring the slip into the mold, stir it gently for a few minutes until it becomes fluid, then pour it. If you pour it without stirring it, the moisture may not be absorbed evenly into the plaster mold, and the slip may form weak or sagging walls. In addition, the extra slip can become too thick to drain easily from the mold.

Pour the slip into the mold carefully, trying not to spill any on the mold (13-13a). Soon after you have filled the mold, you will notice that some of the moisture from the slip is being drawn into the mold walls. As this happens, the level of slip in the mold will drop. At that point, top it off with more slip.

As more water is drawn from the slip into the mold, you will see clay walls begin to form around the edge. Wait until the walls reach the thickness appropriate to what you are casting— thin for a small porcelain bowl, thick for a large sculpture. Remember that the walls will become thinner when the water evaporates from them when they dry. Once the walls reach the desired thickness, pour out the extra slip into a bucket or basin (13-13b). Then, upend the mold over the basin, resting it on two wooden slats, and let the extra slip drain thoroughly out of the mold, usually for 5 to 20 minutes (13-13c).

(c)

Figure 13-13
(a) Myers pours colored porcelain slip into the mold, taking care not to splash the rim. When the slip level drops, she will top it off with more. **(b)** Once walls of the desired thickness have formed around the edge of the mold, Myers pours the extra slip out into a basin. **(c)** She up-ends the mold and places it over a basin to drain out the excess slip.

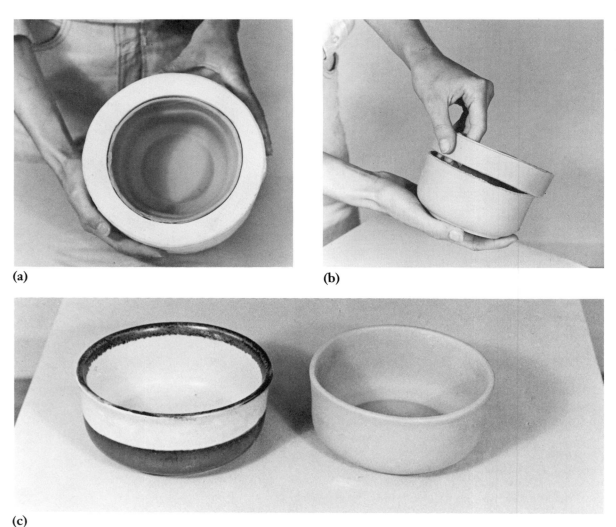

Figure 13-14

(a) As the porous plaster absorbs moisture from the clay, the slip-cast walls begin to pull away from the mold. **(b)** The porcelain cast bowl is removed from the mold, and Myers removes the extra clay of the reservoir mass from the cast. **(c)** The cast bowl is finished, with its rim smoothed, ready for firing. The difference in size between the original and the cast will become even greater when the cast bowl shrinks during drying and firing.

Wait a few minutes, and then reverse the mold and wait until the clay walls begin to pull away from the mold walls (13-14a). Blowing a little **compressed air** around the edge will speed the process. Remove the cast from the mold with care and carefully trim off the extra clay from the reservoir (13-14b). Now you have a replica of your original (13-14c). Note, however, that it is slightly smaller than the object from which you made the mold. It will become even smaller as it dries and when it is fired.

Using Slip Casting Creatively

Slip-casting techniques can be used to create many different types of ceramic objects (13-15 to 13-17 and 13-30, 13-31). In addition to those illus-

Figure 13-16
After assembling the cast sections into a sculpture, Caruso refines the forms, working on the leather-hard clay before firing the final version of *Homage to Tarquinia. Courtesy the artist.*

Figure 13-15
Nino Caruso, Italy, carved the original sections of his sculpture *Homage to Tarquinia* in polystyrene foam. Because there was undercutting on the originals, one-part molds would not have released, so Caruso made two-part molds. Note the registration knobs and sockets on the mold sections. *Courtesy the artist.*

▼ *Figure 13-17*
Heart Teapot: Sharpeville. Yixing Series. Richard Notkin, U.S.A., casts his stoneware Yixing teapots in plaster molds from clay originals that he carves with intricate surface details. Stoneware. 6 × 10⅞ × 5 in. (15 × 28 × 13 cm). *Courtesy the artist and Garth Clark Gallery, NY.*

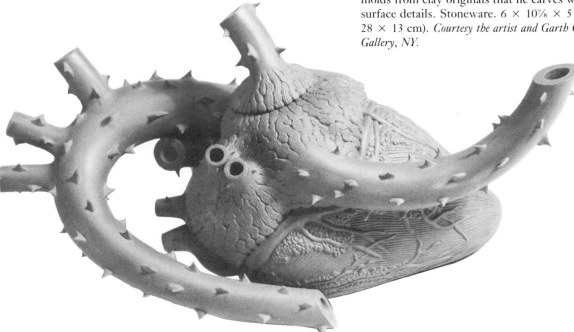

Figure 13-18
Clayton Bailey, U.S.A., made a mold from a real shark's head his son found on the beach. Using slip-casting techniques, he made multiple images of the shark's head, then he altered and individualized each one to create his *Pack of Landsharks* (13-30). Here, Bailey pours slip into the mold through a strainer.

trated in this chapter, look at the assembled sculpture by master mold maker Richard Shaw, for which he made molds from playing cards (8-21). Look also at the heads that Jack Earl and Glenys Barton (8-23 and 8-24), cast in white clay slip, examples of how different artists' concepts lead to totally different treatments. Jindra Viková makes thin slip-cast slabs from which she constructs her portrait heads, then enriches their surfaces with a variety of techniques (15-50, Color plate 22).

Richard Notkin (9-12), who makes molds from clay originals in order to cast his miniature sculptures, says,

> I use the mold as a tool to re-create often used images in a manner that is structurally viable and capable of being altered or combined with other forms. Thus, my growing mold library represents an expanding vocabulary of images, and I add new imagery as each new series of pieces dictates (13-17).

Molds are useful for making repeat components that can be altered to make individual pieces or assembled into grouped works. California artist Clayton Bailey recently made a one-part mold

Figure 13-19
Bailey explains the process of casting and altering the sharks' heads: *Lifting and removing the strainer from the mold after it is filled with slip. Strainer came from a flea market.*

Figure 13-20
After coating the edge of the stiffened cast with slip, Bailey reinforces it with a coil, explaining that *the finished piece will hang on a nail from this edge. The metal band and wooden wedged 'mold clamp' are from the Kohler Company.*

Figure 13-21
Bailey melds the reinforcing coil well into the cast.

Figure 13-22
Reaching through a hole in the ware board to change the contours of the casting.

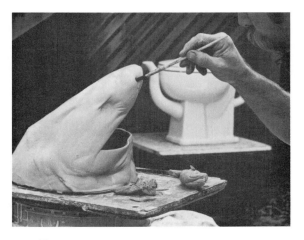

Figure 13-23
After carving holes for mouth and nostrils with a needle, or knife, the edges of the holes are softened with a wet brush and small sponge.

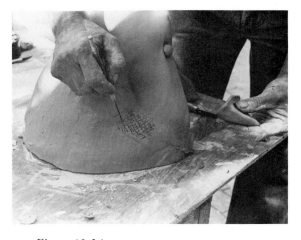

Figure 13-24
Bailey held the ear in place while he outlined the area he would score for attaching it to the head. He then painted some slip on the hatching before pressing the ear in place.

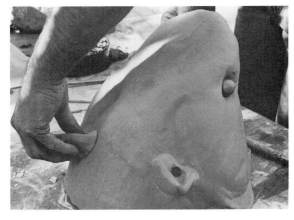

Figure 13-25
Bailey's shark with beady eyes and ears becomes a 'Ratfish.' *Making ears is like pulling handles,* Bailey says. *They have feathered edges so they will easily blend into the head.*

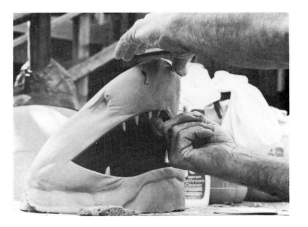

Figure 13-26
Lots of pointed teeth in both upper and lower jaws. They angle inward so it's harder for the victim to get away.

289

Figure 13-28
This shark is transformed into a 'landshark' by a 'skin graft' of lizard skin. Bailey painted the head with slip before applying the lizard skin surface, then *patted it down from the center outwards to drive out air bubbles. The teeth and ears have been made and are 'toughening up' in the air for a few minutes before attaching them.*

Figure 13-27
Bailey cast a slab of "landshark skin" by pouring a thin coat of slip onto a textured slab mold. *The texture of the mold was taken from a 'lizard skin' imprinted plastic purse. A very thin layer of slip is obtained by rocking the bat.*

Figure 13-29
Blending edge of 'lizard skin' into the shark head with a 'pegging tool' that is used by casters at the Kohler Company for sealing cracks in leather-hard ware.

from a real shark's head, then created a family of "landsharks" by altering each of the casts (13-18 to 13-30). In *Flesh and Bones*, a work that used many small cast components, Deborah Horrell cast the bones in Kohler Company porcelain clay and assembled and glued them together (13-31 and page 276) while working in the Arts/Industry Program at the Kohler Company, a program conceived and directed by Ruth Kohler.

Molds can also make it possible to cast a large architectural work in sections. The originals of Carlo Zauli's large wall reliefs are formed of clay, on either a wall or a long table; then a plaster mold reinforced with metal rods is made of the original solid relief. When the sections of the mold are removed from the original, they can be used as press molds, making it possible to make a large, but hollow and relatively light, wall relief (13-32).

Learning to make good molds in which to cast what you wish—from plates, cups, and sculptures to architectural details—will widen the range of what you can make with clay, offering you a wealth of new areas to explore. If you make the effort to learn how to make good molds, the only limit on what you can make with them will be your imagination.

Figure 13-30
A Pack of Landsharks, Clayton G. Bailey, U.S.A. Although all were cast from the same mold, each completed, glazed, and fired Landshark has an individual personality. Slip-cast, low-fire white clay, stain and glaze. Each shark 12 × 12 in. (30 cm × 30 cm). *Courtesy the artist and Joseph Chowning Gallery.*

Figure 13-31
Deborah Horrell, U.S.A., working at the Arts/ Industry program at the Kohler Company, where she cast and built her sculpture *Flesh and Bones*. The figure for Horrell's *Flesh and Bones* was cast in the large flat mold shown in the photo. Behind it, the nest of cast bones has been partially assembled, glued with epoxy over a polystyrene foam form. *Courtesy the artist and the Kohler Company Arts/Industry Program.*

Figure 13-32
Carlo Zauli contemplates a massive sectional plaster mold made over the clay original of one of his clay wall reliefs. After these mold sections have been removed, they will be used as press molds in which he will form the final relief. This will allow the sections to be made hollow, with a network of built-in supports (13-7), lessening the weight of the relief and making it easier to fire and install. *Courtesy the artist.*

14
Installations and Architectural Works

For the "new architecture" a new decoration must evolve to be the worthy corollary of its harmonies, a decoration limitless in organic fluency and plasticity, and in inherent capacity for the expression of thought, feeling and sentiment.

—Louis Sullivan, *Kindergarten Chats*, 1901

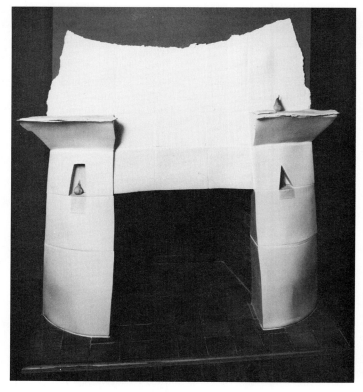

One of the fascinating things about clay is the way the material adapts itself to so many different styles of working and to so wide a range of sizes—from hand-sized fertility figures (1-2) and miniature teapots (9-12) to installations that fill a museum gallery (14-1), and architectural works that can bring "organic fluency and plasticity" to an architectural space (14-12 and Color plates 34, 35, 39, and 42).

Fireplace, Site IV, by Paula Winokur, U.S.A. is a functional, yet expressive, fireplace surround. (See also 14-16), Porcelain, Ht. 68 × W. 55 × 14 in. deep (1.7 m × 1.4 m × 35 cm). *Courtesy Helen Drutt Gallery. Photo: Will Brown.*

292

Figure 14-1
Wabi Sabi Special, by Nobuko Tsutsumi, Japan. Tsutsumi's work combines Japanese folk tale images and the traditional gate that leads into temple enclosures with Western images such as Botticelli's *Birth of Venus*. Tsutsumi poses the question of how Japanese culture will integrate these imported images with the concept of *wabi sabi*—the poetic philosophy surrounding the tea ceremony and its ceramics. Installation in Museum of Modern Arts, Hyogo, Japan. White stoneware, high- and low-fire glazes, china paint and luster. *Courtesy the artist. Photo: Takashi Hatakeyama.*

Historically, ceramists have used their skills to bring color and texture to architecture since the days when sun-dried building bricks were covered with glazed tiles that brought color to the walls and protected them from the weather (2-2) continuing to the present and including the works of late-nineteenth-century architect Louis Sullivan (see page 137), who sheathed his metal-framed buildings with curtain walls of ceramics and enhanced them with rich ornament.

Even during the early and middle decades of the twentieth century when the antiornament philosophy of the International Style was dominant and where a long tradition of using ceramics in architecture had existed, some individual clients and architects continued to call on ceramists to create works for plazas, hospitals, universities, subway stations, and private homes. Today, when more architects show a reawakened interest in ornament, many new opportunities are open for the ceramic artist working in the architectural field.

Creating large-scale sculpture appeals to many ceramists, and even when they have not received

Figure 14-2
Ceramic columns, by John Toki, U.S.A., temporarily installed in an urban plaza. The nearest one, entitled *Earthscape II*, was designed to fit into a landscaped area as if its organic forms grew naturally out of the ground. Following firing, each section of the column was reinforced in the interior with fiber glass and mounted over a steel frame. In a permanent installation, the concrete base would be eliminated. Brown stoneware and colored porcelains; clear glaze. Ht. 15 ft. × 32 in. × 38 in. (4.6 m × 81 cm × 96 cm). *Courtesy the artist. Photo: Scott McCue.*

Figure 14-3
Springwater Fountain, by Fin Lynggaard, Denmark. A fountain made up of brightly glazed, wheel-thrown parts from which the water drips onto a tiled area, giving vitality to a hotel lounge in Copenhagen. *Photo: Mogens S. Koch.*

a commission to create a work for a specific site, they may create large-scale installations for settings that range from temporary gallery exhibits (14-1), to a beach (11-61), to the top of a mountain (Color plate 32), a meadow (Color plate 29), a museum courtyard (Color plate 41), or a public plaza (14-2).

Since such large-scale projects present problems in construction, firing, and installation, if you are a beginner in ceramics you are unlikely to start out by constructing a large fountain (14-3), a tall sculpture for a school entrance (14-4), or a series of columns to brighten a waiting area in an airport (14-5). But because the use of ceramics in architecture is becoming increasingly popular, you should become aware of the possibilities it offers to the more experienced ceramist you may one day become.

SOURCES OF COMMISSIONS

How does the commission process work and how do artists get commissions?

Many countries and a number of American states now have what are known as "percent for art" laws that require them to set aside between ½ and 2 percent of the cost of any new public building to be spent on art. Commissions to create this type of work are usually awarded either by open competition or from the proposals presented by a group of selected artists, who may work in a variety of media. Elisabeth Langsch (14-5), for instance, frequently enters competitions as an in-

Figure 14-4
Eduardo Andaluz, Spain, uses red clay and blue glaze to bring color and warmth to the stark white of the school building for whose entrance it was commissioned. Andaluz says, *My shapes and techniques are conditioned by the dimensions and the architectural spaces.* In this space, the forms had to be simple to balance the elaborate architectural details. Andaluz did not have to worry about freezing and thawing damage to the sculpture in the warm Canary Islands. *Courtesy the artist.*

Figure 14-5
For her commissioned work in the Zürich airport, Elisabeth Langsch, Switzerland, decided that columns ending in organic forms would bring color and animation to the functional surroundings. In planning an architectural work, Langsch tries to anticipate the feelings of those who will use the space and to make their time there more pleasant. She once built a bench heated by a ceramic stove to provide cosy seating for the residents of an elderly people's home. Handmodeled reliefs on columns, colored engobes. Ht. 14 ft. (4.20 m). *Courtesy the artist.*

vited artist, competing for a commission with painters, metal sculptors, or fiber artists.

Corporations and private clients are another source, or a commission might come from the architect who is designing the building and who is familiar with a particular artist's work. Ideally, the ceramic artist would work with the architect from the very beginning to integrate ceramics into the building design. In reality, however, an architect generally does not call on an artist until a building is already planned.

If the commission is awarded before the building has been constructed, it is important for the architect and artist to consult well before building starts in order to agree on the structural changes that may be needed to accommodate the proposed art work. Placing a heavy ceramic work on a wall may mean that the wall will have to be reinforced with steel to support the load, or a free-standing work of sculpture may need a steel-rein-

forced concrete foundation poured as part of the floor, complete with mounting bolts. Since the artist usually bears the expense of installation, arranging for this engineering to be built in from the start will cost less than tearing down a wall or ripping up floors to install the supports later.

On the other hand, it often happens that once a building is finished, the owner will decide that a particular space will be enhanced by a work of art. In this case, the owner may approach an artist directly, through an art consultant whose job it is to find art for the client, or through an artists' representative or gallery that may have approached the owner as a possible purchaser of art.

Whatever method brings the commission and the artist together, carrying out an architectural commission requires an ability on the part of the artist to work with others—architect, engineer, and client. It also requires a flexibility that an artist accustomed to working alone in a studio may find either satisfying or impossible, depending on his or her personality.

BUILDING LARGE-SCALE WORKS

Most of the clay forming techniques demonstrated in earlier chapters can be adapted to large-scale works; the main difference is the difficulty or impossibility of building, firing, and transporting a large-scale work as a single piece. For this reason, a large work must usually be fabricated and fired in sections that will fit together to create the final composition. These smaller clay units can be fired more successfully and transported to the site more easily than single large pieces and can be more easily installed either temporarily or permanently. By using a variety of forming techniques—handforming and modeling, rolling out slabs, pressing clay into molds, or by working on the wheel—a ceramist can construct a work in units to almost any scale, from small wall pieces to an entire wall (14-10 to 14-13 and 14-18 to 14-22).

SITE-SPECIFIC WORKS

The kind of thinking an artist must use to design and carry out a commissioned work is quite different from that needed to create a personal, expressive work that is not planned for a specific place. Thorough planning, from design through installation, is the key factor in creating a work for a commission.

There are many aspects to be considered in making a large-scale work for a specific site; for example, the budget, as it relates to all aspects of construction, must be carefully worked out at the beginning, and installation must be planned from the start because the engineering requirements may necessitate changes in the design. Thus, the artist who works on architectural commissions must either develop some engineering skills or be able to work with an engineer to design the installation of the work. Artists may have to become familiar with the use of engineered steel supports that will keep columns from falling on passersby (14-5), with built-in arrangements for bolts, rods, or brackets with which to attach the heavy sections of a mural, or with the use of construction-grade adhesives to attach sections to a backing. (See Appendix 4B for information on adhesives and installation.)

If an artist is called in to propose a sculpture or ceramic mural for a specific site after a building has been completed, he or she should first of all arrange to see the architect's drawings and construction details. For an interior site, these should include wall-construction details and the electrical plans; for an exterior site, the artist should contact the landscape architect to obtain irrigation plans, and plans showing the location of wiring and lighting outlets, as well as information on the amount of power available. These electrical specifications are especially important if the artist's work requires electrical power for lighting, pumps, or motors, or when digging is necessary to place the foundations for a sculpture in the vicinity of electric cables, gas, or water lines.

Designing for Specific Sites

In designing a work for architecture, the artist must give thought to many other questions, among them, the scale of work that would be most appropriate for a particular building or outdoor environment. For example, an extremely heavy or large mural might dominate and overwhelm a small room, while the same mural could be highly appropriate for an extensive outdoor wall. A school (14-4), an airport waiting area (14-5), a government building wall (14-6), a conference or lecture room (14-7), a remodeled historic building (14-8)—all present unique situations in which the ambience of each site must be retained and the needs of those who will use the spaces should be respected.

Figure 14-6
Untitled #645. Robert Sperry, U.S.A. (standing in front of the mural), won the Honors
Program Award of the King County Arts Commission to create a wall for the County
Administration Building, Seattle. Since he could not see the mural in its entirety until it
was fired, Sperry made full-scale studies using acrylic paints, and he also developed some
of the forms and their relationships in a series of etchings. To create the ceramic images,
he applied the black and white slip freely, sometimes flinging it at the black-glazed
modules, creating explosions of texture and atmosphere that he then stabilized with strong
geometric shapes. Ht. 10½ ft. × 30 ft. (3 m × 9 m). *Courtesy the artist. Photo: Jim Ball.*

Figure 14-7
A relief by Carlo Zauli, Italy, brings a suggestion of the natural world—tidepools?
ploughed fields? a geological formation?—to a conference room at the headquarters of the
organization known as Conosce Italia S. I. in Bologna. Unlike many of Zauli's murals,
this one was formed directly, without molds, with an interior slab-formed network of
supports. Also unlike Zauli's earlier murals (8-14), it is unglazed, colored yellow, orange,
green, and brown, with red-brown clay. Stoneware, 2282 °F/1250 °C. Length 33 ft. (10
m). *Courtesy the artist. Photo: Antonio Masotti.*

Other factors the artist should consider include the following: From what distance or what
angle will the viewer see the work? How will the
space in which the work is installed be used? Under what type of lighting will the work be seen?

The color of the work as it relates to its surroundings is also important. For example, the
brilliantly colored glazes that might be appropriate in an informal restaurant would probably be
out of place in a bank president's office. The scale
of surface texture or the type of glaze treatment
would also appropriately vary according to placement of the work. For instance, an extremely detailed surface would be lost on a work in a tall
lobby where people do not linger but would create interest in an intimate setting or a lounge area

where people would have time to study it (14-13).
If any images are included in the work, these too
would vary according to the use of the site.

Other factors apply to three-dimensional
sculpture. What about the space in which it will
be placed? Will viewers merely look at the work
or will they walk around it, or through it or even
climb on it? When designing work for children's
playgrounds, the artist should consult a play-
ground consultant, who will explain the special
safety considerations that must be taken into account. These include height limitations, planning
the surface treatment so children are protected
from injury from sharp forms or edges, and the
provision of soft material (sand, bark) into which
children may jump or onto which they would

Figure 14-8
Birthplace, a sculpture by Stephen De Staebler, U.S.A., for the historic Old Post Office building in St. Louis. De Staebler, himself born in St. Louis, appropriately chose forms that evoke atavistic symbols of earth, water, and the human figure. The mural was mounted on a support of steel channels and brackets for which holes had been built into the clay sections. The piece was commissioned through the Architecture Program of the General Services Administration; a local committee chose three artists to be reviewed for final choice by the administration. Stoneware; fired in sections in six firings at cone 5. *Courtesy the artist.*

land if they fell from the sculpture. If the work will be accessible to the public, then possible vandalism must also be anticipated; the same is true for the danger of injury to the public that might be caused by structural failure. If the work is intended for outdoor use, the artist must take climate into account; in a mild climate such as that of the Canary Islands (14-4), a mural or sculpture intended for the outdoors will not encounter the same difficulties as it would if installed where winters are harsh. In cold climates, however, if water enters the pores of the fired clay and then alternately freezes and thaws, the work can develop cracks and eventually be destroyed.

Lighting

The lighting arrangement will greatly affect how the viewer will see a work once it is installed. Will the lighting be natural or artificial? Poor lighting has more than once obscured art works that have taken artists months to create, and more than one artist has been shocked to discover unexpected lamps hanging in front of his or her mural. The type of lighting—incandescent, fluorescent, low-voltage, spot lighting—and its placement, should be agreed upon with the architect or client, and the amount of electric current needed to supply the fixtures should be analyzed and agreed on from the start.

These are just some of the factors that the artist who designs work for architecture must deal with.

THE COMMISSION PROCESS

To receive an award for an architectural commission, an artist may decide to enter an open competition or may be asked to prepare a presentation in competition with a few other invited artists. Stephen De Staebler (14-8) was recommended as one of a group of three by a local committee to create a work for the remodeled Old Post Office in St. Louis, Missouri, under the Architecture Program of the General Services Administration. De Staebler's ceramic sculpture *Birthplace* evokes ancient earth forms and forces, but firing the work in De Staebler's "space-age" **ceramic fiber**-insulated kiln was an experience very much of the present.

Once having decided to apply for a commission, the artist must present the proposed work as attractively and as graphically as possible so that the jurors can visualize it. In order to convince the competiton jury, architect, or client that his or her particular design is the most appropriate one for the chosen site, the artist's presentation generally covers concept, design, material, budget, site (placement), time schedule, and installation details. This presentation also often includes a written description, plans, and elevation drawings showing the proposed placement, plus a three-dimensional model of the proposed work. Upon the artist's receipt of the commission, a signed contract between artist and client becomes the final binding document.

Creating A Commissioned Work

American artist Marylyn Dintenfass was invited to prepare a presentation for an art work to be placed in the Superior Court Complex in Enfield, Connecticut. In order to select artists for this and similar commissions, the Connecticut State Commission on the Arts maintains an Artist Bank registry, and for this particular assignment, the commission chose a number of artists to submit proposals and reviewed the finalists' entries to make the final choice. After this review, Dintenfass's proposal was chosen. The illustrations on these pages (14-9 to 14-12) show some of the steps though which Dintenfass proceeded as she designed the work, presented her proposal, constructed the components, and installed them.

Dintenfass says that she was helped in deciding on the concept of her work by the architect's design, which included references to classical architecture, but the building was, she says,

> constructed in contemporary fashion, modularly. The portico, the columns, the oculus and colonnade were all fabricated elsewhere and assembled on site. My response to this was to propose a frieze fragment, over-scaled so it might seem to have come from a monumental building, but built in the con-

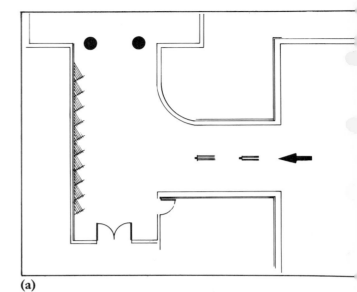

(a)

(b)

Figure 14-9
As an entrant in a nationwide search for an artist to create an art work for the Superior Court Complex at Enfield, Connecticut, Marylyn Dintenfass, U.S.A., studied the architect's plans and aesthetic concepts before submitting plans and drawings proposing her *Diagonal Frieze*. **(a)** Plan of the lobby, showing placement of the frieze on the wall facing the main door. **(b)** View of the entrance to the building and through to the interior wall on which the frieze was installed. *Courtesy the artist.*

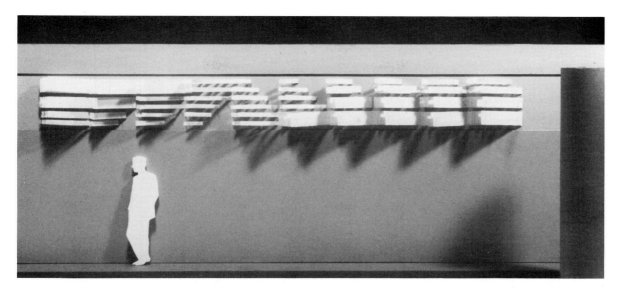

Figure 14-10
Dintenfass constructed a three-dimensional model to show the scale of the proposed work in relation to passersby and to the building. The model also made clear the dimensional quality of the frieze. *Courtesy the artist.*

(a)

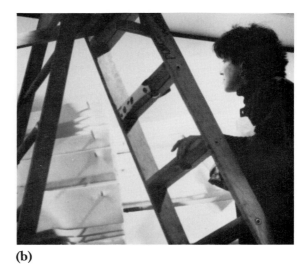

(b)

Figure 14-11
(a) Dintenfass passing porcelain through a slab roller, rolling it to a thickness of ½ inch (1.3 cm). She then hand-rolled it to ¼ inch and ripped and cut the edges of the components, using templates. The curved units were draped over arched bisque forms to support them as they dried and were fired. After firing the sections in an electric kiln to 2150 °F/1176.6 °C, she strengthened them with cotton/polyester cloth laminated onto the back. **(b)** Dintenfass supervises the installation of *Diagonal Frieze.* The wall was specially designed and constructed to support the steel rods for the slabs, while a jig maintained the necessary 63-degree angle for the drilled insertion holes. Slabs were also secured to the wall with silicon adhesive. *Courtesy the artist.*

Figure 14-12
Diagonal Frieze. After months of thought and work, the frieze is finally in place and the appropriateness of Dintenfass's design becomes apparent. Responding to the classical references in the architecture, she comments that *the frieze, while recalling a classical frieze, is quite exaggerated in its scale, suggesting perhaps that it may have come from a monumental structure.* Porcelain slabs, ¼ in. thick, mounted on ⅜-inch threaded steel rods. Ht. 3 ft. × 30 ft. × 17 in. (91 cm × 9 m × 43 cm). Commissioned by the Department of Administrative Services and the Connecticut Commission on the Arts. *Courtesy the artist.* Photo: *Joann Sieburg-Baker.*

temporary way, in units. This is also a requirement for fabricating large scale ceramics work. In fact, I feel the use of clay is particularly appropriate because of both its historical and space age applications. . . . Her work, *Diagonal Frieze,* was conceived to present three distinct perspectives. *The observer approaching from the main entry will see a series of volumetric units; viewed from the left it appears to be two dimensional bands of varying widths; and upon leaving the courthouse the volume disappears and becomes undulating vertical edges.*

In addition to the drawings and model, Dintenfass submitted a statement explaining her concept, a complete list of materials, and a description of her fabrication techniques. She also provided instructions for unpacking the piece,

and once the work was installed, she provided suggestions for maintenance. Since the work was to be installed indoors, hung on a wall well off the floor, and in a secure environment, she was not concerned with the demands of a harsh climate, nor did she need to worry about vandalism.

Commission work can bring both challenge and fulfillment. Ernst Häusermann (14-13), found that creating a mural for a home for the elderly was an emotionally satisfying experience, because in order to decide on a theme for the work he let himself free-associate about what he could remember about his childhood relationship with his grandfather. By doing this, he came to a greater appreciaton of what his grandfather had handed on to him and was able to create a work that was both decorative and expressive.

Ceramist Rita Pagony of Hungary sees a link

Figure 14-13
When Ernst Häusermann, Switzerland, designed a wall for the lounge areas in a home for
the elderly, he drew on childhood memories to create symbols representing what his
grandfather taught him or shared with him. Cutting slabs of clay, he made simplified
representations of birds, tools, fishing equipment, pipes, wine goblets, flowers, and trees.
The mural continues through four stories. Low- and high-fired clay and porcelain; no added
color or glazes. *Courtesy the artist. Photo: Jörg Müller.*

(a)

A SYMBOL OF CERAMICS TRADITONS

(b)

Figure 14-14
(a) Rita Pagony, of Hungary, and her architect husband, Miklós Olasz, created a series of proposals inspired by Pagony's large vessels for the urban planning competition of the Faenza Concorso. **(b)** Using the vessel as an architectural form, they proposed a brick vessel over which water would run down into a fountain in a plaza. Pagony says, *Clay has always been a basic material of architecture and pottery through the ages. This is one of the reasons we propose a huge vase to build up of bricks. . . . And this whole thing with water is pottery again.* Ht. 3 stories. *Courtesy the artist.*

between architecture and sculptural vessels, and working with her architect husband Miklós Olasz, Pagony proposed innovative schemes in which huge vessels made of bricks would be incorporated into buildings. These would function as fountains, with the water flowing down the building into brick-lined basins. Viewing her proposals as both expressions of the art of the Absurd and a way to incorporate ceramics and the concept of the container into the architecture itself rather than applying it to the surface of a building as decoration, she says,

We tried to find an extreme (absurd?) way to unite architectural and sculptural values inseparably (14-14).

In the United States, a group of ceramists and architects in New York joined forces to explore ways to use ceramics in architecture. Among the proposals that emerged were designs for modules to be used in construction or decoration, site-specific projects for vacant lots or redeveloped neighborhoods in Manhattan, and studies for the facades of row houses. The results were shown in an exhibit and a catalogue entitled *Firing the Imagination*. One of the ceramic artists involved, Susan Tunick, comments:

> At a recent conference on public sculpture it became clear that all over the country collaborations are beginning to occur, and that an artist's involvement begins at the initial stages of the project. . . .

Mark Robbins, the architect with whom she collaborated, adds,

> We have tried to get away from the notion that the architect sets the infrastructure and the artist creates a work located in or on it.

Another unusual use of ceramics in architecture has been that of Nader Khalili, who has experimented with firing adobe houses to make safe, affordable shelter—shelter that would not be subject to collapse due to heavy rain. Khalili has actually fired entire buildings, truly integrating architecture and ceramics (see "Further Reading").

Obviously, the planning and carrying out of large projects is a lengthy, time-consuming, and exhausting process. At times, the problems that artists must overcome when creating works for architecture can appear overwhelming, but despite this, many ceramic artists find it both challenging and exciting to work on a large scale and to design for a specific site.

Other Commission Possibilities

In addition to large public or corporate commissions, there are also possibilities for creating smaller works or individual sculptures to be placed in private or public settings. These can range from hand-thrown sinks (12-61) to city benches, to fireplace mantels, to imaginative individual sculptures for public spaces. Karen Park's bollard-supported benches bring color and liveliness to the urban environment (14-15), and in a variation of the traditional use of ceramics for stoves (6-10, 6-11), Paula Winokur creates porcelain fireplace surrounds that are individual works of art (14-16, page 292), while Jan Snoeck's seated or reclining figures brightens the functional settings of hospitals and municipal plazas in which they are placed (14-17).

Figure 14-15
Karen Park, Denmark, known for her fountains and murals, has also created benches to enliven a city street, courtyard, or garden. This one displays a strong black and white spiral pattern reminiscent of designs on prehistoric pottery, yet contemporary. *Courtesy the artist.*

Figure 14-16
Detail of *Fireplace, Site IV*, Paula Winokur, U.S.A. Of her architectural works, Winokur says, *They are planned to relate to the space provided and in some ways to the individual sensibilities of those for whom they were made. The large scale provides me with a format for exploring various aspects of landscape and imagery in one piece.* (See page 292 for illustration of whole fireplace surround.) Porcelain, cast objects, metallic sulfates, ceramic pencil drawings. *Courtesy Helen Drutt Gallery. Photo: Will Brown.*

(a)

(b)

Figure 14-17
(a) Jan Snoeck, the Netherlands. These reclining figures will bring color and humor to a hospital courtyard. Sectioned and fired, they are ready for shipping; note small models that will aid the workers who assemble them on site. Dense, brightly colored glazes protect the surface from freezing and thawing. *Courtesy the artist.* **(b)** Snoeck and one of his seated figures in progress at Struktuur '68. Built solid, it will be cut into sections while still damp, hollowed out, and fired, creating building-block components that will be assembled in a city plaza, park, or outside a public building. *Courtesy Struktuur '68, The Hague.*

Figure 14-18

Pastoral #1. Patrick Siler, U.S.A., uses units made from hand-formed slabs to create large ceramic walls, creating the images with his slip and stencil process (15-17 to 15-19). Fired at cone 5, oxidation. 7 ft. × 13 ft. × 10 in. (2 m × 4 m × 25 cm). *Courtesy the artist.*

Modules

The term *module* is most correctly applied to standardized components that can be used interchangeably, but it is also loosely used to describe any similar units that can be combined to create a larger work. As defined in this way, modules can extend the possibilities of architectural ceramics; they can be grouped to make wall pieces (14-18) to create architectural detailing or can be extended to cover a whole wall. The units can be made by being pushed through the die of an extruder, by using press molds, or by slip casting in molds (14-19). Extruders come in all sizes; Gladding McBean, an architectural ceramic and pipe-manufacturing company in California, has one several stories high that pushes out huge sections of culvert pipe. They also have smaller ones fitted with custom dies that will press out architectural moldings or components with any desired profile. Tile extruders, available for the ceramics studio, take the handwork out of making small modules, while others can make tubes or solid components that can be combined to form architectural works. The industrial extruders that make bricks provide another sort of modular unit. Beate Kuhn, in Germany, Ulla Viotti and Lillemor Petersson in Sweden, and Karen Park in Denmark have all worked at brick companies, where they took ordinary building bricks as they came from the extruder, altered or glazed them, and then assembled them into one-of-a kind reliefs that became part of walls.

Used throughout history, tiles (6-2, 7-7) have been handformed, shaped in press molds, cast in slip molds, or mechanically formed for use as wall

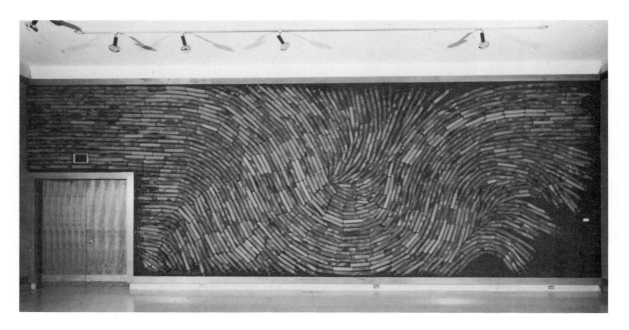

Figure 14-19
Wall installation. Jack Sures, Canada, makes use of unit construction to create a large work. For this mural, Sures designed a large hydraulic extruder with which he formed the 1,300 individual pieces. Planned to link together and hung on nails, the mural sections could be dismantled and reassembled in different configurations. Sprayed with variegated engobes; earthenware, cone 04; fired in electric kiln. Ht. 13 × 38 ft. (4 × 11.6 m.). *Courtesy the artist. Photo: Don Hall.*

decorations. Nowadays, tiles still bring color and texture to walls in the hands of accomplished ceramists. Beth Starbuck and Steven Goldner (14-20), for example, have built up a business that creates custom designs for a select portion of the ceramic tile market. Working with architects, designers, contractors, and homeowners, they design for specific sites or spaces and accommodate their work to particular requirements such as color, texture, thickness, and surface. Rather than compete with mass-produced tile, they use handcraft techniques and design the tiles for specific applications and spaces. Their backgrounds include work at the historic American Moravian Tile Works (7-7), where Starbuck was head ceramist. Some artists make their own tiles (14-21), while others alter commercial greenware or glazed tiles by adding clay relief, by glazing or reglazing them, or by painting on them with under- or over-glazes, transforming these mass-produced modules into the components of highly individual works. James Melchert (Color plate 39), for ex-

ample, has been using glazed commercial tiles on which he paints with glazes and which, after firing, he assembles into wall pieces.

Made in molds taken from his carved plastic foam originals, Nino Caruso's slip-cast modules (14-22) are combined into free-standing columns or for a variety of architectural applications. This suggests another area to which the ceramist could apply his or her skills. The increasing interest in preservation has created a demand for the restoration of terra-cotta decoration on vintage buildings, and since there is now also great interest on the part of some architects in using decorative detail on their buildings, there is a need for well-designed contemporary architectural components.

Considering these possibilities, it appears that ceramic artists will have increasing opportunities to apply their creativity and skill to architectural applications, continuing the tradition started thousands of years ago when glazed tiles were used to cover the sun-dried bricks of palaces and processional gates in the ancient Middle East.

(a)

(b)

(c)

Figure 14-20
Beth Starbuck and Steven Gardner, U.S.A., made the modules for this dimensional relief, *Wedges*, by **(a)** pounding clay into a plaster press mold, then **(b)** scraping off the excess clay. The shaped module was then removed from the mold **(c)**. In this case, the glazed and assembled modules were combined to make a small relief **(d)**, but if desired, the modules could be repeated to cover a complete wall. *Courtesy the artists.*

(d)

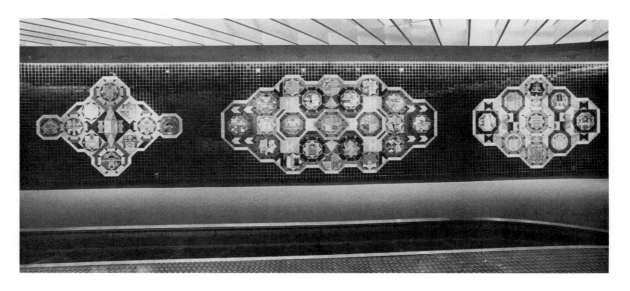

Figure 14-21
Tile works by Joyce Kosloff, U.S.A., in subways and railway stations bring color and decoration to what are often drab surroundings. For the walls of a baggage claim area in the international terminal of the San Francisco Airport, her earthenware medallions set in glass mosaic reflect aspects of Bay Area culture from Victorian to Art Deco to Funk. Underglazes, transparent overglaze. 10 ft. × 53 ft. (3 m × 16 m). *Courtesy the Barbara Gladstone Gallery and the artist. Photo: Gary Sinick.*

◄ *Figure 14-22*
Nino Caruso, Italy, installed terra-cotta framed doors in his exhibit *Homage to the Etruscans.* Caruso carves the originals in plastic foam with a hot wire cutter and then makes a plaster mold in which he casts the terra-cotta sections. He then combines and recombines the modules to form architectural works or installations ranging from single doorways to whole walls. Slip-cast terra-cotta, fired at cone 06. *Courtesy the artist. Photo: M. Ruta.*

15
Surface: Texture, Color, and Glaze

On one side you have technique, on the other the spiritual aspect. If you can bring both sides up together, you have a work of art. If one ascends faster than the other, you have nothing.

—Pierre Bayle, France*

Sleeping Mountain, Kyoko Tonegawa, U.S.A., uses a special traditional technique in which she throws from the inside only in order to preserve the natural exterior texture of the clay. Stoneware, reduction firing, cone 10 to 11. Ht. 15 in. (38 cm). *Courtesy the artist.*

When the word *ceramics* is mentioned, most people tend to think of the shiny surface of a glaze. But there are many other ways to treat the surface of clay to give it an interesting texture, attractive color, or luscious glossy finish before you fire it to permanence. First of all, your choice of clay body will influence the final appearance of the surface, so you will need to anticipate the type of surface treatment you will be giving the clay *before* you choose the clay body. Fine-grained porcelain, for example, will take detailed carving (15-5), while heavily grogged earthenware or stoneware are more appropriate for rougher finishes (see right).

*Contact, Alberta Potters Association, quoted from Le Monde, Paris.

CLAY BODIES KEYED TO GLAZES

Clay bodies, ceramic coloring materials, slips, and glazes make use of many of the same materials. How you use these materials in relationship to each other has a profound effect on the final quality and appearance of your work. Because this relationship is so important, when John Toki formulated some easy-to-make clay bodies for you to mix and test (chapter 10), he planned them as part of a series that proceeds from mixing the clays, and texturing and coloring them to, finally, mixing simple glazes to embellish them. These same clay bodies, given in Appendix 1A, are keyed to colorants and the specially formulated glaze recipes in the same appendix. This series of basic clays and glazes was planned for study purposes to help you develop an understanding of the materials through testing. Additional information that will prove useful to you as you continue—glaze additives; water percentages; clay and glaze colorants; and frit, feldspar, and **opacifier** composition charts—are all located in appendix 1A through 1F, along with some clay, slip, and glaze recipes other ceramists have shared. As you progress in testing, you can try those as well (Appendix 1C). Then, if you wish to go further into analyzing glazes, you may read the section "Calculating Glazes Using Chemical Analysis" in Appendix 3A, always remembering that the clay body itself must be in harmony with the glazes you apply to it.

UNGLAZED SURFACES

Today, many potters and sculptors have become interested in exploring the inherent qualities of the material, leaving the surface of the clay in its natural state (see the photograph that opens this chapter). Others are interested in the effects of the fire on unglazed clay and let the fire create the surface effects (16-16). Still others add texturing material or deliberately develop a texture on the surface.

Of her rough-textured vessels, Kyoko Tonegawa says,

Based on a special traditional technique of throwing on the wheel, I throw from the inside only, without

Figure 15-1
Pompeo Pianezzola, Italy, uses a variety of methods to texture the clay for his wall pieces, among them pressing in beans and rice. This organic material will burn out in the firing, leaving the surface pitted. *Courtesy the artist.*

touching the exterior of the pot. In this way I create untouched surfaces of texture and modify the shape, while allowing natural, earthen textures and colors to express themselves outwardly.

The very earliest potters used no more than their fingers, fingernails, sticks, shells, or other natural objects to scratch, impress, or carve textures onto the surfaces of their pots, frequently showing an innate sensitivity to the relationship of the decoration to the form of the pot (1-3, 1-13, and 1-23).

You may find equally simple materials or objects you can use to alter the surface of the clay (15-1). Look around you, in your home or outdoors, to see what you can discover to stamp, stroke, or stick in the clay to give its surface added interest (15-2). Almost anything, from beans to bolts, or bits

Figure 15-2
Gerd Hjorth Petersen, Denmark, uses a saw to
texture slabs and then presses them into molds to
form slab plates; sometimes she uses an inner tube as
a mold over which she drapes the textured slabs.
Photo: Mogens S. Koch.

Figure 15-3
Erik Gronborg, U.S.A., uses carved wooden printing
blocks, newspaper zinc plates, or textured fabrics to
create texture on the clay. *Courtesy the artist.*

of bark, might give you the surface you want for a
particular pot or piece of sculpture.

You can also use carved wooden or plaster
stamps (15-3) to impress designs into the clay, or
you can model or carve your own stamps from
clay, bisque fire them, and press them into the
damp clay to create positive or negative images.
A stamp modeled in relief will make a negative
impression in the clay surface, while a concave
carving will create a relief when it is impressed on
the clay (2-28).

In addition, if you leave the clay components
of your work unmelded, the method of construction that you use—coils, pellets of clay pressed
together, overlapping slabs—can in itself create
surface interest.

Carving and Incising

The Jōmon potters of ancient Japan combined impressed patterns with carving, giving a
distinctive surface to the unglazed clay, using
both methods effectively on their pottery and on
their sculpture (1-3, 3-23).

There is something very satisfying about
carving into stiff but still damp clay—it is so easy
to put one's mark in it, and even if your marks

don't turn out as you wish, you can usually fill
the gouge and start over again! But as with all
decorative techniques, it is important in carving
to consider the relationship of the carved surface
to the object's clay body and to its shape (15-4, 15-
5). A taller-than-life-sized vessel, looming over
the viewer, calls for deep carving (15-6) while the
overall patterning of a sculptured figure's dress
calls for a more precise incised line (15-7).

Other Surface Treatments

Another technique from the past still sometimes used to create decoration in relief is **sprigging.** By applying pellets, rolls, modeled images,
or cut-outs of clay to the surface, you can create
an overall texture or raised decorations on a pot
or sculpture. This sprigged relief can be added to
the soft clay as you build, or you can first score
and paint a leather-hard surface with slip to be
sure the added relief will adhere.

Burnishing the clay object when it is leather
hard or dry (1-24 and 5-18) also has a long history
and is a tried and true way of altering the surface
of damp clay. Some ceramists prefer to burnish
while the clay is damp, while others prefer to
work on dry clay. To burnish, stroke the surface

(a)

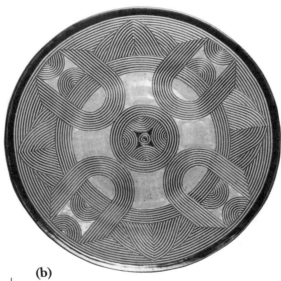

(b)

Figure 15-4
David R. MacDonald, U.S.A., **(a)** carving one of his
large *Nyama* vessels. He bases the designs of his
vessels and plates **(b)** on African patterns inspired by
fabrics, pottery, and body decoration. Stoneware.
Diameter 32 in. (81 cm). *Courtesy the Hanover Gallery
and the artist. Photo: Clifford Oliver.*

with a river-polished stone or any smooth object,
such as the back of a kitchen spoon. Some potters
and sculptors prefer, however, to burnish with a
piece of cloth or chamois. Burnishing works best
when used on a clay body that is not too coarse
or on a fine-particled slip that has been applied
over the clay body.

Carving Dry Clay

You can achieve other effects by scratching,
carving, drilling, chiseling, filing, or sanding the
clay when it is dry rather than leather hard. It is
more difficult to texture or carve dry clay than
leather-hard clay, but the effects you can achieve
by carving dry clay are different. Carving dry
clay that is heavily grogged may result in a
slightly ragged edge. Care must be taken to avoid
chipping edges when carving a smooth body such
as porcelain. Lightly dampening the dry clay before carving can make carving easier.

Avoiding Clay Dust

There is one disadvantage to carving dry
clay—clay dust is hazardous to breathe because

Figure 15-5
Karl Scheid, West Germany, carves his delicate
porcelain bowls and boxes with precise patterns that
are especially appropriate to their material, size, and
shape. Porcelain. Ht. 3½ in. (9 cm). *Courtesy the artist.
Photo: Bernd P. Göbbels, Hirzenhain.*

Figure 15-6
Arnold Zimmerman, U.S.A., carving one of his
mammoth sculptural vessels, is surrounded by others
in various stages of completion. The thick, coil-built
walls (11-2) accept,—almost demand—the deep
carving that becomes an important aspect of their
robust surface (Color plate 41). *Courtesy the artist.*

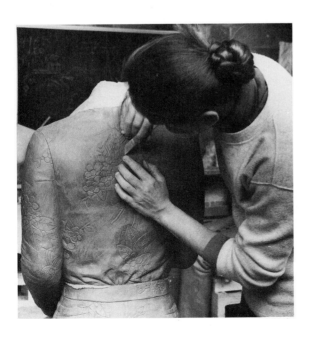

◀ *Figure 15-7*
Marilyn Lysohir, U.S.A., carves a flowered pattern
into the dress of one of the figures for her installation
Bad Manners (15-21, Color plate 15). The clay is
leather hard and smooth, allowing her to incise the
linear designs with which she embellishes its surface.
Courtesy the artist. Photo: A. Okazaki.

the microscopic clay particles that carry free silica (silica that has not combined with the clay molecules) can enter and clog your lungs. You can wear a respirator while carving, but since not only you but everyone else in the studio is exposed to the dust, be sure that there is also adequate active ventilation to remove the dust at its source. Adelaide Robineau (7-5) spent more than a thousand hours carving one of her famous pieces of pottery—unaware of the hazards the process entailed. One can say, "Well, lots of potters lived to ripe old ages doing all the unsafe things you warn against," but they were not exposed to the same amount of pollutants and toxic substances in their daily lives as we are now. It is that cumulative effect that is especially dangerous to us, so that we must be especially wary of exposure to more.

PRECAUTIONS

Since an important purpose of this book is to encourage you to work in clay, we don't want to emphasize the precautions to such a degree that you become fearful of using ceramic materials and give up. If you take the proper precautions, you should be able to work safely and healthily in a ceramic studio unless you have a health problem that would make you especially vulnerable.

Before starting to use *any* coloring materials in clays, underglazes, glazes, or overglazes, please read the section on good studio procedures and the basic health and safety rules that should be posted in any studio (see page 195). Almost all coloring materials offer some degree of hazard, and if you are a smoker, have allergies or asthma, are pregnant, or have a heart condition, be aware that your system cannot tolerate much exposure to toxic materials. Children are also more vulnerable to exposure to such materials.

In appendix 1E, we list the ceramic materials that you will be using in the studio and rate them according to their degree of toxicity as it was known at the time the book was written. Since such information is always being updated, however, it is important that you stay aware of the new information as it is published. In order to be sure you know what you are using, read labels and any warnings carefully and ask the dealer from whom you buy supplies to give you the appropriate material safety data sheet (MSDS) that

reveals any hazardous ingredients, the effects of exposure, and the necessary protection and precaution information. In Appendix 5A we also list organizations where you can find out the current information, and in "Further Reading" you will find publications that will keep you up to date on the latest findings. Here, we repeat some of the basic precautions you should take while working with glaze materials. Make the decision to protect yourself from danger and to take responsibility for your own health.

While working with the materials used in ceramic glazes, you must protect yourself from ingesting them by breathing them as dry ingredients or absorbing them through your mouth or skin. Be especially careful if you have any cuts in your skin. Wear protective gloves while mixing glazes and either use active local ventilation a few inches from the dry materials you are mixing or wear a properly fitting respirator mask with a filter rated for toxic dust. For added protection, you can mix glaze materials in a plastic-covered mixing box with a hole in the side so you can reach in and mix the materials (10-6).

Spray or **air brush** glazes and overglazes only in a properly vented **spray booth**, and wear a respirator rated for mists, acid mists, and fumes (see page 195). Keep your hands away from your face, mouth, and eyes, and to avoid accidental ingestion, do not eat or smoke when using glaze materials. Never hold a dirty glaze brush in your mouth when your hands are occupied! Wear an impermeable protective apron, keep it clean of glaze materials, and leave it in the glaze room when you are finished. It is also a good idea to shower and shampoo so you can remove any glaze materials from your body.

Ventilation is as important in the glaze areas as in the clay-mixing areas, so be sure that the proper standards are followed in those areas and that you turn on the fans or dust collectors before working.

The glaze area should be kept clean. Wet sponge all table surfaces and areas that have been splashed with glaze, and clean the floors either with a wet mop or a wet shop vacuum that has a filter rated to trap the microscopic particles of clay and glaze materials. Glaze materials and glazes should be stored in covered, unbreakable containers and be well labeled.

Although the chemicals and materials list in

Appendix 1E identifies certain materials as particularly toxic, remember that *all* materials in a ceramics studio should be used with care. Take all the necessary precautions, and limit your exposure to the toxic materials as much as possible.

COLOR IN THE CLAY

The simplest way to achieve a variety of clay colors is by wedging together two different clay bodies, varying the percentages of the clays to obtain the color you want. You can change the earth tones of clay to produce different shades by using this blending process. For example, a low-fire white clay wedged with a red terra-cotta (low-fire) will yield a medium reddish-brown, while a high-fire iron-rich stoneware blended with a white porcelain (also high-fire) will yield a medium brown when fired in an electric kiln (it will be darker if fired in reduction). The important point here is that you should choose two clays that have similar maturing temperatures in order to be sure they are compatible in the new clay body.

Coloring Oxides

You can develop a wider palette of clay-body colors by exploring what happens when you blend various oxides in different proportions into the clay (Color plate 33). For example, 2 to 5 percent of red iron added to a clay will give you browns, and ½ to 2 percent cobalt oxide will create blues when blended into porcelain or very light-colored bodies. Different percentages will give you different shades of each color. You will achieve the truest colors when you blend colorants into light or white clay bodies. Remember also that both the temperature to which the clay is fired and the atmosphere in the kiln will also affect the colors, so *test!* You did some tests for color changes in clay bodies in chapter 10, so you know the procedure. You can carry these tests further, creating a wider variety of colors. You will find information about colorants that you can use to color clays in Appendixes 1A and 1F.

Ceramic Stains

Although the most common oxides provide some of the basic colors, commercial stains offer you the possibility of making a wider range of colored clay bodies. These commercially prepared stains, produced primarily for the ceramics industry, not only provide a wide selection of colors but are also in general more color-stable than oxides within specified firing ranges. It is worth it to buy prepared stains; if you wanted to make stains like these in the studio, you would need access to many materials, would need elaborate processing equipment to **calcine** the materials (that is, to heat to the point just below fusing to combine them chemically), and you would also need equipment for washing out the soluble salts, to say nothing of needing a great deal of knowledge and experience. If you want to make it really easy for yourself, you can buy premixed colored clay bodies—one company even offers a kit that includes small amounts of variously colored clays for you to try.

With stains, your color range can extend beyond the basic oxide colors to purples, pinks, yellows, and various shades of blues, grays, greens, maroons, and browns, and in addition the careful processing these stains undergo for industry ensures quality control and color-batch consistency. There is no bright red or orange stain for clay bodies; the brightest red available for clay bodies is maroon. For glazes, cadmium and selenium red and yellow stains are available, but these will not produce color in clay bodies.

Another advantage of using stains in clay bodies is the fact that the color you see in the dry stain will be similar to the color you will obtain when you blend it into the clay. Oxides, on the other hand—cobalt, for example—do not show their true color until they are fired. Until you are experienced and can predict the colors you will get from oxides, using them can be a bit like painting in the dark. As with the oxides, the truest stain colors are achieved when they are blended into light or white clay bodies. The temperature at which the clay is fired can affect a stain just as it does an oxide, so, again, testing is the way to discover what final color you will get.

You can place the dry stain powder on the **wedging table** and wedge moist clay into the color until it is thoroughly blended, or, for greater control of the color tones, you can add the stains to batches of dry clay, carefully controlling the percentage of stain added. The percentage of color you will need to add to the clay body will

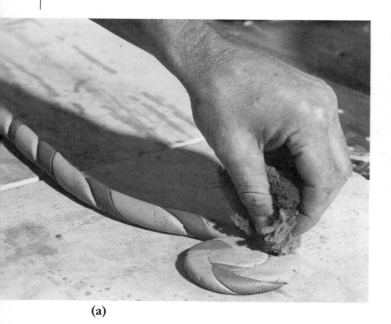

(a)

(b)

Figure 15-8

(a) Using colored clay that he has twined into a rope, Hans Munk Anderson, of Denmark, coils a base for a pot. **(b)** Transferring the rope to a mold, he continues to press the colored clay coils together. The trick is to meld the colored clays enough to keep them from cracking apart but not enough to disturb the pattern. *Photo: Mogens S. Koch.*

be affected by the type of clay body, firing temperature, and atmosphere, so, as always, make tests. In Appendix 1A you will find percentages of some stains and oxides to add to clay bodies to color and test them.

Working with Colored Clay

By using more than one colored clay body and combining them using a variety of methods, the range of effects you can create can extend from a braid-formed bowl (15-8), to tiny agate ware boxes (15-9), to a landscape vessel (15-34). To achieve effects like these, you can simply twist or braid rolls of colored clays together or use a more complex technique in which you combine blocks of colored clays, then cut, layer, and roll them, creating an agate effect. It takes a good deal of practice to make agate ware, because you must keep the various colored clay bodies separate while at the same time melding them enough to

keep cracks from developing at the points where the two colors meet.

Using color in the clay is not, however, simply a matter of picking any color of clay body and combining it with any other clay. Each colorant contributes certain characteristics to the clay, including different shrinkage rates, so when the clay dries or is fired, the colored clays may shrink at different rates and possibly separate. The amount of stain you add to make the colors can also affect the shrinkage rates; in addition, the maturing temperatures of the different clay bodies used must be similar in order for the piece to come through the fire without cracking. On the other hand, the cracks and crevices that develop in the kiln become part of the surface interest, as in John Toki's large wall sculptures (Color plate 33).

Figure 15-9
Paul Philp, England, colored the clay with commercial stains, then used a complex layering, cutting, and pressing process to achieve marbled patterns that he says were often inspired by ones he saw through a microscope. Each tiny box opens to show a different clay pattern in the interior. Stained white earthenware. *Courtesy the artist.*

Surface Color

Oxides   An oxide is a basic element combined with oxygen. Over a geological period of time, almost all the basic elements on earth have formed a chemical combination with oxygen, and the oxides that have resulted have proved of great importance in the history of ceramics. They have been used for coloring clay and glaze and to provide fluxes that help to fuse the clay and the glaze in the kiln.

If you worked through the tests of clay bodies in chapter 10, you already have some idea of the action of oxides in clay bodies. In addition to their usefulness in clay bodies, these chemical compounds can also be used for coloring and decorating the surface of bisque-fired clay in a number of ways. Throughout history, potters applied them with brushes, feathers, twigs, or **slip trailers**. One popular way to use oxides on bisque is to brush or sponge on the oxide (15-10), then wipe it off, enhancing the texture of the clay. You can also apply it using brushes or by dabbing it on with a sponge to create an overall stippled texture.

There are a number of other ways you can apply an oxide—spraying it on, carefully painting it into incised lines—or you can add depth and definition to textures and carved areas by covering the piece with oxide so that it fills the grooves,

Figure 15-10
Oxides can be wiped onto a pot with a sponge, and wiped off again, allowing the texture of the clay body to show through. You can also create a dappled surface if you dab two different colors of oxide on with sponges. *Photo: Alphabet and Image.*

then sponge it off the raised area. You can also apply oxides with **resist** methods, covering up the parts you want to remain uncolored with masking tape, wax, adhesive paper, liquid **latex**, or a stencil (15-19) and then painting over it with the oxide. Even if you were limited to using iron oxide alone, you would be able to enhance the surface of your clay with a considerable variety of effects. By adding another oxide such as cobalt, copper, or manganese to your palette and using the two oxides in combination, you can develop a considerable range of colors.

Normally, you would paint or wipe the oxide decoration onto a pot after the clay has been through a bisque firing, although it is also possible to paint it on damp unfired clay.

Slips and engobes for decoration   A slip is basically a mixture of clay and water. With an added deflocculant, the slip mixture can become a medium for casting in plaster or bisque clay molds (chapter 13). In this chapter, however, the term is used in relation to water-diluted clays that are used for decoration. Correctly, the term *slip* refers to this clay-and-water mixture used for decoration or for casting, while the term **engobe** should only be applied to any slip that covers the whole of a pot or sculpture. However, the two terms *slip* and *engobe* are frequently used interchangeably. White or cream engobes are often used to cover the reddish tone of earthenware clay in order to create a light background suitable for painted decoration. However, an engobe or slip can also be dark.

You will find that slips and engobes do not melt and run in the same way that many glazes do, and the color does not blur. For this reason, a beginner often finds slips easier to use for decoration than glazes. In addition, since slips or engobes are also made of clay, they have a natural visual relationship to the clay body, and with a transparent (or salt) glaze over the whole, a slip or engobe decoration seems particularly appropriate. A number of Picasso's ceramics were painted with white, red, and brown slips, giving these contemporary works a classic Mediterranean quality (15-11) that was not a result of the painting style alone. White slips are often made from white porcelain clay blended into a liquid state, white slips can be colored with the basic oxides or with the

Figure 15-11
Vase with Four Seasons, painted by Pablo Picasso. Picasso incised the vase with sgraffito lines and then painted it with white, red, brown and black slip. Once-fired earthenware. 1954. *Courtesy Museo Internazionale delle Ceramiche, Faenza. Photo: Minarini.*

wider range of colors available in commercial stains (Color plate 26). (See Appendices 1A and 1C for several slip recipes.)

Fitting the engobe or slip   It is usually a good idea to make (or buy) slip or engobe from the same clay body as that used for your pot or sculpture in order to ensure a good "fit" between the slip and the clay body. Since clays vary in their shrinkage rates, an engobe or slip made of a different clay might not have the same rate of shrinkage and may therefore peel off during drying or after firing. Early potters faced this problem when they made their white or cream engobes to cover the red earthenware body, and the pottery found in early sites frequently will show the results of this peeling, with very little of the original color left. If you use a slip of the same clay body as that used for the pot or sculpture, this will not be a problem, but one reason for using a slip or engobe is for color change.

To mix the light-colored engobes and slips, you can use light-colored clay materials such as kaolin, bentonite, and ball clays in varying proportions. Since each of these has a different rate of shrinkage, however, you may have to add flint to counteract shrinkage or borax to help the slip adhere to the pot.

If you have difficulty with a slip or engobe peeling after you have applied it or during firing, then reformulate the slip, engobe, or clay body so they fit each other better. You can also try adding a solution of **gum** to the slip. This may not solve your difficulty completely, but it will help to counteract the tendency to peel. Use a solution of 196 grams of CMC gum or gum tragacanth with 1 gallon of water. If the slip is to be stored for a long time, you *can* add an antispoilant solution to keep the gum from spoiling. Either Dowicide G or formaldahyde (¾ ounce per gallon) will do this. Since both these products are toxic, we suggest, in line with our recommendations to avoid using toxic materials when possible, that you mix only the amount of slip you need for immediate use so you do not have to use an antispoilant. If you do use them, ask the dealer to provide you with a MSDS information sheet giving handling precautions, and follow them.

Running a series of tests of a slip or engobe on test tiles made of the clay you want to cover is the only really *sure* way to see that it will fit and adhere to that particular clay body. In Appendixes 1A and 1C you will find some slip recipes to alter and test on your clay bodies.

Decorating with slip   Early potters devised a number of ways in which to decorate with slips and engobes. Since engobe is opaque, if you apply several coats it can color the whole pot or sculpture with a uniform color, or you can use it to create a variety of decorative effects. In the past, one especially popular method used was trailing the slip onto the damp clay, creating lines, marbeling, or "feathered" effects (7-1). The slip was simply trailed on in patterns, rather as one would write "Happy Birthday" on a cake. Nowadays, potters use variations of the slip-trailing technique to recreate traditional European designs (15-12) or even adapt it to designs based on African scarification (15-13). Robert Sperry, however, uses very direct methods to apply slip to his plates (see page 243) or to his large murals (14-6), sometimes splashing the slip on directly from a bucket.

Sgraffitto   The early use of white slip over reddish clay led to the sgraffitto technique. In this technique, lines were scratched through the light slip to reveal the darker clay beneath (page 115). Contemporary potters now use variations of this method, brushing the slip on thickly and then drawing into it with a sharp-pointed tool (15-14), inlaying slip into sgraffitto lines to suggest the ever-changing ocean (15-15), or using incised lines to capture the spirit of wild creatures in their natural habitats (15-16). Eileen Murphy, who uses incised lines to draw nature subjects, glazes her work in a salt kiln because she wants control over the evenness of the glaze and does not want the incised lines of her drawing to be filled in. She says,

The salt process does let me incise and keep the detail I want, but a misplaced pot, turned (unknowingly) the wrong way can loose the crispness I am after from too much heat, or 'blast'. For salt potters who don't want detail, the blast is what makes the work come alive and become interesting, but for my work I want control over the evenness of the glaze.

Figure 15-12
Trailing slip, using a rubber syringe, in a pattern inspired by early pottery decoration. Slip can be trailed over the surface to create marbled effects like this (7-1) and then "feathered" by drawing across the lines with a toothpick. *Photo: Alphabet and Image.*

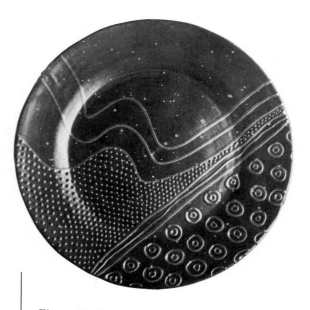

Figure 15-13
Plate: Scarification Series. David R. MacDonald, U.S.A., approaches the traditional method of slip trailing in a free manner, using slip to create patterns inspired by the scarification patterns of Africa. Stoneware. Diameter 22 in. (56 cm). *Courtesy the Hanover Gallery and the artist. Photo: Clifford Oliver.*

Slips and engobes can also be brushed on over a resist material, such as the wax-resist medium that is used to keep the edges of slabs damp or to create **wax-resist** effects with glazes. To do this, you apply the wax to the areas in which you wish to retain the color of the clay body. Then, when you brush the slip over the piece, the slip will adhere only to the unwaxed areas of the pot. The wax will burn off in the fire, and leave the contrasting body color showing in the areas that have been covered with wax. To get sharp-edged color decoration, you can use masking tape, adhesive paper, or a paper stencil. Apply it to the damp clay, paint over the stencil with slip, and then carefully pull off the tape. This method—known as the reserve method because you are *reserving* the color of the pot or sculpture itself—will result in an image that remains the color of the body with the contrasting slip surrounding it. Patrick Siler works with a complex stencil process using two colors of slip to create his figurative images. He uses a black slip over the greenware,

(a)

(b)

Figure 15-15
Inspired by the ocean outside her studio, Eileen Lewenstein, England, created a wavelike effect on her plate with incised lines that she filled with an oxide mixture; she rubbed it off, and then coated the surface with two glazes. Stoneware, press molded. Width 12 in. (30 cm). *Courtesy the artist.*

Figure 15-14
(a) Jens Morrison, U.S.A., builds up the finish on his sculpture using many different surfacing materials—found clays, slips, underglazes, glazes, and lusters. Here, he paints on thick, juicy brushfuls of slip. When it is leather hard, he will draw through it to expose the darker surface beneath. **(b)** *Tea Temple. Farmounian Reliquary.* Detail of the surface shows the incised drawing and the rich encrustment, made up of indigenous clays, underglaze, and glaze. *Courtesy the artist.*

323

Figure 15-17
Patrick Siler cutting out one of the blotting-paper stencils with which he created the series *Clay Works* (see page 189). *I like the contrast between the thick slip impasto and the sharp, severe stencil edge . . . ,* Siler says, *the making of stencils takes about three times what the clay work takes so I initiate the process by drawing and cutting out a whole lot of paper stencils.*

Figure 15-16
To create portrait vessels of the animals that live on her country acreage, Eileen Murphy, U.S.A., first sands her dry greenware (wearing a mask and goggles), then brushes on slips, and incises detail into the dry clay. For a glaze that will not fill the lines, Murphy depends on salt firing to coat, but not destroy, the complex colored surface. Stoneware, slips, stains, and sgraffito. *Courtesy Smith Gallery and the artist. Photo: Richard Walker.*

then applies a light ivory slip thickly over stencils made of blotting paper. After the slip has dried for a few minutes, he peels off the stencils, and the black underslip appears in the protected areas (15-17 to 15-19). Siler's slip recipes are in Appendix 1C.

If they are used alone, without a glaze coating or burnishing, slips and engobes fire with a dry, matt surface, a surface that can be extremely effective. On the other hand, the slip or engobe can be covered with a transparent glaze that, along with protecting the surface, gives it a glossy finish and enriches its color.

Terra sigillata   Terra sigillata is really a slip, made of clays whose particles are extremely

Figure 15-18
First, Siler coats the piece with a heavy covering of black slip; then he dips the stencils in water and attaches them to the stiffened clay with straight pins. *When I reach an arrangement I like, I will then dip the stencils in water and carefully pat them on the surface. Only when the edges of all the stencils are well pressed into the dark underslip will I begin to paint on the light colored overslips. Courtesy the artist.*

fine and that contain micalike minerals such as illite. The glossy red and black of the Greek vases (page 26, 2-20) and the glowing red of the Roman Arrentine ware (2-28) were produced by the use of this fine coating. On the Greek pottery, the black was obtained by reduction. But today, terra sigillata is used to give a much wider range of effects than in classic times. Like slip or engobe— which it basically is—terra sigillata appeals to those who wish to develop an intimate relationship between the surface of their work and its form, and who respond to the way in which the terra sigillata becomes an integral part of the clay body rather than coating the surface like a glaze. Such contemporary ceramists as Pierre Bayle (12-2 and Color plate 9) and Richard Hirsch (15-

Figure 15-19
A group of stencils are attached to one of Siler's three-dimensional pieces in preparation for brushing the second coat of slip. On the left side, the thick, light slip has already been applied over the stencils, and after drying for about five or ten minutes, they have been peeled off. *I like to apply the overslip thick enough to be stucco-like and crack a little in drying. . . . When the piece is thoroughly dry, I will spray on a simple clear glaze and fire the piece up to cone 5. Photos courtesy the artist.*

Figure 15-20
Vessel and Stand #2. Richard Hirsch, U.S.A., says of his smaller vessels, *Their presentation on a tripod stand pursues the feeling of ceremony and develops a monumentality beyond their true dimensions. . . . By purposely raising the pieces on this type of pedestal, I give visual praise to the vessel as an art form.* Despite the small scale of this sculptural vessel, its powerful forms and effective use of negative space give it an imposing character. Its rich surface, produced with a layering of terra sigillata, glazes, and a raku firing, adds to the sense of antiquity. Thrown and handbuilt; blue and green terra sigillata under cone 04 glaze; raku fired. Ht. 8 in. (20 cm). *Courtesy the artist.*

20, Color plate 13) use terra sigillata for sculptural vessels whose rich surfaces are nevertheless subordinated to the strong forms of their work, while Marilyn Lysohir (15-21, Color plate 15) finds that using terra sigillata on the bodies and clothing of her figurative sculpture gives them the warm surface she wants.

Terra sigillata is made by mixing a fine clay with water and water softener, then allowing it to settle—Marilyn Lysohir lets hers settle for at least two weeks. The particles fall to the bottom—first the coarsest, then the finer particles—leaving a layer of water on top. This water is then siphoned off, and only the top layer of very fine slip is applied in thin coats to the dry, unfired clay. Once a pot or a sculpture is coated with the terra sigillata, it can be fired at around 1760°F/960°C.

Applying terra sigillata   Terra sigillata can be brushed or sprayed on; it can then be burnished to achieve a high gloss or left unburnished. A good terra sigillata slip will dry to an attractive

Figure 15-21
Bad Manners, an installation by Marilyn Lysohir, U.S.A. (Color plate 15). Lysohir burnished
four coats of colored terra sigillata to create the rich surface on the figures. She carved the
patterning on the dress of the figure on the right before painting it (15-7). The foods on the
laden table are colored with underglaze (15-24). Clay and wood; terra sigillata and
underglaze; fired at cone 06. 4 ft. × 10 ft. 4 in. × 7 ft. (1.2 m × 3 m × 2 m). *Courtesy
Asher/Faure Gallery, Los Angeles. Collection: Mr. & Mrs. Louis Taubman. Photo: James Reinke.*

sheen, but it can be made even more glossy by
burnishing. Marilyn Lysohir applies three coats
to dry clay; then, on the fourth coat, she starts to
burnish the surface, rubbing just a small area at a
time.

Richard Hirsch also applies his sigillata on
dry clay:

*when the clay is bone dry in two or three coats
brushed on, which I burnish slightly—not a high
gloss. Then I air brush some on to create contrast*

*on the surface—i.e., glossy versus matt—and to
give some detail to the sigillata surface.*

Richard Hirsch gave up using the usual glaze
techniques some years ago and has experimented
with a number of other methods in order to develop a surface that does not interfere with the
formal aspects of his work. He has found that the
use of a white terra sigillata that can be colored
with stains or combined with low-fire glazes formulated to bring out its color enhances and em-

phasizes the forms of his work. Recipes for Hirsch's white and his red terra sigillata are in Appendix 1C, along with percentages of other colorants that can be added to the white.

Coloring terra sigillata   In the same way that the color of clay bodies can be altered using oxides and stains, terra sigillata can also be colored with these materials. A number of ceramic artists have found that colored terra sigillatas lend themselves especially well to the surfaces they wish to develop on their sculptures. Both Hirsch and Marilyn Lysohir find that with "sigs" they can get effects that they can obtain in no other way (Color plates 13 and 15). Hirsch says,

I mix my 'sigs' to get particular colors not obtainable through the use of one stain itself, just like mixing paint.

He then bisque fires the pieces to cone 06 or 05,

never higher than 04 because the color burns out and the sigs get too hard to raku-smoke, post-reduce.

To get the rich surface characteristic of his work, Hirsch also uses a semiopaque glaze to which he adds a variety of coloring materials. These glazes interface well with the terra sigillata beneath them. His base glaze recipe is in Appendix 1C along with the percentages of colorant he uses.

UNDERGLAZES

Underglazes, as the word implies, are used under other glazes. Whether they are applied as oxides or as commercial underglazes, they provide the ceramist with a wide range of decorative effects (Color plates 15 and 16) from which to choose.

Oxides as Underglaze

Historically, oxides have played an extremely important role in the development of ceramic colors and glazes. First, as components of the natural slips and clays, they were frequently part of the decoration of pottery. Then, once glazes were developed and the coloring properties of oxides were better understood, the oxides themselves were isolated and were often used for decorative effects under glazes. In chapter 3 we saw how potters first experimented with copper to produce red underglaze decoration, then abandoned it when the red bled into the glaze. They then turned to cobalt blue, finding it a more satisfactory underglaze color that did not bleed as much as the copper. The Chinese created their blue and white ware with cobalt, inspiring European potters to try to reproduce it (chapter 6). One of the advantages of using oxides under a glaze is that after firing, the color seems to float, suspended in the glaze, giving the decoration a luminous quality. The Chinese cobalt-decorated porcelain was especially noted for this quality; the best of it, made in the imperial kilns (3-18), was so precious that it was kept for the emperor's sole use. On the other side of the world, the American colonial potters used cobalt underglaze to decorate useful stoneware crocks and jugs for farmers, creating simple, direct images appropriate to the ware's use in rural homes (7-3). Oxides can be applied with a variety of brushing techniques, with sponges, or with cords dipped in the oxide and trailed across the object (15-22).

Prepared Underglaze Colors

Commercial opaque underglaze colors are prepared by calcining finely ground oxides, combining them with a flux and a refractory material, and mixing them with gum or some other binder to ensure adhesion. Although it is possible to make your own underglazes, it is difficult to formulate them so that they fit the clay body properly and adhere well. Most ceramists use commercially prepared underglazes for that reason. It is, however, possible to mix oxides and stains with a gum solution and use these as transparent underglazes that you can apply using a watercolor technique. (See Appendix 1A.)

Generally, these prepared underglazes are formulated for low firing, because at higher temperatures the warmer colors such as red and orange will burn out. Underglaze colors can be painted on with brushes as you would use watercolors, but you can also spray diluted underglaze on with an **airbrush**—using a respirator and a

Figure 15-22
Metal oxides are used to color glazes, but they can also be used for underglaze decoration. This plate shows the effects that can be produced by applying oxides with a variety of brushes or cords dipped in the coloring oxides. *Courtesy Alphabet and Image.*

spray booth—blending the colors much as you might on a canvas. Or you can apply underglazes over stencils or masking tape to create hard-edged images or patterns. By using these techniques in combination with other underglaze materials such as pencils and crayons, you can extend the range even further. David Miller, for example, decorates his vessels with a combination of techniques; first he sprays his teapots with slip and bisque-fires them; then he paints them with underglaze colors and slip stains. He adds a small amount of frit to the underglaze to make it less refractory and to help it fuse to the clay body during firing (15-23). Miller outlines areas with copper or cobalt oxide, or sometimes a mixture of both, then gives his vessels a salt firing to coat them with a transparent glaze that will bring out the color.

One of the advantages of using underglaze is that as you paint, the colors appear closer to the way they will look after firing—a factor that makes the final appearance easier to visualize than

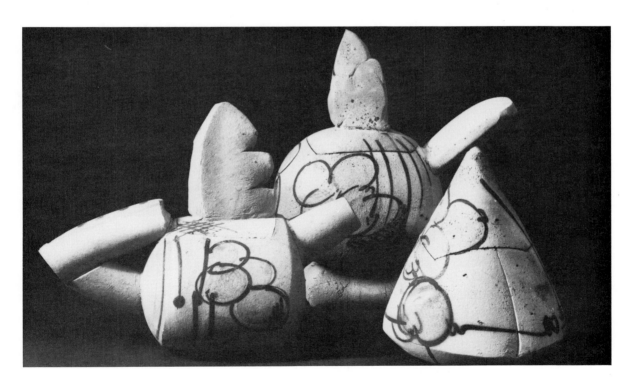

Figure 15-23
David Miller, England, first sprays slip onto his dry pots. He then bisque fires them and colors them with underglaze colors and slip stains to which he has added a small amount of frit to make them less refractory and to help them adhere to the pot. *Courtesy the artist.*

Figure 15-24
Marilyn Lysohir displays the food she made to use in
her installation *Bad Manners*. Here, it has been coated
with underglaze colors and awaits spraying with a
clear cone 05 glaze before firing. *Courtesy the artist.*
Photo: A. Okazaki.

Figure 15-25
James Caswell, U.S.A., slip cast *The Arcade* in one
piece using a five-part mold. He then painted it with
underglazes—aqua greens, deep pinks, yellow, and
purples—and fired it at cone 05. Of his work Caswell
says, *I developed an allergy to roundness and the circle. I
began and continue to work with the opposite—straight lines
and their conjunctions. . . .* Slip-cast earthenware. Ht.
24 in. (61 cm). *Collection, Mr. and Mrs. Alexander Grass.*
Courtesy the artist.

when you use ceramic glazes, whose colors look
dusty and pale until they are fired. Underglaze
pencils and crayons that allow one to draw in detail and shading appeal to many artists, since this
makes it possible to develop an image more easily
(15-31).

Underglaze colors are especially popular today, when many artists are using ceramic materials in ways that were never dreamed of a few
decades ago. Now that the line between vessel
and sculpture is blurred, with art and craft working together to create expressive statements that
redefine traditional ceramic terms, a technique
such as underglazing allows a ceramic artist to
achieve images with almost the same freedom as
a painter working on paper or canvas. Such a

Figure 15-26
Dan Gunderson, U.S.A., makes many sketches from
which he chooses the images he uses on his
underglaze-decorated cones. He draws the images on
the bisque-fired cone with a hard pencil before
starting the process of stenciling on the color with
underglazes.

Figure 15-27
Next, he uses masking tape and adhesive paper to cover
areas that he does not want colored when he sprays the
underglaze. As he proceeds with building up the colors,
he removes sections of the masking tape.

technique is bound to be popular (15-24 to 15-31
and Color plate 16).

Commercial underglazes come in a number of
forms:

- *Liquid*—either opaque or translucent
  colors
- *Pan*—in pans as in a watercolor paint set,
  these will give translucent colors when applied as a wash and opaque colors when
  applied thickly
- *Tube*—as with watercolors
- *Crayon or chalk*—similar to colored chalks
- *Pencil*—used for drawing detail, especially
  on fine-grained clay such as porcelain or
  low-fire white earthenware

Application Methods

Brushing   The traditional method of applying underglaze was with a brush. You may use
any type of brush that will give you the effect you
wish. A few brush types are listed in Appendix
4A.

Sponging   Applying underglaze with a natural or man made sponge is another common
method. With it you can achieve a stippled effect.

Airbrush   In addition to applying underglazes with a brush, you can airbrush it on. To do
this, you may need to add a little additional water

Figure 15-29
With the images completed, Gunderson sprays on a transparent glaze to cover the entire piece before firing it to cone 04. For one of Gunderson's pieces, see Color plate 16. *Courtesy the artist. Photos: Stetson University, Office of Public Relations.*

Figure 15-28
Gunderson airbrushes commercial underglazes thinned with water over a stencil held in place on his piece *Teeter Totter.* Note the original sketch tacked on the spray-booth wall as a guide. Even if you work in a ventilated spray booth, a respirator is recommended for added protection while airbrushing.

and use a coarser tip in the airbrush to allow it to go through.

Silk screen   If the ceramic object to be decorated is flat or nearly flat, you can easily use a **silk-screen** frame to apply underglaze colors directly onto it. If it is not flat enough to allow use of a framed screen, you can sometimes screen colors onto it by unframed taping silk-screen material to the curved surface.

Decals   **Decals** can be printed on transfer paper with underglaze colors. Such decals are not available commercially but they can be made to order. These decals are made with ceramic stains,

a flux, and a vehicle. The image is silk-screened or photo-printed onto special transfer paper using underglaze colors and then is transferred onto the ceramic surface.

Once you have applied underglaze colors—by whatever method you choose—you might wish to cover the piece with a transparent glaze before firing it. This glaze will enhance and protect the rather fragile underglaze colors (15-29). A transparent glaze is not essential as long as durability or solubility is not a problem, and the pastel matt colors that can be achieved by leaving off the glaze may suit your image better. As with every other ceramic technique, through experimentation you may discover a unique way of using un-

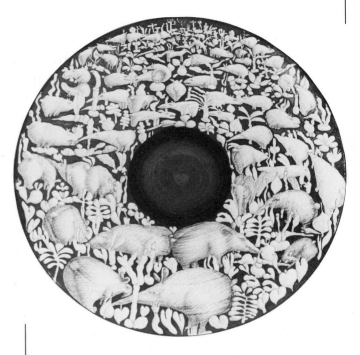

Figure 15-30
Great Egret Teapot, by Annette Corcoran, U.S.A.
Corcoran used an airbrush to spray underglaze stains
onto the elegant bird, drew detail with a brush, then
sprayed a light glaze to set the underglaze. In
addition, she sprayed and brushed on china paint
details and gave the piece multiple firings—sometimes
she does as many as 20 firings, going lower and lower
as she progresses. Although the teapot is made of
porcelain, the top firing temperature was cone 04.
Corcoran says, *I am very aware of the tactile feeling of the
finished piece as well as the visual. I sand the piece at each
stage of firing. I also like the look of an underfired
porcelain—it has a softer quality, not so much like glass!*
Porcelain. 1988. Ht. 9½ in (24.1 cm). *Courtesy the
artist and Dorothy Weiss Gallery. Photo: Lee Hocker.*

Figure 15-31
Bowl, by Jack Sures, Canada, shows the detail one
can achieve using underglaze pencils. Sures plays with
the illusionary space he creates with strong
perspective within the confines of the bowl form.
Engobe, underglaze pencil. Diameter 5 in. (12.5 cm).
*Courtesy Moose Jaw Art Museum and National Exhibition
Centre.*

derglaze that will be particularly appropriate to
your individual style of working.

 ## Precautions

Certain colors used in underglazes do not
pass the standards set up to monitor control the
use of toxic substances in glazes. Because such
colors could be soluble in certain food substances,
if you mix your own underglazes and use them on
any object that could be a container, you should
send them to an independent laboratory for testing to find out if they are safe. Care should also
be taken when working with the colors.

GLAZING YOUR WORK

You may be surprised the first time you see a
glazed pot or sculpture ready for the kiln. Most
people think that the potter has a palette of colors
like a painter's and need only pick out a color from
fired test tiles and paint it on for the pot to look
as it will when it is fired. Instead, there sits a
chalky, grayish-white pot, showing nothing of the
brilliant color or rich gloss that the firing will reveal. Because of the difference between unfired
and fired glaze, it is not always easy to visualize
what the result will be, but once you become accustomed to the transformation that occurs in the
kiln to change the powdery, unfired glaze coating

Figure 15-32
Vase, Edouard Chapallaz, Switzerland. Chapallaz's classic wheel-thrown forms display his perfectly fitted glazes in a pleasing integration of form and color. Stoneware, iron glaze, reduction firing. Ht. 12½ in. (32 cm). *Courtesy the artist. Photo: Rolf Zwillsperger.*

Figure 15-33
Teapot, Susan Ashmore, Canada. Rather than formulate her own glazes, Ashmore reformulates and tests glazes from various sources until she finds the one she likes. She used three glazes on this teapot—a high-fire volcanic ash glaze with tin and copper colorants, a soda feldspar transparent glaze with red iron oxide and rutile colorants, and an overlapping glaze with gold flecks and milky blue and purple accents. Fired to cone 6 in oxidation, with a 2–5 hour final soak. *Courtesy the artist.*

on your bisque-fired ware to a colorful glazed surface, you will understand why the process of **glaze firing** can become so fascinating.

Why Glazes Are Used

Glazes are not only functional, making the fired piece impervious to liquids and giving it a durable, watertight surface; they also add color and visual interest to pottery or sculpture (15-32 and Color plates 22 and 38). Remember, however, that a beautiful glaze cannot transform your work if its forms are not well composed in the first place.

Glazes can be glossy or matt, transparent or opaque, and the color range extends from subdued earth tones to brilliant reds and blues (Color plates 2, 3, 24, 27, and 43).

A glaze can be applied very thinly, allowing the texture of the clay to show through, or so thickly that it develops its own texture (Color plate 44). The decorative effects possible with glazes are many, varying from those that run down the sides (15-33) to carefully controlled applications (Color plates 23, 28, 30, and 38).

Thinking ahead to how you want to use glazes before applying them will help you arrive at more satisfactory final results. Rather than waiting until the bisqued form is ready to glaze, begin to think about the glaze as you are making the piece. Catherine Hiersoux (12-80) speaks of how, as she became more experienced and adopted this way of working, her glazes and decorations improved greatly. Many of the principles you may have learned in a painting or design class can be applied to glazing your work, and if you plan a design and color scheme with watercolors or chalks *before* you start to apply the glaze, you can choose the glazes from your test tiles with greater success.

Choosing a Glaze

As you study the examples of glazes from past and present throughout the book, consider which type would be most appropriate to your work. For example, the delicate green of a celadon glaze can be successful as Harris Deller uses it (Color plate 31), but it would hardly suit a heavily grogged rough-textured piece. If the pot or sculpture to be glazed is heavily carved or modeled, a glossy glaze might destroy the impact of the carving by producing confusing reflections and highlights; on such a piece, a matt surface may be the solution. Deciding on what glaze to use, if any, is one of the important aesthetic and expressive decisions every potter and sculptor has to make, and it usually takes a good deal of experience with glazes before your choices will always be successful (15-33).

The first glazes you use may be school glazes made up in quantity from a formula that has been translated into a batch recipe. Or perhaps you will choose from the many prepared glazes available commercially. You can, for example, choose bright, low-fire glazes to bring animation to your sculpture, or you may want to use a more subdued, high-fire glaze that will fire to a color similar to that on a sample tile you saw in the store. However, if you want to understand why glazes respond as they do to the fire, it is worthwhile to learn how to formulate your own, or at least how to make changes in the formulas given in Appendix 1A, or from magazines and ceramists. There are a number of advantages to mixing your own glazes. One is that you will know exactly what materials are used in them—for example, you can mix them with no toxic ceramic materials and no toxic antispoilants. The main advantage of mixing your own glazes is that, as when you mix clay, you will be able to make changes in the glaze composition, thereby often achieving qualities that are not available commercially. For example, Les Manning could not have combined stoneware and porcelain with a pale, glacier-green glaze on one

Figure 15-34
Snow Bowl by Les Manning, Canada. He laminated stoneware and porcelain to create what he calls a sculptural clayscape. He then gave the porcelain a coating of Leach's clear glaze with 1 percent iron, which, he says *is very icelike and similar in color to the limestone silt-colored lakes in the Canadian Rocky Mountains.* For these landscape bowls, Manning says he uses, *heavily grogged stoneware for the immediate surroundings, medium stoneware for the distant horizon, and porcelain to depict the atmosphere. These natural characteristics of the clays help animate in the pieces the awesome space of the landscape.* Stoneware and porcelain; fired in reduction at cone 8. Ht. 6 in. (15 cm). *Courtesy the artist. Photo: Monte Greenshields.*

piece without having a thorough knowledge of how clay and glaze act and interact in the kiln (15-34). Learning more about the various chemicals that comprise glazes and the materials that provide those chemicals will help you to understand the unique qualities that each component contributes to a glaze. For instance, some materials melt easily in the heat of the kiln, others add color, and still others can change the texture of a glaze. Depending on the ingredients used, some glazes may be pitted and lavalike (7-11) while others are glossy (15-35).

In the past, potters knew nothing about the chemistry of glazes, so they had to learn everything by trial and error. Modern chemistry, however, allows us to analyze the composition of a glaze and to learn exactly what materials are needed to change its composition in order to achieve certain effects. As a result, glaze testing is simpler and faster now, because we can start out with a basic understanding of the chemistry of a glaze. Computer programs now available can make this process easier. Nevertheless, it is still necessary to test, and by so doing you may find that your best glaze is the result of experimentation. Indeed, there is no reason why you cannot make excellent glazes by measuring out the basic ingredients within the generally known proportions, adding or subtracting materials and then testing the glaze. Measuring cups and spoons and a creative approach can be successful for those who wish to avoid the chemistry, and there is no need to be put off by the "mystery" of glazes. Glaze making is not some form of alchemy performed by wizards in peaked hats.

What Makes a Glaze?

Glazes are formulated from three categories of chemical compounds, each of which has a different function in the glaze. These are (A) the *fluxes* that help the glaze to melt in the heat; (B) the *refractories* that increase the viscosity and stability of the glaze in the fire, and (C) the *glass formers* that are what the word implies—the basic components of glaze. These compounds are obtained from a variety of materials. The type and percentage of these materials will vary in accordance with the temperatures at which the ceramist intends to fire the work (usually between 1500° and 2450°F/815.5° and 1343.3°C). Hundreds of glaze formulas that have already been formulated with the correct chemical balance needed to form a glaze are available to the ceramist (a few are given in Appendix 1A and 1C). If, after reading this chapter, you want to go further into the subject of glaze calculation using chemistry, study the information on chemical analysis in Appendix 3A, "Calculating Glazes Using Chemical Analysis," where you will find out more about the role these three basic ingredients play—flux, refractory, and glass former—in making a glaze.

Glass former   A glaze is basically a glassy, impervious coating that is fused to the surface of the clay by heat. As the kiln heat is raised and held at a certain temperature, the separate materials that you have mixed together begin to melt and fuse, eventually combining into a completely new material—the glaze. The oxides of silica, alumina, and others such as calcium, sodium, or zinc also play important roles in the formation of glazes. The main glass-forming ingredient in glazes is silica, which is highly resistant to heat. A glaze could be made of silica alone, but since silica's melting point is so high (3115°F/1713°C), that would be impractical; few clay bodies could withstand such high heat, and few ordinary kilns could fire that high.

Flux   The proportion of silica in a high-fire glaze can be greater than in a low-fire glaze, because at low temperatures too much silica would keep the glaze from melting. Generally, as much silica as possible is used in a glaze, because silica adds durability and helps the fired glaze resist the attack of acids and chemicals. Therefore, in order to lower the melting point of the silica, another ingredient must be added—a flux. The glaze melts as a result of the interaction of the oxides in the glaze materials when they are exposed to heat, and it is one of the basic facts of glaze-making that glaze materials used in such a combination (**eutetic**) melt at lower temperatures than they would if they were used alone. The fusing temperature of a glaze may be lowered considerably depending upon the *combination* of fluxing oxides and their proportions in the glaze in relation to the silica. (At this point, we are talking about oxides as glaze components, not as coloring agents. However, the oxides used to color a glaze, such as iron, can also bring extra fluxing action to the glaze, lowering its melting point even further.)

Refractory   The third ingredient necessary to most glazes is a refractory (high-melting) material, alumina. A common source of alumina is china clay. Alumina increases **viscosity**, helps to

Figure 15-35
Two porcelain vases by Catherine Hiersoux, U.S.A., illustrate the visual effect of different glazes on similar shapes. On the glossy black vase (left), the form as shown in profile becomes dominant as one's eye follows the swelling and narrowing contours, while on the copper-red-glazed vase (right), the eye lingers on the surface before following its profile. Porcelain; reduction; copper red and black glazes. *Courtesy the artist. Photo: Richard Sargent.*

keep the glaze materials suspended as well as helping the glaze stick to the ware. Alumina, even if used in very small amounts, also adds strength and durability to the glaze and helps prevent the glaze from running; without it, the glaze might run down and off the sides of the object during firing. Also, without alumina, glazes tend to crystallize during the cooling process and thus may become opaque. Sometimes the potter wants crystals to develop for decorative reasons; in that

case the alumina content is reduced (Color plate 17).

Each of these three basic glaze ingredients may be introduced to the glaze by adding any of a variety of ceramic materials, and each of these materials has individual properties and reacts in its own way with other materials. In order to understand what happens when you change them, it is extremely important to become familiar with the glaze materials. For example, zinc oxide

(ZnO) acts as a flux at temperatures above 2109°F/ 1154°C. It can also make a glaze matt and opaque if you add it in larger amounts. If used in small amounts, it can add smoothness to a glaze, but if too much is used alone as a flux, the zinc may make the glaze **crawl** on the pot or cause pinholes to develop. Zinc interacts well with copper to help produce bright turquoise, but if used with chrome, it sometimes produces brown rather than chrome green. You can see from this example that in order to make successful glazes you should understand the properties and behavior of each material as well as the effect it will have on the other ingredients in the glaze. Although ceramists today can rely on chemistry more than their predecessors, they must still test their glazes to see how they act on a particular clay or in a particular firing situation.

Frits

A **frit** is a combination of raw glass-forming materials that has been fired, fractured by immersion in water while still molten, and finally ground up in a **ball mill**. Fritting is done to make raw, soluble materials insoluble and to lower the fusion point of the individual materials by combining them. It is these qualities that make frits so useful to ceramists.

Frits are available commercially, and their chemical formulas are also available so that you can see exactly what materials they contain, allowing you to know the exact percentage of silica, alumina, and fluxes present. Produced primarily for the ceramic industry, frits offer the ceramist a wide range of glass-forming compounds, and because their chemical composition is known, it is easier for the user to control the uniformity of a glaze from batch to batch.

There is another reason for fritting. Many raw glaze materials, such as lead, barium, and cadmium, are poisonous, and some, such as borax, potash, and soda ash, are caustic **alkalies** that are soluble in water. Used raw, some of these materials would be toxic or injurious to the person using them. Others, when used in their raw soluble state in a glaze, could be released from the glaze when the finished glazed object is used to hold foods that contain acids like vinegar, wine, coffee, whiskey, and lemon juice. Used in frit form, a number of these materials are safe, or at

least less dangerous, so frits have become standard in the ceramics industry. There is still concern, however, about how safe some of the frits are, both for the person handling the glaze in the studio and the person eating or drinking from a glazed container. There is some controversy, for example, about the safety of handling lead even in frit form, and tests show that dangerous amounts of lead are released from even fritted lead glazes when the glazed object is exposed to acids. For that reason, we recommend that you do not use any lead, even in frits, for glazes on the interior of any container that could be used for foods or beverages. Appendix 1D lists some lead-free frits you may safely use. Have any glaze about which you are uncertain analyzed by a testing laboratory to be sure there is no danger in using it on food containers. You must also consider whether you wish to expose yourself to *any* lead in *any* form.

Another reason for using a frit instead of raw, soluble materials is that in some cases a raw material could be absorbed into the porous surface of the bisque-fired ware, and thus change the chemical composition of the glaze. This would affect the texture, color, or other qualities of the glaze. In addition, dry, soluble materials are hard to store, since they absorb water from the atmosphere and form lumps. It is clear, then, that by using frits you can reduce some of the problems caused by soluble materials and some of the hazards of using raw glaze materials.

Frits also lower the temperature at which the soluble materials can be used, and because of their fluxing qualities, frits are extremely useful in low-fire glazes. In addition, since the materials in a frit have already been melted once, no volatile materials are left to cause pinholes or pits as they burn out, which can happen with raw materials. However, frits in glazes fired above cone 6 may tend to bubble, especially when fired in a reduction atmosphere. Because of this tendency, and also because of the expense of frits, feldspars are generally used as the main flux in high-fire glazes where more flux is needed. (In a low-fire glaze where feldspar is used to introduce alumina, the feldspar acts as a refractory.) Feldspars are naturally formed frits and using them is an economical way to introduce silica and alumina into a high-fire glaze. For example, comparing the composition of Frit 25 and Custer spar, we find that the frit contains 12.1 percent alumina while the Custer has 17.5 percent. When it comes to the silica, however, the difference is greater: the Frit 25 has 49.7 percent but the Custer spar contains a much larger proportion of silica—68.5 percent.

Types of Glazes

Like clay bodies, glazes fall into three types according to their firing ranges: low-fire glazes, medium-fire stoneware glazes, and high-fire stoneware and porcelain glazes. The ceramist can also choose from a variety of specific glaze types such as transparent or opaque, matt or glossy, ash glazes (16-15, Color plate 11), slip glazes, crystalline glazes (Color plate 17), salt glaze (16-19 and 16-20), and raku glazes (16-23, Color plates 13 and 28).

Low-fire glazes (cones 015 to 1)   Ever since the early potters in Egypt and the Middle East developed alkaline and then lead and tin glazes, potters have used low-fire glazes to make earthenware watertight or to add color to household vessels. Today, these glazes are popular with potters and sculptors alike, because they provide bright, smooth colors with which to enliven their work (Color plates 27 and 40).

As the name implies, low-fire glazes melt at low temperatures (1479°F/804°C to 2109°F/1154°C). Low-fire glazes have a much wider range of colors than high-fire glazes and are available as transparent, matt, or opaque glazes. Although most low-fire glazes begin to melt at cone 015 (1479°F/804°C) and mature at around cone 05 (1915°F/1046°C), they can often be fired as high as cone 5 (2185°F/1196°C). With the exception of the bright reds and oranges, most colors will fire at higher-than-expected temperatures with interesting results. Because the glazes tend to become more fluid with the higher heat, it may be necessary to apply less glaze to the surface. Thus, if you usually apply three coats by brushing, then two coats of glaze should be adequate if it is to be fired higher. Low-fire glaze colors tend to darken on stoneware clay bodies when fired to stoneware temperatures that are higher than those for which they were formulated.

It is possible to use low-fire glazes in consecutive firings. For example, you could fire your ware with a high-fire glaze, leave some areas blank, and then, after the first glaze firing, apply low-fire glazes to those areas, then refire to create a high-fire look with low-fire accents. Colors such as red and orange, which would burn out at stoneware temperatures can be added using this technique. Many ceramists layer slips, underglazes and glazes, firing them in successive firings. Richard Hirsch is one of these. He says he sometimes glazes low-fire glazes over the bisqued-on terra sigillata or raku fires the piece.

Finally sometimes I sand blast the glaze surface to reveal the colored terra sigillata underneath. I have now returned to the use of glaze because I think it is appropriate to the layering effect of age I am after. Also I like the hardness vs softness, tactile vs visual play.

Throughout history, two types of fluxes have traditionally been used to give low-fire glazes their low-melting characteristics. Alkaline glazes depend on an alkali such as sodium or potassium to melt them. These alkaline glazes, although they produce brilliant colors when coloring oxides are added to them, are rather soft, and can easily be scratched, so use them for objects that will have little wear. For example, if you want to make glazed tiles for installation in your home, you could use colorful alkaline glazed tiles in a spot that receives relatively little wear and moisture; for heavy-use areas such as a floor you would instead use stoneware clay and high-fire stoneware glazes. Alkaline glazes are difficult to fit to the clay body. They tend to craze, developing small cracks, over their entire surface, because they have a wide range of expansion and contraction in the kiln. This may be decorative, but it weakens the glaze, which may wear or weather off with use. Food containers should never be glazed inside with an alkaline glaze because of the possibility of food getting in the cracks. Use alkaline glazes on nonfunctional pieces only, where their brilliant colors will be decorative but not subjected to wear.

Historically, lead was extremely popular, because glazes made with it melt at a low temperature, fit the clay well, and take color well. Combined with tin, lead made possible the cream-colored glazes that early Italian potters used so successfully on their maiolica ware as background for bright-colored glazed decoration

(6-3, 6-4, Color plate 4). Unfortunately, lead is hazardous to work with, and we know from historical documentation that many workers, including women and children who worked in the decorating rooms of pottery factories, died as a result of lead poisoning. We will never know how many more people throughout history were made ill by eating or drinking from improperly fired lead glazes that were used on food containers.

Using lead in fritted form is an improvement over using it raw, but unfortunately even fritted lead can later be released from the glaze. Improper firing (not high or long enough), improper application (too thick), or the addition of even a small amount of copper to a fritted lead glaze can increase the danger that the lead will be released in contact with acids. Because the public generally does not know about this risk, some people recommend putting a hole in any lead-glazed convex form that might hold liquid to make it impossible for a child to drink from it. To be absolutely sure that what you make in the ceramic studio does not present a possible hazard to others, we recommend that you use only high-fire glazes for anything that could possibly be used for food or liquid consumption.

Medium-fire glazes (cones 2 to 7)   Medium-firing glazes were developed partly as a result of the energy crisis of the 1970s and partly because a good many electric kilns on the market do not heat above cone 6 or 8. Once ceramists started to fire within this range of cone 2 (2124°F/1162°C) to 7 (2264°F/1240°C), they found that the lower firing range often gave more brilliance to their glazes. Certain colors, such as the maroons and yellows, do not hold their color well in high temperatures and in a reduction atmosphere, but these colors, which could be lost in a cone 10 reduction firing, hold their color better in the medium firing range. For these reasons, many ceramists have continued to use the medium-range glazes.

High-fire glazes (cones 8 to 13)   High-fire glazes are formulated to be fired from cone 8 to 13 (2305°F/1263°C to 2455°F/1346°C) and are used on stoneware and porcelain clay bodies (15-34, 15-35). Unlike the low-fire glazes, which always remain as a surface coating on the fired object, properly fired high-fire glazes actually in-

teract and bond with the clay body, creating a buffer layer between the glaze and the body. The advantage of this close bond is that the glaze has a greater resistance to the stresses that cause crazing or peeling. Because of this interaction between clay and glaze, the glaze may pick up "impurities" from the clay body that will cause spots, such as iron spots, or splotches of color to appear in the fired glaze. Whether you consider these spots and splotches desirable or undesirable depends upon your personal taste.

Ash glazes   The ashes that were blown onto the shoulders of the pots from the wood fires in early Chinese and Japanese stoneware kilns often formed accidental glazes on the ware (3-9). Observing this, potters started to experiment, and gradually they developed deliberately applied ash glazes. It was from this experimentation that high-fire glazes developed in China and Japan.

Nowadays, potters continue to use ashes to make attractive and interesting glazes. Since the plant materials that are burned to make the ashes take up minerals from the earth while they are growing, their ashes are rich in glaze-forming ingredients such as potash, lime, alumina, and silica, as well as various oxides that provide color. You can obtain ashes for glazes by burning wood, berry canes, grasses, sawdust, corn cobs, rice hulls, and even fruit pits. If you wish to control the ingredients so that you will be able to replicate the glaze, then you should keep each type of ash separate and test them independently, because each one will have a different chemical composition. For example, the ashes of some plants, such as grass, wheat, and fast-growing weeds, contain more silica than those from slow-growing trees. Therefore, the ashes from grasses and weeds create more stable glazes, while ashes from trees will make runnier glazes. Even the locality where the tree or other material was cut may make a difference, because the minerals in the soil vary.

You can experiment making a glaze using ashes alone, burning any organic material you can gather in sufficient quantity; potters have even gathered ashes from state park barbecue pits, and Ericka Clark Shaw has developed a low-fire glaze in which she uses ashes from charcoal briquettes (Appendix 1C). If you use the ash on a clay body that contains a considerable amount of silica, you may find that it makes an adequate and beautiful glaze without any additions. Or you may want to add feldspar, clay, and perhaps whiting as an additional flux. Generally, the proportions suggested are approximately 40 percent ash, 40 percent feldspar, and 20 percent clay, but the percentages can vary. Some ash glaze recipes are given in Appendix 1C.

To prepare ashes for making glazes, soak them first in water to leach out the soluble materials. The water drained off will contain lye and can burn your skin, so be careful and wear rubber gloves when you pour it off. Even if you mix ashes dry, it is wise to wear gloves. After the ashes have soaked, put them through a sieve and mix them with the other ingredients. Although you can add small percentages of ash to low-fire glazes, the best effects with ashes come with high-firing glazes, to which larger amounts can be added.

To give the effect of an accidental ash glaze, you can sprinkle dry ash directly on the ware before placing it in the kiln, duplicating to a certain extent what happens when ashes fly in a wood-fired climbing kiln (Figure 16-13). Many ceramists have also become interested in the effects that can be achieved with the accidental ash glazes that may form on pots in Japanese-style wood-firing kilns (16-13 and 16-14 and Color plates 8 and 11). These kilns are discussed in chapter 16.

Slip glazes   Some clays or powdered rocks will make a glaze when they are used alone. For example, feldspars are natural frits that could form a glaze if fired at high enough temperature, such as those possible in industrial kilns. But feldspar's melting point is so high it would require additional flux in order to fuse in the average studio kiln. There are, however, natural clays that will form slip glazes in the brown range when fired at the lower temperatures because they contain iron and manganese (15-36). In these, the iron functions as both a flux and a colorant. An example of a natural slip glaze was the terra sigillata that the Greeks and Romans used to create the glossy surface of their pottery. It was formed of fine-grained natural clays that contained micalike substances. The dark-brown-firing Albany slip used by the early stoneware potteries in New York state (7-3) was, until it was recently mined out, also a popular natural slip glaze.

Although some substitutes for Albany slip

Figure 15-36
Ron Judd, U.S.A., first poured natural color Albany slip over the whole surface of this vase, producing a reddish-brown background. He then gave it a second coat of Albany slip with rutile that produced yellowish brown areas. The final glaze, through which the earlier glazes show, is a light tan matt.

are being mined, slip glazes are now more likely to be specially mixed rather than used in their natural forms. They are formulated to provide special qualities—for example, a light hue so that the slip can be colored with stains. Because a slip glaze contracts when it dries, it does not adhere well to a bisque-fired surface, so it is generally applied on damp clay or greenware. This will allow the two clays to shrink at similar rates. Even so, in order to fit well, a slip glaze should be carefully formulated to have the same shrinkage rate as the clay body.

Matt glazes   There may be times when, instead of a glossy surface, you would prefer to use a nonshiny, or matt, glaze. The characteristic satin surface of a high-fire matt glaze is hard and durable, but without strong gloss. The matt effect is produced by large numbers of tiny crystals in the glaze—too small to be seen by the naked eye—which break up the light. Satin-matt glazes, along with "buttery" or "fat" matt glazes, are often sought for certain types of pottery. Introducing a larger amount of clay, such as china clay, into the glaze will increase the alumina and make the glaze more refractory so that it will tend to be under-fired. This underfired quality gives it its matt appearance. Matt glazes can also be produced by incorporating zinc oxide into the glaze, and by increasing the silica, calcium oxide, titanium dioxide, or magnesium, or by underfiring a gloss glaze. A matt glaze produced in this way is usually very porous, so it is used primarily for decorative purposes. Barium carbonate has long been the standard material used to create high-fire matt glazes, but since it is extremely poisonous, many people no longer use it. If it is used great care should be taken in handling it and it should not be used on the inside of food containers.

To produce a matt glaze, it is also important that the cooling rate of the kiln be controlled and the kiln be brought down slowly in order to allow the formation of the crystals responsible for the matt surface. You will find the percentage recipes for several matt glazes in appendix 1C.

Crystalline glazes   Unlike the matt glazes, where the crystals are too small to be seen, in crystalline glazes the crystals are visible to the eye, creating unusual decorative effects on the surface of the pot and often giving a quality of depth to the glaze in which they lie suspended. Although these crystals will form in glazes used on both stoneware and porcelain, usually ceramists use them on porcelain because the crystals show to greater advantage against the white clay background. The crystals catch the light and reflect it, visually breaking up the glaze surface and often creating strong patterns. For this reason, crystalline glazes are best exhibited on simple forms.

The snowflake-like crystals that form in this type of glaze are actually grown, through the use of certain materials, by careful control of the rise and decline of kiln temperature, and by soaking the ware in the kiln. Crystalline glazes are produced by reducing the alumina content and using a variety of materials and chemicals such as zinc oxide, borax, sodium, potassium, rutile, or iron. In order to create crystals, these glazes must contain only a small amount of alumina, so they are very runny, and the glazed ware must be placed on special clay or porcelain supports dusted with alumina to prevent it from sticking to the kiln shelves as the glaze melts.

The creation of crystalline glazes requires a thorough knowledge of glaze materials and firing procedures, but even an expert such as Arnold Zahner (Color plate 17), who has formulated crystalline glazes for a number of years, may open a kiln and find unexpected results. Speaking of the vase illustrated in the color plate, Zahner said,

> *The glaze is a cone 8 glaze, containing 27 percent zinc oxide. Normally, it gives starlike or sunburst crystals of a darker green on a light ground. I fired this vessel in an electric kiln, and introduced propane gas into the kiln during the cooling period. For unknown reasons, the color and the shape of the crystals and their pattern came out quite differently; a typical example of the excitement and adventure of working with crystalline glazes. One has to be willing to experiment carefully, and use the best workmanship possible, but then be ready to accept whatever happens. Very often there are good or bad surprises. This is the rule of the game.*

Since Zahner's glaze recipe is in Appendix 1C, you can try it and see what it does on your clay and in your kiln.

Salt glaze   Salt glazing developed in the Rhine Valley in Germany in the Middle Ages and was used for centuries to create watertight, acid-resistant utilitarian ware in both Europe and colonial America (chapters 6 and 7). Produced when damp salt is introduced into the heated kiln (at a temperature of at least 1940°F/1060°C), the glaze is formed when the sodium is released in the presence of moisture, and as the salt volatizes its vapors fill the kiln. As the heat sends the vapors swirling around, they settle on the pots, the shelves, and on the kiln walls. The sodium combines with the silica and alumina in the clay, forming a thin glaze on everything in the kiln. A salt glaze can be thin and smooth—a surface that is especially effective on pieces that have carving or incised decoration, as it does not fill the lines and obscure the design (15-16)—or it can have a mottled and pitted orange-peel texture caused by the glaze beading on the surface (16-20). Since a salt glaze does not usually penetrate and coat the interior of the pots, some ceramists use another high-fire glaze in the interior. The stonewares produced in New York state (7-3) were glazed inside with Albany slip. Salt glaze is, however, no longer used for traditional forms alone; ceramists are now exploring its effect on sculptural creations (16-19).

Some salt glazers introduce the salt by throwing it in, others insert it carefully on metal rods (16-18), and others wrap it in damp newspaper before putting it in the kiln. In order to see if the glaze is developing satisfactorily, some potters place rings of clay in the kiln where they can reach in and draw them out with a metal rod to check on whether the glaze is developing well.

 Salt releases chlorine and hydrochloric acid fumes when it vaporizes, fumes that are capable of seriously damaging your lungs. Protect yourself when you insert the salt into the kiln and the vapors form. Either stay clear of the vapors (16-17 and 16-18) or wear a respirator rated for acid fumes. Also, take care in placing the kiln. The kiln stack should be high enough to avoid sending these fumes toward humans or buildings.

Other Glaze Materials

Any mineral material has the possibility of providing additives that may create interesting glaze effects. A number of contemporary ceramists have explored the use of mineral materials that they find in their locality. These have included volcanic materials, crushed rocks and gravels, cement, and mine tailings (9-13). If you experiment with unusual materials, test them on small test tiles first.

Since glass is compatible with the glass-forming ingredients of glazes, it can also be used along with glazes. You can used smashed glass bottles (wear gloves and a face shield when breaking them), colored beads, or rods of glass. The glass melts and becomes fused with the glaze, creating small areas of contrasting color within it.

OVERGLAZE TECHNIQUES

After you have fired your pot or sculpture with either high-fire or low-fire glazes, you can carry the process of enriching the surface and color further by using overglazes, enamels, china paints, lusters, and metallic lusters on top of the glaze (Color plate 18).

Overglaze (On-Glaze Decoration)

Sometimes called on-glaze painting, overglazing is a traditional method of decorating, used in Spain, Italy, and the rest of Europe for all low-fire color-decorated pottery until the European potters eventually learned how to imitate the Chinese blue and white underglaze decoration on porcelain (6-1, 6-2). To prepare work for overglazing, one generally applies a base coat of glaze, usually (although not always) white or cream or light gray in color, to the piece to be glazed. Once this base glaze is dry, the piece can be sprayed with a solution of gum (128 grams gum to 1 gallon of water) that will protect it from being disturbed when the overglaze is painted on it. Then, either coloring oxides mixed into some of the original base glaze, ceramic stains, or other glazes can be brushed on with quick strokes, disturbing the base glaze as little as possible (15-37, 15-38). The same method may be used with sulfates or nitrates of different oxides.

China Paint and Enamels (Cone 020 to 016)

With the contemporary interest in complex colored surfaces on ceramic sculpture, overglazes have become popular, and china painting, which used to be associated with Victorian ladies painting flowers on teacups, has become quite a different process in the hands of contemporary ceramic artists.

China paints and **enamels** are basically very low-fire glazes (1175°F/635°C to 1323°F/717°C) that you can apply on top of an already fired glaze. They were used in the past to decorate household china, which is why they are often grouped together and called china paints. However, the word enamel correctly refers to overglaze colors that are opaque, while *china paint* is the correct name for the translucent overglaze.

(a)   (b)

Figure 15-37
(a) Larry Murphy, U.S.A., painted cobalt oxide over a white glaze to test how the oxide would appear on it when fired; he found it too bland and discarded the glaze. (b) Murphy demonstrates using a banding wheel that makes it easier to paint decoration over the glaze.

There are a number of advantages to using china paint and enamels. Aside from the range of colors they produce, they are available in matt or gloss, translucent or opaque forms; they hold their position when they are applied; and they give excellent detail (Color plate 25). In fact, enamels are used to paint faces on porcelain dolls. Since china paints and enamels mature at low temperatures, they are generally used for the final firing, because if you apply another glaze that requires a higher temperature over the china paint, the china paint would be likely to change color in the higher heat. If you want the color to hold, you should fire the highest-firing glaze first, then follow it with a lower-firing glaze, and finally end with the china paint or luster on top of that. On the other hand, some artists have found that they like what happens with china paints or enamels when they are fired at higher temperatures: the china paint burns into the glaze, leaving residues that will be darker in hue and somewhat mottled.

Some transparent overglaze paints are avail-able that are like watercolor paints and can be brushed on in thin washes of color, while opaque oil base overglazes can be mixed with a special paste to produce raised textures. Most colors (as long as they are mixed in the same medium) can be mixed with each other to create new shades. Some, such as reds, pinks, and purples, may not mix well, however, because the various oxides and chemicals that are combined to produce these particular colors of china paint have little tolerance for contamination.

The easiest way to use china paint colors and enamels is to buy them ready-to-use in tubes or pans. If, however, you want to prepare your own, you can buy the colors in powder form, add an oil- or water-base **china paint medium**, and mix the colors with a mortar and pestle or on a glass palette. Whichever type you use, the paint can be brushed on, sprayed on, or applied with a silk screen or as decals. Successive sprayed coats of china paint, usually requiring firing between coats, can create subtle gradations and depth of color. You will find information on firing china paints and enamels in chapter 16.

China paint is not very durable—witness your great-grandmother's teacups, whose carefully applied flowers have worn off—so it is generally used for sculpture, for decorative objects, or the outer edges of dinner plates, where it will receive less wear.

Lusters and Metallics

Lusters and metallic lusters, like china paints, are usually applied on top of a fired glazed surface. Made from metallic salts, the earliest deliberately induced lusters were those used by Persian potters on top of opaque tin glazes (3-32). The technique they developed spread to Spain with the Moslem expansion and then on to Italy and the rest of Europe. The metallic salts in these early lusters were first painted on the fired tin glaze, then were refired in the heavy reducing atmosphere necessary to develop the luster of the metal. As is still the case, the base glaze on which they were painted had to be capable of becoming soft enough at a low temperature to allow the metals to adhere, but it could not become too molten or the color would be ruined. The Persian methods were used until a new, easier luster technique was developed in France involving liquid gold. Although some contemporary ceramists have replicated the ancient Persian and Spanish luster techniques, nowadays most use commercially prepared lusters whose metals are dissolved in oils that provide a local reducing agent. Although traditionally lusters are used on top of a glaze, some contemporary ceramists use them on unglazed pieces (Color plate 18).

Translucent lusters   These are known for their shimmering quality, with colors ranging from shades of blue, green, and orange to pinks, gray, purple, maroon, and pearl. Because they are translucent, the color of the glaze on which they are applied tends to show through, making it possible to create sumptuous effects.

Metallic lusters   Metallics are opaque overglazes available in various shades of gold, platinum, and copper. Gold and platinum are also

Figure 15-38
Brushed-on and resist decoration on glazed ware by Eric Norstad, U.S.A. Norstad's high-fire domestic ware is made in his production pottery workshop where tableware is produced in series—somewhat standardized for control but keeping the quality of individually produced pottery. *Courtesy Eric Norstad.*

available in pens for writing or fine line work. Because of their opacity, metallics are not greatly affected by the color of the glaze on which they are applied. When the oil burns out in firing, the metal becomes fused to the surface of the glaze. For information on firing lusters, see chapter 16.

Applying lusters   Since lusters are easily contaminated, the surface on which you apply them should be clean, dust free, and dry, while the brushes you use for applying lusters and metallics should be clean. Either use a separate brush for each color or plan on cleaning your brush thoroughly between colors with a special non-acetone cleaner. Apply luster with proper local ventilation to remove the fumes (see page 195).

Mayer Shacter (15-39) uses only one brush, but, he cleans the brush thoroughly between colors and finds that

Figure 15-39
Zig-Zag. A nonfunctional teapot provides the "canvas" on which Mayer Shacter, U.S.A.,
creates a rich surface by painting layers of luster colors on unglazed porcelain, firing them
after each layer. The satin surface and subtle color relationships integrate the assembled
forms. (See also Color plate 18.) Unglazed high-fired porcelain. Luster, multiple firing. 9 ×
10 × 3 in. (23 × 25 × 8 cm). *Courtesy the artist. Photo: Charlie Frizzell.*

I can use one brush for all the colors, except for yellow and orange. For those I use separate brushes because they are contaminated easily by the other colors.

A little luster goes a long way. Although Shacter uses it directly out of the bottle, most people pour small amounts into a paint-mixing pan or onto an impervious surface such as a glazed dish or the convex bottom of a glass jar. If any is left over when you finish working, you can cover it with plastic wrap to keep it for future use instead of pouring it back into the bottle. This will prevent possible contamination of the luster in the bottle.

Nowadays, lusters are used not only for decorating pottery and china to give it the luxurious, gleaming look of precious metals, but also to give a distinctive surface to sculptures. Richard Notkin brushed two thick coats of silver-gray luster directly onto the surface of unglazed, vitrified stoneware to achieve a galvanized steel effect on his *Heart Teapot* (13-17), and Mayer Shacter (Color plate 18) has experimented with layering lusters, producing subtly glowing surfaces on his nonfunctional teapots.

I started to experiment with lusters, using them in ways in which they normally are not used. Using them directly on my high-fired, unglazed porcelain body, I found that by a simple, though laborious, process of layering—often four or five layers—and a series of cone 018 firings after each layer, that I could get beautiful surfaces and effects that would not have been possible using the luster over a glaze. For example, a darker color like purple or carmine coated with mother of pearl becomes bleached out, creating a totally new shade that you couldn't get with the usual luster. If a color doesn't work as I want, I may paint a metallic luster over it, or I paint a color on top of a metallic. If I get a total disaster, which doesn't happen often, I can high-fire the piece to obliterate the luster completely. Sometimes I paint over the luster with china paint, perhaps applying a polka dot of bright red, or an orange accent. Or I may use a thinned down orange or other color to get a similar though nonlustrous effect.

Shacter's less-than-orthodox methods of using luster are just one more example of how ce-

ramic techniques are developed and changed through experimentation and testing on the part of individual ceramists who approach their work with a spirit of "try it and see."

Silk Screening Overglazes

Using this transfer method of adding color, image, or detail to the surface of your work requires some background in silk screening. When this technique is used for ceramics, the image is screened directly onto a fired and glazed surface. A silk screen usually consists of a fine mesh of real silk or a synthetic held taut in a wooden or metal frame. A stencil is applied onto the screen (see a book on silk screening for the methods) and china paint is applied through the screen with a squeegee. Obviously, this method works only on flat surfaces. However, it is possible to tape unframed, stenciled silk-screen material directly onto curved or irregular ceramic surfaces and then apply the china paint through it. Photo silk-screening methods can also be used with overglaze materials.

Decals

Decals for ceramics are basically designs printed with china paint that is held in suspension on a special paper between two layers of decalmania lacquer. To apply a decal to a glazed surface, cut out the chosen decal, soak it in water for 15 seconds, and then slip off the decal and transfer the image to the ceramic surface. Once you apply the decal, be sure to remove any excess water from between the decal and the glazed surface by gently blotting the decal with a paper towel, cloth, or squeegee, beginning at the center and working outward. This will get rid of bubbles caused by too much water or insufficient adhesion of the decal. Improper adhesion or bubbles may cause a **blistered** area when the ware is fired.

You can also make your own decals by silk screening, painting, or photo-transferring an image with china paint onto special decal paper on which you have first silk-screened a layer of decalmania lacquer. When the china paint has dried, silk screen another layer of decalmania lacquer

Figure 15-40

For his earthenware wall plates, Patrick Loughran, U.S.A., uses a layering of surface techniques, employing slips, underglazes, glazes, lusters, sgraffito, and wax resist: the fresh and spontaneous-appearing surface is actually carefully controlled as he builds it up (Color plate 20). Loughran considers his display plates to be in the tradition of maiolica (6-3), Bernard Palissy's work (6-15) and decorated giftware, and he also makes decorated functional ware (9-17). *Courtesy the artist.*

over the image; then let the decal dry thoroughly before transferring it to the ceramic surface.

Layering Glazes and Overglazes

As both Richard Hirsch and Mayer Shacter have pointed out, it is possible to achieve extremely rich surfaces by using layering methods. The point to remember in using any overglaze technique is that the glaze that fires highest should be applied first and fired; then the lower-firing ones can be applied and fired in successively lower firings, one over the other. Working in this way, developing the surface of your work in a continuous process, you can produce a great variety of surface enhancements, as seen in the

work of Patrick Loughran (15-40 and Color plate 20) or Benet Ferrer (Color plate 38). However, before using these overglaze methods, it is a good idea to learn more about the base glazes on which you will use them. Testing is the best way to do that.

GLAZE TESTS

In the early days of ceramics, all glaze formulation was based on trial and error. Learning through their successes and failures, the Chinese potters developed their subtle celadon (Color plate 1) and brilliant **flambé** glazes (Color plate 3), the Persian potters created their bright blue-green glazes, and the Europeans perfected colored decoration on tin-glazed earthenware (Color plate 4). Modern chemistry, however, has given the potter considerable information about the components of glaze materials, and many ceramists use the methods of chemical calculation to analyze their glazes.

Then why test glazes? Despite modern chemical analysis, the ultimate test of a glaze is how it fires, so the ceramist still depends on testing to find out how an individual glaze will respond to a particular clay body in a kiln fired at a certain temperature or in a given kiln atmosphere. Testing on small tiles allows you to change the proportion of a material in the glaze and quickly see what will happen to the glaze as a result. Since slight changes in the amount of one ingredient can change a glaze radically, by running tests you can see how these changes will alter the glaze and can gain an understanding of how the chemicals react under controlled conditions. Glaze tests also provide clues that can be useful in formulating special colors and textures or in producing such glaze qualities as viscous or fluid, matt or glossy. The clues to glaze-material behavior that you pick up while doing these tests on tiles in small test kilns will help you when you come to mixing a full batch of the glaze. Remember, however, that the same glaze applied to a larger work and fired in a different kiln may vary from the small tests. The length of firing time, thickness of the clay, position of the glazed work in the kiln, the presence of any residues of oxides in the kiln as dust or absorbed into the kiln bricks from a previous firing, and even the fumes burning off from other glazed ware in the kiln can all affect the outcome of the final glaze firing. As you gain a greater understanding of glaze components and how they react under test conditions, you will be better able to predict how a tested glaze will fire on larger objects in a regular kiln and in varying atmospheres. As you test, keep a notebook to record the formulas and the results of each test. Susan Ashmore, one of whose teapots won a top prize in Japan, says,

> I do many glaze tests but I do not formulate my own glazes. I will find a base formula with certain characteristics and run a series of colour tests with different percentages and combinations. (See Appendix 1C for two examples of glazes Ashmore has tested.)

Formulating Test Glazes

The glazes for tests are generally formulated in batches ranging from 100 grams to 500 grams of dry glaze materials.

To conduct a series of tests, first form test tiles out of the clay body to be glazed. One way to make test tiles is to cut a slab into a series of rectangles and then bend these into L-shaped tiles. You can also throw a low cylinder and slice it into sections. Either type of tile will stand up, allowing you to see how the glaze acts on a vertical surface, or you can fire flat tiles in a rack. Bisque-fire the test tiles after punching a hole in the top so you can hang the tile for easy reference.

Test by changing an ingredient a small amount at a time—in increments of .50 percent to 5 percent—fire the tiles, and record the temperature, the placement in the kiln, and the kiln atmosphere in your notebook. It is also a good idea to write the proportions on the tile with an underglaze pencil or oxide. In this way, you can go back over your records and compare results from several testings.

In Appendix 1A you will find some cone 05, cone 5, and cone 10 glazes formulated for *Hands in Clay* for testing on the white clay body you have already tested. These are simple glazes, easy for a beginner to use, and they contain no toxic materials. If you follow through the process of testing and altering the clays and glazes given in Appendix 1A, you will develop a basic understanding of the composition of clays and glazes and their relationship to each other.

Mixing a Glaze for Tests

Wearing a respirator and following the precautions given at the beginning of this chapter, mix at least a 100-gram batch of your selected glaze. Avoid mixing smaller batches because the possibility of measuring errors increases in small batches. You might begin by mixing 100-gram test batches of several glazes. Through these small tests, you will gain clues to the behavior of the components. Then, when you have narrowed the formulas down to one or two from which you might want to make a glaze, you can then test 500-gram batches in which you refine each glaze by changing the percentage of certain chemicals, by eliminating some chemicals, or by adding others.

If you use oxides such as cobalt, iron, chromium, copper, or nickel for color in the final batches of glaze, you may have to grind the oxides with a mortar and pestle or put them through a ball mill to reduce the particle size. Otherwise, streaks of color may mar the fired glaze. Of course, you may like the streaky effect or specks of color, in which case you need not grind the oxides.

To mix the batch, weigh out the dry ingredients with a balance gram scale and add the water, using the proportion given in the table in Appendix 1A. Put this mixture through a **sieve** with a number 50 to 80 mesh. For the small amount of glaze you are making for tests, mix the ingredients by shaking the glaze in a small covered container. Repeat this mixing as needed as you use the glaze so that you always keep the glaze materials in suspension. Brush some of the base glaze mixture on a tile (or dip it). Fire the test tiles and note the results.

Color Tests

To find out exactly what effect a certain oxide has on the color of a glaze, test it by making changes in its proportions in the glaze. Remember, however, that an oxide that produces a certain color alone may give a totally different color in combination with another oxide. For example, cobalt alone in certain glazes will yield a brilliant blue, but in combination with vanadium it can give a mustardy yellow. Because oxides interact, we recommend that at first you test only one coloring oxide or stain at a time. One color may burn out in the kiln at a particular temperature, while another may hold its color intensity. The kiln atmosphere—whether oxidizing or reducing—also has an important effect on the color, with each oxide reacting differently to varying kiln atmospheres. As an example of the various colors that just one oxide can produce, consider the range of iron. It can yield creams, yellows, red-browns, and also the gray-greens so popular in ancient China. It can also produce the black and brown tenmoku glaze.

The glaze color that each oxide will produce will also vary depending on the color of the clay body under it, on how finely the oxide was ground, on how the glaze was applied, and on the temperature, duration, and kiln atmosphere of the firing.

There are so many factors involved in color formation that the only way you can be sure of how an oxide will perform is to test it in *your* glaze, on *your* clay, in *your* kiln, or even in one section of your kiln. Working in this way, with one oxide at a time, changing its proportions for each test, you will get a good idea of how certain colors develop in glazes. It is a lengthy process, but it will add to your understanding and control of your glazes. Later, when you have tested the single oxides given in Appendix 1A, you can test several oxides, if you wish. To get black, for example, you would use cobalt, iron, and chromium according to the percentages given in the charts.

Not only do all the components making up a glaze affect the color, but the earth elements can vary depending on where they were mined and the industrial processing they have undergone. An anecdote will highlight this situation. One ceramist found color tone differences in batches of glaze stain from a supplier, although they were all labeled with the same name and number. When he asked the salesman why the color varied so much, the man replied, "Oh, the wind could have been blowing hard that day, affecting the heat of the processing furnace and that could have affected the color." Thus, to get color consistency

in one's work over a period of time, it is wise to purchase enough of the same material to ensure that all components of your glaze remain the same for a reasonable period of time. This is especially important if you are going to construct a large mural or make a dinner set that requires a consistent color.

Running a Series of Color Tests

Taking as an example the *Hands in Clay* cone 05 base test glaze in Appendix 1A, start your color testing. Use tiles made of the cone 05 white clay body given in appendix 1A. The recipe for the base glaze in percentage is:

Frit 3195 (3811)	88	88 grams
Kaolin (Georgia)	10	10 grams
Bentonite	2	2 grams
	100%	100 grams

Mix this according to the earlier directions, adding water in the proportion given in the table in Appendix 1A. A batch mixed with 100 grams of glaze material and water will give you about 4 ounces of glaze, an adequate amount for this test. If you want to convert the percentage recipe to other amounts, such as ounces or even pounds, you can use the table in Appendix 2B.

Mix the 100-gram batch; then dip or brush it on a test tile and mark it cone 05 base glaze. Set this tile aside to be fired. For the first colorant, add cobalt. Because cobalt is such a strong colorant, add it in extremely small increments of ½ gram. When you test the other colors you can add them in larger increments.

Next, to the base glaze mixture, add ½ gram cobalt. Dip or brush a tile and mark it ½ percent cobalt.

Repeat this three more times, adding cobalt in ½-gram increments and marking these tiles 1, 1½, and 2 percent cobalt. Fire the tiles at cone 05 in oxidation and see what effects the changes in the cobalt content produce in the glaze.

Continue the testing process with new tiles, adding the other coloring oxides in increments up to the percentage given in the table for the cone 05 test glaze in Appendix 1A. When you finish testing the cone 05 glaze, continue testing through the cone 5 and cone 10 glazes. You may want to fire the cone 10 tests in reduction to see what effect that has on the glaze. By the time you have worked through these tests, you will have a good understanding of glaze materials and you can move on to try some of the glazes from other ceramists in Appendix 1C.

Out of the many tests you do, you may get only one glaze that you like, but in the process you will learn a great deal about colorants that will help you analyze your glazes when they come out of the fire. Eventually, you will build up a body of knowledge that one day will enable you to look at a glaze test and know just why it was successful or what you can do to refine it.

In these tests, you have changed the colorants. In Appendix 3A, you will find an example of changing and testing the flux in a high fireglaze. After working through that, if you want to go into the subject of calculating glazes using chemical analysis, you will find a section on that in Appendix 3B.

Figure 15-41
A balance scale is essential for proper measuring of glaze ingredients. Be sure you place it on a level surface. When handling dry glaze materials, you should have good local ventilation and wear a respirator. If you have any cuts on your hands, wear rubber gloves.

MIXING GLAZES

Now that you have carried out some tests, have decided on a glaze, and are ready to glaze some pieces, you will need to mix your glaze in a batch big enough to coat them. Mixing is a relatively simple process, but be sure to read the precautions at the beginning of this chapter before you mix. Use a balance scale (15-41) to measure the dry ingredients, making sure that you set it on a level surface. Weigh out the dry ingredients and add them to the water. (See Appendix 1A for suggested glaze-water ratio.) Put the mixture through a sieve with number 50 to 80 mesh; then if necessary add water until the glaze is the right consistency for dipping or brushing. Adding gum powder (½ to 1 percent) to a brushing glaze will make it thicker, so you may have to add more water. When you dip a test tile or object in a glaze and a lot of **pinholes** develop on it, the mixture may be too thick. In that case, you will need to add more water. Using a **hydrometer** (15-42) to measure the water content will make it easier to keep it constant so that the glaze will have the same consistency at all times.

Use a container large enough to allow you to

Figure 15-42
The water content of glazes should remain constant to keep viscosity stable. The viscosity affects glaze application, which in turn affects the consistency of color and surface. You can use a **hydrometer** from a ceramics shop to measure the amount of water. This will allow you to calibrate and replace the correct amount of water as it evaporates from the glaze.

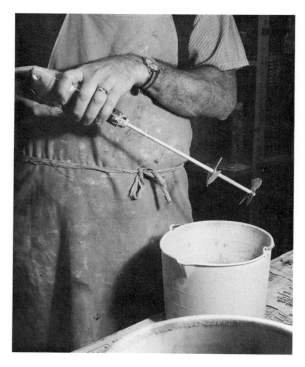

Figure 15-43
A paint-mixer attachment on an electric drill works well to keep small batches of glaze homogenous although a mixer on a stand would be more comfortable for long periods of mixing. If you use an electric mixer, be sure it is grounded.

mix comfortably. Batches of less than a gallon can be mixed with a stick, paddle, or kitchen wire whip; old kitchen blenders have also been used with excellent results for small batches. For batches of more than one gallon, an electric paint mixer can be a help (15-43) but since thorough blending of glaze components often takes ten to twenty minutes, a mixer on a stand is easier to use than one you have to hold. Ball mills can mix glaze materials in the dry or wet state, with the added advantage that they will grind the particles to a very small size. If you do not use a ball mill, screen the mixture through a 50 to 80 mesh sieve in order to eliminate lumps and coarse particles. This is especially important if the glaze is going to be sprayed, as larger particles clog the spray-gun tip. A high-speed **dispersion blender** with a special blade that creates a vortex effect refines the particles even further than an ordinary mixer does and prepares the glaze quickly and thoroughly, blending it rather than mixing it. A glaze blended with this type of mixer will stay in suspension better and melt more evenly in the kiln, because the particle size will be finer and more homogenous throughout. Whatever method you use to mix the glaze, it is extremely important to see that the glaze ingredients stay in suspension rather than falling to the bottom.

Occasionally, however, the heavy material *will* settle on the bottom. If you have that problem, consider doing the following with your next batch. After weighing the proper amount of water, mix the most glutinous materials first—such as the suspending agents, macaloid, bentonite, or gum. (See Appendix 1B for percentages of these materials to add.) Using hot water may help too. Once these materials are well blended, add the clay—such as kaolin or ball clay—followed by feldspar, frits, opacifiers, oxides, and other components, in that order.

Glazes that contain either CMC or gum tragacanth as a binder for brushing may decompose, and as they do, the gum, which also acts as a suspending agent, will lose its effectiveness and cause the glazes to smell like rotting plants, and turn dark. This will affect only the suspension and brushing qualities. Although it is possible to slow decomposition by adding formaldehyde or Dowicide G, since both these substances affect your health adversely, we recommend instead that you mix only the amount of glaze you will use in a reasonably short period of time. In that way, you will not have to use antispoilants.

APPLYING GLAZES

You will probably be applying the glaze to bisque-fired ware. Although it is perfectly possible to apply a glaze to greenware and give it just one firing, in general glazes fire more satisfactorily when they have been applied to bisque-fired ware, so it is best to put your work through a first firing before applying the glaze.

The bisque ware should be free of dust and grease. Handle it with clean hands to prevent leaving oily fingerprints that will resist the glaze. Wipe the ware off with a damp sponge or rinse it

Dipping

Dipping the bisque-fired piece in a bucket of glaze is one way to apply the glaze (15-44). Each person will work out a glaze consistency and method of dipping that is most comfortable or efficient for him or her. Some dip only once, others mix the glaze thinner and double dip, a process that will cover any pinholes that may appear in the first coat. Wear rubber gloves, or use tongs to dip the piece in the glaze. How long you hold the piece in the glaze—usually only a few seconds—and how long you let it dry between dips if you double dip will also affect the way the glaze will turn out. Any marks remaining from holding the piece can be covered by touching up with a brush, but if you hold the piece carefully by the very bottom while dipping, this should not be necessary. After dipping, shake the piece to get rid of the excess.

Figure 15-44
Murphy dips a stoneware teapot into a bucket of glaze. The length of time a piece is held in the glaze and the amount of time allowed between double dips are individual choices, determined by experience. It is a wise precaution to wear gloves when dipping to protect your hands from glaze materials.

Pouring

You can get interesting effects by pouring more than one glaze on the exterior of a piece or by pouring glaze on only part of a piece, allowing some of the clay body or another glaze to show through (15-45). Pouring is also the most efficient way to get the glaze into tall, narrow vases (15-46), and it is also a good way to glaze the inside of a bowl with a glaze different from that on the outside.

Glazes for pouring are usually mixed for one- or two-coat application. If you use a glaze that has been mixed for brushing, you will need to thin it for pouring.

quickly under a tap to dampen it slightly, and clean off the dust. This will also keep it from absorbing too much glaze. Experienced potters can mix glazes to a consistency that does not require the pot to be damp, and they can often dip or pour expertly enough to dispense with damping, but for the less experienced it is usually better to dampen first.

In the kiln, the glaze can run off the bottom of a pot, actually fusing it to the kiln shelf with glaze, often making it impossible to remove the pot without breakage. To avoid this, either dip the bottom and a minimum of ³⁄₁₆ inch up the sides of a pot in melted wax or a wax resist before glazing, or clean the glaze off this area with a sponge after you have applied the glaze.

Which method of applying glaze you will choose depends on personal preference, on the object you are glazing, on the type of glaze used, and on the effect you wish to create on the fired piece.

Brushing

When brushing on a glaze with a wide brush, you can control the thickness of the coat you apply, but it is sometimes difficult to get the coats even. On the other hand, you may be more comfortable using a brushing technique because it is similar to painting, and allows you to vary the brushstrokes or their thickness, to alter textural qualities, or to paint accents on certain areas

◄ *Figure 15-45*
Ron Judd pours a second Albany slip glaze over a large stoneware bowl, creating a varied but subtle combination of colors and surface to be finished with a matt glaze.

▼ *Figure 15-46*
Pouring allows glaze to penetrate into the interior of a narrow vase. **(a)** To lighten the interior color, Judd pours light matt glaze over one coat of Albany slip. **(b)** The vase must be turned constantly to ensure even application as the glaze coats the interior then is poured out.

(15-47). Usually, brushing a glaze evenly requires at least two coats, each applied after the previous coat is dry—which normally takes only a few minutes.

You can also use brushing to add a second or third glaze and to apply decoration over the glaze. You can also trail a second glaze or an oxide over a glaze with a slip syringe (15-48).

Spraying

Before **air compressors** and **spray guns** were developed, potters sprayed glazes or areas of glaze onto their pottery by blowing them through a wooden or metal tube—exposing themselves to hazardous glaze materials. Now that we have spray guns, airbrushes, and ventilated spray booths and respirators, we can protect ourselves more fully from the glaze materials. Do *all* spraying in a booth and wearing a mist-rated respirator (see page 195). If the piece is too large to fit in a booth then glaze it outdoors with the wind blowing the spray *away* from you. Wear a respirator and goggles so that if there is any back spray it doesn't get in your eyes. This is especially important for contact lens wearers. Before spraying, re-read the precautions about using glaze materials.

Spray guns are useful for spraying glazes, engobes, and slips where a wide fanning spray is required to cover the piece and for fast coverage of a large area. Spraying allows you to develop gradations in color, but it takes practice to learn to spray the glaze on evenly, building up the coating gradually. Glazes for spraying should be well sieved or ball milled so that coarse particles will not clog up the spray gun orifices. Usually, 10 to 40 pounds of air pressure will pull the glaze through the spray gun.

Use airbrushes for spraying oxides, ceramic stains, underglazes, lusters, and china paints, and for detail work over small areas. The material

Figure 15-47
Brushing on a glaze can add detail and smooth out small irregularities. Brushing can also be used to apply glaze to a whole pot; in that case it would be applied in two or three coats with a wide brush.

(a)

(b)

▶ *Figure 15-48*
(a) Trailing slip or glaze with a syringe can create contrasting areas over a base glaze. **(b)** The trailing syringe and the slip in a cup.

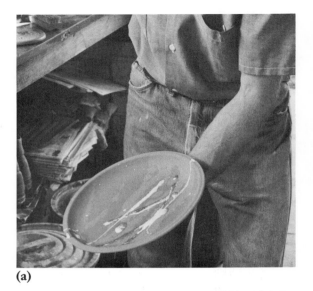

(a)

(b)

(c)

Figure 15-49
(a) Wax resist is applied on a plate that has already been dipped and trailed with two slip glazes. **(b)** The plate is dipped in the third—cobalt blue—glaze. Waxed areas will resist the glaze. **(c)** Only small bubbles of glaze form on the waxed areas, and Judd cleans these off before firing, because he finds that the droplets look messy when fired.

must be sieved, ground fine with a mortar and pestle or in a ball mill. When using oxides or stains in an airbrush, you can add a small amount of gum solution to help them stay in suspension and adhere to the object's surface. The gum solution recipe is in Appendix 1A.

Various orifice sizes are available for spray guns and airbrushes. The coarser, and more viscous the material the larger the orifice it will require. The type of glaze material and the tip size will also affect the amount of air pressure needed to pull it through the brush; 10 to 20 pounds will usually suffice.

Resist Methods

Many decorative effects can be achieved by covering sections of a piece with commercial wax-resist compounds or latex. The covered areas will repel the glaze when the piece is dipped or poured (15-49 and 15-50). You can mask off areas with paper or tape so that parts of the clay body will remain unglazed, or use stencils through which to spray a contrasting image or pattern onto an already glazed area (15-26 to 15-29 and Color plate 16). There are resist materials available that do not require heating; thus, they are safer to use. If

Figure 15-50
The subtle color relationships between the glazes keep the fired plates from looking busy.

you use an electric skillet to heat wax-resist material, keep the skillet set to the lowest possible temperature that will keep the wax melted.

READY TO FIRE

Assuming that you have chosen one of the methods of applying glaze discussed in this section, you are now ready to fire your work. The next chapter discusses loading the kiln, firing temperatures, duration, and kiln atmospheres, all of which will have their effects on your glaze.

When you finally take your fired piece out of the kiln, you may be very happy with the glaze or you may see things in it you want to expand upon or to refine. This is the time to go back over your records, study your tests, and ask yourself some questions. It is only by understanding what happened in the kiln that you can build up a knowledge of glazes that will allow you to go further into this fascinating subject with understanding.

GLAZE DEFECTS

If you have problems with a glaze, it is important to study and analyze your formula, and later your fired glazed pieces, to try to determine why a particular defect appeared when it was fired. Since the way the glaze was formulated, the way it was applied, and the way it was fired may *all* contribute to the problem, it is often difficult to know just what went wrong. To figure out which factor or factors may have caused the problem, it helps to look back over each step in the process leading up to and including the firing. Asking yourself the questions from the following checklist may help you to find the answer:

- *Check the original formula.* Was the glaze correctly weighed and mixed?

- *Were there any chemical substitutions?* This is often the key to defects and is often overlooked.

- *Was the clay body changed since previous tests?* This could affect the color or the fluxing of the glaze.

- *Was the test glaze applied to a different clay body?* Perhaps you used a slightly different clay body than the one you used for your tests.

- *To which cone or temperature was the ware bisque-fired?* If it was bisqued too low (015 to 010) that could cause pinholes to form. Refire at a higher bisque temperature.

- *Were there changes in the firing pattern?* Did you give it a longer or shorter firing?

- *What about its placement in the kiln?* Where was it placed? In a cooler or hotter area?

- *What was the kiln shelf pattern like?* Were the shelves tightly packed or loosely stacked? This can affect the heat rise and cooling of the kiln, which in turn will affect the glaze.

- *What type of fuel was used?* Was it changed or altered?

- *What was fired in the kiln previously?* Clays or glazes containing oxides such as copper can affect a glaze in the next firing because traces remain in the kiln.

- *Does the glaze look thin or washed out?* The glaze mixture may have been thinned to the point where the glaze materials settled. Thus, when you applied the glaze you did not apply all the components equally.

With all these factors in mind, look at the defects that may have appeared on your pieces and see if you can figure out what happened.

Common Glaze Problems

Crazing   Several factors can cause fine cracks to develop in a fired glaze. For example, crazing may be caused by incompatibility between the glaze and clay body owing to different rates of expansion and contraction. Altering the clay body may solve the problem. On the other hand, one person's defect may be another person's decorative effect; then the crazing is called crackle. Chinese potters appreciated the surface cracks and deliberately increased certain ingredients in order to produce them, learning to control the spacing of the cracks, and often rubbing color into them for emphasis. Crazing is characteristic of low-fire alkaline glazes.

Crawling   This defect can occur when there are fingerprints, dust, oil, or grease on the bisque-fired ware, or when the unfired glaze shrinks as it dries. **Crawling,** where glazed areas alternate with areas of bare clay, can also be caused by starting to fire when the glaze is not completely dry or by adding too much of certain materials with high shrinkage rates, such as zinc oxide, to the glaze. The presence of ingredients, such as colemanite, that give off gases when they reach high temperatures in the kiln can also cause pinholes and craters, which in turn may cause the glaze to crawl. Opaque glazes that are more viscous than transparent ones are more prone to crawl. Crawling can also occur when a glaze is applied over areas painted with underglaze, especially if the underglaze has been applied thickly. A low-fire glaze applied to a high-fire porcelain bisque may peel after it is applied or crawl when it is fired owing to differing shrinkage rates. This can sometimes be remedied by adding a few drops of **electrolyte** (Darvan #7) to the glaze.

Pinholes and pits   Sometimes pinholes and pits are caused by applying glaze to a bisque that is too porous, so that during firing, air or moisture escaping from the pores of the clay body may cause these holes to develop in the glaze as the vapor bursts through it. Also during firing, tiny gas bubbles form while the clay body and glaze components break down in the heat, sometimes causing pinholes and pits to come through the glaze and burst on the surface. Tiny pinholes sometimes also appear in glaze that has been intentionally underfired to achieve a matt effect. Too much zinc oxide or rutile can also cause pits in a glaze. Bisque-firing to a higher temperature, adding more flux, applying the glaze less thickly, increasing the heat, soaking the kiln, or lengthening the firing may all help to prevent pinholes.

Blistering   In blistering, the surface looks like a magnified photo of the moon's surface with many little craters. It is usually caused by gases escaping from a glaze fired too rapidly; by applying the glaze too thickly; or, in some low-fire glazes containing frit, by firing them above cone 6.

Refiring and Second Glazing

An already glazed piece that is to be coated with a second or third coat of glaze in order to reglaze it can be warmed first in the kiln to ensure that it will be dry. Adding a small amount of gum to the second application will also help the additional glaze to adhere. When reglazing and refiring high-fire pottery, it is often necessary to reglaze the inside of a pot with one thin coat as well as the outside. This helps to equalize the tensions created on the piece by the second glaze and thus to prevent cracking of the ware on refiring.

If you continue to study and analyze your glazes as you remove your ware from the kiln, you will find that your control over this important aspect of ceramics will increase, and as your knowledge expands so will your satisfaction. You will then be able to concentrate on the form or the image, using, if you wish, many of the techniques shown in this chapter to create works that use color and glaze expressively (15-51).

POST-FIRING PAINT

If, after trying some glazes, you find that finishing your nonfunctional objects or sculpture with glaze is not for you, then there is no reason why you cannot do as many artists do—use paint. There is nothing new about using paint on fired

Figure 15-51
A Different Woman. Jindra Viková, Czechoslovakia, casts porcelain slabs from slip, forms them into her figurative sculptures, and then uses underglazes, overglaze painting, salt, metallic oxides, and transparent glazes to develop her rich surfaces (Color plate 22). Fired at 2372 °F/1300 °C in an electric kiln. 43 × 24 in. (110 × 62 cm). *Courtesy the artist and Art Centrum, Praha. Photo: Pavel Banka.*

Figure 15-52
Shell, by Burton Isenstein, U.S.A. Istenstein studied biology before becoming a ceramist, and many of his works reflect his interest in nature. His sculpture is formed of porcelain, then painted after firing with alkyd oil paint in natural, although not necessarily realistic, colors. 1986. Porcelain. *Courtesy the artist. Photo by Tom Van Eynde.*

Figure 15-53
Gertraud Möhwald, DDR, develops a rich surface on her sculptures by applying shards of glazed pottery, contrasting their glossy colors with the roughly-textured clay. 1986. Stoneware, porcelain, oxides and glaze. Ht. 21¾ in. (55 cm). *Courtesy the artist and Galerie Schneider.*

clay. In fifteenth-century Italy, religious figures sculpted by Dell'Arca and other artists were coated with a thin coat of **gesso** and then painted very realistically, as were many of the portrait busts by such sculptors as Verrocchio in the sixteenth century. Acrylic paints, stains, oil paints, enamels—any coloring material you would use on wood or canvas—may give you just the surface you want on your sculpture or nonfunctional vessel. Louise McGinley, for example (8-18) never glazes her work, but uses acrylic paint either watered down to a transparent stain or left thick for opaque areas. She has found that in the California climate these colors hold up well, even out-doors. Burton Isenstein (15-52) also paints his biologically inspired works after firing.

OTHER SURFACES

Some ceramists—Jamie Walker, Beth Thomas, Joseph Manning, and Gertraud Möhwald (15-53), among others—apply ceramic shards to their sculptures or constructions somewhat in the manner of the Spanish architects Antonio Gaudi and Josep Maria Jugol (Color plate 6). Others sand-blast their glazed pieces in order to change the surface of the glaze. If you do this, be sure to do it only in an isolated area with good ventilation and wearing a respirator.

Now that the definition of an appropriate ceramic finish has been expanded in these ways, you are free to explore and experiment with the surface of your work in any way that you wish.

16
Firing

John Toki, U.S.A., removing shelves and bricks before unloading one of his wall sculptures (Color plate 33). Note how the shelves have been doubled and built up with fire bricks to provide adequate support for heavy sculptures.

Considering the destructive aspects of fire and its ability to transform clay and metal, it is not surprising that early humans believed that fire was a gift from the gods, or that in many early cultures metal workers and potters were considered to be magical or supernatural beings. From the ancient Greeks to contemporary Native Americans, many peoples have created myths in which gods or goddesses teach humanity how to shape metal and harden clay with fire (16-1). Even today in ceramics studios you will usually see a handformed kiln god or goddess seated atop the kiln—a symbol of fire's power, a protective spirit for the ware being fired.

Is it really true that the fire controls the outcome of your hours of work? Yes and no. It depends a great deal on the type of clay you use, the type of glaze, and type of kiln, as well as on your approach to firing. There are those who believe in giving a considerable amount of control to the fire, enjoying the unexpected effects it can create on the contents of the kiln, and responding to the sense of adventure that type of firing gives them. Others are more concerned with retaining their original conceptions, so they try to direct the firing as much as possible.

*Ross Anderson and Barbara Berry, *The Diversions of Keramos, American Clay Sculpture, 1925–1950*. N.Y.: Everson Museum of Art, 1983.

Figure 16-1
In *Watching the Cones Fall*, Patrick Siler, U.S.A., captures the excitement of firing—and the potter lives dangerously as he stares into the depths without goggles and leans too near the flames. Siler used paper stencils and slips to apply the image. Fired in oxidation, cone 5. Diameter 19 in. (48 cm). *Courtesy the artist.*

STARTING TO FIRE

If you carried out the clay-body and glaze tests recommended in chapters 10 and 15, you have already had some experience with a kiln. Firing clay tests, however, although interesting, hardly gives one the same satisfaction as firing one's own pot or sculpture (see page 361 and 16-1). So, let's suppose that now, after many hours of work, you have a hollow piece of sculpture ready to fire or a glaze-coated pot waiting to be miraculously transformed from a chalky gray to rich, glossy color. You have been told that the fire makes its own demands, imposes its own limits, and that it will transform—or destroy—your carefully shaped creation. After investing so many hours of time and effort, you may well wonder what the kiln will do to your pot or sculpture, and you may approach the firing with some trepidation. If you are working in a school situation, you will often place your glazed piece on a shelf, go off to other classes, and come back a few days later to find the pot fired. But even if you get no nearer to the firing than this, it is important for you to know what happens in the kiln, because in ceramics everything works together—clay, glaze, and heat interact so that any change in one area affects the others. It is important to recognize this, for it means that the aesthetics of ceramics continues through the firing process.

Firing Ranges of Clays

How your pot or sculpture will look when it leaves the kiln will depend not only on the type of clay body with which you built it and the glaze with which you may have coated it. It also depends on the fuel that you used in the kiln, and on how high a temperature your kiln can reach burning that fuel.

The type of clay used dictates to a considerable extent the temperature at which finished work is fired. Early earthenware pottery, for example, was usually fired only once to a low temperature, generally in an open fire or a rudimentary kiln. Depending upon the heat and duration of the fire, this pottery was either heated barely beyond the sun-dried state or its low-fire clay was brought to maturity—for most earthenwares this

would be about 920°F/510°C. Later, however, when it was discovered that certain clays became more dense and vitreous at higher temperatures, and high-firing glazes were developed, kilns and their firing became more complex. Today, a bewildering number of firing choices are available to a ceramist. These range from single firing, in which dry greenware is placed in a kiln that is very gradually brought up to the desired temperature, to multiple firings, in which a piece may be given a bisque firing, then a high firing, and possibly additional successive low firings to mature layers of overglaze.

Some examples of the temperature ranges of modern commercial clay bodies include low-fire clays that begin to get hard but not mature at cone 015 (1479°F/803°C) and mature from cone 06 (1830°F/999°C) to cone 1 (2109°F/1154°C); medium range clays that fire between cone 2 (2124°F/1162°C) and 7 (2264°F/1240°C); high-fire stonewares that mature at cone 8 (2305°F/1263°C) to 12 (2419°F/1326°C); and porcelains, whose range is from cone 10 (2381°F/1305°C) to 13 (2455°F/1346°C). The potential range of most clays, however, is considerably wider than labels or recipes may suggest, and you might well find that a clay can go to a higher temperature than you would expect. Be sure, however, to test before you try to fire a special pot beyond the recommended range.

Drying Before Firing

Chapter 11 contains information about drying an object thoroughly before subjecting it to the heat of the kiln. We cannot emphasize strongly enough the importance of drying. Thorough drying is crucial and, especially when a thick-walled piece is to be fired, the drying process cannot be hurried. To be sure that it is completely dry, you can give a thick-walled object extra drying with a space heater or place it near a kiln that is firing, so that it dries as it waits to be loaded.

You can also place it in the kiln with the door left open about five to ten inches while the heat starts to rise. Once the piece is thoroughly heated and dry, you can then close the door and proceed with the firing.

Temperature and Duration

How do you know when the kiln has reached the point at which your clay or glaze has matured? It is important to recognize that clay and glaze need *time* in addition to heat to become fully mature. Thus, firing involves duration as well as temperature. The experienced ceramist can look into the kiln through a peephole and judge the temperature of the kiln by the color of the interior as the temperature rises—from dull red-orange through light orange to white. (See Appendix 2A for a table that shows temperatures and kiln colors.) If you peer into the kiln, always wear special goggles to protect your eyes from the infrared radiation, which has a cumulative effect on the eyes, the damage increasing with frequency of exposure. The goggle shades that will protect your eyes from damage range from #3 for low temperatures to #5 for high firing. Number 5 will protect you through the entire range. A dull red kiln interior is associated with temperatures of around 1200°F/648.8°C, when you would be firing luster and china paint; an orange color is seen during bisque or low firings; yellow appears at the usual temperatures for firing earthenware and medium-fired stoneware; and an intense white glow is seen when the kiln is firing high-fire glazes. The experienced ceramist also knows how long to leave the kiln at the correct heat and how long it would take to bring it down to a temperature low enough for unloading. But until you have fired a good many kilns, to ensure successful firing it is best to use cones and/or a pyrometer or to set a computerized kiln to the appropriate firing program that will control the heat rise and decline over a specified period of time.

Pyrometers

A **pyrometer** is a gauge that measures the temperature inside the kiln. Just as a speedometer indicates the speed of a car, so the pyrometer displays the temperature readings as you raise or lower the heat in the kiln. When a pyrometer is installed in a gas kiln, a special porcelain tube can be placed over the thermocouple to protect its metal from accelerated deterioration. A pyrometer is usually calibrated to show increments of

20°F/−6.6°C. Installed on kilns—gas or electric—a pyrometer allows you to check the temperature as it rises and falls in the kiln. Since the pyrometer is usually installed on the inside wall of a kiln rather than in the middle of the chamber, the readings you get from it will not indicate the temperature throughout the entire kiln; but because the pyrometer shows any temperature change almost immediately, it will indicate if the kiln is heating or cooling too fast. In that case you can slow the rise or fall of the heat. A pyrometer is a useful aid, but since it can only measure the temperature in the kiln, not the effect of time plus temperature, ceramists usually use **pyrometric cones** as well.

Pyrometric Cones

A pyrometric cone on the other hand will show you when both the time and temperature have reached the point at which the clay or glaze has come to maturity. These cones are made of ceramic materials that are formulated to fuse and bend when they have been exposed to a certain amount of heat saturation. This means that rather than simply measuring the temperature, they are also affected by the length of time the kiln has been at a specific temperature; thus they measure the total effect of the heat and time on the clay or glaze materials. In effect, cones are carefully calculated miniature tests (16-11).

American Orton cones and European Seger cones are formulated to bend according to the work done by the heat during a certain temperature rise per hour. The large Orton cones used in the United States cover temperatures from cone 022 (1112°F/600°C) to cone 13 (2455°F/1346°C), with their numbers representing the point at which they bend over. The cone numbers and temperatures used in the text are those for the large Orton cones with a temperature rise of 270°F/150°C per hour (see table in appendix 2A). If you live in a place where Seger cones are used, the same table shows equivalent Seger cones and temperatures. The most commonly used Orton cones run from the lowest number of cone 022 (1112°F/600°C) through cone 020 to 018, used for firing lusters and china paints, up to cone 13 (2455°F/1346°C), used for stonewares and porcelains. The cones below cone 1 are numbered so that the lower the cone temperature, the larger the number—that is, 022 is lower than 019—a fact that sometimes confuses beginners. There are cones as high as 36, but they are used largely for industrial firings.

To use cones in a gas kiln, you would insert three consecutively numbered cones in a series, placing them at an eight-degree angle in a wad of clay or in soft fire bricks cut to support the cones at the correct angle. You can also use specially designed reusable, heat-resistant metal cone holders. You would usually use three cones known as the guide cone, the firing cone, and the guard cone. For example, you might use cones 06 (1830°F/999°C), 05 (1915°F/1046°C), and 04 (1940°F/1060°C), placed in a series. To use cones as guides, you must check on them (wearing special shaded goggles) through the kiln peepholes. Once the first cone has bent, you should begin to check on the middle one every fifteen to forty-five minutes, because at this point the kiln is approaching the desired temperature. As soon as the middle cone bends, stop the heat rise. If the third cone starts to bend, you have overfired. Since there can be a wide difference in heat saturation in a large kiln—as much as several cones' difference—it is best to place several sets of cones at different shelf levels (16-11a).

Kiln Sitters and Electronic Controls

Since the heat of a kiln must be raised slowly to the correct point, firing requires the ceramist's careful attention. Fortunately, kiln sitters eliminate the need to watch an electric kiln constantly. Kiln sitters allow you to place a small cone of the appropriate number in the sitter, set the mechanism, and leave it to the sitter to switch off the kiln mechanically when the clay cone bends and trips a switch that breaks the electric circuit. The cones used in sitters are called junior size, and their response is different from that of the large cones placed in the interior of gas kilns. One of the strong points of kiln sitters is that they help prevent the overfiring of a kiln. Nevertheless, it is recommended that a person firing with a kiln sitter, timer, or other automatic control check the

kiln within an hour or two of the expected firing time, since equipment is not always 100 percent foolproof. If there is any question in your mind about what is happening inside the kiln, or if the equipment seems to be malfunctioning, turn off the kiln manually, let it cool, and check it thoroughly, or call a repair person.

Computers that can be programmed to fire either an electric or gas kiln are now available, relieving the ceramist of a great deal of kiln watching. Some ceramists who have used them say that it takes a good while to learn to trust a computer, but that once you do, firing becomes much easier; others, on the other hand, say they feel they could never trust a computer to monitor their firings.

SAFE KILN INSTALLATION

Gas Kilns

The installation of a gas kiln is a complicated business, not only from the point of view of safety, but also to ensure that the kiln will achieve the proper firing temperature. Not only is it essential to follow the manufacturer's specifications for installing a commercial kiln or, if you are building your own, to refer to books on the subject, but it is also essential to check with your utility company and code officials about local conditions and requirements. For kilns fired with natural or propane gas, many cities require safety controls on the burner system that will cut off the incoming fuel if the flame fails or is blown out. This is to avoid a gas build-up in the firing chamber that might cause an explosion. If you are installing a gas kiln for the first time, you should get help from a person who is knowledgeable about kilns and who knows your requirements. Your dealer, instructor, or other ceramists can probably recommend someone to help with installation.

Electric Kilns

Although an electric kiln does not use open flame, it can still present some installation problems. One does not simply buy an electric kiln and then plug it in. If you are considering purchasing one, you should first study where you will place it, and how to vent it. Have a licensed electrician check any existing wiring against the manufacturer's or supplier's information on requirements. For example, is the existing voltage 110–120 volts, 208 volts, or 220 to 240 volts? Is rewiring necessary to accommodate a kiln that draws more amperage than the wiring will handle? Improperly installed, an electric kiln will not reach full heat and may blow circuit breakers or fuses. Improper wiring can also ruin kiln elements and even cause a fire.

Ventilation

It is essential that any indoor kiln—gas or electric—be well vented. This is done to draw away the gases that are released during firing from the organic materials in clay, the carbon monoxide produced during incomplete combustion (as in reduction firing), and the heavy metal fumes that escape from the kiln during glaze firings. Venting can be done on a gas kiln by building a hood over the kiln, extending it beyond its edges, and installing a fan to pull the fumes and heat away and exhaust them outside. Ready-made venting systems for electric kilns are also available now that actively draw fresh air directly into the kiln, through the chamber, and then exhaust the fumes outside.

The vented kiln must also be placed so that the heat from the vent does not come too near combustible materials; also, the chimney of a gas kiln must be properly installed. Have the installation checked by your local building (plumbing) inspector. Obviously, a gas kiln presents a greater fire hazard from explosion than does an electric kiln, and if the kiln is outside, its chimney must not send hot air too near to dry foliage.

PRECAUTIONS

Remember that while working around a kiln, you are dealing with high heat and, in the case of a gas kiln, an open flame. Around a gas kiln, take the same precautions you would take around any gas appliance or open flame:

- Tie back long hair and loose clothing and keep them under control.
- Protect your eyes from flame and the infrared radiation that can damage your eyes. When looking into a kiln, wear either shaded goggles (#3 to #5) or, a face shield with a #3 to #5 shade that will protect your entire face from infrared radiation and the flames that often escape through the spyholes during reduction.
- Use aramid fiber, heat-resistant gloves (or leather welding gloves) whenever you have to touch the hot parts of a kiln.
- When the time comes to unload the kiln, remember that even if the exterior seems cool, the pots inside will be hot. Curb your desire to grab your glazed pot with your bare hands; it may be hotter than you think. If your gloves start to smoke, it's too hot!

Alternative Fuels and Energy Saving

It is beyond the scope of this book to go into kiln design, but you should be aware that experiments have been made with fuels other than natural gas, propane, or electricity. Some potters, such as Dennis Parks (9-13), have fired successfully with used crankcase oil, others have fired with methane gas from the sludge of a paper mill, and another has managed to fire very small pots in a solar-heated kiln. Some have saved energy by using extra insulation, varying, for example, from a mixture of vermiculite and clay applied to the outside walls of a kiln to a ceramic fiber wrap around the kiln. Such ceramic fiber insulation is most efficient when applied to the *inside* walls of a kiln, where it reflects the heat best, but it still helps hold in some heat if it is used on the outside.

SINGLE FIRING

Let's assume that you now want to preserve and then glaze your first pieces of ceramics. They have been completely dried to the touch and are ready for placing in the kiln as greenware—dried,

Figure 16-2
Bisque firing is often done in an electric kiln even if the glaze firing will be done in a gas or wood kiln. For a bisque firing, a kiln can be loaded tightly with pieces touching each other or even nested.

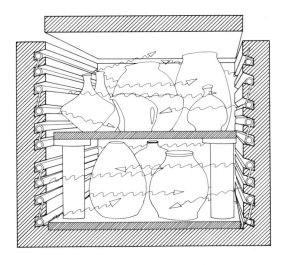

Figure 16-3
The heat in an electric kiln is radiated outward from the elements set in the walls. In the United States, electric kilns are generally used for bisque firings and oxidation firings. In other parts of the world, electric kilns are frequently the only type available to ceramists, so if a reduction atmosphere is needed, it must be produced through the introduction of reduction materials either in the kiln or in individual saggers.

unfired clay objects. You have a choice at this point between glazing the greenware and firing it only once or firing it first unglazed in a bisque firing. Since, in single firing, the ware is only handled once, this can save fuel and labor. Indeed, when the pot or sculpture to be fired is heavy, or when thick walls require a very slow firing, a single firing is preferred in order to eliminate the effort of a second loading.

Bisque Firing

Greenware, however, is fragile, and can easily break while you are handling it or when applying a glaze. Also, if the ware has not been bisqued, the chance is greater that it might blow up in the kiln, causing its glazed fragments to stick to the interior or to other ware. In addition, some glazes are affected by the release of gases from organic materials in the clay bodies that would have been eliminated during a bisque firing. As a result, glazes that have been applied to bisqued ware are generally less likely to be subjected to the bubbling that the escaping gases from these organic materials can cause. Ware that is bisque fired before glazing also tends to have brighter, clearer colors after it is fired. For all these reasons, you will probably choose to bisque fire your work to somewhere between 1661° F/905°C and 1900° F/1037°C before glazing. Bisque firing can be done in any type of kiln, but many prefer to use an electric kiln for the bisque firing, even if they use gas for the glaze firing (16-2, 16-3). In a school studio or a production pottery where a large number of objects must be fired, at least two kilns are a necessity—one for bisque firing and one for glaze or sculpture firing.

A low bisque firing of cone 010 (1661° F/905°C) not only saves fuel but leaves the fired ware more porous. This can be a help in applying certain glazes that require an especially absorbent surface in order to build up the correct thickness. On the other hand, some glazes may develop defects such as excessive pinholes or craters when the clay body has been bisque fired too low. If that happens, try a cone 05 (1915°F/1046°C) bisque.

Loading a Bisque Kiln

It is easier to load a bisque kiln than a glaze kiln, because without any melting glaze to cause the ware to stick together, the pots or sculpture can be tightly stacked, even touching or nested inside each other (16-2). A closely stacked bisque load, however, necessitates a slower firing than one more loosely stacked. It is wise to turn thick-bottomed pots or sculpture upside-down so that the moisture can escape more efficiently. To stack an electric kiln, you would first set the kiln sitter, then load the ware and turn on the kiln. To load a gas kiln, you would first place the ware on the shelves and then insert the cones and set the controls.

In a bisque firing, you would not want the clay to reach full maturity, because the objects to be glazed should remain absorbent enough for the glaze to adhere to them. Once the kiln has reached the desired temperature for the bisque, the kiln must be cooled very slowly, probably overnight, and you should resist the temptation to open the door too soon, or the ware may crack. When you do open it, you will see the clay pieces changed by the action of the fire to a new material—one that can never revert to its original chemical or physical state.

THE FIRING PROCESS

Now that your work is in the kiln, the cones are in place, the controls are set and the door is closed or bricked in, you can begin to raise the heat. As you watch the kiln, you may wonder what is actually happening to your creations behind that closed door. They will go through many transformations before you open the door again.

Physical and Chemical Water Release

By the time the heat in the kiln has slowly increased to a temperature of about 660° F/348° C, most of the physical water that was still left in the clay has been driven out in the form of vapor. This is a tricky time in firing, because if the heat is raised too rapidly during this period, the object can explode as the steam escapes. The more temper there is in the clay, the more porous the clay will be. These spaces between the particles allow the steam and gases to escape. It is for this reason that thick-walled pots or sculpture should be made with a high percentage of grog or other temper—20 to 40 percent.

Now the physical, or free, water has left the clay. As the temperature continues to rise slowly to between 1650° to 2010° F/900° to 1100° C, the chemical water (H_2O) that has combined with the molecular structure of the clay particles is also driven out along with the gases formed by the decomposition of any organic materials remaining in the clay. These gases can cause problems as they escape, so the temperature should be raised slowly at this point. It is essential that the fumes and smoke that will be emitted from the kiln as these organic materials decompose are removed by a well-functioning ventilation system.

CHANGES IN THE KILN

Quartz Inversion

As it is fired, clay undergoes various changes, some visible, some invisible. One invisible change that takes place as the kiln is heated and the silica crystals in the clay change in volume and form, is a phenomenon called **quartz inversion.** As it is heated, the silica contained in the flint, quartz, or sand in the clay first expands gradually; then, at the quartz inversion point—between about 440° F/226.6° C to 1070° F/576.6° C, a series of rapid changes and expansions in the silica take place. After the clay has been fired to maturity and the cooling process begins, the same phenomenon takes place in reverse; and as the kiln temperature is slowly lowered through the quartz inversion point, most of the changes are reversed and the silica begins to revert to its original form. If the

Figure 16-4
Flames escape from the open peephole of a downdraft gas kiln during firing. The peepholes allow observation of the cones during firing. To create a reducing atmosphere, in this kiln the damper would be nearly closed, trapping the air, which would back up and allow less oxygen to enter. The kiln could also be reduced by closing the burner ports so no fresh air could enter.

temperature changes during these expansion and contraction periods are, however, too rapid, they can cause fracturing of the clay body. The same applies to glaze firings during which these stresses can affect the fit of the glaze to the clay.

If you intend to glaze the bisqued ware, store it in a dust-free spot and handle it only with clean hands, because the oil from your fingers can keep the glaze from adhering properly at the spots where you touch it.

Vitrification

The term *maturity* refers to the point at which the clay has been fired as high as possible, before it starts to slump and melt. At maturity, certain clays become vitrified, rocklike and dense. Potters like to fire their high-fire ware to vitrification so that moisture will not seep through the foot of the piece, causing liquids to leak and damage if it is set on wooden furniture. However, even though low-fire clays are said to be vitreous when they are fired to maturity, they are generally not im-

pervious to water. For this reason, to make low-fire ware watertight, the potter will often glaze it on the bottom as well as the inside.

KILN ATMOSPHERES

Before you start to fire a glaze kiln, you will need to know something about kilns and the atmosphere in the kiln. The school studio will frequently have a gas kiln as well as an electric one, and chances are you will be using the gas kiln to fire your glazed ware (16-4).

There are many types of gas kilns—updraft, downdraft, cross-draft, and ones with multiple burners at angles that can create a swirling effect—but the most common types are variations within the two categories of updraft and downdraft kilns. These terms describe the flow of the heat as it enters from the burners or other fuel source and exits through a vent or chimney (16-5, 16-6). The kiln may also have a **muffle** or a **bag wall** in the chamber to protect the ware from the

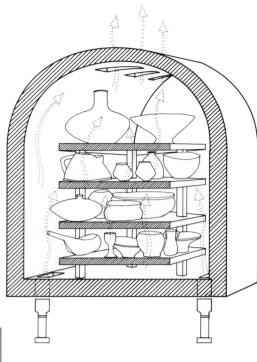

Figure 16-5

In a modern updraft gas kiln the heat from the burners goes up through the ware on the shelves, and is vented out through the top of the kiln. The modern updraft uses the same principle of rising heat that led to the development of early kilns in the Orient (3-4) and the Mediterranean (2-7).

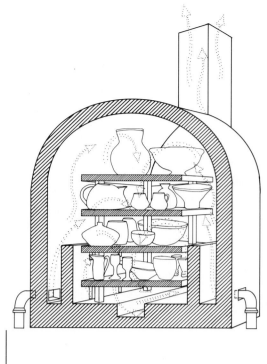

Figure 16-6

A modern downdraft kiln is designed to send the heat from the burners first upward and then down through the ware to the flue at the bottom. Finally, the heat is vented out the stack at the back of the kiln. A bag wall may be built inside the outer walls to direct the flames and heat upward.

direct flame. There are two atmospheres that may develop in a kiln as it fires—oxidation and reduction.

Oxidation

Any burning is the result of oxidation, and if there is plenty of air entering a fire, it will produce an oxidizing atmosphere, in which the fire can burn bright and clear, with full combustion taking place. If you have ever helped a smoky fire to burn well by blowing on it or using a bellows, you were providing the oxygen necessary for full combustion to take place, thereby creating an oxidizing atmosphere.

Reduction

If, however, you were to smother the open fire so that most of the air was shut off, then the incomplete combustion would produce smoke and carbon. This incomplete combustion is what creates a reducing atmosphere, and when such an atmosphere is produced in a kiln, the carbon and carbon monoxide that are formed in the oxygen-starved fire will draw oxygen from the clay body or from the oxides in the glaze. When this happens, some of the oxides in the clay or glaze will lose oxygen; they are then said to be reduced. Depending upon how much oxygen is removed from the oxides, the color of clay or glaze can change color radically when reduced. A dramatic example of what reduction can do to the color of a glaze ingredient is the color change that takes place in copper oxide. Fired in an oxidizing atmosphere, copper oxide becomes green, but in a successful reduction atmosphere it becomes red, proving that the atmosphere of the kiln plays a vital role in creating glaze effects.

Each ceramist develops an individual reduction firing pattern. For example, some begin reducing at cone 05 and maintain that atmosphere all the way to the end of the firing while others reduce two times; once around 1900°F/1038°C for one hour and again during the last hour of firing.

During a reduction firing, there are visible evidences of the reduction process: in an updraft kiln, the flames may have a greenish tinge, and in an up- and downdraft kiln, black carbon forms around the spyholes or door jambs. As the reduction firing is nearing completion with all burners on, the gas pressure up, the air valves open, and the damper adjusted, a sense of excitement builds up. At this point, when the heat is high, a soft roar comes from the kiln, and the flames dance as they leave the chamber. The kiln deity is working its magic while the fire gives the clay a new life.

Depending on the kiln, or on the methods used, you can change the kiln atmosphere from oxidizing to reducing either by controlling the air flow into the kiln or by cutting down on the draft. Closing the damper of a gas kiln, for example, forces the air to back up and prevents new air from entering the kiln; thus, as the oxygen in the kiln is consumed, the fire is forced to draw oxygen from the oxides. Many stoneware and porcelain glazes require reduction to reach their best appearance, but the reduction must be controlled and not become too heavy, or the clay body can become brittle.

In preindustrial societies, potters and sculptors traditionally used any fuel available to them; in arid lands this might be the sparse vegetation or manure from their herds, while in lush tropical areas it might be palm fronds. Starting out with open pits and simple kilns, gradually, over the centuries, potters perfected their kilns to reach higher temperatures and fire more efficiently. The Chinese and Japanese potters developed wood kilns that could fire to porcelain temperatures (chapter 3), while the European potters used wood for low-firing maiolica. Then, when the Europeans learned to fire high-fire stoneware (chapter 6), they fired it in kilns that were fueled with wood, or, later, coal. With these fuels, combustion was not as complete, so it was easier to achieve a reduction atmosphere than an oxidizing atmosphere. By the early 1900s some kilns burned oil; then, finally gas and electric kilns were developed and perfected, making it possible to maintain greater control over the firing process and the kiln atmosphere than with wood or coal.

Reduction in Electric Kilns

You will always get an oxidizing atmosphere in an electric kiln unless you take special steps to change the atmosphere. Where stringent fire regulations prohibit gas kilns in built-up areas, ceramists who want to achieve glazes that require reduction have to reduce in their electric kilns by adding smoke-producing materials. This material may range from excelsior or straw to mustard seeds, seaweed, sawdust, pine needles, or paper—anything that will burn and create a local reducing atmosphere. You can throw the materials directly into the kiln or place your ware in a sagger (a protective container) along with the material. This contrasts sharply with the original use of saggers, which were originally used to protect the delicate ware in the kiln from the effects of flame and carbon (3-16). You can also add reducing material to the clay body itself or the glaze mixture; **silicon carbide** 3F (carborundum) powder is sometimes added to glazes to create reduction.

These methods make it possible to reduce in an electric kiln, but constant reduction firings can wear out the electric elements and wiring connectors, and any reduction material that remains in the kiln after such a firing can spoil certain glazes that you might want to fire in it later. To cut down on wear on the elements and to clean the kiln, it helps to heat an empty kiln to high heat, or fire it under oxidizing conditions, after each reduction firing. Even heavy-duty electric elements, however, will have to be replaced eventually if they are subjected to frequent reduction atmospheres.

LOADING A GLAZE KILN

Assuming that you have bisque fired and have applied glaze to your work (chapter 15) and that the glaze has dried, you are ready for the next firing—the glaze firing. The next step is to load the kiln, using kiln furniture.

Kiln Furniture

Kiln furniture consists of heat-resistant slabs, shelves, and posts that support the ware in the kiln during firing. Kiln shelves are commonly

(a)

(b)

Figure 16-7

Movable fire-resistant shelves, stacked on posts, make it possible to accommodate pots or sculptures of different sizes. Larry Murphy knows the idiosyncracies of his gas kiln, so he can stack it according to which areas get the most heat or are more highly reduced, thus controlling to a degree the firing conditions for each piece. **(a)** With the kiln loaded, Murphy places a series of cones on shelves, positioning them opposite the peepholes. **(b)** The kiln has cooled and the door is unbricked to reveal shelves of glazed ware. The cones show that the kiln fired to a little less than cone 10; at cone 10 the third cone would have bent over.

made of three materials—silicon carbide, high-alumina, and cordierite. Cordierite shelves, ½ to ⅝ inch thick, are commonly used in electric kilns up to cone 8, and 1 inch thick to cone 10. These can withstand the rapid heat rise and decline of electric kilns without cracking. Silicon carbide and high-alumina shelves are used in gas kilns, withstanding without excessive warping the high temperatures needed to fire stoneware and porcelain. Silicon carbide shelves range in thickness from ⅝ inch to 1¼ inch; the higher the temperature and the heavier the load on each shelf, the thicker the shelf you should use. Before loading the kiln, be sure that its interior is clean and that there are no loose fragments in the brick lining that can fall on the ware.

It can take a good deal of ingenuity to arrange the shelves on the posts so that they provide the most space for the varied shapes of work you may want to fire (16-7a). When you start to build up the shelves, use three rather than four posts for each shelf; three points make for a less wobbly support. If a shelf does not sit evenly on three posts, you can shim up one of the posts with a low-shrinkage mixture of buff grog mixed with as small an amount of fire clay as is necessary to bind it blended with water into a stiff, puttylike consistency. You may want to fire wafers of this material to be reused for shimming. For larger pots or sculpture, the shelves may require a structure built up of a number of posts or fire bricks to support their weight (16-12).

Kiln Wash

Most potters and sculptors coat the top surfaces of new kiln shelves with two or three coats of **kiln wash.** This, like the flour in a cake pan, acts as a separator, so that if glaze drips onto the shelves from the ware, the shelves can be easily cleaned. The wash is a mixture of one-half china clay (kaolin) and one-half flint, diluted with only enough water to make it possible to paint it on. Usually, after a dozen or more firings, glaze drippings will need to be scraped off and a new coating of kiln wash applied. Shelves that are heavily coated with glaze and kiln wash may need to be brushed and scraped or sandblasted to clean them thoroughly and then recoated with kiln wash.

Stilts

If you want to make low-fire ceramics watertight by glazing the bottom, then to keep the glaze from sticking to the shelves you will need to use **stilts** to keep the ware up off the shelves. Stilts are triangular supports on which the piece is balanced on the kiln shelf and which leave only small marks in the glaze when they are removed. There are three types of stilts. For low-fire ceramics, the stilts may be made of clay. Generally these are rated to stand heats from 05 (1915°F/1046°C) or lower up to cone 1 (2109°F/1154°C). Clay stilts with metal points inserted in the clay are also good for low firing and leave smaller marks on the foot when they are removed after firing. The sharp edges left after removal can be filed or ground down (wear goggles and a respirator), and the spots can then be touched up with paint, colored epoxy, or marking pens. The third type of stilts are made of special heat-resistant metal that can be fired to cone 10. These are reusable, so they may be well worth the extra cost. It is possible to make your own supports from nichrome wire for low firing and from Kanthal A1 or kiln-element wire for high firing—but don't use coat hanger metal—it will fatigue or disintegrate in high firings.

Because clays that fire above cone 10 (2381°F/ 1305°C)—porcelain and even some high-fire stonewares—soften as they reach the high temperatures at which they mature, anything made

from them will slump and warp if placed on stilts. Therefore, objects made of these clays must be placed flat on the shelf; for that reason they must have unglazed feet. The Chinese potters frequently fired their porcelain bowls upside down to keep them from warping, leaving a band of clay free of glaze around the rim to keep the piece from sticking to the shelf. They turned this glaze-free rim into a decorative feature by covering it with a band of metal.

Loading Glazed Ware

Any pieces of glazed ware, whether high or low fire, will stick together if they touch each other during the firing, so one of the challenges of loading a kiln is to find just the right spot for each piece where it will not touch any other (16-7). It is wise to leave at least ¼ inch between glazed pieces, because when the glaze goes through its maturing process, the glaze bubbling up on pieces that are closer together than that may actually touch, then stick as the kiln cools.

Each kiln—gas, electric, or other fuel—has its idiosyncracies. For example, many kilns have hot spots where certain glazes would be overfired. Once you have become acquainted with a particular kiln, you will know which areas go to a higher heat and which areas get more reduction than others, so you will be able to load the kiln according to the heat and atmosphere each piece requires. When you have loaded everything properly into the kiln, place sets of cones in appropriate places, usually in the middle of the kiln and possibly also at the top and bottom. The number of sets you use will depend upon the size of the kiln and its individual variations (16-7).

GLAZE IN THE KILN

We have seen that the chemical composition of clay or glaze is affected by the heat of the kiln, as well as by the type of fuel used to heat it. It is also important to remember that glazes fired quickly in a small test kiln (for example, about 6 × 6 × 6 inches or 15 × 15 × 15 cm) will yield different results even though its atmosphere is similar to that in which they will be fired in the larger kiln. In general, glazes are brighter and richer in depth when fired in a full-sized kiln.

While the glaze kiln is firing, if you look through the peepholes at the right moment (wearing goggles) you will see the glaze actually melting. In this active stage, the glaze bubbles and boils, and you may wonder if it will ever become the smooth, glossy surface you pictured. It usually does, and the bubbles generally smooth out as the melting process continues—assuming that there are no problems with formulation, fit, application, or firing! But when glazes come out of the kiln with bubbles hardened into them, this is often the result of too-rapid cooling, although it might also be the result of a too-low bisque firing which failed to burn all of the volatile materials out of the clay body. They would then have escaped through the clay pores as gases and have bubbled up through the glaze.

Speed of Temperature Rise

The slower the temperature rise of the kiln, the better. No ware was ever damaged by raising the temperature too slowly, and the speed at which you raise the kiln temperature is especially critical in the initial stages of glazing. Even if the glazed bisque ware appears to be thoroughly dry, there may be some moisture in the clay, and if this is too quickly driven off as vapor through the glaze, it can damage the adhesion of the glaze to the clay surface, causing defects. In general, the kiln is raised at a rate of around 150° F/65.5° C to 210° F/100° C an hour as an average for the firing. How long it will take to bring a kiln to the point at which a particular clay or a glaze will mature will vary from kiln to kiln, from clay to clay, from glaze to glaze, and depend upon the amount of ware in the kiln. If the kiln is tightly packed it will take longer to raise its temperature. The type of objects being fired in the kiln will also influence how quickly the temperature should be raised. For example, some potters will bring a kiln of thrown ware up to cone 10 reduction in ten hours. Sculptors, on the other hand, may preheat the kiln with the sculpture in it for two days before starting to fire it. Other factors may also influence the amount of time needed: a kiln that is outdoors may retain moisture in the porous brick of the firing chamber and require a much slower start to

dry it out. A good rule of thumb is to go slowly until the pyrometer gauge is at 1200° F/648.8° C, or the entire kiln becomes red-orange; then you can go faster. This is where cones are very helpful. Place the cones where they can be seen easily but as far as possible out of the direct flame or draft so that they will give more accurate readings. Then check them often for signs of bending. As the first one bends, monitor the kiln more carefully (every 25 to 45 minutes for an electric kiln, every 15 to 60 minutes for a gas kiln) to be sure that you leave enough time between the bending of the cones.

Using such conservative tuning thirty students (who used and fired about nine or ten tons of clay in a semester) had 100 percent firing success, with no kiln disasters.

The chemical and structural changes that take place in different types of glazes as they are fired are beyond the scope of this book, but it is important to be aware that the speed at which the kiln is heated or cooled at certain points in the firing cycle affects the relationship between the glaze and the clay body and the ultimate fit of the glaze. Changes in the clay and glaze materials taking place under heat and on cooling can cause either desired glaze effects, such as crystalline glazes, or such defects as **dunting**, which is the term used for cracks that go through both the glaze and the clay body.

Soaking

Soaking simply means keeping the kiln at a specific heat, often for about thirty minutes to an hour. Glazes need time to smooth out, and to give them time to do so, the potter often gives the kiln a soaking period, holding the temperature steady while the glaze sits and smooths out. To soak in a gas kiln, once the appropriate firing cone has bent, turn half the burners down to low heat (or to about ⅛ to ½ inch in gas pressure) for about an hour with the damper open. After the soaking time, shut off the kiln, close the damper, and plug all spyholes while the kiln cools.

To soak in an electric kiln, when the cone has bent and the kiln has been shut off by the kiln sitter or electronic controls, turn the kiln back on and set one or all switches to low for about 30 minutes. At the end of the soaking period, shut the kiln off, plug all spyholes, and allow the kiln to cool. Some people never soak, or use an alternative method, firing either an electric or a gas kiln one or two cones higher than usual.

Cooling the Kiln

Careful control of the kiln during cooling is essential to prevent defects in your work or to produce certain effects such as matt and crystalline glazes. In general, the most critical period for glazes is during the first period of cooling, when slow, careful lowering of the temperature is essential. The number of hours it takes depends on the mass of ware in the kiln, how closely it is packed, and the mass of the kiln itself. The time involved depends on so many factors that each firing should be treated individually. To give an electric kiln plenty of cooling time, after the kiln shuts off, wait between nine to twelve hours, then open the peephole. When you feel that the heat coming from the kiln is well below searing hot, then open the lid an inch every 2 to 6 hours. With a large gas kiln, on the other hand, to be sure of giving it adequate cooling time, leave it with everything shut for a minimum of 12 hours, and then open the damper one inch every 3 to 6 hours. These are conservative cooling times, but by cooling this slowly it is possible to have a high success rate in firing. Once the kiln has cooled to about 150°F/65.5°C the door can be opened to reveal the kiln of glazed ware ready to unload (16-7b).

Firing Low-Fire Glazes

Low-fire ware is made of clays that mature at low temperatures and is decorated with glazes that mature between cones 015 (1915°F/1046°C) and cone 1 (2109°F/1154°C). The most common low-fire firings are to cone 07, 06, 05, and 04 (1803°F to 1940°F/984° to 1060°C). Low-fire glazes are frequently fired in an electric kiln, because in order to achieve the clear, bright glaze colors associated with them, they require the clean oxidizing atmosphere characteristic of that type of kiln. If overfired, the red and orange glazes will look splotchy black or clear. In electric kilns, you would generally fire these glazes in the coolest areas of the kiln—usually the very bottom

or the very top. They need a well-ventilated kiln atmosphere, so you may even consider firing with most of the spyholes open. If you are firing reds and oranges, avoid firing any other ware in the same kiln with green glazes or glazes with copper and other metallic oxides that can affect the red or orange colors.

Firing Overglazes (China Paint)

Overglazes are either water- or oil-base enamels that melt at between cone 022 to 018 (1112° to 1323°F/600° to 717°C). Firing overglazes is a much faster process than bisque firing or glaze firing, because overglaze paint melts in a relatively short time at temperatures that need only be high enough to soften the base glaze somewhat so that the china paint or enamel will fuse with it. The firing temperature depends upon the color as well as the glazed surface on which it is painted. The cone to which the ware is fired is determined not only by the melting point of the overglaze, but also by the relation of the clay and the base glaze to the overglaze. For example, china paint over low-fire glazes can be fired at a lower temperature than china paint over high-fire glazes, because it takes less heat to make the base glaze tacky. Thus, china paint on a low-fire glaze can be fired at cone 020 to cone 017, while the same color may need a hotter firing (cone 016) on glazed porcelain ware. China paint is often fired in multiple firings, one color at a time, because many of these colors will be contaminated by touching another color. Also, excessive layers could cause peeling, so a number of coats of paint and multiple firings may be required to build up a particular color effect. These successive coats of china paint can create subtle gradations and depth of color. Because overglazes melt at such low temperatures, the firing process usually takes only about two and a half or three hours from beginning to end (not counting the cooling time).

A clean oxidation atmosphere is crucial to the brilliance of some overglaze colors. To achieve this in an electric kiln, keep all spyholes open through the *entire* firing. Then follow this procedure: turn all switches to low and keep the lid propped open about 2 inches for 30 to 40 minutes.

Turn switches to medium with the lid still propped open about an inch for another 30 to 45 minutes. Then close the lid, turn switches to high, and fire until the kiln sitter shuts off or the cone bends. This usually takes another 1½ hours. Cool for approximately 15 to 20 hours.

Firing Lusters

Although there are ceramists who have researched and duplicated the ancient lusters as they were fired in strong reduction in Persia, the lusters most people use today are commercial oil-base colors that contain their own reduction materials in the glaze medium. Lusters emit toxic fumes during firing that necessitate careful venting of the kiln to prevent anyone nearby inhaling them. All spyhole plugs should be left open during the entire luster firing. Often the kiln lid is also left cracked open an eighth- to a quarter-inch so that the kiln is not trapping the fumes and creating too heavy a reduction atmosphere. This could cause discoloration of the colors or might leave a murky film or residue on the surface.

SCULPTURE IN THE KILN

Although much of the firing information so far can also be applied to sculpture, some special factors must be taken into consideration when firing sculpture.

Loading Sculpture

Loading a large sculpture can be a challenge. First, you have to get it into the kiln, then place it in the best spot for firing (16-8). Large sculptures are not normally bisque fired first, because this would just double the effort and the time needed for the process. Since sculpture is therefore often loaded in the green state, and because a heavy sculpture must often be pushed or fork lifted into a kiln or loaded with a hoist using nylon slings, it should be built to accept the stresses that will be applied to it at that time. Generally, a large sculpture will be constructed in relatively small sections, partly for convenience during building

and partly so that it can be fitted into the kiln more easily. There may be instances, however, when a large sculpture cannot be made in sections, and must be loaded in one piece (16-9). The key to loading large sculpture is careful planning, so before tackling the job, organize your loading equipment to give you as much help as possible, and work out the placement of each piece before you load the kiln. John Toki, whose large sculpture takes careful loading, says,

> *First, I bring everything that I plan to load in the kiln near to the kiln where I can study and measure them. I use a tape measure and make charts, measuring each piece, and deciding where it should go in the kiln; the three key issues are: position in the kiln relates to heat, which in turn affects color. I measure and mark the bricks inside the kiln where the shelf will be positioned, and to show me where each piece will go. I also chart which piece will go in first, second and third and so on, and calculate how many shelves and posts will be needed for each piece. It's only when I have all this worked out that I actually begin to load. If I am working alone, it can take as much as forty hours to load the 100 cubic foot kiln.* (page 361, 16-12)

A level floor and level shelves are important when sliding large work into the kiln. This is where the newspapers you planned to take to the recycling center come in handy—heavy works slide easily on three to six layers of paper (the heavier the work, the more layers needed), especially on the glossy Sunday sections. To help you push large sculpture into a kiln, you can also attach braces to the floor, positioning them so that you can get leverage against them while you push. For extremely heavy pieces, however, no amount of manual work may be enough, and you may have to use a hydraulic hand cylinder with a hose and ram, a scissor-style automobile jack, or a forklift. If you use hydraulic aids to push the sculpture, it is extremely important to pad the surfaces against which the ram will push.

But even the hydraulic alternatives to two-by-fours and leverage frequently require a good deal of physical labor and ingenuity, and one of the most important qualities you must call on at this point is patience. Allow yourself plenty of time. To load one large section, allow anywhere from 2 to 5 hours, and for an entire large sculp-

Figure 16-8
Figuring out the best way to load unusual shapes of sculptures can present a challenge. Marilyn Lysohir, U.S.A., contemplates parts of her *Bad Manners* figures. While they await loading, the sections rest on foam pads, protecting their unfired finish. Lysohir fires her terra-sigillata-coated pieces to cone 06 in a single firing in a downdraft gas kiln. *Courtesy the artist. Photo: Arthur Okazaki.*

Figure 16-9
Stephen De Staebler, U.S.A., used to load his massive thrones into his large gas kiln with the help of a two-by-four used as a lever. Now, however, his sculpture is fired in his ceramic-fiber-insulated car kiln, which gives him access to the kiln floor on three sides. The car rolls directly into the fire chamber, easing the loading process considerably.

ture, the process of loading a 100-cubic foot-kiln can take one person as many as 40 hours. Remember, too, that unloading the sculpture from a large kiln after firing can take a good 12-hour day of effort as well (16-12).

One way to avoid the pushing and pulling required to load a large sculpture is to build the kiln up around the sculpture instead. Maria Kuczynska, who works in Poland and Australia, did this when she constructed one of her draped slab pieces on a larger scale than usual (16-10). Building a temporary kiln around a sculpture takes a knowledge of kiln construction and burner installation, so it is not a job for the inexperienced.

Firing Small Sculpture

The process of firing small pieces of sculpture is basically the same as that used when firing pottery, provided that it was built hollow or was hollowed out and that it was well dried. Because the walls of handbuilt sculpture may be of uneven thickness, it is especially important that it be dried slowly and, to prevent explosion, that the heat in the kiln be brought up extremely slowly.

Before starting to fire a kiln load of sculpture, be sure to preheat it with the kiln door open. This is critical. Follow the preheating by gradually increasing the temperature: in an electric kiln, turn

Figure 16-10
To fire *Icarus*, a larger-than-usual example of her slab sculpture, Maria Kuczynska used a kiln specially built up around the sculpture. Kuczynska's sculptures are built of slabs draped while still damp over an interior hollow clay support that has been allowed to stiffen enough to support the slabs. *Courtesy the artist.*

one switch one notch every 1 or 2 hours until all switches are at the high position; in a gas kiln, adjust the gas pressure by ⅛ inch every 6 to 12 hours until the kiln reaches 1200°F/537.7°C or is dull-orange in color. After that temperature has been reached throughout the entire kiln from top to bottom, you can raise it by ¼ inch gas pressure every 3 to 6 hours. The length of the complete firing will vary depending upon the size and thickness of the sculpture, and how tightly it is loaded. Slip-cast sculpture will generally take less time, because the slip used in the casting process is homogenous.

If a small sculpture has been bisque-fired first, there is no chance that it will blow up during a glaze firing. In an electric kiln the glaze firing may take between 8 to 12 hours to bring it up to the desired cone, and in a gas kiln it may require 8 to 16 hours, depending on the amount of ware and kiln size.

Firing Large Sculpture

Raising the heat of a kiln containing large sculpture that has not been given a preliminary bisque firing to the required firing temperature, then cooling it down slowly after firing, can be a lengthy process. Because a large sculpture is often constructed with varying thicknesses of clay walls, it is crucial to raise the temperature of the kiln gradually and to gauge the firing time correctly in relation to its thickest section. It is also important to preheat a thick piece of sculpture and then to increase the temperature of the kiln very gradually. For example, sections of sculpture 1 to 10 inches thick may take three to five days of firing: about 1½ to 2 days to preheat and about the same time to get up to full heat.

In an electric kiln, you can fire any size of sculpture that will fit in the kiln by turning up each switch one notch every 1 to 4 hours until all switches are in the high position. In a gas kiln, you can adjust the burner by changing the gas pressure by ⅛ inch every 6 to 12 hours until about 1200° F/537.7° C is reached or the kiln interior is red-orange. The temperature could be raised faster with thinner walled sculpture.

Since sculptures vary so much, each firing has to be planned individually depending upon the number of pieces you have placed in the kiln and their thickness. The placement of the work in the kiln is also important, as the heat in different areas of a kiln may vary by several cones (16-11). The final temperature to which you fire the sculpture will, of course, depend upon the clay from which it is built and the type of glaze, if any, you have applied. And just as it was essential to raise the heat slowly, it is equally important to give a kiln loaded with large sculpture a long, slow cooling period. This period can extend from one to three days.

(a)

(b)

Figure 16-11

(a) The cones in place show that the second shelf from the bottom of John Toki's kiln fired considerably hotter than the lowest shelf during a firing that included the sculpture illustrated in Color plate 33. **(b)** The cones are reassembled in the order in which they were placed. From bottom to top they show the wide range of temperatures in the kiln.

Unloading Sculpture

Unloading large fired sculpture is not quite as difficult as loading it into the kiln in the fragile green state, but it can still give you plenty of exercise, since it is often impossible to get hydraulic equipment into the small space of the kiln to help you. One suggestion is to use wooden wedges that can be inserted and tapped under large pieces to lift them enough so that you can slide newspaper under them and then slide them out on the paper (16-12).

If a large sculpture was well constructed in the first place, if it is handled with care and is fired slowly and with patience, you can probably fire it without breakage—at least a percentage of the time. But if your sculpture comes out of the fire in more pieces than when it went in, turn to the section on adhesives in chapter 11.

WOOD FIRING

In recent years, the ancient process of wood firing has regained popularity with Western ceramists. There is, of course, nothing new about using wood to heat a kiln full of pots. Through the centuries, designs of wood-burning kilns showed a progression from the simple pit fire to highly sophisticated structures that maximized efficiency of combustion and heat retention. And today, wood-fired kilns are built to many differing designs, some of which still carry Japanese names. Although in the West the trend started

Figure 16-12
John Toki, U.S.A. Unloading large sculptures can take almost as much ingenuity as loading. Toki finds layers of newspapers, especially the glossy Sunday sections, very useful because they allow him to slide his large wall panels onto the fork lift with a little less effort. Toki now has Stephen De Staebler's old kiln, which has now been firing clay sculpture for nearly twenty-five years.

with the fossil fuel shortage of the 1970s, it was also the result of an interest in Japanese ceramics that led numerous British and American potters to study in Japan. As these ceramists discovered that wood firing achieved effects impossible to achieve in any other way, they came to value the process for itself. Impressed with what they saw in Japan, some of them returned to build their own Japanese-style kilns (16-13, 16-14). Jack Troy is one of the many potters who are building such kilns as more ceramists turn to wood firing to give their work a distinctive surface.

Of his wood-fired pottery, Jack Troy says,

> *The individual pieces I make have evolved to suit this type of firing. Many of my thrown forms are paddled and stacked in groups, so the fire will bump and fumble its way through the pots. . . . As the temperature climbs, the velocity of the flames increases as they thrust themselves through the work on their way to the chimney. Fine-grained stoneware and porcelain clays document the experience they undergo during this strenuous firing, flashing and changing color from one part of a piece to another, depending on their location in the kiln (6-15, Color plate 11).*

In addition to the effect of the fire flashing on the pots, the minerals in the ash that is deposited on their surface may interact with the minerals in the clay, fuse, and form a glaze. These ashes will also affect any slips or glazes applied to the pots, as will the type of wood used for fuel, its degree of seasoning, and even the soil in which it grew and from which it drew minerals.

In the 1970s, after spending a year in Japan, where he studied the history and methods of wood-burning kilns intensively, Paul Chaleff (16-16, Color plate 8), built a large wood-burning kiln in New York state designed specifically for his own work. Speaking of the increasing popularity of wood-firing Chaleff says,

> *One of the reasons I believe that this technique has such allure for potters, beside the obvious excitement of the firing process, is that the finished work imparts a sense of history, a continuum of human emotion. Indeed, I try to preserve that respect for history throughout my work in concept, process and in form.*

Chaleff predicts that the strong Japanese influence in wood firing will wane as individual

Figure 16-13
The chambered climbing kiln at the pottery studio/school Earth, Air, Fire & Water was patterned on the Oriental kilns that were used for centuries in both China and Japan. The heat rises up the hill from chamber to chamber, preheating successive chambers before the wood is introduced. This kiln was built by students, who made the bricks over a period of years from clay they dug nearby and blended with fire clay to make it heat resistant. They mixed the clay in a concrete basin by treading it with their feet. *Courtesy Earth, Air, Fire & Water. Photo: Ann Henry.*

◀   *Figure 16-14*
Jack Troy, U.S.A., at the fire mouth of his *anagama* kiln. When finished, the kiln's single twenty-four-foot chamber contained five stepped levels. Buried in the ground, it takes advantage of the upward slope of the hill, allowing the heat to rise naturally, developing a good draft. Calling it the *kiln of my dreams/nightmares,* Troy says, *Stacking the kiln is an extremely important part of an anagama firing, since each object's placement relative to the others will ultimately determine its identity.* Because each firing takes several days, the stacking and stoking tasks are shared with colleagues, who work in pairs for three-hour shifts. *When the pieces come from the kiln,* says Troy, *I know better than to call them 'mine.' Courtesy the artist. Photo: Schecter Lee.*

Figure 16-15
Jack Troy's wood-fired bottle received a natural glaze from the wood ash on its shoulders, recalling a jar made by a Chinese potter in about 200 B.C. (3-9). Because the heaviest ash particles settle near the port through which the wood is introduced and the kiln temperature may vary as much as eight cones, Troy's placement of his ware in the kiln affects how the glaze develops. Troy says, *My wish is for the work to be discovered on whatever terms seem appropriate to a beholder, in much the same way that I discover my work transformed by the fire.* (See also Color plate 11.) Porcelain. Ht. 14 in. (35 cm). *Courtesy the artist and Helen Drutt Gallery. Photo: Schecter Lee.*

Figure 16-16
Covered jar, Paul Chaleff, U.S.A. Although he uses a Japanese-style wood-firing kiln, Chaleff prefers the terms *kiln-glazed* or *naturally ash glazed*, because he feels that the Oriental methods of wood firing are now being adapted in the West to many ways of working. Chaleff says, *I started with borrowed forms and have eventually developed my own style. . . . This kiln and the materials I have chosen to use in it have allowed me to learn a new language of forms and surfaces.* Wood-fired stoneware; heavy accumulation of ash. Ht. 11 in. (28 cm). *Courtesy the artist. In the Collection of the Everson Museum.* (See also Color plate 8.)

Western artists gradually adapt the process to their own needs. He prefers to apply the terms *fire-glazed* or *kiln-glazed* to his pottery, and he is concerned with adapting the process so that his work reflects his own creativity and the Western society in which he lives rather than attempting to replicate an ancient Oriental style.

Chaleff says he has experimented with and chooses clays that he feels will have good visual and tactile character when fired properly. They are often clays that are difficult to use owing to their extreme shrinkage, impurities and stones, or lack of tooth. Workability, for Chaleff, is now secondary.

> *Quiet strength is the overall effect I try to achieve. Form is the most important element of that effect. Surface quality and color serve to help define the form, interact with it, and of course enhance its character. . . .*

Wood firing of kilns is prohibited in some cities or areas because of the air pollution caused by the smoke. Check your local ordinances before you build a wood-fired kiln.

SALT FIRING

Salt glazing has had a long tradition in Europe, England, and the United States (6-14, 7-3), and proved to be ideally suited for use on containers for domestic use because the glaze that develops when the sodium in the salt combines with the silica in the clay is impermeable to both water and acids. In the days before refrigerators, when many foodstuffs were preserved in brine and vinegar, this was an important feature. It is no wonder that when European and British potters came to the American colonies, they searched for a stoneware clay on which they could use their traditional glaze.

In order for a salt glaze to develop, the clay body must contain the right amount of silica, the silica must be softened enough by the heat of the kiln to be ready to fuse with the sodium, and the salt must be damp in order to form a vapor. When the damp salt is introduced into the kiln at about cone 7 (2264° F/1240° C), the sodium combines with the silica of the clay to produce a transparent glaze.

Salt releases chlorine and hydrocloric acid fumes when it vaporizes, fumes that are capable of seriously damaging the lungs. Thus, special precautions must be taken in placing the kiln and kiln stack so that the gases will not be released too close to people or buildings (16-17 to 16-19). It is also best to insert the salt when there is no wind, and to avoid any fumes as you insert the salt. For added protection, wear a respirator rated for vapors, acid mists, and fumes. There are a variety of ways to place the salt in the kiln. Some people wrap it in damp newspaper and insert it through the burner port. Robert Winokur uses a long angle iron as a "spoon" so that he can stay clear of the fumes, while Walter Keeler places small bowls containing salt on the bag wall of the kiln among his pots.

Because the gases emitted from a salt firing are poisonous, some ceramists are now using more ecologically safe substitutes for salt. Instead of salt, a mixture of dampened borax, pearl ash, soda ash, whiting, lithium, and bentonite may be inserted in the kiln in small packages. In *The Potter's Complete Book of Clays and Glazes*[1], James Chapell

[1]Watson-Guptill Publications, New York, 1977.

Figure 16-17

Robert M. Winokur, U.S.A., adjusting the damper on his salt-glaze kiln to create a reducing atmosphere during salting. Note the chlorine vapor escaping from the chimney—the reason salt kilns must be carefully placed so that the fumes are kept well away from people and houses. *Courtesy the artist.*

suggests the following proportions for this mixture:

Soda ash (Sodium carbonate)	36.0%
Whiting (Calcium carbonate)	48.0%
Borax	3.0%
Pearl ash (Potassium carbonate)	8.0%
Lithium carbonate	4.0%
Bentonite	1.0%

Although it is possible to build a special kiln with a calcium alumina lining that can be used for both bisque and glaze firing as well as infrequent or light salt firings, usually a salt kiln is used only for salt firing. This is because the bricks lining the kiln become glazed at the same time that the objects receive their glaze. If a salt kiln were to be used for bisque firing or ordinary glaze firing after salt-glaze firing, the salt glaze on the bricks would

(a)

(b)

Figure 16-18
(a) Winokur measures out the salt compound, pouring it into an angle iron in preparation for
introducing it into the kiln. **(b)** He inserts the angle iron "spoon" in order to drop the compound
into the firebox. As the salt vaporizes, the sodium will combine with the silica in the clay,
causing a glaze to form on the surface. The angle iron allows him to stand well away from any
vapors that might escape as he inserts the salt. *Courtesy the artist.*

Figure 16-19

Table with Floral Legs and Vase. Robert Winokur, U.S.A., comments, *Ceramic wares throughout history have been concerned mostly with the evolution of the container, and the value of this art form was judged in terms of the function it performed.* . . . Winokur points out that social and technological changes of the past twenty years have eroded this tradition *to the extent that ceramic objects of no particular function have become common and readily accepted, not as sculpture, though they are that, but as an art form with its own distinct characteristics.* Stoneware; blue wood-ash glaze; slips and engobes; salt glazed. Table ht. 33 in. (84 cm); vase ht. 4½ in. (11 cm). *Courtesy Helen Drutt and Esther Saks Galleries and the artist.*

melt again, and cause problems with the newly introduced ware. Electric kilns cannot be used for salt glazing, as the elements would be harmed.

Many potters respond to the surface that salt glazing creates (9-10 and 12-59). Janet Mansfield says,

Salt firing offers me an aesthetic that suits my temperament. Both form and clay quality are enhanced by the glaze texture and every part of the technical processes demands creative attention.

In order to get a combination of smooth areas and the characteristic mottled and textured "orange-peel" glaze that salt can produce, Walter Keeler (16-20) often coats part of a jug or pot with a colored engobe (appendix 1C). Where he sprays the engobe onto the clay, the surface will fire smooth, but where he leaves the clay uncoated, the orange-peel effect appears.

Eileen Murphy, on the other hand, does not want the details of her delicately incised and painted vessels to be obliterated by the orange-peel texture, so she fires her work very carefully, avoiding the "blast" that could destroy the delicacy of the image drawn on the pot (15-16). Of her salt firing Murphy says,

The firing is magic! Especially in the fall when the stars are clear and the air cold and it's dark and time to salt. The salt I throw in wrapped in newspaper and into the fire box (which needs replacing every so often) and then the flames and vapor swirling are spectacular. A kiln god or goddess is always within; a small token made to come through the changes with the pots.

Traditionally, salt ware was fired without added color, and the pots emerged predominately the color of the fired clay body—sometimes brownish, if there was iron in the clay, sometimes gray, if the fire was heavily reducing and the iron content low. The only added color was in the cobalt blue decoration (7-3). Contemporary ceramists, however, use oxides, stains, and glazes to impart color to their salt-glazed objects. Robert Winokur, for example, uses slips and engobes along with ash glazes on his table-vessel constructions (16-19). This is another example of how contemporary ceramists have taken an historical process, experimented with it, expanded its traditional limits, and found ways to adapt it to their needs. This is the same process that continued throughout the history of ceramics as migrations brought potters to new areas, spreading ceramics techniques from one culture to another. The difference now is that the exchanges take place rapidly as we are constantly exposed to information about ceramics from around the world and from every period of history.

Raku Firing

One of the processes that has spread from one culture to another is raku firing, developed in sixteenth century Japan (chapter 3), where raku-fired pots were used in the tea ceremony. Its popularity in the West began in the 1950s and 1960s, when an interest in Zen philosophy developed in the United States and Europe. Linked with a keen appreciation of nature and a recognition of beauty in nonperfection, raku also appealed because of its participatory aspects and the spontaneous and dramatic results it produced. Raku became "in." Now, like many of the processes from around the world that first attracted attention during that period of rapidly expanding interest in ceramics, the raku process has been absorbed, changed, and adapted to Western methods and needs (16-21, 16-22). The sixteenth-century potters of Japan might be startled by the way some raku firings are done today, although they would probably respond to the aesthetic qualities of many contemporary creations.

More significant than the use of new methods and equipment are the aesthetic changes that have taken place as contemporary ceramists around the world have integrated the raku tradition into their own creative lives, using what is applicable and discarding what is inappropriate to their work or their own ceramic traditions.

Before a pot or a sculpture can be fired using the raku process, it should be built of a clay that can withstand the thermal shocks to which it will be subjected (see appendix 1C). The pot should then be bisque fired in any type of kiln and glazed with a low-fire glaze (see appendix 1C). Although the traditional raku kiln was a small wood-burning kiln with an inner sagger in which the ware was fired, you can use any kiln that can be heated quickly to red-hot heat—between 015 (1479°F/804°C) to 08 (1751°F/955°C)—and that provides easy access to its firing chamber. It can be an elec-

Figure 16-20

Walter Keeler, England, created a variation of a traditional metal jug form in salt-glazed clay. Keeler fires his stoneware to cone 10 (Orton), reduces from 1832°F/1000°C, and salts the kiln at cone 9 for an hour, finishing with a half-hour soak. The variation in texture is achieved by coating part of the ware with an engobe, which fires smooth, while the remaining part fires with an "orange-peel" salt texture. Stoneware, gray/gray-blue. Ht. 17 in. (43 cm). *Courtesy the artist.*

Figure 16-21
Contemporary raku equipment can be a far cry from that used in sixteenth-century Japan.
(a) Alan Widenhofer, U.S.A., fires a large glazed bowl by lowering a light-weight wire and
ceramic fiber-insulated gas kiln around it. **(b)** The bowl is removed from the kiln while hot
and placed on a bed of newspaper, which ignites from the heat. **(c)** The bowl was so large it
required a specially built cover of wire and ceramic fiber. Once lowered, the ring was
immediately covered with sheet metal to smother the fire and cause reduction. *Courtesy the
artist.*

Figure 16-22
Elke Blodgett, Canada, built her wood-firing raku kiln at the edge of the woods. Of it she says, *Best kiln ever. My favorite. Very atypical design: cross-draft, updraft, and downdraft. So I call it my circular-draft kiln.* As the kiln is stoked, the bisqued ware can be warmed above the stoking hole or on top of the firing chamber, thus reducing the thermal shock when it is placed in the red-hot kiln. *Courtesy the artist.*

goggles when you look into the fire. Depending upon the design of the kiln, as the firing progresses, you may be able to look in and see the glaze actually maturing on the ware.

As soon as the glaze matures, remove the pot and leave it to cool rapidly or treat it in one of several ways. You can place it immediately in a heat-resistant container of sawdust, charcoal, newspapers, seaweed—anything that will burn and create a reducing atmosphere when the container is covered. Reduction will cause iridescent luster areas to appear, and fire marks that enrich the surface will often develop. Most raku develops crackles in the glaze, but if you want more crackle, you can plunge the piece into water while it is hot.

Traditionally, the glazes used for raku firing were lead glazes, because lead was a readily available flux that made it possible for the glaze to be melted at the low temperature the kilns achieved. Nowadays, however, for health reasons, lead is generally avoided, and the raku-fired pots, with their pitted, cracked glazes, are not considered hygenic for use as containers for food.

The experience of pulling a pot from the kiln and plunging it into sawdust, or seaweed and water can be exhilarating for those new to clay. But raku firing techniques, when developed by an artist to meet his or her individual artistic requirement, become an expressive tool, used not just for the excitement of the process but for the results that can be obtained with it (16-23). One artist who uses raku in a highly expressive manner is Richard Hirsch (15-20, Color plate 13).

Hirsch uses a combination of terra sigillata and low-fire glazes to surface his tripod vessel forms (see chapter 15 and appendix 1C for details). Of his raku firing method, Hirsch says,

> the piece is removed while very hot (1400° F/760° C approx.) and sprayed with several metallic salts (i.e., copper, iron). I use a mask when spraying outdoors and never do this indoors because the fumes are toxic.

(Note: the respirator you use should be rated for toxic fumes.) Hirsch continues this process for several removals and sprayings to build up the surface. His final step is removing the piece from

tric or gas kiln, a wood kiln built outdoors (16-22), or a specially constructed space-age insulated one (16-21), and it can be fired with whatever fuel is available. Since the process involves placing the preheated pot directly in the hot firing chamber and then withdrawing it, the interior should be accessible so that you can easily insert and withdraw the pots. Be sure you use tongs and protective gloves when you do this, and wear shaded

Figure 16-23

Portrait of Linda by Susan and Steven Kemenyffy, U.S.A. The Kemenyffys work together, with potter Steven responsible for building and firing their large raku-fired wall pieces, while Susan, trained as a printmaker, creates the incised drawings and does the glazing. The clay they use is a special body mixed to allow the work to survive the raku process to which it is subjected (see Appendix 1C for their clay-body recipe). Approx. 36 × 32 in. (91 × 81 cm). 1988. *Courtesy the artists.*

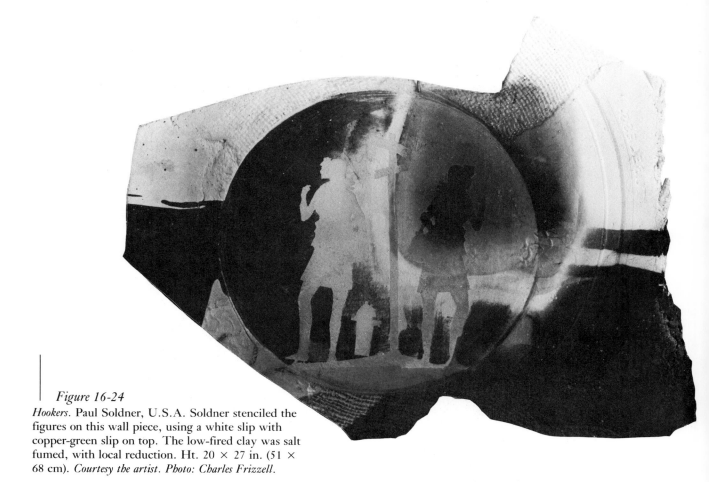

Figure 16-24

Hookers. Paul Soldner, U.S.A. Soldner stenciled the figures on this wall piece, using a white slip with copper-green slip on top. The low-fired clay was salt fumed, with local reduction. Ht. 20 × 27 in. (51 × 68 cm). *Courtesy the artist. Photo: Charles Frizzell.*

 the hot kiln and placing it in straw for the post-firing reduction. Hirsch says this

> *further enhances the visual depth of the surface and changes the coloration of the salts and sigs. The results are a colored patination that expresses age and history which is an integral aspect of my work. (Color plate 13).*

Raku firing, with its unexpected results, appeals to many people for its spontaneity. Nevertheless, there are health and safety precautions you should follow when working with flaming materials and red-hot objects. Keep a hose or bucket handy; don't go barefoot, and wear safety shoes to protect you against burning straw or a dropped pot. Keep the area around the kiln free of combustibles, and if you reduce in a container also keep the area around it clear of loose straw or paper. Lift the lid of the reducing container carefully so that any flames will be directed away from yourself or other people. And, as Hirsch said, if you spray metallic salts on your ware, use a respirator.

POST-FIRING SMOKING

A number of artists use postfiring smoking and fuming techniques to give a rich, smoky quality to their pots or sculptures without subjecting them to the stresses of the raku method. By using this process, they can also achieve interesting reduction effects without damaging the elements of their electric kilns. There are various ways to do this, but basically it is a matter of exposing the already fired piece to the effects of a reduction atmosphere. Glenys Barton, in England, smoked her poetic figurative wall plaques because she felt they would not stand the raku process, while Paul Soldner used a salt fuming and local reduction to give his wall piece its misty night-time quality (16-24). Do not fume or smoke your pieces by

Figure 16-25
A group pit firing on a beach can be a rewarding experience, especially if the fire is good to your ware and creates the colored surface you desire. Here, Carol Molly Prier sprinkles copper carbonate on some of the pots that have been buried in sawdust at the bottom of the pit and then covered with seaweed.

(b)

Figure 16-26
(a) After the pots have been covered with cow dung and wood, and after a ritual scattering of cornmeal over them, the fire begins to play its part. **(b)** After the fire has burned down, the pots emerge surrounded by the ashes, which hold the shape of the dung until they are disturbed. The hardest part of pit firing is not digging the pit or lugging the wood and dung, but waiting until the ashes are cool enough so that you can remove and study your pots.

 burning straw soaked in salts without wearing a respiratory rated for protection against toxic fumes.

PIT FIRING

The earliest potters fired in open firings on the top of the ground or in shallow pits. This tradition has continued throughout history and to the present in non-industrialized areas around the world—Africa (4-12), the American Southwest (5-19), Mexico (5-8), and Fiji (1-33), for example. This type of firing produces a porous type of earthenware that is not watertight, an adavantage in hot countries where drinking water is cooled in earthenware water jars by evaporation. Contemporary potters, entranced with the fire marks and other effects that can be achieved with pit firing, have experimented with firings ranging from sawdust and peat in an open-top brick kiln to pit firing on a beach. Each person has a favorite way of conducting this type of firing, so it is impossible to generalize about the method. For example, some people use only earthenware clay for objects to be pit fired, feeling that it will survive the stress of the firing better than high fire clays, but Carol Molly Prier (16-25 to 16-27) has fired every type of clay in pit fires—from low-fire to porcelain—and finds that no clay seems to crack more or less than another. Since her vessels are usually burnished, she chooses clay with no grog. At one

Figure 16-27
On a windy beach within sound of the surf, the fire, the clay, and human artistry unite to create an elegant vessel using a firing method as old as the art of ceramics. Pit-fired, burnished vessel by Carol Molly Prier, U.S.A. *Courtesy the artist. Photo: Charles Frizzell.*

group pit firing, held on a beach, the ware was partially buried in a layer of sawdust with seaweed and driftwood placed over it to provide salt and other minerals. The pots were then sprinkled with copper carbonate, covered with cow dung, and prepared for firing by piling wood on top of the cushioning of the dung (16-25, 16-26, 16-27). With everyone pitching in to dig the pit, to gather driftwood and seaweed, and to place their pots in a layer of sawdust, the sense of community effort gave this group of contemporary clay crafters a vivid sense of identification with early potters.

CHOOSING *YOUR* MEANS OF EXPRESSION

Never in the history of ceramics has the person working in clay had such a wide choice of techniques or such an extensive range of available materials. The alternatives open to you today de-

mand that you make aesthetic choices as well as learn techniques for forming, coloring, and firing clay. Ceramics can be a seductive medium in which to work, offering processes that in themselves are fascinating. As a result, the craft or technique sometimes becomes an end in itself. Nobody would deny that craft is a vital part of ceramics, but craft without artistic sensibility will never form a beautiful pot or build an expressive piece of sculpture. Nurturing your creativity, fostering your imagination, developing your aesthetic awareness, and learning to trust them is as much a part of your development in ceramics as is mastering the process.

If you make the choice to join those who have spent their lives making useful and beautiful objects from clay, you will become part of a tradition that not only stretches back to the earliest days of human history, but reaches ahead into the future and will continue as long as there is earth for human hands to shape and fire to transform it.

393

APPENDIXES

The information in these appendixes is designed to supplement the information in the main text. It includes a series of clay and glaze tests that you can follow in progression, using the accompanying charts. If you work through the clay and glaze tests in Appendix 1, you will develop a basic understanding of both the composition and the qualities of different clay bodies and glazes. Appendix 2 gives you information you will find useful when you fire your tests and ware. If you want to go deeper into testing and glaze calculation, Appendix 3 provides an example of changing the flux in a glaze, and follows a potter calculating, testing, and modifying a high-fire glaze. It also includes charts of chemical information you will need. Other appendixes supplement the text with additional useful information and sources of information on many aspects of pottery and sculpture.

1A
Clays and Glazes Formulated for Testing

The following clay body and glaze recipes were formulated for *Hands In Clay* to provide a guide for mixing and testing as a learning experience. The clay recipes will produce clay bodies with various qualities and firing temperatures, while the glaze recipes will give you practice in changing the color of a base glaze. Testing is only a means to extend your creativity in clay. What makes a successful ceramic technician and artist? He or she must maintain a bright spirit, solid determination, and hope for a dash of luck!

CLAY BODIES FOR TESTING

Although the clay body-tests were fired at cone 05, cone 5, and cone 10, allowing for a wide range of firing temperatures, the actual range of the cones and temperatures for these tests is less rigid than the charts imply. For example, the low-fire white clay can be fired as low as cone 010 and as high as cone 1, while the cone 5 porcelain develops a richer sheen when fired at cone 7, or even as high as cone 10. Changes in firing temperatures will affect the shrinkage and color of the clay, and changes in components will affect the workability of the body. While you are developing your own clay bodies through tests, it is wise to be flexible about material substitutes, temperatures, and kiln atmospheres. Each of these factors will subtly affect the outcome of your tests, adding to the excitement as you proceed. Do not be discouraged from mixing clays or glazes if the names of the materials listed in the following recipes are not the same as those in your area. For example, the names of fire clays, ball clays, and feldspars will vary depending on where you live. You will just have to test the substitutes thoroughly.

The following clay bodies were mixed in 300 gram batches. The clays were first blended dry; then they were mixed with water into a slip. For the smooth clay bodies, the water content was about 20 percent of the batch, while the bodies with 20 percent grog required roughly 13–15 percent water content per batch. The slip was poured onto a plaster bat and left 5 or 10 minutes or until enough moisture had been absorbed to bring the clay to the right consistency for wedging. The base recipes for these clay bodies were formulated to total 100 percent. Coloring oxides and stains were added to the base clay in varying percentages. The letters and numbers in parentheses refer to the poster illustrating test tiles. Be sure that you follow the precautions given in Chapter 10 for handling dry clay.

Clay Bodies Formulated for Use in Color and Glaze Tests

Hands in Clay white cone 05, 5, and 10 clay bodies (CL1, CL2, CL3)

Components	Percent		
	Cone 05 (CL1)	*Cone 5 (CL2)*	*Cone 10 (CL3)*
Kentucky ball clay OM4	50.0	21.0	20.0
Kaolin (Georgia)		27.0	28.0
Fire clay (Lincoln)			
Feldspar (Custer)			25.0
Feldspar (Nepheline syenite)		25.0	
Silica 200 mesh (flint)		25.0	25.0
Talc	50.0		
Macaloid		2.0	2.0

Notes.
White base clay bodies in oxidation: (CL1 to CL3)
Cone 05—smooth, warm-white body. (CL1)
Cone 5—smooth, slightly off-white. (CL2)
Cone 10—smooth, slightly off-white. (CL3)
   White base clay bodies in reduction:
Cone 10—smooth, light gray. (CL4)

Substitutions for the materials and chemicals listed in the recipes will cause changes in the color, texture and firing range of the clays. If you substitute, you will need to carry out additional tests. Some possible substitutes:

- *Kaolin:* EPK or Grolleg or other kaolin may be substituted for Georgia.
- *Feldspar:* Locally available feldspars may be substituted for Custer, a potash feldspar.
- *Fire clay (Lincoln):* Other fire clays such as IMCO#400 or #800 Cedar Heights, Goldart, Pine Lake or Missouri may be substituted for Lincoln.

- *Macaloid:* assists in giving plasticity to some clays; it may be eliminated for test purposes, or Vee gum or bentonite can be substituted.
- *Any red earthenware,* such as Newman earthenware or Cedar Heights REDART terra-cotta can be substituted for the Red Horse clay.
- *Stains:* Other pink or yellow glaze or body stains may be substituted, as can other color stains. Be aware of the maximum cone or temperature range of whatever stain you substitute because some colors fade at high temperatures (D-320 pink and #378 tin-vanadium yellow are both high temperature stains).

Coloring Clay Bodies with Natural Clays (CL5 to CL8)

To make subtle changes in the color of a clay body, you may simply wedge two colors of clay together to create a lighter or darker shade. However, the following clays for testing were mixed dry, and then water was added to make a slip that was poured onto a plaster bat to absorb the water and stiffen the clay. (See the general instructions for mixing clay bodies in Chapter 10.)

Components	Percent		
	Cone 05 (CL5)	*Cone 5 (CL6)*	*Cone 10 (CL7)*
Kentucky ball clay (OM4)	30.0		35.0
Earthenware (Red Horse)	50.0	50.0	
Fire clay (Lincoln)		50.0	65.0
Talc	20.0		

Notes.
Coloring white clay bodies with natural clays:
Cone 05—warm light red, smooth (would burnish well.) (CL5)
Cone 5—rust-red, slightly grainy. (CL6)
Cone 10 oxidation—gray-buff, smooth. (CL7)
Cone 10 reduction—warm brown, smooth. (CL8)

Texturing Clay Bodies with Grog/Fillers/Temper (CL9 to CL12)

To give differing textures to clay bodies, you can introduce various types of grog or filler in place of the buff grog (30–70 mesh) or the molochite. You can also blend the texturing materials in combinations, adding even greater tooth and openness to the clay body. For example, for a sculpture body use half sand, half grog, or a variety of mesh sizes of ione grain, or sand and grog and pearlite in combination.

Components	Percent			
	Cone 05 (CL9)	*Cone 5 (CL10)*	*Cone 10A (CL11)*	*Cone 10B (CL12)*
Kentucky ball clay (OM4)	40.0	50.0	28.0	25.0
Kaolin (Georgia)				20.0
Fire clay (Lincoln)		30.0	52.0	
Feldspar (Custer)				20.0
Silica 200 mesh				20.0
Talc	40.0			
Macaloid				2.0
Grog (buff 30–70 mesh)	20.0	20.0	20.0	
Molochite				13.0

*Silica sand   (30–90 mesh)   5–10%
Ione grain   (30–150 mesh)   5–20%
Red grog   (9–30 mesh)   5–20%
Pearlite   (fine or coarse) 1–5%

(Sand in some clay bodies fired to around cone 10 may form a gritty surface.)
Notes.
Texturing clay bodies with grog/tempers:
Cone 05—white, slightly rough surface. (CL9)
Cone 5—off-white, rough surface. (CL10)
Cone 10A oxidation—gray-buff, slightly rough surface. (CL11)
Cone 10B reduction—warm brown, lighter speckles, rough surface. (CL12)

White Cone 10 Stoneware Clay Body (WS1, WS2)
A textured stoneware body for general use.

Components	Percent
Kentucky ball clay (OM4)	25.0
Silica 200 mesh (flint)	20.0
Georgia China clay	20.0
Custer feldspar	20.0
Macaloid	2.0 (WS1) Oxidation
Molochite	13.0 (WS2) Reduction

Shrinkage Test

If you are planning to make a large sculpture or even a series of thrown wine goblets, you will want to know how much the clay will shrink on drying and during firing. Since clay bodies have different rates of shrinkage, when you formulate a clay body it is important to test the amount of shrinkage. For example, the white 05 clay used in these tests shrank about 5 percent from wet to dry and about 6 percent from dry to fired state. One way to measure the amount of shrinkage of a clay is to cast a block of plaster, carve lines into it one inch apart, and number the lines from 1 to 10. To make a clay test tile, simply press a slab of clay onto the block to imprint the pattern of lines and numbers in the clay, then dry and fire the slab. You can then measure how much the clay shrinks after drying and firing by comparing its measurement before and after with the plaster ruler that you made, or with a plastic **shrink ruler.**

CASTING SLIP

Hands in Clay Low-Fire (Cone 05) White Casting Slip (SL1)
Batch formula: for 128 fluid ounces (1 gallon)

Components	Amount	Percent
Kentucky ball clay (OM4)	2,027.25 gr	50
Talc	2,027.25 gr	50
		100 total percent
Additives		
Soda ash	4.46 gr (fluid wt)	.11
Sodium silicate (N)	18.65 gr (fluid wt)	.46
Water	1,900.60 gr (67 fluid oz.)	1.65 fluid oz. water
		100 gram batch

Notes.

Weigh the sodium silicate and soda ash on a gram scale and mix with water. Add talc and ball clay and mix for 30 minutes, then screen the slip through a 40 to 60 mesh sieve. Accurate measurement and mixing time are crucial to suspension and fluidity, and screening is essential for smoothness. Immediately before casting, slip should be mixed again for 1–2 minutes. See Chapter 13 for pouring directions.

Hands in Clay White Porcelain Cone 5–7 Casting Slip (Electric Kiln) (SL2)
Batch formula: for 128 fluid ounces (1 gallon)

Components	Amount	Percent
Kaolin (Georgia)	1,380.0 gr	25.0
Feldspar (Custer)	552.0 gr	10.0
Feldspar (Nepheline syenite)	1,656.0 gr	30.0
Silica 325 mesh	552.0 gr	10.0
Kentucky ball clay (OM4)	1,380.0 gr	25.0
		100 total percent
Additives		
Soda ash	5.52 gr	.10
Sodium silicate (N)	22.08 gr (fluid wt.)	.40
Darvan #7	13.80 gr (fluid wt.)	.25
Water	1,564.92 gr (55.20 oz.)	2.0 oz. water per
		gram batch

Notes.

Follow the same measuring and mixing directions as for the cone 05 slip. For casting an object with fine detail, it is a good idea to put the slip through a ball mill. You may also want to use up to an 80 mesh sieve to screen the slip. In that case, you will probably have to push the slip through with a flexible spatula. One way to check the amount of water needed in the casting slips is to measure out one pint of slip and weigh it. If it weighs less than 26 to 28.5 ounces for the low-fire slip, or less than 28.5 to 32 ounces for high-fire slips, your mixture has too much water. This could cause settling.

Hands in Clay White Porcelain Cone 10–11 Casting Slip (for Gas or Electric Kiln) (SL3)
Batch formula: for 128 fluid ounces (1 gallon)

Components	Amount	Percent
Kaolin (Grolleg) (English china clay)	1,951.20 gr	40.0
Feldspar (Custer)	1,219.50 gr	25.0
Silica 325 mesh	975.60 gr	20.0
Kentucky ball clay (OM4)	731.70 gr	15.0
		100 total percent
Additives		
Soda ash	6.09 gr	.125
Sodium silicate (N)	19.51 gr (fluid wt.)	.40
Darvan #7	19.51 gr (fluid wt.)	.40
Water	1,936.0 gr (68.29 oz.)	1.40 ounces water per 100 gram batch

Notes.
Fired in oxidation, this is a white slip, in reduction it will be gray. Follow the same measuring and mixing directions as for the cone 05 slip. For casting an object with fine detail, it is a good idea to put the slip through a ball mill. You may also want to use up to an 80 mesh sieve to screen the slip. In that case, you will probably have to push the slip through with a flexible spatula.

EGYPTIAN PASTE

White Egyptian Paste (Cone 015) (EP1)
The components of this clay body form an integral glaze
on its surface as it is fired. (See Chapter 2 for historical
information on Egyptian paste.)

Components	Percent
Nepheline syenite	25.0
Frit 3134	15.0
Silica 200 mesh	20.0
Silica sand 70 mesh	8.0
Kentucky ball clay OM4	24.0
Soda ash	3.0
Borax (powder)	3.0
Macaloid	2.0
	100 total percent

Notes.
Mix the dry components, then add enough water to
form a stiff paste. Shape it into whatever small object
you wish, then dry it slowly until soluble salts form
on the surface. Fire it at cone 015. Although the
Egyptian objects made of this type of clay were
usually turquoise, nowadays, ceramists add other
colorants to produce a wider range of colors. Once
you mix the base white body, you can experiment
with a variety of stains and oxides. The following
percentages will give you a starting point for your
testing.

Colorants
Turquoise: Copper carbonate   2.50%(EP2)
Blue: Cobalt carbonate   .75%(EP3)
Soft Lavender: D320 pink stain   3.00%(EP4)
              Cobalt carbonate   .15%

Speckling
Granular ilmenite: forms tiny black specks
Silicon carbide (36 grit): forms prominent black specks

COLORING CLAY BODIES WITH OXIDES AND STAINS (CS1 to CS4)

The dry stains can be mixed directly into the dry
clay. In the following tests of cone 05, cone 5, and cone
10 clay in oxidation, the same percentages of stain were
used, so only one chart is given below with notes on
the colors achieved in each clay.

Stains and Oxides Added to all the White Clays

Colorants	Percent					
	Blue (CS1)	Medium Brown (CS2)	Green (CS3)	Pink (CS4)	Yellow (CS5)	Dark Brown (CS6)
Cobalt oxide	3.0					1.0
Iron oxide (Red)		5.0				4.0
Chromium oxide			3.0			2.0
Manganese oxide						3.0
Pink stain (D320)				5.0		
Tin vanadium yellow					5.0	

Notes.
Coloring code 05 white clay body with oxides and stains (oxidation) (CS1 to CS6):
Blue—a light, rather watery blue. (CS1)

Red-brown—a light reddish brown, the color of flower pots. (S2)
Green—pale leaf green, no blue tones. (CS3)
Pink—very pale pink, almost off-white. (CS4)
Yellow—pale, beige-yellow. (CS5)
Brown—more gray than brown. (CS6) On this clay, the low-fire clear glaze (formula on page 405) has a milky appearance.

If you like a matt finish, fire the test without a glaze, but if you want to deepen and intensify the color and add a glossy finish, apply a clear glaze.

Coloring cone 5 white clay with stains and oxides (oxidation) (CS1 to CS6):
Blue—rich deep blue with very slight purple tinge. (CS1)
Medium brown—warm brown (CS2)
Green—dark leaf green. (CS3)
Pink—light pink, flesh color. (CS4)
Yellow—earthtone yellow; not clear lemon yellow. (CS5)
Dark brown—rich chocolate brown. (CS6)

Applying the clear glaze over these clays does not intensify the color, but adds a glossy surface.

Coloring cone 10 white base clay body (oxidation) (CS1 to CS6):
Blue—very dark blue, slightly purplish tone. (CS1)
Medium brown—cold gray/brown. (CS2)
Green—yellow green. (CS3)
Pink—paler than cone 5 pink. (CS4)
Yellow—slightly yellower than cone 5 yellow. (CS5)
Dark brown—rich chocolate brown. (CS6)

GUM SOLUTION FOR TRANSPARENT UNDERGLAZE STAIN OR OXIDES USED ON WHITE CLAY BODY

If you would like to make your own transparent water base underglazes, you can mix oxides and ceramic stains using a solution of CMC gum in water:

Basic Stain Solution

Water	CMC gum
1 gallon	130.66 grams
or	
1 pint	16.33 grams

SURFACE COLORS/UNDERGLAZES, STAINS

Colorants (Stains and Oxides) for Use on White Clay Body

Colorant		Solution	Color: cone 05	Color: cone 5	Color: cone 10
Cobalt	5 grams	3 oz.	Matt gray blue (S1)	Dark blue, slight gloss (S5)	Dark blue, slight gloss (S9)
Yellow stain	5 grams	3 oz.	Bright yellow (S3)	Pale yellow (S7)	Pale yellow (S11)
Iron	8 grams	3 oz.	Matt red brown (S4)	Dark matt brown (S8)	Dark matt brown (S12)
Chromium	5 grams	3 oz.	Matt leaf green (S2)	Dark leaf green (S6)	Dark leaf green (S10)

Apply thinly in one coat; otherwise any glaze you use over the underglaze may crawl. You may brush, spray, or paint on the underglaze. The test underglazes applied with this solution were fired from cone 05 up to cone 10 in oxidation. The oxides and stain tested held their colors at these cones. You will need to make more tests to see which proportion of coloring agents will work best for you, depending upon your clay and the temperature at which you fire the tests. If you plan to keep the solution for later use you may add a few drops of formaldehyde, but rather than use formaldehyde we recommend that you mix only enough solution for immediate use. Formaldehyde can produce allergic reactions. With a coat of transparent glaze over the underglaze the colors are generally brighter (ST1 to ST2).

GLAZES FORMULATED FOR TESTING

The following glazes were tested on the base white clay body. Since a glaze consists of a combination of chemicals that fuse and adhere to a clay body under proper application and firing, both the clay body and the firing are equally important in developing successful glazes, and the two must work in a symbiotic relationship. The glazes in this section were formulated to be used on the clays that you have already tested (page 397). The cone 05 glaze fits that clay, the cone 5 glaze fits the cone 5 clay, and the cone 10 glaze fits the white cone 10 clay.

How you apply the glaze and the type of kiln and atmosphere in which you fire it will also affect the final result. Make notes as you test so that you can make changes based on what happened in your tests. Devise a system of displaying or storing your test tiles so that they are easily available for reference. Our notes following the clay and glaze recipes describe the appearance of the test tiles after firing in a test kiln. Your tests may differ from these descriptions, and the colors or textures as they appear on these small test tiles may also look quite different on a piece of sculpture or a pot.

Water Ratio

The amount of water you add to the glaze materials must be controlled because it affects glaze material suspension as well as application properties. The percentages in the following chart indicate the water-to-glaze ratio for the glaze test formulas in Appendix 1A. The chart should be used only as a guide when formulating your own test glazes. In our testing, the glazes were applied with two to three brushed-on applications. For dipping or pouring, more water would be needed. The varying porosity of bisque ware affects the water ratio. For example, Murphy's cone 10 glaze needs 3.40 ounces of water per 100 grams of glaze for dipping. For brushing two coats will usually suffice, for dipping it takes one to two dips.

Once the water content for a glaze has been established through testing, if settling occurs, try reducing the amount of water, and refer to the glaze suspension chart in appendix 1B. Start by adding .50 to 2 percent of bentonite or macaloid. Purified bentonite was used for the tests in this appendix. The addition of gums, which will thicken a glaze, may necessitate increased amounts of water.

Water Proportions for Hands in Clay Glazes

Glaze	Per 100 Grams Glaze Material	Per 100 Grams Glaze and Colorant
Hands in Clay Cone 05	2.5 oz.	2.5 oz.
Hands In Clay Cone 5	2.5 oz.	3.0 oz.
Cone 10	3.4 oz.	4.0 oz.

Fluidity Test

Mark your glaze tiles with a line lightly scored into the clay or with a black underglaze pencil, halfway or a third of the way down the test tile. (The lower section is useful for marking the cone number, glaze components, glaze number, or firing atmosphere; e.g., OX for oxidation, RE for reduction.) If the glaze when fired travels past the line, you can see how much it flowed. It is a good idea to fire your tiles set on end at about a 10-degree angle.

Opacity Test

To test the opacity of the glazes, make a mark on each tile with a dark-colored underglaze pencil prior to glazing and firing. In this way you can observe the opacity of the glaze when fired by noting how clearly the dark pencil mark shows through the glaze.

GLAZE RECIPES TO MIX AND TEST

Hands in Clay Cone 05 Glaze Recipe (For Testing Only)

Components	Percent							
	Clear Base (G1)	*White (G2)*	*Blue (G3)*	*Brown (G4)*	*Green (G5)*	*Black (G6)*	*Pink (G7)*	*Yellow (G8)*
Frit 3195 (3811)	88.0	88.0	88.0	88.0	88.0	88.0	88.0	88.0
Kaolin (Georgia)	10.0	10.0	10.0	10.0	10.0	10.0	10.0	10.0
Bentonite	2.0	2.0	2.0	2.0	2.0	2.0	2.0	2.0
Added Colorants								
	Clear Base (G1)	*White (G2)*	*Blue (G3)*	*Brown (G4)*	*Green (G5)*	*Black (G6)*	*Pink (G7)*	*Yellow (G8)*
Tin oxide		12.0						
Cobalt oxide			2.0			2.0		
Iron oxide (red)				6.0		4.0		
Chromium oxide					6.0	2.5		
D 320 pink stain							7.0	
#378 Tin vanadium yellow								7.0

Notes.
Cone 05 tests fired in a small test kiln in oxidation:
Clear—good clear glaze, no crackle; pencil shows. (G1)
White—glossy, almost opaque, but black underglaze pencil shows through slightly. (G2)
Blue—deep blue with attractive mottling; covers pencil. (G3)
Brown—rich, opaque dark brown with golden brown areas; covers pencil. (G4)
Green—opaque shiny green, completely covers clay surface and underglaze pencil. (G5)
Black—brownish-black, slight pinholing; covers pencil. (G6)
Pink—pale pink, underglaze pencil runs, but shows clearly. (G7)
Yellow—glossy yellow, more opaque than the pink, underglaze pencil shows somewhat. (G8)

Hands in Clay Cone 5 Glaze Recipe and Colorant Percentages (For Testing Only)

Components	Percent								
	Clear Base (G9)	White (G10)	Blue (G11)	Brown (G12)	Green (G13)	Black (G14)	Pink #1 (G15A)	Pink #2 (G15B)	Yellow (G16)
Calcium carbonate (whiting)	3.0	3.0	3.0	3.0	3.0	3.0	3.0	3.0	3.0
Kaolin (Georgia)	13.0	13.0	13.0	13.0	13.0	13.0	13.0	13.0	13.0
Gerstley borate	27.0	27.0	27.0	27.0	27.0	27.0	27.0	27.0	27.0
Nepheline syenite	45.0	45.0	45.0	45.0	45.0	45.0	45.0	45.0	45.0
PV clay (plastic vitrox)	10.0	10.0	10.0	10.0	10.0	10.0	10.0	10.0	10.0
Bentonite (purified)	2.0	2.0	2.0	2.0	2.0	2.0	2.0	2.0	2.0
Added Colorants									
	Clear Base (G9)	White (G10)	Blue (G11)	Brown (G12)	Green (G13)	Black (G14)	Pink #1 (G15A)	Pink #2 (G15B)	Yellow (G16)
Tin oxide		12.0							
Cobalt oxide			2.0			2.0			
Iron oxide (red)				6.0		4.0			
Chromium oxide					6.0	2.5			
D—320 Pink stain #1 test*							7.0		
F—444 Pink stain #2 test*								7.0	
#378 Tin vanadium yellow									7.0

*This test was run first with the Pink stain D320 in the same proportion as in the cone 05 glaze. Since no pink color showed, a new test was run with Pink stain F444 substituted, which produced a true pink at cone 5. This shows that a stain that gives true color at one cone may not hold color in another cone range. For this reason, it is important to run tests at a number of temperature ranges, using other colors of stains to see which colors hold true.

Notes.
Cone 5 glaze tests fired in a small test kiln (oxidation):
Clear—smooth, clear, with some crackling; pencil shows. (G9)
White—semiopaque white, pencil shows slightly. (G10)
Blue—rich, smooth, and glossy dark blue; pencil covered. (G11)
Light brown—translucent golden brown; some crackle; underglaze pencil shows. (G12)
Green—shiny green, slightly darker than in cone 05 firing; covers body and pencil completely. (G13)
Black—shiny; almost a true black with only slight brown tone; covers pencil. (G14)
Pink #1—no pink color using stain D320; milky white matt; pencil shows through, blurry. (G15A)
Pink #2—stain F444 gave a true pink at this cone. (G15B)
Yellow—runny and slightly more transparent than in cone 05; pencil blurred, but shows more. (G16)

Larry Murphy's (Hands in Clay) Matt Cone 10 Glaze Recipe
(Very slightly changed from the proportions given for this glaze in Appendix 3). (G17 to G32)

Components	Percent							
	Matt Base (G17)	*White (G18)*	*Blue (G19)*	*Brown (G20)*	*Green (G21)*	*Black (G22)*	*Pink (G23)*	*Yellow (G24)*
Kaolin (Georgia)	28.0	28.0	28.0	28.0	28.0	28.0	28.0	28.0
Silica (flint)	13.0	13.0	13.0	13.0	13.0	13.0	13.0	13.0
Feldspar (Custer)	35.0	35.0	35.0	35.0	35.0	35.0	35.0	35.0
Calcium carbonate (whiting)	24.0	24.0	24.0	24.0	24.0	24.0	24.0	24.0
Added Colorants								
	Matt Base (G17)	*White (G18)*	*Blue (G19)*	*Brown (G20)*	*Green (G21)*	*Black (G22)*	*Pink (G23)*	*Yellow (G24)*
Tin oxide		12.0*						
Cobalt oxide			2.0			2.0		
Iron oxide				6.0		4.0		
Chrome oxide					6.0	2.5		
D370 Pink							7	
#378 Tin vanadium yellow								7

*Varying quantities of tin oxide may affect glaze smoothness and will affect opacity.

Notes.
Cone 10 glaze tests fired in small test kiln in *oxidation*
Murphy formulated this to be a cone 10 matt. The surface is smooth and pleasantly matt, the colors more subtle as a result. The glaze was applied on the *Hands In Clay* cone 10 white test clay given on page 397 rather than on Murphy's stoneware clay because the white clay provided a better background for testing color.

Clear—semiopaque. (G17)
White—completely opaque. (G18)
Blue—handsome, matt blue, softer color than when shiny. (G19)
Brown—still golden brown tinge, but darker than at cone 5; slightly rough surface. (G20)
Green—porch-furniture green. (G21)
Black—truer black than either of the other glazes. (G22)
Pink—the brightest pink of all! Semi-opaque with the underglaze pencil fuzzy but quite clear. (G23)
Yellow—soft, almost golden yellow; pencil shows. (G24)

Cone 10 glaze tests fired in gas kiln in *reduction*:
Clear base—semimatt white, underglaze pencil shows. (G25)
White—yellowish pale beige (G26)
Blue—deep blue, matt, slightly mottled. (G27)
Brown—yellowish brown. (G28)
Green—semimatt green. (G29)
Black—semimatt black. (G30)
Pink—pale pink; underglaze pencil shows. (G31)
Yellow—turned gray with some white speckles, which came from the clay. (G32)

1B

Glaze Additives in Relation to Suspension and Application

The quantity and type of glaze additive is related to the composition of the glaze. Testing is essential.

For Glaze Suspension		For Glaze Fluidity		Gums	
Components	Percent	Components	Percent	Components	Percent
Bentonite (Wyoming)	½–3	Darvan #7	1/10	CMC gum (synthetic) (Carboxymethl-cellulose)	1–3
Bentonite (ferro-purified)	½–3	Dispersal	1/10		
Macaloid	½–2	Sodium silicate N	1/10	Gum tragacanth (Natural gum)	1–3
Vee gum	½–2			Gum Arabic	1–3
Calcium chloride	½				
Magnesium carbonate	1				
Magnesium sulfate (Epsom salts)	2/10				
Setit A	½–2				
Dextrin	3				

Notes.
Bentonite is a sticky clay; 2% is commonly used as a suspending agent to keep glaze components from settling. The purified bentonite has greater suspending properties than the Wyoming.

Macaloid and *Vee gum* have greater suspending properties than bentonite, so smaller quantities are needed.

Note.
These act as deflocculants in glazes that tend to become thixotrophic (viscous). Useful for glazes that are to be sprayed.

Notes.
1% gum is usually added to glazes to delay drying and to alleviate brush drag. Also helps to keep glazes, underglaze, engobes, and slips from dusting or crumbling; assists in suspension of glaze components and adhesion of glaze to ware. Hardens the glaze surface, and, in solution, can be sprayed over oxides or underglazes to keep them from smearing during handling prior to firing.

Gum tragacanth and *gum arabic* are natural gums, often used with stains or oxides sensitive to contamination, such as low-fire red and orange glazes with cadmium or selenium stains where CMC gum may cause discoloration.

1C
Clay, Slip, and Glaze Recipes from Ceramists

The following recipes shared with us by a number of ceramists were included to offer you a wider range of clays, slips, and glazes to test. Some of the recipes came originally from other ceramists through personal sharing, books, or magazine articles—an example of how information now spreads throughout the clay community. In the past, recipes were often kept secret, and it usually took hundreds of years for ceramics information to travel from one area of the world to another, while frequently the necessary materials were unknown or unavailable. For example, after Chinese porcelain arrived in Europe, it was many years before potters there found the right components and discovered how to make fine porcelain.

The recipes are given in percentages; in some cases the recipe does not total 100 percent or exceeds 100 percent. These small percentage differences will only slightly affect the quantity of the batch by weight. In some cases, we changed the percentages slightly to bring them closer to 100 percent. We did not test any of these formulas. Remember to observe precautions when mixing glazes. See Chapter 15 for mixing directions.

CLAY RECIPES FROM CERAMISTS

Susan and Steven Kemenyffy, Pennsylvania, need a clay that will allow them to subject their large wall panels to the stress of raku firing. The following formula is for the clay body they use:

Raku Clay

Components	Percent
Kyanite (35 mesh)	33.3
Cedar Heights Goldart	33.3
Frederick fire clay	33.3
Traces of Barium carbonate *(toxic)*	———
	99.9

Mary Parisi, California, offers her modification to Jerry Rothman's low-shrinkage clay for building thick, solid sculpture walls (up to or exceeding 10 inches). Like Rothman, she is able to fire steel in her sculpture without the piece cracking. She says that the different sizes of ione grain grog fill up more space in the clay body than particles of only one size, lessening the shrinkage as well as contributing to the openness of the body. *The clay dries better and fires easier. Bentonite is used to give plasticity, but since it increases shrinkage, it is used in a small amount. . . . The grog can be increased or decreased to reduce graininess or increase plasticity. Water should be carefully controlled; the wetter the clay, the greater amount of shrinkage.*

White Low-Shrinkage Cone 06 Clay

Components	Percent
C-1 Clay (Pfizer Co)	14.0
Calcined kaolin	7.0
Talc	7.0
Nepheline syenite	21.0
Ione grain grog #400	14.0
Ione grain grog #412 or #414	14.0
Ione grain grog #420	14.0
Wollastonite	7.0
Bentonite	1.4
Chopped fiber glass (optional)	1.4
	100.0

(Mary Parisi, continued)

Buff Low-Shrinkage Cone 6 Clay

Components	Percent
Bentonite	1.68
C-1 clay (Pfizer)	16.8
Calcined kaolin	8.4
Fire clay	16.8
Ione grain #400	8.4
Ione grain grog #412 or #414	16.8
Ione grain grog #420	8.4
Wollastonite	8.4
Spodumene	12.6
Chopped fiber glass (optional)	1.68
Red iron oxide (optional)	.84
	100.80

Note.
With red iron oxide, clay is reddish.

William Daley, Pennsylvania, builds his vessel forms using the following clay body and fires them in oxidation.

Cone 6 Clay

Components	Percent
Valentine fire clay	20.0
Kentucky ball clay (OM4)	20.0
Missouri fire clay	20.0
Red Art Clay	40.0
	100.0
Additive	
Medium grog 10%	

Karen Massaro, California, contributes a clay along with a compatible glaze. These were shared with her when she was a graduate student at the University of Wisconsin, Madison, by Dennis Caffrey, who had studied with Fred Bauer in Seattle—a good example of how information is shared and spreads. Massaro says, *This is a beautiful porcelain surface. Some shrinkage, some crackling. A bit tricky, but interesting for throwing smaller pieces. Very responsive.*

Cone 9 Porcelain

Components	Percent
Kaolin (EPK)	40.0
Custer feldspar	30.0
Silica	20.0
Nepheline syenite	10.0
	100.0

Gary Holt, California, throws his stoneware clay on the wheel as well as using it to form slab plates. He says that this lightly grogged clay fires to a toasty brown in reduction and is very strong and durable. The white stoneware clay body contains no grog and fires to a gray-white. Holt says, *It throws easily. I use it for both my large slab platters and for functional pieces—casseroles, dinner plates, etc.*

Cone 10 Stoneware

Components	Percent
IMCO #800 clay	25.0
Kaiser Missouri fire clay	25.0
Kentucky ball clay (OM4)	25.0
Silica 200 mesh (flint)	9.0
Custer feldspar	7.0
Ione grain grog #420	7.0
Talc	2.0
Macaloid (200 mesh)	1.0
	101.0

Cone 10 White Stoneware

Components	Percent
6-Tile Kaolin	45.0
Custer feldspar	20.0
Silica 200 mesh (flint)	15.0
C-1 clay (Pfizer)	10.0
Kentucky ball clay (OM4)	10.0
Bentonite	1.5
Macaloid	.05
	101.55

Walter Keeler, England, throws his jugs using a clay body consisting of stoneware, ball clay, and sand. He then coats part of the jug with an engobe and salt glazes the jugs.

Cone 10 Stoneware (for Salt Glazing)

Components	Percent
Dorset ball clay	60.72
Staffordshire stoneware clay	30.36
Sand (80 mesh)	9.20
	100.28

Frank Boyden, Oregon, says this porcelain body for wood firing is translucent if thinly thrown. He suggests that for firing in an *anagama* kiln where the pieces will be stacked on each other, one should avoid brittle, thin shapes; cylinders do well, as do large, thick, flat plates.

Cone 13 to 14 Porcelain Clay

Components	Percent
Kaolin (EPK)	37.50
PV clay (plastic vitrox)	11.25
Custer feldspar	26.25
Silica 200 mesh (flint)	22.50
Pyrophyllite	2.25
Macaloid	.75
	100.50

SLIP RECIPES FROM CERAMISTS

Gary Holt offers two slips. The white slip is to be used on damp ware, *not on bisque*. The other slip, Holt says is *particularly well suited for use on a glassy glaze like my Amber glaze. Applied over the glaze, it melts in when fired, giving caramel orange/browns, tans, and occasionally bluish purple.* Since Albany slip is no longer available, you might try a slip mined in Washington called Seattle slip or Sheffield slip from Massachusetts, both offered as substitutes for Albany. This slip recipe came from Jack Troy through Leon Paulos.

Cone 8 to 10 White Slip (Damp Ware)

Components	Percent
Kaolin (EPK)	25.0
Kentucky ball clay (OM4)	25.0
Nepheline syenite	15.0
Talc	7.0
Silica (flint)	20.0
Zircopax	5.0
	97.0

Cone 8 to 10 Troy Slip

Components	Percent
Albany slip	75.0
Rutile	10.0
Red iron oxide	10.0
Custer feldspar	5.0
	100.0

Note.
Ball mill for 1 or 2 hours for even consistency and better flowing characteristics.

John Toki, California, offers an engobe/slip for stoneware decoration.

Cone 6–10 Stoneware Engobe

Components	Percent
China clay	21.0
Kentucky ball clay (OM4)	21.0
Silica 200 mesh	29.0
Nepheline syenite	24.0
Borax (powder)	5.0
	100.0
Colorants	
Red: iron	6.0%
Blue: cobalt	2.0%
Green: chrome	3.0%

Patrick Siler, Washington, stencils black and white images on greenware using these slips. Then, before firing, he covers the slip with a sprayed-on clear glaze. Single-firing to cone 5.

Cone 5 Black Slip

Components	Percent
Lincoln fire clay	66.6
Kentucky ball clay (OM4)	33.3
	99.9
Colorants	
Black stain	15.0%
Red iron	15.0%

(Patrick Siler, continued)

Cone 5 Ivory Slip

Components	Percent
Lincoln clay	33.3
Kaolin	33.3
OM4 ball clay	33.3
	99.9

Walter Keeler, England, applies an engobe to the lower part of his salt glazed jugs in order to achieve a contrast between the characteristic "orange peel" salt glaze surface and the smooth engobe. He then sprays on color mixed with a little engobe to prevent it from brushing off the unfired pot when it is handled. He salt glazes, firing to 2336°F/1280°C (Orton cone 10), salts at 2280°F/1250°C (Orton cone 9), then soaks for half an hour.

Keeler Engobe for Salt Glaze

Components	Percent
Feldspar	60.0
China clay	40.0
	100.0
Colorants	
Mixtures of oxides and/or stains—for example, Chrome oxide and cobalt oxide Black stain Black stain and cobalt or manganese dioxide and iron.	

Ericka Clark Shaw, California, offers a crackle slip that, she says . . . *is a lot like Bob Sperry's. It can be applied over green or bisque ware, either under or over a glaze.*

Crackle Slip

Components	Percent
Nepheline syenite	50.0
Magnesium carbonate	50.0
	100.0
Additives	
Gum for working consistency Stains for color (except lilac)	

Richard Hirsch, New York, uses terra sigillata combined with low-fire glazes to develop the rich patina of his vessel forms. He colors his white terra sigillata with stains, then may intermix the terra sigillatas themselves. He says the firing limit for good color is cone 04, and the color values can be changed by varying the percentages of the stain in the white base. The frit helps in hardness and color.

White Terra Sigillata

Components	Percent
Kentucky (OM4) or Tenn. #5 ball clay	20.0
Frit 3110	.5
H_2O (water)	80.0
Calgon	1.0
	101.5
Colorants	
Medium blue: Medium blue stain	10.0%
Medium green: Medium green stain	10.0%
Orange: Saturn orange stain	10.0%
Purple: Red and medium blue sigillatas mixed	

Red Terra Sigillata

Components	Percent
Kentucky ball clay (OM4)	50.0
Iron oxide	50.0
Calgon	5.0
	105.0
Water (H_2O)	61.0 grams

GLAZE RECIPES FROM CERAMISTS

Low to Mid-Range Glazes

Richard Hirsch, New York, uses a low-fire cone 04 base glaze to which he adds a variety of colorants to create semiopaque glazes that interface well with the terra sigillata beneath, creating a patina and layering effect. The cone 04 limit assures good color.

Cone 04 Base Glaze, for Use with Terra Sigillatas

Components	Percent
Gerstley borate	31.54
Lithium carbonate*	8.30
Nepheline syenite	4.15
Kaolin (EPK)	4.15
Silica (flint)	34.86
Whiting	16.60
	99.60

Colorants	
Blue-green: leave out lithium, add	
Copper carbonate	4.0%
Yellow-blue-green	
Copper carbonate	4.0%
Rutile	4.0%
Red-rust	
Rutile	10.0%
Golden Ambrosia stain	3.0%
Orange-rust	
Red iron oxide	6.0%
Rutile	4.0%
Saturn orange stain	2.0%

The Richmond Art Center, uses a raku glaze that develops a coppery luster. Ceramic instructor Larry Henderson says, *After the glaze bubbles and then flattens out and turns glossy, I take the pots out and place them in a covered garbage can with sawdust for 10 minutes, then remove them from the can and spray them with water.*

Clear Raku Glaze (Cone 09–07)

Components	Percent
Colemanite (Gerstley borate)	79.0
Nepheline syenite	21.0
	100.0

Colorants for Black/Copper Luster	
Iron oxide	4.0%
Cobalt	2.5%
Copper carbonate	3.0%

Ericka Clark Shaw, California, contributes a low-fire ash glaze made from the ashes of charcoal briquettes. She suggests you pass the ashes two or three times through a kitchen sieve.

Charcoal Briquette Ash Glaze

Components	Percent
Charcoal briquette ash	40.0
Potash spar	40.0
Kaolin (EPK)	20.0
Whiting	15.0
	115.0

To provide some additional low-fire glazes for you to test, *Hands In Clay* offers two more cone 05 glazes. The clear glaze fires to a clear gloss over white clay, and clear glossy with a white granulated mottle when applied over red clay. For a clear 05 crackle glaze, eliminate the copper carbonate used as colorant in the green crackle glaze. For other colors, test it with glaze stains instead of the copper.

Hands In Clay *Cone 05 Clear Glaze*

Components	Percent
Gerstley borate	65.0
Kaolin (Georgia)	15.0
Silica 325 mesh (flint)	18.0
Bentonite	2.0
	100.0

Notes: Clear glaze
On white clay body—clear gloss.
On red clay body—white granulated mottle.

Hands in Clay *Cone 05 Green Crackle Glaze*

Components	Percent
Frit #25	85.0
Kaolin (Georgia)	13.0
Bentonite	2.0
Copper carbonate	5.0
	105.0

Notes: Crackle glaze
On cone 05 white clay body—blue-green, medium crackle.
On cone 05 red body—dark olive green, medium crackle.
On cone 5 clay body—olive-green, transparent with small crackles.
On porcelain at cone 5—at this temperature, the glaze runs.

Roslyn Myers, California, contributes a low-fire texture glaze to which she added silicon carbide, molochite, steel and brass shaving, etc., in order to produce unusual textures.

Low-Fire Texture Glaze

Components	Percent
Borax (Powder)	30.0
Kaolin (Georgia)	10.0
Feldspar (Custer)	20.0
Soda ash	18.0
Silica 325 mesh (flint)	20.0
Bentonite	2.0
	100.0

Additives: for varying texture effects on white clay: use .5 to 1½%, either sprinkled over the tile or mixed in the glaze.
Notes.
Silicon carbide (36–100 grit)—white background, widely spaced dark gray texture.
Silica sand (30–60 mesh)—30 mesh gives white texture, large granules.
Ilmenite (granulated)—small brown granules catch the light and give golden sparkles.
Ione grain #420—very rough gray texture.
Molochite—similar to silica sand, but smaller granules, overall texture.
Steel grindings—very rough, shiny, black lava effect.
Stainless steel grindings—particles did not melt and flow at cone 05, leaving sharp tooth, dark gray.
Brass—mottled light and dark green, flowed, but clear spaces remain.

Medium-Range Glazes

Susan Ashmore, Canada, offers a glaze from Emanuel Cooper's *The Potter's Book of Glaze Recipes.* She finds it an excellent base glaze for overlap experiments with other glazes, and fires it at a wide range of temperatures, from cone 05 to 8. Of the Zakin glaze, Ashmore says: *I found this in* Electric Kiln Ceramics *by Richard Zakin. I fire with an electric kiln so these two glazes have been tested only under those conditions. I do try to achieve long soaking periods at cone 6 to 7.*

Cooper's Cone 05 to 8 Clear Base Glaze

Components	Percent
Soda Feldspar (Kona F-4)	38.0
Whiting	14.0
Zinc oxide	12.0
Kentucky ball clay (OM4)	6.0
Silica (flint)	30.0
	100.0

Zakin Medium-Range Glaze

Components	Percent
Nepheline syenite	40.0
Dolomite	18.0
Silica (flint)	18.0
Kaolin	12.0
Bone ash	6.0
Lithium carbonate	2.0
Zinc oxide	4.0
	100.0
Colorant	
Copper carbonate	2%

Two Cone 5 Glazes

To add more medium-ranges glazes for you to test, John Toki formulated and tested two cone 5 glazes, one of which is an example of how radically a glaze may vary when fired in oxidation or in reduction. For this reason, he called the matt glaze "Night and Day."

Cone 5 "Night and Day" Matt Glaze

Components	Percent
Dolomite	18.0
Gerstley borate	10.0
Kona F4 feldspar	15.0
Nepheline syenite	23.0
Kentucky ball clay (OM4)	18.0
Silica (flint)	10.0
Titanium dioxide	6.0
	100.0

Notes.
Matt glaze
Oxidation—pale warm yellow gloss glaze.
Reduction—handsome granite gray, dry matt.

Cone 5 Japanese Wood Ash Glaze

Components	Percent
Ash	16.0
Silica (flint)	33.0
Custer feldspar	21.0
Gerstley borate	4.0
Kentucky ball clay (OM4)	7.0
Dolomite	10.0
Iron oxide (Spanish red)	9.0
	100.0

Wood ash glaze
Oxidation—reddish brown, pebbly.
Reduction—rich, glossy brown/black.
At cone 10—matt, purplish.

Cone 6 Matt Glaze (Oxidation)

Components	Percent
Feldspar Custer	33.0
Gerstley borate	5.0
Silica (flint)	25.0
Whiting	24.0
Kaolin (Georgia)	11.0
Bentonite	2.0
	100.0

Notes.
A buttery, white, translucent matt glaze with no toxic ingredients that would be good for the inside of food containers.

High-Fire Glazes

Gary Holt, California, uses the following high-fire glaze mainly on stoneware. *On my stoneware, with a medium to heavy reduction it will fire to a honey brown color. Takes iron oxide decoration well. It will craze on white stoneware or porcelain.*

Cone 9 to 10 Amber Glaze

Components	Percent
Feldspar (Custer)	52.00
Whiting	18.25
Silica (flint)	16.75
Kaolin (EPK)	10.0
Tin oxide	1.30
Rutile	1.70
	100.0

Frank Boyden, Oregon, applies this Shino-type glaze to porcelain, which he fires to high temperature in his wood-fired *anagama* kiln. Boyden says, *This is not my own glaze, but Tom Coleman's, I think. I use it along with many others. Most Shino glazes will fire extremely high.* He recommends avoiding delicate brushwork and strong stains containing cobalt, chrome, and copper.

Cone 13 to 14 Shino-Type Glaze

Components	Percent
Feldspar Kona F4	15.0
Spodumene	13.0
Soda ash	3.0
Nepheline syenite	50.0
Kentucky ball clay (OM4)	16.0
Kaolin (EPK)	3.0
	100.0
Additive	
Iron oxide	⅛ to ¼%

Karen Massaro, California, sends a clear glaze that came originally from Fred Bauer. It is compatible with the clay body recipe she gave earlier (see page 410), and she says it is good in oxidation or in reduction. *For celadon, you may add 1 to 3 percent iron oxide to yield a lovely blue-green color.* Of the barium matt glaze, Massaro says, *Colorants can be added singly or in combination. Results are interesting; the richer hues with varied undertones come when using two or more oxides. Single oxide gives flatter color.*

Cone 9 to 10 Clear Glaze

Components	Percent
Silica (flint)	14.56
Cornwall stone	66.37
Whiting	12.41
Colemanite	2.49
Zinc oxide	2.49
Magnesium carbonate (or 2% bentonite)	1.72
	100.04

Colorants	
Red iron oxide	2–5%
Copper carbonate	5–5%
Nickel oxide	1–3%
Manganese dioxide	2–8%

Cone 10 Dry Barium Matt* Glaze
(Not for food containers)

Components	Percent
Nepheline syenite	44.93
Kentucky ball clay (OM4)	6.69
Barium carbonate *(toxic)*	35.37
Rutile	8.60
Flint	2.61
Bentonite	1.91
	100.11

(Karen Massaro, continued)

Cone 8 to 10 Matt Black Glaze

Components	Percent
Nepheline syenite	17.51
Dolomite	13.98
Cornwall stone	25.23
Whiting (calcium)	3.80
Talc	14.36
Kaolin	21.50
Silica (flint)	3.83
	100.21

Colorants Add All for Black	
Iron chromate	4.00%
Iron oxide	6.01%
Cobalt oxide	2.00%
Nickel oxide	2.00%
Ilmenite (powder)	3.51%
Bentonite	2.00%

Ernst Haüsermann, Switzerland, glazed the bowl shown in the text (page 278) with the following simple ash glaze fired to 2462°F/1350°C. It fires on stoneware to a matt, clear, gray. Haüsermann's feldspar comes from Norway and is similar to Custer feldspar. The ashes he uses in his glazes come from the wood he burns in his ceramic-tile heating stove.

Ash Glaze

Components	Percent
K-feldspar	30.0
Mixed ash	30.0
Kaolin	26.0
White stoneware clay	14.0
	100.0

Harris Deller, Illinois, says, *A heavy reduction beginning at cone 010 all the way to a hot cone 10 is very important for this cone 10 Chun celadon glaze,* adding, *I clear the kiln atmosphere at the end of the firing for five to ten minutes by oxidizing.*

Cone 10 Chun Celadon Glaze

Components	Percent
Feldspar* Potash	42.1 to 37.1*
China clay	1.8
Silica* (flint)	27.2 to 32.2*
Whiting	2.6
Colemanite	8.8
Dolomite	8.8
Zinc oxide	1.7
Barium carbonate *(toxic)*	4.4
Iron oxide	2.6
(Total will vary)	100.0

Colorants	
Green-blue: Spanish red iron oxide**	1.5%
Green: Spanish red iron oxide	2–3%
Red: Copper carbonate	.50%

*Adjustments may be made in feldspar and/or flint to control crazing. (Custer feldspar is a potash spar.)

**I use Spanish red iron oxide because it's a finer mesh iron with a good consistency from batch to batch. Some red iron oxide, because of larger particle size, will cause the glaze to have freckles or iron spots." Since this glaze contains* (toxic) *barium, it should not be used on the interior of food containers, and you should protect yourself against exposure to barium when mixing it.*

Larry Henderson, California, uses this glaze with salt-glaze firing. It requires a strong dose of salt to make it shiny, Because salt vapor does not penetrate the inside of pots readily, to achieve full gloss, use glaze only on outside of objects.

Cone 8 to 10 Salt Glaze

Components	Percent
Feldspar (Custer)	53.41
Wollastonite	10.90
Gerstley borate	5.45
Silica (flint)	22.89
Kentucky ball clay (OM4)	5.45
Bentonite	2.18
	100.28

Colorants	
Iron oxide (red)	4.36%
Cobalt	.55%

William S. Holoway, California, offers a purple semi-matt glaze, saying, *This glaze must be screened and mixed thoroughly to ensure a smooth consistency and must be applied relatively thick to ensure a good all-over violet to purple.* Stable, will hardly drip or move in the kiln.

Cone 8 Purple Semi-Matt

Components	Percent
Nepheline syenite	22.5
Colemanite (Gerstley borate)	12.1
Wollastonite	6.8
Macaloid	6.4
Dolomite	5.4
Kentucky ball clay (OM4)	11.3
Silica (flint)	35.3
	99.8

Colorant	
Cobalt	3.0%

Arnold Zahner, Switzerland, sends a crystaline glaze. He says that to develop crystals the exact weight of the components is not so important; the control of temperature, cooling, etc., is of decisive influence.

Cone 10 to 12 Crystaline Glaze

Components	Percent
K-feldspar	25.0
Kaolin	5.0
Silica (quartz)	20.0
Barium carbonate *(toxic)*	5.0
Lithium carbonate	5.0
Frit	13.0
Zinc oxide	27.0
	100.0

Colorant	
Copper carbonate	4%

1D
Percentage Charts: Clays, Frits, Feldspars, and Opacifiers

Percentage Composition of Clays and Chemicals

Clay	Percent											
	SiO_2	Al_2O_3	Fe_2O_3	CaO	MgO	TiO_2	K_2O	Na_2O	P_2O_5 & F	SO_3	Alkaline	Ig Loss*
EPK kaolin	45.91	38.71	.42	.09	.12	.34	.22	.04				14.15
Grolleg kaolin	47.70	37.20	.60	.10	.25	.03	1.92	1.92				12.60
Georgia kaolin	44.90	38.90	.40	.10	.10	1.30	.20	.20				14.21
PV clay	78.70	12.80	.09	.28	Trace		.28	.28				4.42
Talc	56.29	1.07	.43	9.26	28.31		.57	.69				3.49
Kentucky ball clay (OM4)	53.8	30.00	.90	.30	.30	1.70	1.10	.30				11.80
Tennessee ball clay	52.90	31.10	.80	.20	.20	1.60	1.20	.40				11.60
Sagger clay	59.40	27.20	.70	.60	.20	1.60	.70	.30				9.40
Pyrophyllite	73.00	20.40	.50			.50	.20					3.50
Spodumene	63.60	26.50	.64	.30			.50	.30	.43			.55
C-1 clay	75.60	15.80		.80			1.55					4.84
Lincoln fire clay	52.57	29.41	2.90									11.51
Missouri/fire clay	53.41	30.41	1.61									11.22
Goldart	57.32	28.50	1.23	.08	.22	1.98	.88	.30	SO_2/.24			9.39
Pine Lake	70.4	24.8	1.35	.27	.29	2.03	.86	.86			.17	N/A
Red Horse clay	67.46	21.99	6.61	.45	.62		1.20	.30				1.18
REDART	64.27	16.41	7.04	.23	1.55		4.07	.40	.17			4.78
Jordan clay	67.19	20.23	1.73								2.23	6.89

Ignition loss, or loss on ignition (LOI). This phrase indicates the loss of weight on ignition that results from the carbonates being burned off when the clay or mineral is heated to from 1832° to 2012°F/1000° to 1100°C. This change in the weight of the material is shown as a percentage of the dry weight in the "Ig Loss" column.

Percentage Composition of Leadless Frits

Leadless Frits	Na$_2$O	Na$_2$F$_2$	NaKO	K$_2$O	Li$_2$O	CaO	CaF$_2$	CdO	ZnO	B$_2$O$_3$	Al$_2$O$_3$	SiO$_2$	F	Sb$_2$O$_3$	MgO
P-25	14.70			5.40		.50			.70	16.90	12.10	49.70	1.80		
P-283	16.30					.30					5.90	76.50			.70
3124	5.60			.60		14.50				12.50	10.00	56.80			
3134	10.20					20.10				23.20		46.50			
3195	5.70					11.30				22.40	12.00	48.50			
2106			21.67			3.42			3.60	13.00	9.13	45.20		3.98	

Notes.

Leadless frits   We included a small selection of leadless frits. Other frits are available that contain the chemicals for which no percentages are listed. The numbers of equivalent frits that can be substituted are listed below.

Frit equivalents   The composition of these equivalent frits may vary slightly from those on the chart above: P-25 = 3269; 3124 = 90 = 311; 3195 = 3811; P-283 = 3293; 3134 = 14 = P54.

Percentage Composition of Feldspars

Feldspars	Percent								
	Na$_2$O	*K$_2$O*	*Al$_2$O$_3$*	*SiO$_2$*	*Fe$_2$O$_3$*	*CaO*	*MgO*	*P$_2$O$_5$ & F*	*Ig Loss**
Custer	3.00	10.40	17.50	68.50	.08	.30	trace		.30
Kona F-4 (#56)	6.90	4.80	19.60	66.80	.04	1.70	trace		.20
G-200	3.20	10.36	19.28	65.76	.06	.98	trace		.20
Nepheline syenite	4.60	9.80	23.60	60.40	.08	.70	trace		.70
Cornwall stone	4.00	3.81	14.93	72.90	.13	2.06	.25	1.40	.61

*See note to chart of clays and chemicals, page 418.

Percentage Composition of Opacifiers

Opacifier	Percent						
	ZrO$_2$	*ZrSiO$_4$*	*SiO$_2$*	*TiO$_2$*	*Fe$_2$O$_3$*	*Al$_2$O$_3$*	*Other Components*
Zircopax		96.00		0.25	0.10		
Ultrox	65.00		35.00				
Superpax		93.40		0.25	0.10		
Zircon G milled		98.60		0.20	0.04		
Calcium zirconium silicate	50.50		26.70				CaO 18.80
Magnesium zirconium silicate	53.60		27.50				MgO 17.40
Zinc zirconium silicate	46.40		24.20				ZnO 28.60

1E
Chemicals and Materials

This list includes the main oxides used in glaze forming and coloring as well as the materials that yield them. Colorants and opacifiers are listed separately.

Use all these materials with great care and proper protection. The precautions that should be taken when using all ceramics materials are discussed in Chapter 10. The bold letters in front of each material indicates its degree of toxicity. However, new findings may change these ratings, so it is important that you keep up to date on current information. See Appendix 5A for sources of information on health and safety.

H = highly toxic
M = moderately toxic
S = slightly toxic
N = nuisance

H Alumina (Al_2O_3)   A refractory material that increases the vicosity of glazes, making them less runny, and that helps to control the melting point of a glaze. The main sources of alumina are china clay and ball clay. Because of its high melting point, only a small amount of alumina is needed—the proportion can be higher in a high-fire glaze. The quantity of alumina is increased for a matt surface and decreased if a crystalline glaze is desired. Alumina also helps to make glazes more durable.

H Antimony oxide (Sb_2O_3)   Infrequently used to produce light yellow.

H Barium carbonate ($BaCO_3$)   A source of barium oxide for glazes.

H Barium oxide (BaO)   A refractory, but in high-fire glazes it acts as a flux. Helps produce a matt surface. Adds brilliance to certain colors.

Bentonite ($Al_2O_3 \cdot 4SiO_2 \cdot 9H_2O$)   A colloidal clay of volcanic origin that increases plasticity of other clays. Used in glazes to keep glaze particles in suspension. Formula varies according to source.

Bone ash ($Ca_3(PO_4)_2$) **(Tricalcium phosphate)** Made from animal bones. Formulas will vary. A source of calcium and phosphate. A plasticizer for clay bodies.

Used in clay bodies such as bone china, it lowers maturing point, increases translucency. In glazes, gives texture and acts as opacifier.

M Borax ($Na_2O \cdot 2B_2O_3 \cdot 10H_2O$)   Generally used in fritted form, since it is soluble in water. A low-fire flux, but small amounts in high-fire glazes can help a glaze melt more smoothly. Source of sodium and boric oxides.

M Borix oxide (B_2O_3)   A useful flux that operates at both high and low temperatures. Helps produce a smooth glaze and increases brilliance of colors. Although a glass-forming material, it is also a strong flux at high temperatures. With iron, it may produce opalescent blues.

Boron   See **Boric oxide.**

H Cadmium sulfide (CdS)   Used with selenium in stains and low-fire frits for overglazes to produce red and orange. It can be released into food, so do not use on food containers.

N Calcium oxide (CaO)   A useful glaze ingredient. Glazes with calcium are durable and resistant to acids. Has a high melting point, but is a very active flux at high temperatures. For this reason, is used especially in porcelain glazes. In low-fire glazes, usually combined with other fluxes. See **Whiting.**

China clay   See **Kaolin.**

H Chromium oxide (Cr_2O_3)   In glazes without zinc, it yields green; with zinc, browns and tans. With tin, under proper conditions, it may produce pink. Reduction darkens the green color.

H Clay (theoretical formula $Al_2O_3 \cdot 2SiO_2 \cdot 2H_2O$) Clay bodies are made up of various types of clays and range from low-fire to porcelain. In glazes, clay is generally used in the form of kaolin or ball clay to provide alumina and silica. Amounts will vary according to the particular clay used. In a glaze it helps to keep the ingredients suspended and helps the glaze adhere to the ware.

M Cobalt oxide (CoO) and **cobalt carbonate** ($CoCO_3$)   Formulas vary. Strong blue colorants that do not burn out. Used for centuries for decoration, cobalt can be fired from low to high temperatures. Cobalt alone gives rather strong blues that can be softened by adding manganese, iron, rutile, or nickel. A combination of cobalt oxide, chrome oxide, and manganese oxide will produce a strong black.

M Colemanite ($2CaO \cdot 3B_2O_3 \cdot 5H_2O$) (Calcium borate)   A source of boric oxide in insoluble form, it also produces calcium oxide. Acting as a flux in both high- and low-fire glazes, it is also popular for the effects it produces in glazes—with rutile, for example, it gives a mottled appearance and may also give a milky blue. (See **Gerstley borate**.)

M Copper oxide (CuO) and **copper carbonate** ($CuCO_3$)   Copper gives greens, blues, or reds depending on the other ingredients in the glaze and the atmosphere in the kiln. In reduction it produces reds in certain glazes; in oxidation copper gives greens, and in alkaline glazes it gives turquoise. Copper was used in China to produce the famous red oxblood and peach-bloom glazes.

H Cornish stone (Cornwall stone) (theoretical formula $K_2O \cdot Al_2O_3 \cdot 8SiO_2$)   Formula varies. An English feldspathic material that requires high temperatures to fuse. Shrinks less than kaolin and feldspar, so it is less subject to glaze defects. Helps form tough, hard glazes. Used as a source of silica, Cornish stone contains varying amounts of silica as well as potassium and sodium. In ancient China, a similar rock, called *petuntze*, made possible the development of porcelain.

Cryolite (Na_3AlF_6)   A natural source of sodium. Can be used when both sodium and alumina are needed. Gives brilliant colors, but sometimes glazes containing it are subject to pits.

S Dolomite ($CaCO_3 \cdot MgCO_3$)   A natural source of magnesium and calcium oxides. Used as a flux in stoneware glazes, it helps produce smooth matt surfaces and can help in crystal formation.

H Feldspar (also spelled **felspar**)   Yields alumina and silica. Feldspars vary in composition and availability, with some containing potash, and others, soda. The formula of a commercial feldspar is usually available from the supplier, so you can see which oxides are present. (see Appendix 1D) At high temperatures, some feldspars melt with no additional flux at 2280°F/ 1250°C. At lower temperatures, talc, dolomite, gerstley borate, or whiting are added to lower their melting point. Used in porcelain clay bodies.

Ferric oxide, ferrous oxide and **ferro-ferric oxide** See **Iron.**

H Flint (SiO_2)   Also called quartz, this is the main source of silica in glazes and combines with a variety of fluxes to fuse at lower temperatures. In glazes it in-

creases viscosity and hardness. In clay bodies, use coarser mesh (around 200); for glazes, use finer grind (around 300 mesh).

H Fluospar (CaF_2) (Calcium fluoride)   Used in some glazes as a source of calcium, it fluxes at a lower temperature than most calcium compounds. Helps develop blue-greens of copper in oxidation firing. *Toxic fumes of fluorine gas are released in firing.*

Gerstley borate ($2CaO \cdot 3B_2O_3 \cdot 5H_2O$)   A source of boric oxide. Used as a flux, it is more stable than colemanite, another source of boric oxide. (see **Colemanite**)

Ilmenite ($FeO \cdot TiO_2$)   An ore in granular or powder form, contains both iron and titanium. Added to glazes, the granular form gives specks of dark color. May also encourage crystals in glazes.

Iron   Varying amounts of iron are responsible for the buff and reddish colors of natural earthenware clays, where its fluxing action lowers their firing temperatures. Iron is also used in glazes to give warm cream or yellowish tones, tans, red-browns, and black; in reduction it gives grays, blue-greens, and black. (See "Colorants and Opacifiers" on page 424). Most commonly used forms are:

N Ferric oxide (Fe_2O_3)   Red iron oxide or hematite
Ferrous oxide (FeO)   Black iron oxide
Ferro-ferric oxide (Fe_3O_4)   Magnetite

H Iron chromate ($FeCrO_4$)   Usually gives grays and browns. With copper, it will yield black, with tin it may give pink or red-brown.

H Kaolin (theoretical formula $Al_2O_3 \cdot 2SiO_2 \cdot 2H_2O$)   Also called china clay. The main source of alumina and silica in glazes. Since it contains only traces of iron, it is also used in white clay bodies. (For example, EP Kaolin contains .42 percent iron; English .60 percent iron, and Georgia .40 percent iron.)

H Lead oxide (PbO)   A very active flux at low temperatures, used for this purpose for many centuries in the Near East, Europe, and the United States until its toxicity was understood. When fritted with silica, the danger of handling this poisonous material is lessened, but even fritted lead is suspect. *We do not recommend the use of lead*, but if you do use a commercial lead frit in a glaze, you must fire it properly to avoid releasing lead into food, and the frit should be checked to make sure there is enough silica in proportion to the lead—at least in the proportion of ($PbO \cdot 2SiO_2$). If in doubt, get a laboratory to test. *Red lead and white lead are highly toxic raw materials.*

M Lepidolite ($LiF \cdot KF \cdot Al_2O_3 \cdot 3SiO_2$)   Formula varies. Used in china bodies and as a flux in some high-fire glazes. It contains lithium and helps make most glazes brighter than soda or potash feldspars, but it can cause pitting.

Lime   See **Calcium oxide** and **Whiting**

M Lithium carbonate (Li_2CO_3)   A source of lithium in glazes, at high temperatures it is an active flux, allowing the use of more alumina and silica in alkaline glazes to increase their hardness. It widens the firing range and brightens the colors, as well as having low expansion and contraction coefficients, helping the glaze fit.

Macaloid   A suspending agent in glazes similar in effect to bentonite. Also a plasticizer in clay bodies.

Magnesium carbonate ($MgCO_3$)   Provides magnesia oxide. Often introduced into glazes as a high-fire flux and matting agent.

Magnesium oxide (MgO)   Acting as a flux at high temperatures, magnesium is a refractory in lower firings. Increases viscosity, improves the adhesion of glazes, and at high temperatures it gives a smooth surface. At lower temperatures, it helps produce matt, opaque surfaces.

Magnetite (Fe_3O_4)   The mineral form of black iron oxide. Produces speckling in clays or glazes.

H Manganese dioxide (MnO_2)   Gives purple when used with alkaline fluxes (sodium, potassium, and lithium), but usually brown in most glazes. Used with cobalt, depending on the other ingredients, purple or black may develop. A strong flux.

Manganese carbonate ($MnCO_3$)   A strong flux. Produces light browns; in alkaline glazes gives a purplish color.

H Nepheline syenite ($K_2O \cdot 3Na_2O \cdot 4Al_2O_3 \cdot 9SiO_2$)   A potash feldspar. Since it has more potassium and sodium, it melts at lower temperatures, and is particularly useful in medium-range temperatures in both clays and glazes. Mutes the color of bright colorants in glazes. The formula varies depending on sources.

M Nickel carbonate ($NiCO_3$)   Used as a colorant, it produces muted brown, blues, grays, greens, and yellows.

M Nickel oxide (NiO)   Refractory. Will dull down other colors in a glaze. Produces muted colors such as browns, grays, and greens. Produces lime green when applied as a stain to bisque-fired porcelain and glaze fired.

Opax   One of several commercial opacifiers. See **Tin oxide.**

H Pearl ash   See **Potassium carbonate.**

H Petalite ($Li_2O \cdot Al_2O_3 \cdot 8SiO_3$)   A lithium feldspar used in clay bodies and glazes to reduce thermal expansion.

H Potassium carbonate (K_2CO_3)   Used in frits as a source of potassium. Soluble material that is highly toxic in the raw state.

H Potassium dichromate ($K_2Cr_2O_7$)   Acts as a green colorant with boric acid. Soluble and poisonous in raw state. In a frit, with tin in low-fire glazes, it develops red and orange.

H Potassium oxide (K_2O)   An active flux that operates at all temperatures. It has a high coefficient of thermal expansion than can cause crazing if used in large amounts. A component of feldspars and commercial frits.

Pyrophyllite ($Al_2O_3 \cdot 4SiO_2 \cdot H_2O$) (Aluminum silicate)   By decreasing thermal expansion, shrinkage and cracking it extends the firing range of clay bodies.

H Quartz   See **Flint**

N Rutile (TiO_2) (Titanium dioxide)   An ore that contains titanium and some iron. When fired in oxidation, it gives tans and browns, often in streaks. In reduction, it can give blues and orange. In glazes with copper, cobalt, chrome, or iron, it may produce subtle grayed colors. Promotes the growth of crystals.

Seattle slip   A slip glaze mined in Washington state. Offered as a substitute for Albany slip.

Sheffield slip   A slip glaze mined in Massachusetts. Offered as a substitute for Albany slip.

H Silica (flint) (SiO_2)   The essential glass-forming oxide. It is the high silica content in high-fire glazes that causes them to be more durable and have greater resistance to chemicals, so the more silica used in a glaze the harder it will be. Requires high temperatures to fuse. At lower temperatures it is necessary to bring down the melting point of silica with a flux. *Free silica is extremely damaging to the lungs.*

H Silicon carbide (SiC)   A chief ingredient in heat-resistant kiln furniture. In powder form, used in glazes to produce local reduction with copper oxide. In granular form it adds specks to glazes.

H Soda ash   See **Sodium carbonate.**

H Sodium carbonate (Na_2CO_3)   Also called *soda ash.* An active glaze flux, usually used only in frit form because it is soluble. Also a deflocculant and, when used in a clay body for slip casting, it reduces the amount of water needed.

Sodium oxide (Na_2O)   Used widely in low-fire glazes as a flux. It can also be used in high-fire glazes; when introduced into a kiln at at least 1940°F/1060°C, it will combine with the silica in clay to form a glaze. Has a high expansion coefficient that can cause crazing. Glazes high in sodium are apt to weather and flake off. Most useful if used with other fluxes. *Fumes of sodium when released in salt glaze firing are caustic.*

M Sodium silicate ($Na_2 \cdot SiO_2$)   Varies in formula. Used as a deflocculant in casting slips, where it helps to keep the particles in suspension, and increases fluidity reducing the amount of water needed to form the slip, thus reducing shrinkage. Also used in producing crystalline glazes.

M Spodumene ($Li_2O \cdot Al_2O_3 \cdot 4SiO_2$)   A source of lithium in glazes. If used instead of feldspar, it lowers the fusing temperature and helps to eliminate crazing.

H Talc ($3MgO \cdot 4SiO_2 \cdot H_2O$) (Magnesium silicate) Formula varies. Used widely in low-fire clay bodies, it can also be used as an opacifier in glazes. As a source of magnesium, it acts as an effective high-fire glaze flux as well as lowering the melting temperatures of ball clays, feldspars, and kaolin in clay bodies. *Contains asbestos, which is harmful to the lungs.*

S Tin oxide (SnO_2)   Gives opaque and semiopaque white. Has been used for centuries to create opaque glazes to cover the reddish tones of earthenware. Since it is relatively expensive, many ceramists now use commercial products such as **Zircopax, Superpax,** and **Opax** to take its place.

   Titanium oxide (TiO_2)   An opacifier that also helps create a somewhat matt surface. Gives white and cream opaque glazes. Used in frit form or combined with other chemicals. (Rutile is a source of titanium that also contains iron.)

H Vanadium pentoxide (VaO_5)   Alone, it gives light yellow; with tin, it gives a bright yellow. Reduced, it can produce blue-gray.

   Whiting ($CaCO_3$) (Calcium carbonate)   The main source of calcium oxide in glazes and an important high-fire flux. Small amounts can be added to low-fire alkaline glazes to increase durability.

M Wollastonite ($CaSiO_3$) (Calcium silicate)   Used in clays and glazes as a source of calcium oxide. Reduces shrinkage and increases strength. Often introduced into clays and glazes for ware that may need to resist thermal shock, such as ovenware.

S Zinc oxide (ZnO)   A high-fire flux that reduces thermal expansion. Increases strength of glazes and helps produce smooth surfaces. Often used as a substitute for lead. In small amounts it helps create matt glazes; too much, however, causes glazes to become dry, to pit, or to crawl.

S Zirconium oxide (ZrO_2)   An opacifier, usually fritted with other oxides. Not as strong as tin, but cheaper.

   Zircopax ($ZrSi_4$)   A commercial zirconium opacifier. Generally used where semiopaque glaze is desired.

1F
Colorants and Opacifiers

 Many of these materials are toxic and precautions must be taken when using them. The relative toxicity is indicated by the following letters;

H = **highly toxic**
M = **moderately toxic**
S = **slightly toxic**
N = **nuisance**

Colorant	Colors Yielded	Percent
H Antimony oxide Sb_2O_3	Below cone 1 or 2, infrequently used for light yellows.	10–20
H Cadmium sulfide CdS	In low-fire overglazes, produces red. Disappears if fired over cone 010. Usually combined with selenium in stain.	10–20
M Chromium oxide Cr_2O_3	Greens; with tin, pinks; with zinc, browns. In reduction, may darken or blacken colors.	1–6
M Cobalt carbonate $CoCO_3$ **M Cobalt oxide** CoO	Blues; with magnesium, purple. Higher percent gives blue-black. Powerful colorant, frequently used with iron, rutile, manganese, or nickel to soften harsh color. Withstands high firing. Carbonate with manganese, iron, or ochre gives black tones.	.01–2
M Copper carbonate $CuCO_3$ **M Copper oxide** CuO	Blue and turquoise in alkaline glazes. In lead glazes, gives soft greens (copper facilitates release of toxic lead in contact with acidic foods). In some high-fire glazes, copper gives blues; in others, browns. In certain formulations and firing conditions, produces the red oxblood and peachbloom glazes of ancient China.	1–5
Ilmenite $FeO \cdot TiO_2$	Gives brown specks and spots.	1–7
Iron **Ferric oxide** Fe_2O_3 (red) **Ferrous oxide** FeO **Ferro-ferric oxide** Fe_3O_4 **H Iron chromate** $FeCrO_4$	Iron can produce a wide range of colors in clay or glaze. In most glazes, from tans to reddish brown to black. With other oxides it modifies their brilliance. Under correct firing conditions, produces the Japanese tenmoku or the famous gray-green celadon of China.	1–10

Colorant	Colors Yielded	Percent
H Manganese carbonate MnCO₃		
H Manganese dioxide MnO₂	In alkaline glazes, gives purples; with cobalt, produces violets. In high-fire reduction, brown. With cobalt, yields violets.	2–10
N Nickel oxide NiO	Browns and grays. Used mostly to modify other oxides. In some reduction glazes with zinc, it *may* yield yellows or blues, but results are uncertain.	1–3
H Potassium dichromate (bichromate) K₂Cr2O₇	Soluble, used in frit form. In low-fire glazes with boric oxide, gives greens, with tin, gives reds and oranges.	1–10
N Rutile TiO₂	Tans and browns. With cobalt, and sometimes with iron, gives blues and oranges. Produces streaks and mottled effects.	2–10
S Tin oxide SnO₂	Gives soft, opaque whites. Used as opacifier in early Persian, Spanish, and Italian glazes. Higher percent gives opaque glaze; lower percent yields semiopaque glaze.	5–12
Titanium dioxide TiO₂	Whites and creams.	5–15
H Vanadium oxide (pentoxide) V₂O₅	Generally used in frit, with tin. Gives opaque yellows.	5–10

In addition to these colorants, many glaze stains are available commercially. Check ceramic supply catalogs to see the range of colors.

Opacifiers	
Tin oxide	5.0–12.0%
Titanium dioxide	5.0–15.0%
Zircopax	5.0–15.0%
Superpax	5.0–15.0%
Ultrox	5.0–15.0%

Notes.
Tin oxide provides white when introduced into glazes in oxidation firing, or off-white in reduction firing. It also possesses strong opacifying properties, and therefore usually a smaller percentage is necessary when formulating a glaze. Since tin is substantially more expensive than the other opacifiers listed, Ultrox and Zircopax are commonly used instead, or along with a smaller percentage of tin oxide. Titanium dioxide generally yields soft cream whites and may be combined with the other opacifiers to develop a range of white glazes.

2A

Comparative Temperatures, Centigrade and Fahrenheit; Orton and Seger Cones

Comparative Temperatures, Centigrade and Fahrenheit; Orton and Seger Cones (Large Cones, Rise of 270°F/132.2°C per Hour); Kiln Interior Colors; Maturing Points of Clays and Glazes

Kiln Interior	Seger Cone	Degrees C	Degrees F	Orton Cone	Clays	Glazes
Black		400				
		605	1112	022	Clay	Lusters
		615	1137	021	dehydrates	China paint
Dull red-orange		635	1175	020		(020–016)
		683	1261	019		
	019	685	1265			
	018	705	1301			
		717	1323	018		
	017	730	1346			
		747	1377	017		
	016	755	1391			
	015a	780	1436			
		792	1458	016		
		804	1479	015		
Red-orange		838	1540	014		Raku glazes
		852	1566	013		(014–05)
		884	1623	012		
		894	1641	011		
		905	1661	010	Bisque ware	
		923	1693	09	(010–05)	
	09a	935	1715			
Orange	08a	955	1751	08		Low-fire glazes
	07a	970	1778			(015–1)
		984	1784	07		

426

Kiln Interior	Seger Cone	Degrees C	Degrees F	Orton Cone	Clays	Glazes
Orange (continued)	06a	990	1803			
		999	1830	06	Low-fire	
	05a	1000	1832		(015–1)	
	04a	1025	1847			
		1046	1915	05		
	03a	1055	1931			
		1060	1940	04		
	02a	1085	1955			
		1101	2014	03		
	01a	1105	2021			
Yellow		1120	2048	02		
	1a	1125	2057			
		1137	2079	01		
	2a	1150	2102			
		1154	2109	1	Stoneware	
		1162	2124	2	mid-range	Stoneware glazes
		1168	2134	3	(2–7)	(mid-range)
	3a	1170	2138			(2–7)
		1186	2167	4		
	4a	1195	2183			
		1196	2185	5		
	5a	1215	2219			
		1222	2232	6		Salt glaze
	6a	1240	2264	7		(8–11)
	7	1260	2300			
		1263	2305	8	Stoneware	Stoneware glazes
	8	1280	2336	9	(8–12)	(8–12)
	9	1300	2372			
		1305	2381	10	Porcelain	Porcelain-glazes
White		1315	2399	11	(9–13)	(9–13)
	10	1320	2408			
		1326	2419	12		
	11	1340	2444			
		1346	2455	13		

427

BISQUE AND
SINGLE FIRING

Kiln Temperature Rise per Hour Based on Cone 05 (1915°F/1046°C)

Use the following chart only as a guide in establishing firing patterns for ware. Differing clay types—such as a smooth-body porcelain or a heavily grogged stoneware—will have varying firing patterns, even though the objects have the same thickness of walls. Coarse clays can generally be fired faster, and kiln size and fuel difference will also have an effect on temperature rise. In addition, different types of kiln brick, or a ceramic fiber interior, will affect the heat saturation of ware per hour of temperature rise. Variations in moisture content of the ware when it is placed in the kiln will also affect the temperature rise per hour pattern. This chart is based on establishing a firing pattern in relation to the thickest portion of a work. The temperature ranges are *averages* based on the total number of hours required to fire the ware to cone 05.

Temperature Rise per Hour	Type and Thickness of Object to be Fired
25 to 40°F/-6.4 to 4.4°C	¾–6 in. Massive sculpture or handbuilt
40 to 60°F/4.4 to 15.5°C	⅜–¾ in. Handbuilt, wheel thrown
60 to 100°F/15.5 to 37.7°C	3/16–⅜ in. Small handbuilt, wheel thrown
100 to 210°F/37.7 to 98.8°C	⅛–3/16 in. Slip cast ware, thin wheel thrown, thin handbuilt

Converting Fahrenheit to Centigrade and Centigrade to Fahrenheit

To convert Fahrenheit to centigrade (Celsius), subtract 32 degrees, multiply by 5, divide by 9.

To convert centigrade (Celsius) to Fahrenheit, multiply by 9, divide by 5, add 32 degrees.

2B

Useful Measurements and Equivalents in U.S.A. and Metric Systems

USA	Equivalent	Metric
Liquids		
1 fluid ounce		29.573 milliliters
1 fluid pint	16 fluid ounces	.473 liter
1 quart	2 fluid pints	.946
1 gallon	4 fluid quarts	3.785 liters
2.1134 pints		1 liter
1.0567 quarts		1 liter
0.26418 gallon		1 liter
Length		
1 inch		2.54 centimeters
.3937 inch		1 centimeter
1 foot	12 inches	0.3048 meter
1 yard	36 inches	.9144 meter
39.37 inches		1 meter
Weight		
1 dram		1.772 grams
1 ounce		28.350 grams
1 pound	16 ounces	453.592 grams
2.2046 pounds		1000 grams = 1 kilogram
35.274 ounces		1000 grams = 1 kilogram
Volume		
1 cubic inch		16.38716 cubic centimeters
.0616234 cubic inch		1 cubic centimeter
1 cubic foot	17228 cubic inches	.028317 cubic meter
1 cubic yard	27 cubic feet	.76456 cubic meter
1.30794 cubic yards		1 cubic meter

3A
Changing the Flux in a Glaze

In the tests that you did earlier, you changed only the colorants in some glazes. Colorants are not, of course, the only glaze components that can be changed and tested. Changing the amount of flux in a glaze, then running a series of tests on it, will prepare you for the testing you will do if you work through the example of calculating glazes using chemical analysis in Appendix 3B.

The following series of tests alters the type and amount of flux in a cone 10 glaze, while the accompanying table shows a similar glaze formulated for low, medium, and high firings, allowing you to test those as well. (They are given for test purposes only.) If you test all three firing ranges, you will then have a good idea of how fluxes work in a wide range of temperatures, and also a good cross reference between cone 05, cone 5, and cone 10 glazes. Although the cone 10 glaze is a reduction glaze, for test purposes you can use an electric kiln in oxidation—the results will just be different.

Components	Percent		
	Cone 05	*Cone 5*	*Cone 10*
Potash Feldspar			35.0
Nepheline syenite		45.0	
Whiting		3.0	24.0
Frit 3195 (or 3811)	88.0		
Kaolin (Georgia)	10.0	13.0	28.0
Bentonite	2.0	2.0	
Silica 325 mesh (flint)			13.0
Gerstley borate		27.0	
PV clay		10.0	

In this example, the formula is expressed in percentages, giving the option of mixing the batch in any amount. This means that the 35 parts of feldspar could be 35 grams, pounds, or tons, but the relationship remains the same. To get 500 grams, you would multiply each number by 5, although actually you are multiplying each percentage by 500 to get the following:

Potash feldspar	35% (.35)		175
Whiting	24% (.24)	× 500	120
Kaolin (Georgia)	28% (.28)		140
Silica 325 mesh (flint)	13% (.13)		65
	100%		100 grams

First mix the cone 10 glaze. Then add coloring materials in the following proportions. (If you wish to use another colorant, find the correct percentage in the chart in Appendix O):

Rutile	8% (.08)	× 500	40 grams
Tin	1% (.01)		5 grams

Dip a tile and mark it; then add to the mixture:

Talc   25 grams

In this instance, talc is used as a high-fire flux. It can also be an opacifier. Dip a tile in this mixture and mark it. Add 25 more grams of talc, dip and mark another tile, and repeat the additions for 2 or 3 more tiles. Fire the test tiles at cone 10.

Repeat the tests for the cone 5 and cone 05 glazes, fire these tiles at the appropriate cone, and compare the results of the tests to see how changing the proportions of the flux affected the glaze.

3B
Calculating Glazes Using Chemical Analysis

For generations, potters made glazes using an experimental approach. Based on the knowledge handed down from earlier potters, they tried out various combinations of materials much as you followed the progression of clay and glaze tests in Appendix 1. By working in this way, a ceramist can develop a clear sense of what each material does in combination with others without necessarily knowing the exact chemical composition of each material in the glaze—as potters did for centuries before the development of modern chemistry. You may wish to continue working in this way, trying and testing. But if you want to go into the chemistry of glazes in greater depth, in this appendix you can follow a potter who works with high-fire stoneware glazes as he goes about analyzing, calculating, and testing a glaze. The method is the same whether the glaze is high-fire or low-fire, matt or glossy, transparent or opaque. By working through this step-by-step process, you will learn how to apply the basics of glaze calculation to any glaze.

Modern chemistry enables one to break down glaze materials into their chemical components and to work out formulas that represent the chemical, rather than the physical, proportions of its components. Using such chemical formulas, it is possible to analyze and compare glazes in a more detailed manner. The chemical structure as well as the behavior of ceramic materials in the kiln has now been analyzed, tested, observed, and recorded, and rules have been established to express their chemical relationships, making it easier for the ceramist to supply the needed chemical components of a glaze from the available ceramic materials. This method of calculation involves some understanding of chemistry and of the basic atomic and molecular composition of glaze materials. A calculator is also helpful and computer software is now available that makes glaze calculation easier.

ELEMENTS AND COMPOUNDS

Before going further with the calculations, it is important to understand something about the chemical composition of the minerals used in glaze making. The earth's crust, from which these materials come, is made up of elements and compounds. An element is a substance that cannot be separated into substances different from itself by ordinary chemical means; it contains only one kind of atom. The atoms of the 106 known elements have been assigned weights in relation to the lightest element—hydrogen—which was given the weight of 1. In order to calculate glazes, you must use the atomic weights of the elements.

The elements, however, rarely exist in pure form, but rather exist in compounds. Made up of combinations of different elements in a definite proportion, these compounds have been formed by natural forces and may exist as gases, liquids, or solids. The compounds with which the potter is mainly concerned are oxides produced when various elements become chemically combined with the oxygen that is so plentiful in our environment.

ATOMS AND MOLECULES

Molecules are the smallest particles of a compound that retain chemical identity with a substance in mass. The weight of a molecule consists of the total combined weights of all the atoms in that molecule. For example, water, which is made up of two atoms of hydrogen to one atom of oxygen, is written as H_2O. Since the atomic weight of one atom of hydrogen is 1, the weight of two atoms is 2. Add that 2 to the atomic weight of one atom of oxygen, which is 16, and you have a total molecular weight of 18. It is this concept of molecular weight that you will be concerned with in glaze calculation.

It helps to remember that the gram weight is the actual physical weight of the materials you will use when mixing a glaze, while the molecular weight is the chemical weight based on the atomic structure of the molecules. When making changes in a glaze, which is made up of different compounds, it is necessary to convert all calculations to molecular weights, since the weight of a compound in molecular terms differs markedly from its physical weight. If you simply mixed by gram weight, you would not achieve the desired result. Here we are concerned with the chemical reactions determined by the *proportion* of molecules of the various substances, rather than with the gross amounts of the substances.

EXAMPLE OF GLAZE CALCULATION

Now let's follow a potter through a calculation*:

I need to calculate a cone 10 glaze for the interior of casseroles and cups. I want a glaze that is glossy and either colorless or a very light gray or off-white. Most glazes that don't have glaze-coloring oxides (such as cobalt, iron, or copper oxide) added to them turn out to be clear or light gray. I will test a glaze without coloring oxides, fire it, and see what it looks like. Later I can add a colorant or an opacifier if I wish and test again. Experience has given me some basic knowledge as a starting point. I know, for instance, that most cone 10 glazes have ingredients, by weight, in the following very general proportions:

Feldspar (either soda or potash	35–50%
Clay (china clay or ball clay)	5–20%
Additional flux for texture (whiting, colemanite, talc, dolomite, etc.)	15–30%
Silica 325 mesh (flint or quartz)	5–25%

Each of these ingredients functions in one or more ways in a glaze:

Feldspar 35–50%   This is an extremely useful and important material that is present in most glazes. In high-fire glazes it is usually the main flux because feldspars have a relatively low melting point (around 2264°F/1240°C). Feldspar lowers the point at which the silica fuses and will also bring some additional silica and alumina to the glaze. Used with another flux, the fusing point can be lowered even more.

*In this edition the glaze has been recalculated to use Custer feldspar than the original Kingman feldspar, which is no longer available.

Clay (china clay, or ball clay) 5–20%   This is the main source of the refractory, alumina, in a glaze. China clay is white, so for my particular glaze, I would use china clay rather than ball clay, which fires to a gray or cream. The clay, along with the feldspar, will generally supply all the alumina needed in a glaze.

Additional flux 15–30%   One of several high-fire fluxing materials can be used, such as talc, whiting, dolomite, or colemanite. The additional flux may lower the melting point of the glaze by a cone or two, or even more if large quantities are added, and will also bring other oxides to the glaze. Talc, for instance, contains magnesia and silica, while colemanite yields calcium and boric oxide. When you use feldspar alone as a flux, the fired glaze surface is usually "glassy." If additional fluxes are used, the surface of the fired glaze changes. Potters use terms like *buttery, satin,* or *soft matt* to describe these glaze surfaces.

Silica (flint) 5–25%   Flint (or quartz) is the main source of silica, the glass-forming oxide. It is best to use as much silica as possible in order to give a glaze the desired qualities of durability, hardness, and resistance to acids.

Using these proportions as a rough guide, I'll select the ingredients I'll use from those available to me, mix a glaze by gram weight, and test it. These are the proportions I choose:

Custer feldspar Because it is the principal and most efficient flux material, used to lower the melting point of silica.	45% (.45)
China clay Because it is the source of the refractory and it is whiter than ball clay.	15% (.15)
Talc Because in combination with the feldspar it acts as a stoneware flux that promotes highly glossy textures at cone 9 or 10, as well as being an opacifier.	15% (.15)
Silica (flint) is the source of silica, the glass former.	25% (.25)
	100%

Since I want to have enough glaze to dip the tiles, I'll mix up a batch of 500 grams. To do this, I'll multiply the above proportions by 500, to get the following amounts in grams:

Feldspar	225 grams
China clay	75 grams
Talc	75 grams
Silica (flint)	125 grams
	500 grams

Now I measure out these ingredients on my balance scale and add them to enough water to form a soupy mixture (Chapter 15). This mixture is the basic glaze. After mixing these ingredients, I dip some test tiles in the glaze and put them in the kiln with pottery I am ready to fire to cone 10.

After I have fired the kiln and looked at the test tiles, I can see that the glaze has some characteristics that I want to change. I'm unhappy with its rather bland, glassy, and uninteresting texture. I feel it lacks the smooth, rich quality I like in a stoneware glaze, so I decide to make some alterations in the glaze ingredients.

Since the proportions of feldspar, china clay, and silica are constants in most stoneware glazes, I decide not to change them. This means I'll have to make my alterations in the additional flux, which in this case is talc. But in order to decide how much to change the proportions of the talc, I have to get involved in some chemistry. I'll have to examine the molecular makeup of the glaze, as well as take into consideration certain known limits of amounts of materials, altering the formula of the glaze accordingly. Before I do that, I'll explain some basic procedures that apply to glaze calculation.

EMPIRICAL FORMULA

For the purposes of glaze calculation, the materials used in a glaze are divided into three categories, according to their function in glazes. In Table 1, these categories are arranged in columns. The fluxes (both high- and low-fire) are listed under the heading RO/R_2O (also called bases); the refractory materials are listed under the heading R_2O_3 (also called neutrals); and the main glass former is listed under the heading RO_2 (also called acid). In this method of listing the ingredients, the R symbol represents the element and the O represents oxygen.

Notice that the oxides in the flux column (RO/R_2O) are all made up of one or two atoms of the element for each atom of oxygen (for example, MgO, PbO, Na_2O). Some of these fluxes, like lead, are only effective in low-fire glazes. The second column (R_2O_3) contains the oxides that make up the refractory ingredients in the glaze. Notice that these oxides are all formed with two atoms of the element to three atoms of the oxygen. The third column, which contains the glass-forming agent (silica), is called the RO_2 column because the oxide in it consists of the element combined with two atoms of oxygen.

This arrangement of glaze materials in three columns is called the empirical method, and glaze formulas that list ingredients in the same three-column arrangement are called empirical formulas. Later, when we discuss the unity formula and limit formulas, we will see that the three-column (empirical) method of writing formulas provides a convenient format for checking the proper proportions of glaze ingredients.

Table 1   Glaze Oxides

A Flux	B Refractory	C Glass Former
RO/R$_2$O (Bases)	*R$_2$O$_3$ (Neutrals)*	*RO$_2$ (Acid)*
Oxides of:		
Lead, PbO**	Alumina, Al$_2$O$_3$	Silica, SiO$_2$
Sodium, Na$_2$O	Boric oxide, B$_2$O$_3$*	
Potassium, K$_2$O**		
Zinc, ZnO		
Calcium, CaO		
Magnesium, MgO		
Barium, BaO**		
Lithium, Li$_2$O		
Strontium, SrO		

*This is a neutral that can function as an acid or a base. It is an effective flux in both low- and high-fire glazes.

**Highly toxic (see Appendix 1E for toxicity of ceramic materials)

ATOMIC AND MOLECULAR WEIGHT

As we have seen, because ceramic materials vary so widely in weight, you cannot merely take so many grams of that material or so many grams of this. If you did, you might get many more molecules of the heavier material than you wanted. Unless you know the weight of the molecules in each of the materials you cannot select 1 or 20 or 500 or 10,000 molecules.

Each of the 106 known elements has been assigned an atomic weight in relation to hydrogen (see Appendix 3C.) Since the atomic weight of hydrogen is 1 and oxygen 16, calcium 40, and silica 28, this means that the atomic weight of oxygen is 16 times the weight of hydrogen, while calcium is 40 times the weight of hydrogen, and silica is 28 times the weight of hydrogen. Unfortunately, ceramic materials are not conveniently made up of pure elements, but rather combinations of elements. In order to find the molecular weight of each material, I must first refer to its chemical symbol in Appendix 1E, to see the kind and number of atoms that compose the material. For example, the symbol for silica (or flint) is SiO_2, and that, I know, means that silica consists of 1 atom of silicon (Si) and 2 atoms of oxygen (O_2). By looking at Appendix 3C, I can see that the atomic weight of silicon is 28 and the atomic weight of oxygen is 16. Doing some arithmetic, I can figure out the molecular weight of flint. To do this, I first multiply the atomic weight of silicon by 1 atom:

Silicon: $28 \times 1 = 28$

Then I multiply the atomic weight of oxygen by 2 atoms:

Oxygen: $16 \times 2 = 32$

Added together these come to 60, which gives me the weight of one molecule of silica (that is, the molecular weight of SiO_2). However, I don't have to go through this arithmetic each time, for the molecular weights are listed in Appendix 3D.

EQUIVALENT WEIGHTS

You will notice that there is also a column of equivalent weights in Appendix 3D, and that for some of the materials, the equivalent weight is not the same as the molecular weight. The reason for this is that some materials are structured in such a way that they would yield more or less than one molecule of the desired oxide. In these cases, an altered, or equivalent, weight has been assigned to the material in order to introduce one molecule of the desired oxide into the glaze formula (and other oxides in proportion). In these cases, the equivalent weight should be used because it will yield precise quantities for the purposes of glaze calculation.

THE UNITY FORMULA

Before I do the necessary calculations to change my glaze, I must explain one more procedure. You have seen the reason for the empirical formula and the three-column arrangement, and also how to express the materials in molecular weights. However, in a formula based on the relationship between three groups of materials, there must always be one constant for the purpose of comparison. Remember, it is the *relative* amount of the materials that is important in formulating a glaze. So, arbitrarily, it has been decided that the RO/R_2O column will always represent 1—or *unity*. By accepting this, and by comparing this column to the other two columns, the relationships of the materials in a glaze will always be clear. Remember my glossy white glaze? Its original recipe was

Custer feldspar	45%
China clay	15%
Talc	15%
Silica (flint)	25%
	100%

In order to be able to work with molecules, I will divide these percentages of the materials by their molecular weights (or their equivalent weights). By consulting Appendix 3C, I see that the molecular weight of Custer feldspar is 694, that of China clay is 258, that of talc is 379, and that of silica is 60.

Now, taking each material in turn, I do the necessary arithmetic to find out the existing proportional amounts of the glaze ingredients:

Components	Molecular Proportions
Custer feldspar	$45 \div 694 = .065$
China clay	$15 \div 258 = .058$
Talc	$15 \div 379 = .039$
Silica (flint)	$25 \div 60 = .417$

The numbers in the right-hand column express the molecular proportions.

Now I can consult Appendix 3D and Appendix 3E for the formulas of each of my ingredients. I know which materials I am using and the molecular proportion of each one in this particular glaze. The formula for talc, for example, is $3MgO \cdot 4SiO_2 \cdot H_2O$, and I have already worked out that its molecular proportion in this glaze is .039. With this information, I can now construct a chart of my own glaze, which will give me a clear picture of its contents and the relationship of the parts to each other. I can do this by multiplying the molecular proportion of each raw material by the quantity of each oxide in its formula. For example, in the case of talc, which has 3 parts of magnesium, I multiply 3 by .039. This shows me that the talc will contribute .117 parts of magnesium oxide to this glaze $(3 \times .039 = .117)$.

There is one complication. Feldspars are composed of many oxides, so I must be sure to have the correct formula for the type of feldspar I use. Ceramic material suppliers usually provide the necessary information about the composition of various feldspars, but these formulas may vary somewhat depending on where the feldspar is mined. Also, they usually have to be brought to unity. I have worked out that the empirical formula for Custer feldspar is

RO/R$_2$O	R$_2$O$_3$	RO$_2$
Na$_2$O, .300	Al$_2$O$_3$, 1.04	SiO$_2$, 6.94
K$_2$O, .670		
CaO, .030		
FeO$_2$, trace*		

*Small amounts can be ignored.

This means that there are .300 parts of sodium oxide and .670 parts of potassium oxide and .030 parts of calcium in the Custer feldspar formula, as well as 1.04 parts of alumina and 6.94 parts of silica.

Now I draw up a table in which I arrange the ingredients down the left side, next to the molecular proportions for my particular glaze (see Table 2). Across the top I list the oxides that my materials will yield. This table makes it possible for me to see very clearly the quantity of each oxide that is present in my white glaze. Since water and gases burn away or change in the firing, they are not included in the calculations, nor are the small amounts of other elements in the feldspar.

Now, again using the three columns, I arrange my oxides according to the empirical formula:

RO/R$_2$O		R$_2$O$_3$		RO$_2$	
K$_2$O,	.044	Al$_2$O$_3$,	.126	SiO$_2$,	1.139
Na$_2$O,	.020				
CaO	.002				
MgO,	.117				
Totals	.183		.126		1.139

As I said before, I want to make a unity formula by expressing the RO/R$_2$O column as a unit of one. Now it adds up to .183. How do I fix this? By dividing everything in the above formula by .183, I get a true unity formula. Here it is:

RO/R$_2$O		R$_2$O$_3$		RO$_2$	
K$_2$O,	.241	Al$_2$O$_3$,	.688	SiO$_2$,	6.224
Na$_2$O,	.109/.108				
MgO,	.639				
CaO	.011				
Totals	1.00		.685		6.224

LIMIT FORMULAS

Now I can see my glaze expressed in a unity formula that can easily be analyzed and compared to other glazes. The amount of each oxide in the glaze can also be checked easily against the limits suggested on page 436. These limit formulas have been worked out as guides to show the amount of each oxide that occurs in a particular type of glaze maturing at a particular tem-

Table 2

Material	Molecular Proportions	Oxides					
		K$_2$O	CaO	Na$_2$O	Al$_2$O$_3$	MgO	SiO$_2$
Custer feldspar	.065	.044	.002	.020	.068		.45
China clay	.058			.058	.116		
Talc	.039				.117	.156	
Silica (flint)	.417					.417	
Totals		.044	.002	.020	.126	.117	1.139

perature range. Remember, however, that although limit formulas are generally accurate, there are many glazes that exceed either the upper or lower limits but which can still be successful glazes. These limits should be taken only as broad guidelines and should not keep you from experimenting. However, in order to solve my problems with this particular glaze, it will help me to look at the proportions of the materials in the unity formula of my glaze and compare them to the limits suggested in the limit formula for stoneware or porcelain glazes in the cone 8 to 12 range.

Cone 8 to 12 Stoneware Limit Formula

KNaO	.2–.40	Al_2O_3	.3–.5	SiO_2	3.0–5.0
CaO	.4–.70	B_2O_3	.1–3		
MgO	0–.35				
ZnO	0–.30				
BaO*	0–.30				

*Highly toxic

When I look at the two sets of numbers and compare the formula of my glaze with the limit formula, several facts become apparent.

1. My sodium and potassium are within limits. I combine these two ingredients by addition to get the total of the KNaO:

K_2O	.241
Na_2O	.109/.108
CaO	.011

    .361 versus a limit of .2–.40

2. My magnesium is very high: .639 versus a limit of .35.

3. My alumina is high: .688 versus a limit of .5.

4. My silica is high: 6.224 versus a limit of 5.0.

So now I can figure out that the combination of high silica and high flux made a very shiny, glassy glaze, but it did not run off the test tile because the alumina was also high.

ANALYZING THE GLAZE

I now examine the glaze ingredients closely in view of their functions. This will give me some information about how to change the glaze so that it may suit my purposes better. After firing, I saw that the glaze was glossy. This means that despite the fact that the silica was high, the actual proportion of glass (silica) to glass melters (feldspar and talc) was all right. If there

had been too much silica and not enough flux, the final product would have been underfired, rough, and granular. On the other hand, if there had been too much flux, the glaze would have run down off the wall of the test tile into a pool at the base of the tile. Also, I see that the glaze is not brittle, nor is it crazing, crackling, or shivering off the clay body. This means that the proportion of the refractory (alumina) must be all right. Too little alumina would cause the glaze to be brittle and probably shiver, while if there is too much alumina, the glaze surface will be matt and dull.

The ony thing I find wrong with this glaze for my purposes is that I don't care for the texture. I know that texture is controlled largely by the oxides in the optional fluxes (such as calcium, magnesium, zinc, or barium). So, considering the high proportion of magnesium (.611 versus a limit of .35), my decision is to reduce the magnesium to bring it within the usual limits. I'll then substitute another flux for the quantity of magnesium I remove. (Remember that I am still testing, and all experimentation at this point can be modified according to the results that show after the tiles have been fired in the kiln.)

I decide to reduce the magnesium by .30 to a total of .311 and to substitute .339 molecules of calcium. I choose calcium for several reasons: it is easily available in whiting, a staple in most pottery studios; it is known to provide a smooth, matt surface in some glazes; and it is a proven trouble-free stoneware flux. Also, when calcium is added in the form of whiting, it will promote a light color in the glaze, suiting my purpose.

After I have made the substitution, my formula looks like this:

K_2O	.241	Al_2O_3	.688	SiO_2	6.224
Na_2O	.109				
MgO	.311				
CaO	.339				

CONVERTING FROM EMPIRICAL FORMULA TO BATCH RECIPE

Now that I have decided how to alter my empirical formula to achieve the desired results, I must find a way to supply the ingredients from the dry materials. I do this by constructing another table with the ceramic materials and their formulas on the left and the oxides of my empirical formula running across the top (Table 3). Starting with the oxides that come from single-oxide materials, I continue with the materials that have two or more oxides, putting the silica last. Under each oxide

Table 3   From Empirical Formula to Batch Recipe

Materials	Proportional Requirement	Remarks	CaO .311	MgO .339	Na₂O .108/.109	K₂O .241	Al₂O₃ .688	SiO₂ 6.224
Whiting, $CaCO_3$	.311	I need .3 parts of CaO. Whiting has 1 part CaO, so I divide .3 by 1 to get my proportional requirement.	Satisfied by $1 \times .3 =$ .3 (still needs .011)					
Talc, $3\ MgO \cdot 4\ SiO_2$	.113	I need .339 MgO. Talc has 3 MgO. The materials proportion is thus .346 ÷ 3 = .113. I multiply each part in talc by this figure. Magnesium is satisfied, but we need more silica.		Satisfied by $3 \times .113 = .339$				$4 \times .113 = .452$ (Still need 5.772)
Custer feldspar, .30 $Na_2O \cdot$ .67 $K_2O \cdot$ .03 CaO $1.04\ Al_2O_3 \cdot$ $6.94\ SiO_2$	.361	I need .108/.109 Na_2O. There is .30 Na_2O available in the feldspar. I divide .108 by .30 to get .361. Then I multiply each part in the feldspar formula by this figure. I find I still need more Al_2O_3 and SiO_2.	Satisfied by $.03 \times .361$ = .011		Satisfied by $.30 \times .361 =$ .108	Satisfied by $.67 \times .361 =$ .241	$1.04 \times .361 =$ .375 (Still need .313)	$6.94 \times .361 =$ 2.505 (Still need 3.267)
China clay, $Al_2O_3 \cdot 2\ SiO_2$	.313	.313 Al_2O_3 is needed. There is one part Al_2O_3 available in china clay. .313 ÷ 1 = .313, which is the materials proportion still needed of alumina. China clay satisfies .626 silica. I still need 2.641 silica.					Satisfied by $1 \times .313 =$ .313	$2 \times .305 = .610$ (Still need 2.355)
Silica (flint), SiO_2	2.641	Remaining silica needed satisfied by 2.641 of flint.						Satisfied by $1 \times 2.641 = 2.641$

I enter the desired proportional amount needed as I determined them for my altered formula. Table 3 includes notes and comments to clarify the process for the reader. Of course, I would not add these notes if I were working alone in my workshop.

To determine the required amounts of each material, I must fill in the table using the amounts I found in my empirical formula and which I have listed across the top of the table. Starting with the oxides that come from the materials that have only one oxide in them, I determine the required amounts by using the following equation:

Proportional requirements
of materials

$$= \frac{\text{Amount wanted in formula}}{\text{Amount present in material}}$$

For example, I want .3 CaO. Whiting has one part CaO, so I divide .3 by 1, which of course gives me .3. (If there were any other elements in whiting, I would have to multiply them all by .3, since that is how much I will use of the entire material.) As you can see, my needs for CaO are thus satisfied entirely by the whiting. I can now go on to calculate the proportional figures for the remaining materials.

I need .339 MgO and I find that talc has 3 MgO in its formula. Therefore, I divide .339 by 3 to arrive at the proportional figure of .113 for talc. I then multiply each oxide in the talc formula by .113, which gives me .339 of MgO (satisfying my needs) and 1.452

of SiO_2. I subtract that amount of SiO_2 from my needed amount of 6.224 and put the remaining needed amount (5.772) in parentheses.

The next material listed in my empirical formula at the top of the chart is Na_2O and I need .108/.109 parts of it. In the Custer feldspar formula I see that there is .30 available. To get my proportional figure, I divide .108/.109 by .30 and get .361. I then multiply each part in the feldspar formula by .361 to get the equivalent amounts of each part contained in my empirical formula. So I get .109 Na_2O (satisfying the amount needed), .241 K_2O (also satisfying that amount needed), .375 Al_2O_3, which I subtract from the needed amount of .688, and I put the remaining amount needed (.313) in parentheses. Finally I get 2.505 SiO_2 and subtract that from the needed amount of 5.772 and put the remainder (3.267) in parentheses.

Now I have satisfied all my needs except for the remaining amounts of Al_2O_3 and SiO_2. I can complete my alumina needs with china clay by using .313 of it, since it contains one part of Al_2O_3. However, there are two parts of SiO_2 in china clay, and when I multiply by .313, I get .626. I subtract this amount from the needed 3.267, leaving me with 2.641 parts of silica still needed. I complete my remaining requirements by adding the needed amount (2.641) with flint, which is a nearly pure form of silica.

Now that I have determined the proportions required of each material, I simply multiply this amount by the molecular (or equivalent) weights for each ingredient. The molecular or equivalent weights of the most common materials are listed in Appendix 3D. Thus, I have:

Ingredient	Material (Proportional Amount)	×	Molecular Weight (or Equivalent Weight)	=	Batch Amount (Grams)	Percent
Whiting	0.311	×	100	=	31.1	6
Talc	0.113	×	378	=	42.7	8
Feldspar	0.361	×	694	=	250.5	44
China clay	0.313	×	258	=	180.8	14
Silica (flint)	2.641	×	60	=	158.5	28
					563.6 (grams)	

A batch recipe is what I started with, and now I have another batch recipe of the altered glaze ready to mix, test, and fire.

Once again I will mix a batch of 500 grams of the glaze, dip some test tiles in the batch, and fire them to cone 10. It is a good idea to dip several tiles and place them in different locations in the kiln. In this way you will see if small variations in kiln atmosphere will affect the glaze.

The fired result of the test is a glaze that has changed somewhat. Its glossy finish has a softer texture that suits my purpose as a liner glaze. If I decide to alter it later, I could add a little Zircopax (2 to 10 percent) to try to introduce some opacity and whiteness to the glaze, or I could add some other colorants.

What I have followed here is the basic method for testing glazes using chemical analysis, using most of the procedures required in order to go from batch recipe to molecular formula and back to batch again. If you have followed this example through these procedures, you now have seen the basic process of calculating and analyzing glazes.

As you proceed to work with more complex materials and to formulate more sophisticated and elaborate glazes, the calculations can become more complex. However, no amount of knowledge of chemistry can substitute for patient testing and retesting of trial formulas in your own kiln, with your own clay body, and with the available materials. The use of chemistry answers many technical questions and gives you a method of formulating a glaze, but experience, patience, hard work, and aesthetic sensitivity are what really create beautiful glazes.

3C
Atomic Weights of Elements Used in Ceramics

The relative toxicity of these materials in shown in Appendix 1E.

Element	Symbol	Atomic Weight
Aluminum	Al	26.98
Antimony	Sb	121.75
Barium	Ba	137.34
Bismuth	Bi	208.98
Boron	B	10.81
Cadmium	Cd	112.40
Calcium	Ca	40.08
Carbon	C	12.01
Chlorine	Cl	35.45
Chromium	Cr	51.99
Cobalt	Co	58.93
Copper	Cu	63.54
Fluorine	F	18.99
Gold	Au	196.96
Hydrogen	H	1.00
Iridium	Ir	192.22
Iron	Fe	55.84
Lead	Pb	207.20
Lithium	Li	6.94
Magnesium	Mg	24.30
Manganese	Mn	54.93
Nickel	Ni	58.71

Element	Symbol	Atomic Weight
Nitrogen	N	14.00
Oxygen	O	15.99
Phosphorus	P	30.97
Platinum	Pt	195.09
Potassium	K	39.10
Selenium	Se	78.96
Silicon	Si	28.08
Silver	Ag	107.86
Sodium	Na	22.98
Strontium	Sr	87.62
Sulphur	S	32.06
Tin	Sn	118.69
Titanium	Ti	47.90
Uranium	U	238.02
Vanadium	V	50.94
Zinc	Zn	65.37
Zirconium	Zr	91.22

3D
Molecular and Equivalent Weights

 The relative toxicity of these materials is shown in Appendix 1E.

Material	Formula	Molecular Weight	Equivalent Weight
Alumina	Al_2O_3	101.9	101.9
Antimony oxide	Sb_2O_3	291.5	291.5
Barium oxide	BaO	153.4	153.4
Barium carbonate	$BaCO_3$	197.4	197.4
Bone ash	$Ca_3(PO_4)_2$	310.3	103.0
Borax	$Na_2O \cdot 2B_2O_3 \cdot 10H_2O$	381.4	381.4
Boric acid (Boron)	$B_2O_3 \cdot 3H_2O$	123.7	123.7
Boric oxide	B_2O_3	69.6	69.6
Calcium borate (colemanite)	$2CaO \cdot 3B_2O_3 \cdot 5H_2O$	412.0	206.0
Calcium carbonate (whiting)	$CaCO_3$	100.09	100.1
China clay (Kaolin)	$Al_2O_3 \cdot 2SiO_2 \cdot 2H_2O$	258.1	258.1
Chromium oxide	Cr_2O_3	152.0	152.0
Cobalt carbonate	$CoCO_3$	118.9	118.9
Cobalt oxide	CoO	74.9	74.9
Copper carbonate	Cu_2CO_3	187.0	187.0
Copper oxide (cupric)	CuO	79.57	79.57
Copper oxide (cuprous)	Cu_2O	143.0	80.0
Cornish stone	$\begin{matrix} CaO \cdot 304 \\ Na_2O \cdot 340 \\ K_2O \cdot 356 \end{matrix}\Big\}\ \begin{matrix} Al_2O_3 \\ 1.075 \end{matrix}\Big\}\ \begin{matrix} SiO_2 \\ 8.10 \end{matrix}$	667.0	667.0
Cryolite (soda)	Na_3AlF_6	210.0	420.0
Dolomite	$CaCO_3\ MgCO_3$	184.4	184.4
*Feldspar (potash)	$K_2O \cdot Al_2O_3 \cdot 6SiO_2$	556.8	556.8
*Feldspar (soda)	$Na_2O \cdot Al_2O_3 \cdot 6SiO_2$	524.5	524.5
*Feldspar (lime)	$CaO \cdot Al_2O_3 \cdot 2SiO_2$	278.6	
Flint	SiO_2	60.06	60.06

*Feldspar formulas vary. See Appendix 3E.

Material	Formula	Molecular Weight	Equivalent Weight
Ilmenite	$FeO \cdot TiO_2$	151.74	151.74
Iron chromate (ferrous-ferric)	$FeCrO_4$	172.0	172.0
Iron oxide, red (ferric)	Fe_2O_3	159.7	159.7
Iron oxide, black (ferrous)	FeO	71.8	71.8
Kaolin (calcined)	$Al_2O_3 \cdot 2SiO_2$	222.0	222.0
Lead carbonate (white lead)	$2PbCO_3 \cdot Pb(OH)_2$	775.6	223.0
Lead oxide (red)	Pb_3O_4	685.6	228.0
Lead oxide	PbO	223.2	223.2
Lithium carbonate	Li_2CO_3	73.9	73.9
Magnesium carbonate	$MgCO_3$	84.3	84.3
Magnesium oxide	MgO	40.3	40.3
Manganese carbonate	$MnCO_3$	114.9	114.9
Manganese dioxide	MnO_2	86.9	86.9
Nepheline syenite	$\begin{cases} K_2O \cdot 25 \\ Na_2O \cdot 75 \\ 0 \cdot 75\ Na_2O \end{cases}\ \begin{matrix} Al_2O_3 \\ 1 \cdot 11 \\ 4 \cdot 65\ SiO_2 \end{matrix}\ \begin{matrix} SiO_2 \\ 4 \cdot 65 \end{matrix}$	462	462
Nickel oxide	NiO	74.7	74.7
Potassium carbonate (pearl ash)	K_2CO_3	138.2	138.2
Quartz (silica)	SiO_2	60.0	60.0
Rutile	TiO_2	79.1	79.1
Silica (flint)	SiO_2	60.1	60.1
Sodium carbonate (soda ash)	Na_2CO_3	106.0	106.0
Sodium silicate	Na_2SiO_3	122.1	122.1
Spodumene	$Li_2O \cdot Al_2O_3 \cdot 4SiO_2$	372.2	372.2
Talc (magnesium silicate)	$3MgO \cdot 4SiO_2 \cdot H_2O$	378.96	378.96
Tin oxide	SnO_2	150.7	150.7
Titanium oxide	TiO_2	80.1	80.1
Vanadium pentoxide	V_2O_5	181.9	181.9
Whiting	$CaCO_3$	100.1	100.1
Wollastonite	$Ca \cdot SiO_3$	116.0	116.0
Zinc oxide	ZnO	81.4	81.4
Zirconium oxide	ZrO_2	123.2	123.2
Zirconium silicate (Zircopax)	$ZrO_2 \cdot SiO_2$	182.9	182.9

3E
Formulas of Some Feldspars

The formulas and molecular weights may vary slightly depending on area mined and other factors.

Feldspar	Formula	Molecular Weight
Cornwall stone	$.356 \ K_2O \cdot 1.075 \ Al_2O_3 \cdot 8.10 \ SiO_2$ $.340 \ Na_2O$ $.304 \ CaO$	667
Custer	$.67 \ K_2O \cdot 1.04 \ Al_2O_3 \cdot 6.94 \ SiO_2$ $.30 \ Na_2O$ $.03 \ CaO$	694
Kona F-4 (56)	$.58 \ NaO \cdot 1.00 \ Al_2O_3 \cdot 5.79 \ SiO_2$ $.26 \ K_2O$ $.16 \ CaO$	518
Lepidolite	$.39 \ K_2O \cdot 1.00 \ Al_2O_3 \cdot 3.74 \ SiO_2$ $.06 \ Na_2O$ $.55 \ Li_2O$	383
Nepheline syenite	$.75 \ Na_2O \cdot 1.11 \ Al_2O_3 \cdot 4.65 \ SiO_2$ $.25 \ K_2O$	462
Oxford	$.58 \ K_2O \cdot 11.07 \ Al_2O_3 \cdot 1.07 \ SiO_2$ $.42 \ Na_2O$	556
Petalite	$1.00 \ Li_2O \cdot 1.00 \ Al_2O_3 \cdot 8.00 \ SiO_2$	612
Plastic vitrox	$.61 \ K_2O \cdot 1.33 \ Al_2O_3 \cdot 14.00 \ SiO_2$ $.34 \ Na_2$ $.05 \ CaO$	1051
Spodumene	$1.00 \ Li_2O \cdot 1.00 \ Al_2O_3 \cdot 4.00 \ SiO_2$	372
Volcanic ash	$.47 \ KNaO \cdot 1.09 \ Al_2O_3 \cdot 9.52 \ SiO_2$ $.17 \ CaO$ $.25 \ MgO$ $.11 \ FeO$	720

4A
Additional Useful Information, Equipment, and Terms

Brushes
  a. Shader: glazing and decorating with underglaze.
  b. Bamboo: glazing and decorating with underglaze.
  c. Flat oxhair: glazing.
  d. Flat camel hair: glazing, china paint, luster.
  e. Liner (sable): detail, lines; use with underglaze, oxides, stains, and overglazes.
  f. Flat (red sable): china paint.
  g. Shader quills and French pointers: china paint.
  h. Hake: wide, soft brush, glazing and washes.
  i. Glass brush: a brush with fine glass bristles used for burnishing and polishing fired gold.

China paint
  a. Mortar and pestle: for grinding and mixing colors.
  b. Glass palette frosted on one side: for mixing.
  c. Palette knife: for mixing.
  d. French fat oil: Thinned with turpentine and mixed to painting consistency, this is used for outlining and fine pen work. Can also be used as thickener for oil base china painting medium.
  e. Lavender oil and Balsam of Copaiba; used for thinning oil china paint medium.

Clay
  Additives, to open pores, add strength, reduce thermal expansion, etc.
  a. Grog
  b. Ione grain grog: available in various sized particles.
  c. Nylon fiber
  d. Pearlite
  e. Vermiculite
  f. Sawdust, straw, and other organic materials that burn out in the kiln.

  g. Silica sand, 30 to 90 mesh: adds tooth and texture. (Do not inhale; use local ventilation and respirator.)
  h. Molochite
  i. Pyrophyllite: reduces thermal expansion.

  Flower clay, for making small applied decorations.
  a. Use glycerin in the clay body to keep it from cracking on drying.

Deflocculants
  a. Darvan #7.
  b. Sodium silicate "N."

Drill bits for ceramics
  a. Diamond core.
  b. Carbide tip.
  c. With drills use abrasive drilling compound as cutting vehicle.

Gas
  Pressure and volume
  a. It is important to provide correct pressure *and* volume of gas, usually around 4 to 6 pounds at the kiln.
  b. "Water column pressure" indicates the amount of gas pressure to the kiln.

  Gas burners
  a. Propane: orifice drill size, #38 to #50.
  b. Natural gas: orifice drill size, #28 or #32.

Glazes, underglazes, and overglazes
  Spraying
  a. Underglazes: use airbrush.
  b. Glazes: use spray gun.
  c. Use air compressor for airbrush and spray gun.
  d. For oil base paints you may need a moisture trap to catch moisture in the air-supply line, and a regulator for air-pressure control.

  Gums, add to glazes to make them adhere and to eliminate brush drag in brushing glazes.

a. CMC; carboxymethal cellulose.
b. Tragacanth.
c. Gum arabic.
d. Syrup.
e. Molasses.

Kilns
Kiln brick
a. Firebrick K20, K23, K26.
b. Hardbrick.

Kiln flue
a. Triple wall, stainless steel.

Kiln installation
a. Ceramic kiln insulation for barrel raku kilns. To attach insulation, purchase special refractory studs, or make your own porcelain buttons and attach them with nichrome wire threaded through them, through the insulation and holes in the metal barrel.

Kiln controls
a. Stepless control: electric kiln.
b. Kiln sitter: electric kiln.
c. Pyrometer: gas kiln and electric.
d. Electronic kiln controls:
   (1) Digital pyrometers show temperature.
   (2) Various types of analog and digital controls will give temperature and shut down the kiln when desired temperature is reached; some will shut down the kiln if burner goes out accidentally.

Patching compound, for patching kiln wall brick and kiln floor.
a. Kiln cement.
b. Castable refractories, for filling large holes, or for insulation.

Cleaning kiln, use silicon carbide rubbing stone or fragment of silicon carbide kiln shelf.

Lusters
a. Luster resist: for covering desired negative areas.
b. Marbelizing liquid: creates marbelized effect when added to lusters.
c. Gold and luster essence: add sparingly to thin lusters and use as brush cleaner.
d. Luster essence and lavender oil: a small amount will thin lusters that have congealed.
e. Gold eraser: an abrasive stick eraser for removal of fired gold, metallics, and lusters.
f. Liquid remover: a chemical remover for gold.

Plaster
Mold separators
a. Mold soap (for plaster to plaster separation for slip casting molds).

b. Petroleum jelly.
c. Motor oil.
d. Liquid dishwashing soap.
e. Waterbase lubricating jellies.
f. Formula used for calculating proportions of casting plaster for mold (Chapter 13). Length $\times$ width $\times$ height $\div$ 81 $\times$ 2 = lb of water $\times$ 2.75 = lb of plaster.

Rubber stamps
a. Use a solution of glycerin with cobalt carbonate to stamp letters on ware in blue before firing. Will fire blue.

Saws for cutting ceramics
a. Diamond blade (for high-fired ware)
b. Carbide blade (for soft bisque, terra cotta)

Sealers, to protect unglazed fired work from dust, fingerprints, and moisture as well as to heighten color use:
a. Acrylic spray sealer.
b. Spray varnish (tends to yellow with age).
c. Spray shellac (tends to yellow with age).
d. Water base concrete sealer.
e. Linseed oil.

Sieves
Brass mesh types, recommended meshes
a. Slip: 40–60 mesh.
b. Glaze: 50–100 mesh.
c. Underglaze: 80 mesh.
d. Engobe: 50–80 mesh.
e. Powdered materials: 30–80 mesh.

Sponges
a. Silk: for throwing.
b. Elephant ear: throwing.
c. Sea wool: plaster mold soaping.
d. Man-made: clean-up.

Unusual materials to test in glazes
a. Cement.
b. Cleaning powders.
c. Toothpaste.
d. Mine tailings.
e. Crushed glass or glass chunks (handle with care. Use goggles, gloves).
f. Crushed rocks.
g. Crushed sea shells.

Water (H_2O)
a. Mineral content varies in different parts of country. Water quality affects the amount of deflocculants needed in slip and can affect clay and glazes if it contains inordinate amounts of salts.
b. Water temperature makes a difference to setting time of plaster: the hotter the water the faster the setting time.

4B

Types of Plaster and Their Uses

Plaster Type	Parts Water per 100 lb Plaster	Setting Time	Density	Uses	Notes
Casting	67–80	20–25 min.**	soft	a, b, c, d, h, k	All-purpose; harder, somewhat coarser than Pottery Plaster #1
Pottery plaster #1	67–70	20–25 min.**	softer	a, b, c, g	Slip casting; excellent detail, produces high quality casting molds.***
Hydrocal (white) TM*	38–42	20–30 min.**	hard	d, e	Sculpture and carving
Hydrocal A-11 TM*	42–44	16–20 min.**	hard	h, j	Original model making
Hydrostone TM*	28–32	17–20 min.**	hardest	d, e, h, i	One of the hardest gypsum cements; used for molds, casting, finished art works.
Ultracal 30 TM*	35–38	25–30 min.**	hard	f, h, j	Super strength gypsum cement; often used for original model making and splash-cast molds.

USES Letter Code

a. Plaster bats, wedging table tops
b. Press molds
c. Slip casting molds
d. Sculpting and carving
e. Casting art works
f. Splash-cast molds
g. Molds for jiggering
h. Case for supporting flexible molds
i. Ram press dies
j. Template models
k. Waste molds

*Trademarks owned by United States Gypsum Company.

**Time varies according to age of material, temperature of water and atmospheric conditions, ratio of water to material, quantity of batch, and mixing methods.

***Density will be affected by water to material ratio and mixing methods.
Soft = Can be easily sanded, chiseled, carved or drilled.
Hard = Can be filed, drilled, chiseled, and sanded.
Hardest = Can be filed, chiseled and drilled.

4C
Repair and Installation of Ceramics; Adhesives and Colorants

Greenware
  a. If a large section (more than ¼ inch thick) breaks off of an unfired piece, you can often repair it by wrapping the two pieces in saturated cotton rags, thus gradually dampening them, and then scoring and rebonding them with water or slip.
  b. For smaller pieces, if you dampen the two areas with water, water and vinegar, or plain vinegar, you may be able to rescore and bond them again before firing.

Bisque repair   There are commercial products that are advertised for repair of greenware and bisque ware before refiring. Ericka Clark Shaw shares her formula for what she calls "bisque glue"

White glue	50%
Sodium silicate	50%

She says, "Add EPK (kaolin) and water until it becomes the consistency of mayonnaise" and apply. Can be fired to cone 10.

Acrylic adhesives and mastics   Single part adhesives for fired ware. For interior or exterior use. Use these adhesives to glue ceramics where dampness is present: showers, kitchen floors, and walls; to glue ceramic to ceramic; to bond ceramic sections with relatively flat surfaces with gluing gaps under ¼ inch. Useful for gluing sculpture or light wall pieces, such as thin slabs installed indoors. Follow manufacturers instructions.

Epoxy tile-setting adhesives consist of two-part epoxy resin and hardener that is blended with a cement/sand filler. Usually gray or white. White can be tinted with glaze stains to match sculpture colors for repair and postfiring construction. Especially good where resistance to physical abuse or salts, dilute acids, and/or cleaning agents is necessary. Bonds ceramic to ceramic, ceramic to wood (interior only unless protected from weather and with properly prepared un-

derstructure), ceramic to concrete, terrazo, vinyl, steel, stone, or gypsum board (interior only). Epoxy should only be used with **gloves and adequate ventilation to draw its fumes away from the worker, and with a respirator rated by NIOSH for toxic fumes.** Follow manufacturers instructions.

For works to be installed in public places, consult a structural engineer before starting to build.

Gluing glazed surfaces   For glazed areas glued to glazed areas, silicon or epoxy will work for nonstructural, lightweight areas. For larger works, for outdoor work, or work coming in contact with moisture or water, before gluing it is essential to prepare the glaze by grinding until the clay is visible. It is also strongly recommended that you make a physical bond using metal bolts or wooden dowels in conjunction with adhesive between parts.

Proper surface preparation is essential when gluing ceramic to ceramic or to other surfaces for installation of ceramic works. Clean each surface thoroughly. Both should be dry, dust free, and free of scale or loose parts. Painted surfaces should be sanded or wire brushed until raw material is visible; metal surfaces such as steel, galvanized metal, aluminum, sheet brass, or bronze should be cleaned, sanded, or ground until shiny. Mild steel is adequate for interior installation. For outside installation it must be painted, or use stainless steel, galvanized metal, aluminum, brass, bronze, or other rust-resistant materials.

PLANNING FOR INSTALLATION

Light to medium interior works   For interior installations, interior or exterior plywood is adequate for panels on which to assemble the work before attaching it to the wall. For outdoor installation, water must not penetrate the wood; use high grade exterior or marine-grade plywood. For light pieces, sanded wood backing is adequate for surface bonding. For bonding heavier sections, score the wood and the ceramic sections to increase gripping power of adhesive. Inserting screws, nails, or bolts through clay sections and wood will assure a safe bond.

Large works   Preplanning before or while the work is in the damp stage is helpful, and avoids tiresome re-working and grinding later. Score damp surfaces that are to be glued after firing. Drill holes for screws or bolts in the leather-hard clay or greenware. Drill holes approximately 15 to 20 percent larger than final bolt size to allow for shrinkage in the kiln. Countersink holes, so that after firing and assembling they can be plugged with colored epoxy, grout, adhesive, or mortar and hide the hardware. Sections may be mounted directly on the wall or attached to plywood panels then mounted on the wall. Be sure that the plywood is dry; free of oil, grease, or other chemicals that could affect the adhesive; and that the wall construction will handle the weight.

Connectors/Nuts and bolts   Mild steel or plated steel is adequate for interior installation but for outdoor installation use stainless steel, galvanized metal, brass, bronze or other rust-resistant materials. Consult a structural engineer for information on which of these materials is appropriate for your application.

COLOR ADDITIVES FOR EPOXY

The following coloring materials can be mixed with epoxy to color repaired areas or to glue sections. Because these colors are not fired, almost any powdered color, such as tempera or oil base paint will work. Universal tinting colors can also be used, and many intermediate colors can be mixed. Stains available in other parts of the country will work as well, but have not been tested for color results. Since many of the ceramic stains and oxides contain materials that are **toxic,** they should be used with **proper precautions.** When using epoxy, **wear neoprene gloves,** have **adequate ventilation** to draw its fumes away, and wear a **respirator** NIOSH rated for toxic fumes.

Color Desired	Additive
Clear	Epoxy resin.
Red brown	Red iron oxide, concrete colors, Red Horse clay, Neuman red clay.
Browns	Brown ceramic stain, concrete colors, burnt umber, raw umber, ball clay, Jordan clay, manganese dioxide, Barnard clay.
Light browns/tans	EPK Kaolin, fire clay (Lincoln), cement, rutile.
Light tans	Talc, white cement, dolomite.
Black	Black ceramic stain (K470), lamp black, black iron, oxide, cobalt oxide, concrete colors, black ink concentrate.
Blue-greens	Blue ceramic stain (#100), Turquoise blue stain (G490).
Blues	Dark blue ceramic stain (#1166), blue resin dye.
Yellows	Yellow ceramic stain (F222A), cadmium yellow, yellow ochre, tin vanadium.
Oranges	Universal tint (yellow-orange), Universal tint (raw sienna), orange enamel paint.
White	Tin oxide.
Off-white	Talc, dolomite, Zircopax, Ultrox.

(chart continued on page 450)

Color Desired	Additive
Green	Victorian green ceramic stain (B211), chrome oxide.
Pink	Pink ceramic stain (D-320).
Red	Apple red ceramic stain (#7464), cadmium red (highly toxic), red enamel paint.
Purple	Ceramic stains; mix pink and blue.
Silver	Aluminum paint.
Gold	Gold paint.

5A

Sources of Health and Safety Information

Art Hazards Project,
Center for Occupational Hazards Inc.
5 Beekman St.
New York, NY 10038
(212) 227-6220

This center is not only a source of pamphlets and bibliographies on the subject of art hazards, but it will also provide lecturers to conduct workshops at art schools and professional organizations of artists and teachers. Its Art Hazards Information Center answers telephoned or written inquiries, and publishes the *Art Hazards News Letter*. In addition, the Center runs a Consultation Program that will conduct health hazard surveys in schools and arts centers, and that provides consultation services to institutions that are building or renovating studio space.

The Art and Craft Materials Institute, Inc.
715 Boylston St.
Boston, MA 02116

The Institute provides toxicological evaluation of art materials, and compiles brand-name lists of art materials that are judged by the Institute to be non-toxic.

ASTM Committee on Standards, American
Society for Testing and Materials (ASTM)
1916 Race St.
Philadelphia, PA 19103

This organization sets standards for hazard labeling in art materials that are revised automatically every five years and more often if needed. Write for a copy of the standards.

The American Lung Association issues pamphlets explaining how to protect yourself against health hazards in the arts and crafts, with particular emphasis on dusts, fumes, and gases. Contact your local chapter.

The National Institute for Occupational Safety and Health (NIOSH) is primarily concerned with safety in the workplace, but many of their standards also apply to ceramic studios.

Local and state health departments, labor unions, and industrial relations organizations are sources of health and safety information, as are occupational health clinics, poison centers, and toxic information centers at local hospitals.

Occupational Safety and Health Administrations (OSHA) run by the states are primarily concerned with safety in the workplace, but are sources of information for studio standards.

The Cancer Information Service of the **National Cancer Institute** provides information on related subjects, while the **American Heart Association** is also concerned with occupational hazards that may affect heart patients. They will give information on this aspect of art hazards. Contact your local chapters.

In the Yellow Pages of your local telephone directory, you will find local and national safety equipment companies, many of which issue catalogs describing safety and health protection equipment. These catalogs are often a source of information on respirators, gloves, dust collectors, supplied air systems, and other protective equipment. In addition, many of the catalogs of the ceramic equipment and supply companies listed in Appendix 5B include information on protective measures and equipment.

Safety Equipment Catalogs

Direct Safety Company
7815 South 46th St.
Phoenix, AZ 85044

E. D. Bullard Co.
P.O. Box 187
White Oak Pike, Cynthiana, KY 41031-0187
(800) 227-04230

5B
Sources of Equipment and Material

The following are some of the largest suppliers. For local sources, check the Yellow Pages in your area under Ceramic Equipment and Supplies as well as advertisements in ceramics magazines.

A.R.T., 1555 Louis Ave., Elk Grove Village, IL 60007

Alaska Clay Supply Inc., P.O. Box 196577, Anchorage, AK 99519

American Art Clay Co., Inc., 4717 West 16th St., Indianapolis, IN 46222

Bailey Ceramic Supply, CPO 1577, Kingston, NY 12401

Bluebird Mfc. Co. Inc., P.O. Box 2307, Ft. Collins, CO 80522

Brent Equipment, 4717 West 16th St., Indianapolis, IN 46222

Cerami Corner Inc., P.O. Box 516, Azusa, CA 91702

Ceramic Fiber Fabrication Inc., 56828 Skyline Ranch Rd., Yucca Valley, CA 92284

Ceramics Hawaii Ltd., 501 Kokea St., Bldg. A6, Honolulu, HI 96817

Columbus Clay Co., 1049 W. Fifth Ave., Columbus, OH 43212

Cutter Ceramics, 47 Athletic Field Rd., Waltham, MA 02154

Griffin Earthworks Inc., P.O. Box 4057, 1006 Lee Hill Rd., Boulder, CO 80306

Hammill & Gillespie, Inc., P.O. Box 104, Livingston, NJ 07039

Jack D. Wolfe Co., 2130 Bergen St., Brooklyn, NY 11233

Kemper Tools, P.O. Box 696, Chino, CA 91710

Kickwheel Pottery Supply, 6477 Peachtree Industrial Blvd., Atlanta, GA 30360

Leslie Ceramic Company, 1212 San Pablo, Berkeley, CA 94706

Marjon Ceramics Inc., 3434 W. Earll Dr., Phoenix, AZ 85017

Miami Clay Co., 270 N.E. 183rd St., Miami, FL 33179

Mid-South Ceramic Supply Co., 1230 4th Ave. North, Nashville, TN 37208

Midwest Clay, 1800 West Cornelia, Chicago, IL 60057

Mile Hi Ceramics Inc., 77 Lipan, Denver, CO 80223-1580

Minnesota Clay, 8001 Grand Ave. South, Bloomington, MN 55420

Ohio Ceramic Supply, P.O. Box 630, Kent, OH 44240

Randall Pottery, P.O. Box 774, Alfred, NY 14802

Seattle Pottery Supply Inc., 35 South Hanford, Seattle, WA 98134

Shimpo West, 3500 Devon Ave., Lincolnwood, IL 60659

Skutt Ceramic Products, 2618 S.E. Steele St., Portland, OR 97202

Standard Ceramic Supply Co., P.O. Box 4435, Pittsburgh, PA 15205

Stratford Clay Supply Ltd., P.O. Box 344, Stratford, Ontario, N5A 6T3, Canada

Tucker Pottery Supplies, 15 West Pearce St., #7, Richmond Hill, Ontario, L4B 1H6, Canada

West Coast Ceramic Supply, 756 N.E. Lombard, Portland, OR 97211

Westwood Ceramic Supply Co., 14400 Lomitas Ave., City of Industry, CA 91746-0305

Software

INSIGHT ceramic chemistry software:

IMC, 134 Upland Dr., Medicine Hat, Alberta, T1A 3N7 Canada

Glossary

Acids In glaze calculation, the term refers to glaze chemicals that combine with **bases** and **neutrals** under heat, interacting in the formation of glazes. Silica is the most important acid. Acids are represented by the symbol RO_2. (See Appendix 3B.)

Air brush An atomizer that uses compressed air to spray a liquid. In ceramics, used for spraying oxides, underglazes, glaze stains, china paint, and lusters.

Air compressor A device that compresses air to below atmospheric pressure. In the studio, used to activate spray guns and airbrushes.

Albany slip A natural slip glaze made of clay that was mined near Albany, New York. It was used for glazing stoneware in the United States until recently, when it became unobtainable.

Alkalies Mainly sodium and potassium, but also lime, lithium, and magnesia. They act as fluxes in certain glazes.

Alkaline glazes Glazes in which the fluxes are alkalies (mainly sodium and potassium). The earliest glazes developed in the Near East were alkaline.

Amphora An ancient Greek vase form used there for transporting liquids and for prize presentations to Olympic games winners.

Antefix An ornament placed to cover the ends of tiles on the roofs of Greek and Etruscan temples.

Armature A framework of any rigid material used as a support while building clay sculpture. Most armatures must be removed before firing.

Ashes In ceramics, ashes from trees, plants, or animal bones may provide fluxes for use in glazes. Ashes contain varying amounts of silica and alumina, as well as potash, iron, magnesia, phosphorus, and lime. Oriental glazes such as the temmoku frequently used rice straw ash, naturally high in silica. Tree and plant ashes are still popular glaze ingredients, while bone ash is used in making china.

Aventurine glaze A glaze which, when cooled slowly, crystallizes and produces small spangles that catch the light. Generally high in iron.

Bag wall A wall built inside a down-draft kiln to separate the firing chamber from the fire. It directs the flames upward, producing even circulation, and also protects the ware from direct contact with the flame.

Ball clay A plastic fine-grained, secondary clay. Often containing some organic material, it is used in clay bodies to increase plasticity, and in glazes to add alumina. Ball clay fires to a grayish or buff color.

Ball mill A rotating porcelain jar filled approximately half full with flint pebbles or porcelain balls that revolve and grind dry or wet glaze materials or pigments into powder or refined liquid state.

Banding wheel A turntable that can be revolved with one hand to turn a piece of pottery or sculpture while decorating it with the other hand.

Basalt ware A black, unglazed stoneware first developed by Josiah Wedgewood in eighteenth-century England.

Bases Glaze oxides that combine under heat with the **acids,** acting as fluxes. Represented in glaze calculation by the symbol RO. (See Appendix 3B.)

Bas-relief Three-dimensional modeling that is raised only slightly above a flat background.

Bat A plaster disk or square slab usually ¾ to 1½ inches thick on which a pot is thrown or is placed to dry when removed from the wheel. Also used when handbuilding.

Batch A mixture of glaze materials or ingredients that have been weighed in certain proportions to obtain a particular glaze or clay body.

Bisque (bisquit) Unglazed ceramic ware that has been fired at a low temperature to remove all moisture from the clay body and to make handling easier during glazing.

Bisque firing The process of firing ware at a low temperature, usually from cone 010 to 05, to produce bisque ware.

Bizen ware Produced in Japan in wood-fired kilns in which the pots are stacked along with straw that is high in silica content. Its combustion causes fire markings, and ashes from the fire may also create glazed areas. Traditionally used in Japan to create ware for tea ceremony, modifications of the technique are now popular with potters elsewhere.

Blistering A pitted, craterlike surface of a glaze

caused by gases bursting through the glaze as it is fired, often caused by too-rapid firing, or over-firing.

Blunger   A machine with revolving paddles used to mix slips or glazes.

Body (clay body)   Any blend of clays and nonplastic ceramic materials that is workable and that has certain firing properties. Clay bodies are formulated to serve particular purposes and to achieve maturity at various firing temperatures. See **earthenware, stoneware,** and **porcelain.**

Bone ash   Calcium phosphate ash made from animal bones. Used in a clay body for making **bone china.**

Bone china   Ware made of clay to which bone ash has been added to lower its maturing point. Produced mainly in England, it matures at lower temperatures—usually around 2270°F/1240°C) than true porcelain.

Burner (gas, propane, oil)   The system through which fuel, combined with air (which is usually controlled by a butterfly valve or air shutter), is fed into the kiln, creating the necessary mixture for combustion.

Burnishing   Rubbing leather-hard or dry clay with any smooth tool to polish it, tighten the clay surface, and compress the clay particles.

Calcine (calcining)   To heat a substance to a high temperature, but below its melting point, causing loss of moisture.

Caliper   An instrument used to measure the inside and outside diameter of an object.

Casting   The process of forming pottery or sculpture by pouring liquid clay (slip) into absorbent plaster or, historically, into terra cotta molds.

Celadon   The western name for a type of glaze first used in China on stoneware and porcelain in an attempt to imitate the color and texture of jade. Its colors, ranging from shades of green to gray-green tones, depend on the percentage of iron it contains. Historically, celadon has been fired in a reducing atmosphere, but celadon colors may now be attained in an electric kiln.

Centering   The act of forcing a lump of clay by hand into a symmetrical form at the center of a spinning potter's wheel in preparation for throwing pottery.

Centrifugal force   The force that tends to impel an object or material outward from the center of rotation. It acts on the clay while it rotates on a potter's wheel, and the action of the potter's hands in conjunction with this force causes the walls to rise.

Ceramic-fiber   Refractory materials developed for the space exploration program. When exposed to the heat range for which each one is designed, they reflect heat and are resistant to thermal shock, are light in weight, and are excellent insulating materials. Used for kiln insulation.

Ceramic-fiber rigidizer   A liquid that can be applied to ceramic fiber to harden the surface, make it more rigid, and help eliminate the dust that it releases when handled. There is also a form of ceramic-fiber cement that will stiffen the material even more when applied to the surface.

Ceramics   Objects made from earthy materials with the aid of heat, or the process of making these objects.

Chambered kiln   A type of kiln developed in the Orient, built on a slope with several separate firing chambers opening into each other. Sometimes called a climbing kiln.

China   A term usually applied to any white ware fired at a low porcelain temperature. It was developed in Europe to compete with the expensive imported Chinese porcelain.

China clay   Primary clay, or kaolin, that is white, refractory, and not very plastic.

China paint   An opaque overglaze paint that is fired onto already-fired glazed ware at various low-range temperatures. Because of the low temperatures used, colors like red or orange do not burn out. Sometimes called overglaze enamel.

China paint medium   A substance in which china paint pigment is ground so that it can be applied like paint. China paint may have either an oil or water base.

Chinoiserie   Decoration used in eighteenth-century Europe inspired by the newly imported Chinese crafts. The motifs were used on furniture, china, and other objects.

Clay   A variety of earthy materials formed by the decomposition of granite. In the process, these may have been combined with a variety of other materials, forming clay bodies with differing maturing points. See also **primary clay** and **secondary clay.**

Clay body   See **body.**

Coiling   A method of forming pottery or sculpture from rolls of clay melded together to create the walls.

CMC   A synthetic **gum** used as a binder for pigments.

Compressed air   See **air compressor.**

Cone   See **Pyrometric cone.**

Cornish stone (Cornwall stone)   A feldspathic material found in England, containing silica and various fluxes. Similar to the Chinese *petuntze* used in the first porcelains.

Crackle glaze   A glaze with deliberate crazing that forms a decorative surface. Color may be rubbed into the cracks to emphasize them or the ware may be soaked in tea or coffee.

Crawling Crawling is characterized by bare, unglazed areas on fired ceramic ware alternating with thickened glazed areas. Usually caused by surface tension in the molten glaze pulling it away from areas of grease or dust on the surface of the bisque ware. Also may occur in glaze applied over underglazed areas, or low-fire glaze containing gum applied to high-fire porcelain bisque, or through use of a glaze solution containing too much gum.

Crazing Unintentional cracks that occur over the entire glaze surface because the glaze expands and contracts more than the clay body to which it is applied. Caused by improper "fit" of glaze to clay.

Crystalline glazes Glazes in which crystals are formed, causing the light to reflect. Large crystals may be caused to grow, creating a deliberately sought decorative effect. Slow cooling helps to produce crystals in glazes that are low in alumina.

Cuenca An Hispano-Moresque technique in which designs for tiles or pottery were impressed into damp clay, forming ridges that acted as barriers between glaze colors, keeping them from running into each other.

Cuerda seca A technique used by Hispano-Moresque potters in which they drew lines around the designs on tiles or pottery, using a mixture of manganese and grease. This barrier kept the multicolored glazes from melding together and provided a dark outline to the areas.

Decal An image or design printed with ceramic material on a special paper so that it can be transferred to bisque ware or glazed surface and fired to permanency.

Deflocculant Material such as sodium carbonate or sodium silicate, used in slip for casting to aid in maintaining the fluidity of the slip. Less water is needed to produce a slip containing deflocculant, thus less shrinkage will occur in drying the cast object. See Appendix 4A.

Die A pattern made of steel, acrylic, or wood for cutting or stamping clay, or pressing it through an **extruder** in order to produce the desired form.

Dipping Applying glaze or slip to the body by immersing the piece and shaking off excess glaze.

Dispersion blender A type of high speed (vortex) blender useful in mixing glazes. Reduces glaze particle size and blends glaze more thoroughly and efficiently than traditional propeller blades.

Drape mold A support (such as a stretched cloth, a wooden frame, or rope network) in or over which a clay slab is draped to shape as it stiffens. The term is also sometimes used for a **hump mold** over which slabs of clay are stiffened.

Draw To take fired ware from the kiln.

Drill For drilling holes in ceramics, a carbide tip drill bit will penetrate soft bisque. For high-fired ceramics, use a diamond core drill bit with water. See Appendix 4A.

Dunting The cracking of pots during cooling, caused by too-rapid cooling of the kiln, by drafts reaching the ware as it cools in the kiln, or by removing the ware from the kiln before it is cool enough.

Earthenware Pottery that has been fired at low temperature (below cone 2) and is porous and relatively soft. Usually red or brown in color. Used worldwide for domestic ware, glazed or unglazed.

Electrolyte A substance, usually alkaline, that changes the electrical charges in clay particles so that they repel rather than attract each other, thus maintaining them in suspension in water. See **deflocculant** and Appendix 1B.

Enamels Low-temperature opaque or translucent glazes that are usually painted over higher fired glazed surfaces. More commonly called **china paints.**

Engobe Originally, the term referred to slip that is applied over the entire surface of a piece of pottery or sculpture to change the color and/or texture of the clay body. The term now often refers to slip used for decoration.

Epoxy An adhesive made from a thermosetting resin. Often used in ceramic repair. May be colored with a variety of coloring additives. Ultraviolet light may affect the color over an extended period of time. See Appendix 4C.

Eutetic A combination of two or more ceramic materials whose melting point when combined is always lower than that of any one of the materials used alone.

Extruder A mechanical aid for forming moist clay by pressing it through a **die.** This causes the clay to take the shape of the die. Extruders can form clay quickly into many forms, from tubes to tiles to sewer pipes.

Faience From the French name for the Italian town Faenza, where much tin-glazed earthenware (maiolica ware) was made. Frequently a general term for any pottery made with a colored, low-fire clay body covered with opaque base glaze and decorated with colored glazes.

Feathering A method of making a decorative feather pattern with slip or glaze.

Feldspar Any of a group of common rock-forming minerals containing silicates of aluminum, along with potassium, sodium, calcium, and occasionally barium. Used extensively in stoneware and porcelain bodies and in glazes as a flux. Feldspars melt at a range of temperatures between 2192°F/

1200°C and 2372°F/1300°C depending on their composition. See Appendix 1D.

Ferric oxide and **ferrous oxide**   The red and black iron oxides that produce reddish and brown colors in clay bodies and glazes, as well as acting as fluxes. They also produce the greens of celadon glazes when fired in a reducing atmosphere. See Appendix 1E.

Fettle   The thin extrusion of clay left on a slip-cast form at the line where the mold sections were joined.

Fettling knife   A long, tapered knife used for trimming clay, and removing the **fettle** from a cast.

Fiber glass   A material consisting of glass fibers in resin. Sometimes called spun glass, it is used as an additive to clay bodies to strengthen them, or as a reinforcing material in a matrix of epoxy or resin applied to sculpture after firing.

Firebox   The part of the kiln into which fuel is introduced and where combustion takes place.

Fire clays (refractory clays)   Clays that withstand high temperatures. Used in kiln bricks and also as ingredients in stoneware bodies or in clay bodies for handbuilding or sculpture.

Firing   Heating pottery or sculpture in a kiln or open fire to bring the clay or glaze to maturity. The temperature needed to mature a specific clay or glaze varies.

Fit   The adjustment of the glaze composition to the composition of a clay body so that it will adhere to the surface of the ware.

Flambé glaze   A high-fire red and purple-red glaze produced by firing copper in a reducing atmosphere.

Flocculant   A material, such as calcium chloride or hydrated magnesium sulfate (Epsom salts), that aids in keeping clay particles together. Used in suspension of glazes or for thinning slip. See Appendix 1B.

Flues   The passageways in a kiln designed to carry the heat from the chamber to the chimney or vent.

Flux   A substance that lowers the melting point of another substance. Oxides such as those of iron, sodium, potassium, calcium, zinc, lead, boric oxide and others that combine with the silica and other heat-resistant materials in a glaze, helping them to fuse.

Foot   The base of a piece of pottery. Usually left unglazed in high-fired ware; occasionally glazed in low-fire, in which case the ware must be put on stilts to keep it from sticking to the shelf.

Frit (Fritt)   A glaze material that is formed when any of several soluble materials are melted together with insoluble materials, cooled rapidly, and splintered in cold water, then ground into a powder.

This renders them less soluble and less likely to release toxic materials. Feldspar is a natural frit.

Galena   Lead sulfide, formerly used in Europe to glaze earthenware. No longer used because of its toxicity.

Gesso   A mixture of plaster and gum used as a base for painting.

Glaze   Any vitreous coating that has been melted onto a clay surface by the use of heat. Made of fine-ground minerals that, when fired to a certain temperature, fuse into a glassy coating. Glazes may be matt or glossy, depending on their components.

Glaze firing (also glost firing)   The firing during which glaze materials melt and form a vitreous coating on the clay body surface.

Glaze stain   Commercial blends formulated with various coloring oxides that produce a wide range of colors when used in glazes or clay bodies.

Glost   Ware that has been glazed. *Glost firing* is another term for glaze firing.

Greenware   Unfired pottery or sculpture.

Grog   Crushed or ground particles of fired clay graded in various sizes of particles. Added to the clay body to help in drying, to add texture, and to reduce shrinkage and warpage.

Gum   A viscous material, such as gum tragacanth, that is exuded from certain trees, or a chemically formulated substance; used as a binder for pigments. See Appendix 1A.

Hard paste   True porcelain made of a clay body containing kaolin, traditionally fired between 2370° to 2640°F/1300° to 1450°C. It is white, vitrified, and translucent. See **porcelain.**

Hematite   Iron oxide (Fe_2O_3) used as coloring on much early pottery.

High-fire   Describes clays or glazes that are fired from cone 2 on up to cone 10 or 13. Ware fired at cone 2 and up is usually considered to be **stoneware.**

Hispano-Moresque   Term used to describe tin-lead glazed earthenware produced in Spain in the Middle Ages. Frequently decorated with luster, its style exhibited influences from both Islam and Christian Europe.

Hump mold   A mold of plaster or terra cotta, or a found object such as a rounded rock, an upended bowl or a bag of sand, foam padding or crumpled newspaper over which a slab of clay can be laid to shape as it stiffens.

Hydrometer   An instrument that determines specific gravity. In ceramics, used to monitor the proportion of water in a slip or a glaze.

In-glaze decoration   Decoration applied on top of a glaze before firing. The colors ink into the glaze during firing.

Ione grain   Hard, fired kaolin clay that has been crushed to various mesh sizes. White to grayish, its sharp particle shape adds tooth to clay bodies. Used for handbuilding and wheel clay bodies. Increases workability and strength, and reduces shrinkage in proportion to the amount added.

Jiggering   A method of forming multiples rapidly. Soft clay is placed in a mold, pressed into or onto the mold walls either mechanically or by hand, then trimmed to size by hand or with a **jolley.** The Greeks and Romans used hand-jiggering methods to make utilitarian ware, and potters today use modifications of this method. Mechanical jiggering is used in ceramics factories. In industry, kerosene is used as a lubricant instead of water.

Jolley   The mechanical arm and template used to shape clay as it turns on a jigger machine or on a potter's wheel.

Kaolin   (Also called **china clay.**)   A white-firing natural clay that withstands high temperatures. An essential ingredient in porcelain, its presence in large quantities in China allowed the potters there to develop their fine white porcelain.

Kaowool   Trademark of an insulating material for kilns. See **ceramic-fiber materials.**

Keramos   A Greek word meaning *earthenware*, from which our term *ceramics* is derived.

Kiln   A furnace or oven built of heat-resistant materials for firing pottery or sculpture, sometimes referred to as a *kil*.

Kiln flues   See **flues** and Appendix 4A.

Kiln furniture   Heat-resistant shelves, posts, and slabs that support the ware in the kiln during firing. Kiln shelves may warp in firing if they are not well supported.

Kiln hood   The metal hood containing a venting system permanently built over a kiln or lowered over a kiln during firing to exhaust the heat and gases that are released from clays and glazes during firing. It is extremely important that all kilns be vented properly and to building codes.

Kiln wash   A coating of refractory materials (half flint and half kaolin) painted onto the kiln floor and the top side of shelves to keep the melting glaze from fusing the ware onto the shelves.

Latex   An emulsion of rubber or plastic material with water. Used in ceramics as a resist material in applying glazes; also a material for making flexible molds for plaster, wax, or concrete casting.

Lead   Until recently lead was used extensively in a variety of forms as a flux for low- or medium-temperature glazes. Although the dangers of handling toxic lead were known quite early, it solubility in acid foods and liquids was not understood until comparatively recently. Lead glazes should not be used on food containers. See Appendix 1E.

Leather-hard   The condition of a clay body when much of the moisture has evaporated and shrinkage has just ended, but the clay is not totally dry. Carving, burnishing, or joining slabs are often done at this stage.

Low-fire   The range of firing of clays and glazes in which the kiln temperature reached is usually in the cone 015 to cone 1 range.

Luster (lustre)   A thin film of metallic salts usually, although not always, applied to a glazed surface, then refired at a low temperature in reduction. Modern luster mediums include a reducing material, so no further reduction is necessary, but the early lusters developed in Persia and brought to Europe by the Moors required a reducing atmosphere in the kiln to develop their characteristic sheen.

Luster resist   A special water-base resist material used like **wax resist** for luster resist decoration.

Luting   The method of joining two parts of a still-damp clay object. Used for constructing both pottery and sculpture, especially large objects that cannot be made in one piece.

Maiolica (Majolica)   The Italian name for tin-glaze ware that was sent from Spain to Italy via the island of Majorca. Later, local styles of decoration were developed in Italian pottery towns such as Faenza and Deruta. Now a general term for any earthenware covered with a tin-lead glaze.

Matt glaze   A glaze that has a dull, non-glossy finish due to its deliberate composition. Barium carbonate (toxic) or alumina added to the glaze, along with a slow cooling, assists the formation of matt glazes.

Maturing point (maturity)   Refers to the temperature and time in firing at which a clay or glaze reaches the desired condition of hardness and density. Both clays and glazes have differing maturing points, depending on their composition.

Model   The original form in clay, plaster, wood, plastic, metal or other material from which a mold is made.

Mold   Any form that can be used to shape fluid or plastic substances. In ceramics, usually the negative form from which pottery or sculpture can be cast by pouring or pressing methods using either liquid slip or damp clay. Molds can be made in one piece or in multiple sections. See also **hump mold.**

Molochite   Crushed, fired white porcelain. Added to clay bodies, it assists in reducing shrinkage, cracking, and warping.

Muffle   A kiln, or section of a kiln, in which ceramics can be fired without direct contact with the flame.

Mullite   An additive material available in raw or **cal-**

cined form. Acting as a heavy-duty refractory, it aids in producing strong clay bodies with high resistance to thermal shock, cracking, warping, or other deformations.

Mullite crystals   Crystals of aluminum silicate that start to form in clay as it is fired between 1850° and 2200°F/1010° and 1204°C. These crystals strengthen stoneware and porcelain when fully developed at high temperatures and also help in the interaction that unites high-fire glazes and high-fire clay bodies.

Neutral atmosphere   The point at which the atmosphere in a kiln is balanced between oxidation and reduction.

Neutrals   Materials that are neutral and can react as either an acid or a base. Also called *amphoteric*, they are represented in glaze calculation by the symbol R_2O_3. See Appendix 3B.

Nylon fiber   Synthetic fiber added to a clay body for strength.

Opacifier   A material that causes a glaze to become opaque by producing minute crystals. Tin, zirconium, and titanium oxides are used as opacifiers in combination with various oxides. See Appendix 1F.

Open firing   Firing that is not done in an enclosed kiln.

Over-fire   To fire a clay body or glaze above its maturing point.

Overglaze   A low-temperature ceramic enamel painted on a previously glazed and fired surface, then fired for a second time at a lower temperature, usually as the final firing process. Bright colors like red and orange that would burn out at high temperatures will be maintained in the lower firing (around 1300°F/705°C). Often called **enamel** or **china paint.**

Oxidation (oxidizing firing)   The firing of a kiln or open fire with complete combustion so that the firing atmosphere contains enough oxygen to allow the metals in clays and glazes to produce their oxide colors. Electric kilns always produce oxidizing firings unless reducing materials are added. Bright and clear low-fire colors are often associated with glazes and clays fired in an oxidation atmosphere.

Oxide   A combination of an element with oxygen. In ceramics, oxides are used in formulating glazes and for coloring glazes and clays. They are also used for decorating ware.

Parallel-flue kiln   A rectangular kiln used by Roman and later potters in which parallel flues were placed under the perforated floor.

Peephole   A hole in the door or wall of a kiln through which the ceramist can watch the pyrometric cones, the color of heat in the kiln, and the process of the firing. (Always wear goggles of the proper shade (#3 to #5) when peering into a kiln through a peephole.)

Petuntze   A type of feldspar rock in China from which, with kaolin, the Chinese formed their porcelains. In Europe and the United States it is called Cornish stone, Cornwall stone, or china stone.

Piece mold   A mold for casting that is made in sections so that it can be removed easily from the cast object without distortion. Generally used to cast an object that has undercuts and that therefore can not be removed from a one-piece mold.

Pinholes   Small holes in a glaze caused by the bursting of blisters formed by gases as they escape through the glaze during firing.

Pithos (plural, *pithoi*)   A Greek term for a large storage jar made of earthenware.

Plastic clay   See **Plasticity.**

Plasticity   The ability of a damp clay body to yield under pressure without cracking and to retain the formed shape after the pressure is released.

Porcelain   A translucent, nonabsorbent body fired at high temperature. White and hard, it was first developed in China. Traditionally fired in the 2370° to 2640°F/1300° to 1450°C range, some porcelain bodies have been developed that mature in the 2230 to 2340°F/1220° to 1280°C range.

Pottery   Originally a term for earthenware, now loosely used to refer to any type of ceramic ware, as well as to the workshop where it is made.

Press mold   Any mold made from plaster, fired clay, or a found object into which damp clay can be pressed to reproduce the shape of the mold.

Primary clay   Clay found in nature that was formed in place rather than transported by the action of water. Also called residual clay. Kaolin is a primary clay.

Proto-porcelain (proto-porcelaneous)   Refers to an early high-fire ware developed in China as kilns became more efficient and capable of reaching higher temperatures. It preceded true porcelain.

Pug mill   A machine used to blend clay into a moist, workable consistency. Also used to recycle clay scraps and, when equipped with a vacuum pump system, to de-air clay.

Pyrometer   A device for measuring and recording the exact interior temperature of a kiln throughout the firing and cooling process.

Pyrometric cones   Small pyramids of ceramic materials formulated to bend over and melt at designated temperatures. Orton cones in the United States and Seger cones in England and Europe have different ranges. In addition to the brown and white Orton cones that range from cone 022 to cone 42 (for industrial use), there are now cones that contain color coding to avoid confusion. See Appendix 2A.

Quartz inversion point The point at which the silica crystals in clay change in structure and volume during the rise and fall of the temperature in the kiln. This development influences the fit of glaze to clay body.

Raku Originally a name used by a Japanese family that has made tea ceremony ware since the seventeenth century. Now refers to both the process of raku firing and to ware glazed in such a firing. Soft and porous, traditional raku ware was lead-glazed, placed in a red-hot kiln, and quickly withdrawn when the glaze melted. In the West, lead is now rarely used in raku glazes. Leadless frits and Gerstley borate are now commonly used fluxes in place of lead. Raku ware is often reduced after firing by burying it in straw, sawdust, paper, or other combustible material, then covering it with an airtight lid to create a reducing atmosphere that aids in producing luster or opalescent colors.

Raw glaze Glaze that does not contain fritted material.

Reduction (reducing firing, reduction atmosphere) A firing in which insufficient air is supplied to the kiln for complete combustion. Under these conditions, the carbon monoxide in the kiln combines with the oxygen in the oxides of the clay body and glaze, causing the oxides to change color. Commonly associated with high-fire stoneware, porcelain, raku, and lusters.

Refractory Resistance to heat and melting. Refractory materials are used in porcelain and stoneware. Also used for building kilns and kiln furniture, and in combination with other materials, as kiln insulation.

Reserve A technique of painting *around* an area, reserving it so that it remains the color of the clay body or glaze while the painted area around it fires a different color. Used on Greek red-figure ware, and still in use today, as when using a stencil to mask areas.

Resist A method of applying a covering material such as wax, latex, or special luster resist to bisque or glazed ware, then coating the piece with a glaze or a second glaze. The resist material will not accept the glaze so that on firing, the color of the covered area will remain intact.

Roulette A carved or textured wheel that imprints repeated motifs or texture when run over a damp clay surface.

Saggar A refractory container in which glazed ware is placed during firing to protect it from the kiln fire. Saggers are also used to introduce local reducing material by placing leaves, seaweed, cow dung or other organic material in the sagger with the ware.

Salt glaze A glaze formed by introducing salt into a hot kiln. The vaporized salt combines with the silica in the clay body, forming a sodium silicate glaze on the surface. It also combines with the silica in the kiln bricks, coating them with a glaze that will be transferred to any ware fired in the kiln later. Salt glazing releases noxious and toxic fumes.

Sandblasting A method of etching the surface of a fired object or kiln shelves by directing a blast of air carrying fine sand onto the surface at high velocity. Since sand is largely silica and is extremely harmful to the lungs, aluminum oxide is a recommended substitute. Use a sand blasting booth or wear a supplied air respirator that covers your head.

Sang de boeuf The French name for the oxblood red glazes of China.

Sealers See Appendix 4A.

Secondary clay Natural clay that has been moved by water or wind from its source and settled elsewhere in deposits.

Setting Placing the ware in the kiln in preparation for firing.

Sgraffito Decoration of pottery made by scratching through a layer of colored slip to the differently colored clay body underneath.

Shard A broken piece of pottery. From these fragments, archaeologists can learn much about ancient cultures.

Shivering The flaking off of slivers of glaze due to poor glaze fit, frequently due to greater shrinkage of the clay body than the glaze.

Short Clay that is not plastic. Cracks will form on handling after brief manipulation.

Shrink ruler A scale ruler used to calculate the percent of shrinkage of clay during firing.

Sieve A utensil of wire mesh (usually brass to resist rust) used to strain liquids or powdered materials. See Appendix 4A for sizes of mesh used in ceramics.

Silica Oxide of silicon, SiO_2. Found in nature as quartz or flint sand, it is the most common of all ceramic materials. See Appendix 1E.

Silicate of soda A solution of sodium silicate that is used as a **deflocculant** to help in the suspension of clay materials in slip.

Silicon carbide Used in a glaze (as 3-F powder) to produce local reduction in an electric kiln. Also used in making kiln furniture for high-fire ware.

Silk-screening The process of transferring an image to a surface by forcing paint through a fine screening material, such as silk or polyester, on which a stencil of the image has been applied. In ceramics, it is generally used for applying china paint.

Sintering   The stage in glaze firing during which the heat converts a powder into a cohesive mass before melting it into a glassy material.

Slab roller   A mechanical device for rolling out slabs to a set, consistent thickness.

Slaking   The process of chemically combining a material, such as plaster, with water.

Slip   A suspension of clay in water used for casting pottery or sculpture in molds. Slip (sometimes called **engobe**) can also be used for painted decoration or for the **sgraffito** technique. Often contains sodium silicate "N" and soda ash, or Darvan #7, to help keep the particles in suspension and for fluidity.

Slip casting   Forming objects by pouring slip into a plaster mold. The mold absorbs the water in the slip so that solid clay walls are formed to create a positive of the original.

Slip glaze   A glaze that contains a large proportion of clay. Generally one that contains enough flux to form a glaze with few or no additives. Albany slip was widely used as slip glaze in traditional American potteries. Substitutes now offered to replace it are Sheffield (Massachusetts) and Seattle slip clays.

Slip trailer   A rubber syringe used to apply decorations of slip on ware.

Soaking   Maintaining a certain temperature in the kiln for a period of time to achieve heat saturation.

Sodate retarder   A material that can be added to plaster (in proportions of ¼ to 2 teaspoons to 100 pounds of plaster) to slow its setting time by ten minutes to an hour.

Soft paste   A porcelain body that fires at a lower temperature than true porcelain.

Soluble   Capable of being dissolved in a fluid.

Spray booth   A ventilated booth that removes chemicals and fumes from the air so that the worker does not inhale them while spraying glazes, underglazes, or overglazes.

Spray gun   A gun-like device through which compressed air passes, forcing the substance into a fine mist for application. Used for spraying glazes.

Sprigging   The process of attaching low-relief decorations of damp clay onto already-formed greenware.

Stilts   Triangular supports with either clay (for low-fire) or heat-resistant metal points (for low- or high-fire), used to support pieces of glazed pottery during glaze firing. They support the ware above the shelves to keep the glaze from sticking the ware

to the shelf. Small stilt marks can be filed, sanded or ground smooth.

Stoneware   A type of clay body fired to a temperature at which the body becomes vitrified, dense, and nonabsorptive, but not translucent. Natural stoneware clay is usually brownish in color because of the presence of iron, but there are formulated white stoneware bodies. Usually matures at temperatures above 2192°F/1200°C.

Temper   Any material, such as sand, mica, or crushed fired pottery fragments (**grog**), added to a clay body to make it more porous, and less likely to shrink and warp.

Template   A wooden, metal, or plastic pattern used as a guide for shaping clay. A template can be used on the inside or outside of a pot as it turns on the wheel, in a process called **jiggering.**

Tenmoku (temmoku)   High-fired, saturated iron glaze; black, brown, and yellowish. Used by the Chinese and Japanese, especially on tea ware. Still a popular glaze.

Terra-cotta   A low-fire, porous, reddish clay body, frequently containing grog or other temper. Used throughout history for common, utilitarian ware; also used for sculpture.

Terra sigillata   A fine slip glaze used by the Greeks, Etruscans, and Romans to coat their pottery. It fired black or red according to the kiln atmosphere. Now used in a wide variety of colors by many potters and sculptors to surface their ware or sculpture.

Thermal shock   The stress to which ceramic material is subjected when sudden changes occur in the heat during firing or cooling.

Throwing   Forming objects on the potter's wheel using a clay body with plastic qualities (see **plasticity**).

Tin enamel   A low-fire overglaze containing tin.

Tin glaze   A low-fire, opaque glaze containing tin oxide.

Trailing   A method of decorating in which a slip or glaze is squeezed out of a syringe. Historically, decoration trailed from a quill inserted in a narrow-necked clay cup.

Undercut   A negative space in a solid form, creating an overhang. Casting a form with undercutting requires a multipart mold in order to release the mold from the cast.

Underfire   To fire clay or glaze—accidentally or deliberately—to a point below its maturing point. Underfiring can turn a normally glossy glaze into a matt surface.

Viscosity   The ability to resist running or flow. A glaze must have enough viscosity to avoid flowing off the ware when it is melted under heat. China clay in a glaze assists in stabilizing it.

Vitreous Pertaining to or having the nature of glass. In ceramics, a vitreous glaze or clay body has been fired to a dense, hard, and nonabsorbent condition. High-fire glazes vitrify and combine with the glassy particles that form in the high-fire clay body as it approaches vitrification. This results in a glaze that is united with the clay body as compared to a low-fire glaze that merely coats the surface of the fired clay.

Ware A general term applied to any ceramic—earthenware, stoneware, or porcelain—in the green, bisqued, or fired state.

Warping Changes in the form of a clay body. Warping of ware can occur during drying or firing if the walls are built unevenly or if drying or firing is uneven or ware is improperly supported during firing.

Waster (kiln waster) A piece of pottery discarded due to slumping, warping, or breaking in the kiln. Many wasters have been found during excavations at ceramic sites such as Faenza, Italy, or early New England potteries, helping archaeologists date styles and types of ware.

Wax resist A method of decoration in which melted wax or oil emulsion is painted onto the clay body or onto a glazed piece. See **resist.**

Wedging Any one of various methods of kneading a mass of clay to expel the air, get rid of lumps, and prepare a homogenous material.

Wedging table A table of plaster, wood, or concrete, often covered with canvas, on which clay can be wedged. A stretched wire attached to the table allows one to cut the clay to check for air bubbles, lumps, or lack of homogeneity.

Further Reading

PERIODICALS
General

American Ceramics. 15 West 44th St., New York, N.Y. 10036.

Ceramica. Apartado 70008, Acacias 9, Madrid, Spain.

Ceramic Review. 21 Carnaby St., London, W1V1PH, England.

Ceramics Monthly. 1609 Northwest Blvd., Columbus, Ohio 43212.

Crafts Magazine. 8 Waterloo Place, London SW1Y4AT, England.

La Revue de la Céramique. 61 Rue Marconi, 62880 Vendin-le-Vieil, France.

L'Atelier des Métiers d'Art. 18 Rue Wurtz, Paris, France.

New Zealand Potter. Box 12-162, Wellington, New Zealand.

Pottery in Australia. 48 Burton St., Darlinghurst, 2010, NSW, Australia.

Studio Potter. P.O. Box 172, Warner, N.H. 03278.

Health and Safety

Art Hazard News. Center for Occupational Hazards, 5 Beekman St., New York, N.Y. 10038.

BOOKS: PART 1
SHAPING THE PAST
General

Charleston, Robert J. *World Ceramics*. New York: McGraw-Hill, 1968.

Cooper, Emanuel. *A History of World Pottery*. 2d ed. New York: Larousse, 1981/England: Batsford.

Kingery, David W., and Vandiver, Pamela. *Ceramic Masterpieces: Art, Structure and Technology*. New York: Free Press, 1986.

Rice, Prudence M. *Pots and Potters: Current Approaches in Ceramic Archaeology*. Los Angeles: University of California Press Institute of Archaeology, 1984.

Savage, George. *Porcelain Through the Ages*. Baltimore, Md.: & Harmondsworth, England: Penguin, 1954.

The Mediterranean World

Near East

Hodges, Henry. *Technology in the Ancient World*. New York: Knopf, 1970.

Kingery, W. D., ed. *Ceramics and Civilization: Technology and Style*. Columbus: American Ceramic Society, 1985.

Mellaart, James. *Earliest Civilizations of the Near East*. New York: McGraw-Hill, 1966.

Greece, Rome, Etruria

Bendel, Otto J. *Etruscan Art*. Harmondsworth, England and New York: Penguin, 1978.

Bibke, Joseph V. *The Techniques of Painted Attic Pottery*. New York: Watson-Guptill, 1965.

Boardman, John. *Athenian Black-Figure Vases*. London, New York, Toronto: Oxford University Press, 1975.

Herbert, S. *The Red Figure Pottery*. Athens: American School of Classical Studies, 1977.

Peacock, D. P. S. *Pottery in the Roman World*. New York: Longman, 1982.

Europe and England

Barton, K. J. *Pottery in England from 3500 B.C.–A.D. 1730*. South Brunswick/New York: Barnes, 1975.

Brears, Peter C. D. *The English Country Pottery. Its History and Techniques*. Rutland, Vt.: Tuttle.

Guidotti, Ravanelli Carmen. *Ceramiche Occidentali del Museo Civico Medievale di Bologna*. Bologna: Museo Civico Medievale, 1985.

Lewis, Griselda. *A Collector's History of English Pottery*. New York: Viking, 1970.

Liverani, Guiseppe. *Five Centuries of Italian Majolica*. New York: McGraw-Hill, 1960.

Neuwirth, Waltraud. *Wiener Werkstatte Keramik: Origi-*

nal Ceramics, 1920–31. Cincinnati: Seven Hills, 1981.

Ramié, Georges. *Ceramics of Picasso.* Poughkeepsie, N.Y.: Apollo.

The Orient

Koyana, Fujio, and Figges, John. *Two Thousand Years of Oriental Ceramics.* New York: Abrams, 1961.

China

Hetherington, A., and Hobson, R. L. *The Art of the Chinese Potter.* Magnolia, Mass.: Peter Smith, 1983.

Medley, Margaret. *The Chinese Potter.* Ithaca, N.Y.: Cornell University Press, 1982.

———. *Yuan Porcelain and Stoneware.* London: Faber & Faber, 1974.

Korea

d'Argencé, Réne-Yvon Lefebvre, ed. *5000 Years of Korean Art.* Asian Art Museum of San Francisco, 1979.

Asia Society. *The Art of the Korean Potter: Silla, Koryo, Yi.* New York: Asia Society, 1968.

Japan

Cort, Louise. *Shigaraki Potter's Valley.* New York: Kodansha, 1980.

Jenyns, Soame. *Japanese Pottery.* London: Faber & Faber, London, 1960; New York: Praeger, 1971.

Leach, Bernard. *Hamada, Potter.* New York: Kodansha, 1975.

———. *A Potter in Japan.* London: Faber & Faber, 1960.

Munsterberg, Hugo. *The Ceramic Art of Japan.* Rutland, Vt.: Tuttle, 1964.

Peterson, Susan. *Shoji Hamada: A Potter's Way and Work.* New York: Kodansha, 1984.

Rhodes, Daniel. *Tamba Potter: The Timeless Art of a Japanese Village.* New York: Kodansha, 1982.

Saint-Giles, Amaury. *Earth 'n 'Fire: A Survey Guide to Contemporary Japanese Ceramics.* Tokyo: Shufunotomo, 1981.

Sanders, Herbert H., and Tomimoto, Kenkichi. *The World of Japanese Ceramics.* Tokyo: Kodansha, 1983.

Islam

Atil, Esin. *Ceramics from the World of Islam.* Washington, D.C.: Freer Gallery of Art, 1973.

Caiger-Smith, Alan. *Lustre Pottery: Technique, Tradition and Innovation in Islam and the Western World.* London: Faber & Faber, 1985.

Mitsukuni, Yoshida. *In Search of Persian Pottery.* New York: Weatherhill, 1972.

Wilkinson, Charles K. *Iranian Ceramics.* New York: Asia House, 1963.

———, ed. *Nishapur, Pottery of the Early Islamic Period.* New York: Metropolitan Museum of Art, 1974.

India

Philadelphia Museum of Art. *Unknown India. Ritual Art in Tribe and Village.* Philadelphia, Pa.: Philadelphia Museum of Art, 1968.

Singh, Gurcharan. *Pottery in India.* New York: Advent, 1979.

Africa

Cardew, Michael. *Pioneer Pottery.* New York: St. Martin's, 1976.

Clark, C., and Wagner, L. *Potters of Southern Africa.* New York: Hacker, 1974.

d'Azevedo, Warren L., ed. *The Traditional Artist in African Societies.* Bloomington: University of Indiana Press, 1973.

Fagg, William, and Picton, John. *The Potter's Art in Africa.* London: The British Museum, 1970.

Gardi, Rene. *African Crafts and Craftsmen.* New York: Van Nostrand Reinhold, 1969.

Gebauer, Paul. *Art of Cameroon.* Portland and New York: Portland Art Museum and Metropolitan Museum of Art, 1979.

Wahlman, Maude. *Contemporary African Arts.* Chicago: Field Museum of Natural History, 1974.

The Americas

MesoAmerica and South America

Bushnell, Geoffrey H. *Ancient Arts of the Americas.* New York: Praeger, 1965.

Lackey, Luana M. *The Pottery of Acatlan: A Changing Mexican Tradition.* Tucson: University of Arizona Press, 1982.

Litto, Gertrude. *South American Folk Pottery.* New York: Watson-Guptill, 1976.

Monti, Franco. *Precolumbian Terracottas.* New York: Hamlyn, 1969.

North America

Brody, J.; Scott, Catherine J.; and Le Blanc, Steven A. *Mimbres Pottery: Ancient Art of the American Southwest.* New York: Hudson Hills, 1983.

Harlow, Francis, H., and Frank, Larry. *Historic Pueblo Indian Pottery*. Santa Fe: Museum of New Mexico, 1967.

Lister, Robert H., and Lister, Florence C. *Anasazi Pottery*. Albuquerque: University of New Mexico Press, 1978.

Peterson, Susan. *The Living Tradition of Maria Martinez*. New York: Kodansha, 1981.

The United States

Barber, Edwin Atlee. *Tulip Ware of the Pennsylvania–German Potters*. New York: Dover Publications, Inc., 1970.

Barret, Richard Carter. *Bennington Pottery and Porcelain*. New York: Crown, 1958.

Blasberg, Robert W., and Carpenter, J. W. *George Ohr and His Biloxi Art Pottery*. Port Jarvis, N.Y.: J. W. Carpenter, 1973.

Burrison, John. *Brothers in Clay: The Story of Georgia Folk Pottery*. Athens: University of Georgia Press, 1983.

Clark, Garth. *American Potters: The Work of Twenty Modern Masters*. New York: Watson-Guptill, 1981.

Clark, Garth, and Hughto, Margie. *A Century of Ceramics in the United States 1878–1978*. New York: Dutton and Everson Museum of Art, 1981.

Ferriday, Virginia Guest. *Last of the Handmade Buildings: Glazed Terra Cotta in Downtown Portland*. Portland: Mark Publishing, 1984.

Ferris, William. *Afro-American Folk Arts and Crafts*. Boston: Hall, 1983.

Greer, Georgeanna H. *American Stoneware: The Art and Craft of Utilitarian Potters*. West Chester, Pa.: Schiffer, 1981.

Henzke, Lucile. *Art Pottery of America*. West Chester, Pa.: Schiffer, 1982.

Levin, Elaine. *The History of American Ceramics*. New York: Abrams, 1988.

Poor, Henry Varnum. *A Book of Pottery: From Mud into Immortality*. Englewood Cliffs, N.J.: Prentice-Hall, 1958.

Sweesy, Nancy. *Raised in Clay*. Washington, D.C.: Smithsonian Institution Press, 1984.

Vlach, John. *The Afro-American Tradition in Decorative Arts*. Cleveland, Ohio: Cleveland Museum of Art, 1978.

Watkins, Lura Woodsie. *New England Potters and Their Wares*. Cambridge, Mass.: Harvard University Press, 1968.

Webster, Donald Blake. *Decorated Stoneware Pottery of North America*. Rutland, Vt.: Tuttle, 1970.

Zug, Charles G., III. *Turners and Burners: The Folk Potters of North Carolina*. Chapel Hill: University of North Carolina Press, 1986.

BOOKS: PART 2
SHAPING THE PRESENT
General and Aesthetics

Anderson, Bruce, and Hoare, John. *Clay Statements: Contemporary Australian Pottery*. Darling Downs Institute Press, Australia, 1985.

Axel, Jan, and McCreary, Karen. *Porcelain: Traditions and New Visions*. New York: Watson-Guptill, 1981.

Berensohn, Paulus. *Finding One's Way With Clay*. New York: Simon & Schuster, 1972.

Birks-Hay, Tony. *Art of the Modern Potter*. New York: Van Nostrand Reinhold, 1977; London: Hamlyn, 1976.

————. *Hans Coper*. New York and Sherborne, England: Harper & Row/Alphabooks, 1983.

————. *Lucie Rie*. Sherborne, England: Alphabooks, 1988.

Casson, Michael. *The Craft of the Potter*. England: Barron, 1979.

Dormer, Peter. *The New Ceramics: Trends and Traditions*. New York: Thames & Hudson, 1986.

Hopper, Robin. *The Ceramic Spectrum*. Radnor, Pa.: Chilton, 1983.

————. *Functional Pottery: Form and Aesthetic in Pots of Purpose*. Radnor, Pa.: Chilton, 1986.

Khalili, Nader. *Racing Alone*. New York: Harper & Row, 1983.

Lane, Peter. *Ceramic Form*. New York: Rizzoli, 1987.

Nance, John. *The Mud Pie Dilemma: A Master Potter's Struggle to Make Art and Ends Meet*. Portland: Timber, 1978.

Needleman, Carla. *The Work of Craft*. New York: Avon, 1979.

Nigrosh, Leon. *Claywork: Form and Idea in Ceramic Design*. 2d ed. Worcester, Mass.: Davis, 1986.

Nordness, Lee. *The Genesis and Triumphant Survival of an Ohio Artist*. Racine, Wis.: Perimeter, 1985.

Rawson, Philip. *Ceramics*. Philadelphia: University of Pennsylvania Press, 1984.

Richards, M. C. *Centering in Pottery, Poetry and the Person*. Middletown, Conn.: Wesleyan University Press, 1964.

Wildenhain, Marguerite. *The Invisible Core: A Potter's Life and Thoughts*. Palo Alto, Calif.: Pacific, 1973.

Wood, Beatrice. *I Shock Myself*. Ojai, Calif.: Dillingham.

Technical
General

Cowley, David. *Molded and Slip Cast Pottery and Ceramics*. New York: Scribner's, 1973.

Coyne, John., ed. *The Penland School of Craft Book of Pottery.* New York: Rutledge, 1975.

Fournier, Robert., ed. *Illustrated Dictionary of Practical Pottery.* New York: Van Nostrand Reinhold, 1976.

Hamer, Frank, and Hamer, Janet. *The Potter's Dictionary of Materials and Techniques.* New York: Watson-Guptill, 1986.

Hamilton, David. *Thames & Hudson Manual of Architectual Ceramics.* New York: Thames & Hudson, 1978.

———. *Thames & Hudson Manual of Pottery and Ceramics.* New York: Thames & Hudson, 1982.

———. *Thames & Hudson Manual of Stoneware and Porcelain.* New York: Thames & Hudson, 1982.

Holden, A. *The Self- Reliant Potter.* Black, 1986.

Nelson, Glenn C. *Ceramics, A Potter's Handbook.* New York: Holt, Winston & Rheinhart, 1984.

Rogers, Mary. *Mary Rogers on Pottery and Porcelain: A Handbuilder's Approach.* New York and Sherborne, England: Watson-Guptill/Alphabooks, 1979.

Speight, Charlotte F. *Images in Clay Sculpture. Historical and Contemporary Techniques.* New York: Harper & Row, 1983.

Clays, Glazes, and Firing

Chappell, James. *The Potter's Complete Book of Clay and Glazes.* New York and London: Watson-Guptill: Pitman, 1977.

Conrad, J. W. *Contemporary Ceramic Formulas.* New York: Macmillan, 1981.

Cooper, Emanuel, and Royle, Derek. *Glazes for the Studio Potter.* Batsford, England: David & Charles, 1986.

Dickerson, John. *Raku Handbook: A Practical Approach to Ceramic Art.* New York: Van Nostrand Reinhold, 1972.

Fournier, Robert. *Illustrated Dictionary of Practical Pottery.* New York: Van Nostrand Reinhold, 1973.

Fraser, Harry. *Glazes for the Craft Potter.* London: Pitman; New York: Watson-Guptill, 1974.

Green, David. *Pottery Materials and Techniques.* New York: Praeger, 1967; London: Faber & Faber, 1963.

Hamer, Frank. *The Potter's Dictionary of Materials and Techniques.* New York and London: Watson-Guptill/Pitman, 1975.

Lane, Peter. *Studio Porcelain.* Radnor, Pa.: Chilton, 1980.

Mason, Ralph. *Native Clays and Glazes for the North American Potter.* Portland: Timber, 1981.

McKee, Charles. *Ceramics Handbook: A Guide to Glaze Calculation, Material and Processes.* Belmont, Calif.: Star, 1973.

Memmott, Harry. *An Artist's Guide to the Use of Ceramic Oxides.* Burwood, Australia: Victoria College Press, 1988.

Nigrosh, Leon. *Low Fire: Other Ways to Work in Clay.* Worcester, Mass.: Davis, 1980.

Parks, Dennis. *A Potter's Guide to Raw Glazing and Oil Firing.* New York: Scribner's, 1980.

Parmelee, Cullen W. *Ceramic Glazes.* Chicago: Industrial Publications, 1951.

Reigger, Hal. *Primitive Pottery.* New York: Van Nostrand Reinhold, 1972.

———. *Raku: Art and Techniques.* New York: Van Nostrand Reinhold, 1972.

Rhodes, Daniel. *Clay and Glazes for the Potter.* Radnor, Pa.: Chilton, 1973.

———. *Stoneware and Porcelain.* Radnor, Pa.: Chilton, 1973.

Sanders, Herbert. *Glazes for Special Effects.* New York: Watson-Guptill, 1974.

Sutherland, Brian. *Glazes from Natural Sources: A Working Handbook for Potters.* England: Batsford, 1987.

Tichane, Robert. *Ching-Te-Chen.* Painted Post, N.Y.: New York Glaze Institute, 1983.

———. *Reds, Reds, Copper Red.* Painted Post, N.Y.: New York Glaze Institute, 1985.

———. *Those Celadon Blues.* Painted Post, N.Y.: New York Glaze Institute, 1983.

Troy, Jack. *Salt Glazed Ceramics.* New York: Watson-Guptill, 1972.

Tyler, Christopher, and Hirsch, Richard. *Raku: Techniques for Contemporary Potters.* New York: Watson-Guptill, 1975; London: Pitman.

Zakin, Richard. *Electric Kiln Ceramics: A Potter's Guide to Clay and Glazes.* Radnor, Pa.: Chilton, 1980.

Kilns

Colson, Frank A. *Kiln Building with Space-Age Materials.* New York: Van Nostrand Reinhold, 1975.

Olsen, Frederick. *The Kiln Book.* Bassett, Calif.: Keramos Books, 1973.

Rhodes, Daniel. *Kilns.* Radnor, Pa.: Chilton, 1974.

Specialized Techniques

Cowley, David. *Molded and Slip Cast Pottery and Ceramics.* New York: Scribner's, 1973.

Frith, Donald E. *Mold Making for Ceramics.* Radnor, Pa.: Chilton, 1985.

Khalili, Nader. *Ceramic Houses: How to Build Your Own.* New York: Harper & Row, 1986.

Kosloff, Albert. *Photographic Screen Printing.* Cincinnati: The Signs of the Times, 1972.

———. *Ceramic Screen Printing.* 2d ed. Cincinnati: The Signs of the Times, 1984.

Whitford, Philip, and Wong, Gordon. *Handmade Potter's Tools.* New York: Kodansha, 1986.

Health and Safety

Barazani, Gail Coningsby. *Ceramics Health Hazards*. rev. ed. Occupational Safety and Health for Artists and Craftsmen, 1984.

Center for Occupational Hazards. (5 Beekman St., New York, NY). *Ventilation Handbook for the Arts*. New York: Center for Occupational Hazards, 1984.

Cutter, Thomas, and McGrane, Jean-Ann. *Ventilation: A Practical Guide*. New York: Center for Occupational Hazards.

McCann, Michael. *Artist Beware! The Hazards and Precautions in Working with Art and Craft Materials*. New York: Watson-Guptill, 1979.

——. *Health Hazards Manual for Artists*. New York: Nick Lyons Books, 1985.

Occupational Health Guidelines for Chemical Hazards. Cincinnati: NIOSH, 1981.

Perry, Rosemary. *Potter's Beware*. This is a booklet available from Rosemary Perry, 865 Cashmere Rd., Christchurch 3, New Zealand.

Rosso, Monona. *Ceramics and Health*. Articles compiled from Ceramic Scope. New York: Center for Occupational Hazards, 1984.

Safe Practices in the Arts and Craft. A Studio Guide. New York: College Art Association of America, no date.

Seeger, Nancy. *A Ceramists's Guide to the Safe Use of Materials*. Chicago: School of the Art Institute of Chicago, 1984.

Data Sheets from the Art Hazards Project, Center for Occupational Hazards: *Ceramics, Respirators, Silica Hazards*.

Note: This list includes only a few of the books and pamphlets that are available on the subject of Health and Safety. New material appears frequently. Up-to-date information lists are available through the Art Hazards Project of The Center for Occupational Hazards, 5 Beekman St., New York, NY 10038, as well as local chapters of The American Lung Association.

Index

The index lists only the most important individual ceramics materials. A complete listing of these materials appears in Appendixes 1E and 1F.

Page numbers of illustrations and color plate numbers appear in bold type.